1996

READING *for* DIFFERENCE

Texts on Gender, Race, and Class

Melissa E. Barth

Thomas McLaughlin

James A. Winders

HARCOURT BRACE JOVANOVICH COLLEGE PUBLISHERS

Fort Worth   Philadelphia   San Diego   New York   Orlando   Austin   San Antonio
Toronto   Montreal   London   Sydney   Tokyo

Publisher	*Ted Buchholz*
Acquisitions Editor	*Stephen T. Jordan*
Developmental Editor	*Cathlynn Richard*
Project Editors	*Dawn Youngblood/Angela Williams*
Production Manager	*Erin Gregg*
Book Designer	*Melinda Huff*

ISBN: 0-15-500216-3

Library of Congress Cataloging-in-Publication Number: 92-071247

Copyright © 1993 by Harcourt Brace Jovanovich, Inc.

Address for editorial correspondence:
301 Commerce Street, Suite 3700
Fort Worth, TX 76102

Address for orders:
6277 Sea Harbor Drive
Orlando, FL 32887
1-800-782-4479 outside Florida
1-800-433-0001 inside Florida

PRINTED IN THE UNITED STATES OF AMERICA

2 3 4 5 6 7 8 9 0 1   090   9 8 7 6 5 4 3 2 1

Copyright acknowledgments continued on page 611.

PREFACE

Reading for Difference invites students to think about themselves and their experiences in what is probably a new way—as participants in a complex and diverse social world. The readings in this book address some of the issues that surround gender, race, and class differences in our society. As editors our attitude toward those differences is affirmative. We want to acknowledge and celebrate diversity and to help students see themselves within our diverse cultural scene. We provide material by writers who occupy very different social positions, writers from both marginalized and socially powerful groups, so that students will recognize their own experience somewhere in this variety. We hope this will establish that *all* writing comes from individuals who have to deal with their gender, race, and class identities. The book also provides students with opportunities and suggestions for writing activities to help them enter the process of self-exploration and self-definition.

Most of the writings are nonfiction, though some are stories or poems. Most were written by professional writers, though some were written by ordinary people in the midst of an extraordinary experience that required them to write it down. The authors are men and women, rich and poor, members of many different ethnic and racial groups, all reflecting on issues central to their identity. You will see in this anthology workers analyzing the conditions of their labor, members of minority groups confronting the stereotypes that oppress them, women dealing with such controversial issues as abortion and rape, men trying to come to terms with their masculinity, heterosexuals and homosexuals reflecting on their experience in society, blacks and whites opposing racism, members of elite classes dealing with their own privileges, and writers from around the world dealing with many of these same issues within their own societies.

The book's organization allows students to explore various reading and writing experiences. Section I, on personal narrative, provides accounts by various writers of experience that taught them something about their social and personal identity. Writing suggestions in this section call for students to explore their own experiences, often in narrative form. Section II includes more controversial and argumentative readings. It asks students to share in the examination of these controversies and includes readings on compelling current issues that each member of our society must examine critically. We believe that analysis and interpretation of what they read will help students construct arguments that express their own positions on these issues.

The close relationship between reading and writing in this book makes it usable in any course where students are exploring our culture and their place in it. The experience of researching and assembling this project came out of our commitment to interdisciplinary work. And we believe that teachers of English, Women's Studies, Interdisciplinary Studies, History, Anthropology, and any multicultural courses will find this textbook useful in getting students to write about issues central to their experiences.

The selections here represent not only the experiences of women and minority groups but males and members of privileged groups as well. The result is a portrait of the diversity of American culture. Writers such as Jo Carson depict the world of the working class in the South, while writers like Paul Fussell see the world from a more elite perspective. Writers as different as Alice Walker and James T. Farrell deal with issues of race in America. This anthology presents various positions on such controversial topics as AIDS, abortion, and sexual preference. Many of the key cultural questions that face our country today are confronted by a wide variety of authors.

For help and support in the development of this project we would like to thank our colleagues and administrators at Appalachian State University, especially George Antone, Loyd Hilton, Bill Byrd, and Don Sink. We would also like to thank our student assistants, Pat Anderson, John Brown, and Carole Lassiter. Early opportunities to explore the philosophy behind this book were provided by the Gender Studies Conference at Lewis and Clark College and by the Center for the Development of Social Responsibility, and we are grateful for those opportunities. We also benefitted from the help of the library staffs at Appalachian State University, the University of North Carolina at Chapel Hill, the University of Georgia, and the Schomburg Center for Research in Black Culture. Reviewers whose valuable comments and suggestions assisted in the development of this book included Carol Cyganowski, DePaul University-Lincoln Park; Ramola Gereben, University of San Francisco; and Madeline Picciotto, Oglethorpe University. We also want to express our appreciation to the following editors and staff members at Harcourt Brace Jovanovich: Eleanor Garner, Erin Gregg, Melinda Huff, Stephen Jordan, Stuart Miller, Marlane Miriello, Cathlynn Richard, and Dawn Youngblood.

For their personal support we want to thank Joan, Nora, Kate, Julia; Becky, Jacob, Ben; Tigger, Jeff, Loretta Lynn, Spook, Skeeter, Duffy, Tootsie, Mr. Finch, and Mr. Foonman.

Melissa E. Barth
Thomas McLaughlin
James A. Winders

CONTENTS

PART II: ISSUES 247

INTRODUCTION TO
READING FOR DIFFERENCE
Texts on Gender, Race, and Class

We live in a very diverse society. In fact, when people say "American society," it's hard to know exactly what they have in mind. Are they thinking of the men and women of influence that we see on TV who appear to have political and social power? Or are they thinking of street people, skinheads, Rastafarians, lesbian separatists, bikers, yuppies, New Agers, fundamentalists, labor union members, Native American activists, etc.—members of what seems like the endless list of subcultures that blend (or collide) to make up our society? Of one thing we can be fairly certain: Living in contemporary America means encountering and dealing with difference. It's a rare experience for most people to go through the day meeting only people like themselves. We have to deal with different races, different classes, different genders. And each encounter that crosses the boundaries of these categories—and others, such as religion, politics, geography, and age—calls for a complex set of negotiations.

Think of a young black woman on welfare who has an appointment with a white male doctor. If these two people are to get along, they are going to have to negotiate a lot of differences. There is every likelihood that the doctor might treat the woman in an overbearing way, since his position in society is usually defined as being higher than hers. He might talk down to her or keep her waiting at his convenience. She might come in to the appointment with a chip on her shoulder, expecting him to act like a superior, and so take offense when none is intended. In this case the costs of failing to reach mutual respect are high. The doctor might not pay enough attention to the woman's analysis of her symptoms; the woman might not trust the doctor enough to listen to his advice. Both must learn how to cross the boundaries that separate them, how to respect their differences and still communicate.

Our lives are made up of such encounters, although most of them are not as obvious as this. We go to school, work, and shop with people of various religious, ethnic, racial, and social backgrounds. We cross the boundaries of gender and racial and class divisions every day. Some of us have learned to fear these differences, for what seems strange to us may also seem dangerous. Others have learned to revere and enjoy difference, seeking out the diversity in our culture, enjoying the music, the food, and the traditions and rituals of various groups. Either way, one of the most important factors in coming to know ourselves is seeing how we differ from others. One way this sometimes is played out is that members of one group define themselves as superior to others. Males may feel superior to females. Whites may feel superior to non-whites. The rich may feel superior to the poor. But it is also possible to think about these differences without establishing a hierarchy among them. A man, for example, can learn to respect gender differences without assuming that the qualities he has been taught are superior to those that women learn. One of our goals in this book is to encourage this kind of respect for differences. We believe that the diversity of our culture demands this mutual regard if we are to survive together.

In America we are taught from earliest childhood that we are all unique. This belief can keep us from recognizing that we are also members of social groups. No one can simply escape from the definitions our society has developed for these groups. Take gender again as an example. Traditionally our society assumes that interest in athletics is a male trait. This attitude is changing, of course, but many people still make the association. When a young girl is interested in athletics, she has to learn to deal with the fact that she is engaged in an activity many people define as masculine. There are many ways she can do this. She may adopt, for example, a very "feminine" style of dress so that she won't be mistaken for a tomboy. Or she may defy other people's expectations and adopt a very "masculine" appearance.

Whatever her response, she is learning to create a personal identity out of her membership in social groups. As members of gender and racial and social class groups, we constantly engage in this process. We see the differences between ourselves and others, and we learn who we are by comparing ourselves with those who are not like us. Of course we are all unique, but our personal identity itself is a function of our membership in groups that define our differences.

We believe that gender, race, and class are the most recognizable and important of those categories in our culture. They are also the most controversial. Very little is settled within these categories. Not everyone agrees on what it means to be male or female, white or a person of color, or rich or poor. The result of all these differences of opinion is a great deal of freedom in how an individual negotiates the differences. Each of us must decide how we will deal with gender, racial, and class definitions. We have the right—and many people exercise it—to reject those definitions that don't suit us. But gender, race, and class never disappear. Even if we reject the standard definitions, they continue to influence us because others might well think of us in conventional terms.

The texts in this collection represent writers who are positioned very differently within these groups: rich white women, middle-class black men, working-class women, and others—as many of the combinations as we could find and fit in. Some of these writers accept the conventional definitions applied to their particular group; some resist the definitions with a passion. As a result, you will probably find someone very much like yourself in this anthology, but you will also find many others who are very different.

You will find other kinds of differences among these texts. Some are examples of "literature" in the narrow sense—poems and stories. Many others are essays, journals, autobiographies, calls to action. In all these forms, people reflect on the issues raised in this book. Some of the authors are professional writers, but others are people who needed to express themselves under the pressure of extraordinary events. Their writing may not be as *"polished," but it is often just as effective and moving. Most of the texts are relatively mod-*

ern, and most are written by Americans, because we felt that such texts would be easier to

identify with. You will also see pieces drawn from earlier periods of American history as well

as from other cultures. Issues of gender, race, and class are not new, nor are they limited to

an American cultural experience.

No matter who the writer is or what form the writing takes, it is possible to see in these

works traces of the writer's gender, racial, and class identities. When writers sit down to ex-

press their ideas, they do not set aside their social identity. Take as an example the following

letter, written in 1911 by Alice Hamilton, a pioneering woman doctor. She took as her par-

ticular work the job of cleaning up factories in what were then called "the dangerous trades,"

particularly those that handled toxic materials like lead. In this letter Hamilton, who was

brought up in an upper-class home, is addressing a Mr. Foster, the foreman of a factory.

The letter crosses a number of social boundaries. Hamilton has the authority conferred by

being from a higher social class, but as a woman she is aware that Mr. Foster may not accept

her as an authority. Watch how she adjusts her style and rhetoric in order to negotiate those

differences:

To Mr. Foster

Philadelphia, Pa.
May 22, 1911

My Dear Mr. Foster:

   I have just been writing to Mr. Wetherill about our conversation of last Friday, as he asked me to put my recommendations down on paper. Now I want
to write you also, because I feel that you are really the one upon whom the re-
forms depend. The factory which is safe and clean, is the factory which has a
foreman who wishes it to be safe and clean. He is the most important factor, for
he is there all the time. That is why I am sending you, as well as Mr. Wetherill,
a list of the things that I think ought to be done.

   1.   There ought to be a rule against any white lead which is dry, being exposed to draughts of air, especially on the floor in rooms where men are working, except of course the dry pan room where it cannot be helped. As long as
your roller room has piles of white lead on the floor and in open trucks, you will
always be having lead poisoning. You see you will never be able to make your
men careful under those circumstances, for they get so used to dust and untidi-

ness, that they do not know it when they see it. Make a rule that the floor must be kept clean and all white lead covered up. I know two white lead factories, old ones at that, where you would not know what was being made in the place, where the floor is so clean you could eat your dinner off it, and no white lead is to be seen anywhere. This should be the rule for every white lead factory.

Keep at the men all the time about the dust. Teach them to watch each other, and when you see a man raising dust, tell the other men that he is poisoning them and they must watch him. Make them wear respirators and overalls which does not mean only trousers. It will be slow work, but it can be done. They have done it at John T. Lewis. I have been able to find only three cases from John T. Lewis for 1910, and twenty-seven from Wetherill, yet both factories employ about the same number of men, both use the old Dutch process, both have an oxide department.

There is one matter that I want to speak about: the widow of one of your fatal cases told me that her husband contracted lead poisoning very quickly because he was doing an unusually dangerous piece of work. He was packing barrels and he was induced by the promise of extra pay to ram down the white lead in the barrel so as to be able to pack in an extra quantity. I hope this is no longer done at Wetherill's. There could not possibly be a more dangerous piece of work.

It is slow work and difficult to train a lot of foreigners to take care of themselves, but I know you can do it and I am sure there is no man in the white lead business who is more genuinely anxious to protect his men than you are.

I shall be very grateful if you will let me know later on, whether any changes have been made in the factory.

Yours sincerely,

Hamilton manages to make this man feel his own importance, while she simultaneously establishes her experience and expertise in the field. She writes as an upper-class woman, but gets her message across effectively, even though her reader is very different from her. Every one of the writers in this book is engaged in a similar process. And some of the questions that we ask about the readings will get you to think about these writers in terms of how they get their ideas across to their—perhaps very different—readers.

The readings in the anthology are organized into two large sections: One deals with individuals' experiences of gender, race, and class: the other deals with issues associated with these social forces. The book begins with writings about personal experiences, those that help individuals define their own identity as members of social groups, and those that teach them about the identity of others. We then turn to writings about controversial issues, writings that raise forceful arguments and offer analysis. Because we assume that all of these texts will invite your own written responses, each selection is followed by suggestions for writing, so that you can make these concerns relevant to your own situation. Writing is a process of exploration, and we believe that these readings will help you begin your own explorations of social identity.

Part I
EXPERIENCES

In this section you will read about personal experiences that can best be understood within the social categories of gender, race, and class. There are three chapters in the section: The first presents experiences that helped some individual define his or her identity; the second incudes writings by people attempting to accept their identity and understand themselves; the third deals with experiences that helped some person understand or define another. Our premise is that we define ourselves and others in terms of the groups to which we and they belong. We understand ourselves in terms of our similarities to and differences from others, and we understand others in terms of their similarities to and differences from us. In this section you will read about moments when people learn about the consequences of belonging to a group—what others think of them for being who they are. And you will read about moments when individuals encounter others, who perhaps are radically different from themselves, and come—or fail to come—to terms with and understand that other person.

We will ask you to think and write about yourself and the different people you have encountered. The writing you do will be based primarily on your experience. But this writing will also encourage you to think about your identity in terms of how you relate to others and to think about your experiences with others, about how you negotiate differences.

1

LEARNING ABOUT YOURSELF

No one is born with a fully developed identity. Of course we are born with qualities and tendencies we inherit from our parents and their parents, but that potential has to be made real over the course of a lifetime. Identity is made, not given. We construct our identity in the circumstances in which we find ourselves. Those circumstances are social, as well as personal. No one chooses the historical moment, the social class, the gender, the race he or she is born into. Those factors are givens, and they greatly influence the self we are to become.

Let's take gender as our first example. Our culture has devised elaborate sets of roles for females and males. These roles are taught to us from earliest infancy, adding onto whatever natural tendencies come with biological sex a set of expectations for behavior and self-image. Little boys and girls are generally raised differently, see different images of themselves in the media, and are treated differently in school; as a result of these and a thousand other influences, both obvious and subtle, boys and girls come to hold different images of themselves. This is not to say that all boys or girls are identical—there are a lot of ways to negotiate our identity within those gender roles. Pee Wee Herman is not Arnold Schwarzenegger. Yet no boy or girl negotiates an identity outside those roles, as though they did not exist. The socially defined roles of gender behavior are a principal part of the social matrix within which we produce our identity.

Just as inescapable are the social roles and expectations surrounding racial differences. In some societies, most visibly in South Africa, racial differences are subjected to legal restrictions, as they were in America until the successes of the civil rights movement of the 1950s and 1960s. Now most of these legal constraints are gone, but there are still social roles and expectations that make life very different for people of different races in our society. Because we live in a white-dominated society, the category of race strongly influences a black person's efforts to create an identity. He or she does not have the luxury of disregarding race. Whites may think they can take their racial identity for granted, but there are situations that remind them that social definitions of race are a part of their identity, too. Take, for example, a moment when a white person fails to recognize the meaning of a phrase of black slang. At that moment it is clear that a whole range of experience lies outside the knowledge of most white people, and that all members of our society have to contend with socially defined racial differences as part of the terrain in which we construct our self-image.

Perhaps the most difficult to recognize of these social categories is social class. We have been taught to enjoy equal opportunity, equal protection under the law, and an equal chance at economic success. Social classes seem like concepts from older, more rigid societies, but social class is nevertheless an important factor in how we define ourselves. Of course, social class is a difficult concept to define. Membership in a given class is not simply a matter of economics, although sheer differences in wealth and the different opportunities available to rich and poor are important factors in making an identity. The sons and daughters of the privileged classes who attend exclusive private schools live within a different social environment than those who can only afford a public school that might offer limited educational options. Social class is a matter of money, but it also involves education, job status, religion, geographical location, and many other factors. A truck driver might make more money than a computer programmer, but the programmer's status—the social ranking of his or her profession's importance and public image—is probably higher. The social class an individual grows up in is another important element in the social reality he or she inhabits.

Social class, race, gender—no one can escape them or think about themselves outside their categories. To create an identity, to define the terms of your individual style, is to negotiate these categories. There are many ways to be black, to be female, to be working-class.

The range of options is vast, maybe infinite. But the fact that these categories exist is undeniable. It is within their bounds that we make our choices and find ourselves.

The essays, stories, and poems in this section display this process. In them we see individuals face experiences that teach them about themselves and help them find an identity within that social world. We have focused particularly on the experiences of young people—on the moment, for example, when a young boy learns what it means to be black, or on the moment when a young person has to decide whether to follow the definitions of behavior imposed on a group he or she belongs to. In the writing projects we suggest, you will explore that same process, reflecting on how these writers, and how you yourself, work out a personal and social identity.

THE SKY IS GRAY

Ernest J. Gaines

Ernest J. Gaines (b. 1933) is a significant contemporary African-American writer. His works include novels, short fiction, plays, and children's stories. He is best known for his novels The Autobiography of Miss Jane Pittman *and* A Gathering of Old Men. *Like the boy in this story, Gaines grew up in Louisiana during the 1930s and 1940s. At that time, people in the rural Deep South were living much as they had for at least a half century, that is, since the waning of Reconstruction (1865–1876) and the institution of the so-called "Jim Crow laws." These were state laws that, much like the apartheid system of South Africa, systematically deprived African-Americans of fundamental civil liberties and equal protection under the law. In short, they undercut the formal, legal emancipation of the slaves, which dated officially from 1863. At the time of this story, the injustice of Jim Crow was heightened by the severe economic dislocation of the Great Depression (1929–1939) and its social consequences. In desperate times, the black family provided resources of nurture, solidarity, and resistance, the very qualities that were to surface heroically during the civil rights movement of the 1950s and 1960s.*

The narrator of "The Sky is Gray" is called upon to play the "little man" as he accompanies his mother and bears with her the brunt of public Southern racism. As he learns about race, he also gets an early lesson in what it means to be a man.

I

Go'n be coming in a few minutes. Coming round that bend down there full speed. And I'm go'n get out my handkerchief and wave it down, and we go'n get on it and go.

I keep on looking for it, but Mama don't look that way no more. She's looking down the road where we just come from. It's a long old road, and far's you can see you don't see nothing but gravel. You got dry weeds on both sides, and you got trees on both sides, and fences on both sides, too. And you got cows in the pastures and they standing close together. And when we was coming out here to catch the bus I seen the smoke coming out of the cows's noses.

I look at my mama and I know what she's thinking. I been with Mama so much, just me and her, I know what she's thinking all the time. Right now it's home—Auntie and them. She's thinking if they got enough wood—if she left enough there to keep them warm till we get back. She's thinking if it go'n rain and if any of them go'n have to go out in the rain. She's thinking 'bout the hog—if he go'n get out, and if Ty and Val be able to get him back in. She always worry like that when she leaves the house. She don't worry too much if she leave me there with the smaller ones, 'cause she know I'm go'n look after them and look after Auntie and everything else. I'm the oldest and she say I'm the man.

I look at my mama and I love my mama. She's wearing that black coat and that black hat and she's looking sad. I love my mama and I want to put my arm round her and tell her. But I'm not supposed to do that. She say that's weakness and that's crybaby stuff, and she don't want no crybaby round her. She don't want you to be scared, either. 'Cause Ty's scared of ghosts and she's always whipping him. I'm scared of the dark, too, but I make 'tend I ain't. I make 'tend I ain't 'cause I'm the oldest, and I got to set a good sample for the rest. I can't ever be scared and I can't ever cry. And that's why I never said nothing 'bout my teeth. It's been hurting me and hurting me close to a month now, but I never said it. I didn't say it 'cause I didn't want to act like a crybaby, and 'cause I know we didn't have enough money to go have it pulled. But, Lord, it been hurting me. And look like it wouldn't start till at night when you was trying to get yourself a little sleep. Then soon's you shut your eyes—ummm-ummm, Lord, look like it go right down to your heartstring.

"Hurting, hanh?" Ty'd say.

I'd shake my head, but I wouldn't open my mouth for nothing. You open your mouth and let that wind in, and it almost kill you.

I'd just lay there and listen to them snore. Ty there, right 'side me, and Auntie and Val over by the fireplace. Val younger than me and Ty, and he sleeps with Auntie. Mama sleeps round the other side with Louis and Walker.

I'd just lay there and listen to them, and listen to that wind out there, and listen to that fire in the fireplace. Sometimes it'd stop long enough to let me get little rest. Sometimes it just hurt, hurt, hurt. Lord, have mercy.

II

Auntie knowed it was hurting me. I didn't tell nobody but Ty, 'cause we buddies and he ain't go'n tell anybody. But some kind of way Auntie found out. When she asked me, I told her no, nothing was wrong. But she knowed it all the time. She told me to mash up a piece of aspirin and wrap it in some cotton and jugg it down in that hole. I did, but it didn't do no good. It stopped for a little while, and started right back again. Auntie wanted to tell Mama, but I told her, "Uh-uh." 'Cause I knowed we didn't have any money, and it just was go'n make her mad again. So Auntie told Monsieur Bayonne, and Monsieur Bayonne came over to the house and told me to kneel down 'side him on the fireplace. He put his finger in his mouth and made the Sign of the Cross on my jaw. The tip of Monsieur Bayonne's finger is some hard, 'cause he's always play-ing on that guitar. If we sit outside at night we can always hear Monsieur Bay-onne playing on his guitar. Sometimes we leave him out there playing on the guitar.

Monsieur Bayonne made the sign of the Cross over and over on my jaw, but that didn't do no good. Even when he prayed and told me to pray some, too, that tooth still hurt me.

"How you feeling?" he say.

"Same," I say.

He kept on praying and making the Sign of the Cross and I kept on praying, too.

"Still hurting?" he say.

"Yes, sir."

Monsieur Bayonne mashed harder and harder on my jaw. He mashed so hard he almost pushed me over on Ty. But then he stopped.

"What kind of prayers you praying, boy?" he say.

"Baptist," I say.

"Well, I'll be—no wonder that tooth still killing him. I'm going one way and he pulling the other. Boy, don't you know any Catholic prayers?"

"I know 'Hail Mary,' " I say.

"Then you better start saying it."

"Yes, sir."

He started mashing on my jaw again, and I could hear him praying at the same time. And, sure enough, after awhile it stopped hurting me.

Me and Ty went outside where Monsieur Bayonne's two hounds was and we started playing with them. "Let's go hunting," Ty say. "All right," I say; and we went on back in the pasture. Soon the hounds got on a trail, and me and Ty followed them all 'cross the pasture and then back in the woods, too. And then they cornered this little old rabbit and killed him, and me and Ty made them get back, and we picked up the rabbit and started on back home. But my tooth had started hurting me again. It was hurting me plenty now, but I wouldn't tell Monsieur Bayonne. That night I didn't sleep a bit, and first thing in the morning Auntie told me to go back and let Monsieur Bayonne pray over me some more. Monsieur Bayonne was in his kitchen making coffee when I got there. Soon's he seen me he knowed what was wrong.

"All right, kneel down there 'side that stove," he say. "And this time make sure you pray Catholic. I don't know nothing 'bout that Baptist and I don't want know nothing 'bout him."

III

Last night Mama say, "Tomorrow we going to town."

"It ain't hurting me no more," I say. "I can eat anything on it."

"Tomorrow we going to town," she say.

And after she finished eating, she got up and went to bed. She always go to bed early now. 'Fore Daddy went in the Army, she used to stay up late. All of us sitting out on the gallery or round the fire. But now, look like soon's she finish eating she go to bed.

This morning when I woke up, her and Auntie was standing 'fore the fireplace. She say: "Enough to get there and back. Dollar and a half to have it pulled. Twenty-five for me to go, twenty-five for him. Twenty-five for me to come back, twenty-five for him. Fifty cents left. Guess I get little piece of salt meat with that."

"Sure can use it," Auntie say. "White beans and no salt meat ain't white beans."

"I do the best I can," Mama say.

They was quiet after that, and I made 'tend I was still asleep.

"James, hit the floor," Auntie say.

I still made 'tend I was asleep. I didn't want them to know I was listening.

"All right," Auntie say, shaking me by the shoulder. "Come on. Today's the day."

I pushed the cover down to get out, and Ty grabbed it and pulled it back.

"You, too, Ty," Auntie say.

"I ain't getting no teef pulled," Ty say.

"Don't mean it ain't time to get up," Auntie say. "Hit it, Ty."

Ty got up grumbling.

"James, you hurry up and get in your clothes and eat your food," Auntie say. "What time y'all coming back?" she say to Mama.

"That 'leven o'clock bus," Mama say. "Got to get back in that field this evening."

"Get a move on you, James," Auntie say.

I went in the kitchen and washed my face, then I ate my breakfast. I was having bread and syrup. The bread was warm and hard and tasted good. And I tried to make it last a long time.

Ty came back there grumbling and mad at me.

"Got to get up," he say. "I ain't having no teefs pulled. What I got to be getting up for?"

Ty poured some syrup in his pan and got a piece of bread. He didn't wash his hands, neither his face, and I could see that white stuff in his eyes.

"You the one getting your teef pulled," he say. "What I got to get up for. I bet if I was getting a teef pulled, you wouldn't be getting up. Shucks; syrup again. I'm getting tired of this old syrup. Syrup, syrup, syrup. I'm go'n take with the sugar diabetes. I want me some bacon sometime."

"Go out in the field and work and you can have your bacon," Auntie say. She stood in the middle door looking at Ty. "You better be glad you got syrup. Some people ain't got that—hard's time is."

"Shucks," Ty say. "How can I be strong."

"I don't know too much 'bout your strength," Auntie say; "but I know where you go'n be hot at, you keep that grumbling up. James, get a move on you; your mama waiting."

I ate my last piece of bread and went in the front room. Mama was standing 'fore the fireplace warming her hands. I put on my coat and cap, and we left the house.

IV

I look down there again, but it still ain't coming. I almost say, "It ain't coming yet," but I keep my mouth shut. 'Cause that's something else she don't like. She don't like for you to say something just for nothing. She can see it ain't coming. I can see it ain't coming, so why say it ain't coming. I don't say it, I turn and look at the river that's back of us. It's so cold the smoke's just raising up from the water. I see a bunch of pool-doos not too far out—just on the other side the lilies. I'm wondering if you can eat pool-doos. I ain't too sure, 'cause I ain't never ate none. But I done ate owls and blackbirds, and I done ate redbirds, too. I didn't want to kill the redbirds, but she made me kill them. They had two of them back there. One in my trap, one in Ty's trap. Me and Ty was go'n play with them and let them go, but she made me kill them 'cause we needed the food.

"I can't," I say. "I can't."

"Here," she say. "Take it."

"I can't," I say. "I can't. I can't kill him, Mama, please."

"Here," she say, "Take this fork, James."

"Please, Mama, I can't kill him," I say.

I could tell she was go'n hit me. I jerked back, but I didn't jerk back soon enough.

"Take it," she say.

I took it and reached in for him, but he kept on hopping to the back.

"I can't, Mama," I say. The water just kept on running down my face. "I can't," I say.

"Get him out of there," she say.

I reached in for him and he kept on hopping to the back. Then I reached in farther and he pecked me on the hand.

"I can't, Mama," I say.

She slapped me again.

I reached in again, but he kept on hopping out my way. Then he hopped to one side and I reached there. The fork got him on the leg and I heard his leg pop. I pulled my hand out 'cause I had hurt him.

"Give it here," she say, and jerked the fork out of my hand.

She reached in and got the little bird right in the neck. I heard the fork go in his neck, and I heard it go in the ground. She brought him out and helt him right in front of me.

"That's one," she say. She shook him off and gived me the fork. "Get the other one."

"I can't Mama," I say. "I'll do anything, but don't make me do that."

She went to the corner of the fence and broke the biggest switch over there she could find. I knelt 'side the trap, crying.

"Get him out of there," she say.

"I can't, Mama."

She started hitting me 'cross the back. I went down on the ground, crying.

"Get him," she say.

"Octavia?" Auntie say.

'Cause she had come out of the house and she was standing by the tree looking at us.

"Get him out of there," Mama say.

"Octavia," Auntie say, "explain to him. Explain to him. Just don't beat him. Explain to him."

But she hit me and hit me and hit me.

I'm still young—I ain't no more than eight; but I know now; I know why I had to do it. (They was so little, though. They was so little. I 'member how I picked the feathers off them and cleaned them and helt them over the fire. Then we all ate them. Ain't had but a little bitty piece each, but we all had a little bitty piece, and everybody just looked at me 'cause they was so proud.) Suppose she had to go away? That's why I had to do it. Suppose she had to go away like Daddy went away? Then who was go'n look after us? They had to be somebody left to carry on. I didn't know it then, but I know it now. Auntie and Monsieur Bayonne talked to me and made me see.

V

Time I see it I get out my handkerchief and start waving. It's still 'way down there, but I keep waving anyhow. Then it come up and stop and me and Mama get on. Mama tell me go sit in the back while she pay. I do like she say, and the people look at me. When I pass the little sign that say "White" and "Colored," I start looking for a seat. I just see one of them back there, but I don't take it, 'cause I want my mama to sit down herself. She comes in the back and sit down, and I lean on the seat. They got seats in the front, but I know I can't sit there, 'cause I have to sit back of the sign. Anyhow, I don't want to sit there if my mama go'n sit back here.

They got a lady sitting 'side my mama and she looks at me and smiles little bit. I smile back, but I don't open my mouth, 'cause the wind'll get in and make that tooth ache. The lady take out a pack of gum and reach me a slice, but I shake my head. The lady just can't understand why a little boy'll turn down gum, and she reach me a slice again. This time I point to my jaw. The lady understands and smiles a little bit, and I smile little bit, but I don't open my mouth, though.

They got a girl sitting 'cross from me. She got on a red overcoat and her hair's plaited in one big plait. First, I make 'tend I don't see her over there, but then I start looking at her little bit. She make 'tend she don't see me, either, but I catch her looking that way. She got a cold, and every now and then she h'ist that little handkerchief to her nose. She ought to blow it, but she don't. Must think she's too much a lady or something.

Every time she h'ist that little handkerchief, the lady 'side her say something in her ear. She shakes her head and lays her hands in her lap again. Then I catch her kind of looking where I'm at. I smile at her a little bit. But think she'll smile back? Uh-uh. She just turn up her little old nose and turn her head. Well, I show her both of us can turn us head. I turn mine too and look out at the river.

The river is gray. The sky is gray. They have pool-doos on the water. The water is wavy, and the pool-doos go up and down. The bus go round a turn, and you got plenty trees hiding the river. Then the bus go round another turn, and I can see the river again.

I look toward the front where all the white people sitting. Then I look at that little old gal again. I don't look right at her, 'cause I don't want all them people to know I love her. I just look at her little bit, like I'm looking out that window over there. But she knows I'm looking that way, and she kind of look at me, too. The lady sitting 'side her catch her this time and she leans over and says something in her ear.

"I don't love him nothing," that little old gal says out loud.

Everybody back there hear her mouth, and all of them look at us and laugh. "I don't love you, either," I say. "So you don't have to turn up your nose, Miss."

"You the one looking," she say.

"I wasn't looking at you," I say. "I was looking out that window, there."

"Out that window, my foot," she say. "I seen you. Everytime I turned round you was looking at me."

"You must of been looking yourself if you seen me all them times," I say.

"Shucks," she say, "I got me all kind of boyfriends."

"I got girlfriends, too," I say.

"Well, I just don't want you getting your hopes up," she say.

I don't say no more to that little old gal 'cause I don't want to have to bust her in the mouth. I lean on the seat where Mama sitting, and I don't even look that way no more. When we get to Bayonne, she jugg her little old tongue out at me. I make 'tend I'm go'n hit her, and she duck down 'side her mama. And all the people laugh at us again.

VI

Me and Mama got off and start walking in town. Bayonne is a little bitty town. Baton Rouge is a hundred times bigger than Bayonne. I went to Baton Rouge once—me, Ty, Mama, and Daddy. But that was 'way back yonder, 'fore Daddy went in the Army. I wonder when we go'n see him again. I wonder when. Look like he ain't ever coming back home. . . . Even the pavement all cracked in Bayonne. Got grass shooting right out the sidewalk. Got weeds in the ditch, too; just like they got at home.

It's some cold in Bayonne. Look like it's colder than it is home. The wind blows in my face, and I feel that stuff running down my nose. I sniff. Mama says use that handkerchief. I blow my nose and put it back.

We pass a school and I see them white children playing in the yard. Big old red school, and them children just running and playing. Then we pass a café, and I see a bunch of people in there eating. I wish I was in there 'cause I'm cold. Mama tells me keep my eyes in front where they belong.

We pass stores that's got dummies, and we pass another café, and then we pass a shoe shop, and that bald-head man in there fixing on a shoe. I look at him and I butt into that white lady, and Mama jerks me in front and tells me stay there.

We come up to the courthouse, and I see the flag waving there. This flag ain't like the one we got at school. This one here ain't got but a handful of stars. One at school got a big pile of stars—one for every state. We pass it and we turn and there it is—the dentist office. Me and Mama go in, and they got people sitting everywhere you look. They even got a little boy in there younger than me.

Me and Mama sit on that bench, and a white lady come in there and ask me what my name is. Mama tells her and the white lady goes on back. Then I hear somebody hollering in there. Soon's that little boy hear him hollering, he starts hollering, too. His mama pats him and pats him, trying to make him hush up, but he ain't thinking 'bout his mama.

The man that was hollering in there comes out holding his jaw. He is a big old man and he's wearing overalls and a jumper.

"Got it, hanh?" another man asks him.

The man shakes his head—don't want open his mouth.

"Man, I thought they was killing you in there," the other man says. "Hollering like a pig under a gate."

The man don't say nothing. He just heads for the door, and the other man follows him.

"John Lee," the white lady says. "John Lee Williams."

The little boy juggs his head down in his mama's lap and holler more now. His mama tells him go with the nurse, but he ain't thinking 'bout his mama. His mama tells him again, but he don't even hear her. His mama picks him up and takes him in there, and even when the white lady shuts the door I can still hear little old John Lee.

"I often wonder why the Lord let a child like that suffer," a lady says to my mama. The lady's sitting right in front of us on another bench. She's got on a white dress and a black sweater. She must be a nurse or something herself, I reckon.

"Not us to question," a man says.

"Sometimes I don't know if we shouldn't," the lady says.

"I know definitely we shouldn't," the man says. The man looks like a preacher. He's big and fat and he's got on a black suit. He's got a gold chain, too.

"Why?" the lady says.

"Why anything?" the preacher says.

"Yes," the lady says. "Why anything?"

"Not us to question," the preacher says.

The lady looks at the preacher a little while and looks at Mama again.

"And look like it's the poor who suffers the most," she says. "I don't understand it."

"Best not to even try," the preacher says. "He works in mysterious ways—wonders to perform."

Right then little John Lee bust out hollering, and everybody turn they head to listen.

"He's not a good dentist," the lady says. "Dr. Robillard is much better. But more expensive. That's why most of the colored people come here. The white people go to Dr. Robillard. Y'all from Bayonne?"

"Down the river," my mama says. And that's all she go'n say, 'cause she don't talk much. But the lady keeps looking at her, and so she says, "Near Morgan."

"I see," the lady says.

VII

"That's the trouble with the black people in this country today," somebody else says. This one here's sitting on the same side me and Mama's sitting, and he is kind of sitting in front of that preacher. He looks like a teacher or somebody that goes to college. He's got on a suit, and he's got a book that he's been reading. "We don't question is exactly our problem," he says. "We should question and question and question—question everything."

The preacher just looks at him a long time. He done put a toothpick or something in his mouth, and he just keeps on turning it and turning it. You can see he don't like that boy with that book.

"Maybe you can explain what you mean," he says.

"I said what I meant," the boy says. "Question everything. Every stripe, every star, every word spoken. Everything."

"It 'pears to me that this young lady and I was talking 'bout God, young man," the preacher says.

"Question Him, too," the boy says.

"Wait," the preacher says, "Wait now."

"You heard me right," the boy says. "His existence as well as everything else. Everything."

The preacher just looks across the room at the boy. You can see he's getting madder and madder. But mad or no mad, the boy ain't thinking 'bout him. He looks at that preacher just's hard's the preacher looks at him.

"Is this what they coming to?" the preacher says. "Is that what we educating them for?"

"You're not educating me," the boy says. "I wash dishes at night so that I can go to school in the day. So even the words you spoke need questioning."

The preacher just looks at him and shakes his head.

"When I come in this room and seen you there with your book, I said to myself, 'There's an intelligent man.' How wrong a person can be."

"Show me one reason to believe in the existence of a God," the boy says.

"My heart tells me," the preacher says.

" 'My heart tells me' " the boy says. " 'My heart tells me.' Sure, 'My heart tells me.' And as long as you listen to what your heart tells you, you will have only what the white man gives you and nothing more. Me, I don't listen to my heart. The purpose of the heart is to pump blood throughout the body, and nothing else."

"Who's your paw, boy?" the preacher says.

"Why?"

"Who is he?"

"He's dead."

"And your mom?"

"She's in Charity Hospital with pneumonia. Half killed herself, working for nothing."

"And 'cause he's dead and she's sick, you mad at the world?"

"I'm not mad at the world. I'm questioning the world. I'm questioning it with cold logic sir. What do words like Freedom, Liberty, God, White, Colored mean? I want to know. That's why *you* are sending us to school, to read and to ask questions. And because we ask these questions, you call us mad. No sir, it is not us who are mad."

"You keep saying 'us'?"

" 'Us.' Yes—us. I'm not alone."

The preacher just shakes his head. Then he looks at everybody in the room—everybody. Some of the people look down at the floor, keep from looking at him. I kind of look 'way myself, but soon's I know he done turn his head, I look that way again.

"I'm sorry for you," he says to the boy.

"Why?" the boy says. "Why not be sorry for yourself? Why are you so much better off than I am? Why aren't you sorry for these other people in here? Why not be sorry for the lady who had to drag her child into the dentist office? Why not be sorry for the lady sitting on that bench over there? Be sorry for them. Not for me. Some way or the other I'm going to make it."

"No, I'm sorry for you," the preacher says.

"Of course, of course," the boy says, nodding his head. "You're sorry for me because I rock that pillar you're leaning on."

"You can't ever rock the pillar I'm leaning on, young man. It's stronger than anything man can ever do."

"You believe in God because a man told you to believe in God," the boy says. "A white man told you to believe in God. And why? To keep you ignorant so he can keep his feet on your neck."

"So now we the ignorant?" the preacher says.

"Yes," the boy says. "Yes." And he opens his book again.

The preacher just looks at him sitting there. The boy done forgot all about him. Everybody else make 'tend they done forgot the squabble, too.

Then I see that preacher getting up real slow. Preacher's great big old man and he got to brace himself to get up. He comes over where the boy is sitting. He just stands there a little while looking down at him, but the boy don't raise his head.

"Get up, boy," preacher says.

The boy looks up at him, then he shuts his book real slow and stands up. Preacher just hauls back and hit him in the face. The boy falls back 'gainst the wall, but he straightens himself up and looks right back at that preacher.

"You forgot the other cheek," he says.

The preacher hauls back and hit him again on the other side. But this time the boy braces himself and don't fall.

"That hasn't changed a thing," he says.

The preacher just looks at the boy. The preacher's breathing real hard like he just run up a big hill. The boy sits down and opens his book again.

"I feel sorry for you," the preacher says. "I never felt so sorry for a man before."

The boy makes 'tend he don't even hear that preacher. He keeps on reading his book. The preacher goes back and gets his hat off the chair.

"Excuse me," he says to us. "I'll come back some other time. Y'all, please excuse me."

And he looks at the boy and goes out the room. The boy h'ist his hand up to his mouth one time to wipe 'way some blood. All the rest of the time he keeps on reading. And nobody else in there say a word.

VIII

Little John Lee and his mama come out the dentist office, and the nurse calls somebody else in. Then little bit later they come out, and the nurse calls another name. But fast's she calls somebody in there, somebody else comes in the place where we sitting, and the room stays full.

The people coming in now, all of them wearing big coats. One of them says something 'bout sleeting, another says he hope not. Another one says he think it ain't nothing but rain. 'Cause, he says, rain can get awful cold this time of year.

All round the room they talking. Some of them talking to people right by them, some of them talking to people clear 'cross the room, some of them talking to anybody'll listen. It's a little bitty room, no bigger than us kitchen, and I can see everybody in there. The little old room's full of smoke, 'cause you got two old men smoking pipes over by that side door. I think I feel my tooth thumping me some, and I hold my breath and wait. I wait and wait, but it don't thump me no more. Thank God for that.

I feel like going to sleep, and I lean back 'gainst the wall. But I'm scared to go to sleep. Scared 'cause the nurse might call my name and I won't hear her. And Mama might go to sleep, too, and she'll be mad if neither one of us heard the nurse.

I look up at Mama. I love my mama. I love my mama. And when cotton come I'm go'n get her a new coat. And I ain't go'n get a black one, either. I think I'm go'n get her a red one.

"They got some books over there," I say. "Want read one of them?"

Mama looks at the books, but she don't answer me.

"You got yourself a little man there," the lady says.

Mama don't say nothing to the lady, but she must've smiled, 'cause I seen the lady smiling back. The lady looks at me a little while, like she's feeling sorry for me.

"You sure got that preacher out here in a hurry," she says to that boy.

The boy looks up at her and looks in his book again. When I grow up I want to be just like him. I want clothes like that and I want keep a book with me, too.

"You really don't believe in God?" the lady says.

"No," he says.

"But why?" the lady says.

"Because the wind is pink," he says.

"What?" the lady says.

The boy don't answer her no more. He just reads in his book.

"Talking 'bout the wind is pink," that old lady says. She's sitting on the same bench with the boy and she's trying to look in his face. The boy makes 'tend the old lady ain't even there. He just keeps on reading. "Wind is pink," she says again. "Eh, Lord, what children go'n be saying next?"

The lady 'cross from us bust out laughing.

"That's a good one," she says. "The wind is pink. Yes sir, that's a good one."

"Don't you believe the wind is pink?" the boy says. He keeps his head down in the book.

"Course I believe it, honey," the lady says. "Course I do." She looks at us and winks her eye. "And what color is grass, honey?"

"Grass? Grass is black."

She bust out laughing again. The boy looks at her.

"Don't you believe grass is black?" he says.

The lady quits her laughing and looks at him. Everybody else looking at him, too. The place is quiet, quiet.

"Grass is green, honey," the lady says. "It was green yesterday, it's green today, and it's go'n be green tomorrow."

"How do you know it's green?"

"I know because I know."

"You don't know it's green," the boy says. "You believe it's green because someone told you it was green. If someone had told you it was black you'd believe it was black."

"It's green," the lady says. "I know green when I see green."

"Prove it's green," the boy says.

"Sure, now," the lady says. "Don't tell me it's coming to that."

"It's coming to just that," the boy says. "Words mean nothing. One means no more than the other."

"That's what it all coming to?" the old lady says. That old lady got on a turban and she got on two sweaters. She got a green sweater under a black sweater. I can see the green sweater 'cause some of the buttons on the other sweater's missing.

"Yes ma'am," the boy says. "Words mean nothing. Action is the only thing. Doing. That's the only thing."

"Other words, you want the Lord to come down here and show Hisself to you?" she says.

"Exactly, ma'am," he says.

"You don't mean that, I'm sure?" she says.

"I do, ma'am," he says.

"Done. Jesus," the old lady says, shaking her head.

"I didn't go 'long with that preacher at first," the other lady says; "but now—I don't know. When a person say the grass is black, he's either a lunatic or something's wrong."

"Prove to me that it's green," the boy says.

"It's green because the people say it's green."

"Those same people say we're citizens of these United States," the boy says.

"I think I'm a citizen," the lady says.

"Citizens have certain rights," the boy says. "Name me one right that you have. One right, granted by the Constitution that you can exercise in Bayonne."

The lady don't answer him. She just looks at him like she don't know what he's talking 'bout. I know I don't.

"Things changing," she says.

"Things are changing because some black men have begun to think with their brains and not their hearts," the boy says.

"You trying to say these people don't believe in God?"

"I'm sure some of them do. Maybe most of them do. But they don't believe that God is going to touch these white people's hearts and change things tomorrow. Things change through action. By no other way."

Everybody sit quiet and look at the boy. Nobody says a thing. Then the lady 'cross the room from me and Mama just shakes her head.

"Let's hope that not all your generation feel the same way you do," she says.

"Think what you please, it doesn't matter," the boy says. "But it will be men who listen to their heads and not their hearts who will see that your children have a better chance than you had."

"Let's hope they ain't all like you, though," the old lady says. "Done forgot the heart absolutely."

"Yes ma'am, I hope they aren't all like me," the boy says. "Unfortunately, I was born too late to believe in your God. Let's hope that the ones who come after will have your faith—if not in your God, then in something else, something definitely that they can lean on. I haven't anything. For me the wind is pink, the grass is black."

IX

The nurse comes in the room where we all sitting and waiting and says the doctor won't take no more patients till one o'clock this evening. My mama jumps up off the bench and goes up to the white lady.

"Nurse, I have to go back in the field this evening," she says.

"The doctor is treating his last patient now," the nurse says. "One o'clock this evening."

"Can I at least speak to the doctor?" my mama asks.

"I'm his nurse," the lady says.

"My little boy's sick," my mama says. "Right now his tooth almost killing him."

The nurse looks at me. She's trying to make up her mind if to let me come in. I look at her real pitiful. The tooth ain't hurting me at all, but Mama says it is, so I make 'tend for her sake.

"This evening," the nurse says, and goes on back in the office.

"Don't feel 'jected, honey," the lady says to Mama. "I been round them a long time— they take you when they want to. If you was white, that's something else; but we the wrong color."

Mama don't say nothing to the lady, and me and her go outside and stand 'gainst the wall. It's cold out there. I can feel that wind going through my coat. Some of the other people come out of the room and go up the street. Me and Mama stand there a little while and we start walking. I don't know where we going. When we come to the other street we just stand there.

"You don't have to make water, do you?" Mama says.

"No ma'am," I say.

We go on up the street. Walking real slow. I can tell Mama don't know where she's going. When we come to a store we stand there and look at the dummies. I look at a little boy wearing a brown overcoat. He's got on brown shoes, too. I look at my old shoes and look at his'n again. You wait till summer, I say.

Me and Mama walk away. We come up to another store and we stop and look at them dummies, too. Then we go on again. We pass a café where the white people in there eating. Mama tells me keep my eyes in front where they belong, but I can't help from seeing them people eat. My stomach starts to growling 'cause I'm hungry. When I see people eating, I get hungry; when I see a coat, I get cold.

A man whistles at my mama when we go by a filling station. She makes 'tend she don't even see him. I look back and I feel like hitting him in the mouth. If I was bigger, I say; if I was bigger, you'd see.

We keep on going. I'm getting colder and colder, but I don't say nothing. I feel that stuff running down my nose and I sniff.

"That rag," Mama says.

I get it out and wipe my nose. I'm getting cold all over now my face, my hands, my feet, everything. We pass another little café, but this'n for white people, too, and we can't go in their, either. So we just walk. I'm so cold now I'm 'bout ready to say it. If I knowed where we was going I wouldn't be so cold, but I don't know where we going. We go, we go, we go. We walk clean out of Bayonne. Then we cross the street and we come back. Same thing I seen when I got off the bus this morning. Same old trees, same old walk, same old weeds, same old cracked pave—same old everything.

I sniff again.

"That rag," Mama says.

I wipe my nose real fast and jugg that handkerchief back in my pocket 'fore my hand gets too cold. I raise my head and I can see David's hardware store. When we come up to it, we go in. I don't know why, but I'm glad.

It's warm in there. It's so warm in there you don't ever want to leave. I look for the heater, and I see it over by them barrels. Three white men stand round the heater talking in Creole. One of them comes over to see what my mama want.

"Got any axe handles?" she says.

Me, Mama and the white man start to the back, but Mama stops me when we come up to the heater. She and the white man go on. I hold my hands over the heater and look at them. They go all the way to the back, and I see the white man pointing to the axe handles 'gainst the wall. Mama takes one of them and shakes it like she's trying to figure how much it weighs. Then she rubs her hand over it from one end to the other end. She turns it over and looks at the other side, then she shakes it again, and shakes her head and puts it back. She gets another one and she does it just like she did the first one, then she shakes her head. Then she gets a brown one and do it that, too. But she don't like this one, either. Then she gets another one, but 'fore she shakes it or any-thing, she looks at me. Look like she's trying to say something to me, but I don't know what it is. All I know is I done got warm now and I'm feeling right smart better. Mama shakes this axe handle just like she did the others, and shakes her head and says something to the white man. The white man just looks at his pile of axe handles, and when Mama pass him to come to the front, the white man just scratch his head and follows her. She tells me come on and we go on and start walking again.

We walk and walk, and no time at all I'm cold again. Look like I'm colder now 'cause I can still remember how good it was back there. My stomach growls and I suck it in to keep Mama from hearing it. She's walking right 'side me, and it growls so loud you can hear it a mile. But Mama don't say a word.

X

When we come up to the courthouse, I look at the clock. It's got quarter to twelve. Mean we got another hour and a quarter to be out here in the cold. We go and stand 'side a building. Something hits my cap and I look up at the sky. Sleet's falling.

I look at Mama standing there. I want stand close 'side her, but she don't like that. She say that's crybaby stuff. She say you got to stand for yourself, by yourself.

"Let's go back to that office," she says.

We cross the street. When we get to the dentist office I try to open the door, but I can't. I twist and twist, but I can't. Mama pushes me to the side and she twist the knob, but she can't open the door, either. She turns 'way from the door. I look at her, but I don't move and I don't say nothing. I done seen her like this before and I'm scared of her.

"You hungry?" she says. She says it like she's mad at me, like I'm the cause of everything.

"No, ma'am," I say.

"You want eat and walk back, or you rather don't eat and ride?"

"I ain't hungry," I say.

I ain't just hungry, but I'm cold, too. I'm so hungry and cold I want to cry. And look like I'm getting colder and colder. My feet done got numb. I try to work my toes, but I don't even feel them. Look like I'm go'n die. Look like I'm go'n stand right here and freeze to death. I think 'bout home. I think 'bout Val and Auntie and Ty and Louis and Walker. It's 'bout twelve o'clock and I know they eating dinner now. I can hear Ty making jokes. He done forgot 'bout getting up early this morning and right now he's probably making jokes. Always trying to make somebody laugh. I wish I was right there listening to him. Give anything in the world if I was home round the fire.

"Come on," Mama says.

We start walking again. My feet so numb I can't hardly feel them. We turn the corner and go on back up the street. The clock on the courthouse starts hitting for twelve.

The sleet's coming down plenty now. They hit the pave and bounce like rice. Oh, Lord; Oh, Lord, I pray. Don't let me die, don't let me die, don't let me die, Lord.

XI

Now I know where we going. We going back of town where the colored people eat. I don't care if I don't eat. I been hungry before. I can stand it. But I can't stand the cold.

I can see we go'n have a long walk. It's 'bout a mile down there. But I don't mind. I know when I get there I'm go'n warm myself. I think I can hold out. My hands numb in my pockets and my feet numb, too, but if I keep moving I can hold out. Just don't stop no more, that's all.

The sky's gray. The sleet keeps on falling. Falling like rain now—plenty, plenty. You can hear it hitting the pave. You can see it bounding. Sometimes it bounces two times 'fore it settles.

We keep on going. We don't say nothing. We just keep on going, keep on going.

I wonder what Mama's thinking. I hope she ain't mad at me. When summer come I'm go'n pick plenty cotton and get her a coat. I'm go'n get her a red one.

I hope they'd make it summer all the time. I'd be glad if it was summer all the time—but it ain't. We got to have winter, too. Lord, I hate the winter. I guess everybody hate the winter.

I don't sniff this time. I get out my handkerchief and wipe my nose. My hands's so cold I can hardly hold the handkerchief.

I think we getting close, but we ain't there yet. I wonder where everybody is. Can't see a soul but us. Look like we the only two people moving round today. Must be too cold for the rest of the people to move round in.

I can hear my teeth. I hope they don't knock together too hard and make that bad one hurt. Lord, that's all I need, for that bad one to start off.

I hear a church bell somewhere. But today ain't Sunday. They must be ringing for a funeral or something.

I wonder what they doing at home. They must be eating. Monsieur Bayonne might be there with his guitar. One day Ty played with Monsieur Bayonne's guitar and broke one of the strings. Monsieur Bayonne was some mad with Ty. He say Ty wasn't go'n ever 'mount to nothing. Ty can go just like Monsieur Bayonne when he ain't there. Ty can make everybody laugh when he starts to mocking Monsieur Bayonne.

I used to like to be with Mama and Daddy. We used to be happy. But they took him in the Army. Now, nobody happy no more. . . . I be glad when Daddy comes home.

Monsieur Bayonne say it wasn't fair for them to take Daddy and give Mama nothing and give us nothing. Auntie say, "Shhh, Etienne. Don't let them hear you talk like that." Monsieur Bayonne say, "It's God truth. What they giving his children? They have to walk three and a half miles to school hot or cold. That's anything to give for a paw? She's got to work in the field rain or shine just to make ends meet. That's anything to give for a husband?" Auntie say, "Shhh, Etienne, Shhh." "Yes, you right," Monsieur Bayonne say. "Best don't say it in front of them now. But one day they go'n find out. One day." "Yes, I suppose so," Auntie say. "Then what, Rose Mary?" Monsieur Bayonne say. "I don't know, Etienne," Auntie say. "All we can do is us job, and leave everything else in His hand. . . ."

We getting closer, now. We getting closer. I can even see the railroad tracks.

We cross the tracks, and now I see the café. Just to get in there, I say. Just to get in there. Already I'm starting to feel a little better.

XII

We go in. Ahh, it's good. I look for the heater; there 'gainst the wall. One of them little brown ones. I just stand there and hold my hands over it. I can't open my hands too wide 'cause they almost froze.

Mama's standing right 'side me. She done unbuttoned her coat. Smoke rises out of the coat, and the coat smells like a wet dog.

I move to the side so Mama can have more room. She opens out her hands and rubs them together. I rub mine together, too, 'cause this keep them from hurting. If you let them warm too fast, they hurt you sure. But if you let them warm just little bit at a time, and you keep rubbing them, they be all right every time.

They got just two more people in the café. A lady back of the counter, and a man on this side the counter. They been watching us ever since we come in.

Mama gets out the handkerchief and count up the money. Both of us know how much money she's got there. Three dollars. No, she ain't got three dollars 'cause she had to pay us way up here. She ain't got but two dollars and a half left. Dollar and a half to get my tooth pulled, and fifty cents for us to go back on, and fifty cents worth of salt meat.

She stirs the money round with her finger. Most of the money is change 'cause I can hear it rubbing together. She stirs it and stirs it. Then she looks at the door. It's still sleeting. I can hear it hitting 'gainst the wall like rice.

"I ain't hungry, Mama," I say.

"Got to pay them something for the heat," she says.

She takes a quarter out the handkerchief and ties the handkerchief up again. She looks over her shoulder at the people, but she still don't move. I hope she don't spend the money. I don't want her spending it on me. I'm hungry, I'm almost starving I'm so hungry, but I don't want her spending the money on me.

She flips the quarter over like she's thinking. She's must be thinking 'bout us walking back home. Lord, I sure don't want walk home. If I thought it'd do any good to say something, I'd say it. But Mama makes up her own mind 'bout things.

She turns 'way from the heater right fast like she better hurry up and spend the quarter 'fore she change her mind. I watch her go toward the counter. The man and the lady look at her. She tells the lady something and the lady walks away. The man keeps on looking at her. Her back's turned to the man and she don't even know he's standing there.

The lady puts some cakes and a glass of milk on the counter. Then she pours up a cup of coffee and sets it 'side the other stuff. Mama pays her for the things and comes on back where I'm standing. She tells me sit down at the table 'gainst the wall.

The milk and the cake's for me; the coffee's for Mama. I eat slow and I look at her. She's looking outside at the sleet. She's looking real sad. I say to myself, I'm go'n make all this up one day. You see, one day, I'm go'n make all this up. I want say it now; I want tell her how I feel right now; but Mama don't like for us to talk like that.

"I can't eat all this," I say.

They ain't got but just three little old cakes there. I'm so hungry right now, the Lord knows I can eat a hundred times three, but I want my mama to have one.

Mama don't even look my way. She knows I'm hungry, she knows I want it. I let it stay there a little while, then I get it and eat it. I eat just on my front teeth, though, 'cause if cake touch that back tooth I know what'll happen. Thank God it ain't hurt me at all today.

After I finish eating I see the man go to the juke box. He drops a nickel in it, then he just stand there a little while looking at the record. Mama tells me keep my eyes in front where they belong. I turn my head like she say, but then I hear the man coming toward us.

"Dance, pretty?" he says.

Mama gets up to dance with him. But 'fore you know it, she done grabbed the little man in the collar and done heaved him 'side the wall. He hit the wall so hard he stop the juke box from playing.

"Some pimp," the lady back of the counter says. "some pimp."

The little man jumps up off the floor and starts toward my mama. 'Fore you know it, Mama done sprung open her knife and she's waiting for him.

"Come on," she says. "Come on. I'll gut you from your neighbo to your throat. Come on."

I go up to the little man to hit him, but Mama makes me come and stand 'side her. The little man looks at me and Mama goes on back to the counter.

"Some pimp," the lady back of the counter says. "Some pimp." She starts laughing and pointing at the little man. "Yes sir, you a pimp, all right. Yes sir-ree."

XIII

"Fasten that coat, let's go," Mama says.

"You don't have to leave," the lady says. Mama don't answer the lady, and we right out in the cold again, I'm warm right now—my hands, my ears, my feet—but I know this ain't go'n last too long. It done sleet so much now you got ice everywhere you look.

We cross the railroad tracks, and soon's we do, I get cold. That wind goes through this little old coat like it ain't even there. I got on a shirt and a sweater under the coat, but that wind don't pay them no mind. I look up and I can see we got a long way to go. I wonder if we go'n make it 'fore I get too cold.

We cross over to walk on the sidewalk. They got just one sidewalk back here, and it's over there.

After we go just a little piece, I smell bread cooking. I look, then I see a baker shop. When we get closer, I can smell it more better. I shut my eyes and make 'tend I'm eating. But I keep them shut too long and I butt up 'gainst a telephone post. Mama grabs me and see if I'm hurt. I ain't bleeding or nothing and she turns me loose.

I can feel I'm getting colder and colder, and I look up to see how far we still got to go. Uptown is 'way up yonder. A half mile more, I reckon. I try to think of something. They say think and you won't get cold. I think of that poem, "Annabel Lee." I ain't been to school in so long—this bad weather—I reckon they done passed "Annabel Lee" by now. But passed it or not, I'm sure Miss Walker go'n make me recite it when I get there. That woman don't never forget nothing. I ain't never seen nobody like that in my life.

I still getting cold. "Annabel Lee" or no "Annabel Lee," I'm still getting cold. But I can see we getting closer. We getting there gradually.

Soon's we turn the corner, I seen a little old white lady up in front of us. She's the only lady on the street. She's all in black and she's got a long black rag over head.

"Stop," she says.

Me and Mama stop and look at her. She must be crazy to be out in all this bad weather. Ain't got but a few other people out there, and all of them's men.

"Y'all done ate?" she says.

"Just finish," Mama says.

"Y'all must be cold then?" she says.

"We headed for the dentist," Mama says. "We'll warm up when we get there."

"What dentist?" the old lady says. "Mr. Bassett?"

"Yes, ma'am," Mama says.

"Come on in," the old lady says. "I'll telephone him and tell him y'all coming."

Me and Mama follow the old lady in the store. It's a little bitty store, and it don't have much in there. The old lady takes off her head rag and folds it up.

"Helena?" somebody calls from the back.

"Yes, Alnest?" the old lady says.

"Did you see them?"

"They're here. Standing beside me."

"Good. Now you can stay inside."

The old lady looks at Mama. Mama's waiting to hear what she brought us in here for. I'm waiting for that, too.

"I saw y'all each time you went by," she says. "I came out to catch you, but you were gone."

"We went back of town," Mama says.

"Did you eat?"

"Yes, ma'am."

The old lady looks at Mama a long time, like she's thinking Mama might just be saying that. Mama looks right back at her. The old lady looks at me to see what I have to say. I don't say nothing. I sure ain't going 'gainst my mama.

"There's food in the kitchen," she says to Mama. "I've been keeping it warm."

Mama turns right around and starts for the door.

"Just a minute," the old lady says. Mama stops. "The boy'll have to work for it. It isn't free."

"We don't take no handout," Mama says.

"I'm not handing out anything," the old lady says. "I need my garbage moved to the front. Ernest has a bad cold and can't go out there."

"James'll move it for you," Mama says.

"Not unless you eat," the old lady says. "I'm old, but I have my pride, too, you know."

Mama can see she ain't go'n beat this old lady down, so she just shakes her head.

"All right," the old lady says. "Come into the kitchen.

She leads the way with that rag in her hand. The kitchen is a little bitty little old thing, too. The table and the stove just 'bout fill it up. They got a little room to the side. Somebody in there laying 'cross the bed—'cause I can see one of his feet. Must be the person she was talking to: Ernest or Alnest—something like that.

"Sit down," the old lady says to Mama. "Not you," she says to me. "You have to move the cans."

"Helena?" the man says in the other room.

"Yes, Alnest?" the old lady says.

"Are you going out there again?"

"I must show the boy where the garbage is, Alnest," the old lady says.

"Keep your shawl over your head," the old man says.

"You don't have to remind me, Alnest. Come, Boy," the old lady says.

We go out in the yard. Little old back yard ain't no bigger than the store or the kitchen. But it can sleet here just like it can sleet in any big back yard. And 'fore you know it, I'm trembling.

"There," the old lady says, pointing to the cans. I pick up one of the cans and set it right back down. The can's so light. I'm go'n see what's inside of it.

"Here," the old lady says. "Leave that can alone."

I look back at her standing there in the door. She's got that black rag wrapped round her shoulders, and she's pointing one of her little old fingers at me.

"Pick it up and carry it to the front," she says. I go by her with the can, and she's looking at me all the time. I'm sure the can's empty. I'm sure she could've carried it herself—maybe both of them at the same time. "Set it on the sidewalk by the door and come back for the other one," she says.

I go and come back, and Mama looks at me when I pass her. I get the other can and take it to the front. It don't feel a bit heavier than that first one. I tell myself I ain't go'n be nobody's fool, and I'm go'n look inside this can to see just what I been hauling. First, I look up the street, then down the street. Nobody coming. Then I look over my shoulder toward the door. That little old lady done slipped up there quiet's a mouse, watching me again. Look like she knowed what I was go'n do.

"Ehh, Lord," she says. "Children, children. Come in here, boy, and go wash your hands."

I follow her in the kitchen. She points toward the bathroom, and I go in there and wash up. Little bitty old bathroom, but it's clean, clean. I don't use any of her towels; I wipe my hands on my pants legs.

When I come back in the kitchen, the old lady done dished up the food. Rice, gravy, meat—and she even got some lettuce and tomato in a saucer. She even got a glass of milk and a piece of cake there, too. It looks so good. I almost start eating 'fore I say my blessing.

"Helena?" the old man says.

"Yes, Alnest?"

"Are they eating?"

"Yes," she says.

"Good," he says. "Now you'll stay inside."

The old lady goes in there where he is and I can hear them talking. I look at Mama. She's eating slow like she's thinking. I wonder what's the matter now. I reckon she's thinking 'bout home.

The old lady comes back in the kitchen.

"I talked to Dr. Bassett's nurse," she says. "Dr. Bassett will take you as soon as you get there."

"Thank you, ma'am," Mama says.

"Perfectly all right," the old lady says. "Which one is it?"

Mama nods toward me. The old lady looks at me real sad. I look sad, too.

"You're not afraid, are you?" she says.

"No, ma'am," I say.

"That's a good boy," the old lady says. "Nothing to be afraid of. Dr. Bassett will not hurt you."

When me and Mama get through eating, we thank the old lady again.

"Helena, are they leaving?" the old man says.

"Yes, Alnest."

"Tell them I say good-bye."

"They can hear you, Alnest."

"Good-bye both mother and son," the old man says. "And may God be with you."

Me and Mama tell the old man good-bye, and we follow the old lady in the front room. Mama opens the door to go out, but she stops and comes back in the store.

"You sell salt meat?" she says.

"Yes."

"Give me two bits worth."

"That isn't very much salt meat," the old lady says.

"That's all I have," Mama says.

The old lady goes back of the counter and cuts a big piece off the chunk. Then she wraps it up and puts it in a paper bag.

"Two bits," she says.

"That looks like awful lot of meat for a quarter," Mama says.

"Two bits," the old lady says. "I've been selling salt meat behind this counter twenty-five years. I think I know what I'm doing."

"You got a scale there," Mama says.

"What?" the old lady says.

"Weigh it," Mama says.

"What?" the old lady says. "Are you telling me how to run my business?"

"Thanks very much for the food," Mama says.

"Just a minute," the old lady says.

"James," Mama says to me. I move toward the door.

"Just one minute, I said," the old lady says.

Me and Mama stop again and look at her. The old lady takes the meat out of the bag and unwraps it and cuts 'bout half of it off. Then she wraps it up again and juggs it back in the bag and gives the bag to Mama. Mama lays the quarter on the counter.

"Your kindness will never be forgotten," she says. "James," she says to me.

We go out, and the old lady comes to the door to look at us. After we go a little piece I look back, and she's still there watching us.

The sleet's coming down heavy, going now, and I turn up my coat collar to keep my neck warm. My mama tells me turn it right back down.

"You not a bum," she says. "You a man." 🖋

SUGGESTIONS FOR WRITING

1. One way to think about this story is to reflect on the relationship of mothers and their sons. Describe and analyze the emotions this son feels for his mother and her responses.

2. Discuss your own experience or observation of mother-son relationships. Compare them with those depicted in *The Sky is Gray*.

3. In this story, what aspects of the characters' behavior have to do with the realities of race? What aspects of their behavior have to do with gender roles and expectations?

4. Narrate an incident from your childhood in which you became aware of racial or ethnic prejudice and conflict.

LOST VOICES

Maxine Hong Kingston

If you grew up in a home in which English was spoken and whose traditions were those of the dominant western European culture, then you probably were the "same person" at home that you were at school. It has only been recently that the American educational system began looking at our culture from a multiple perspective: Not everyone is white, not everyone is Christian, not everyone's ancestors came from Europe, and so on. This shift in attitude makes a big difference to a child whose family is not like the household in a traditional television situation comedy.

A challenge for education today is to reflect the multicultural nature of American society by including the achievements and histories of the many people who live in this country. Although textbooks and classroom activities teach children about who is and who is not important, the playground is often where we learn whether or not we "fit in." Students who are a member of a minority, whether it's ethnic, religious, political, or some other category, may well feel different, set apart, and even excluded.

As a child of Chinese immigrants who ran a laundry in Stockton, California, **Maxine Hong Kingston** *(b. 1940), grew up at a time when almost everyone who was not of white European descent was on the outside looking in. Her autobiography,* The Woman Warrior: Memories of a Childhood Among Ghosts *(1975), examines her experiences as a Chinese-American child growing up in a culture that had no place for her. Of equal importance, Kingston explores the many ways in which she differs from her parents, in particular from her mother. They were raised in China and never fully adapted to the ways of their new country.*

Besides The Woman Warrior, *Kingston has also written* China Men *(1980), which deals with her father's and grandfather's journeys to America, and* Tripmaster Monkey: His Fake Book *(1988), a novel.*

Long ago in China, knot-makers tied string into buttons and frogs, and rope into bell pulls. There was one knot so complicated that it blinded the knot-maker. Finally an emperor outlawed this cruel knot, and the nobles could not order it anymore. If I had lived in China, I would have been an outlaw knot-maker.

Maybe that's why my mother cut my tongue. She pushed my tongue up and sliced the frenum. Or maybe she snipped it with a pair of nail scissors. I don't remember her doing it, only her telling me about it, but all during childhood I felt sorry for the baby whose mother waited with scissors or knife in hand for it to cry—and then, when its mouth was wide open like a baby bird's, cut. The Chinese say "a ready tongue is an evil."

I used to curl up my tongue in front of the mirror and tauten my frenum into a white line, itself as thin as a razor blade. I saw no scars in my mouth. I thought perhaps I had had two frena, and she had cut one. I made other children open their mouths so I could compare theirs to mine. I saw perfect pink membranes stretching into precise edges that looked easy enough to cut. Sometimes I felt very proud that my mother committed such a powerful act upon me. At other times I was terrified—the first thing my mother did when she saw me was to cut my tongue.

"Why did you do that to me, Mother?"

"I told you."

"Tell me again."

"I cut it so that you would not be tongue-tied. Your tongue would be able to move in any language. You'll be able to speak languages that are completely different from one another. You'll be able to pronounce anything. Your frenum looked too tight to do those things, so I cut it."

"But isn't 'a ready tongue an evil'?"

"Things are different in this ghost country."

"Did it hurt me? Did I cry and bleed?"

"I don't remember. Probably."

She didn't cut the other children's. When I asked cousins and other Chinese children whether their mothers had cut their tongues loose, they said, "What?"

"Why didn't you cut my brothers' and sisters' tongues?"

"They didn't need it."

"Why not? Were theirs longer than mine"

"Why don't you quit blabbering and get to work?"

If my mother was not lying she should have cut more, scraped away the rest of the frenum skin, because I have a terrible time talking. Or she should not have cut at all, tampering with my speech. When I went to kindergarten and had to speak English for the first time, I became silent. A dumbness—a shame—still cracks my voice in two, even when I want to say "hello" casually, or ask an easy question in front of the check-out counter, or ask directions of a bus driver. I stand frozen, or I hold up the line with the complete, grammatical sentence that comes squeaking out at impossible length. "What did you say?" says the cab driver, or "Speak up," so I have to perform again, only weaker the second time. A telephone call makes my throat bleed and takes up that day's courage. It spoils my day with self-disgust when I hear my broken voice come skittering out into the open. It makes people wince to hear it. I'm getting better, though. Recently I asked the postman for special-issue stamps; I've waited since childhood for postmen to give me some of their own accord. I am making progress, a little every day.

My silence was thickest—total—during the three years that I covered my school paintings with black paint. I painted layers of black over houses and flowers and suns, and when I drew on the blackboard, I put a layer of chalk on top. I was making a stage curtain, and it was the moment before the curtain parted or rose. The teachers called my parents to school, and I saw they had been saving my pictures, curling and cracking, all alike and black. The teachers pointed to the pictures and looked serious, talked seriously too, but my parents did not understand English. ("The parents and teachers of criminals were executed," said my father.) My parents took the pictures home. I spread them out (so black and full of possibilities) and pretended the curtains were swinging open, flying up, one after another, sunlight underneath, mighty operas.

During the first silent year I spoke to no one at school, did not ask before going to the lavatory, and flunked kindergarten. My sister also said nothing for three years, silent in the playground and silent at lunch. There were other quiet Chinese girls not of our family, but most of them got over it sooner than we did. I enjoyed the silence. At first it did not occur to me I was supposed to talk or to pass kindergarten. I talked at home and to one or two of the Chinese kids in class. I made motions and even made some jokes. I drank out of a toy saucer when the water spilled out of the cup, and everybody laughed, pointing at me, so I did it some more. I didn't know that American's don't drink out of saucers.

I liked the Negro students (Black Ghosts) best because they laughed the loudest and talked to me as if I were a daring talker too. One of the Negro girls had her mother coil braids over her ears Shanghai-style like mine; we were Shanghai twins except that she was covered with black like my paintings. Two Negro kids enrolled in Chinese school, and the teachers gave them Chinese names. Some Negro kids walked me to school and home, protecting me from the Japanese kids, who hit me and chased me and stuck gum in my ears. The Japanese kids were noisy and tough. They appeared one day in kindergarten, released from concentration camp, which was a tic-tac-toe mark, like barbed wire, on the map.

It was when I found out I had to talk that school became a misery, that the silence became a misery. I did not speak and felt bad each time that I did not speak. I read aloud in first grade, though, and heard the barest whisper with little squeaks come out of my throat. "Louder," said the teacher, who scared the voice away again. The other Chinese girls did not talk either, so I knew the silence had to do with being a Chinese girl.

Reading out loud was easier than speaking because we did not have to make up what to say, but I stopped often, and the teacher would think I'd gone quiet again. I could not understand "I." The Chinese "I" has seven strokes, intricacies. How could the American "I," assuredly wearing a hat like the Chinese, have only three strokes, the middle so straight? Was it out of politeness that this writer left off strokes the way a Chinese has to write her own name small and crooked? No, it was not politeness; "I" is a capital and "you" is lower-case. I stared at that middle line and waited so long for its black center to resolve into tight strokes and dots that I forgot to pronounce it. The other troublesome word was "here," no strong consonant to hang on to, and so flat, when "here" is two mountainous ideographs. The teacher, who had already told me every day how to read "I" and "here," put me in the low corner under the stairs again, where the noisy boys usually sat.

When my second grade class did a play, the whole class went to the auditorium except the Chinese girls. The teacher, lovely and Hawaiian, should have understood about us, but instead left us behind in the classroom. Our voices were too soft or nonexistent, and our parents never signed the permission slips anyway. They never signed anything unnecessary. We opened the door a crack and peeked out, but closed it again quickly. One of us (not me) won every spelling bee, though.

I remember telling the Hawaiian teacher, "We Chinese can't sing 'land where our fathers died.'" She argued with me about politics, while I meant because of curses. But how can I have that memory when I couldn't talk? My mother says that we, like the ghosts, have no memories.

After American school, we picked up our cigar boxes, in which we had arranged books, brushes, and an inkbox neatly, and went to Chinese school, from 5:00 to 7:30 P.M. There we chanted together, voices rising and falling, loud and soft, some boys shouting, everybody reading together, reciting together and not alone with one voice. When we had a memorization test, the teacher let each of us come to his desk and say the lesson to him privately, while the rest of the class practiced copying or tracing. Most of the teachers were men. The boys who were so well behaved in the American school played tricks on them and talked back to them. The girls were not mute. They screamed and yelled during recess, when there were no rules; they had fistfights. Nobody was afraid of children hurting themselves or of children hurting school property. The glass doors to the red and green balconies with the gold joy symbols were left wide open so that we could run out and climb the fire escapes. We played capture-the- flag in the auditorium, where Sun Yat-sen and Chiang Kai-shek's pictures hung at the back of the stage, the Chinese flag on their left and the American flag on their right. We climbed the teak ceremonial chairs and made flying leaps off the stage. One flag headquarters was behind the glass door and the other on stage right. Our feet drummed on the hollow stage. During recess the teachers locked themselves up in their office with the shelves of books, copybooks, inks from China. They drank tea and warmed their hands at a stove. There was no play supervision. At recess we had the school to ourselves, and also we could roam as far as we could go—downtown, Chinatown stores, home—as long as we returned before the bell rang.

At exactly 7:30 the teacher again picked up the brass bell that sat on his desk and swung it over our heads, while we charged down the stairs, our cheering magnified in the stairwell. Nobody had to line up.

Not all of the children who were silent at American school found voice at Chinese school. One new teacher said each of us had to get up and recite in front of the class, who was to listen. My sister and I had memorized the lesson perfectly. We said it to each other at home, one chanting, one listening. The teacher called on my sister to recite first. It was the first time a teacher had called on the second-born to go first. My sister was scared. She glanced at me and looked away; I looked down at my desk. I hoped that she could do it because if she could, then I would have to. She opened her mouth and a voice came out that wasn't a whisper, but it wasn't a proper voice either. I hoped that she would not cry, fear breaking up her voice like twigs underfoot. She sounded as if she were trying to sing though weeping and strangling. She did not pause or stop to end the embarrassment. She kept going until she said the last word, and then she sat down. When it was my turn, the same voice came out, a crippled animal running on broken legs. You could hear splinters in my voice, bones rubbing jagged against one another. I was loud, though. I was glad I didn't whisper. There was one little girl who whispered.

You can't entrust your voice to the Chinese, either; they want to capture your voice for their own use. They want to fix up your tongue to speak for them. "How much less can you sell it for?" we have to say. Talk the Sales Ghosts down. Make them take a loss.

We were working at the laundry when a delivery boy came from the Rexall drugstore around the corner. He had a pale blue box of pills, but nobody was sick. Reading the label we saw that it belonged to another Chinese family, Crazy Mary's family. "Not ours," said my father. He pointed out the name to the Delivery Ghost, who took the pills back. My mother muttered for an hour, and then her anger boiled over. "That ghost! That dead ghost! How dare he come to the wrong house?" She could not concentrate on her marking and pressing. "A mistake! Huh!" I was getting angry myself. She fumed. She made her press crash and hiss. "Revenge. We've got to avenge this wrong on our future, on our health, and on our lives. Nobody's going to sicken my children and get away with it." We brothers and sisters did not look at one another. She would do something awful, something embarrassing. She'd already been hinting that during the next eclipse we slam pot lids together to scare the frog from swallowing the moon. (The word for "eclipse" is *frog-swallowing-the-moon*.) When we had not banged lids at the last eclipse and the shadow kept receding anyway, she'd said, "The villagers must be banging and clanging very loudly back home in China."

("On the other side of the world, they aren't having an eclipse, Mama. That's just a shadow the earth makes when it comes between the moon and the sun."

"You're always believing what those Ghost Teachers tell you. Look at the size of the jaws!")

"Aha!" she yelled. "You! The biggest." She was pointing at me. "You go to the drugstore."

"What do you want me to buy, Mother?" I said.

"Buy nothing. Don't bring one cent. Go and make them stop the curse."

"I don't want to go. I don't know how to do that. There are no such things as curses. They'll think I'm crazy."

"If you don't go, I'm holding you responsible for bringing a plague on this family."

"What am I supposed to do when I get there?" I said, sullen, trapped. "Do I say, 'Your delivery boy made a wrong delivery'?"

"They know he made a wrong delivery. I want you to make them rectify their crime."

I felt sick already. She'd make me swing stinky censers around the counter, at the druggist, at the customers. Throw dog blood on the druggist. I couldn't stand her plans.

"You get reparation candy," she said. "You say, 'You have tainted my house with sick medicine and must remove the curse with sweetness.' He'll understand."

"He didn't do it on purpose. And no, he won't, Mother. They don't understand stuff like that. I won't be able to say it right. He'll call us beggars."

"You just translate." She searched me to make sure I wasn't hiding any money. I was sneaky and bad enough to buy the candy and come back pretending it was a free gift.

"Mymotherseztagimmesomecandy," I said to the druggist. Be cute and small. No one hurts the cute and small.

"What? Speak up. Speak English," he said, big in his white druggist coat.

"Tatatagimme somecandy."

The druggist leaned way over the counter and frowned. "Some free candy," I said. "Sample candy."

"We don't give sample candy, young lady," he said.

"My mother said you have to give us candy. She said that is the way the Chinese do it."

"What?"

"That is the way the Chinese do it."

"Do what?"

"Do things." I felt the weight and immensity of things impossible to explain to the druggist.

"Can I give you some money?" he asked.

"No, we want candy."

He reached into a jar and gave me a handful of lollipops. He gave us candy all year round, year after year, every time we went into the drugstore. When different druggists or clerks waited on us, they also gave us candy. They had talked us over. They gave us Halloween candy in December, Christmas candy around Valentine's day, candy hearts at Easter, and Easter eggs at Halloween. "See?" said our mother. "They understand. You kids just aren't very brave." But I knew they did not understand. They thought we were beggars without a home who lived in back of the laundry. They felt sorry for us. I did not eat their candy. I did not go inside the drugstore or walk past it unless my parents forced me to. Whenever we had a prescription filled, the druggist put candy in the medicine bag. This is what Chinese druggists normally do, except they give raisins. My mother thought she taught the Druggist Ghosts a lesson in good manners (which is the same word as "traditions").

My mouth went permanently crooked with effort, turned down on the left side and straight on the right. How strange that the emigrant villagers are shouters, hollering face to face. My father asks, "Why is it I can hear Chinese from blocks away? Is it that I understand the language? Or is it they talk loud?" They turn the radio up full blast to hear the operas, which do not seem to hurt their ears. And they yell over the singers that wail over the drums, everybody talking at once, big arm gestures, spit flying. You can see the disgust on American faces looking at women like that. It isn't just the loudness. It is the way Chinese sounds, chingchong ugly, to American ears, not beautiful like Japanese sayonara words with the consonants and vowels as regular as Italian. We make guttural peasant noise and have Ton Duc Thang names you can't remember. And the Chinese can't hear Americans at all; the language is too soft and western music unhearable. I've watched a Chinese audience laugh, visit, talk-story, and holler during a piano recital, as if the musician could not hear them. A Chinese-American, somebody's son, was playing Chopin, which has no punctuation, no cymbals, no gongs. Chinese piano music is five black keys. Normal Chinese women's voices are strong and bossy. We American-Chinese girls had to whisper to make ourselves American-feminine. Apparently we whispered even more softly than the Americans. Once a year the teachers referred my sister and me to speech therapy, but our voices would straighten out, unpredictably normal, for the therapists. Some of us gave up, shook our heads, and said nothing, not one word. Some of us could not even shake our heads. At times shaking my head no is more self-assertion than I can manage. Most of us eventually found some voice, however faltering. We invented an American-feminine speaking personality, except for that one girl who could not speak up even in Chinese school.

She was a year older than I and was in my class for twelve years. During all those years she read aloud but would not talk. Her older sister was usually beside her; their parents kept the older daughter back to protect the younger one. They were six and seven years old when they began school. Although I had flunked kindergarten, I was the same age as most other students in our class; my parents had probably lied about my age, so I had had a head start and came out even. My younger sister was in the class below me; we were normal ages and normally separated. The parents of the quiet girl, on the other hand, protected both daughters. When it sprinkled, they kept them home from school. The girls did not work for a living the way we did. But in other ways we were the same.

We were similar in sports. We held the bat on our shoulders until we walked to first base. (You got a strike only when you actually struck at the ball.) Sometimes the pitcher wouldn't bother to throw to us. "Automatic walk," the other children would call, sending us on our way. By fourth or fifth grade, though, some of us would try to hit the ball. "Easy out," the other kids would say. I hit the ball a couple of times. Baseball was nice in that there was a definite spot to run to after hitting the ball. Basketball confused me because when I caught the ball I didn't know whom to throw it to. "Me. Me," the kids would be yelling. "Over here." Suddenly it would occur to me I hadn't memorized which ghosts were on my team and which were on the other. When the kids said "Automatic walk," the girl who was quieter than I kneeled with one end of the bat in each hand and placed it carefully on the plate. Then she dusted her hands as she walked to first base, where she rubbed her hands softly, fingers spread. She always got tagged out before second base. She would whisper-read but not talk. Her whisper was as soft as if she had no muscles. She seemed to be breathing from a distance. I heard no anger or tension.

I joined in at lunchtime when the other students, the Chinese too, talked about whether or not she was mute, although obviously she was not if she could read aloud. People told how *they* had tried *their* best to be friendly. *They* said hello, but if she refused to answer, well, they didn't see why they had to say hello anymore. She had no friends of her own but followed her sister everywhere, although people and she herself probably thought I was her friend. I also followed her sister about, who was fairly normal. She was almost two years older and read more than anyone else.

I hated the younger sister, the quiet one. I hated her when she was the last chosen for her team and I, the last chosen for my team. I hated her for her

China doll hair cut. I hated her at music time for the wheezes that came out of her plastic flute.

One afternoon in the sixth grade (that year I was arrogant with talk, not knowing there were going to be high school dances and college seminars to set me back), I and my little sister and the quiet girl and her big sister stayed late after school for some reason. The cement was cooling, and the tetherball poles made shadows across the gravel. The hooks at the rope ends were clinking against the poles. We shouldn't have been so late; there was laundry work to do and Chinese school to get to by 5:00. The last time we had stayed late, my mother had phoned the police and told them we had been kidnapped by bandits. The radio stations broadcast our descriptions. I had to get home before she did that again. But sometimes if you loitered long enough in the schoolyard, the other children would have gone home and you could play with the equipment before the office took it away. We were chasing one another through the playground and in and out of the basement, where the playroom and lavatory were. During air raid drills (it was during the Korean War, which you knew about because every day the front page of the newspaper printed a map of Korea with the top part red and going up and down like a window shade), we curled up in this basement. Now everyone was gone. The playroom was army green and had nothing in it but a long trough with drinking spigots in rows. Pipes across the ceiling led to the drinking fountains and to the toilets in the next room. When someone flushed you could hear the water and other matter, which the children named, running inside the big pipe above the drinking spigots. There was one playroom for girls next to the girls' lavatory and one playroom for boys next to the boys' lavatory. The stalls were open and the toilets had no lids, by which we knew that ghosts have no sense of shame or privacy.

Inside the playroom the lightbulbs in cages had already been turned off. Daylight came in x-patterns through the caging at the windows. I looked out and, seeing no one in the schoolyard, ran outside to climb the fire escape upside down, hanging on to the metal stairs with fingers and toes.

I did a flip off the fire escape and ran across the schoolyard. The day was a great eye, and it was not paying much attention to me now. I could disappear with the sun; I could turn quickly sideways and slip into a different world. It seemed I could run faster at this time, and by evening I would be able to fly. As the afternoon wore on we could run into the forbidden place—the boys' big yard, the boys' playroom. We could go into the boys' lavatory and look at the urinals. The only time during school hours I had crossed the boys' yard was when a flatbed truck with a giant thing covered with canvas and tied down with ropes had parked across the street. The children had told one another that it was a gorilla in captivity; we couldn't decide whether the sign said "Trail of the Gorilla" or "Trial of the Gorilla." The thing was as big as a house. The teachers couldn't stop us from hysterically rushing to the fence and clinging to the wire mesh. Now I ran across the boys' yard clear to the Cyclone fence and thought about the hair that I had seen sticking out of the canvas. It was going to be summer soon, so you could feel that freedom coming on too.

I ran back to the girls' yard, and there was the quiet sister all by herself. I ran past her, and she followed me into the girls' lavatory. My footsteps rang hard against cement and tile because of the taps I had nailed into my shoes. Her footsteps were soft, padding after me. There was no one in the lavatory but the two of us. I ran all around the rows of twenty-five open stalls to make sure of that. No sisters. I think we must have been playing hide-and-go-seek. She was not good at hiding by herself and usually followed her sister; they'd hide in the same place. They must have gotten separated. In this growing twilight, a child could hide and never be found.

I stopped abruptly in front of the sinks, and she came running toward me before she could stop herself, so that she almost collided with me. I walked closer. She backed away, puzzlement, then alarm in her eyes.

"You're going to talk," I said, my voice steady and normal, as it is talking to the familiar, the weak, and the small. "I am going to make you talk, you sissy-girl." She stopped backing away and stood fixed.

I looked into her face so I could hate it close up. She wore black bangs, and her cheeks were pink and white. She was baby soft. I thought that I could put my thumb on her nose and push it bonelessly in, indent her face. I could poke dimples into her cheeks. I could work her face around like dough. She stood still, and I did not want to look at her face anymore; I hated fragility. I walked around her, looked her up and down the way the Mexican and Negro girls did when they fought, so tough. I hated her weak neck, the way it did not support her head but let it droop; her head would fall backward. I stared at the curve of her nape. I wished I was able to see what my own neck looked like from the back and sides. I hoped it did not look like hers; I wanted a stout neck. I grew my hair long to hide it in case it was a flower-stem neck. I walked around to the front of her to hate her face some more.

I reached up and took the fatty part of her cheek, not dough, but meat, between my thumb and finger. This close, and I saw no pores. "Talk," I said. "Are you going to talk?" Her skin was fleshy, like squid out of which the glassy blades of bones had been pulled. I wanted tough skin, hard brown skin. I had callused my hands; I had scratched dirt to blacken the nails, which I cut straight across to make stubby fingers. I gave her face a squeeze. "Talk." When I let go, the pink rushed back into my white thumbprint on her skin. I walked around to her side. "Talk!" I shouted into the side of her head. Her straight hair hung, the same all these years, no ringlets or braids or permanents. I squeezed her other cheek. "Are you? Huh? Are you going to talk?" She tried to shake her head, but I had hold of her face. She had no muscles to jerk away. Her skin seemed to stretch. I let go in horror. What if it came away in my hand? "No, huh?" I said, rubbing the touch of her off my fingers. "Say 'No,' then," I said. I gave her another pinch and a twist. "Say 'No.'" She shook her head, her straight hair turning with her head, not swinging side to side like the pretty girls'. She was so neat. Her neatness bothered me. I hated the way she folded the wax paper from her lunch; she did not wad her brown paper bag and her school papers. I hated her clothes—the blue pastel cardigan, the white blouse with the collar that lay flat over the cardigan, the homemade flat, cotton skirt she wore when everybody else was wearing flared skirts. I hated pastels; I would wear black always. I squeezed again, harder, even though her cheek had a weak rubbery feeling I did not like. I squeezed one cheek, then the other, back and forth until the tears ran out of her eyes as if I had pulled them out. "Stop crying," I said, but although she habitually followed me around, she did not obey. Her eyes dripped; her nose dripped. She wiped her eyes with her papery fingers. The skin on her hands and arms seemed powdery-dry, like tracing paper, onion skin. I hated her fingers. I could snap them like breadsticks. I pushed her hands down. "Say 'Hi,' " I said. " 'Hi.' Like that. Say your name. Go ahead. Say it. Or are you stupid? You're so stupid, you don't know your own name, is that it? When I say, 'What's your name?' you just blurt it out, O.K.? What's your name?" Last year the whole class had laughed at a boy who couldn't fill out a form because he didn't know his father's name. The teacher sighed, exasperated, and was very sarcastic, "Don't you notice things? What does your mother call him?" she said. The class laughed at how dumb he was not to notice things. "She calls him father of me," he said. Even we laughed, although we knew that his mother did not call his father by name, and a son does not know his father's name. We laughed and were relieved that our parents had had the foresight to tell us some names we could give the teachers. "If you're not stupid," I said to the quiet girl, "what's your name?" She shook her head, and some hair caught in the tears; wet black hair stuck to the side of the pink and white face. I reached up (she was taller than I) and took a strand of hair. I pulled it. "Well, then, let's honk your hair," I said. "Honk. Honk." Then I pulled the other side—"ho-o-n-k"— a long pull; "ho-o-n-n-nk"—a longer pull. I could see her little white ears, like white cutworms curled underneath the hair. "Talk!" I yelled into each cut-worm.

I looked right at her. "I know you talk," I said. "I've heard you." Her eye-brows flew up. Something in those black eyes was startled, and I pursued it. "I was walking past your house when you didn't know I was there. I heard you yell in English and in Chinese. You weren't just talking. You were shouting. I heard you shout. You were saying, 'Where are you?' Say that again. Go ahead, just the way you did at home." I yanked harder on the hair, but steadily, not jerking. I did not want to pull it out. "Go ahead. Say, 'Where are you?' Say it loud enough for your sister to come. Call her. Make her come help you. Call her name. I'll stop if she comes. So call. Go ahead."

She shook her head, her mouth curved down, crying. I could see her tiny white teeth, baby teeth. I wanted to grow big strong yellow teeth. "You do have a tongue," I said. "So use it." I pulled the hair at her temples, pulled the tears out of her eyes. "Say, 'Ow,' " I said. "Just 'Ow.' Say, 'Let go.' Go ahead. Say it. I'll honk you again if you don't say, 'Let me alone.' Say, 'Leave me alone,' and I'll let you go. I will. I'll let go if you say it. You can stop this anytime you want to, you know. All you have to do is tell me to stop. Just say 'Stop.' You're just asking for it, aren't you? You're just asking for another honk. Well then, I'll have to give you another honk. Say, 'Stop.' " But she didn't. I had to pull again and again.

Sounds did come out of her mouth, sobs, chokes, noises that were almost words. Snot ran out of her nose. She tried to wipe it on her hands, but there was too much of it. She used her sleeve. "You're disgusting," I told her. "Look at you, snot streaming down your nose, and you won't say a word to stop it. You're such a nothing." I moved behind her and pulled the hair growing out of her weak neck. I let go. I stood silent for a long time. Then I screamed, "Talk!" I would scare the words out of her. If she had had little bound feet, the toes twisted under the balls, I would have jumped up and landed on them—crunch!—stomped on them with my iron shoes. She cried hard, sobbing aloud, "Cry, 'Mama,'" I said. "Come on. Cry, 'Mama.' Say, 'Stop it.'"

I put my finger on her pointed chin. "I don't like you. I don't like the weak little toots you make on your flute. Wheeze. Wheeze. I don't like the way you don't swing at the ball. I don't like the way you're the last one chosen. I don't like the way you can't make a fist for tetherball. Why don't you make a fist? Come on. Get tough. Come on. Throw fists." I pushed at her long hands; they swung limply at her sides. Her fingers were so long, I thought maybe they had an extra joint. They couldn't possibly make fists like other people's. "Make a fist," I said. "Come on. Just fold those fingers up; fingers on the inside, thumbs on the outside. Say something. Honk me back. You're so tall, and you let me pick on you.

"Would you like a hanky? I can't get you one with embroidery on it or crocheting along the edges, but I'll get you some toilet paper if you tell me to. Go ahead. Ask me. I'll get it for you if you ask." She did not stop crying. "Why don't you scream, 'Help'?" I suggested. "Say, 'Help.' Go ahead." She cried on. "O.K. O.K. Don't talk. Just scream and I'll let you go. Won't that feel good? Go ahead. Like this." I screamed, not too loudly. My voice hit the tile and rang it as if I had thrown a rock at it. The stalls opened wider and the toilets wider and darker. Shadows leaned at angles I had not seen before. It was very late. Maybe a janitor had locked me in with this girl for the night. Her black eyes blinked and stared, blinked and stared. I felt dizzy from hunger. We had been in this lavatory together forever. My mother would call the police again if I didn't bring my sister home soon. "I'll let you go if you say just one word," I said. "You can even say, 'a' or 'the,' and I'll let you go. Come on. Please." She didn't shake her head anymore, only cried steadily, so much water coming out of her. I could see the two duct holes where the tears welled out. Quarts of tears but no words. I grabbed her by the shoulder. I could feel bones. The light was coming in queerly through the frosted glass with the chicken wire embedded in it. Her crying was like an animal's—a seal's—and it echoed around the basement. "Do you want to stay here all night?" I asked. "Your mother is wondering what happened to her baby. You wouldn't want to have her mad at you. You'd better say something." I shook her shoulder. I pulled her again. I squeezed her face. "Come on! Talk! Talk! Talk!" She didn't seem to feel it anymore when I pulled her hair. "There's nobody here but you and me. This isn't a classroom or a playground or a crowd. I'm just one person. You can talk in front of one person. Don't make me pull harder and harder until you talk." But her hair seemed to stretch; she did not say a word. "I'm going to pull harder. Don't make me pull anymore, or your hair will come out and you're going to be bald. Do you want to be bald? You don't want to be bald, do you?"

Far away, coming from the edge of town, I heard whistles blow. The cannery was changing shifts, letting out the afternoon people, and still we were here at school. It was a sad sound—work done. The air was lonelier after the sound died.

"Why won't you talk?" I started to cry. What if I couldn't stop and everyone would want to know what happened? "Now look what you've done," I scolded. "You're going to pay for this. I want to know why. And you're going to tell me why. You don't see I'm trying to help you out, do you? Do you want to be like this, dumb (do you know what dumb means?), your whole life? Don't you ever want to be a cheerleader? Or a pompon girl? What are you going to do for a living? Yeah, you're going to have to work because you can't be a housewife. Somebody has to marry you before you can be a housewife. And you, you are a plant. Do you know that? That's all you are if you don't talk. If you don't talk, you can't have a personality. You'll have no personality and no hair. You've got to let people know you have a personality and a brain. You think somebody is going to take care of you all your stupid life? You think you'll always have your big sister? You think somebody's going to marry you, is that it? Well, you're not the type that gets dates, let alone gets married. Nobody's going to notice you. And you have to talk for interviews, speak right up in front of the boss. Don't you know that? You're so dumb. Why do I waste my time on you?" Sniffling and snorting, I couldn't stop crying and talking at the same time. I kept wiping my nose on my arm, my sweater lost somewhere (probably not worn because my mother said to wear a sweater). It seemed as if I had spent my life in that basement, doing the worst thing I had yet done to another person. "I'm doing this for your own good," I said. "Don't you dare tell anyone I've been bad to you. Talk. Please talk."

I was getting dizzy from the air I was gulping. Her sobs and my sobs were bouncing wildly off the tile, sometimes together, sometimes alternating. "I don't understand why you won't say just one word," I cried, clenching my teeth. My knees were shaking, and I hung on to her hair to stand up. Another time I'd stayed too late, I had had to walk around two Negro kids who were bonking each other's head on the concrete. I went back later to see if the concrete had cracks in it. "Look. I'll give you something if you talk. I'll give you my pencil box. I'll buy you some candy. O.K.? What do you want? Tell me. Just say it, and I'll give it to you. Just say, 'Yes,' or, 'O.K.,' or, 'Baby Ruth.' " But she didn't want anything.

I had stopped pinching her cheek because I did not like the feel of her skin. I would go crazy if it came away in my hands. "I skinned her," I would have to confess.

Suddenly I heard footsteps hurrying through the basement, and her sister ran into the lavatory calling her name. "Oh, there you are," I said. "We've been waiting for you. I was only trying to teach her to talk. She wouldn't cooperate, though." Her sister went into one of the stalls and got handfuls of toilet paper and wiped her off. Then we found my sister, and we walked home together. "Your family really ought to force her to speak," I advised all the way home. "You mustn't pamper her."

The world is sometimes just, and I spent the next eighteen months sick in bed with a mysterious illness. There was no pain and no symptoms, though the middle line in my left palm broke in two. Instead of starting junior high school, I lived like the Victorian recluses I read about. I had a rented hospital bed in the living room, where I watched soap operas on t.v., and my family cranked me up and down. I saw no one but my family, who took good care of me. I could have no visitors, no other relatives, no villagers. My bed was against the west window, and I watched the seasons change the peach tree. I had a bell to ring for help. I used a bedpan. It was the best year and a half of my life. Nothing happened.

But one day my mother, the doctor, said, "You're ready to get up today. It's time to get up and go to school." I walked about outside to get my legs working, leaning on a staff I cut from the peach tree. The sky and trees, the sun were immense—no longer framed by a window, no longer grayed with a fly screen. I sat down on the sidewalk in amazement—the night, the stars. But at school I had to figure out again how to talk. I met the poor girl I had tormented. She had not changed. She wore the same clothes, hair cut, and manner as when we were in elementary school, no make-up on the pink and white face, while the other Asian girls were starting to tape their eyelids. She continued to be able to read aloud. But there was hardly any reading aloud anymore, less and less as we got into high school.

I was wrong about nobody taking care of her. Her sister became a clerk-typist and stayed unmarried. They lived with their mother and father. She did not have to leave the house except to go to the movies. She was supported. She was protected by her family, as they would normally have done in China if they could have afforded it, not sent off to school with strangers, ghosts, boys. ✐

SUGGESTIONS FOR WRITING

1. Examine why Kingston behaved as she did to the "shy" sister. In what ways is this other girl like Kingston herself? What contributed to making both children silent at school?

2. Some children are treated as outcasts by their peers and are never given a chance to become part of the group. Describe one such outcast in your school. Analyze what it was about that person that make him or her "different." How did the others in your school treat that person? How did this treatment cause the outsider to behave? Describe your reactions to this person.

3. If you come from a home whose traditions or language differ from the predominant ones where you grew up, describe the ways in which your family differed—economically, ethnically, religiously and so forth—and how that made you feel outside of your home. Describe how your classmates treated you. What did you learn about your cultural group in the lessons at school?

IMPRESSIONS OF AN INDIAN CHILDHOOD

Zitkala-Sä
(Gertrude Simmons Bonnin)

Zitkala-Sä, *also known as Gertrude Simmons Bonnin and Red Bird (1876–1938), was the child of a Sioux mother and a white father. Raised as a Sioux until she was eight, Zitkala-Sä was sent to a Quaker school for Indians in Wabash, Indiana. As an adult, she returned to work on the Sioux Standing Rock Reservation. With her husband, she spent much of her life working for Indian rights and to preserve the heritage of Native American peoples. Zitkala-Sä lectured and published on issues of concern to Native Americans, including articles and two books:* Old Indian Legends *(1901) and* American Indian Stories *(1921).*

Zitkala-Sä's story reveals the fascination of faraway places for those who have not travelled there, particularly when visitors from another part of the world capture their imagination with stories of what life there is like. Of course, as naive children we remain unaware of the double-edged nature of a foreign culture: Not only does it have marvels, but it also differs from what we are used to. The distant and therefore romantic place exerts an attraction that is sometimes hard to resist.

In the following selection, Zitkala-Sä describes her and her mother's reactions to American missionaries, who can send her East to learn their ways.

The first turning away from the easy, natural flow of my life occurred in an early spring. It was in my eighth year; in the month of March, I afterward learned. At this age I knew but one language, and that was my mother's native tongue.

From some of my playmates I heard that two paleface missionaries were in our village. They were from that class of white men who wore big hats and carried large hearts, they said. Running direct to my mother, I began to question her why these two strangers were among us. She told me, after I had teased much, that they had come to take away Indian boys and girls to the East. My mother did not seem to want me to talk about them. But in a day or two, I gleaned many wonderful stories from my playfellows concerning the strangers.

"Mother, my friend Judéwin is going home with the missionaries. She is going to a more beautiful country than ours; the palefaces told her so!" I said wistfully, wishing in my heart that I too might go.

Mother sat in a chair, and I was hanging on her knee. Within the last two seasons my big brother Dawée had returned from a three years' education in the East, and his coming back influenced my mother to take a farther step from her native way of living. First it was a change from the buffalo skin to the white man's canvas that covered our wigwam. Now she had given up her wigwam of slender poles, to live, a foreigner, in a home of clumsy logs.

"Yes, my child, several others besides Judéwin are going away with the pale-faces. Your brother said the missionaries had inquired about his little sister," she said, watching my face very closely.

My heart thumped so hard against my breast, I wondered if she could hear it.

"Did he tell them to take me, mother?" I asked, fearing lest Dawée had forbidden the palefaces to see me, and that my hope of going to the Wonderland would be entirely blighted.

With a sad, slow smile, she answered: "There! I knew you were wishing to go, because Judéwin has filled your ears with the white men's lies. Don't believe a word they say! Their words are sweet, but, my child, their deeds are bitter. You will cry for me, but they will not even sooth you. Stay with me, my little one! Your brother Dawée says that going East, away from your mother, is too hard an experience for his baby sister."

Thus my mother discouraged my curiosity about the lands beyond our eastern horizon; for it was not yet an ambition for Letters that was stirring me. But on the following day the missionaries did come to our very house. I spied them coming up the footpath leading to our cottage. A third man was with them, but he was not my brother Dawée. It was another, a young interpreter, a paleface who had a smattering of the Indian language. I was ready to run out to meet them, but I did not dare to displease my mother. With great glee, I jumped up and down on our ground floor. I begged my mother to open the door, that they would be sure to come to us. Alas! They came, they saw, and they conquered!

Judéwin had told me of the great tree where grew red, red apples; and how we could reach out hands and pick all the red apples we could eat. I had never seen apple trees. I had never tasted more than a dozen red apples in my life; and when I heard of the orchards of the East, I was eager to roam among them. The missionaries smiled into my eyes, and patted my head. I wondered how mother could say such hard words against them.

"Mother, ask them if little girls may have all the red apples they want, when they go East," I whispered aloud, in my excitement.

The interpreter heard me, and answered: "Yes, little girl, the nice red apples are for those who pick them; and you will have a ride on the iron horse if you go with these good people."

I had never seen a train, and he knew it.

"Mother, I'm going East! I like big red apples, and I want to ride on the iron horse! Mother, say yes!" I pleaded.

My mother said nothing. The missionaries waited in silence; and my eyes began to blur with tears, though I struggled to choke them back. The corners of my mouth twitched, and my mother saw me.

"I am not ready to give you any word," she said to them. "To-morrow I shall send you my answer by my son."

With this they left us. Alone with my mother, I yielded to my tears, and cried aloud, shaking my head so as not to hear what she was saying to me. This was the first time I had ever been so unwilling to give up my own desire that I refused to hearken to my mother's voice.

There was a solemn silence in our home that night. Before I went to bed I begged the Great Spirit to make my mother willing I should go with the missionaries.

The next morning came, and my mother called me to her side. "My daughter, do you still persist in wishing to leave your mother?" she asked.

"Oh, mother, it is not that I wish to leave you, but I want to see the wonderful Eastern land," I answered.

My dear old aunt came to our house that morning, and I heard her say, "Let her try it."

I hoped that, as usual, my aunt was pleading on my side. My brother Dawée came for mother's decision. I dropped my play, and crept close to my aunt.

"Yes, Dawée, my daughter, though she does not understand what it all means, is anxious to go. She will need an education when she is grown, for then there will be fewer real Dakotas, and many more palefaces. This tearing her away, so young, from her mother is necessary, if I would have her an educated woman. The palefaces, who owe us a large debt for stolen lands, have begun to pay a tardy justice in offering some education to our children. But I know my daughter must suffer keenly in this experiment. For her sake, I dread to tell you my reply to the missionaries. Go, tell them that they may take my little daughter, and that the Great Spirit shall not fail to reward them according to their hearts."

Wrapped in my heavy blanket, I walked with my mother to the carriage that was soon to take us to the iron horse. I was happy. I met my playmates, who were also wearing their best thick blankets. We showed one another our new beaded moccasins, and the width of the belts that girdled our new dresses. Soon we were being drawn far away by the white man's horses. When I saw the lonely figure of my mother vanish in the distance, a sense of agony weighed heavily upon me. I felt suddenly weak, as if I might fall limp to the ground. I was in the hands of strangers whom my mother did not fully trust. I no longer felt free to be myself, or to voice my own feelings. The tears trickled down my cheeks, and I buried my head in the folds of my blanket. Now the first step, parting me from my mother, was taken. . . .

We crossed the Missouri in the evening. Then riding . . . a few miles eastward, we stopped before a massive brick building. I looked at it in amazement, and with a vague misgiving, for in our village I had never seen so large a house. Trembling with fear and distrust of the palefaces, my teeth chattering from the chilly ride, I crept noiselessly in my soft moccasins along the narrow hall, keeping very close to the bare wall. I was as frightened and bewildered as the captured young of a wild creature. 🖊

SUGGESTIONS FOR WRITING

1. Although Zitkala-Sä fantasizes about having all of the red apples she can eat at the mission school, analyze the conditions she will face in the white person's world.

2. People often think that because someone does things differently, he or she is doing them "wrong." You may have experienced a different culture, even in your home country. Analyze in what ways the behaviors that you observed startled you or made you feel uncomfortable or out of place. How did you resolve these feelings?

3. You may have known some people who were different from your friends in school. Examine how they differed, your reactions to them, and their ways of either maintaining or altering their "unconventional" behaviors.

BATTLE ROYAL

Ralph Ellison

Few experiences are as unsettling as finding yourself in a situation in which you expected to be treated with respect, only to discover that the others see you merely in terms of your racial or sexual categories. The narrator of this story anticipated a ceremony honoring his abilities as an orator. Instead he and the other black youths are treated as racial caricatures and are forced to participate in humiliating activities to entertain their white male hosts.

"Battle Royal" is the first chapter of Invisible Man, *the 1952 novel by Ralph Ellison (b. 1914) that many critics consider one of the finest novels written by an American in the twentieth century. He is also the author of* Shadow and Act (1964). *In the eloquent prologue to his first novel, Ellison explained the title "Invisible Man" by asserting that the dominant white culture does not see the reality of black existence. If whites see at all, they see only the racist stereotypes they have created.*

It goes a long way back, some twenty years. All my life I had been looking for something and everywhere I turned someone tried to tell me what it was. I accepted their answers too, though they were often in contradiction and even self-contradictory. I was naïve. I was looking for myself and asking everyone except myself questions which I, and only I, could answer. It took me a long time and much painful boomeranging of my expectations to achieve a realization everyone else appears to have been born with: That I am nobody but myself. But first I had to discover that I am an invisible man!

And yet I am no freak of nature, nor of history. I was in the cards, other things having been equal (or unequal) eighty-five years ago. I am not ashamed of my grandparents for having been slaves. I am only ashamed of myself for having at one time been ashamed. About eighty- five years ago they were told that they were free, united with others of our country in everything pertaining to the common good, and, in everything social, separate like the fingers of the hand. And they believed it. They exulted in it. They stayed in their place, worked hard, and brought up my father to do the same. But my grandfather is the one. He was an odd old guy, my grandfather, and I am told I take after him. It was he who caused the trouble. On his deathbed he called my father to him and said, "Son, after I'm gone I want you to keep up the good fight. I never told you, but our life is a war and I have been a traitor all my born days, a spy in the enemy's country ever since I give up my gun back in the Reconstruction. Live with your head in the lion's mouth. I want you to overcome 'em with yesses, undermine 'em with grins, agree 'em to death and destruction, let 'em swoller you till they vomit or bust wide open." They thought the old man had gone out of his mind. He had been the meekest of men. The younger children were rushed from the room, the shades drawn and the flame of the lamp turned so low that it sputtered on the wick like the old man's breathing. "Learn it to the younguns," he whispered fiercely; then he died.

But my folks were more alarmed over his last words than over his dying. It was as though he had not died at all, his words caused so much anxiety. I was warned emphatically to forget what he had said and, indeed, this is the first time it has been mentioned outside the family circle. It had a tremendous effect upon me, however. I could never be sure of what he meant. Grandfather had been a quiet old man who never made any trouble, yet on his deathbed he had called himself a traitor and a spy, and he had spoken of his meekness as a dangerous activity. It became a constant puzzle which lay unanswered in the back of my mind. And whenever things went well for me I remembered my grandfather and felt guilty and uncomfortable. It was as though I was carrying out his advice in spite of myself. And to make it worse, everyone loved me for it. I was praised by the most lily-white men of the town. I was considered an example of desirable conduct—just as my grandfather had been. And what puzzled me was that the old man had defined it as *treachery*. When I was praised for my conduct I felt a guilt that in some way I was doing something that was really against the wishes of the white folks, that if they had understood they would have desired me to act just the opposite, that I should have been sulky and mean, and that that really would have been what they wanted, even though they were fooled and thought they wanted me to act as I did. It made me afraid that some day they would look upon me as a traitor and I would be lost. Still I was more afraid to act any other way because they didn't like that at all. The old man's words were like a curse. On my graduation day I delivered an oration in which I showed that humility was the secret, indeed, the very essence of progress. (Not that I believed this—how could I, remembering my grandfather?—I only believed that it worked.) It was a great success. Everyone praised me and I was invited to give the speech at a gathering of the town's leading white citizens. It was a triumph for our whole community.

It was in the main ballroom of the leading hotel. When I got there I discovered that it was on the occasion of a smoker, and I was told that since I was to be there anyway I might as well take part in the battle royal to be fought by some of my schoolmates as part of the entertainment. The battle royal came first.

All of the town's big shots were there in their tuxedoes, wolfing down the buffet foods, drinking beer and whiskey and smoking black cigars. It was a large room with a high ceiling. Chairs were arranged in neat rows around three sides of a portable boxing ring. The fourth side was clear, revealing a gleaming space of polished floor. I had some misgivings over the battle royal, by the way. Not from a distaste for fighting, but because I didn't care too much for the other fellows who were to take part. They were tough guys who seemed to have no grandfather's curse worrying their minds. No one could mistake their toughness. And besides, I suspected that fighting a battle royal might detract from the dignity of my speech. In those pre-invisible days I visualized myself as a potential Booker T. Washington. But the other fellows didn't care too much for me either, and there were nine of them. I felt superior to them in my way, and I didn't like the manner in which we were all crowded together into the servants' elevator. Nor did they like my being there. In fact, as the warmly lighted floors flashed past the elevator we had words over the fact that I, by taking part in the fight, had knocked one of their friends out of a night's work.

We were led out of the elevator through a rococo hall into an anteroom and told to get into our fighting togs. Each of us was issued a pair of boxing gloves and ushered out into the big mirrored hall, which we entered looking cautiously about us and whispering, lest we might accidentally be heard above the noise of the room. It was foggy with cigar smoke. And already the whiskey was taking effect. I was shocked to see some of the most important men of the town quite tipsy. They were all there—bankers, lawyers, judges, doctors, firechiefs, teachers, merchants. Even one of the more fashionable pastors. Something we could not see was going on up front. A clarinet was vibrating sensuously and the men were standing up and moving eagerly forward. We were a small tight group, clustered together, our bare upper bodies touching and shining with anticipatory sweat; while up front the big shots were becoming increasingly excited over something we still could not see. Suddenly I heard the school superintendent, who had told me to come, yell, "Bring up the shines, gentlemen! Bring up the little shines!"

We were rushed up to the front of the ballroom, where it smelled even more strongly of tobacco and whiskey. Then we were pushed into place. I almost wet my pants. A sea of faces, some hostile, some amused, ringed around us, and in the center, facing us, stood a magnificent blonde—stark naked. There was dead silence. I felt a blast of cold air chill me. I tried to back away, but they were behind me and around me. Some of the boys stood with lowered heads, trembling. I felt a wave of irrational guilt and fear. My teeth chattered, my skin turned to goose flesh, my knees knocked. Yet I was strongly attracted and looked in spite of myself. Had the price of looking been blindness, I would have looked. The hair was yellow like that of a circus kewpie doll, the face heavily powdered and rouged, as though to form an abstract mask, the eyes hollow and smeared a cool blue, the color of a baboon's butt. I felt a desire to spit upon her as my eyes brushed slowly over her body. Her breasts were firm and round as the domes of East Indian temples, and I stood so close as to see the fine skin texture and beads of pearly perspiration glistening like dew around the pink and erected buds of her nipples. I wanted at one and the same time to run from the room, to sink through the floor, or to go to her and cover her from my eyes and the eyes of the others with my body; to feel the soft thighs, to caress her and destroy her, to love her and murder her, to hide from her, and yet to stroke where below the small American flag tattooed upon her belly her thighs formed a capital V. I had a notion that of all in the room she saw only me with her impersonal eyes.

And then she began to dance, a slow sensuous movement; the smoke of a hundred cigars clinging to her like the thinnest of veils. She seemed like a fair bird-girl girdled in veils calling to me from the angry surface of some gray and threatening sea. I was transported. Then I became aware of the clarinet playing and the big shots yelling at us. Some threatened us if we looked and others if we did not. On my right I saw one boy faint. And now a man grabbed a silver pitcher from a table and stepped close as he dashed ice water upon him and stood him up and forced two of us to support him as his head hung and moans issued from his thick bluish lips. Another boy began to plead to go home. He was the largest of the group, wearing dark red fighting trunks much too small to conceal the erection which projected from him as though in answer to the insinuating low-registered moaning of the clarinet. He tried to hide himself with his boxing gloves.

And all the while the blonde continued dancing, smiling faintly at the big shots who watched her with fascination, and faintly smiling at our fear. I noticed a certain merchant who followed her hungrily, his lips loose and drooling. He was a large man who wore diamond studs in a shirtfront which swelled with the ample paunch underneath, and each time the blonde swayed her undulating hips he ran his hand through the thin hair of his bald head and, with his arms upheld, his posture clumsy like that of an intoxicated panda, wound his belly in a slow and obscene grind. This creature was completely hypnotized. The music had quickened. As the dancer flung herself about with a detached expression on her face, the men began reaching out to touch her. I could see their beefy fingers sink into the soft flesh. Some of the others tried to stop them and she began to move around the floor in graceful circles, as they gave chase, slipping and sliding over the polished floor. It was mad. Chairs went crashing, drinks were spilt, as they ran laughing and howling after her. They caught her just as she reached a door, raised her from the floor, and tossed her as college boys are tossed at a hazing, and above her red, fixed-smiling lips I saw the terror and disgust in her eyes, almost like my own terror and that which I saw in some of the other boys. As I watched, they tossed her twice and her soft breasts seemed to flatten against the air and her legs flung wildly as she spun. Some of the more sober ones helped her to escape. And I started off the floor, heading for the anteroom with the rest of the boys.

Some were still crying and in hysteria. But as we tried to leave we were stopped and ordered to get into the ring. There was nothing to do but what we were told. All ten of us climbed under the ropes and allowed ourselves to be blindfolded with broad bands of white cloth. One of the men seemed to feel a bit sympathetic and tried to cheer us up as we stood with out backs against the ropes. Some of us tried to grin. "See that boy over there?" one of the men said. "I want you to run across at the bell and give it to him right in the belly. If you don't get him, I'm going to get you. I don't like his looks." Each of us was told the same. The blindfolds were put on. Yet even then I had been going over my speech. In my mind each word was as bright as flame. I felt the cloth pressed into place, and frowned so that it would be loosened when I relaxed.

But now I felt a sudden fit of blind terror. I was unused to darkness. It was as though I had suddenly found myself in a dark room filled with poisonous cottonmouths. I could hear the bleary voices yelling insistently for the battle royal to begin.

"Get going in there!"

"Let me at that big nigger!"

I strained to pick up the school superintendent's voice, as though to squeeze some security out of that slightly more familiar sound.

"Let me at those black sonsabitches!" someone yelled.

"No, Jackson, no!" another voice yelled. "Here, somebody, help me hold Jack."

"I want to get at that ginger-colored nigger. Tear him limb from limb," the first voice yelled.

I stood against the ropes trembling. For in those days I was what they called ginger-colored, and he sounded as though he might crunch me between his teeth like a crisp ginger cookie.

Quite a struggle was going on. Chairs were being kicked about and I could hear voices grunting as with a terrific effort. I wanted to see, to see more desperately than ever before. But the blindfold was tight as a thick skin-puckering scab and when I raised my gloved hands to push the layers of white aside a voice yelled, "Oh, no you don't, black bastard! Leave that alone!"

"Ring the bell before Jackson kills him a coon!" someone boomed in the sudden silence. And I heard the bell clang and the sound of the feet scuffling forward.

A glove smacked against my head. I pivoted, striking out stiffly as someone went past, and felt the jar ripple along the length of my arm to my shoulder. Then it seemed as though all nine of the boys had turned upon me at once. Blows pounded me from all sides while I struck out as best I could. So many blows landed upon me that I wondered if I were not the only blindfolded fighter in the ring, or if the man called Jackson hadn't succeeded in getting me after all.

Blindfolded, I could no longer control my motions. I had no dignity. I stumbled about like a baby or a drunken man. The smoke had become thicker and with each new blow it seemed to sear and further restrict my lungs. My saliva became like hot bitter glue. A glove connected with my head, filling my mouth with warm blood. It was everywhere. I could not tell if the moisture I felt upon my body was sweat or blood. A blow landed hard against the nape of my neck. I felt myself going over, my head hitting the floor. Streaks of blue light filled the black world behind the blindfold. I lay prone, pretending that I was knocked out, but felt myself seized by hands and yanked to my feet. "Get going, black boy! Mix it up!" My arms were like lead, my head smarting from blows. I managed to feel my way to the ropes and held on, trying to catch my breath. A glove landed in my mid-section and I went over again, feeling as though the smoke had become a knife jabbed into my guts. Pushed this way and that by the legs milling around me, I finally pulled erect and discovered that I could see the black, sweat-washed forms weaving in the smoky-blue atmosphere like drunken dancers weaving to the rapid drum-like thuds of blows.

Everyone fought hysterically. It was complete anarchy. Everybody fought everybody else. No group fought together for long. Two, three, four, fought one, then turned to fight each other, were themselves attacked. Blows landed below the belt and in the kidney, with the gloves open as well as closed, and with my eye partly opened now there was not so much terror. I moved carefully, avoiding blows, although not too many to attract attention, fighting from group to group. The boys groped about like blind, cautious crabs crouching to protect their mid-sections, their heads pulled in short against their shoulders, their arms stretched nervously before them, with their fists testing the smoke-filled air like the knobbed feelers of hypersensitive snails. In one corner I glimpsed a boy violently punching the air and heard him scream in pain as he smashed his hand against a ring post. For a second I saw him bent over holding his hand, then going down as a blow caught his unprotected head. I played one group against the other, slipping in and throwing a punch then stepping out of range while pushing the others into the melee to take the blows blindly aimed at me. The smoke was agonizing and there we no rounds, no bells at three minute intervals to relieve our exhaustion. The room spun round me, a swirl of lights, smoke, sweating bodies surrounded by tense white faces. I bled from both nose and mouth, the blood spattering upon my chest.

The men kept yelling, "Slug him, black boy! Knock his guts out!"

"Uppercut him! Kill him! Kill that big boy!"

Taking a fake fall, I saw a boy going down heavily beside me as though we were felled by a single blow, saw a sneaker-clad foot shoot into his groin as the two who had knocked him down stumbled upon him. I rolled out of range, feeling a twinge of nausea.

The harder we fought the more threatening the men became. And yet, I had begun to worry about my speech again. How would it go? Would they recognize my ability? What would they give me?

I was fighting automatically when suddenly I noticed that one after another of the boys was leaving the ring. I was surprised, filled with panic, as though I had been left alone with an unknown danger. Then I understood. The boys had arranged it among themselves. It was the custom for the two men left in the ring to slug it out for the winner's prize. I discovered this too late. When the bell sounded two men in tuxedoes leaped into the ring and removed the blindfold. I found myself facing Tatlock, the biggest of the gang. I felt sick at my stomach. Hardly had the bell stopped ringing in my ears than it clanged again and I saw him moving swiftly toward me. Thinking of nothing else to do I hit him smash on the nose. He kept coming, bringing the rank sharp violence of stale sweat. His face was a black blank of a face, only his eyes alive—with hate of me and aglow with a feverish terror from what had happened to us all. I became anxious. I wanted to deliver my speech and he came at me as though he meant to beat it out of me. I smashed him again and again, taking his blows as they came. Then on sudden impulse I struck him lightly and as we clinched, I whispered, "Fake like I knocked you out, you can have the prize."

"I'll break your behind," he whispered hoarsely.

"For *them?*"

"For *me*, sonofabitch!"

They were yelling for us to break it up and Tatlock spun me half around with a blow, and as a joggled camera sweeps in a reeling scene, I saw the howling red faces crouching tense beneath the cloud of blue-gray smoke. For a moment the world wavered, unraveled, flowed, then my head cleared and Tatlock bounced before me. That fluttering shadow before my eyes was his jabbing left hand. Then falling forward, my head against his damp shoulder, I whispered,

"I'll make it five dollars more."

"Go to hell!"

But his muscles relaxed a trifle beneath my pressure and I breathed, "Seven?"

"Give it to your ma," he said, ripping me beneath the heart.

And while I still held him I butted him and moved away. I felt myself bombarded with punches. I fought back with hopeless desperation. I wanted to deliver my speech more than anything else in the world, because I felt that only these men could judge truly my ability, and now this stupid clown was ruining my chances. I began fighting carefully now, moving in to punch him and out again with my greater speed. A lucky blow to his chin and I had him going too—until I heard a loud voice yell, "I got my money on the big boy."

Hearing this, I almost dropped my guard. I was confused: Should I try to win against the voice out there? Would not this go against my speech, and was not this a moment for humility, for nonresistance? A blow to my head as I danced about sent my right eye popping like a jack-in-the-box and settled my dilemma. The room went red as I fell. It was a dream fall, my body languid and fastidious as to where to land, until the floor became impatient and smashed up to meet me. A moment later I came to. A hypnotic voice said FIVE emphatically. And I lay there, hazily watching a dark red spot of my own blood shaping itself into a butterfly, glistening and soaking into the soiled gray world of the canvas.

When the voice drawled TEN I was lifted up and dragged to a chair. I sat dazed. My eye pained and swelled with each throb of my pounding heart and I wondered if now I would be allowed to speak. I was wringing wet, my mouth still bleeding. We were grouped along the wall now. The other boys ignored me as they congratulated Tatlock and speculated as to how much they would be paid. One boy whimpered over his smashed hand. Looking up front, I saw attendants in white jackets rolling the portable ring away and placing a small square rug in the vacant space surrounded by chairs. Perhaps, I thought, I will stand on the rug to deliver my speech.

Then the M.C. called to us, "Come on up here boys and get your money."

We ran forward to where the men laughed and talked in their chairs, waiting. Everyone seemed friendly now.

"There it is on the rug," the man said. I saw the rug covered with coins of all dimensions and a few crumpled bills. But what excited me, scattered here and there, were the gold pieces.

"Boys, it's all yours," the man said. "You get all you grab."

"That's right, Sambo," a blond man said, winking at me confidentially.

I trembled with excitement, forgetting my pain. I would get the gold and bills, I thought. I would use both hands. I would throw my body against the boys nearest me to block them from the gold.

"Get down around the rug now," the man commanded, "and don't anyone touch it until I give the signal."

"This ought to be good," I heard.

As told, we got around the square rug on our knees. Slowly the man raised his freckled hands as we followed it upward with our eyes.

I heard, "These niggers look like they're about to pray!"

Then, "Ready," the man said. "Go!"

I lunged for a yellow coin lying on the blue design of the carpet, touching it and sending a surprised shriek to join those rising around me. I tried frantically to remove my hand but could not let go. A hot, violent force tore through my body, shaking me like a wet rat. The rug was electrified. The hair bristled up on my head as I shook myself free. My muscles jumped, my nerves jangled, writhed. But I saw that this was not stopping the other boys. Laughing in fear and embarrassment, some were holding back and scooping up the coins knocked off by the painful contortions of the others. The men roared above us as we struggled.

"Pick it up, goddamnit, pick it up!" someone called like a bass-voiced parrot. "Go on, get it!"

I crawled rapidly around the floor, picking up the coins, trying to avoid the coppers and to get greenbacks and the gold. Ignoring the shock by laughing, as I brushed the coins off quickly, I discovered that I could contain the electricity—a contradiction, but it works. Then the men began to push us onto the rug. Laughing embarrassedly, we struggled out of their hands and kept after the coins. We were all wet and slippery and hard to hold. Suddenly I saw a boy lifted into the air, glistening with sweat like a circus seal, and dropped, his wet back landing flush upon the charged rug, heard him yell and saw him literally dance upon his back, his elbows beating a frenzied tattoo upon the floor, his muscles twitching like the flesh of a horse strung by many flies. When he finally rolled off, his face was gray and no one stopped him when he ran from the floor amid booming laughter.

"Get the money," the M.C. called. "That's good hard American cash!"

And we snatched and grabbed, snatched and grabbed. I was careful not to come too close to the rug now, and when I felt the hot whiskey breath descend upon me like a cloud of foul air I reached out and grabbed the leg of a chair. It was occupied and I held on desperately.

"Leggo, nigger! Leggo!"

The huge face wavered down to mine as he tried to push me free. But my body was slippery and he was too drunk. It was Mr. Colcord, who owned a chain of movie houses and "entertainment palaces." Each time he grabbed me I slipped out of his hands. It became a real struggle. I feared the rug more than I did the drunk, so I held on, surprising myself for a moment by trying to topple *him* upon the rug. It was such an enormous idea that I found myself actually carrying it out. I tried not to be obvious, yet when I grabbed his leg, trying to tumble him out of the chair, he raised up roaring with laughter, and, looking at me with soberness dead in the eye, kicked me viciously in the chest. The chair leg flew out of my hand and I felt myself going and rolled. It was as though I had rolled through a bed of hot coals. It seemed a whole century would pass before I would roll free, a century in which I was seared through the deepest levels of my body to the fearful breath within me and the breath seared and heated to the point of explosion. It'll all be over in a flash, I thought as I rolled clear. It'll all be over in a flash.

But not yet, the men on the other side were waiting, red faces swollen as though from apoplexy as they bent forward in their chairs. Seeing their fingers coming toward me I rolled away as a fumbled football rolls off the receiver's fingertips, back into the coals. That time I luckily sent the rug sliding out of place and heard the coins ringing against the floor and the boys scuffling to pick them up and the M.C. calling, "All right, boys, that's all. Go get dressed and get your money."

I was limp as a dish rag. My back felt as though it had been beaten with wires.

When we had dressed the M.C. came in and gave us each five dollars, except Tatlock, who got ten for being last in the ring. Then he told us to leave. I was not to get a chance to deliver my speech, I thought. I was going out into the dim alley in despair when I was stopped and told to go back. I returned to the ballroom, where the men were pushing back their chairs and gathering in groups to talk.

The M.C. knocked on a table for quiet. "Gentlemen," he said, "we almost forgot an important part of the program. A most serious part, gentlemen. This boy was brought here to deliver a speech which he made at his graduation yesterday . . ."

"Bravo!"

"I'm told that he is the smartest boy we've got out there in Greenwood. I'm told that he knows more big words than a pocket-sized dictionary."

Much applause and laughter.

"So now, gentlemen, I want you to give him your attention."

There was still laughter as I faced them, my mouth dry, my eye throbbing. I began slowly, but evidently my throat was tense, because they began shouting, "Louder! Louder!"

"We of the younger generation extol the wisdom of that great leader and educator," I shouted, "who first spoke these flaming words of wisdom: 'A ship lost at sea for many days suddenly sighted a friendly vessel. From the mast of the unfortunate vessel was seen a signal: "Water, water; we die of thirst!" The answer from the friendly vessel came back: "Cast down your bucket where you are." The captain of the distressed vessel, at last heeding the injunction, cast down his bucket, and it came up full of fresh sparkling water from the mouth of the Amazon River.' And like him I say, and in his words, 'To those of my race who depend upon bettering their condition in a foreign land, or who underestimate the importance of cultivating friendly relations with the Southern white man, who is his next-door neighbor, I would say: "Cast down your bucket where you are"—cast it down in making friends in every manly way of the people of all races by whom we are surrounded . . .' "

I spoke automatically with such fervor that I did not realize that the men were still talking and laughing until my dry mouth, filling up with blood from the cut, almost strangled me. I coughed, wanting to stop and go to one of the tall brass, sand-filled spittoons, to relieve myself, but a few of the men, especially the superintendent, were listening and I was afraid. So I gulped it down, blood, saliva and all, and continued. (What powers of endurance I had during those days! What enthusiasm! What a belief in the rightness of things!) I spoke even louder in spite of the pain. But still they talked and still they laughed, as though deaf with cotton in dirty ears. So I spoke with greater emotional emphasis. I closed my ears and swallowed blood until I was nauseated. The speech seemed a hundred times as long as before, but I could not leave out a single word. All had to be said, each memorized nuance considered, rendered. Nor was that all. Whenever I uttered a word of three or more syllables a group of voices would yell for me to repeat it. I used the phrase "social responsibility" and they yelled:

"What's that word you say, boy?"

"Social responsibility," I said.

"What?"

"Social . . ."

"Louder."

". . . responsibility."

"More!"

"Respon—"

"Repeat!"

"—sibility."

The room filled with the uproar of laughter until, no doubt, distracted by having to gulp down my blood, I made a mistake and yelled a phrase I had often seen denounced in newspaper editorials, heard debated in private.

"Social . . ."

"What?" they yelled.

". . . equality—"

The laughter hung smokelike in the sudden stillness. I opened my eyes, puzzled. Sounds of displeasure filled the room. The M.C. rushed forward. They shouted hostile phrases at me. But I did not understand.

A small dry mustached man in the front row blared out. "Say that slowly, son!"

"What, sir?"

"What you just said!"

"Social responsibility, sir," I said.

"You weren't being smart, were you, boy?" he said, not unkindly.

"No, sir!"

"You sure that about 'equality' was a mistake?"

"Oh, yes, sir," I said. "I was swallowing blood."

"Well, you had better speak more slowly so we can understand. We mean to do right by you, but you've got to know your place at all times. All right, now, go on with your speech."

I was afraid. I wanted to leave but I wanted also to speak and I was afraid they'd snatch me down.

"Thank you, sir," I said, beginning where I had left off, and having them ignore me as before.

Yet when I finished there was a thunderous applause. I was surprised to see the superintendent come forth with a package wrapped in white tissue paper, and gesturing for quiet, address the men.

"Gentlemen, you see that I did not overpraise this boy. He makes a good speech and some day he'll lead his people in the proper paths. And I don't have to tell you that that is important in these days and times. This is a good, smart boy, and so to encourage him in the right direction, in the name of the Board of Education I wish to present him a prize in the form of this . . ."

He paused, removing the tissue paper and revealing a gleaming calfskin brief case.

". . . in the form of this first-class article from Shad Whitmore's shop."

"Boy," he said, addressing me, "take this prize and keep it well. Consider it a badge of office. Prize it. Keep developing as you are and some day it will be filled with important papers that will help shape the destiny of your people."

I was so moved that I could hardly express my thanks. A rope of bloody saliva forming a shape like an undiscovered continent drooled upon the leather and I wiped it quickly away. I felt an importance that I had never dreamed.

"Open it and see what's inside," I was told.

My fingers a-tremble, I complied, smelling the fresh leather and finding an official-looking document inside. It was a scholarship to the state college for Negroes. My eyes filled with tears and I ran awkwardly off the floor.

I was overjoyed; I did not even mind when I discovered that the gold pieces I had scrambled for were brass pocket tokens advertising a certain make of automobile.

When I reached home everyone was excited. Next day the neighbors came to congratulate me. I even felt safe from grandfather, whose deathbed curse usually spoiled my triumphs. I stood beneath his photograph with my brief case in hand and smiled triumphantly into his solid black peasant's face. It was a face that fascinated me. The eyes seemed to follow everywhere I went.

That night I dreamed I was at a circus with him and that he refused to laugh at the clowns no matter what they did. Then later he told me to open my brief case and read what was inside and I did, finding an official envelope stamped with the state seal; and inside the envelope I found another and another, endlessly, and I thought I would fall of weariness. "Them's years," he said, "Now open that one." And I did and in it I found an engraved document containing a short message in letters of gold. "Read it, " my grandfather said. "Out loud!"

"To Whom It May Concern," I intoned. "Keep This Nigger-Boy Running."

I awoke with the old man's laughter ringing in my ears.

(It was a dream I was to remember and dream again for many years after. But at that time I had no insight into its meaning. First I had to attend college.)

SUGGESTIONS FOR WRITING

1. Recall an occasion on which you were the victim of stereotyping. Describe the event and the feelings it produced in you.

2. Are the actions of the white men in the story specific to their social class, or would they be typical of any racist whites? Explain your reasoning.

3. Could such an incident as that described in "Battle Royal" happen today? How would your react to it if you were present?

4. Compare the treatment of the dancer in the story with the treatment of the black youths.

LESSONS

Maya Angelou

We are all shaped by the family in which we grew up. In some cases, our home life provided us with all the "tools" we needed to get along in the world; in others, it may have limited our vision or our options . . . or so we thought when we were young. Sometimes families can be a source of embarrassment when we're growing up because they don't live up to our expectations. At the same time, someone in our community may provide us with an especially powerful example or give us encouragement at exactly the moment when we need it most.

American author, actress, singer, dancer, and producer **Maya Angelou** *(b. 1928) spent some of her childhood in the care of her paternal grandmother—the Momma mentioned in the following selection. The first volume of Angelou's autobiography,* I Know Why the Caged Bird Sings *(1970), describes the time she spent with her brother and Momma in Stamps, Arkansas, as well as her life with her mother and father. Angelou has written two other volumes of autobiography:* Gather Together in My Name *(1974) and* Singin' and Swingin' and Gettin' Merry Like Christmas *(1976), as well as several volumes of poetry. She now lives in North Carolina, where she teaches at Wake Forest University.*

In the following selection from I Know Why the Caged Bird Sings, *Angelou describes two women who influenced the direction of her life.*

For nearly a year, I sopped around the house, the Store, the school and the church, like an old biscuit, dirty and inedible. Then I met, or rather got to know, the lady who threw me my first life line.

Mrs. Bertha Flowers was the aristocrat of Black Stamps. She had the grace of control to appear warm in the coldest weather, and on the Arkansas summer days it seemed she had a private breeze which swirled around, cooling her. She was thin without the taut look of wiry people, and her printed voile dresses and flowered hats were as right for her as denim overalls for a farmer. She was our side's answer to the richest white woman in town.

Her skin was a rich black that would have peeled like a plum if snagged, but then no one would have thought of getting close enough to Mrs. Flowers to ruffle her dress, let alone snag her skin. She didn't encourage familiarity. She wore gloves too.

I don't think I ever saw Mrs. Flowers laugh, but she smiled often. A slow widening of her thin black lips to show even, small white teeth, then the slow effortless closing. When she chose to smile on me, I always wanted to thank her. The action was so graceful and inclusively benign.

She was one of the few gentlewomen I have ever known, and has remained throughout my life the measure of what a human being can be.

Momma had a strange relationship with her. Most often when she passed on the road in front of the Store, she spoke to Momma in that soft yet carrying voice, "Good day, Mrs. Henderson." Momma responded with "How you, Sister Flowers?"

Mrs. Flowers didn't belong to our church, nor was she Momma's familiar. Why on earth did she insist on calling her Sister Flowers? Shame made me want to hide my face. Mrs. Flowers deserved better than to be called Sister. Then, Momma left out the verb. Why not ask, "How *are* you, *Mrs.* Flowers?" With the unbalanced passion of the young, I hated her for showing her ignorance to Mrs. Flowers. It didn't occur to me for many years that they were as alike as sisters, separated only by formal education.

Although I was upset, neither of the women was in the least shaken by what I thought an unceremonious greeting. Mrs. Flowers would continue her easy gait up the hill to her little bungalow, and Momma kept on shelling peas or doing whatever had brought her to the front porch.

Occasionally, though, Mrs. Flowers would drift off the road and down to the Store and Momma would say to me, "Sister, you go on and play." As I left I would hear the beginning of an intimate conversation. Momma persistently using the wrong verb, or none at all.

"Brother and Sister Wilcox is sho'ly the meanest—" "Is," Momma? "Is"? Oh, please, not "is," Momma, for two or more. But they talked, and from the side of the building where I waited for the ground to open up and swallow me, I heard the soft-voiced Mrs. Flowers and the textured voice of my grandmother merging and melting. They were interrupted from time to time by giggles that must have come from Mrs. Flowers (Momma never giggled in her life). Then she was gone.

She appealed to me because she was like people I had never met personally. Like women in English novels who walked the moors (whatever they were) with their loyal dogs racing at a respectful distance. Like the women who sat in front of roaring fireplaces, drinking tea incessantly from silver trays full of scones and crumpets. Women who walked over the "heath" and read morocco-bound books and had two last names divided by a hyphen. It would be safe to say that she made me proud to be Negro, just by being herself.

She acted just as refined as whitefolks in the movies and books and she was more beautiful, for none of them could have come near that warm color without looking gray by comparison.

It was fortunate that I never saw her in the company of powhitefolks. For since they tend to think of their whiteness as an evenizer, I'm certain that I would have had to hear her spoken to commonly as Bertha, and my image of her would have been shattered like the unmendable Humpty-Dumpty.

One summer afternoon, sweet-milk fresh in my memory, she stopped at the Store to buy provisions. Another Negro woman of her health and age would have been expected to carry the paper sacks home in one hand, but Momma said, "Sister Flowers, I'll send Bailey up to your house with these things."

She smiled that slow dragging smile, "Thank you, Mrs. Henderson. I'd prefer Marguerite, though." My name was beautiful when she said it. "I've been meaning to talk to her, anyway." They gave each other age-group looks.

Momma said, "Well, that's all right then. Sister, go and change your dress. You going to Sister Flowers's."

The chifforobe was a maze. What on earth did one put on to go to Mrs. Flowers' house? I knew I shouldn't put on a Sunday dress. It might be sacrilegious. Certainly not a house dress, since I was already wearing a fresh one. I chose a school dress, naturally. It was formal without suggesting that going to Mrs. Flowers' house was equivalent to attending church.

I trusted myself back into the Store.

"Now, don't you look nice." I had chosen the right thing, for once.

"Mrs. Henderson, you make most of the children's clothes, don't you?"

"Yes, ma'am. Sure do. Store-bought clothes ain't hardly worth the thread it takes to stitch them."

"I'll say you do a lovely job, though, so neat. That dress looks professional."

Momma was enjoying the seldom-received compliments. Since everyone we knew (except Mrs. Flowers, of course) could sew competently, praise was rarely handed out for the commonly practiced craft.

"I try, with the help of the Lord, Sister Flowers, to finish the inside just like I does the outside. Come here, Sister."

I had buttoned up the collar and tied the belt, apronlike, in the back. Momma told me to turn around. With one hand she pulled the strings and the belt fell free at both sides of my waist. Then her large hands were at my neck, opening the button loops. I was terrified. What was happening?

"Take it off, Sister." She had her hands on the hem of the dress.

"I don't need to see the inside, Mrs. Henderson, I can tell . . ." But the dress was over my head and my arms were stuck in the sleeves. Momma said, "That'll do. See here, Sister Flowers, I French-seams around the armholes." Through the cloth film, I saw the shadow approach. "That makes it last longer. Children these days would bust out of sheet-metal clothes. They so rough."

"That is a very good job, Mrs. Henderson. You should be proud. You can put your dress back on, Marguerite."

"No ma'am. Pride is a sin. And 'cording to the Good Book, it goeth before a fall."

"That's right. So the Bible says. It's a good thing to keep in mind."

I wouldn't look at either of them. Momma hadn't thought that taking off my dress in front of Mrs. Flowers would kill me stone dead. If I had refused, she would have thought I was trying to be "womanish" and might have remembered St. Louis. Mrs. Flowers had known that I would be embarrassed and that was even worse. I picked up the groceries and went out to wait in the hot sunshine. It would be fitting if I got sunstroke and died before they came outside. Just dropped dead on the slanting porch.

There was a little path beside the rocky road, and Mrs. Flowers walked in front swinging her arms and picking her way over the stones.

She said, without turning her head, to me, "I hear you're doing very good school work, Marguerite, but that it's all written. The teachers report that they have trouble getting you to talk in class." We passed the triangular farm on our left and the path widened to allow us to walk together. I hung back in the separate unasked and unanswerable questions.

"Come and walk along with me, Marguerite." I couldn't have refused even if I wanted to. She pronounced my name so nicely. Or more correctly, she spoke each word with such clarity that I was certain a foreigner who didn't understand English could have understood her.

"Now no one is going to make you talk—possibly no one can. But bear in mind, language is man's way of communicating with his fellow man and it is language alone which separates him from the lower animals." That was a totally new idea to me, and I would need time to think about it.

"Your grandmother says you read a lot. Every chance you get. That's good, but not good enough. Words mean more than what is set down on paper. It takes the human voice to infuse them with the shades of deeper meaning."

I memorized the part about the human voice infusing words. It seemed so valid and poetic.

She said she was going to give me some books and that I not only must read them, I must read them aloud. She suggested that I try to make a sentence sound in as many different ways as possible.

"I'll accept no excuse if you return a book to me that has been badly handled." My imagination boggled at the punishment I would deserve if in fact I did abuse a book of Mrs. Flowers'. Death would be too kind and brief.

The odors in the house surprised me. Somehow I had never connected Mrs. Flowers with food or eating or any other common experience of common people. There must have been an outhouse, too, but my mind never recorded it.

The sweet scent of vanilla had met us as she opened the door.

"I made tea cookies this morning. You see, I had planned to invite you for cookies and lemonade so we could have this little chat. The lemonade is in the icebox."

It followed that Mrs. Flowers would have ice on an ordinary day, when most families in our town bought ice late on Saturdays only a few times during the summer to be used in the wooden ice-cream freezers.

She took the bags from me and disappeared through the kitchen door. I looked around the room that I had never in my wildest fantasies imagined I would see. Browned photographs leered or threatened from the walls and the white, freshly done curtains pushed against themselves and against the wind. I wanted to gobble up the room entire and take it to Bailey, who would help me analyze and enjoy it.

"Have a seat, Marguerite. Over there by the table." She carried a platter covered with a tea towel. Although she warned that she hadn't tried her hand at baking sweets for some time, I was certain that like everything else about her the cookies would be perfect.

They were flat round wafers, slightly browned on the edges and butter-yellow in the center. With the cold lemonade they were sufficient for childhood's lifelong diet. Remembering my manners, I took nice little lady-like bites off the edges. She said she had made them expressly for me and that she had a few in the kitchen that I could take home to my brother. So I jammed one whole cake in my mouth and the rough crumbs scratched the insides of my jaws, and if I hadn't had to swallow, it would have been a dream come true.

As I ate she began the first of what we later called "my lessons in living." She said that I must always be intolerant of ignorance but understanding of illiteracy. That some people, unable to go to school, were more educated and even more intelligent than college professors. She encouraged me to listen carefully to what country people called mother wit. That in those homely sayings was couched the collective wisdom of generations.

When I finished the cookies she brushed off the table and brought a thick, small book from the bookcase. I had read A Tale of Two Cities and found it up to my standards as a romantic novel. She opened the first page and I heard poetry for the first time in my life.

"It was the best of times and the worst of times . . ." Her voice slid in and curved down through and over the words. She was nearly singing. I wanted to look at the pages. Were they the same that I had read? Or were there notes, music, lined on the pages, as in a hymn book? Her sounds began cascading gently. I knew from listening to a thousand preachers that she was nearing the end of her reading, and I hadn't really heard, heard to understand, a single word.

"How do you like that?"

It occurred to me that she expected a response. The sweet vanilla flavor was still on my tongue and her reading was a wonder in my ears. I had to speak.

I said, "Yes, ma'am." It was the least I could do, but it was the most also.

"There's one more thing. Take this book of poems and memorize one for me. Next time you pay me a visit, I want you to recite."

I have tried often to search behind the sophistication of years for the enchantment I so easily found in those gifts. The essence escapes but its aura remains. To be allowed, no, invited, into the private lives of strangers, and to share their joys and fears, was a chance to exchange the Southern bitter wormwood for a cup of mead with Beowulf or a hot cup of tea and milk with Oliver Twist. When I said aloud, "It is a far, far better thing that I do, than I have ever done . . ." tears of love filled my eyes at my selflessness.

On that first day, I ran down the hill and into the road (few cars ever came along it) and had the good sense to stop running before I reached the Store.

I was liked, and what a difference it made. I was respected not as Mrs. Henderson's grandchild or Bailey's sister but for just being Marguerite Johnson.

Childhood's logic never asks to be proved (all conclusions are absolute). I didn't question why Mrs. Flowers had singled me out for attention, nor did it occur to me that Momma might have asked her to give me a little talking to. All I cared about was that she had made tea cookies for me and read to me from her favorite book. It was enough to prove that she liked me.

Momma and Bailey were waiting inside the Store. He said, "My, what did she give you?" He had seen the books, but I held the paper sack with his cookies in my arms shielded by the poems.

Momma said, "Sister, I know you acted like a little lady. That do my heart good to see settled people take to you all. I'm trying my best, the Lord knows, but these days . . ." Her voice trailed off. "Go on in and change your dress."

In the bedroom it was going to be a joy to see Bailey receive his cookies. I said, "By the way, Bailey, Mrs. Flowers sent you some tea cookies—"

Momma shouted, "What did you say, Sister? You, Sister, what did you say?" Hot anger was crackling in her voice.

Bailey said, "She said Mrs. Flowers sent me some—"

"I ain't talking to you, Ju." I heard the heavy feet walk across the floor toward our bedroom. "Sister, you heard me. What's that you said?" She swelled to fill the doorway.

Bailey said, "Momma." His pacifying voice—"Momma, she—"

"You shut up, Ju. I'm talking to your sister."

I didn't know what sacred cow I had bumped, but it was better to find out than to hang like a thread over an open fire. I repeated, "I said, 'Bailey, by the way, Mrs. Flowers sent you—' "

"That's what I thought you said. Go on and take off your dress. I'm going to get a switch."

At first I thought she was playing. Maybe some heavy joke that would end with, "You sure she didn't send me something?" but in a minute she was back in the room with a long, ropy, peach-tree switch, the juice smelling bitter at having been torn loose. She said, "Get down on your knees. Bailey, Junior, you come on, too."

The three of us knelt as she began, "Our Father, you know the tribulations of your humble servant. I have with your help raised two grown boys. Many's the day I thought I wouldn't be able to go on, but you gave me the strength to see my way clear. Now, Lord, look down on this heavy heart today. I'm trying to raise my son's children in the way they should go, but, oh, Lord, the Devil try to hinder me on every hand. I never thought I'd live to hear cursing under this roof, what I try to keep dedicated to the glorification of God. And cursing out of the mouths of babes. But you said, in the last days brother would turn against brother, and children against their parents. That there would be a gnashing of teeth and a rendering of flesh. Father, forgive this child, I beg you, on bended knee."

I was crying loudly now. Momma's voice had risen to a shouting pitch, and I knew that whatever wrong I had committed was extremely serious. She had even left the Store untended to take up my case with God. When she finished we were all crying. She pulled me to her with one hand and hit me only a few times with the switch. The shock of my sin and the emotional release of her prayer had exhausted her.

Momma wouldn't talk right then, but later in the evening I found that my violation lay in using the phrase "by the way." Momma explained that "Jesus was the Way, the Truth, and the Light," and anyone who says "by the way" is really saying, "by Jesus," or "by God" and the Lord's name would not be taken in vain in her house.

When Bailey tried to interpret the words with: "Whitefolks use 'by the way' to mean while we're on the subject," Momma reminded us that "whitefolks' mouths were most in general loose and their words were an abomination before Christ." ✒

SUGGESTIONS FOR WRITING

1. Reflect on your childhood and see if there wasn't someone who affected you in the way that Mrs. Flowers did Maya Angelou. Describe this person and examine what lessons they helped you to learn about yourself and about life.

2. When we are children, and sometimes into later life, our parents can embarrass us by the way they act. Examine the ways in which Momma behaves in this essay and discuss why Angelou was ashamed.

Selections from
GLIMPSES OF FIFTY YEARS:
THE AUTOBIOGRAPHY OF
AN AMERICAN WOMAN

Frances E. Willard

*This section of **Frances E. Willard's** autobiography describes a moment
known to many women, when her tomboyish youth is set aside in favor of a
more conventional notion of womanhood. Willard (1839–1898), who was
at one time the leader of the immensely powerful Women's Christian Tem-
perance Union, published this autobiography in 1889. At that time in our
cultural history, the rules of gender definition were very definite. What it
meant to be "feminine" was absolutely clear, right down to specifics of dress
and hair style. Young Frances might be allowed to follow her older brother
into "masculine" activities like woodworking and shooting a gun, but once
puberty occurred, even her liberal mother demanded that Frances conform to
the social rules. In this passage, especially in the journal entries she quotes,
the pain Frances felt at giving up her freedom comes through very clearly.
The adult Willard draws a parallel between this loss of personal freedom and
the lack of political freedom inherent in women's lack of voting rights.
Willard's account of this moment is a striking example of how the development of personal identity can run afoul of socially defined gender roles.*

Another rich experience that came to my sister and me was following the
"breaking plow" in spring. Just after the prairie fire had done its work and the
great field was black with the carpet it had spread, came the huge plow, three
times as large as that generally used, with which the virgin soil was to be turned
upward to the sun. Nowadays in the far West, that keeps going farther every
year, they use steam plows. Just think of a locomotive out in the boundless prairie, going so fast and far that one wouldn't dare tell how many miles it gets over
in a day! But away back in the forties and fifties, so distant from these wonderful eighties in which we live, we thought that nothing could go beyond the
huge plow, with steel "mould-board" so bright that you could see your face in
it; "beam" so long that we two girls could sit upon it for a ride and have space
for half a dozen more; formidable "colter"—a sharp, knife-like steel that went
before the plowshare to cut the thick sod—and eight great branch-horned
oxen sturdily pulling all this, while one man held the plow by its strong, curving handles, and another cracked a whip with lash so long it reached the heads
of the head oxen away at the front. As father generally held the plow, and Oliver, who was very kind to animals, the whip, Mary and I used to enjoy running
along and balancing ourselves on the great black furrow, as it curved over from
the polished mould-board and lay there smooth and even as a plank. Some-

times the plow would run against a snag in the shape of a big "red-root"; for, strange to say, the prairie soil, where no tree was in sight, had roots, sometimes as large as a man's arm, stretching along underground. Then would come a cheery, "Get up, Bill! Halloa there, Bright! Now's your time, Brindle!" The great whip would crack above their heads; the giant creatures would bend to the yoke; "snap" would go the red-root and smooth would turn the splendid furrow with home and school and civilization gleaming from its broad face, and happy children skipping, barefooted, along its new-laid floor. These were "great times" indeed! As the sun climbed higher and the day grew warm, we would go to the house, and compound a pail of "harvest drink," as father called it, who never permitted any kind of alcoholic liquor in his fields or at his barn-raisings. Water, molasses and ginger were its ingredients, and the thirsty toilers, taking it from a tin dipper, declared it "good enough to set before a king."

Later on, we girls were fitted out with bags of corn, of beans, onion, turnip or beet seed, which we tied around our waists, as, taking hoe in hand, we helped do the planting, not as work, but "just for fun," leaving off whenever we grew tired. We "rode the horse" for Oliver when he "cultivated corn"; held trees for father when he planted new ones, which he did by scores each spring; watched him at "grafting time" and learned about "scions" and "seedlings"; had our own little garden beds of flowers and vegetables, and thought no blossoms ever were so fair or dishes so toothsome as those raised by our own hands. Once when I was weeding onions with my father, I pulled out along with the grass, a good-size snake by the tail, after which I was less diligent in that department of industry. The flower-garden was a delight to people for miles around, with its wealth of rare shrubs, roses, tulips and clambering vines which mother and her daughters trained over the rambling cottage until it looked like some great arbor. I had a seat in the tall black oak near the front gate, where I could read and write quite hidden from view. I had a box with lid and hinges, fastened beside me, where I kept my sketches and books, whence the "general public" was warned off by the words painted in large, black letters on a board nailed to the tree below: "The Eagle's Nest, Beware!" Mary had her own smaller tree, near by, similarly fitted up.

Oliver thought all this was very well, but he liked to sit betimes on the roof of the house, in the deep shade, or to climb the steeple on the big barn, by the four flights of stairs, and "view the landscape o'er," a proceeding in which his sisters, not to be outdone, frequently imitated him. Indeed, Oliver was our forerunner in most of our outdoor-ish-ness, and but for his bright, tolerant spirit, our lives, so isolated as they were, would have missed much of the happiness of which they were stored full. For instance, one spring Oliver had a freak of walking on stilts; when, behold, up went his sisters on stilts as high as his, and came stalking after him. He spun a top; out came two others. He played marbles with the Hodge boys; down went the girls and learned the mysteries of "mibs," and "alleys," and the rest of it. He played "quoits" with horseshoes; so did they. He played "prisoner's-base" with the boys; they started the same game immediately. He climbed trees; they followed after. He had a cross-gun; they got him and Loren to help fit them out in the same way, and I painted in capitals along the side of mine its name, "Defiance," while Mary put on hers, plain "Bang Up!" After awhile he had a real gun and shot muskrats, teal, and once a long-legged loon. We fired the gun by "special permit" with mother looking on, but were forbidden to go hunting and didn't care to, anyway. Once, however, Oliver "dared" me to walk around the pasture ahead of him and his double-barreled gun when it was loaded and both triggers lifted. This I did, which was most foolhardy, and we two "ne'er-do-weels," whose secret no one knew but Mary, came home to find her watching at the gate with tear-stained face, and felt so ashamed of ourselves that we never repeated the sin—for it was nothing less. Oliver was famous at milking cows; his sisters learned the art, sitting beside him on three-legged stools, but never carried it to such perfection as he, for they were very fond of milk and he could send a stream straight into their mouths, which was greater fun than merely playing a tuneful tattoo into a tin pail, so they never reached distinction in the latter art. They did, however, train the cat to sit on the cow's back through milking time. Oliver could harness a horse in just about three minutes; his sisters learned to do the same, and knew what "hames" and "tugs" and "hold-backs" were, as well as "fetlock," "hock," and "pastern."

There were just four things he liked that we were not allowed to share— hunting, boating, riding on horseback and "going swimming." But at this distance it looks to this narrator as if hunting was what he would better not have done at all, and for the rest, it was a pity that "our folks" were so afraid "the two forest nymphs" might drown, that they didn't let them learn how not to— which boating and swimming lessons would have helped teach; and as for horseback-riding, it is one of the most noble sports on earth for men and women both. We proved it so when (after the calf-taming episode) it was permitted us, by the intercession of our mother, who had been a fine rider in her younger years.

Happy the girls of the period who practice nearly every outdoor sport that is open to their brothers; wear gymnastic suits in school, flee to the country as soon as vacation comes, and have almost as blessed a time as we three children had in the old days at Forest Home. It is good for boys and girls to know the same things, so that the former shall not feel and act so overwise. A boy whose sister knows all about the harness, the boat, the gymnastic exercise, will be far more modest, genial and pleasant to have about. He will cease to be a tease and learn how to be a comrade, and this is a great gain to him, his sister, and his wife that is to be. . . .

No girl went through a harder experience than I, when my free, out-of-door life had to cease, and the long skirts and clubbed-up hair spiked with hair-pins had to be endured. The half of that down-heartedness has never been told and never can be. I always believed that if I had been let alone and allowed as a woman, what I had had as a girl, a free life in the country, where a human being might grow, body and soul, as a tree grows, I would have been "ten times more of a person," every way. Mine was a nature hard to tame, and I cried long and loud when I found I could never again race and range about with freedom. I had delighted in my short hair and nice round hat, or comfortable "Shaker bonnet," but now I was to be "choked with ribbons" when I went into the open air the rest of my days. Something like the following was the "state of mind" that I revealed to my journal about this time:

This is my birthday and the date of my martyrdom. Mother insists that at last I must have my hair "done up woman-fashion." She says she can hardly forgive herself for letting me "run wild" so long. We've had a great time over it all, and here I sit like another Samson "shorn of my strength." That figure won't do, though, for the greatest trouble with me is that I never shall be shorn again. My "back" hair is twisted up like a corkscrew; I carry eighteen hair-pins; my head aches miserably; my feet are entangled in the skirt of my hateful new gown. I can never jump over a fence again, so long as I live. As for chasing the sheep, down in the shady pasture, it's out of the question, and to climb to my "Eagle's-nest" seat in the big burr-oak would ruin this new frock beyond repair. Altogether, I recognize the fact that my "occupation's gone."

Something else that had already happened, helped to stir up my spirit into a mighty unrest. This is the story as I told it to my journal:

This is election day and my brother is twenty-one years old. How proud he seemed as he dressed up in his best Sunday clothes and drove off in the big wagon with father and the hired men to vote for John C. Frémont, like the sensible "Free-soiler" that he is. My sister and I stood at the window and looked out after them. Somehow, I felt a lump in my throat, and then I couldn't see their wagon anymore, things got so blurred. I turned to Mary, and she, dear, little innocent, seemed wonderfully sober, too. I said, "Wouldn't you like to vote as well as Oliver? Don't you and I love the country just as well as he, and doesn't the country need our ballots?" Then she looked scared, but answered, in a minute, " 'Course we do, and 'course we ought,—but don't you go ahead and say so, for then we would be called strong-minded."

These two great changes in my uneventful life made me so distressed in heart that I had half a mind to run away. But the trouble was, I hadn't the faintest idea where to run to. Across the river, near Colonel Burdick's, lived Silas Hayner and several of his brothers, on their nice prairie farms. Sometimes Emily Scoville, Hannah Hayner, or some other of the active young women, would come over to help mother when there was more work than usual; and with Hannah, especially, I had fellowship, because, like myself, she was venturesome in disposition; could row a boat, or fire a gun, and liked to be always out-of-doors. She was older than I, and entered into all my plans. So we two foolish creatures planned to borrow father's revolver and go off on a wild-goose chase, crossing the river in a canoe and launching out to seek our fortunes. But the best part of the story is that we were never so silly as to take a step beyond the old home-roof, contenting ourselves with talking the matter over in girlish phrase, and very soon perceiving how mean and ungrateful such an act would be. Indeed, I told Mary and mother all about it, after a little while, and that ended the only really "wild" plan that I ever made, except another, not unlike it, in my first months at Evanston, which was also nothing but a plan.

"You must go to school, my child, and take a course of study; I wish it might be to Oberlin"—and this was my mother's quiet comment on the confession. "Your mind is active; you are fond of books and thoughts, as well as of outdoors; we must provide them for you to make up for the loss of your girlish good times;" so, without any scolding, this Roman matron got her daughter's aspirations into another channel. To be busy doing something that is worthy to be done is the happiest thing in all this world for girl or boy, for old or young. ✒

SUGGESTIONS FOR WRITING

1. Many people think that the rules for women's behavior have relaxed in our time. Do you agree? Compare the rules for socially acceptable women's behavior in our time with those depicted in Willard's account.

2. Is there a comparable moment in the lives of boys, when they must give up their "little-girlish" ways in order to become socially acceptable adult males? If so, describe what is involved in the change. If not, what does that tell us about the different socialization processes for men and women?

3. Are little boys in our society allowed more freedom than little girls? Describe some specific freedoms that are limited to boys.

4. Is life easier now for a "tomboyish" girl? Is it easier for an "effeminate" boy? Why or why not?

An Awakening . . .
Summer 1956

Nicholasa Mohr

*If you have ever visited a foreign country or even a different area of your own
country, you may have noticed that people there don't always talk or behave in
ways that you are used to. In its extreme, the difference between what you are
used to and what is happening in the new environment can make you feel uncomfortable and very aware that you are an outsider. This is sometimes referred
to as culture shock. Part of the excitement derived from exploring new environments comes from recognizing and evaluating these differences.*

*But not all cultural differences will be pleasant or make the outsider feel
welcome, especially when visitors unwittingly trigger a negative response simply because they are not native to the area. Prejudices are not universally
shared;* **Nicholasa Mohr** *explores what happens when a young woman
from Puerto Rico is stranded in a small Texas town where people with Latin
American features are not always welcome.*

*Mohr (b. 1935) writes and often illustrates young adult novels and short
stories about life in New York's Puerto Rican barrio:* Nilda *(1973),* El
Bronx Remembered: A Novella and Stories *(1977), and* Felita *(1979).
Her work has earned numerous awards, and she has contributed material to
many anthologies and magazines. Mohr has been writer- and artist-in-resi-
dence at colleges, universities, and schools.*

The young woman looked out of the window as the Greyhound bus sped by the
barren, hot, dry Texas landscape. She squinted, clearing her vision against the
blazing white sunlight. Occasionally, she could discern small adobe houses
clumped together like mushrooms, or a gas station and diner standing alone
and remote in the flat terrain. People were not visible. They were hiding, she
reasoned, seeking relief indoors in the shade. How different from her native
Puerto Rico, where luscious plants, trees and flowers were abundant. Green
was the color of that Island, soothing, cool, inviting. And people were seen everywhere, living, working, enjoying the outdoors. All of her life had been spent
on her beloved land. For more than a decade she had been in service of the
church. Now, this was a new beginning. After all, it had been her choice, her
sole decision to leave. At the convent school where she had been safe and
loved, they had reluctantly bid her farewell with an open invitation to return.
Leaving there had been an essential part of working it all out, she thought, one
had to start somewhere. Still, as she now looked out at all the barrenness before
her, she felt a stranger in a foreign land and completely alone.

She was on her way to spend the summer with her good friend Ann. They
were going to discuss the several directions in which she might continue to

work. After all, she had skills; her degrees in elementary education and a master's in counseling. There was also the opportunity offered her of that scholarship toward a doctorate in Ohio. The need to experience the world independently, without the protection of the church, was far more compelling than her new apprehension of the "unknown."

The young woman checked her wristwatch.

"On time . . ." she whispered, and settled back in her seat.

Her friend Ann was now a social worker with the working poor and the Mexican American community in a small town in rural Texas. The invitation to spend most of this summer with Ann and her family had appealed to the young woman, and she had accepted with gratitude.

"You know you are welcome to stay with us for just as long as you want," Ann had written. "You will be like another member of the family."

The knowledge that she would once more be with her good friend, discussing ideas and planning for the future, just as they had done as co-workers back home, delighted and excited her.

"Clines-Corners . . ." the bus driver announced. The next stop would be hers.

"Now, please wait at the bus depot, don't wander off. Promise to stay put, in case of a change in schedule, and we will pick you up," Ann had cautioned in her last letter.

"Sentry!" the bus driver shouted as the bus came to a sudden halt. She jumped down and the bus sped off barely missing a sleeping dog that had placed itself comfortably under the shade of a large roadside billboard. The billboard picture promised a cool lakeside ride on a motorboat, if one smoked mentholated cigarettes.

She found herself alone and watched a cloud of dust settle into the landscape as the bus disappeared into the horizon. She approached the depot building where two older Mexican men and a young black man, laborers, sat shaded on a wooden porch, eating lunch. She smiled and waved as she passed them. They nodded in response.

Inside the ticket booth, a tall man with very pink skin peered out at her from under a dark green sun visor.

"Good day," she cleared her throat. The man nodded and waited. "I was wondering . . . eh, if there was some message for me?"

"What?" he asked.

Feeling self-conscious and embarrassed, she repeated her question, adding. "I'm sorry, but it is that my English is not too perfect. I am not used to speaking English very often."

"What's you name? I can't know if there's a message for you if I don't know your name." She told him, speaking clearly and spelling each letter with care.

"Nope," he shook his head, "ain't nothing here for nobody by that name." The man turned away and continued his work.

The young woman stood for a moment wondering if her friends had received her wire stating she would arrive several hours earlier than expected. Checking the time she realized it was only twelve thirty. They were not expecting her until five in the late afternoon. She walked to the pay phone and dialed Ann's number. She waited as it rang for almost two full minutes before she replaced the receiver. Disappointed, she approached the clerk again.

"Excuse me, sir . . . can I please leave my luggage for a while? There is not an answer where my friends are living."

The man motioned her to a section of luggage racks.

"Cost you fifty cents for the first three hours, and fifteen cents for each hour after that. Pay when you come back." He handed her a soiled blue ticket.

"Thank you very much. Is there a place for me to get a cold drink? It's very hot . . . and I was riding on the bus for a long time."

"There's a Coke machine by the garage, right up the street. Can't miss it."

"Well, I would like a place to sit down. I think I saw a small restaurant up on the main street when I got off the bus."

"Miss, you'd be better off at the Coke machine. Soda's nice and cold. You can come back and drink it in here if you like." He looked at the young woman for a moment, nodded, and returned once more to his work.

She watched him somewhat confused and shrugged, then walked out into the hot empty street. Two mangy, flea-bitten mutts streaked with oil spots walked up to her wagging their tails.

"Bueno . . ." she smiled, "you must be my welcoming committee." They followed her as she continued up the main street. The barber shop and the hardware store were both closed. Out to lunch, she said to herself, and a nice siesta . . . now that's sensible.

Playful shouts and shrieking laughter emanated from a group of Mexican children. They ran jumping and pushing a large metal hoop. She waved at them. Abruptly, they stopped, looking with curiosity and mild interest at this stranger. They glanced at each other and, giggling, quickly began once more to run and play their game. In a moment they were gone, heading into a shaded side street.

The red and white sign above the small store displayed in bold printed letters: NATHANS FOOD AND GROCERIES—EAT IN OR TAKE OUT. On the door a smaller sign read, OPEN. Thankful, she found herself inside, enjoying the coolness and serenity of the small cafe. Two tables set against the wall were empty and except for a man seated at the counter, all the stools were unoccupied. No one else was in sight. She took a counter seat a few stools away from the man. After a minute or two, when no one appeared, the young woman cleared her throat and spoke.

"Pardon me . . . somebody. Please, is somebody here?" She waited and before she could speak again, she heard the man seated at the counter shout:

"ED! Hey Ed, somebody's out here. You got a customer!"

A middle-aged portly man appeared from the back. When he saw the young woman, he stopped short, hesitating. Slowly he walked up to her and silently stared.

"Good day," she said. "How are you?" The man now stood with his arms folded quite still without replying. "Can I please have a Pepsi-Cola." Managing a smile, she continued, "It is very hot outside, but I am sure you know that . . ."

He remained still, keeping his eyes on hers. The young woman glanced around her not quite sure what to do next. Then, she cleared her throat and tried again.

"A Pepsi-Cola, cold if you please . . ."

"Don't have no Pepsi-Colas," he responded loudly.

She looked around and saw a full fountain service, and against the rear wall, boxes filled with Pepsi-Colas.

"What's that?" she asked, confused.

The man gestured at the wall directly behind her. "Can't you read English."

Turning, she saw the sign he had directed her to. In large black letters and posted right next to the door she read:

NO COLOREDS
NO MEXICANS
NO DOGS
WILL BE SERVED ON THESE
PREMISES

All the blood in her body seemed to rush to her head. She felt her tongue thicken and her fingers turn as cold as ice cubes. Another white man's face appeared from the kitchen entrance and behind him stood a very black woman peering nervously over his shoulder.

The silence surrounding her stunned her as she realized at the moment all she was—a woman of dark olive complexion, with jet black hair; she spoke differently from these people. Therefore, she was all those things on that sign. She was also a woman alone before these white men. Jesus and the Virgin Mary . . . what was she supposed to do? Colors flashed and danced before her embracing the angry faces and cold hateful eyes that stared at her daring her to say another word. Anger and fear welled up inside her, and she felt threatened even by the shadows set against the bright sun; they seemed like daggers menacing her very existence. She was going to fight, she was not going to let them cast her aside like an animal. Deeply she inhaled searching for her voice, for her composure and without warning, she heard herself shouting.

"I WOULD LIKE A PEPSI-COLA, I SAID! AND, I WANT IT NOW . . . RIGHT NOW!!" The words spilled out in loud rasps. She felt her heart lodged in her throat, and swallowed trying to push it back down so that she could breathe once more.

"Can't you read . . . girl?" the man demanded.

"I WANT A PEPSI, DAMN IT . . . NOW!" With more boldness, this time her voice resounded, striking the silence with an explosion. Taking out her change purse she slammed several coins on the counter. "NOW!" she demanded staring at the man. "I'm not leaving until I get my drink."

As the young woman and the middle-aged portly man stared, searching each others' eyes, that moment seemed an eternity to her. All she was, all she would ever be, was here right now at this point in time. And so she stood very still, barely blinking and concentrated, so that not one muscle in her body moved.

He was the first to move. Shaking his head, he smiled and with slow deliberate steps walked over to the cases by the wall and brought back a bottle of

Pepsi-Cola, placing it before her. As she picked up the bottle, she felt the heat of the liquid; it was almost too hot to hold.

"Very well," she said, surprised at the calmness in her voice. "May I please have an opener?"

"Girl . . . we ain't got no openers here. Now you got your damned drink . . . that's it. Get the hell out of here!" He turned, ignoring her, and began to work arranging cups behind the counter.

Her eyes watched him and just for an instant the young woman hesitated before she stood, grabbed the bottle and lifted it high above her bringing it down with tremendous force and smashing it against the counter edge. Like hailstones in a storm, pieces of glass flew in every direction, covering the counter and the space around her. The warm bubbling liquid drenched her. Her heavy breathing sucked in the sweetness of the cola.

"KEEP THE CHANGE!" she shouted. Quickly she slammed the door behind her and once again faced the heat and the empty street.

She walked with her back straight and her head held high.

"BITCH!" she could hear his voice. "YOU DAMNED MEXICAN COLORED BITCH! CAN'T TREAT YOU PEOPLE LIKE HUMAN BEINGS . . . you no good . . ."

His voice faded as she walked past the main street, the bus depot and the small houses of the town. After what seemed a long enough time, she stopped, quite satisfied she was no longer in that town near that awful hateful man. The highway offered no real shade, and so she turned down a side road. There the countryside seemed gentler, a few trees and bushes offered some relief. A clump of bushes up on a mound of earth surrounded a maple tree that yielded an oasis of cool shade. She climbed up the mound and sat looking about her. She enjoyed the light breeze and the flight of large crows that dotted the sky in the distance. The image of the man and what had happened stirred in her a sense of humiliation and hurt. Tears clouded her view and she began to cry quietly at first, and then her sobs got louder. Intense rage overtook her and her sobbing became screams that pierced the quiet countryside. After a while, her crying subsided and she felt a sharp pain in her hand. She looked down and realized she still clenched tightly the neck of the broken Pepsi-Cola bottle. The jagged edges of glass had penetrated in between her thumb and forefinger; she was still bleeding. Releasing her grip, the young woman found a handkerchief in her pocket. Carefully she pressed it to the wound and in moments the bleeding stopped. Exhausted, she closed her eyes, leaned against the tree, and fell asleep.

She dreamt of that cool lakeside and the motorboat on the billboard, that might take her back home to safety and comfort. Friends would be there, waiting, protection hers just for the asking.

"Wake up . . . it's all right. It's me, Ann." She felt a hand on her shoulder and opened her eyes. Ann was there, her eyes filled with kindness and concern. Again, the young woman cried, openly and without shame, as she embraced her friend.

"I know, we got your wire, but only after we got home. By then it was late, around three o'clock, and we went looking for you right away. This is a very small town. You caused quite a stir. I should have warned you about things out here. But I thought it would be best to tell you when we were together. I'm so sorry . . . but don't worry . . . you are safe and with us. We are proud of you . . . the way you stood up . . . but, never mind that now. Let's get you home where you can rest. But, you were wonderful . . . ."

In the weeks that followed, the young woman worked with Ann. She made lifetime friends in the small Texas community. There were others like her and like Ann, who would fight against those signs. Civil rights had to be won and the battles still had to be fought. She understood quite clearly in that summer of 1956, that no matter where she might settle, or in which direction life would take her, the work she would commit herself to, and indeed her existence itself, would be dedicated to the struggle and the fight against oppression. Consciously for the very first time in her life, the young woman was proud of all she was, her skin, her hair and the fact that she was a woman.

Riding back East on the bus, she looked at her hand and realized the wound she had suffered had healed. However, two tiny scars remained, quite visible.

"A reminder . . . should I ever forget," she whispered softly.

Settling back, she let the rhythmic motion of the large bus lull her into a sweet sleep. The future with all its uncertainties was before her; now she was more than ready for this challenge. 🖋

SUGGESTIONS FOR WRITING

1. Every area has its outcast group or groups; they can be identified by ethnic background, social class, neighborhood, and so on. Persons from this "marked" group are treated as outsiders, shunned, and otherwise made to feel inferior. What group in your hometown filled this niche? Examine their "differences" and how these people were treated. See if you can determine why they were looked down upon.

2. At some time you may have witnessed an act of blind prejudice such as the one Mohr described. Describe what happened, the reactions of the people involved, and your own response.

3. If you attended public schools, you more than likely had classmates from a variety of ethnic and social backgrounds. Examine what effect this diversity had on your "education." If you did not attend an ethnically or culturally diverse school, explore what it meant to attend a school where everyone was pretty much like you.

2

COMING TO TERMS
WITH YOURSELF

The process of developing an identity does not stop at the end of childhood. It is a lifelong process of growth, adjustment, defiance, acceptance. At different moments we either accept the social definitions of the groups we belong to, or we rebel against them, claiming the right to define ourselves. In adulthood it no longer surprises us that people stereotype and prejudge others, and we learn how to cope with what they might think of us. Many people learn to be proud of who they are, even if they belong to groups that others despise. Social definitions of the categories of gender, race, and class do not go away. If we accept our identity as a member of such groups, these definitions become a stable part of who we are. And even if we reject those definitions, we still have to spend much of our lives defying others who would impose the definitions on us.

All societies, for example, produce definitions of masculinity. A man must negotiate that definition for himself. In our society, perhaps the dominant image of the masculine is macho, which requires the man to be powerful, controlling, rational, and unemotional. But this is not the only image available. Even mass-media images of men are more various. There are men who show emotion and refuse to dominate others. There is Clint Eastwood, but there are also Woody Allen and Phil Donohue and Spike Lee and Richard Simmons and Bill Cosby—each of these men suggesting another role for men to follow. There are so many possibilities, in fact, that the "dominant" stereotype no longer seems so powerful. Men continue to come to terms with themselves as men throughout their lives. The matter is never settled. And for each individual, a similar process goes on in terms of race, social class, and all the other factors that determine a social identity.

This section of the book offers texts that describe this adult process of coming to terms with oneself. Among the texts are stories about dealing with prejudice, essays in praise of the groups the writer belongs to, and accounts of the writers' refusal to accept social definitions. You will be asked to write about how you are engaged in this process as well. This exercise will ask you to deal with the effort that we all make to understand and define our personal experience in the terms that society makes available to us. We expect that you will know yourself better because of the work you put into reading and writing about the experiences that this section presents.

BLUE BLOOD BLUES

E. Digby Baltzell

This brief essay from 1989 comes to the defense of George Bush, who had been characterized by his opponents as a "wimp," in part because of his up-bringing in the highest American social class. Baltzell recounts the historical role of that class in American political leadership and points to Bush's back-ground as a source of pride and tradition. Baltzell is clearly a part of the class he defends with such energy. He has had a lifelong academic interest as a so-ciologist in the elite groups—mainly Eastern, upper-class, Protestant, Ivy League-educated—that Bush is a part of. As a result, the essay seems to be as much a defense of Baltzell's own identity as it is of Bush. Baltzell's essay can also be seen as a defense of the accomplishments of white men, in the context of a moment when the contributions of women and ethnic groups are being emphasized.

Baltzell (b. 1915) is the author of such books as The Philadelphia Gen-tleman *(1958),* The Protestant Establishment *(1964), and* Puritan Bos-ton and Quaker Philadelphia.

In our rootless and resentful age of increasingly classless bureaucracy, George Bush purportedly has a "class problem" which I should like to look at here from a historical perspective.

Throughout most of this so-called Century of the Common Man, the sub-ject of class in America has had much the same closed-closet status as mastur-bation and fornication: ladies and gentlemen simply did not talk about such things in mixed company or in public. Since the '60s, however, when every damned thing was dragged out of the closet, and ladylike and gentlemanly manners were dismissed as elitist, everybody has been free to talk about any-thing, anywhere at anytime, few suspecting that a world without closets might already be well on its way to barbarism. In this new climate of opinion, I should not have been taken by surprise when one of my students at Penn during the '70s came up to me after class and asked: "What's *your* class background, pro-fessor?" "None of your business, my boy," I replied with a smile. Nor should I have been enraged as I watched Diane Sawyer rudely ask George Bush, in front of millions of TV viewers, to explain why people thought of him as a wimp. Had I been Bush, I would have kicked her, but Bush did his best to answer her patiently and politely. I suspect that Sawyer hardly remembers that people like her once thought of Franklin Roosevelt as the equivalent of a wimpy preppy (or featherduster), although the term "wimp" was not coined until our present unisexual age, and the term "preppy" was never used, especially when referring to a graduate of Groton School, where Roosevelt was educated in the British tradition of the Christian gentleman by his headmaster and later lifelong friend, Endicott Peabody, who *never* referred to Groton as a prep school.

Even Walter Lippmann, the George Will of his age, was somewhat deceived by FDR's accent and easy patrician charm. In his now famous column in the *Herald Tribune*, Lippmann wrote of candidate Roosevelt, in 1932, as a "a highly impressionable person . . . without very strong convictions. . . . He is an amiable man with many philanthropic impulses, but he is not the dangerous enemy of anything." All too eager to please and too cautious to take political risks, Roosevelt, Lippmann concluded, was merely "a pleasant man who, without any important qualifications for the office, would very much like to be president." What Lippmann and many others failed to take into account, according to Lippmann's biographer, Ronald Steel, was Roosevelt's "tenacious will." Perhaps we should remember that George Bush also possesses a tenacious will beneath his obvious good manners.

In spite of our cherished "Log Cabin" myth, President Bush is now part of a long tradition of aristocratic and patrician presidents. Washington, the two Adamses, Jefferson, Madison, Monroe, and the two Harrisons, in the 18th and 19th centuries, and the two Roosevelts, Taft, Wilson, and Kennedy, in the 20th, were all born to families of the very highest social status in their respective communities; Washington was one of the wealthiest men of his day.

But of course everybody knows that wealth and privilege are a great help to anyone seeking high office in America; less obvious, however, is the fact that high performance in office is also correlated with privileged origins. Thus, of our six greatest presidents—Lincoln, Franklin Roosevelt, Washington, Jefferson, Theodore Roosevelt, and Wilson—all save Lincoln were born to privilege. On the other hand, of the five presidents—Lincoln, Eisenhower, Fillmore, Andrew Johnson, and Nixon—born with the least advantages, only Lincoln and Eisenhower performed above average in office, while Fillmore, Andrew Johnson, and Nixon were well below average, if not outright failures.

George Bush is also part of a venerable WASP establishment tradition of Skull and Bones men in the nation's service: President William Howard Taft, his son, Senator Robert Taft, Henry Stimson, Averell Harriman, Justice Potter Stewart, William and McGeorge Bundy, and the late Malcolm Baldrige. Stimson—who served in high appointive offices under Theodore Roosevelt, Taft, Wilson, Coolidge, Hoover, Franklin Roosevelt, and Truman—was Andover Academy's most distinguished alumnus when he gave the graduation address to George Bush's class of 1942.

Traditions are produced by a cumulation of successful experiments down through the ages. Or as Oliver Wendell Holmes Jr. once wrote: "A page of history is worth a volume of logic." The patriarchal family, for instance, has proved to be an empirically successful through hundreds of generations, while the egalitarian family is largely the reasoned product of our age alone. And, from all historical evidence, Bush's privileged class origins should have been, from the beginning, an asset rather than a liability; indeed, perhaps the preppy, wimpy, elitist issue has been a problem for media intellectuals alone. By and large I have always assumed that liberal intellectuals have resented *other* people's privileges far more than the average man on the street, or on the factory floor. Thus, Frank Greer, a Democratic consultant, was quoted by *Newsweek* as saying during the presidential campaign: "If I were managing Bush, I wouldn't be filming commercials in Kennebunkport, I'd be in the working-class neighborhoods of Houston. . . ."

Fortunately, intellectuals are sometimes divided on issues, and *Newsweek* also noted that Faith Popcorn, a social trend analyst of some wit, thought that "the elitist thing is just the ticket" for George Bush. "Money could be his flag—how everyone can aspire to getting some," Popcorn continued. "And, after all, there is a return to fashion of good families, good schools, quality. The Kennedys didn't hide it. Why should he? If Ralph Lauren can sell the Polo line to the country, why can't Bush sell polo to the masses . . .? But he needs a style of his own. Maybe he needs a Scottie." It is my impression that the political forecasters would have profited far more from Popcorn's wit than from Greer's elitist and patronizing conventional wisdom.

Finally, if one may be allowed to bare one's private fantasies, I should suggest that if all the young girls growing up in America today were to marry the first boy they ever kissed, in the style of our First Lady, our beleaguered land would be well on its way to solving its tragic problems of poverty, AIDS, and abortion.

SUGGESTIONS FOR WRITING

1. In your opinion, does George Bush exhibit the style of the upper class? Analyze the elements of his leadership style and his appearance on TV that suggest his elite background and those that do not.

2. Examine the tone of Baltzell's essay. Is he angry? Defensive? Use specific examples of his language that express his tone.

3. Describe your attitudes toward the wealthy and toward members of elite social groups. What is there in your background and experience that accounts for that attitude?

4. Describe the behavior of the elite social and economic group in your town. How do they differ from your social group? If you were brought up in an elite group, describe how you felt about these differences.

DRESSING FOR SEXESS

Margaret Kent

"Dressing for Sexess" is a chapter from **Margaret Kent**'s book, How to
Marry the Man of Your Choice (1984). *The book came out of Kent's series of seminars on this theme, which had grown out of her familiarity with
women who had been divorced and were anxious about finding a new mate.
The premise of the book is that women can take active steps to find and win
in marriage the kind of man they desire. In this chapter she outlines the decisions a woman should make about her personal appearance if her goal is to
attract men to her. Kent uses the word "manipulation," which usually has a
negative connotation, to describe this process of controlling men's responses.
But the argument of the book is that the goal of marriage is so important that
it requires women to make a conscious effort to achieve that end.*

When you go out to meet men, do you go "as is"? Or do you take a shower, fix
your hair, put on makeup, and dress in a way you think will enhance your appeal? Are you, in fact, planning your appearance? If so, you are already using
your looks to "manipulate" men. This chapter will help you learn how to use
this form of manipulation more effectively.

Don't let the power of clothing pass you by, for it can be a major asset in attracting men. If you are afraid to read further because you have limited funds
or a body that's not quite fit for fashion, don't worry. As you will see, you don't
need thin thighs to marry the man of your choice. The use of clothing to attract
men has nothing to do with fashion or size.

Don't feel guilty about using your appearance to manipulate men. You are
not going to create a relationship under false pretenses. By being noticed by
men, and, most important, by *not* scaring them off, you'll give your new relationships a chance to prosper.

FOR WHOM DO YOU DRESS?

Answer this question honestly. For whom do you really dress? If your answer is
"other women," then you are not dressing in a manner that appeals to men. If
you dress to impress other women, your clothes are working against you, not for
you, in your quest for a mate.

You are dressing to please other women if you buy the expensive fashions of
many of the prominent designers. Some designers, but not all, do their best to
distort the female form; it's as if they view the female body as unappealing.
Women who wear those outfits often appear to men as unfriendly and unavailable for dating. If you wear designer garments, select your designer with a great

deal of care. Some fashions can enhance your appearance, but it is hard for most women to know which ones have a positive effect on men.

Chances are, you were first taken shopping by your mother and waited on by a saleswoman. If this is your situation, you probably do not know which clothing appeals to men.

If you dress for other women, these other women may be impressed by the sophistication of the design, the creativity of the designer, or the money you spent. These factors, however, do not impress most men.

If you dress for "business," your business clothes probably emulate men's clothing. The major difference between your suits and a man's suits is that his have pants and yours probably have skirts. If this is your situation, you need a separate social wardrobe.

Many women dress properly for men when they're not paying attention to their clothing. When these women are not focusing on their clothes, they may wear, for instance, a solid color cotton T-shirt and simple straight skirt. In contrast, when they dress for a date, they look like mannequins wrapped in lace or in unnatural nightwear.

Select your wardrobe carefully, as it can be a real plus in attracting men. Your goal in dressing for a man should be to dress "friendly." Dressing friendly does *not* mean wearing a wet T-shirt or a see-through blouse. Stir his sexual imagination without satisfying his curiosity about your body.

If you want to dress to please men, follow these twenty simple principles.

1. Cleanliness Is Especially Important

If you have the clean, fresh look that a recent shower gives, you can wear a potato sack and still be desirable.

2. Follow the Form of Your Body

What do you think when you see a man in a plaid suit, polka-dot tie, and white socks? You view him as a nerd and reject him. Yet this man may be expending a great deal of effort to meet women, and may dress as he does to gain your attention.

It may surprise you, but women can make the same type of errors in their wardrobe. Women can be nerds, too.

To avoid being a nerd, wear clothing that follows the natural form of your body. Keep the waistline at the waist. Avoid the waistband under the bosom (the Empire style) or at the hips (the Twenties style). Avoid huge puffy sleeves that make the upper arms appear enormous. Avoid frills, pleats, or gathers that distort your neck, breasts, arms, legs, or thighs. You're better off draping a sheet over your head and tying it at your waist than wearing these uncomplimentary styles.

3. Color

Wear clothing that has a solid color, or at most a small print or stripes that will not detract from the contours of your body.

An outfit that looks busy is like the picture game in which you must find ten things that are wrong. If there are too many distracting items, it will take too much effort to "figure" out your body's shape. Your goal in selecting clothing is enhancement of your appeal. Don't hide your female attributes with confusing patterns.

The basic colors—black, white, red, yellow, and blue—are usually the best. Pink should be avoided unless the style is very sophisticated, because it often connotes that the wearer is a girl, not a woman. Green, orange, and purple are usually less attractive than the basic colors.

4. Fabrics

Consider sex as an electrical force and clothing as the body's insulation. Wear a fabric that "insulates" sexually, but does not create a stiff barrier. Choose a fabric that is soft to the touch and transmits some body warmth. Most natural fabrics—such as silk and soft cottons—and some artificial fabrics—such as silk-like polyesters—are acceptable. Above all, avoid rough, scratchy materials such as metallics, corduroy, or nubby wools.

5. Undergarments

Tight undergarments such as corsets and girdles are a misery of the past. If you own any such instruments of torture, toss them out! No matter how large a woman you are, you are more appealing if your body is unconstricted and natural. If you're bound up in a girdle, you'll look like you're in a body cast or brace. Even if you do look ten pounds thinner, these garments are *not* effective in attracting men.

6. Shirts and Blouses

When you select a blouse, choose one that has an open neckline and small collar. Your blouse should draw attention to your breasts, but not be revealing. Wear a shirt-type blouse or other blouse with buttons in front. These blouses show easy access to your breasts even if the blouse is not the slightest bit revealing. Let the man fantasize even though you don't give him permission to touch.

T-shirts are great. It doesn't take much male imagination to know that in less than five seconds they are off over your head.

7. Skirts

Skirt lengths should be short, but within the normal range for where you live. Skirts that are too short are associated with hookers. If you are sufficiently thin, you can wear a skirt that hugs your sexy body contours. If you are not model thin, though, wear skirts that loosely outline the body and appear easy to raise. Pleats, stiff materials, uneven hemlines, and other devices distort the body to sexlessness. Skirts that button up the front are fine because they stir the imagination.

8. Pants

Men generally prefer to see women in skirts or dresses, not slacks. If you *do* wear slacks, a solid color is best. Avoid plaids and pleats. Jeans are likely to get a positive response because they are snug and outline the body; they also represent casualness and comfort. If you wear slacks other than jeans, wear white or blue or black, not orange or yellow.

9. Shorts

Men like shorts on women. Short shorts are especially appealing, but be sure they are within the norms of your community before you wear them in public. Your shorts should be relatively snug, yet provide you with enough range of movement for your active life. Avoid pleats, even when pleats are in style, as they distort your figure. Select a solid color, not a busy pattern.

10. Bathing Suits

You don't need a bikini—or a bikini figure—to lure men. But if you do decide to wear one, a solid color is usually the best, and be sure the top and bottom match. Make sure your bikini is not the skimpiest, and be sure to stay within the norms of society. And don't go to the other extreme and wear a bathing suit that has a skirt or ruffles.

11. Shoes

Your legs look more attractive if you wear shoes with heels. A slight lift accentuates the calves and creates graceful leg lines. Avoid high heels, though, so that you don't look awkward when you walk or run. Clumsiness isn't sexy. Wear shoes that slip off easily, not shoes with ankle straps.

12. Panty Hose

Garters have been relegated to the category of sexual aides or props; they are no longer items of clothing. When you wear hose, always wear hose that reach high on the thighs. The last thing you want is an elastic stocking band that interrupts a man's imagination as his eyes glide up your leg. Avoid white hose. Natural-color panty hose is preferable, but there are occasions when black net hose may be called for.

13. Hair

Your hair can be an important asset. The style you choose should make a man want to run his fingers through your hair. You don't need beautiful hair—it's "touchability" that attracts most men. You needn't spend much time on your hair. In fact, most women would do better with men if they fussed with it less. Fix your hair for the man's point of view. Cleanliness and softness are the keys.
Ten specific guidelines:

1. Avoid extreme styles—unless you are looking for a man who is an extremist. Stay away from punk.
2. Avoid hair that is too short. Here is a rule of thumb that really is a rule of thumb: Have hair at least as long as your thumb.

3. If you use hair spray, avoid the three S's: hair spray that is smelly or sticky or makes your hair stiff.
4. Make sure your hair looks soft, not brittle.
5. Once your hair starts to turn gray, the right hair coloring can be a real beauty enhancer. Most men do not like gray hair because it generally makes a woman look older. If you color your hair, be consistent and make sure that roots don't show. Black roots make blonde hair look phony.
6. Don't wear a hat indoors, and don't wear a hat outdoors unless it is absolutely necessary because of the weather. Men love to see a woman's hair.
7. Do not wear curlers in your hair when you are with your man.
8. Avoid frizzy perms.
9. Get rid of those split ends.
10. Get yourself a hairdo that's fun for him to fondle. Keep your hair free of snarls and knots.

14. Jewelry

Are you looking to meet new men, or are you looking to strengthen your present relationship? Your answer to this question should determine the way you wear jewelry, and even the jewelry you wear.

A man looks at your jewelry—or lack of it—as a sign of your availability to him. In particular, he will glance at your hands. If he sees even one ring, he may assume you're not available.

The age-old custom of a man giving an engagement ring and a wedding ring to his woman has a present-day purpose. These rings are designed as barriers to intimidate other men. The single most common mistake widows in search of companionship make is not taking off their wedding rings.

If you are still looking for the man of your choice, avoid rings until you find him. A man views every ring you wear as a commitment ring, given by some other man with whom you have a relationship. You may have bought the ring yourself, or it may have been your grandmother's, but the man you are hoping to meet does not know its origin. Keep your heirlooms in the vault, not on your fingers. When you meet the right man, let him buy you new rings.

A watch is the only jewelry you should wear on your hands or arms (and wear only one watch at a time). Avoid bracelets, as they detract from the man's image of caressing your arms. Also, men generally dislike the noise they make.

There are times when wearing jewelry is appropriate. If you are invited to a gala event where all that glitters is gold, you would feel out of place wearing only your functional watch. For these occasions, the best jewelry is a necklace, especially if it hints at sexuality. A necklace that is tight around your neck may appear unfriendly to the man, as well as uncomfortable for you. Circular necklaces, especially those made of beads, are often a turnoff. Your best bet is to wear a necklace that looks triangular or "plunging," with larger jewels in the center. You will do better wearing one attractive necklace that enhances you than a few different and dissimilar necklaces that distract from your form.

Pendants should be avoided, because they indicate commitment to another man. If you wear a pendant, avoid anything that looks like a locket, or anything shaped like a heart, or a pendant with one single jewel. Also avoid diamond pendants. If you do wear a pendant, wear a pendant with more than one gem.

Avoid wearing visible religious symbols unless you want to attract a man who shares the religious belief that the symbol connotes.

Earrings can be a detriment, especially if they detract from your hair. A man will envision himself nibbling at your ear lobes, and will view earrings that are physically sharp or look like mobiles as barriers. Smaller earrings are preferable to large ones.

There are times at which you should wear no jewelry at all. Do not wear jewelry at the beach, on casual dates, to sporting events, or on the job.

Men look at a woman's jewelry to determine if she is overly materialistic. If a woman shows too strong an interest in jewelry, and wears jewelry when it is inappropriate, she will turn off most men. Diamonds, therefore, are often not a girl's best friend when it comes to attracting men. Perhaps they are even her worst enemy! Never wear diamonds in a way that could lead a man to think you are committed to someone else. You may be better off with emerald, topaz, amethyst, aquamarine, or other gems.

And one final note: Junk jewelry is just that—junk. Junk is cute on a teeny-bopper, but not on a grown woman. If you wear jewelry, it should be the real thing or nothing at all.

15. Nails

Forget about growing long fingernails. They may impress other women, but they do not appeal to men. Long nails may indicate to many men that the woman is unwilling to do household tasks and is unavailable for recreational activities. Also, men view long fingernails as "claws." Keep your nails clean, at a working length, and without jagged edges.

If you must paint your nails, use clear nail polish or a shade in the red family. Men are more comfortable with painted fingernails on women than they are with painted toenails. If you use nail polish on your toes, limit yourself to clear polish.

You may want long fingernails for gala events, but don't grow your nails just for these occasions. Since you don't want long nails all the time, rely on artificial ones instead.

16. Makeup

One major error that many women make is the excessive and incorrect use of makeup. You are better off with no makeup than with the wrong makeup.

The sexiest part of a woman is her face. If you are looking to attract men, your face needs to look kissable. This does not mean that you are giving a stranger *permission* to kiss you, but you do want him to *think* about kissing you. Unless you select your makeup very carefully, it will hinder rather than enhance your appeal.

Don't surround your eyes with circles of purple. If your eye makeup is obvious to the man, it is excessive.

Men are not eager to rub cheeks with a woman who is caked with powder or foundation. Many men have tasted face powder, and not one has enjoyed it, so minimize its use.

When you wear lipstick, be sure it does not smear. Also: Men prefer to kiss a woman who is wearing lipstick that is in the red family, not some more exotic color.

Careful use of makeup can keep you from looking too young and sexless, or too old and haggard. Older women generally need more makeup than younger women, so your makeup strategy may need to be updated from time to time.

17. Perfume

Excessive use of perfume makes a woman *less* desirable. As with makeup, it is better to use no perfume at all than too much.

If you seek an aroma, choose a cologne or toilet water rather than a perfume, as it has a more pleasant aftereffect.

And don't expect a man to share your interest in perfumes. He is highly unlikely to know or care about the brand names, but will be offended by a perfume named after an illicit drug.

18. Teeth

You kiss with your lips, of course, but you also kiss with your teeth. Make sure your teeth are appealing.

1. Food particles between the teeth, especially the front teeth, are highly undesirable. Use dental floss if you need it, but not in public.
2. Good dental care is essential, but a man isn't going to be interested in your cavities, caps, and fillings unless he is a dentist. Make sure that your teeth look natural. Avoid looking like a mine waiting to be excavated for gold and silver.
3. If you are missing teeth, get dentures. Missing teeth are a definite turn-off.

19. Overweight?

Are you too fat? Are you worried about your weight? Then here is some good news: A few extra pounds will rarely cost you the relationship. In fact, you are much more likely to lose a man by extreme dieting, especially if the diet involves self-denial. Don't be overly conscious of your weight, or you will make *him* conscious of it.

Do not delay your quest for a mate with the excuse that you must diet. You don't have to choose between love and food.

However, if you weigh twenty percent more than the standard weight for your height, you will lose a few men. Your losses will climb dramatically if you weigh an extra fifty percent. If your weight is double the standard weight, it will be quite difficult to find anyone to date. Of course, if you are truly obese, weight reduction is in order. If you are under five feet tall and weigh more than three hundred pounds, make weight reduction your priority. More than dating is at stake here.

20. Eyeglasses

Are you wearing glasses to see or to be seen? A carefully chosen pair of glasses will make you more attractive. But how you deal with people also depends upon how well you see them. If your vision is inadequate, you will lose out. No man wants to date someone who fumbles and stumbles.

Contact lenses are not necessary and are not always preferable to glasses. Here are some hints for selecting eyeglasses:

1. Select the thinnest lens that gives you the optical correction you require.
2. Avoid glasses that are too trendy or extreme.
3. A man must be able to make eye contact with you, so avoid reflecting glasses, prism glasses, and other glasses that hide your eyes.

FIRST IMPRESSIONS

First impressions are the strongest and are often irreversible. The first impression you make on a man types you. You don't know what man is waiting around the corner to meet you or is observing you from afar, so act at all times as if you believe in yourself. Do not act like a loser or otherwise allow yourself to exhibit any feelings of inferiority. Present yourself as a winner, and soon you will become one. ✐

SUGGESTIONS FOR WRITING

1. Write a "Dress for Sexess" for men. Describe how men would have to dress and rearrange themselves if they were to conform to women's ideas of what makes men attractive.

2. Who holds the power in the process that Kent describes? She talks about women "manipulating" men, but she also argues that women should make themselves look how men want them to look. If a woman followed Kent's suggestions, in what ways would she gain or lose power?

3. How much does physical appearance contribute to our personal identity? Describe the ways that you adjust your personal appearance to the desires of others.

4. What kinds of personal appearance advice do magazines give to women of college age? How important is it for college women to follow that advice?

IN CELEBRATION OF
MY UTERUS

Anne Sexton

For much of her life, the great American poet **Anne Sexton** *(1928–1974)
was the victim of severe depression and was under the care of psychiatrists,
in and out of psychiatric hospitals. As a part of her early therapy she joined a
writing group and began producing poetry. Sexton was not afraid to voice
her own fears and concerns in her poetry, even when the subject matter
touched on the most intimate details of her life and her sexuality. Sexton
wrote about herself, in particular about herself as a woman, but the issues
that she explores are of concern to both women and men. The female body
often provides Sexton with a basis from which to explore who she is as a
woman, and she writes frankly about such things as drug addiction, suicide,
menstruation, incest, abortion, adultery, and masturbation. Unable to conquer the impulse that drove her toward self-destruction, Sexton committed
suicide in 1974.*

In the poem In Celebration of My Uterus, *Sexton examines her body
and her femaleness. By focusing on that which marks her as a woman—her
uterus, Sexton reaches toward an appreciation of what being female can
mean. Her vision is not that there is only one way to "be" female, but that a
multiplicity of avenues exist for women to express their female nature.*

Everyone in me is a bird.
I am beating all my wings.
They wanted to cut you out
but they will not.
They said you were immeasurably empty
but you are not.
They said you were sick unto dying
but they were wrong.
You are singing like a school girl.
You are not torn.

Sweet weight,
in celebration of the woman I am
and of the soul of the woman I am
and of the central creature and its delight
I sing for you. I dare to live.
Hello, spirit. Hello, cup.
Fasten, cover. Cover that does contain.
Hello to the soil of the fields.
Welcome, roots.

Each cell has a life.
There is enough here to please a nation.
It is enough that the populace own these goods.
Any person, any commonwealth would say of it,
"It is good this year that we may plant again
and think forward to a harvest.
A blight had been forecast and has been cast out."
Many women are singing together of this:
one is in a shoe factory cursing the machine,
one is at the aquarium tending a seal,
one is dull at the wheel of her Ford,
one is at the toll gate collecting,
one is tying the cord of a calf in Arizona,
one is straddling a cello in Russia,
one is shifting pots on the stove in Egypt,
one is painting her bedroom walls moon color,
one is dying but remembering a breakfast,
one is stretching on her mat in Thailand,
one is wiping the ass of her child,
one is staring out the window of a train
in the middle of Wyoming and one is
anywhere and some are everywhere and all
seem to be singing, although some can not
sing a note.

Sweet weight,
in celebration of the woman I am
let me carry a ten-foot scarf,
let me drum for the nineteen-year-olds,
let me carry bowls for the offering
(if that is my part).
Let me study the cardiovascular tissue,
let me examine the angular distance of meteors,
let me suck on the stems of flowers
(if that is my part).
Let me make certain tribal figures
(if that is my part).
For this thing the body needs
let me sing
for the supper,
for the kissing,
for the correct
yes.

SUGGESTIONS FOR WRITING

1. Examine your responses to Sexton's poem. In particular, analyze how you reacted to her awareness of and description of her uterus.

2. In some families females are often taught to be ashamed—or at least secretive—about their menstrual cycle; in other families it is a celebrated event. Analyze these two responses and examine your own feelings. Would you respond differently than your family did?

3. Do you agree that in our society women tend to be more shy about their bodies than men? What in our culture accounts for this difference?

WHY I SMELL LIKE THIS

Roy Blount, Jr.

Roy Blount, Jr. (b. 1941) is one of America's most successful and funniest humorists. His essays have been collected in such books as About Three Bricks Shy of a Load, What Men Don't Tell Women, Not Exactly What I Had in Mind, *and* Now, Where Were We?, *in which this essay appears. Blount's goofy story illustrates the lengths to which a guy will go to explain why he is doing something that doesn't seem very masculine, in this case shopping for scent. The story is set in Bloomingdale's, a store that always attempts to make shopping an elegant and sensuous experience. Blount feels hopelessly out of place there, but that's where the fun comes from.*

I burst into the last place on earth where I would go willingly—the men's fragrance department in Bloomingdale's—exclaiming, "I want to smell better."

Which was a lie.

The Board Room is what Bloomingdale's calls the place where it pushes men's aromas: a confined passage maybe ten yards long and three yards wide between two counters, with a little alcove in one corner. The walls and ceiling are chrome and black. Hanging on the walls are photographs of fragrances. Fragrances—men's, especially—are hard to capture visually. Several of these photographs show blown-up decanterlike bottles, bottles looking heavy enough to brain intruders with, yet bottles that glow. Bottles containing dynamic, masculine fragrances. Some of their names: Grey Flannel. Gruene. Quorum. Entrepreneur.

Rife—not to mention ripe—as this areaway is with scent, it seems even rifer, both behind and in front of the counters, with salespersons. Watching your movements. Making eye contact. Saying, "Citrus, of course. And black pepper. With a base of musk." Or, "Can I borrow your nose?"

I say "watching your movements," but I assume you have never been there. Who would go there? What was I doing there? I have a dynamic, masculine explanation. The only conceivable one.

I was scared.

Unless fear has an odor, I felt I smelled okay. Generally, all I feel I need to keep me fresh enough is baking soda. Some kind of product with baking soda in it. There is this toothpaste I have been able to find only in the South and the Midwest, called Peak, that has baking soda in it, and there is Shower to Shower body powder, which has baking soda and cornstarch in it.

I am not a shill for the baking soda and cornstarch industries. I am just saying these things meet my needs. So far as I can tell. And who wants to dwell too much on how he smells?

I have no business being in a store such as Bloomingdale's. It is not my scene. It makes me exude a slow, clinging, heavier-than-liquid sweat. But I went there out of the kindness of my heart, to buy a present. I was . . . shopping.

Once I met a woman who, in filling out a form for a computer dating service, had put down under hobbies, "Shopping and crying."

I am not like that. I will cry if I have to, but I would rather not, and I am the same way about shopping.

Well, I like to shop for groceries, because you don't have to try on groceries. And in grocery stores, they don't squirt things on you. They don't run out at you, shouting, "Here! Here! wouldn't you like some of this cheese stuff on your tongue?"

Bloomingdale's is so intense. There are so many people in there who—you can tell by the looks on their faces—promised themselves that they wouldn't go in there. Promised themselves, their parents, their spouses, their accountants: They wouldn't go in there for the rest of the month, at least. But there they are, again, driven by mindless need. They are shopping. And when they get home, they will cry.

And while they are in Bloomingdale's, they are being called to by sirens. People of both sexes line the aisles, brandishing hot-on-the-market unguents, emollients, wrinkle erasers, aura enhancers, antistaleness agents, musk elicitors, liquid talcs, essences of black orchid and teak.

And these sirens are not content just to tout their products. They try to get some on you. The air is full of their sprays, and if they can get ahold of your hand, they will squeeze creams out onto it.

And the names of these products! Niosôme. You know what Niosôme is? It is, according to a leaflet that was thrust into my hands, "beyond a cream or a lotion to a first-of-its-kind système." It is "a complex of . . . microscopic, multilayered spheres that are totally unique in their composition and action. In a phenomenon called biomimitism, these spheres mimic the skin's intercellular support organization."

Do you want a phenomenon like that going on, on your skin?

And what does the word "niosôme" (if "word" is the word for it) look like, at first, to you? To me, it looks like "noisome."

They give these products offensive-looking names! They make you think. Perhaps I'm noisome!

"Why don't you try some B.O.?" said one of the six or eight or ten salespersons in Bloomingdale's men's fragrance department, which, as I have said, is called the Board Room.

"What? You're going to spray *body odor* on me? *Whose?*" I cried.

"No, no," said the salesperson. "V.O."

"Whiskey? You're going to spray whiskey on me?"

"No, no. V.O. Eau de Toilette Homme." V.O. stands for Version Originale.

It's all foreign names in these tony smell parlors, you know. You don't see your basic green American skin bracers; you see things named for princesses, and I don't mean Fergie. I thought exotic princesses spent their time trying not to get caught on mattresses with peas under them, but no, not today! Today, they crank out effluvia for men!

You think I was oversensitive to this V.O. reference? You think I'm leaping to the conclusion that fragrance names seek to evoke *fear?*

Okay, then, why was there a beautiful woman standing in a Bloomingdale's aisle under a sign that said "POISON"? Poison! She was standing there trying to put Poison on people and then looking cranky when they didn't buy some!

"Poison?" I said to her.

"No, no," she said semi-indulgently. *"Pwa-zawnh.* It is French." And she showed me on the sample that she was trying to get within squirting distance of my wrist: "NEW POISON CRÈME SOMPTUEUSE."

"Are you sure that's right?" I asked. "Are you sure it's not supposed to be spelled *poisson,* which I happen to know means 'fish'?"

"No, no," she said less indulgently. *"Pwa-zawnh.* It is a French word meaning 'beautiful woman.' "

"I see," I said. A dab of it had appeared on the back of my hand. It smelled all right, I guess, but it looked like bird-doo.

"Rub it in," she urged.

I ran. Because I was desperate. Poison wasn't enough, I needed something stronger. And that is how I found myself in the Board Room.

Where, as I say, there must have been at least eight salespersons behind the counters. And each of them wanted to spray me with something. And I let them! I even sprayed things on myself! Eight, ten, twelve different things, containing cardamom, galbanum, *lavande, bois de rose, moussse de chêne, cannelle,* cumin, patchouli, geranium, wood notes, leather, tobacco, oak moss, and citrus.

And vanilla. Do you know those ads in which several people are pictured in a grainy naked heap, always with an extra leg or so that you can't quite tell the sex or owner of? Those ads for . . . that's right: Obsession. (Why would something called Obsession *need* to advertise?) Well, there is an Obsession fragrance, which laces all manner of creams and splashes, and then there is Obsession for Men, which aromatizes balms (a balm called Obsession?) and all sorts of "body products" (I'll tell you what's a body product: sweat) for men. Often, today's women, according to the salespersons in the Board Room, prefer Obsession for Men. And do you know what the difference between Obsession and Obsession for Men is? According to one of those salespersons?

Obsession for Men has less vanilla in it.

Vanilla! Now, I have heard of people (not tony people, though) *drinking* vanilla extract and then doing things they felt sheepish about afterward, but I have never heard of anyone being swept up into disorienting activity by the *smell* of vanilla.

But did I spray on myself or allow to be sprayed on myself Obsession and countless other men's fragrances? Yes. Not only that, but I kept sniffing at myself, all up and down both forearms. And I smelled salespersons' arms! "Here, smell me," a salesman said. "It's already mellowed out on my skin."

I was smelling a strange guy's arm!

I even bought things! At $25, $35 per bottle, and let me tell you, those bottles aren't as big as they look in the photographs, thank God. Things that, when I smelled them, it was like biting into strange new pickles: I had no way of knowing whether they had gone bad or not. I had to buy them, because the Board Room does not take kindly to fragrance leeches. The salespersons seem to sniff them out. A harmless old guy in a safari jacket came through while I was there, cadging spritzes and trying to talk to people in either French or German about his experiences in Europe during the Second World War, and since he did not buy anything, he was discouraged from lingering.

I had to linger. I had to take on all the fragrances I could.

For this reason. The only possible honorable reason.

Here's what happened.

Shortly after I'd entered Bloomingdale's, I'd dropped some change and bent over to pick it up. And you know how sometimes you're backed up farther against a counter or something than you realize, so when you stand up, your behind hits the counter or whatever at a certain angle and you pitch forward suddenly?

That happened to me, and it caused me to tackle this guy. Inadvertently. I'd never seen him before in my life. Why would anyone tackle a complete stranger in Bloomingdale's?

That's what made it look so bad. Well, that was one of the things.

The guy was lying in the aisle, outraged. And he was swarthy, wore sunglasses, and was huge. Weight-lifter arms and shoulders, in this tank top.

And his nose curled as I disengaged (I had some beer and Vietnamese fish sauce on me from lunch, and some spot remover from just after breakfast, and I was sweating), and he shouted, "I'll get you, you son of a bitch! You'll never get out of this store alive! I'd recognize you anywhere!"

And he was blind. 🖋

SUGGESTIONS FOR WRITING

1. Why does Blount feel so out of place in Bloomingdale's? Contrast the atmosphere of the place with the personality that Blount exhibits.

2. Do women enjoy shopping more than men? Why or why not?

3. Examine some advertisements for women's perfumes and men's colognes. How do they differ? How are they similar? What does this analysis tell us about how advertisers think about gender differences?

ALL THINGS ARE
NOTHING TO ME

James T. Farrell

*Racism, religion, ethnic loyalty, education, family conflict—these are the
tangled issues in this story of the Irish American working class by **James T.
Farrell**. Joe Doyle, the main character, lives in the 1930s, a time when
there were still many barriers against social and economic mobility for Irish
Americans. Getting an education and becoming a successful lawyer or politician required the ability to overcome the prejudices of the many Americans
who considered the Irish to be lazy, drunk, and unreliable. Farrell's story
touches some of the pain of the American immigrant experience, showing
that the journey upward in social and economic status is not always a happy one.*

*Farrell (1904–1979) spent his whole life as a writer of novels, short sto-
ries, and essays, most of them dealing with the Irish of Chicago. He is best
known for his trilogy of Studs Lonigan novels of the 1930s. His father was
a teamster and his mother a domestic. He moved from the Irish neighborhood
of Chicago into the life of a student at the prestigious University of Chicago.
His life parallels Joe Doyle's in many ways.*

I

"Who was the jigg I seen you talking with?" Jim Doyle asked Cousin Joe.

"That must have been Lincoln. He was on the track team with me in high school.
He's a crack sprinter, and we have a class together this quarter. He lives near here."

"He does, huh? That goddamn nigger! He's living around here, huh?"

"Why shouldn't he?" Joe asked.

"Why should he!" Jim stormed, becoming so angry that he paused, inarticulate, his face bloating with his wrath. "What are you, a nigger lover? Did that
A.P.A. University do that to you too?" Jim turned to his younger brother,
Tommy, who joined them in the musty and dim parlor. "He's starting to love
niggers now."

"I suppose that next he'll be taking out a black dame," Tommy said with
heated sarcasm.

"I wouldn't put it past him," Jim said.

"I don't see why we should think that we're any better than they are because
our skin is a different color," Joe said calmly.

"You wouldn't. That's what comes of reading all those books the atheistic
college professors tell you to read," Jim said.

"And I suppose you like a nigger's stink. Well, I don't. I worked with them,
and I know how they smell. If you like their smell, you're welcome to it. They're
animals, just like dogs. They ain't human," Tommy said with confidence.

"A white man can have perspirational odors."

"Never mind using them big words. Can that highbrow stuff!" Jim shouted.

"For Christ sake, talk American!" Tommy sneered.

"Well, what's the matter with them?" Joe asked.

"I'll tell you. Look at your aunt out there in the kitchen now, cooking your supper. She's getting old, and this building is all she has in the world. What are the niggers doing to its value? They're trying to come into a good white man's neighborhood, spoiling and degrading property values. They're robbing your aunt of the value of her building, and it's her bread and butter. Just to love niggers I suppose you'd even see her in the poorhouse," Jim bawled.

"He's got no appreciation or gratitude after all she's done for him. She took him as an infant when his mother died, and raised him, and that's all the gratitude he shows," Tommy said.

"I always said he never should have gone to that damn school," Jim said proudly.

II

"Hello, Unc," Joe said, smiling as they sat down to supper, and Unc's creased, unshaven face tensed into a scowl, his glasses set down toward the center of his nose.

"Stop plaguin' him," said Aunt Maggie, a stout, bovine, sad-faced woman with gray hair.

"Just because you think you're smart and educated, you don't have to be acting superior to him. There's plenty of people in the world smarter than you are, and they didn't go to an atheistic university to get their education, either," Jim said.

"I was only saying hello to Unc, that's all," Joe said, and Unc ate, heedless of their talk.

"Unc and me saw a movie last night, *Broken Hearts,* and I tell you it's a shame what these modern girls and women are doing with their smoking and drinking and cutting up something shameful," Aunt Maggie said as she cut a slice of meat.

"And those bobbed-haired dolls over on the campus, they're not slow," Tommy said.

"Don't be picking up with any of that trash," Aunt Maggie said with a mouthful, looking at her nephew.

"Yeah, you! Nix on the running around with the dames. You're going over there to get an education," Tommy said.

"You know, you can't get an education and make the most of your time if you go chasing after those shameless she-devils, with their bobbed hair and their cigarettes, and hardly a stitch of clothing to hide themselves. You got to mind your studies," Aunt Maggie said.

"What do you think, Unc? Think that bald head of yours would make the flappers fall for you?"

"Shut up!" Unc whined, scowling.

"Now, Joe, I told you to stop plaguin' him!" Aunt Maggie said.

"Well, I just thought the girls might like Unc's whiskers."

"You think you're wise, don't you!" Tommy said.

"If I was wise, I wouldn't have to go to school," Joe said.

"All that University does is make him half-baked like the professors he's got," Tommy said.

"I hear that Mrs. Swanson down the street is sick, and that her daughter has bobbed hair, and is cutting up something fierce. Poor woman, I seen her on the street two weeks ago, and I told myself that now there was a woman who should be home and in bed. And today I met Mrs. O'Neill and she told me."

Unc spilled gravy on the white tablecloth.

"It'll soon be spring, and all the trees will be green. I guess I'll have to fix a nice garden in the back yard," Unc said.

"And mother will be able to take some nice drives on Sundays soon," Jim said.

"I hope not next Sunday. I was planning on usin' the car," Tommy said.

"You're always planning on using the car," Jim said angrily.

"Why shouldn't I when it's idle in the garage?" Tommy quickly and hotly retorted.

"That car is mother's. And any time she wants to go riding you can forget about using it as a taxi service for them hoodlum friends of yours," Jim said.

"Boys, please, now, don't be quarreling!" said Mrs. Doyle.

"Hey, for Christ sake!" Jim yelled as Joe collected the plates. "Hey, don't be pulling such stunts. Take a few at a time and never mind a load like that. We don't want you breaking those dishes. They're a wedding present of your aunt's."

"All right, Coz" Joe said from the kitchen as he set the soiled plates on the board by the sink.

He brought in coffee and cake.

"I suppose he'd like it better now if he was eating with a nigger," Tommy sneered.

"Sure and glory be! He isn't going with the black ones, is he? What will be the end of it with him going to that school! And wasn't his father, Mike, telling me only the other day that Joe O'Reilley, the lawyer, wouldn't let his nephew go there because they hate the Catholics. And didn't I know from the start that no good could come out of that school where they have abandoned the word of God," complained Aunt Maggie.

"He could have gone to Saint Vincent's night school like Tommy O'Reilley, and he would get just as good an education," Jim said.

"He wanted the frills," Aunt Maggie said.

"What's wrong with the Jesuit university?" Tommy belligerently asked Joe.

"It's too far out on the north side," Joe said.

"It would have been better than that A.P.A. dump across the park," Tommy said.

"That house of the devil," Aunt Maggie added.

"Aunt Margaret, sure 'tis a terrible place, I tell you. Why they take every Catholic student who goes there and lock him up in one of the towers of the main library building and keep him there until he promises he'll become an atheist," Joe said.

"Nix, wise guy! Never mind making fun of your aunt," Jim said.

"Somebody ought to kick his pants," Tommy said.

"I'd like to see one of your half-baked professors stand up to a priest like Father Shannon, the missionary, and give the arguments they use, weaning inexperienced half-baked students like yourself away from the faith. Those professors wouldn't know whether they were coming or going when Father Shannon got through with them," Jim said boastfully, as if he could take credit for the priest's abilities.

"If Father Shannon went over there he'd be locked up in a tower, too, and held until he swore to become an atheist," Joe said, drawing looks of disgust from the whole table.

"Some people talks too much," Unc said laconically.

"Why don't you go and try to give some of your arguments to Father Gilhooley?" Tommy challenged.

"He'd ask me for a contribution to the next Coal Collection," Joe said.

"He's even disrespectful of priests. See! I told you what would happen to him when he went over to that dump on the Midway," Jim gloated.

"Indeed, 'tis a bad business!" Aunt Maggie sighed.

"Well, he'll learn some day when he gets older and has to face life," Tommy said, arising and dropping his unfolded napkin beside his plate.

Jim frowned as Mrs. Doyle arose and followed her son out of the room. He shouted a warning for her not to be giving him any money, and nervously wrung and fingered his napkin. He arose, dropped it, left the room. Looking at Unc's stolid and unilluminated face, Joe heard shouting and cursing. He shook his head and thought of Edgar Guest's poem on the home which he had once read somewhere.

"Hop in the bowl!" he heard Tommy yell before slamming the door as he went out.

"But he's my son," he heard his aunt saying in answer to long and loud recriminations from Jim.

"Well, he'll be drunk again," Jim said, raising his voice.

"God forbid! He said he only wanted to see a show, and that he'd be in early and up in the morning to look for a job."

Joe cleared the table and washed the dishes. Unc, complacently smoking his corn-cob pipe, dried them.

"The grass and the trees will be green again soon."

"Yes, Unc. The grass will be green, and there will be leaves on the trees. That's indisputable," Joe idly said as he hung the dishpan on a hook above the sink.

III

The house was quiet now, with Aunt Maggie and Unc gone to see another movie at the Prairie Theatre and Jim out to see his girl. And always when he was alone in the house, Joe felt queer, with a vague unhappiness trickling through him. He had the feeling of being in a tomb that had been turned into a museum. The lights were dim. The parlor was stuffy and musty, and hardly ever used since his uncle, Aunt Maggie's husband, had died. He had the feeling that nothing could be touched, nothing disturbed, that most of the chairs were not to be sat in, that the victrola could not be played. Music, life, these were held without the door. He sat striving conscientiously to study his Pol Sci notebook, carefully proceeding through the notes he had so diligently scribbled down from his readings and from the classroom discussions and lectures, struggling as he read to retain as much as possible in his memory. The winter quarter exams were only a week off, and he was anxious and uncertain, because he always worried before his examinations, no matter how hard he studied. He lacked confidence in himself. And he felt that he knew why. His home, his background. It was only after having started at the University that he had become aware of the poverty in his home life, his background, his people, a poverty not only of mind, but of spirit, even a poverty of the senses, so that they could scarcely even look at many things and enjoy them. And he, too, he had been afflicted with this poverty. He wanted to live more, he wanted to know more, he wanted to see and enjoy more of life, and this limitation of his background was like a hook pulling the confidence out of him. And now, when he was preparing for his examinations, he worried more than he should. For the University had unleashed in him a kind of hunger. Doors to unimagined possibilities in life had been opened to him on every side, and here he stood, surrounded by all these opened doors and lacking confidence to enter them, trying to substitute intense determination for this deficiency. He bent over his notebook, gritting himself to grind on in his study. And stray thoughts intruded. He became restive. He discovered again and again that he was losing track of what he read and letting his mind float through vagrant thoughts and fancies. And he would pull himself back to the books, not even aware of what had been the content of his thoughts and fancies. And then again his mind resisted concentration, and he dreamily tried to imagine himself after the exams, free, feeling that so much more accomplished in his university career had been put behind him. But to do that he had to study. And tonight, study was hard.

Suddenly he gave up the struggle, left his study table, and donning a cap and old sweater went out for a walk. The night was clear in Washington Park, and the early March winds were stiff and invigorating. In the distance the lagoon glittered as he walked toward it over the hard, choppy ground. Once outside the house, he lost that sense of gloomy constriction. He was no longer restless. He could walk slowly, think. And these days, what he needed to do more than anything else was to think. And he scarcely had the time for it. He had three classes, and had to study two hours a day for each of them. Then there was the work on term papers, field work in sociology, daily work-out with the squad for the track teams, and the housework he had to do at home. He was turning into a machine, and just at the time when he had to think, and think hard.

Here he was, twenty-one now, and he was just discovering how he had been brought up and educated on lies. All these years, at home, in church, in grammar school and high school, they had built up his brain on a foundation of prejudices, of things that were not true. Now he was seeing, learning how they had turned him into a walking pack of lies. And how was he going to go on? Was he going to pretend that he still believed in all these lies, or wasn't he? Because if he wasn't, it meant a break, it meant that scenes like the one tonight were only the merest dress rehearsal. He had one foot still in the world of lies. He carried it with him wherever he went, in memories and nostalgias, in ties that bound him by invisible threads. He was sunken in it, in the world of Fifty-eighth Street, and no matter what he did, he felt that he would always carry it with him, as a sense of pain, as a wound in his memory. And it was stupid and prejudiced, and he no longer felt as if he fitted into it. He did not want to be insincere, a liar. And how could he retain his sincerity and live in it? He wanted to be honest, and honesty was impossible in a life builded upon lies. And they all believed in lies, would live for them, even perhaps sacrifice their lives for them. His aunt, and his father, and his cousins, and his brothers, and friends, they all lived benignly in these lies and stupidities. And he had to, or else he would wound and hurt them, fight with them. They would not let him attain his freedom. He had to pay a price for it, and the price was they. And now that his eyes were opened, what would he do?

He had never expected that such problems would face him when he had started in at the University. He had gone there thinking that he would acquire the knowledge that would make him a success in life, the same way that Joe O'Reilley, the lawyer, and Barney McCormick, the politician, were successes. And now, after five quarters in college, he was all at sea. Every truth in life seemed to have been ripped out of him, as teeth are pulled. The world was all wrong, and he felt that he should help to make it right, and not continue agreeing that it was all right, plucking profit out of wrongs and lies.

He felt, too, as if reading more books and studying was not going to help him unless he made up his mind. No book could really help him very much now. Will power alone could. For what he must do was to make up his mind. He must cast these lies out of him, cut them out as if with a knife. And he realized now that that meant that he would be forever estranged from the world of Fifty-eighth Street, and that never again could he be in rapport with its people, and its people were his people. He was saddened, and he stood still, thinking, idly listening to the wind as it shaved nearby bushes like a razor. His bonds were broken, or would be, once he announced his changed convictions without any equivocation. They would all look at him as a traitor, a stool pigeon. They would think that he had lost his mind. And because he liked them, yes, loved them, it would hurt him. And he would be alone, without moorings. Everything that he believed, held as truth, all that he had been brought up in . . . was gone. And again he heard the wind as if it were a melancholy song.

It was not just that they, his people, could not accept him. He could no longer really accept them. Worlds had been placed between them both. At best, he would go on, and his love would turn to pity for them. The very fact that he was going to college made them suspect him, as his cousins had shown at the supper table. And he had thought, too, that when a young man had tried seriously to work his way though school and win an education for himself, the world would applaud and praise and help him, and that, at least, his closest relatives would give him all the encouragement and assistance they could. In the abstract, they all favored the idea. In the concrete, in his case, he was met with distrust, envy, suspicion. They nagged him. They seemed to try and hinder him at every turn. Every day, almost, it seemed that they strove to discourage him by telling him that he was wasting his time, and that he would be a failure.

It was jealousy, envy, spite. And it was fear. And hatred, the hatred begotten from narrowness, bigotry, ignorance. They hated knowledge. It was something mysterious and dangerous. Knowledge in politics would disturb the politicians with their hands in the grab bag. And the politicians were leaders, models, heroes, in the Irish milieu that had been his. Even his cousins, Jim and Tommy, fancied themselves to be politicians. Like two weeks ago, when Tommy had seen people looking at the vacant apartment over them and talking with these people he had said that he was in the political game. He was a politician because he wore a badge on election days and handed out cards asking people to vote Democratic. And Jim acted as a kind of assistant precinct captain and had a minor political job. So they, too, were politicians, and they had their fingers in the political grab bag. And they knew all that was to be known about politics. Knowledge in politics disturbed their petty little grabs, and their egos. It destroyed faith in the Church, and the Church was the heart of their world, and so many of the hopes that they saw frustrated in this life— these would be fulfilled in the Heaven of which the priests preached. Now he could see clearly why the Church had carried on such a relentless warfare against science, why priests attacked the University. And also, next summer, he would have to read through that book of White's.

He had talked with Schwartz about these problems, Schwartz who had read so much more than he, who had attained his freedom so much earlier. And Schwartz had told him about a book, *The Ego and His Own*, by Max Stirner. Schwartz had quoted one of the statements made in the book, and Joe had been so impressed by it that he had copied it down and memorized it. Now, thinking of the Church, of politics, he quoted it to himself:

If an age is imbued with an error, some always derive advantage from that error, while the rest have to suffer from it.

And these last quarters at the University he was learning how his own age was so imbued with errors, and how some profited from them, and how so many who did not profit from them wanted to. They were even suffering from the very errors out of which they wanted to snatch a profit. Like Jim and Tommy, and their being in the political game. And that was what he had planned to do, enter politics after he passed his bar examinations. Now if he did, he knew that it meant failure, or profiting out of errors, injustices, dishonesties. It would make him a crook and a liar. It would make Jim a crook. Jim was naturally good and honest and hard working, and he worked hardest to become part of a whole system of graft. And he was stupid, and in his own stupidity he wanted to keep others that way. Joe again asked himself, was that his ideal?

And still, he wondered why did they hate knowing things so? It brought to his mind an incident that had recently happened at home. Tommy had asked him a question about the Civil War. He had been reading about it in a history book, and he had handed the volume to Tommy, showing him the answer to the question, contained in two pages. Tommy had flung the book on the floor, sneered, and hadn't even spoken to Joe for several days. Such reactions made him want to give up and let them go their own way. At first he had tried to explain to them, to help them, to tell them the things he was learning so that they could learn, too. He had wanted to correct their errors, cut down the margins of their ignorance, break down their prejudices, such as the ones they held against Negroes and Jews. He had tried to tell them that the poor were not always poor because of laziness, that men out of work often could not find jobs, and even with the example of Tommy before them who would not work, they had condemned the shiftlessness of others and contended that there was some kind of a job for anybody who wanted to work. The same way, he had, after his field trips in sociology to Italian districts, tried to tell them that the foreigners were the same as any other people and wanted just to live as others did, and be happy. And it had only precipitated another of those stupid and hot-tempered quarrels. Knowing so little, they acted as if they knew everything. Nothing, it seemed, could be done to dent such self-conscious ignorance.

He stopped by the wrinkling lagoon where an aisle of moonlight reflected over the surface to the wooded island. He thought of how the last time his father had been up, he had looked so very old. His father was the same, though. He had worked for forty years in a railroad office. And during the Wilson administration, he had gotten a raise. So Wilson was the touchstone to all knowledge with him. But at the table his father's hand had shaken noticeably, and now the memory of it saddened Joe. It meant that perhaps soon his father would be dead. And what had the poor man gotten out of life? In a clear-cut focus Joe sensed and visioned his father's life for these last many years. His wife dying at Joe's birth. The family split up. The father living in a succession of rooming houses, ruining his stomach in cheap restaurants, lonely with his family separated. And soon now the father would be pensioned off to die. His hopes were centered in Joe. In him, he saw the triumph, the success, the happiness, that he had never sucked out of living. A beaten, frustrated old man now, waiting for his son to make amends for him. All he had ever seemed to have gotten out of life were those occasional drunks he went on. And even when drunk, the old man seemed sad and usually ended up in a crying jag. Joe shook his head. Because he saw clearly what it would mean for him to hurt his father. And hurt him he must, or capitulate. And could he surrender himself as a sacrifice for such things, the contentment of a few people, the broken dreams of an old man? Even if they were his people, his father? It was so damned unfair, too. And needless, if they could only be intelligent. If! His Aunt Maggie, too, she looked for him to do big things. And she, poor woman, had had her troubles. Her husband, a good man, had been a heavy drinker. And now Tommy, drinking, not ever working. And they would be so hurt. It would leave them bewildered, with a wound cutting them to the core of their consciousness. They would feel betrayed as he now felt betrayed. And the whole situation made him see so clearly how life was not something soft, something harmonious, something that was without contradictions. It was hard, stern, and demanded sternness.

He walked on. He knew that he could no longer aspire as they wanted him to, believe as they expected that he would. He could no longer retain his faith in their God, their church, their ideals of success and goodness. He had tried to, these last days. And now he was at the end of his resistance. To continue as he had meant compromising himself, and going on meant turning his whole life into lies and hypocrisy. And at home, their suspicions were not justified. They sensed it, all right, just as they had shown tonight at the supper table. And soon, if he told them of his loss of faith, he could imagine the scenes, the scorn they would pour on him. And at times it seemed also that they wanted to drive him to it, so that they could indulge themselves in self-righteousness and self-justification at his expense, so that they could stand superior to him. He shrugged his shoulders. It was all coming. He would have to tell them. He would have to show he had changed, and build his life on truer foundations. Because he was choking with hypocrisy. How could he go on like this much longer, pretending, going to church on Sundays, kneeling to a God in Whom he did not believe, pretending, faking, saying yes as if he agreed with so much of their self-assertive ignorance.

He had an impulse to pity himself. Here he was with no belief, no God, a world inside of himself twisted into a chaos. He often, these days, had the feeling that nothing mattered. Just like the statement he had heard Schwartz quoting from that Stirner book.

All things are nothing to me.

Again he stood by the dark waters of the lagoon with the wind sweeping them. A sense of mystery seemed to settle over them, pervade them. He was without words. He felt that beyond these waters there must be something. Beyond life, there must be something. This living as men did, all this suffering, all this defeat, and unhappiness, and self-inflicted pains and poverty, it could not be all that there was. If so, everything was useless. And if there was no God? And there was none. He could not believe in Him. He suddenly hurled a stone into the waters, and listened to the splash and watched the widening ripples in the moonlight. He hurled another stone, and turned his back to walk home.

He thought of how he would some day die, and there was no God. He was living in a world of death, and if he did not free himself from it he would die twice, many times. He would never have any honesty in his own life. And a pervasive pity seeped through him. He could not hate them, his people. He could only feel sorry for them. How could he hate his father, sitting at the dining-room table, his hands palsied, thin and sunken-cheeked, that ghostly dried-up look to his face? How could he hate his own past, even though it was part of a world that would kill anything that was honest within himself?

And he remembered how, as a boy, he had played in this park where he now walked. He had raced,wrestled, played football, chase-one-chase-all, run-sheep-run, looked at girls who reduced him to flustering shyness and speechlessness. Long and sunny days of boyhood idleness, and they now fell through the dark reaches of his brooding mind like sunlight filtering a feeble warmth on the cold stones of a cellar. Now he wished for them back, wished for their obliviousness to doubts, their acceptance of the stupidities he must now vomit out of himself, their faith. And it was just in those days that he had been betrayed. It was all through those years that false faiths had been implanted in him, that the threads knitting him to what he must now destroy, had been sewn. And yet, he wished, if only things were just simple again.

He heard footsteps behind him, and turned to see a stout familiar figure approaching.

"Hello, Mr. Coady."

The park policeman was older, slower now on his flat feet, than when Joe had been a boy.

"Out looking for them tonight?" Joe asked.

"Oh, hello! Hello, boy! How are ye, Joe?"

"Fine, Mr. Coady. How are you feeling these fine days?"

"Well, Joe, me feet, they ain't what they used to be."

"It's nice out tonight, Mr. Coady."

"Grand, Joe, grand, but still a little chilly for a man when he gets to be my age."

"I was taking a walk."

"Well, it's grand if ye don't catch a chill."

"Pretty soon it will be nice, all green. My uncle is getting ready to start his garden."

"Sure, and it will be spring in another month or so."

There was a moment of silence.

"And what are ye doing now, Joe?"

"Studying at the University."

"Fine. And study and apply yourself well, me boy, and make something of yourself, instead of becoming the same as the likes of them that's always about the boathouse in the summer looking for trouble. And I suppose it's the law you'll be going into."

"Yes."

"Well, work hard, boy, and apply yourself."

Joe turned toward home. No use thinking or brooding. And anyway, he had better be getting back to his studying. He suddenly crouched into a sprinting position and shot off, tearing fleetly away. He pulled up, crouched again, sprinted, exulting in unthinking muscular release, feeling his body as a well-developed instrument that would do his bidding, expending himself in a way that was release, was like a clean wind blowing through him. It made him feel better. He stopped, a trifle breathless, the joy of running and motion ebbing in him. He hastened out of the park. Back to his studies. And he had to keep his mind on them this time. Only . . . no, he had to keep his mind on them.

IV

As Joe walked up the steps of the building, he heard drunken shouting down at the corner, and saw some of the neighborhood hoodlums yelling with a female bum in their midst. And he heard Tommy's drunken voice rising. He went inside to study.

SUGGESTIONS FOR WRITING

1. Characterize your responses to Joe's quarrels with his family. In what ways are his family's objections to him valid? Is his rejection of them fair?

2. Anyone who goes to college will be changed by the experience. Describe the conflicts you have had with your family on account of your college experience.

3. Analyze the role of racism in this story. What effect does education have on racial attitudes?

4. What does "success" mean to Joe Doyle? Analyze how definitions of success differ for people of different social classes.

CHILDREN OF LONELINESS

Anzia Yezierska

The conflict in this short story could not be more basic. A daughter of im-
migrant Jewish parents has gotten herself educated and learned the ways of
American society. The parents hold on desperately to the ways of the old
world and their traditions. For the daughter, what comes to symbolize this
conflict is something as simple as eating habits. This intense and personal
story dramatizes in a very intimate way the conflicts that can occur within a
family when one of its members becomes educated and rises in social status.

*   **Anzia Yezierska** (ca. 1880–1970) lived a life very similar to the one*
she depicts in this story. She was born in eastern Europe, emigrated to this
country in the 1890s with her family, fought hard to educate herself, became
alienated from her family and community, and spent her life as an author
writing about the complex emotional experience of immigrant life in Amer-
ica. She published such novels as Salome of the Tenements *(1922) and*
Arrogant Beggar *(1927), and several collections of short stories, including*
Children of Loneliness *(1923), from which our selection comes. She also*
worked as a Hollywood screenwriter.

I

"Oh Mother, can't you use a fork?" exclaimed Rachel as Mrs. Ravinsky took
the shell of the baked potato in her fingers and raised it to her watering mouth.

"Here, *Teacherin* mine, you want to learn me in my old age how to put the
bite in my mouth?" The mother dropped the potato back into her plate, too
wounded to eat. Wiping her hands on her blue-checked apron, she turned her
glance to her husband, at the opposite side of the table.

"Yankev," she said bitterly, "stick your bone on a fork. Our *teacherin* said you
dassn't touch no eating with the hands."

"All my teachers died already in the old country," retorted the old man. "I
ain't going to learn nothing new no more from my American daughter." He
continued to suck the marrow out of the bone with that noisy relish that was
so exasperating to Rachel.

"It's no use," stormed the girl, jumping up from the table in disgust; "I'll
never be able to stand it here with you people."

" 'You people?' What do you mean by 'you people?' " shouted the old man,
lashed into fury by his daughter's words. "You think you got a different skin
from us because you went to college?"

"It drives me wild to hear you crunching bones like savages. If you people
won't change, I shall have to move and live by myself."

Yankev Ravinsky threw the half-gnawed bone upon the table with such vehemence that a plate broke into fragments.

"You witch you!" he cried in a hoarse voice tense with rage. "Move by yourself! We lived without you while you was away in college, and we can get on without you further. God ain't going to turn his nose on us because we ain't got table manners from America. A hell she made from this house since she got home."

"Shah! Yankev leben," pleaded the mother, "the neighbors are opening the windows to listen to our hollering. Let us have a little quiet for a while till the eating is over."

But the accumulated hurts and insults that the old man had borne in the one week since his daughter's return from college had reached the breaking-point. His face was convulsed, his eyes flashed, and his lips were flecked with froth as he burst out in a volley of scorn:

"You think you can put our necks in a chain and learn us new tricks? You think you can make us over for Americans? We got through till fifty years of our lives eating in our own old way—"

"Wo is me, Yankev leben!" entreated his wife. "Why can't we choke ourselves with our troubles? Why must the whole world know how we are tearing ourselves by the heads? In all Essex Street, in all New York, there ain't such fights like by us."

Her pleadings were in vain. There was no stopping Yankev Ravinsky once his wrath was roused. His daughter's insistence upon the use of a knife and fork spelled apostasy, Anti- Semitism, and the aping of the Gentiles.

Like a prophet of old condemning unrighteousness, he ran the gamut of denunciation, rising to heights of fury that were sublime and godlike, and sinking from sheer exhaustion to abusive bitterness.

"Pfui on all your American colleges! Pfui on the morals of America! No respect for old age. No fear for God. Stepping with your feet on all the laws of the holy Torah. A fire should burn out the whole new generation. They should sink into the earth, like Korah."

"Look at him cursing and burning! Just because I insist on their changing their terrible table manners. One would think I was killing them."

"Do you got to use a gun to kill?" cried the old man, little red threads darting out of the whites of his eyes.

"Who is doing the killing? Aren't you choking the life out of me? Aren't you dragging me by the hair to the darkness of past ages every minute of the day? I'd die of shame if one of my college friends should open the door while you people are eating."

"You—you—"

The old man was on the point of striking his daughter when his wife seized the hand he raised.

"Mincha! Yankev, you forgot Mincha!"

This reminder was a flash of inspiration on Mrs. Ravinsky's part, the only thing that could have ended the quarreling instantly. Mincha was the prayer just before sunset of the orthodox Jews. This religious rite was so automatic with the old man that at his wife's mention of Mincha everything was immediately shut out, and Yankev Ravinsky rushed off to a corner of the room to pray.

"*Ashrai Yoshwai Waisahuh!*"

"Happy are they who dwell in Thy house. Ever shall I praise Thee. *Selah!* Great is the Lord, and exceedingly to be praised; and His greatness is unsearchable. On the majesty and glory of Thy splendor, and on Thy marvelous deeds, will I meditate."

The shelter from the storms of life that the artist finds in his art, Yankev Ravinsky found in his prescribed communion with God. All the despair caused by his daughter's apostasy, the insults and disappointments he suffered, were in his sobbing voice. But as he entered into the spirit of his prayer, he felt the man of flesh drop away in the outflow of God around him. His voice mellowed, the rigid wrinkles of his face softened, the hard glitter of anger and condemnation in his eyes was transmuted into the light of love as he went on:

"The Lord is gracious and merciful; slow to anger and of great loving-kindness. To all that call upon Him in truth He will hear their cry and save them."

Oblivious to the passing and repassing of his wife as she warned anew the unfinished diner, he continued:

"Put not your trust in princes, in the son of man in whom there is no help." Here Reb Ravinsky paused long enough to make a silent confession for the sin of having placed his hope on his daughter instead of on God. His whole body bowed with the sense of guilt. Then in a moment his humility was transfigured into exaltation. Sorrow for sin dissolved in joy as he became more deeply aware of God's unfailing protection.

"Happy is he who hath the God of Jacob for his help, whose hope is in the Lord his God. He healeth the broken heart, and bindeth up their wounds."

A healing balm filled his soul as he returned to the table, where the steaming hot food awaited him. Rachel sat near the window pretending to read a book. Her mother did not urge her to join them at the table, fearing another outbreak, and the meal continued in silence.

The girl's thoughts surged hotly as she glanced from her father to her mother. A chasm of four centuries could not have separated her more completely from them than her four years at Cornell.

"To think that I was born of these creatures! It's an insult to my soul. What kinship have I with these two lumps of ignorance and superstition? They're ugly and gross and stupid. I'm all sensitive nerves. They want to wallow in dirt."

She closed her eyes to shut out the sight of her parents as they silently ate together, unmindful of the dirt and confusion.

"How is it possible that I lived with them and like them only four years ago? What is it in me that so quickly gets accustomed to the best? Beauty and cleanliness are as natural to me as if I'd been born on Fifth Avenue instead of the dirt of Essex Street."

A vision of Frank Baker passed before her. Her last long talk with him out under the trees in college still lingered in her heart. She felt that she had only to be with him again to carry forward the beautiful friendship that had sprung up between them. He had promised to come shortly to New York. How could she possibly introduce such a born and bred American to her low, ignorant, dirty parents?

"I might as well tear the thought of Frank Baker out of my heart" she told herself. "If he just once sees the pigsty of a home I come from, if he just sees the table manners of my father and mother, he'll fly through the ceiling."

Timidly, Mrs. Ravinsky turned to her daughter.

"Ain't you going to give a taste the eating?"

No answer.

"I fried the 'lotkes special' for you—"

"I can't stand your fried, greasy stuff."

"Ain't even my cooking good no more either?" Her gnarled, hard-working hands clutched at her breast. "God from the world, for what do I need yet any more my life? Nothing I do for my child is no use no more."

Her head sank; her whole body seemed to shrivel and grow old with the sense of her own futility.

"How I was hurrying to run by the butcher before everybody else so as to pick out the grandest, fattest piece of *brust!*" she wailed, tears streaming down her face. "And I put my hand away from my heart and put a whole fresh egg into the *lotkes*, and I stuffed the stove full of coal like a millionaire so as to get the *lotkes* fried so nice and brown; and now you give a kick on everything I done—"

"Fool woman," shouted her husband, "stop laying yourself on the ground for your daughter to step on you! What more can you expect from a child raised up in America? What more can you expect but that she should spit in your face and make dirt from you?" His eyes, hot and dry under their lids, flashed from his wife to his daughter. "The old Jewish eating is poison to her; she must have *trefa* ham—only forbidden food."

Bitter laughter shook him.

"Woman, how you patted yourself with pride before all the neighbors, boasting of our great American daughter coming home from college! This is our daughter, our pride, our hope, our pillow for our old age that we were dreaming about! This is our American *teacherin!* A Jew-hater, an Anti-Semite we brought into the world, a betrayer of our race who hates her own father and mother like the Russian Czar once hated a Jew. She makes herself so refined, she can't stand it when we use the knife or fork the wrong way; but her heart is that of a brutal Cossack, and she spills her own father's and mother's blood like water."

Every word he uttered seared Rachel's soul like burning acid. She felt herself becoming a witch, a she-devil, under the spell of his accusations.

"You want me to love you yet?" She turned upon her father like an avenging fury. "If there's any evil hatred in my soul, you have roused it with your cursed preaching."

"Oi-i-i! Highest One! pity Yourself on us!" Mrs. Ravinsky wrung her hands. "Rachel, Yankev, let there be an end to this knife-stabbing! *Gottuniu!* my flesh is torn to pieces!"

Unheeding her mother's pleading, Rachel rushed to the closet where she kept her things.

"I was a crazy idiot to think that I could live with you people under one roof." She flung on her hat and coat and bolted for the door.

Mrs. Ravinsky seized Rachel's arm in passionate entreaty.

"My child, my heart, my life, what do you mean? Where are you going?"

"I mean to get out of this hell of a home this very minute," she said, tearing loose from her mother's clutching hands.

"Wo is me! My child! We'll be to shame and to laughter by the whole world. What will people say?"

"Let them say! My life is my own; I'll live as I please." She slammed the door in her mother's face.

"They want me to love them yet," ran the mad thoughts in Rachel's brain as she hurried through the streets, not knowing where she was going, not caring. "Vampires, bloodsuckers fastened on my flesh! Black shadows blighting every ray of light that ever came my way! Other parents scheme and plan and wear themselves out to give their child a chance, but they put dead stones in front of every chance I made for myself."

With the cruelty of youth to everything not youth, Rachel reasoned:

"They have no rights, no claims over me like other parents who do things for their children. It was my own brains, my own courage, my own iron will that forced my way out of the sweatshop to my present position in the public schools. I owe them nothing, nothing, nothing."

II

Two weeks already away from home. Rachel looked about her room. It was spotlessly clean. She had often said to herself while at home with her parents: "All I want is an empty room, with a bed, a table, and a chair. As long as it is clean and away from them, I'll be happy." But was she happy?

A distant door closed, followed by the retreating sound of descending footsteps. Then all was still, the stifling stillness of a rooming-house. The white, empty walls pressed in upon her, suffocated her. She listened acutely for any stir of life, but the continued silence was unbroken save for the insistent ticking of her watch.

"I ran away from home burning for life," she mused, "and all I've found is the loneliness that's death." A wave of self-pity weakened her almost to the point of tears. "I'm alone! I'm alone!" she moaned, crumpling into a heap.

"Must it always be with me like this," her soul cried in terror, "either to live among those who drag me down or in the awful isolation of a hall bedroom? Oh, I'll die of loneliness among these frozen, each-shut-in-himself Americans! It's one thing to break away, but, oh, the strength to go on alone! How can I ever do it? The love instinct is so strong in me; I can not live without love, without people."

The thought of a letter from Frank Baker suddenly lightened her spirits. That very evening she was to meet him for dinner. Here was hope—more than hope. Just seeing him again would surely bring the certainty.

This new rush of light upon her dark horizon so softened her heart that she could almost tolerate her superfluous parents.

"If I could only have love and my own life, I could almost forgive them for bringing me into the world. I don't really hate them; I only hate them when they stand between me and the new America that I'm to conquer."

Answering her impulse, her feet led her to the familiar Ghetto streets. On the corner of the block where her parents lived she paused, torn between the desire to see her people and the fear of their nagging reproaches. The old Jewish proverb came to her mind: "The wolf is not afraid of the dog, but he hates his bark." "I'm not afraid of their black curses for sin. It's nothing to me if they accuse me of being an Anti-Semite or a murderer, and yet why does it hurt me so?"

Rachel had prepared herself to face the usual hail-storm of reproaches and accusations, but as she entered the dark hallway of the tenement, she heard her father's voice chanting the old familiar Hebrew psalm of "The Race of Sorrows":

"Hear my prayer, O Lord, and let my cry come unto Thee.

For my days are consumed like smoke, and my bones are burned as an hearth.

I am like a pelican of the wilderness.

I am like an owl of the desert.

I have eaten ashes like bread and mingled my drink with weeping."

A faintness came over her. The sobbing strains of the lyric song melted into her veins like a magic sap, making her warm and human again. All her strength seemed to flow out of her in pity for her people. She longed to throw herself on the dirty, ill-smelling tenement stairs and weep: "Nothing is real but love— love. Nothing so false as ambition."

Since her early childhood she remembered often waking up in the middle of the night and hearing her father chant this age-old song of woe. There flashed before her a vivid picture of him, huddled in the corner beside the table piled high with Hebrew books, swaying to the rhythm of his Jeremiad, the sputtering light of the candle stuck in a bottle throwing uncanny shadows over his gaunt face. The skull-cap, the side-locks, and the long gray beard made him seem like some mystic stranger from a far-off world and not a father. The father of the daylight who ate with a knife, spat on the floor, and who was forever denouncing America and Americans was different from this mystic spirit stranger who could thrill with such impassioned rapture.

Thousands of years of exile, thousands of years of hunger, loneliness, and want swept over her as she listened to her father's voice. Something seemed to be crying out to her to run in and seize her father and mother in her arms and hold them close.

"Love, love—nothing is true between us but love," she thought.

But why couldn't she do what she longed to do? Why, with all her passionate sympathy for them, should any actual contact with her people seem so impossible? No, she couldn't go in just yet. Instead, she ran up on the roof, where she could be alone. She stationed herself at the air-shaft opposite their kitchen window, where for the first time since she had left in a rage she could see her old home.

Ach! what sickening disorder! In the sink were the dirty dishes stacked high, untouched, it looked, for days. The table still held the remains of the last meal. Clothes were strewn about the chairs. The bureau drawers were open, and their contents brimmed over in mad confusion.

"I couldn't endure it, this terrible dirt!" Her nails dug into her palms, shaking with the futility of her visit. "It would be worse than death to go back to them. It would mean giving up order, cleanliness, sanity, everything that I've striven all these years to attain. It would mean giving up the hope of my new world—the hope of Frank Baker."

The sound of the creaking door reached her where she crouched against the air-shaft. She looked again into the murky depths of the room. Her mother had entered. With arms full of paper bags of provisions, the old woman paused on the threshold, her eyes dwelling on the dim figure of her husband. A look of pathetic tenderness illumined her wrinkled features.

"I'll make something good to eat for you, yes?"

Reb Ravinsky only dropped his head on his breast. His eyes were red and dry, sandy with sorrow that could find no release in tears. Good God! never had Rachel seen such profound despair. For the first time she noticed the grooved tracings of withering age knotted on his face and the growing hump on her mother's back.

"Already the shadow of death hangs over them," she thought as she watched them. "They're already with one foot in the grave. Why can't I be human to them before they're dead? Why can't I?"

Rachel blotted away the picture of the sordid room with both hands over her eyes.

"To death with my soul! I wish I were a plain human being with a heart instead of a monster of selfishness with a soul."

But the pity she felt for her parents began now to be swept away in a wave of pity for herself.

"How every step in advance costs me my heart's blood! My greatest tragedy in life is that I always see the two opposite sides at the same time. What seems to me right one day seems all wrong the next. Not only that, but many things seem right and wrong at the same time. I feel I have a right to my own life, and yet I feel just as strongly that I owe my father and mother something. Even if I don't love them, I have no right to step over them. I'm drawn to them by something more compelling than love. It is the cry of their dumb, wasted lives."

Again Rachel looked into the dimly lighted room below. Her mother placed food upon the table. With a self-effacing stoop of humility, she entreated, "Eat only while it is hot yet."

With his eyes fixed almost unknowingly, Reb Ravinsky sat down. Her mother took the chair opposite him, but she only pretended to eat the slender portion of the food she had given herself.

Rachel's heart swelled. Yes, it had always been like that. Her mother had taken the smallest portion of everything for herself. Complaints, reproaches, upbraidings, abuse, yes, all these had been heaped by her upon her mother; but always the juiciest piece of meat was placed on her plate, the thickest slice of bread; the warmest covering was given to her, while her mother shivered through the night.

"Ah, I don't want to abandon them!" she thought; "I only want to get to the place where I belong. I only want to get to the mountaintops and view the world from the heights, and then I'll give them everything I've achieved."

Her thoughts were sharply broken in upon by the loud sound of her father's eating. Bent over the table, he chewed with noisy gulps a piece of herring, his temples working to the motion of his jaws. With each audible swallow and smacking of the lips, Rachel's heart tightened with loathing.

"Their dirty ways turn all my pity into hate." She felt her toes and her fingers curl inward with disgust. "I'll never amount to anything if I'm not strong enough to break away from them once and for all." Hypnotizing herself into her line of self-defense, her thoughts raced on: "I'm only cruel to be kind. If I went back to them now, it would not be out of love, but because of weakness—because of doubt and unfaith in myself."

Rachel bluntly turned her back. Her head lifted. There was iron in her jaws.

"If I haven't the strength to tear free from the old, I can never conquer the new. Every step a man makes is a tearing away from those clinging to him. I must get tight and hard as rock inside of me if I'm ever to do the things I set out to do. I must learn to suffer and suffer, walk through blood and fire, and not bend from my course."

For the last time she looked at her parents. The terrible loneliness of their abandoned old age, their sorrowful eyes, the wrung-dry weariness on their faces, the whole black picture of her ruined, desolate home, burned into her flesh. She knew all the pain of one unjustly condemned, and the guilt of one with the spilt blood of helpless lives upon his hands. Then came tears, blinding, wrenching tears that tore at her heart until it seemed that they would rend her body into shreds.

"God! God!" she sobbed as she turned her head away from them, "if all this suffering were at least for something worth while, for something outside myself. But to have to break them and crush them merely because I have a fastidious soul that can't stomach their table manners, merely because I can't strangle my aching ambitions to rise in the world!"

She could no longer sustain the conflict which raged within her higher and higher at every moment. With a sudden tension of all her nerves she pulled herself together and stumbled blindly down stairs and out of the house. And she felt as if she had torn away from the flesh and blood of her own body.

III

Out in the street she struggled to get hold of herself again. Despite the tumult and upheaval that racked her soul, an intoxicating lure still held her up— the hope of seeing Frank Baker that evening. She was indeed a storm-racked ship, but within sight of shore. She need but throw out the signal, and help was nigh. She need but confide to Frank Baker of her break with her people, and all the dormant sympathy between them would surge up. His understanding would widen and deepen because of her great need for his understanding. He would love her the more because of her great need for his love.

Forcing back her tears, stepping over her heart-break, she hurried to the hotel where she was to meet him. Her father's impassioned rapture when he chanted the Psalms of David lit up the visionary face of the young Jewess.

"After all, love is the beginning of the real life," she thought as Frank Baker's dark, handsome face flashed before her. "With him to hold on to, I'll begin my new world."

Borne higher and higher by the intoxicating illusion of her great destiny, she cried:

"A person all alone is but a futile cry in an unheeding wilderness. One alone is but a shadow, an echo of reality. It takes two together to create reality. Two together can pioneer a new world."

With a vision of herself and Frank Baker marching side by side to the conquest of her heart's desire, she added:

"No wonder a man's love means so little to the American woman. They belong to the world in which they are born. They belong to their fathers and mothers; they belong to their relatives and friends. They are human even without a man's love. I don't belong; I'm not human. Only a man's love can save me and make me human again."

It was the busy dinner-hour at the fashionable restaurant. Pausing at the doorway with searching eyes and lips eagerly parted, Rachel's swift glance circled the lobby. Those seated in the dining-room beyond who were not too absorbed in one another, noticed a slim, vivid figure of ardent youth, but with dark, age-old eyes that told of the restless seeking of her homeless race.

With nervous little movements of anxiety, Rachel sat down, got up, then started across the lobby. Half-way, she stopped, and her breath caught.

"Mr. Baker," she murmured, her hands fluttering toward him with famished eagerness. His smooth, athletic figure had a cock-sureness that to the girl's worshipping gaze seemed the perfection of male strength.

"You must be doing wonderful things," came from her admiringly, "you look so happy, so shining with life."

"Yes,"—he shook her hand vigorously,—"I've been living for the first time since I was a kid. I'm full of such interesting experiences. I'm actually working in an East Side settlement."

Dazed by his glamorous success, Rachel stammered soft phrases of congratulation as he led her to a table. But seated opposite him, the face of this untried youth, flushed with the health and happiness of another world than that of the poverty-crushed Ghetto, struck her almost as an insincerity.

"You in an East Side settlement?" she interrupted sharply. "What reality can there be in that work for you?"

"Oh," he cried, his shoulders squaring with the assurance of his master's degree in sociology, "it's great to get under the surface and see how the other half live. It's so picturesque! My conception of these people has greatly changed since I've been visiting their homes." He launched into a glowing account of the East Side as seen by a twenty-five-year-old college graduate.

"I thought them mostly immersed in hard labor, digging subways or slaving in sweat-shops," he went on. "But think of the poetry which the immigrant is daily living!"

"But they're so sunk in the dirt of poverty, what poetry do you see there?"

"It's their beautiful home life, the poetic devotion between parents and children, the sacrifices they make for one another—"

"Beautiful home life? Sacrifices? Why, all I know of is the battle to the knife between parents and children. It's black tragedy that boils there, not the pretty sentiments that you imagine."

"My dear child,"—he waved aside her objection,—"you're too close to judge dispassionately. This very afternoon, on one of my friendly visits, I came upon a dear old man who peered up at me through horn-rimmed glasses behind his pile of Hebrew books. He was hardly able to speak English, but I found him a great scholar."

"Yes, a lazy old do-nothing, a bloodsucker on his wife and children."

Too shocked for remonstrance, Frank Baker stared at her.

"How else could he have time in the middle of the afternoon to pour over his books?" Rachel's voice was hard with bitterness. "Did you see his wife? I'll bet she was slaving for him in the kitchen. And his children slaving for him in the sweat-shop."

"Even so, think of the fine devotion that the women and children show in making the lives of your Hebrew scholars possible. It's a fine contribution to America, where our tendency is to forget idealism."

"Give me better a plain American man who supports his wife and children and I'll give you all those dreamers of the Talmud."

He smiled tolerantly at her vehemence.

"Nevertheless," he insisted, "I've found wonderful material for my new book in all this. I think I've got a new angle on the social types of your East Side."

An icy band tightened about her heart. "Social types," her lips formed. How could she possibly confide to this man of the terrible tragedy that she had been through that very day? Instead of the understanding and sympathy that she had hoped to find, there were only smooth platitudes, the sightseer's surface interest in curious "social types."

Frank Baker talked on. Rachel seemed to be listening, but her eyes had a far-off, abstracted look. She was quiet as a spinning-top is quiet, her thoughts and emotions revolving within her at high speed.

"That man in love with me? Why, he doesn't see me or feel me. I don't exist to him. He's only stuck on himself, blowing his own horn. Will he ever stop with his 'I,' 'I,' 'I'? Why, I was a crazy lunatic to think that just because we took the same courses in college, he would understand me out in the real world."

All the fire suddenly went out of her eyes. She looked a thousand years old as she sank back wearily in her chair.

"Oh, but I'm boring you with all my heavy talk on sociology." Frank Baker's words seemed to come to her from afar. "I have tickets for a fine musical comedy that will cheer you up, Miss Ravinsky—"

"Thanks, thanks," she cut in hurriedly. Spend a whole evening sitting beside him in a theater when her heart was breaking? No. All she wanted was to get away—away where she could be alone. "I have work to do," she heard herself say. "I've got to get home."

Frank Baker murmured words of polite disappointment and escorted her back to her door. She watched the sure swing of his athletic figure as he strode away down the street, then she rushed up-stairs.

Back in her little room, stunned, bewildered, blinded with her disillusion, she sat staring at her four empty walls.

Hours passed, but she made no move, she uttered no sound. Doubled fists thrust between her knees, she sat there, staring blindly at her empty walls.

"I can't live with the old world, and I'm yet too green for the new. I don't belong to those who gave me birth or to those with whom I was educated."

Was this to be the end of all her struggles to rise in America, she asked herself, this crushing daze of loneliness? Her driving thirst for an education, her desperate battle for a little cleanliness, for a breath of beauty, the tearing away from her own flesh and blood to free herself from the yoke of her parents— what was it all worth now? Where did it lead to? Was loneliness to be the fruit of it all?

Night was melting away like a fog: through the open window the first lights of dawn were appearing. Rachel felt the sudden touch of the sun upon her face, which was bathed in tears. Overcome by her sorrow, she shuddered and put her hand over her eyes as tho to shut out the unwelcome contact. But the light shone through her fingers.

Despite her weariness, the renewing breath of the fresh morning entered her heart like a sunbeam. A mad longing for life filled her veins.

"I want to live," her youth cried. "I want to live, even at the worst."

Live how? Live for what? She did not know. She only felt she must struggle against her loneliness and weariness as she had once struggled against dirt, against the squalor and ugliness of her Ghetto home.

Turning from the window, she concentrated her mind, her poor tired mind, on one idea.

"I have broken away from the old world; I'm through with it. It's already behind me. I must face this loneliness till I get to the new world. Frank Baker can't help me; I must hope for no help from the outside. I'm alone; I'm alone till I get there.

"But am I really alone in my seeking? I'm one of the millions of immigrant children, children of loneliness, wandering between worlds that are at once too old and too new to live in."

SUGGESTIONS FOR WRITING

1. Why do her parents' eating habits become such an important issue for Rachel? How could Rachel have dealt with her parents more compassionately? Is it possible to change your social class without becoming alienated from your family?

2. We are now in a new period of immigration, with more arrivals from Korea, Vietnam, Russia, and Latin America, among others. What signs have you seen of the kind of conflicts that Yezierska described in this story?

3. How difficult is it for immigrants to be accepted into American society? What kinds of changes do immigrants have to go through in order to be accepted?

ONLY DAUGHTER

Sandra Cisneros

In this personal narrative, **Sandra Cisneros** *tells us about coming to terms with her father. She and her father are divided by many differences in beliefs and values, but they are deeply connected too. Issues of ethnic identity, gender definition, and social status play important roles in this story about how Cisneros feels about herself as a writer. Cisneros (b. 1954) is the author of* The House of Mango Street *(1984),* My Wicked Wicked Ways *(1987), and* Woman Hollering Creek *(1991). This autobiographical account is part of her exploration of Chicano culture and personal identity.*

Once, several years ago, when I was just starting out my writing career, I was asked to write my own contributor's note for an anthology I was part of. I wrote: "I am the only daughter in a family of six sons. *That* explains everything."

Well, I've thought about that ever since, and yes, it explains a lot to me, but for the reader's sake I should have written: "I am the only daughter in a *Mexican* family of six sons." Or even: "I am the only daughter of a Mexican father and a Mexican-American mother." Or: "I am the only daughter of a working-class family of nine." All of these had everything to do with who I am today.

I was/am the only daughter and *only* a daughter. Being an only daughter in a family of six sons forced me by circumstance to spend a lot of time by myself because my brothers felt it beneath them to play with a *girl* in public. But that aloneness, that loneliness, was good for a would-be writer—it allowed me time to think and think, to imagine, to read and prepare myself.

Being only a daughter for my father meant my destiny would lead me to become someone's wife. That's what he believed. But when I was in the fifth grade and shared my plans for college with him, I was sure he understood. I remember my father saying, *"Que bueno, ni'ja,* that's good." That meant a lot to me, especially since my brothers thought the idea hilarious. What I didn't realize was that my father thought college was good for girls—good for finding a husband. After four years in college and two more in graduate school, and still no husband, my father shakes his head even now and says I wasted all that education.

In retrospect, I'm lucky my father believed daughters were meant for husbands. It meant it didn't matter if I majored in something silly like English. After all, I'd find a nice professional eventually, right? This allowed me the liberty to putter about embroidering my little poems and stories without my father interrupting with so much as a "What's that you're writing?"

But the truth is, I wanted him to interrupt. I wanted my father to understand what it was I was scribbling, to introduce me as "My only daughter, the writer." Not as "This is only my daughter. She teaches." *Es maestra*—teacher. Not even *profesora.*

In a sense, everything I have ever written has been for him, to win his approval even though I know my father can't read English words, even though my father's only reading includes the brown-ink *Esto* sports magazines from Mexico City and the bloody *¡Alarma!* magazines that feature yet another sighting of *La Virgen de Guadalupe* on a tortilla or a wife's revenge on her philandering husband by bashing his skull in with a *molcajete* (a kitchen mortar made of volcanic rock). Or the *fotonovelas*, the little picture paperbacks with tragedy and trauma erupting from the characters' mouths in bubbles.

My father represents, then, the public majority. A public who is uninterested in reading, and yet one whom I am writing about and for, and privately trying to woo.

When we were growing up in Chicago, we moved a lot because of my father. He suffered bouts of nostalgia. Then we'd have to let go our flat, store the furniture with mother's relatives, load the station wagon with baggage and bologna sandwiches and head south. To Mexico City.

We came back, of course. To yet another Chicago flat, another Chicago neighborhood, another Catholic school. Each time, my father would seek out the parish priest in order to get a tuition break, and complain or boast: "I have seven sons."

He meant *siete hijos*, seven children, but he translated it as "sons." "I have seven sons." To anyone who would listen. The Sears Roebuck employee who sold us the washing machine. The short-order cook where my father ate his ham-and-eggs breakfasts. "I have seven sons." As if he deserved a medal from the state.

My papa. He didn't mean anything by that mistranslation, I'm sure. But somehow I could feel myself being erased. I'd tug my father's sleeve and whisper: "Not seven sons. Six! and *one daughter*."

When my oldest brother graduated from medical school, he fulfilled my father's dream that we study hard and use this—our heads, instead of this—our hands. Even now my father's hands are thick and yellow, stubbed by a history of hammer and nails and twine and coils and springs. "Use this," my father said, tapping his head, "and not this," showing us those hands. He always looked tired when he said it.

Wasn't college an investment? And hadn't I spent all those years in college? And if I didn't marry, what was it all for? Why would anyone go to college and then choose to be poor? Especially someone who had always been poor.

Last year, after ten years of writing professionally, the financial rewards started to trickle in. My second National Endowment for the Arts Fellowship. A guest professorship at the University of California, Berkeley. My book, which sold to a major New York publishing house.

At Christmas, I flew home to Chicago. The house was throbbing, same as always; hot *tamales* and sweet *tamales* hissing in my mother's pressure cooker, and everybody—my mother, six brothers, wives, babies, aunts, cousins—talking too loud and at the same time, like in a Fellini film, because that's just how we are.

I went upstairs to my father's room. One of my stories had just been translated into Spanish and published in an anthology of Chicano writing, and I wanted to show it to him. Ever since he recovered from a stroke two years ago, my father likes to spend his leisure hours horizontally. And that's how I found him, watching a Pedro Infante movie on Galavisión and eating rice pudding.

There was a glass filmed with milk on the bedside table. There were several vials of pills and balled Kleenex. And on the floor, one black sock and a plastic urinal that I didn't want to look at but looked at anyway. Pedro Infante was about to burst into song, and my father was laughing.

I'm not sure if it was because my story was translated into Spanish, or because it was published in Mexico, or perhaps because the story dealt with Tepeyac, the *colonia* my father was raised in and the house he grew up in, but at any rate, my father punched the mute button on his remote control and read my story.

I sat on the bed next to my father and waited. He read it very slowly. As if he were reading each line over and over. He laughed at all the right places and read lines he liked out loud. He pointed and asked questions: "Is this So-and-so?" "Yes," I said. He kept reading.

When he was finally finished, after what seemed like hours, my father looked up and asked: "Where can we get more copies of this for the relatives?"

Of all the wonderful things that happened to me last year, that was the most wonderful. 🪶

SUGGESTIONS FOR WRITING

1. What does Cisneros mean by saying that she felt "erased" when her father told people that he had seven sons?

2. Analyze the ending of the narrative. What does it tell us about Cisneros's feeling for her father and her family?

3. Cisneros's father believes that the purpose of a college education for a girl is that it gives her the opportunity to find a husband. Does this belief still exist? Doe you know any women who *have* come to college for that purpose?

4. Which is the most important factor in Cisneros's identity as it is discussed in this narrative: being female, being Mexican-American, or being from a working-class family? Explain and defend your choice.

MANZANAR

Frank Chuman

*During most major wars in American history, fundamental civil liberties
have been curtailed by emergency legislation enacted in an atmosphere of
war hysteria. World War II was no exception. The most famous example
from this war was certainly the official policy of internment for Japanese-
Americans.*

*While no evidence exists that Japanese-Americans were pleased by the
Japanese attack on Pearl Harbor December 7, 1941, they were regarded
with mounting suspicion by the large number of Americans who were convinced of the imminent danger of a full-scale Japanese assault on the American mainland.*

*Early in 1942, military evacuation was ordered for first- and second-gen-
eration (Issei and Nisei) Japanese-Americans from "Military Zone A," as
the West Coast was designated. That spring, 110,000 Issei and Nisei were
transported from their homes (which were confiscated) to internment camps
in remote desert locations. Conditions in the camps were rather grim, but in-
mates set about making new lives for themselves. By 1943, military recruitment began in the camps. Amazingly, large numbers of Japanese-American
men enlisted, and many saw combat in Europe. The internment of Japanese-
Americans officially ended in 1944.*

*Fifty years later, most Americans are shocked and embarrassed by this ep-
isode. Official apologies have been issued. In some cases, reimbursement has
been made for the confiscation of property. Disturbing questions remain
about the racist aspects of the internment policy. Why were Japanese-Americans treated this way, but not Americans of German descent? Was it because the German Americans seemed much less conspicuous to the majority
white American populace? Most unsettling of all is the fear that such
an abuse of human rights could take place again at a time of national
"emergency."*

*The experiences of the detainees have produced a rich store of art, mem-
oirs, and oral interviews, of which the following narrative is an example.
Manzanar was one of the best-known internment camps. It was later the
subject of a fine example of photojournalism, through the collaboration of
photographer Ansel Adams and writer John Hersey in the book* Manzanar.
Frank Chuman—*a Nisei, or second-generation Japanese-American—
described his Manzanar internment for John Tateishi, who included the
account in his* And Justice For All: An Oral History of the Japanese
American Detention Camps *(New York: Random House, 1984).*

I was born April 29, 1917, in the town of Montecito outside of Santa Barbara,
California. My father was the caretaker of a very large estate, for a wealthy fam-

ily who would come to Montecito every year as a summer resort area. When I was three, my father felt there was no future for us in Montecito, so we came down to Los Angeles in about 1920. He was a gardener there in those days. In 1927, I believe it was, he purchased a dry cleaning business in Los Angeles and worked there with Mother helping him. Los Angeles was the place where I lived while I was getting all my education.

On December 7, my sister and I had just come back home after attending the morning worship service at St. Mary's Episcopal Church. All of us sat down to lunch—my father, my mother, my sister, and myself—when there was a radio announcement that Pearl Harbor had been bombed and that we were at war with Japan. I was tremendously shocked, and my immediate reaction was that Japan had done a very foolish thing. This was my very first objective, cold reaction to Japan's bombing of Pearl Harbor. My parents' reactions were a little different. Their reaction was, Now that we are at war and we are of Japanese ancestry, we don't know what's going to happen to us; and in order to protect ourselves we should dispose of everything that has to do with any affiliations or associations with Japan.

There were certain awards that my father had gotten when he was with the Kagoshima *Kenji-Kai* ("prefecture association")—Kagoshima is where he came from. There were many letters, and pictures from Japan of members of my father's and mother's families. They pretty much destroyed all of that. I believe my father took them in the backyard, put these papers into an incinerator, and burned them. They kept very carefully all of the documents that pertained personally to themselves in Japan, for example, their Japanese scholastic records and graduation certificates. The graduation certificates and report cards of my sister, brother and myself. Everything that pertained to America, and especially pertained to themselves as a family originating in Japan or us as sons and daughters they were able to keep. It didn't amount to very much, maybe a little box full of documents. But they were able to take that with them when they went up to Manzanar. The only earthly material possessions that they saved were their own family records and ours. Nothing else.

As family heirlooms my father had two swords he had brought from Japan when he came to America in 1906. Of course, since I was very small, I never really knew he had those swords until I was about fourteen or fifteen. Then he showed me these two swords. One was a rather large sword, maybe five feet long, the other one was about two and a half feet. As I remember now, the outside scabbards of the swords were a deep maroon color, ceramic in texture, with little flowers. They were ornamental swords, not for combat, decorated all over with petaled flowers. The hand parts of them were woven with some very fancy twine and then they had very fancy sword guards, with handguards on them. My father said to me then that he wanted to give those swords to me because I was the oldest son. My sister was older than I was, but I was the oldest son; I had a younger brother, George.

When the war broke out on December 7, my father and I took out these swords, which he had placed in a closed drawer, and we then went outside into the backyard. My father proceeded to separate the component parts of the sword. He removed the steel handguard and left the bare, naked steel sword blade itself. He did that with both the swords while I watched him. He then thrust the naked blades of both of the swords deep into the ground, not flat, down into the ground as deep as they would go and covered them so that they couldn't be seen from the surface. Then he threw away the scabbards.

I thought to myself, how stupid of Japan to go to war with the United States. I felt that my relationship with Japan as a nation, as a people, maybe even emotionally, would end with the outbreak of the war. This, of course, was very naïve thinking, but that's the way I thought. And the symbolic act of dismantling the sword and burying it sort of severed any emotional feeling I had at that time for Japan. It's almost like trying to bury a very unpleasant thought: you get it out of your sight and then it's out of your mind. Of course, there was another practical consideration, I think, on the part of my father. I never suggested to my father that he destroy the swords, but I'm sure that he was also thinking of the practical side: any swords, cameras, radios, pistols, rifles, were considered contraband. I believe from the news reports that if he was found in possession of Japanese swords he might have been considered suspect or something. I think this shook him up.

All my father and mother had were these swords, but I'm sure that other families had things as precious or more so in terms of not only intrinsic value, but also of actual monetary value. I'm sure that a lot of families had beautiful cloisonné vases or ceramic objects, paintings. I'm sure that they had hand scrolls, for instance, *kakemonos* ("wall scrolls"). I'm sure that there were just hundreds and thousands of Japanese families that brought these things from Japan, and I'm sure that in the panic that followed many families destroyed those things. Even today, I still have a sort of ache in my heart, because I would be very proud to display those swords in my home.

While there were a lot of things in the newspapers and on the radio during that period of time from December 7 to March, when I went to Manzanar, I was not really the object, personally, or directly, of any anti-Japanese feelings. Maybe a lot of people did get the full brunt of the anti-Japanese hostility, but I didn't. In the first place, I was attending school and I was also working forty hours a week in the Los Angeles County Probation Department, and I kept the job with the county until the Board of Supervisors gave an order to all department heads in the county department similar to those given in the city and state and federal governments to discharge all Japanese Americans. But even in the probation department, I didn't really get anti-Japanese venom directed toward me. I knew most of the people in the probation department, I knew the students, being a student myself at USC Law School, and I wasn't often around the house or the business where my father was operating, so I really didn't get the impact of that.

When the order came from the Board of Supervisors to the acting chief probation officer to discharge me, I being the only Japanese American in the department, the officer called me into his office and said, "Frank, I do not have any legal cause nor any personal cause to terminate you, to fire you." He said, "I'm supposed to fire you. I'm not going to do that. But I have to let you go. You can't work here anymore. I will give you a leave of absence." So, I got a leave of absence. The leave of absence remained in effect all the way through evacuation.

So I didn't get the full brunt of the anti-Japanese hostility which was a hell of a good thing, because when I went to Manzanar there was a delayed reaction for me. What the hell am I doing in camp? I thought. While I was very busy working in the hospital, I said to myself, Why should the United States Government doubt our loyalty to the United States? We haven't done anything to justify this kind of treatment. Certainly not myself and certainly none of the others that I know of. And yet here I am in a camp of ten thousand people— men, women, and children. So I began to think to myself, because I had studied law—constitutional law and constitutional rights and due process and equal protection and all the rest of it—Jesus Christ, we've been deprived of our constitutional rights. There's been no accusations against me, and yet I'm suspect and I'm arbitrarily told to go into a camp. It's completely in violation of my rights. And I began to get goddamned upset. I thought, what the hell is the government doing, to put us away like this and incarcerate us and consider us disloyal and think that we're going to sabotage the United States' war efforts or anything else? What is it with the United States Government that has brought this to pass? And I really got angry and very, very upset at the United States Government for doing this kind of thing to not only me, but all Japanese Americans. I really got upset.

The Army recruiting team came into Manzanar around the early part of 1943. We had a big meeting in this mess hall of all persons eligible for military duty with two white soldiers and a person of Japanese ancestry, and this guy was trying to persuade us all to volunteer for the Army, and I'm not too sure whether I got up and spoke back to him or whether I said it in my own mind, but I said, "Why should we fight for the United States Government as soldiers, when the United States Government distrusts us? Why do they now want us to serve when they consider us to be disloyal? Why do they want us to serve when they have taken us out of our homes and schools and businesses, and now they want us to become loyal to the United States? It doesn't make sense, and so far as I'm concerned I'm not going to do anything to go into the United States Army until the United States Government does something to remedy this unjust situation." I cannot remember whether I stood up and said it or whether I felt it.

In any event, that's the way it was. In the latter part of 1943, this questionnaire came out sponsored by the WRA, and in that questionnaire it had something like "request for relocation" as well as the questionnaire. It was in two parts. And there were these questions 27 and 28, "Are you willing to foreswear any allegiance to any foreign potentate and say that you are loyal to the United States?" and, "Are you willing to bear arms for the United States?" The first answer that I gave to both questions was no. I was so goddamned mad at that questionnaire. It was insulting, impugning without any evidence, just from the top down that there was something that made us Japanese Americans suspect in loyalty, allegiance, that we wouldn't fight for the government and saying now you're going to fight. They don't have to push it down my throat—are you willing to bear arms to defend the United States? That's so goddamned obvious that I would do that that it just really made me angry.

So out of a feeling of anger and disappointment in the United States Government's attitude towards us and their unwarranted suspicion, and the way they treated us to make us all get out of our homes without any real basis for it made me so goddamned angry that for the record I wanted the government to know that I was angry. So I said, "No-no, just shove it up your ass." It was completely impulsive. I was pretty hotheaded back in those days. But pretty damn hotheaded towards things which involved injustice, things which I considered to be not fair. You know, on those kind of issues I have a tendency to get very hot and indignant.

I did not remain a no-no, because all of a sudden I thought to myself, after I had said that, I regretted it, because it wasn't my true feelings. There was no way that I could hate the United States Government, but I was goddamned angry at them for doing things like that about us. I got to thinking to myself that maybe I should do something about changing it and get the record straight as to what my real feelings were. I knew the project director, Ralph Merritt, and I was very close to him, because as administrator of the hospital I had to go down and see him about many, many things—the procurement of medical supplies and trying to take care of the sick and so forth. At least I had considerable personal contact with him.

So I went to Ralph Merritt and I said to him, "You know I regret that I gave the answers no-no." And he said, "Yeah, I think so." He said, "I don't think you really meant that, but you've already said it and put in on the record. It's been filed back in Washington with the WRA." I said, "Well, is there some way I can erase those answers?" He said, "God, that's tough. That is very, very difficult." But he said, "I'll tell you what, I'm in Washington many, many times as project director of Manzanar and I will do everything I can to see if I can get those answers changed for you. But I can't promise, because they were ordered by the military although it's on WRA paper."

So over a period of three or four months, he'd go to Washington and then he would call me in and he'd say, "I went to see such and such who was an officer in the United States Army." And he said, "The officer who has your answers is absolutely adamant about not doing anything about it. You knew what you were doing and when you answered that way, that became your answer." The officer said, "I have no sympathy with Chuman. He knows what the hell he's supposed to say and if he didn't say it, too bad." So Merritt said to me, "The first overture to try to erase the record has not been successful, but I'll try again through somebody else."

I found out later that he had gone almost to the top of the military hierarchy that had anything to do with the WRA questionnaire which really went out to all Japanese American persons of military age. That's what it was for, it was really a draft questionnaire, which later was used for men and women in the relocation camps as a general loyalty questionnaire. I know that Ralph Merritt took this matter about me as a personal crusade. Ralph Merritt gathered together all my background. He checked my background, he checked my school, my church, my Boy Scouts, my community activities up to that time; he checked with different persons who were my character references from the prewar days which we all had to list; and I know that he checked with the camp officials, he checked with people on the hospital staff who were Caucasians. He did a hell of a lot of work on that.

I didn't know that all of our mail was monitored. I was writing to a lot of people. Goddamnit, they were monitoring that. These people would write to me and I would write to them. If I had said anything that was hotheaded or anti-American, I was dead. But that didn't happen, I didn't write in that vein. So he had gathered all these papers together and next time he was in Washington he persuaded somebody who was high up that Frank Chuman was born in the United States, that he had never been to Japan, that from ages seven to eleven he was growing up at a grammar school; then junior high, high school, and so forth; that he was varsity debater and he was on the track team, he was captain; he was Boy's Senior Board at L.A. High School; UCLA; he was YMCA; Bruin Club, Boy Scouts, Eagle Scout; and all the rest of that stuff. While he was at Manzanar he was working diligently in the hospital, and he had said nothing derogatory about the United States Government.

Ralph Merritt said, "When I go to Washington the next time, write me a letter why you think you ought to have your answers changed." I did write that letter and wrote that, out of disgust for the United States Government's policy towards us, I thought it was unjust, I thought it was unfair, and so forth. He persuaded the powers that be that Chuman had just said that out of impulse and out of anger and disappointment rather than out of maliciousness and out of real feelings of hostility. So they changed me back to yes-yes.

The American Friends Service Committee in Philadelphia established the National Student Relocation Council. Many people were in it. I remember some of their names, Tom Emlen and Betty Emlen, a recently married young couple who had both graduated from Haverford College in Pennsylvania. I know that there were several others from other schools, but the only direct contact I had was with Betty and Tom Emlen. So I wrote to the National Student Relocation Council and said, "I'm interested in continuing law school if I can. I have no money. Can you help me?" Within a couple of weeks while the Emlens were on their regular circuit to different relocation camps, they came in to see me, and I told them what my plight was. I had to interrupt law school right in the middle of a semester and lose my credits because of it. I had no money and could not return to USC. I didn't know any other law schools outside of California. So they said, "Fine, we'll try to do something for you." And they made all kinds of efforts to find a suitable law school for me. They reported back to me that they had found a Valparaiso Law School in Indiana, Drake University, Boston College in Boston, and the University of Michigan among others. I said I would like to enter the University of Michigan Law School at Ann Arbor. So the Emlens were the ones who arranged for the transcripts, dormitory housing, and so forth.

The dean of the University of Michigan Law School wrote to me saying they were happy to accept me for the fall 1943 semester. Following that letter, about a week later, came this letter from the president of the university, saying, "I understand that you've been accepted into the Law School at the University of Michigan. I regret to say that you cannot enter the University of Michigan

Law School because it is the policy of the University that no Japanese Americans are accepted into any department of the University, professional or undergraduate, because we are involved in sensitive war defense work." So that pulled the rug from under that. To go to Boston College Law School, which had already accepted me, required at that time, a clearance to enter the Eastern Defense Command. I did not have that clearance. It would probably never come or it would probably take months and months and I would be out as far as trying to attend beginning with the fall semester of 1943.

So among the schools in the Midwest and not within the Eastern Defense Command was the University of Toledo, which was found for me by Betty and Tom Emlen. I consulted with Ralph Merritt, who suggested that I go to the Midwest, and enter the University of Toledo. "After that," Ralph Merritt said, "there is nobody, not even military authorities that can prevent a United States citizen from going into the Eastern Defense Command without the clearance." He said, "You're free to travel throughout the United States. The idea is to get out of Manzanar with your clearance. There's nothing to prevent you from going out of camp because I'm the one that will allow you to go out and go to the Midwest. After that you're free to go into any college along the Eastern Defense Command. Nobody can stop you constitutionally or legally." So that's what I did, I went to the University of Toledo.

Before I left Manzanar for Toledo, I talked about continuing school with my parents—that I wanted to leave, that I didn't know what my future was, that I at least wanted to finish law school instead of going out to find work.

My father dug way underneath the cot where he slept. He pulled out a sack, a fabric sack, I can't remember exactly, but it was kind of a deep stocking sack, and he dug way in there and he pulled out of that sack $150, and he gave it to me. He said, "This is all I have left from the evacuation. We lost our dry cleaning business, equipment, big heavy equipment, and dryer, all kinds of things, furniture and household properties. All we've got is $150." But he said, "You take it. You need it. There's no more money. We don't have any more money. We cannot help you anymore on money; but we want you to finish your school if that's what you want. Don't worry about us, we're here in camp."

There had been some turmoil while we were at Manzanar. On December 7, 1942, a riot broke out. As a matter of fact there were two riots that were going on at the same time. I was in my offices at about seven that night when it happened. One of the riots took place in the northern part of the camp, mess hall 24 or something like that, where a lot of the primarily pro-Japanese, anti-JACL elements were having a meeting where they were denouncing the JACLers for either informing on some of the Japanese or for being too much in favor of the United States Government. I don't know whether it was by coincidence that it was on the first anniversary of Pearl Harbor or not, but anyway it was December 7, 1942. So this group were getting all heated up and excited, and they were all saying, "Well, let's go out and kill these guys." Apparently the anti-JACL elements dispersed and were scouring the camp looking for these people (JACLers) really with the intention of either killing them or doing them great harm.

In the meantime, at the opposite end of the camp, at the guard entrance, a group of persons had congregated because one of the evacuees who was working in the warehouse had accused the warehouse supervisor, a Caucasian, of diverting sugar from the delivery supplies for the camp evacuees and selling it on the black market. I know that the Japanese American was then summarily removed from the camp and put into a temporary jail in Lone Pine. When word got around that this Japanese American was arrested, some of the residents who knew of it gathered at the gate to lodge a protest at the administration building. The evacuees demanded that this person in jail be returned to the camp because he had done no wrong. As I understand it there were several hundred who had gathered at the gate beside the building. The evacuees were getting very riotous; they were saying a lot of bad things about the government, about the camp administration, and against this Caucasian warehouse supervisor, and they were getting very heated emotionally about the unfair arrest of this evacuee.

The project director then ordered the military police to come and restore some order at the entrance. The story I got, although it was told by many people with different versions, depending upon where they were at the time, is that the military police were lined up facing the crowd. The evacuees were coming closer and closer to the military police. The military police had shotguns. The information I had was that there were three military guards there. They ordered the crowd to disperse. Suddenly, as some of the crowd were turning around to leave, there was a shot or a sound as if a shot had been fired. Later I was told that a light bulb had been thrown by an evacuee towards the military guard, and it shattered on the pavement, which was asphalt, causing a shotlike sound. Anyway, the military police were pretty goddamned scared; I'm sure they had been instilled with a lot of anti-Japanese feelings anyway, and so while some of the crowd were trying to leave on orders of the military, other evacuees were sort of approaching the military police. When this noise that sounded like a shot was heard, the military police panicked. They thought that they were being shot at, and as a result they fired their shotguns into the crowd. The result was two dead and nine injured.

It was seven at night; it was dark, about dusk. A telephone call came in to me at my office in the hospital saying that a riot had taken place and that a lot of people were dead or injured; the voice on the phone said he didn't know how many. I immediately told the ambulance drivers who were on duty at the hospital to go down to the place to pick up these injured people.

I sent runners around to get the hospital doctors, nurses, and orderlies who were off duty, plus the warehouse staff to come to the hospital at once because I didn't know the nature and extent of the injuries. The ambulances went out to the entrance to the camp, and they brought the injured and, as we later discovered, some of the dead back to the hospital.

At the same time the riot at the northern part of the camp, around Block 24 which was across the firebreak across from the hospital, was in full progress. The rioters were searching for Tokutaro Slocum and Joe Masaoka and Fred Tayama and some others. There were a lot of people who were being sought out by the rioters. There was turmoil going on all over the camp.

As the ambulance was bringing up the injured and the dead from the entranceway, the military police followed the first two ambulances and came up to the hospital entrance. I was there, and I was only allowing the hospital personnel to come in, although the crowd from the entrance were sort of belligerent toward me. They were saying, "Let us in, let us in," like they were going to beat me up. But I stood on the steps and said, "No, nobody can come in except those who work in the hospital." They respected this, and they quieted down. The injured were lined up along the corridors inside the hospital.

The doctors came and looked at the ones lying on the stretchers in the corridors. Two were dead. The nine who were wounded were immediately brought into the surgical room, examined, and operated on as necessary. The Board of Inquiry from the Army headquarters in San Francisco came down and tried to whitewash the military police shooting incident. They tried to get the evacuee doctors and nurses and all the other witnesses to say that the evacuees who died or were injured were threatening or were in the process of attacking the military police and, therefore, it was justified for the military police to fire upon the evacuees. However, the medical examination, the records, and the trajectory of the bullets showed that the victims had been either shot in the side or in the back. Dr. Goto, who was chief of the medical staff and was the chief surgeon at that time, conducted the surgery and was asked to change his testimony and records to show that the bullets fired by the military police came from the front. He refused to do that, and I know specifically that as a result, his services were terminated the following day as chief of the medical staff. He was sent out of the hospital to some other relocation center.

The government didn't give us a chance. The government just automatically said, You're part of the enemy. We consider you disloyal. We think you're going to commit sabotage. We know you're going to commit espionage because of your bloodline.

I can never justify this evacuation based upon law. It was clearly unconstitutional, regardless of the Yasui, the Hirabayashi, and the Korematsu cases; to me it was a flagrant disregard of individual rights, personal rights, constitutional rights, and it was a violation of due process. They never gave us a chance to show that we could still take our place in society, although at that time I think it would have been a very great travail for us to be in that kind of a society.

I believe that under all the circumstances, even if it were not the military policy, the Japanese and the Japanese Americans would have been evacuated anyway eventually. I think this because there were the politicians, plus economic interests, plus in some parts of the community, the anti-Japanese feeling was so strong.

I have no remaining anger towards the government for what they did. I believe I understand it. I have no lingering, festering animosity that makes me sour towards America. It's funny that I say so. I not only understand, but I can forgive the U.S. government for what they did. And despite all the hardships—and there's no way you can get away from all that—I understand that, and I think I can forgive the U.S. government for the tremendous miscalculation of us as a people in the society.

Am I left with a sense of betrayal? Yes, in this sense: the government did not really protect basic human rights, nor the basic legal procedural and substantive protective rights of individuals. Yes, I think in that sense the government, from President Roosevelt down through the secretary of war, the military commanders, and the politicians—the total forces for the evacuation—engaged, even if not intentionally, in a tremendous conspiratorial activity of maligning persons of Japanese ancestry. From that standpoint, the government and its proponents of the evacuation trampled upon our rights and definitely violated our rights, human as well as constitutional rights. ✒

SUGGESTIONS FOR WRITING

1. Describe Chuman's attitude toward the country whose government implemented this policy. What obligations do you believe you owe your country? How would these be changed by such a radical change in the way you were treated by your government?

2. Chuman reveals real ambivalence about his experiences. Describe and explain some of the complexities and contradictions of what he went through. How much was his age (25) at the time of his detention a factor in his behavior? How would he have behaved differently if he had been significantly younger or older?

3. Among American minority groups, Japanese Americans have not been the only ones in recent years to argue in favor of reparations for wrongs they suffered in the past. According to this logic, justice demands that contemporary Americans have an obligation to compensate others for the misdeeds of their ancestors. How do you feel about this principle?

4. Compare attitudes toward Japanese Americans today with those evident from this episode from half a century ago. If we felt threatened as a nation today, what group or groups might our government decide to detain?

TWICE AN OUTSIDER: ON BEING JEWISH AND A WOMAN

Vivian Gornick

Sometimes a person can be the object of two kinds of prejudice. Jewish women, existing within an ancient patriarchal tradition, have frequently commented on the dual nature of the prejudices they face. **Vivian Gornick,** *however, has little to say about her own direct experience of anti-Semitism. Instead she uses her memory of the bigoted insults her father endured to explore the kinds of sexist insults that make her own spirit "shrivel."*

    Vivian Gornick (b. 1935) is an American feminist and social critic with a wide range of interests and political involvements. Her books include The Romance of American Communism *(1977),* Essays in Feminism *(1978),* Women in Science *(1983), and* Fierce Attachments *(1987). She lives in New York City.*

My father had to be Jewish; he had no choice. When he went downtown he heard "kike." I live downtown, and I do not hear "kike." Maybe it's there to be heard and I'm not tuned in, but it can't be there all that much if I don't hear it. I'm out in the world, and this is what I *do* hear:

I walk down the street. A working-class man puts his lips together and makes a sucking noise at me.

I enter a hardware store to purchase a lock. I choose one, and the man behind the counter shakes his head at me. "Women don't know how to use that lock," he says.

I go to a party in a university town. A man asks me what I do. I tell him I'm a journalist. He asks if I run a cooking page. Two minutes later someone asks me not if I have a husband but what my husband does.

I go to another party, a dinner party on New York's Upper West Side. I'm the only woman at the table who is not there as a wife. I speak a few sentences on the subject under discussion. I am not responded to. A minute later my thought is rephrased by one of the men. Two other men immediately address it.

Outsiderness is the daily infliction of social invisibility. From low-grade humiliation to life-threatening aggression, its power lies in the way one is seen, and how that in turn affects the way one sees oneself. When my father heard the word "kike," the life-force within him shriveled. When a man on the street makes animal-like noises at me, or when a man at a dinner table does not hear what I say, the same thing happens to me. This is what makes the heart pound and the head fill with blood. This is how the separation between world and self occurs. This is outsiderness alive in the daily way. It is here, on the issue of being a woman, not a Jew, that I must make my stand and hold my ground.

This invisibility once made Jews manic and blacks murderous. It works on women in a variety of ways.

I leaned across the counter in the hardware store and said to the man who had told me women didn't know how to use the lock I'd chosen, "Would you say that to me if I were black?" He stared lightly at me for a long moment. Then he nodded. "Gotcha," he said.

To the man at the university party I explained my work in great and careful detail. The man, a 60-year-old Ivy Leaguer, was frankly puzzled at why I spoke of something fairly simple at such excessive length. I knew this was the first time he had heard what I was *really* saying, and I didn't expect it to sink in. What I did expect was that the next time he heard a woman speak these words, they would begin to take hold.

At the dinner party in New York I made a scene. I brought harmless sociability to an end. I insisted that everyone see that the little social murders committed between men and women were the real subtext of the evening, and that civilized converse was no longer possible unless this underlying truth was addressed. I did this because these were liberal intellectuals. They had heard it all before, many times, and *still* they did not get it. It was as terrible for me to go home that evening with the taste of ashes in my mouth as it was for everyone else—we had all come expecting the warm pleasures of good food and good conversation—but I couldn't have lived with myself that night if I hadn't spoken up. Just as I would have had to speak up if the conversation had suddenly turned politely anti-Semitic. Which it would not have in this company.

The Jewishness inside me is an education. I see more clearly, can think more inventively, because I can think analogously about "them" and "us." That particular knowledge of being one among the many is mine twice over. I have watched masters respond to "them" and "us," and I have learned. 🖋

SUGGESTIONS FOR WRITING

1. The author describes a friendly social occasion in which she was taken aback by the open expression of strong, if unwitting, sexism by a companion. She chose to confront the person immediately and directly. How would you have handled the situation?

2. The author almost seems to suggest that the unconscious sexism she encountered among her friends and acquaintances is worse than the very blatant and threatening gesture made to her by the man on the street. Do you agree?

3. The writer says that anti-Semitism, which her father had faced in direct ways, may still be "out there" in her day and age, but that she doesn't come into contact with it. Does this mean that people are more tolerant of Jews today? Are you aware of any openly anti-Semitic statements? Describe one from your own experience.

4. There are various ways in which a person can be made to feel like an outsider. Describe an occasion or event that made you feel this way.

Selections from
STORIES I AIN'T
TOLD NOBODY YET

Jo Carson

*Actress/writer **Jo Carson** (b. 1946) talks about the working people she knows in east Tennessee and the southern Appalachian Mountains. Her work reads like poetry, yet she says that what it really represents is a reproduction of what she has heard from other people. The everyday world is her resource, and her poetry/dialogues provide a rich texture of individual voices as they express their fears, victories, and regrets. Carson is particularly skilled at touching on issues both regional and universal: the fear of losing one's job, the effects of prejudice, the pain—and triumph—of an ended marriage.*

Carson grew up in Appalachia: Johnson City, Tennessee. She left for New York when she was twenty. After two years she returned to her home, where she writes plays, poems, and short stories about her native region.

1. Mountain people
   can't read,
   can't write,
   don't wear shoes,
   don't have teeth,
   don't use soap,
   and don't talk plain.
   They beat their kids,
   beat their friends,
   beat their neighbors,
   and beat their dogs.
   They live on cow peas,
   fatback and twenty acres
   straight up and down.
   They don't have money.
   They do have fleas,
   overalls,
   tobacco patches,
   shacks,
   shotguns,
   foodstamps,
   liquor stills,
   and at least six junk cars in the front yard.
   Right?

Well, let me tell you:
I am from here,
I'm not like that
and I am damned tired of being told I am.

2. The first time I sat in a restaurant
   where blacks were not served
   Martin Luther King was still alive.
   I knew I would not be served;
   I knew it would be me who served
   time in jail. I had taken a shower
   and eaten my lunch in preparation.
   When I came to consciousness
   I had vomited my lunch,
   I had been beaten and handcuffed
   to the bars of a cell in the city jail.
   I stayed in that position for a week.
   I had a wound in my head
   that needed medical attention.
   It was not the last time I sat
   where blacks were not served.
   I did it until I was sentenced
   to the federal pen or the U.S. Army,
   my choice, and I served in Vietnam.

   M.L.K. was murdered twenty years ago.
   My daughter is almost the age I was
   and we were sitting in a restaurant
   where blacks are not served.
   There was no sign that said white only,
   there was a waitress who behaved
   as though she could not see us.
   "We're color blind in America,"
   my daughter said and we walked out.
   Black people already know this story
   and who else do I think might listen—
   the woman who refused to see us?
   the couple who came in after we did
   who were served when we were not?
   This story is not newsworthy, nobody
   needed stitches, but this is the same story
   as the one that cracked my head open.
   The only thing that changed is the law.

3. My daughter got divorced
   and she and her little boy
   has moved back in with me.
   For the time being.

   And everything she goes to do,
   she's got a book.

   Gonna cook something,
   she looks up in the book
   to see what she wants
   and then when we ain't got it,
   she's got to run out to the grocery store.

   "I'll just be gone a minute, Mama, you keep Chip."

   Now, we got hamburger meat
   and we got beans
   and all the rest of the stuff
   you put up from a garden,
   and there's been many a soul
   to make it through this world
   without ever tastin' veal scallopini.
   I could have done without it.

   And she made herself a dress.
   First she read the book of sewing machine directions,
   then she's got this other book
   that tells her how to make things.
   Took two days for something
   that might of taken me two hours.
   I said that.

   "But I did it right," she says.

   Then Chip put a towel down the flush commode,
   and she read *The Reader's Digest Fix-it Book*
   while the damn thing flooded up the bathroom.

   "I didn't know how," she said.

   You see, that book
   don't tell about straightening out a coat hanger
   and fishing something out.

   "Not everything's got a book written about it," I told her.

   "I know that, Mama, there wasn't a book written about my marriage.
   I might not be here if there had a' been."

   Now what am I supposed to say to that?

4. Twenty-one years,
   long enough to grow one of two children
   to the age of her majority,
   I scheduled the machines, the space
   and the people on the floor for Kingsport Press,
   and when they terminated me
   they sent a man who had been there
   two and a half months
   to thank me for my years of service.
   All I could think to say was
   I resent this.
   Now, I can think of plenty more.

   I was terminated because I earned too much.
   They will re-name my job—
   they cannot do without it—
   and pay some new man less to do it.
   It is a complicated responsibility
   and for a while, he will lose them more money
   than I cost. But not for long enough.
   The valuable employee awards I got—
   the last one was last year—
   have turned into a bad joke.

   Now, I get the opportunity to clean out my office.

   I get severance pay if I sign a form that says I will not sue.

   I get what I contributed to my retirement, no more.

   I get to write a resume.

   I have never felt so faceless or so used.

   For the next person who pats me on the back
   to say a rotten deal, a crying shame,
   or some other easy whitewash
   that does not say what happened
   I have some new words: try injustice,
   say abuse out loud.
   And to those who will not look at me
   because somehow fired and failed
   are too close together,
   bend over this barrel, friend,
   your turn is likely to be next.
   And for all who've never thought to ask it,
   a question I never thought to ask till now:
   who decided money is more valuable than people,
   and why did all the rest of us agree to work that way?

SUGGESTIONS FOR WRITING

1. Like the man in "Twenty-one years," many people identify themselves at least in part by the job they do, the career they follow. Examine yourself or someone whom you know well and determine in what ways you or they are shaped by work.

2. Every area of the world has stereotypes associated with it, like those catalogued in the piece "Mountain people." Select a group or a geographic area you know well and examine the stereotypes attributed to it in the same way that Carson has done. Explore both how you feel about these labels and reasons why you believe they developed.

3. In "The first time I sat in a restaurant" Carson makes a strong statement about prejudice and change. Explore her point of view, examine on what grounds she draws these conclusions, and decide whether you agree with her.

4. Examine in what ways the woman speaking in "My daughter got divorced" differs from her daughter in terms of practical knowledge. Carson seems to be making a point about something more crucial than the best way to cook or clean. Respond to what the last three stanzas say about the differences between the mother and her daughter.

3

COMING TO TERMS
WITH OTHERS

Sometimes we refer to ourselves in our social existence as if we were fully formed individuals to be distinguished clearly from the others who make up our intricate social networks. A moment's reflection, however, is sufficient to make us realize that what and who we are expresses the sum total of our interactions with the myriad "others" we encounter in life: from the original "significant others" who make up our families to the social, racial, physical, and sexual "others" from which we attempt, consciously or not, to distinguish ourselves. In traditional societies, one's "others" were the human beings who populated the daily round of existence. In the late twentieth century, the image of the other is perhaps more commonly summoned from our all-pervasive electronic media. Many observers suggest that, for better or worse, the media-generated stereotypes of our social "others" are more persuasive than the responses gained from direct contact.

Much of writing is characterized by the act of representing "others." In the phases of cultural history dominated by books, literary representations played a formative role in constituting social "others." In the age of electronic media, films, videos, and advertisements shape our conscious and unconscious senses of ourselves and others. In the selections that make up this section, "others" are identified and characterized as they both clarify and challenge one's sense of autonomy. The experiences of others throw self-awareness more sharply into relief. These selections also show how a sense of one's own limits often can be gained through encounters with sometimes hostile "others," who direct their prejudices toward the "other" they perceive. In a more positive sense, it also becomes clear that the sense of selfhood un-

dergoes significant modification and even enhancement through interaction with others. Sometimes these differences become assimilated.

The following selections feature situations in which individuals perceive their lives or act on the basis of their notions of themselves in relation to others. Sometimes, as in the case of Lillian Smith's memoir, they are jolted into a new recognition of themselves and their place in the world through an unprecedented awareness of otherness. A sense of self-definition or categorization imposed from without may lead to stubborn resistance, as Paul Fussell shows by commenting on class, that great American "unmentionable." The painfulness of disappointed class expectations demonstrated by Katy Butler's "Pâté Poverty" echoes Fussell's theme. Multiple senses of otherness may converge in some contexts, as in James T. Farrell's "For White Men Only," with its simultaneous exploration of themes of gender and race. It is even possible, as we see in Gary Soto's "Like Mexicans," for the "other" to grow so familiar that it dissolves into oneself. If our experience of others is rich enough, it becomes difficult to distinguish our own identities from those who have made a great impression on us. This can be one of life's welcome complexities. 🖋

WHEN I WAS A CHILD

Lillian Smith

*Racism may not have been as dangerous to Southern whites as it was to blacks, but it nevertheless had its damaging effects. Most damaging of all perhaps was the slow absorption from early childhood of a complex set of social practices that would take the place of a child's natural impulses of friendly association with potential playmates, regardless of race. In her autobiographical account of this initiation into the Jim Crow world of segregation, **Lillian Smith** (1897-1966) shows us a child's first confrontation with racial prejudice.*

Smith was a Southern writer known for her strong opposition to the institutional racism of her region, expressed most eloquently in her 1949 book Killers of the Dream, *from which this selection is taken. She took her stand against segregation at a time when few whites dared to join blacks in this struggle. For this, her house was bombed and burned to the ground three times. Smith was also a sexual outlaw by the prevailing standards. Her lesbianism was fiercely denied by her family, who must surely have caused her acute suffering when, as she lay dying in 1964 from cancer, they would not permit her longtime companion Paula Snelling to pay her a last visit.*

Even its children know that the South is in trouble. No one has to tell them; no words said aloud. To them, it is a vague thing weaving in and out of their play, like a ghost haunting an old graveyard or whispers after the household sleeps—fleeting mystery, vague menace, to which each responds in his own way. Some learn to screen out all except the soft and the soothing; others deny even as they see plainly, and hear. But all know that under quiet words and warmth and laughter, under the slow ease and tender concern about small matters, there is a heavy burden on all of us and as heavy a refusal to confess it. The children know this "trouble" is bigger than they, bigger than their family, bigger than their church, so big that people turn away from its size. They have seen it flash out like lightning and shatter a town's peace, have felt it tear up all they believe in. They have measured its giant strength and they feel weak when they remember.

This haunted childhood belongs to every southerner. Many of us run away from it but we come back like a hurt animal to its wound, or a murderer to the scene of his sin. The human heart dares not stay away too long from that which hurt it most. There is a return journey to anguish that few of us are released from making.

We who were born in the South call this mesh of feeling and memory "loyalty." We think of it sometimes as "love." We identify with the South's trouble as if we, individually, were responsible for all of it. We defend the sins and sorrows of three hundred years as if each sin had been committed by us alone and each sorrow had cut across our heart. We are as hurt at criticism of our region as if our own name were called aloud by the critic. We have known guilt without understanding it, and there is no tie that binds men closer to the past and each other than that.

It is a strange thing, this umbilical cord uncut. In times of ease, we do not feel its pull, but when we are threatened with change, suddenly it draws the whole white South together in a collective fear and fury that wipe our minds clear of reason and we are blocked off from sensible contact with the world we live in.

To keep this resistance strong, wall after wall has been thrown up in the southern mind against criticism from without and within. Imaginations close tight against the hurt of others; a regional armoring takes place to keep out the "enemies" who would make our trouble different—or maybe rid us of it completely. For it is a trouble that we do not want to give up. We are as involved with it as a child who cannot be happy at home and cannot bear to tear himself away, or as a grown-up who has fallen in love with his own disease. We southerners have identified with the long sorrowful past on such deep levels of love and hate and guilt that we do not know how to break old bonds without pulling our lives down. *Change* is the evil word, a shrill clanking that makes us know too well our servitude. *Change* means leaving one's memories, one's sins, one's ancient prison, the room where one was born. How can we do this when we are tied fast!

The white man's burden is his own childhood. Every southerner knows this. Though he may deny it even to himself, yet he drags through life with him the heavy weight of a past that never eases and is rarely understood, of desire never appeased, of dreams that died in his heart.

In this South I was born and now live. Here it was that I began to grow, seeking my way, as do all children, through the honeycomb cells of our life to the bright reality outside. Sometimes it was as if all doors opened inward. . . . Sometimes we children lost even the desire to get outside and tried only to make a comfortable home of the trap of swinging doors that history and religion and a war, man's greed and his guilt had placed us in at birth.

It is not easy to pick out of such a life those strands that have to do only with color, only with Negro-white relationships, only with religion or sex, for they are knit of the same fibers that have gone into the making of the whole fabric, woven into its basic patterns and designs. Religion . . . sex . . . race . . . money . . . avoidance rites . . . malnutrition . . . dreams—no part of these can be looked at and clearly seen without looking at the whole of them. For, as a painter mixes colors and makes of them new colors, so religion is turned into something different by race, and segregation is colored as much by sex as by skin pigment, and money is no longer a coin but a lost wish wandering through a man's whole life.

A child's lessons are blended of these strands however dissonant a design they make. The mother who taught me what I know of tenderness and love and compassion taught me also the bleak rituals of keeping Negroes in their place. The father who rebuked me for an air of superiority toward schoolmates from the mill and rounded out his rebuke by gravely reminding me that "all men are brothers," trained me in the steel-rigid decorums I must demand of every colored male. They who so gravely taught me to split my body from my feelings and both from my "soul," taught me also to split my conscience from my acts and Christianity from southern tradition.

Neither the Negro nor sex was often discussed at length in our home. We were given no formal instruction in these difficult matters but we learned our lessons well. We learned the intricate system of taboos, of renunciations and compensations, of manners, voice modulations, words, feelings, along with our prayers, our toilet habits, and our games. I do not remember how or when, but by the time I had learned that God is love, that Jesus is His Son and came to give us more abundant life, that all men are brothers with a common Father, I also knew that I was better than a Negro, that all black folks have their place and must be kept in it, that sex has its place and must be kept in it, that a terrifying disaster would befall the South if ever I treated a Negro as my social equal and as terrifying a disaster would befall my family if ever I were to have a baby outside of marriage. I had learned that God so loved the world that He gave His only begotten Son so that we might have segregated churches in which it was my duty to worship each Sunday and on Wednesday at evening prayers. I had learned that white southerners are a hospitable, courteous, tactful people who treat those of their own group with consideration and who as carefully segregate from all the richness of life "for their own good and welfare" thirteen million people whose skin is colored a little differently from my own.

I knew by the time I was twelve that a member of my family would always shake hands with old Negro friends, would speak gently and graciously to members of the Negro race unless they forgot their place, in which event icy peremptory tones would draw lines beyond which only the desperate would dare take one step. I knew that to use the word "nigger" was unpardonable and no well-bred southerner was quite so crude as to do so; nor would a well-bred southerner call a Negro "mister" or invite him into the living room or eat with him or sit by him in public places.

I knew that my old nurse who had patiently cared for me through long months of illness, who had given me refuge when a little sister took my place as the baby of the family, who comforted me, soothed, fed me, delighted me with her stories and games, let me fall asleep on her deep warm breast, was not worthy of the passionate love I felt for her but must be given instead a half-smiled-at affection similar to that which one feels for one's dog. I knew but I never believed it, that the deep respect I felt for her, the tenderness, the love, was a childish thing which every normal child outgrows, that such love begins with one's toys and is discarded with them, and that somehow—though it seemed impossible to my agonized heart—I too, must outgrow these feelings. I learned to give presents to this woman I loved, instead of esteem and honor. I learned to use a soft voice to oil my words of superiority. I learned to cheapen with tears and sentimental talk of "my old mammy" one of the profound relationships of my life. I learned the bitterest thing a child can learn: that the human relations I valued most were held cheap by the world I lived in.

From the day I was born, I began to learn my lessons. I was put in a rigid frame too intricate, too complex, too twisting to describe here so briefly, but I learned to conform to its slide-rule measurements. I learned that it is possible to be a Christian and a white southerner simultaneously; to be a gentlewoman and an arrogant callous creature in the same moment; to pray at night and ride a Jim Crow car the next morning and to feel comfortable in doing both. I learned to believe in freedom, to glow when the word *democracy* is used, and to practice slavery from morning to night. I learned it the way all of my southern people learn it: by closing door after door until one's mind and heart and conscience are blocked off from each other and from reality.

I closed the doors. Or perhaps they were closed for me. Then one day they began to open again. Why I had the desire or the strength to open them or what strange accident or circumstance opened them for me would require in the answering an account too long, too particular, too stark to make here. And perhaps I should not have the insight or wisdom that such an analysis would demand of me, nor the will to make it. I know only that the doors opened, a little; that somewhere along that iron corridor we travel from babyhood to maturity, doors swinging inward began to swing outward, showing glimpses of the world beyond, of that clear bright thing we call "reality."

I believe there is one experience in my childhood which pushed these doors open, a little. And I am going to tell it here, although I know well that to excerpt from a life and family background one incident and name it as a "cause" of a change in one's life direction is a distortion and often an irrelevance. The profound hungers of a child and how they are filled have too much to do with the way in which experiences are assimilated to tear an incident out of a life and look at it in isolation. Yet, with these reservations, I shall tell it, not because it was in itself so severe a trauma, but because it became for me a symbol of buried experiences that I did not have access to. It is an incident that has rarely happened to other southern children. In a sense, it is unique. But it was an acting-out, a special private production of a little script that is written on the lives of most southern children before they know words. Though they may not have seen it staged this way, each southerner has had his own dramatization of the theme.

I should like to preface the account by giving a brief glimpse of my family and background, hoping that the reader, entering my home with me, will be able to blend the ragged edges of this isolated experience into a more full life picture and in doing so will see that it is, in a sense, everybody's story.

I was born and reared in a small Deep South town whose population was about equally Negro and white. There were nine of us who grew up freely in a rambling house of many rooms, surrounded by big lawn, back yard, gardens, fields, and barn. It was the kind of home that gathers memories like dust, a place filled with laughter and play and pain and hurt and ghosts and games. We were given such advantages of schooling, music, and art as were available in the South, and our world was not limited to the South, for travel to far places seemed a simple, natural thing to us, and usually there was one of the family in a remote part of the earth.

We knew we were a respected and important family of this small town but beyond this knowledge we gave little thought to status. Our father made money in lumber and naval stores for the excitement of making and losing it— not for what money can buy nor the security which it sometimes gives. I do not remember at any time wanting "to be rich" nor do I remember that thrift and saving were ideals which our parents considered important enough to urge upon us. Always in the family there was an acceptance of risk, a mild delight even in burning bridges, an expectant "what will happen now!" We were not irresponsible; living according to the pleasure principle was by no means our way of life. On the contrary we were trained to think that each of us should do something that would be of genuine usefulness to the world, and the family thought it right to make sacrifices if necessary, to give each child adequate preparation for this life's work. We were also trained to think learning important, and books, but "bad" books our mother burned. We valued music and art and craftsmanship but it was people and their welfare and religion that were the foci around which our lives seemed naturally to move. Above all else, the important thing was what we "planned to do with our lives." That each of us must do something was as inevitable as breathing for we owed a "debt to society which must be paid." This was a family commandment.

While many of our neighbors spent their energies in counting limbs on the family tree and grafting some on now and then to give symmetry to it, or in reliving the old bitter days of Reconstruction licking scars to cure their vague malaise, or in fighting each battle and turn of battle of that Civil War which has haunted the southern conscience so long, my father was pushing his nine children straight into the future. "You have your heritage," he used to say, "some of it good, some not so good; and as far as I know you had the usual number of grandmothers and grandfathers. Yes, there were slaves, far too many of them in the family, but that was your grandfather's mistake, not yours. The past has been lived. It is gone. The future is yours. What are you going to do with it?" Always he asked this question of his children and sometimes one knew it was but an echo of the old question he had spent his life trying to answer for himself. For always the future held my father's dreams; always there, not in the past, did he expect to find what he had spent his life searching for.

We lived the same segregated life as did other southerners but our parents talked in excessively Christian and democratic terms. We were told ten thousand times that status and money are unimportant (though we were well supplied with both); we were told that "all men are brothers," that we are a part of a democracy and must act like democrats. We were told that the teachings of Jesus are real and important and could be practiced if we tried. We were told also that to be "radical" is bad, silly too; and that one must always conform to the "best behavior" of one's community and make it better if one can. We were taught that we were superior not to people but to hate and resentment, and that no member of the Smith family could stoop so low as to have an enemy. No matter what injury was done us, we must not injure ourselves further by retaliating. That was a family commandment too.

We had family prayers once each day. All of us as children read the Bible in its entirety each year. We memorized hundreds of Bible verses and repeated them at breakfast, and said "sentence prayers" around the family table. God was not someone we met on Sunday but a permanent member of our household. It never occurred to me until I was fourteen or fifteen years old that He did not see every act and thought and chalk up the daily score on eternity's tablets.

Despite the strain of living so intimately with God, the nine of us were strong, healthy, energetic youngsters who filled our days with play and sports and music and books and managed to live much of our lives on the careless level at which young lives should be lived. We had our times of profound anxiety of course, for there were hard lessons to be learned about the body and "bad things" to be learned about sex. Sometimes I have wondered how we ever learned them with a mother so shy with words.

She was a wistful creature who loved beautiful things like lace and sunsets and flowers in a vague inarticulate way, and took good care of her children. We always knew this was not her world but one she accepted under duress. Her private world we rarely entered, though the shadow of it lay at times heavily on our hearts.

Our father owned large business interests, employed hundreds of colored and white laborers, paid them the prevailing low wages, worked them the prevailing long hours, built for them mill towns (Negro and white), built for each group a church, saw to it that religion was supplied free, saw to it that a commissary supplied commodities at a high price, and in general managed his affairs much as ten thousand other southern businessmen managed theirs.

Even now, I can hear him chuckling as he told my mother how he won his fight for Prohibition. The high point of the campaign was election afternoon, when he lined up the entire mill force of several hundred (white and black), passed out a shining silver dollar to each one of them, marched them in and voted liquor out of our county. It was a great day in his life. He had won the Big Game, a game he was always playing with himself against all kinds of evil. It did not occur to him to scrutinize the methods he used. Evil was a word written in capitals; the devil was smart; if you wanted to win you outsmarted him. It was as simple as that.

He was a practical, hardheaded, warmhearted, high-spirited man born during the Civil War, earning his living at twelve, struggling through bitter decades of Reconstruction and post-Reconstruction, through populist movement, through the panic of 1893, the panic of 1907, on into the twentieth century accepting his region as he found it, accepting its morals and its mores as he accepted its climate, with only scorn for those who held grudges against the North or pitied themselves or the South; scheming, dreaming, expanding his business, making and losing money, making friends whom he did not lose, with never a doubt that God was always by his side whispering hunches as to how to pull off successful deals. When he lost, it was his own fault. When he won, God had helped him.

Once while we were kneeling at family prayers the fire siren at the mill sounded the alarm that the mill was on fire. My father did not falter from his prayer. The alarm sounded again and again—which signified that the fire was big. With quiet dignity he continued his talk with God while his children sweated and wriggled and hearts beat out of their chests in excitement. He was talking to God—how could he hurry out of the presence of the Most High to save his mills! When he finished his prayer, he quietly stood up, laid the Bible carefully on the table. Then, and only then, did he show an interest in what was happening in Mill Town. . . . When the telegram was placed in his hands telling of the death of his beloved favorite son, he gathered his children together, knelt down, and in a steady voice which contained no hint of his shattered heart, loyally repeated, "God is our refuge and strength, a very present help in trouble. Therefore we will not fear, though the earth be removed, and though the mountains be carried into the midst of the sea. On his deathbed, he whispered to his old Business Partner in Heaven: "I have fought the fight; I have kept the faith."

Against this backdrop the drama of the South was played out one day in my life:

A little white girl was found in the colored section of our town, living with a Negro family in a broken-down shack. This family had moved in only a few weeks before and little was known of them. One of the ladies in my mother's club, while driving over to her washerwoman's, saw the child swinging on a gate. The shack, as she said, was hardly more than a pigsty and this white child was living with ignorant and dirty and sick-looking colored folks. "They must have kidnapped her," she told her friends. Genuinely shocked, the clubwomen busied themselves in an attempt to do something, for the child was very white indeed. The strange Negroes were subjected to a grueling questioning and finally grew frightened and evasive and refused to talk at all. This only increased the suspicion of the white group, and the next day the clubwomen, escorted by the town marshal, took the child from her adopted family despite their tears.

She was brought to our home. I do not know why my mother consented to this plan. Perhaps because she loved children and always showed tenderness and concern for them. It was easy for one more to fit into our ample household and Janie was soon at home there. She roomed with me, sat next to me at the table; I found Bible verses for her to say at breakfast; she wore my clothes, played with my dolls and followed me around from morning to night. She was dazed by her new comforts and by the interesting activities of this big lively family; and I was as happily dazed, for her adoration was a new thing to me; and as time passed a quick, childish, and deeply felt bond grew up between us.

But a day came when a telephone message was received from a colored orphanage. There was a meeting at our home, whispers, shocked exclamations. All afternoon the ladies went in and out of our house talking to Mother in tones too low for children to hear. And as they passed us at play, most of them looked quickly at Janie and quickly looked away again, though a few stopped and stared at her as if they could not tear their eyes from her face. When my father came home in the evening Mother closed her door against our young ears and talked a long time with him. I heard him laugh, heard Mother say, "But Papa, this is no laughing matter!" And then they were back in the living room with us and my mother was pale and my father was saying, "Well, work it out, honey, as best you can. After all, now that you know, it is pretty simple."

In a little while my mother called my sister and me into her bedroom and told us that in the morning Janie would return to Colored Town. She said Janie was to have the dresses the ladies had given her and a few of my own, and the toys we had shared with her. She asked me if I would like to give Janie one of my dolls. She seemed hurried, though Janie was not to leave until next day. She said, "Why not select it now?" And in dreamlike stiffness I brought in my dolls and chose one for Janie. And then I found it possible to say, "Why? Why is she leaving? She likes us, she hardly knows them. She told me she had been with them only a month."

"Because," Mother said gently, "Janie is a little colored girl."

"But she can't be. She's white!"

"We were mistaken. She is colored."

"But she looks—"

"She is colored. Please don't argue!"

"What does it mean?" I whispered.

"It means," Mother said slowly, "that she has to live in Colored Town with colored people."

"But why? She lived here three weeks and she doesn't belong to them, she told me she didn't."

"She is a little colored girl."

"But you said yourself that she has nice manners. You said that," I persisted.

"Yes, she is a nice child. But a colored child cannot live in our home."

"Why?"

"You know, dear! You have always known that white and colored people do not live together."

"Can she come over to play?"

"No."

"I don't understand."

"I don't either," my young sister quavered.

"You're too young to understand. And don't ask me again, ever again, about this!" Mother's voice was sharp but her face was sad and there was no certainty left there. She hurried out and busied herself in the kitchen and I wandered through that room where I had been born, touching the old familiar things in it, looking at them, trying to find the answer to a question that moaned in my mind like a hurt thing. . . .

And then I went out to Janie, who was waiting, knowing things were happening that concerned her but waiting until they were spoken aloud.

I do not know quite how the words were said but I told her that she was to return in the morning to the little place where she had lived because she was colored and colored children could not live with white children.

"Are you white?" she said.

"I'm white," I replied, "and my sister is white. And you're colored. And white and colored can't live together because my mother says so."

"Why?" Janie whispered.

"Because they can't," I said. But I knew, though I said it firmly, that something was wrong. I knew my father and mother whom I passionately admired had done that which did not fit in with their teachings. I knew they had betrayed something which they held dear. And I was shamed by their failure and frightened, for I felt that they were no longer as powerful as I had thought.

There was something Out There that was stronger than they and I could not bear to believe it. I could not confess that my father, who had always solved the family dilemmas easily and with laughter, could not solve this. I knew that my mother who was so good to children did not believe in her heart that she was being good to this child. There was not a word in my mind that said it but my body knew and my glands, and I was filled with anxiety.

But I felt compelled to believe that they were right. It was the only way my world could be held together. And, like a slow poison, it began to seep through me: *I was white. She was colored. We must not be together. It was bad to be together. Though you ate with your nurse when you were little, it was bad to eat with any colored person after that. It was bad just as other things were bad that your mother had told you. It was bad that she was to sleep in the room with me that night. It was bad. . . .*

I was suddenly full of guilt. For three weeks I had done things that white children are not supposed to do. And now I knew these things had been wrong.

I went to the piano and began to play, as I had always done when I was in trouble. I tried to play Paderewski's *Minuet* and as I stumbled through it, the little girl came over and sat on the bench with me. Feeling lonely, lost in these deep currents that were sweeping through our house that night, she crept closer and put her arms around me and I shrank away as if my body had been uncovered. I had not said a word, I did not say one, but she knew, and tears slowly rolled down her little white face. . . .

And then I forgot it. For more than thirty years the experience was wiped out of my memory. But that night, and the weeks it was tied to, worked its way like a splinter, bit by bit down to the hurt places in my memory and festered there. And as I grew older, as more experiences collected around that faithless time, as memories of earlier, more profound hurts crept closer and closer drawn to that night as if to a magnet, I began to know that people who talked of love and Christianity and democracy did not mean it. That is a hard thing for a child to learn. I still admired my parents, there was so much that was strong and vital and sane and good about them and I never forgot this; I stubbornly believed in their sincerity, as I do to this day, and I loved them. Yet in my heart they were under suspicion. Something was wrong.

Something was wrong with a world that tells you that love is good and people are important and then forces you to deny love and to humiliate people. I knew, though I would not for years confess it aloud, that in trying to shut the Negro race away from us, we have shut ourselves away from so many good, creative, honest, deeply human things in life. I began to understand so slowly at first but more and more clearly as the years passed, that the warped, distorted frame we have put around every Negro child from birth is around every white child also. Each is on a different side of the frame but each is pinioned there. And I knew that what cruelly shapes and cripples the personality of one is as cruelly shaping and crippling the personality of the other. I began to see that though we may, as we acquire new knowledge, live through new experiences, examine old memories, gain the strength to tear the frame from us, yet we are stunted and warped and in our lifetime cannot grow straight again any more than can a tree, put in a steel-like twisting frame when young, grow tall and straight when the frame is torn away at maturity.

As I sit here writing, I can almost touch that little town, so close is the memory of it. There it lies, its main street lined with great oaks, heavy with matted moss that swings softly even now as I remember. A little white town rimmed with Negroes, making a deep shadow on the whiteness. There it lies, broken in two by one strange idea. Minds broken in two. Hearts broken. Conscience torn from acts. A culture split in a thousand pieces. That is segregation. I am remembering: a woman in a mental hospital walking four steps out, four steps in, unable to go further because she has drawn an invisible line around her small world and is terrified to take one step beyond it. . . . A man in a Disturbed Ward assigning "places" to the other patients and violently insisting that each stay in his place. . . . A Negro woman saying to me so quietly, "We cannot ride together on the bus, you know. It is not legal to be human in Georgia."

Memory, walking the streets of one's childhood . . . of the town where one was born. ✒

SUGGESTIONS FOR WRITING

1. "When I Was a Child" provides an account of a white child's instruction in the rules of Southern racism. How would a black child have been instructed?

2. Can you recall a time when your sense of your parents was transformed through an encounter with a larger social or cultural issue?

3. Can you remember the first time you learned about racism? What did your parents teach you about race?

MY FATHER'S LIFE

Raymond Carver

The inadequacies of a parent frequently haunt the child long after the parent has departed. In particular, it seems that creative people find themselves wrestling with the ghost, so to speak, of one parent or another. The following reflection by a son on his father's life examines the bleakness of that life with honesty, while seeking to restore some of the dignity and respect his father deserved.

Raymond Carver (1938–1988) was an American writer known for his explorations of the loneliness of contemporary culture, as well as for portraying, in finely crafted short stories and poems, the violent physical challenges and self-destructiveness of masculine culture. He won several major awards for his fiction and taught at a number of colleges and universities. His books include What We Talk About When We Talk About Love *(1981),* Cathedral *(1984), and* Where I'm Calling From *(1988). Much of his writing concerns his alcoholism and features male characters undone by that and other obsessions.*

My dad's name was Clevie Raymond Carver. His family called him Raymond and friends called him C. R. I was named Raymond Clevie Carver Jr. I hated the "Junior" part. When I was little my dad called me Frog, which was okay. But later, like everybody else in the family, he began calling me Junior. He went on calling me this until I was thirteen or fourteen and announced that I wouldn't answer to that name any longer. So he began calling me Doc. From then until his death, on June 17, 1967, he called me Doc, or else Son.

When he died, my mother telephoned my wife with the news. I was away from my family at the time, between lives, trying to enroll in the School of Library Science at the University of Iowa. When my wife answered the phone, my mother blurted out, "Raymond's dead!" For a moment, my wife thought my mother was telling her that I was dead. Then my mother made it clear *which* Raymond she was talking about and my wife said, "Thank God. I thought you meant *my* Raymond."

My dad walked, hitched rides, and rode in empty boxcars when he went from Arkansas to Washington State in 1934, looking for work. I don't know whether he was pursuing a dream when he went out to Washington. I doubt it. I don't think he dreamed much. I believe he was simply looking for steady work at decent pay. Steady word was meaningful work. He picked apples for a time and then landed a construction laborer's job on the Grand Coulee Dam. After he'd put aside a little money, he bought a car and drove back to Arkansas to help his folks, my grandparents, pack up for the move west. He said later that they were about to starve down there, and this wasn't meant as a figure of speech. It was during that short while in Arkansas, in a town called Leola, that my mother met my dad on the sidewalk as he came out of a tavern.

"He was drunk," she said. "I don't know why I let him talk to me. His eyes were glittery. I wish I'd had a crystal ball." They'd met once, a year or so before, at a dance. He'd had girlfriends before her, my mother told me. "Your dad always had a girlfriend, even after we married. He was my first and last. I never had another man. But I didn't miss anything."

They were married by a justice of the peace on the day they left for Washington, this big, tall country girl and a farmhand-turned-construction worker. My mother spent her wedding night with my dad and his folks, all of them camped beside the road in Arkansas.

In Omak, Washington, my dad and mother lived in a little place not much bigger than a cabin. My grandparents lived next door. My dad was still working on the dam, and later, with the huge turbines producing electricity and the water backed up for a hundred miles into Canada, he stood in the crowd and heard Franklin D. Roosevelt when he spoke at the construction site. "He never mentioned those guys who died building that dam," my dad said. Some of his friends had died there, men from Arkansas, Oklahoma, and Missouri.

He then took a job in a sawmill in Clatskanie, Oregon, a little town alongside the Columbia River. I was born there, and my mother has a picture of my dad standing in front of the gate to the mill, proudly holding me up to face the camera. My bonnet is on crooked and about to come untied. His hat is pushed back on his forehead, and he's wearing a big grin. Was he going in to work or just finishing his shift? It doesn't matter. In either case, he had a job and a family. These were his salad days.

In 1941 we moved to Yakima, Washington, where my dad went to work as a saw filer, a skilled trade he'd learned in Clatskanie. When war broke out, he was given a deferment because his work was considered necessary to the war effort. Finished lumber was in demand by the armed services, and he kept his saws so sharp they could shave the hair off your arm.

After my dad had moved us to Yakima, he moved his folks into the same neighborhood. By the mid-1940s the rest of my dad's family—his brother, his sister, and her husband, as well as uncles, cousins, nephews, and most of their extended family and friends—had come out from Arkansas. All because my dad came out first. The men went to work at Boise Cascade, where my dad worked, and the women packed apples in the canneries. And in just a little while, it seemed—according to my mother—everybody was better off than my dad. "Your dad couldn't keep money," my mother said. "Money burned a hole in his pocket. He was always doing for others."

The first house I clearly remember living in, at 1515 South Fifteenth Street, in Yakima, had an outdoor toilet. On Halloween night, or just any night, for the hell of it, neighbor kids, kids in their early teens, would carry our toilet away and leave it next to the road. My dad would have to get somebody to help him bring it home. Or these kids would take the toilet and stand it in somebody else's backyard. Once they actually set it on fire. But ours wasn't the only house that had an outdoor toilet. When I was old enough to know what I was doing, I threw rocks at the other toilets when I'd see someone go inside. This was called bombing the toilets. After a while, though, everyone went to indoor plumbing until, suddenly, our toilet was the last outdoor one in the neighborhood.

I remember the shame I felt when my third-grade teacher, Mr. Wise, drove me home from school one day. I asked him to stop at the house just before ours, claiming I lived there.

I can recall what happened one night when my dad came home late to find that my mother had locked all the doors on him from the inside. He was drunk, and we could feel the house shudder as he rattled the door. When he'd managed to force open a window, she hit him between the eyes with a colander and knocked him out. We could see him down there on the grass. For years afterward, I used to pick up this colander—it was as heavy as a rolling pin—and imagine what it would feel like to be hit in the head with something like that.

It was during this period that I remember my dad taking me into the bedroom, sitting me down on the bed, and telling me that I might have to go live with my Aunt LaVon for a while. I couldn't understand what I'd done that meant I'd have to go away from home to live. But this, too—whatever prompted it—must have blown over, more or less, anyway, because we stayed together, and I didn't have to go live with her or anyone else.

I remember my mother pouring his whiskey down the sink. Sometimes she'd pour it all out and sometimes, if she was afraid of getting caught, she'd only pour half of it out and then add water to the rest. I tasted some of his whiskey once myself. It was terrible stuff, and I don't see how anybody could drink it.

After a long time without one, we finally got a car, in 1949 or 1950, a 1938 Ford. But it threw a rod the first week we had it, and my dad had to have the motor rebuilt.

"We drove the oldest car in town," my mother said. "We could have had a Cadillac for all he spent on car repairs." One time she found someone else's tube of lipstick on the floorboard, along with a lacy handkerchief. "See this?" she said to me. "Some floozy left this in the car."

Once I saw her take a pan of warm water into the bedroom where my dad was sleeping. She took his hand from under the covers and held it in the water. I stood in the doorway and watched. I wanted to know what was going on. This would make him talk in his sleep, she told me. There were things she needed to know, things she was sure he was keeping from her.

Every year or so, when I was little, we would take the North Coast Limited across the Cascade Range from Yakima to Seattle and stay in the Vance Hotel and eat, I remember, at a place called the Dinner Bell Cafe. Once we sent to Ivar's Acres of Clams and drank glasses of warm clam broth.

In 1956, the year I was to graduate from high school, my dad quit his job at the mill in Yakima and took a job in Chester, a little sawmill town in northern California. The reasons given at the time for his taking the job had to do with a higher hourly wage and the vague promise that he might, in a few years' time, succeed to the job of head filer in this new mill. But I think, in the main, that my dad had grown restless and simply wanted to try his luck elsewhere. Things had gotten a little too predictable for him in Yakima. Also, the year before, there had been the deaths, within six months of each other, of both his parents.

But just a few days after graduation, when my mother and I were packed to move to Chester, my dad penciled a letter to say he'd been sick for a while. He didn't want us to worry, he said, but he'd cut himself on a saw. Maybe he'd got a tiny sliver of steel in his blood. Anyway, something had happened and he'd had to miss work, he said. In the same mail was an unsigned postcard from somebody down there telling my mother that my dad was about to die and that he was drinking "raw whiskey."

When we arrived in Chester, my dad was living in a trailer that belonged to the company. I didn't recognize him immediately. I guess for a moment I didn't want to recognize him. He was skinny and pale and looked bewildered. His pants wouldn't stay up. He didn't look like my dad. My mother began to cry. My dad put his arm around her and patted her shoulder vaguely, like he didn't know what this was all about, either. The three of us took up life together in the trailer, and we looked after him as best we could. But my dad was sick, and he couldn't get any better. I worked with him in the mill that summer and part of the fall. We'd get up in the mornings and eat eggs and toast while we listened to the radio, and then go out the door with our lunch pails. We'd pass through the gate together at eight in the morning, and I wouldn't see him again until quitting time. In November I went back to Yakima to be closer to my girlfriend, the girl I'd made up my mind I was going to marry.

He worked at the mill in Chester until the following February, when he collapsed on the job and was taken to the hospital. My mother asked if I would come down there and help. I caught a bus from Yakima to Chester, intending to drive them back to Yakima. But now, in addition to being physically sick, my dad was in the midst of a nervous breakdown, though none of us knew to call it that at the time. During the entire trip back to Yakima, he didn't speak, not even when asked a direct question. ("How do you feel, Raymond?" "You okay, Dad?") He'd communicate if he communicated at all, by moving his head or by turning his palms up as if to say he didn't know or care. The only time he said anything on the trip, and for nearly a month afterward, was when I was speeding down a gravel road in Oregon and the car muffler came loose. "You were going too fast," he said.

Back in Yakima a doctor saw to it that my dad went to a psychiatrist. My mother and dad had to go on relief, as it was called, and the county paid for the psychiatrist. The psychiatrist asked my dad, "Who is the President?" He'd had a question put to him that he could answer. "Ike," my dad said. Nevertheless, they put him on the fifth floor of Valley Memorial Hospital and began giving him electroshock treatments. I was married by then and about to start my own family. My dad was still locked up when my wife went into this same hospital, just one floor down, to have our first baby. After she had delivered, I went upstairs to give my dad the news. They let me in through a steel door and showed me where I could find him. He was sitting on a couch with a blanket over his lap. *Hey*, I thought. *What in hell is happening to my dad?* I sat down next to him and told him he was a grandfather. He waited a minute and then he said, "I feel like a grandfather." That's all he said. He didn't smile or move. He was in a big room with a lot of other people. Then I hugged him, and he began to cry.

Somehow he got out of there. But now came the years when he couldn't work and just sat around the house trying to figure what next and what he'd done wrong in his life that he'd wound up like this. My mother went from job to crummy job. Much later she referred to that time he was in the hospital, and those years just afterward, as "when Raymond was sick." The word *sick* was never the same for me again.

In 1964, through the help of a friend, he was lucky enough to be hired on at a mill in Klamath, California. He moved down there by himself to see if he could hack it. He lived not far from the mill, in a one-room cabin not much different from the place he and my mother had started out living in when they went west. He scrawled letters to my mother, and if I called she'd read them aloud to me over the phone. In the letters, he said it was touch and go. Every day that he went to work, he felt like it was the most important day of his life. But every day, he told her, made the next day that much easier. He said for her to tell me he said hello. If he couldn't sleep at night, he said, he thought about me and the good times we used to have. Finally, after a couple of months, he regained some of his confidence. He could do the work and didn't think he had to worry that he'd let anybody down ever again. When he was sure, he sent for my mother.

He'd been off from work for six years and had lost everything in that time—home, car, furniture, and appliances, including the big freezer that had been my mother's pride and joy. He'd lost his good name too—Raymond Carver was someone who couldn't pay his bills—and his self-respect was gone. He'd even lost his virility. My mother told my wife, "All during that time Raymond was sick we slept together in the same bed, but we didn't have relations. He wanted to a few times, but nothing happened. I didn't miss it, but I think he wanted to, you know."

During those years I was trying to raise my own family and earn a living. But, one thing and another, we found ourselves having to move a lot. I couldn't keep track of what was going down in my dad's life. But I did have a chance one Christmas to tell him I wanted to be a writer. I might as well have told him I wanted to become a plastic surgeon. "What are you going to write about?" he wanted to know. Then, as if to help me out, he said, "Write about stuff you know about. Write about some of those fishing trips we took." I said I would, but I knew I wouldn't. "Send me what you write," he said. I said I'd do that, but then I didn't. I wasn't writing anything about fishing, and I didn't think he'd particularly care about, or even necessarily understand, what I was writing in those days. Besides, he wasn't a reader. Not the sort, anyway, I imagined I was writing for.

Then he died. I was a long way off, in Iowa City, with things still to say to him. I didn't have the chance to tell him goodbye, or that I thought he was doing great at his new job. That I was proud of him for making a comeback.

My mother said he came in from work that night and ate a big supper. Then he sat at the table by himself and finished what was left of a bottle of whiskey, a bottle she found hidden in the bottom of the garbage under some coffee grounds a day or so later. Then he got up and went to bed, where my mother joined him a little later. But in the night she had to get up and make a bed for herself on the couch. "He was snoring so loud I couldn't sleep," she said. The next morning when she looked in on him, he was on his back with his mouth open, his cheeks caved in. *Graylooking*, she said. She knew he was dead—she didn't need a doctor to tell her that. But she called one anyway, and then she called my wife.

Among the pictures my mother kept of my dad and herself during those early days in Washington was a photograph of him standing in front of a car, holding a beer and a stringer of fish. In the photograph he is wearing his hat back on his forehead and has this awkward grin on his face. I asked her for it and she gave it to me, along with some others. I put it up on my wall, and each time we moved, I took the picture along and put it up on another wall. I looked at it carefully from time to time, trying to figure out some things about my dad, and maybe myself in the process. But I couldn't. My dad just kept moving further and further away from me and back into time. Finally, in the course of another move, I lost the photograph. It was then that I tried to recall it, and at the same time make an attempt to say something about my dad, and how I thought that in some important ways we might be alike. I wrote the poem when I was living in an apartment house in an urban area south of San Francisco, at a time when I found myself, like my dad, having trouble with alcohol. The poem was a way of trying to connect up with him.

Photograph of My Father in His Twenty-Second Year

October. Here in this dank, unfamiliar kitchen
I study my father's embarrassed young man's face.
Sheepish grin, he holds in one hand a string
of spiny yellow perch, in the other
a bottle of Carlsberg beer.

In jeans and flannel shirt, he leans
against the front fender of a 1934 Ford.
He would like to pose brave and hearty for his posterity,
wear his old hat cocked over his ear.
All his life my father wanted to be bold.

But the eyes give him away, and the hands
that limply offer the string of dead perch
and the bottle of beer. Father, I love you,
yet how can I say thank you, I who can't hold my liquor either
and don't even know the places to fish.

The poem is true in its particulars, except that my dad died in June and not October, as the first word of the poem says. I wanted a word with more than one syllable to it to make it linger a little. But more than that, I wanted a month appropriate to what I felt at the time I wrote the poem—a month of short days and failing light, smoke in the air, things perishing. June was summer nights and days, graduations, my wedding anniversary, the birthday of one of my children. June wasn't a month your father died in.

After the service at the funeral home, after we had moved outside, a woman I didn't know came over to me and said, "He's happier where he is now." I stared at this woman until she moved away. I still remember the little knob of a hat she was wearing. Then one of my dad's cousins—I didn't know the man's name—reached out and took my hand, "We all miss him," he said, and I knew he wasn't saying it just to be polite.

I began to weep for the first time since receiving the news. I hadn't been able to before. I hadn't had the time, for one thing. Now, suddenly, I couldn't stop. I held my wife and wept while she said and did what she could do to comfort me there in the middle of that summer afternoon.

I listened to people say consoling things to my mother, and I was glad that my dad's family had turned up, had come to where he was. I thought I'd remember everything that was said and done that day and maybe find a way to tell it sometime. But I didn't. I forgot it all, or nearly. What I do remember is that I heard our name used a lot that afternoon, my dad's name and mine. But I knew they were talking about my dad. *Raymond*, these people kept saying in their beautiful voices out of my childhood. *Raymond.*

SUGGESTIONS FOR WRITING

1. How would you describe the tone of Carver's reminiscence?

2. Was embarrassment Carver's primary reaction to his father? If not, what was his primary reaction?

3. Narrate an episode from your childhood that illustrates your relationship with your father.

4. How does Carver's "My Father's Life" encourage you to think about the role that social class plays in a child's view of a parent?

FOR WHITE MEN ONLY

James T. Farrell

*During the early decades of the twentieth century, as Southern blacks mi-
grated northward to such large cities as Chicago, they expected, along with
decent jobs, to escape the overt racial prejudice with which Southern culture
was infused. As **James T. Farrell**'s story shows, they were sometimes
sadly disappointed. In "For White Men Only," Alfred's defiance of a racist
swimming policy collides head-on with the collective will of the young white
swimmers.*

*Much of Farrell's fiction, set in early twentieth-century Chicago, pro-
vides similar examples of ethnic groups residing uneasily together. Farrell
(1904–1979) skillfully portrays his own ethnic background in the Irish
immigrant community of Chicago. He is known primarily for his* Studs
Lonigan *trilogy of novels (1932, 1934, 1935).*

I

"Boy, I tell you, don' you go there," Booker Jones, a small and yellowish Negro,
said.

"Booker, there is no white man alive who's gonna tell me where I is to go
swimming, and where I isn't. If I wants to go swimming this lake here at Jackson Park, that's where I'm going swimming." Alfred, a tall and handsome
broad-shouldered and coppery Negro, replied.

They were shirtless, wearing blue swimming suits and old trousers, and they
walked eastward along Fifty-seventh Street.

"Oh, come on, Alfred, let's go to Thirty-ninth Street," Booker said with intended persuasiveness as they passed across Dorchester after they had ambled
on for a block in silence.

"You go! Me, I'm going swimming over in Jackson Park, whether there's
white men there or not," Alfred said, his face hardening, his voice
determined.

"Alfred, you is always courtin' trouble, and just because you want to show
off before that no-account mulatto gal . . ."

"What you say, nigger?"

"Well, no, I'm sorry, Alfred," Booker cringed. "But some day, you'll go
courtin' trouble, and trouble is just gonna catch right on up with you and it's
gonna say, 'Well, Alfred, you been courtin' me, so here I is with my mind made
up to give you plenty of me'."

"Shut up, black boy!" Alfred said curtly.

Booker shook his head with disconsolate wonder. As they passed under the
Illinois Central viaduct, Booker again suggested that they go down to the
Thirty-ninth Street beach, and Alfred testily told him that Thirty-ninth Street

wasn't a beach at all, just a measly, over-crowded pile of stones. The black man had no beach. But he was aiming to go swimming where he had some space without so many people all around him. He added that if the Negro was to go on being afraid of the white man, he was never going to get anywhere, and if the Negro wanted more space to swim in, he just had to go and take it. And he had told that to Melinda, and she had laughed at him, but she was not going to laugh at him again. Booker just shook his head sadly from side to side.

They entered Jackson Park where the grass and shrubbery and tree leaves shimmered and gleamed with sunlight. The walks were crowded with people, and along the drive, a succession of automobiles hummed by. Alfred walked along with unconcerned and even challenging pride. Booker glanced nervously about him, feeling that the white men were thrusting contemptuous looks at him. He looked up at Alfred, admiring his friend's courage, and he wished that he were unafraid like Alfred.

Turning by the lake, they passed along the sidewalk which paralleled the waters. Sandy beach ran down from the sidewalk to the shore line, and many were scattered along it in bathing suits. Down several blocks from them, they could see that the regular beach was crowded. More white people frowned at them, and both of them could sense hate and fear in these furtive, hasty glances. Alfred's lips curled into a surly expression.

Halfway along toward the regular beach Alfred jumped down into the sand, tagged by Booker. He gazed around him, nonchalant, and then removed his trousers. He stood in his bathing suit, tall and impressively strong, graceful. Booker jittered beside him, hesitating until Alfred, without turning his head, taunted him into haste. Booker removed his trousers, and stood skinny beside Alfred whose arms were folded and whose gaze was sphinx-like on the waters. They heard a gentle and steady rippling against the shore line.

Nearby, white bathers stared with apprehension. A group of three fellows and two young girls who had been splashing and ducking close to the shore saw them, and immediately left the water and walked down a hundred yards to re-enter it. Alfred seemed to wince, and then his face again became hard and intent. Booker saw various white bathers picking up their bundles and moving away from them, and still afraid of these white men, he hated them.

Alfred trotted gracefully to the shore line, again plunged into the water, followed by Booker. They cut outward, and Alfred suddenly paddled around and playfully ducked Booker. They again hit outward. Catching his breath and plunging beside his companion, Booker told Alfred that they had made a mistake coming out here where they were two against a mob. Alfred retorted that he was not going to whine and beg the white man for anything. Some black men had to be the first to come, if they wanted to have the right of a place to swim. And he wasn't scared anyway. Booker shook a pained head, caught a mouthful of water, and splashed to keep himself up. Alfred dove under water and reappeared a number of yards away, laughing, snorting, glorying in the use of his body. After they had swum around, Booker again chattered that he was afraid.

"Here is one black boy that's not going to be mobbed," Alfred said.

II

Buddy Coen and his friends emerged from the water laughing, shaking their wet bodies and heads. They found a space of sand within the enclosure of the regular beach and dropped down, hunting for the cigarettes they had hidden.

"Well, boys, I was just going to say, if you lads want to provide the bottle, I'm all set for a bender tonight," Buddy said after lighting a cigarette.

"If you'd go back driving a hack, you'd have dough enough for your own liquor," fat Marty Mulligan said.

"What the hell have I got a wife working as a waitress for? So that I can drive a taxi all night. See any holes in my head, Irish?" Buddy said tauntingly.

"After the fight Buddy started last Saturday night with two dicks, I should think he'd stay sober once in a while and see how it feels," Morris said.

"Say, there's plenty of neat pickups around here, even if most of them are Polacks," the big Swede said.

"Boys, my girl is out of town tonight, and I'm dated up with a married woman I met out on my territory. Her husband works nights, and brother, she's the stuff," Marty bragged, following his statement with an anatomical description of her contours, charms and sexual technique.

The big Swede began talking about the old days, and Marty told anecdotes of how he used to get drunk when he was going to Saint Stanislaus high school. They talked on until suddenly from a group close to them they heard a lad say:

"There's niggers down a way on the beach."

They became tense, and Buddy asked was that straight stuff.

"Bad enough having Polacks dirtying up the lake without diseased shines," the big Swede said in hate.

"A few weeks ago, a coal-black bastard tried to get into the lockers here, but he was told that there weren't any free. Then a couple of us boys just talked to him outside, you know, we talked, and used a little persuasion, and he's one black bastard that knows his place, and knows that this is a white man's park and a white man's beach," Buddy said.

"Say, I just need to sock somebody to make the day exciting and put me in good spirits for my date tonight," Marty Mulligan said.

"Well, then, what the hell are you guys waiting for?" Buddy said, jumping to his feet.

They followed Buddy to the water, swam out around the fencing that extended along the formal beach limits and walked along the shore line in search of the Negroes.

"I know I don't mind pounding a few black bastards full of lumps," Norton said.

"Me now, I ain't sloughed anybody since Christ knows when, and I need a little practice," Morris said.

III

"Alfred, I'm tired," Booker said.

"Nigger, shut up! Nobody's going to hurt you," Alfred said.

"Well, I is, just the same," Booker said, his voice breaking into a whine.

Ignoring Booker, Alfred turned over on his back and floated with the sun boiling down upon his coppery limbs. Booker paddled after him, afraid to go in alone. He turned and looked back along the avenue of sand, filled with so many white people. Blocks and blocks of sand, populated with all these whites. The fears of a mob assailed him. He wished that he had never come. He thought of Negroes lynched in the South, and of many who had been beaten and mobbed in the Chicago race riots of 1919. He remembered as a boy in those times how he had seen one of his race, dead, hanging livid from a telephone post in an alley. He was afraid, and with his fear was hate, hatred of the white man, hatred because of the injustices to him, to his race, hatred because he was afraid of the white man. Again he glanced along the avenue of sand filled with white men and each small figure along it was a potential member of a mob to beat him and Alfred. He turned and again looked at his friend who was floating, unconcerned. He wished that he had Alfred's courage. With chattering teeth, he shook his head slowly and sadly, feeling, sensing, knowing that they were going to pay dearly for this venture. He trod water waiting for Alfred, wishing that he was out of it. He saw a group of white bathers stand at the shore and look out over the water. He had a premonition.

IV

"There they are," Buddy said, curtly nodding his head toward the water, and they saw two kinky heads and two Negro faces, diminished by distance.

"Let's drown the bastards!" Morris said.

Buddy said that they would walk off a little ways and wait until the two shines came in. They moved a few yards away, and waited, keen and eager. Buddy lashed out contemptuous remarks, keeping them on edge, and Marty remarked that they had driven the white man out of Washington Park, and that if things went on, soon the whole South Side would be black.

"If they want Jackson Park, they got to fight for it!" Buddy sneered.

"Just think! Look at all these white girls bathing around here. With niggers on the beach, it ain't safe for them," Morris said.

"And do you fellows know, my sister nearly came out here swimming today?" Morris said.

They saw the two Negroes coming in and heard the smaller one trying to convince the bigger one about something, but they could not catch enough of what he said. The two Negroes walked slowly toward their small bundles of clothing, their wet bodies glistening in the sunlight. After they had sat down, Buddy arose and led the group toward them. Seeing the white folks approaching, Booker grabbed his clothes and ran. Four of the white lads pursued him, yelling to stop that nigger.

With a sulky expression on his face, Alfred arose at the approach of Buddy and Morris.

"The water nice?" Buddy asked, his voice constrained and threatening.

"Passable," Alfred answered, his fists clenched.

"Been out here before?" Buddy continued.

"No. . . . Why?" Alfred said with unmistakable fearlessness.

A crowd gathered around, and excitement cut through the beach like an electric current because of the shouts and chase after Booker. A white bather tripped him as he ran and joined the four other pursuers in cursing and punching him, mercilessly disregarding his pleas to be let alone. They dragged him to his feet, knocked him down, kicked him, dragged him up, knocked him over again while he continued to emit shrill and helpless cries.

"Anybody ever tell you that this is a white man's beach?" Morris asked Alfred.

"You know we don't want niggers here!" Buddy said.

Buddy went down from a quick and surprising punch on the jaw, and Alfred countered Morris' left swing with a thudding right that snapped the white lad's head back. Buddy sat down, rubbed his jaw, shook his dazed head, leaped to his feet, and went into Alfred swinging both hands. While the Negro fought off the two of them, others dragged back the howling Booker to the fight scene. The big Swede broke through the crowd of spectators and clipped Alfred viciously on the side of the head. Two other white bathers smashed into the attack. Defending himself, Alfred crashed Morris to the sand and was then battered off his feet. A heel was brought against his jaw, and as he struggled to arise, five white bodies piled onto him, punching, scratching, kneeing him. Spectators shouted, females screamed and encouraged the white lads, and Alfred was quickly and severely punished. Booker opened his mouth to beg for mercy, and a smashing fist brought blood from his lips, and another wallop between the eyes toppled him over backward.

A bald-headed Jewish man with a paunchy stomach protested, and a small pretty blonde girl screamed that he must be a nigger lover. A middle-aged woman with a reddish bovine face called in an Irish brogue for them to hit the black skunks, while a child strained at her waist and shouted.

A park policeman hurriedly shoved through the spectators, and the slugging ceased. The two Negroes sat in the sand, their faces cut and bleeding.

"You fellows better go home!" the policeman said roughly, sneering as he spoke.

They slowly got up, and Booker tried to explain that they had done nothing.

"Don't be giving me any lip," the policeman said. "I said you better go home or do your swimming down at Thirty-ninth if you don't want to be starting riots. Now move along!"

He shoved Booker.

"And you, too," he said to Alfred who had not moved.

Booker hurriedly put his trousers on and Alfred did likewise slowly, as if with endless patience. They wiped their bleeding faces with dirty handkerchiefs, and Booker sniffled.

"Go ahead now!" the policeman roughly repeated.

"We will, but we'll come back!" Alfred said challengingly.

The crowd slowly dispersed, and the six fellows stood there near the policeman.

"Shall we follow them?" asked Marty.

"They ain't worth hitting, the skunks, and the dirty fighting they do, kicking me that way," said Collins, limping.

They turned and walked heroically back toward the enclosed beach.

"That black bastard had the nerve to hit me," Buddy said, pointing to his puffed eye.

"Like all niggers, they were yellow," said Morris.

"Well, we did a neat job with them," Norton bragged.

"Boy, I caught that big one between his teeth. Look at my hand," Marty said, showing his swollen knuckles.

"Look at that, fellows! There's somethin'. I say there, sisters!" the Swede said to three girls who were coquetting on the sand.

Looking covertly at legs and breasts, they leered.

SUGGESTIONS FOR WRITING

1. How does the racial conflict in the story play itself out in relation to the gender relationships? Can you think of similar examples in which race and gender converge?

2. Who is the focus of this story, the two black youths or the whites?

3. Would urban gangs of today behave in ways similar to the white "gang" portrayed in "For White Men Only"? In your opinion, is racial conflict more or less likely today? Narrate an episode from your experience that supports your argument.

JUST WALK ON BY: A BLACK MAN PONDERS HIS POWER TO ALTER PUBLIC SPACE

Brent Staples

Brent Staples (b. 1951) is an assistant metropolitan editor of The New York Times *and has worked at a variety of other newspapers, including the* Chicago Sun Times. *He earned a Ph.D. in psychology from the University of Chicago.*

As a black male, Staples describes what it is like to feel like an outsider. Walking down the street and being allowed to mind their own business is something that most people in America would like to take for granted, but because of stereotypes associated with race and crime, Staples can't. This essay describes how social categorizations can affect the way a person lives.

My first victim was a woman—white, well dressed, probably in her early twenties. I came upon her late one evening on a deserted street in Hyde Park, a relatively affluent neighborhood in an otherwise mean, impoverished section of Chicago. As I swung onto the avenue behind her, there seemed to be a discreet, uninflammatory distance between us. Not so. She cast back a worried glance. To her, the youngish black man—a broad six feet two inches with a beard and billowing hair, both hands shoved into the pockets of a bulky military jacket—seemed menacingly close. After a few more quick glimpses, she picked up her pace and was soon running in earnest. Within seconds she disappeared into a cross street.

That was more than a decade ago. I was 22 years old, a graduate student newly arrived at the University of Chicago. It was in the echo of that terrified woman's footfalls that I first began to know the unwieldy inheritance I'd come into—the ability to alter public space in ugly ways. It was clear that she thought herself the quarry of a mugger, a rapist, or worse. Suffering a bout of insomnia, however, I was stalking sleep, not defenseless wayfarers. As a softy who is scarcely able to take a knife to a raw chicken—let alone hold it to a person's throat—I was surprised, embarrassed, and dismayed all at once. Her flight made me feel like an accomplice in tyranny. It also made it clear that I was indistinguishable from the muggers who occasionally seeped into the area from the surrounding ghetto. That first encounter, and those that followed, signified that a vast, unnerving gulf lay between nighttime pedestrians—particularly women—and me. And I soon gathered that being perceived as dangerous is a hazard in itself. I only needed to turn a corner into a dicey situation, or crowd some frightened, armed person in a foyer somewhere, or make an errant move after being pulled over by a policeman. Where fear and weapons meet—and they often do in urban America—there is always the possibility of death.

In that first year, my first away from my hometown, I was to become thoroughly familiar with the language of fear. At dark, shadowy intersections in Chicago, I could cross in front of a car stopped at a traffic light and elicit the *thunk, thunk, thunk, thunk* of the driver—black, white, male, or female—hammering down the door locks. On less traveled streets after dark, I grew accustomed to but never comfortable with people who crossed to the other side of the street rather than pass me. Then there were the standard unpleasantries with police, doormen, bouncers, cab drivers, and others whose business it is to screen out troublesome individuals *before* there is any nastiness.

I moved to New York nearly two years ago and I have remained an avid night walker. In central Manhattan, the near-constant crowd cover minimizes tense one-on-one street encounters. Elsewhere—visiting friends in SoHo, where sidewalks are narrow and tightly spaced buildings shut out the sky—things can get very taught indeed.

Black men have a firm place in New York mugging literature. Norman Podhoretz in his famed (or infamous) 1963 essay, "My Negro Problem—And Ours," recalls growing up in terror of black males; they "were tougher than we were, more ruthless," he writes—and as an adult on the Upper West Side of Manhattan, he continues, he cannot constrain his nervousness when he meets black men on certain streets. Similarly, a decade later, the essayist and novelist Edward Hoagland extols a New York where once "Negro bitterness bore down mainly on other Negroes." Where some see mere panhandlers, Hoagland sees "a mugger who is clearly screwing up his nerve to do more than just *ask* for money." But Hoagland has "the New Yorker's quick-hunch posture for broken-field maneuvering," and the bad guy swerves away.

I often witness that "hunch posture," from women after dark on the warrenlike streets of Brooklyn where I live. They seem to set their faces on neutral and, with their purse straps strung across their chests bandolier style, they forge ahead as though bracing themselves against being tackled. I understand, of course, that the danger they perceive is not a hallucination. Women are particularly vulnerable to street violence, and young black males are drastically overrepresented among the perpetrators of that violence. Yet these truths are no solace against the kind of alienation that comes of being ever the suspect, against being set apart, a fearsome entity with whom pedestrians avoid making eye contact.

It is not altogether clear to me how I reached the ripe old age of 22 without being conscious of the lethality nighttime pedestrians attributed to me. Perhaps it was because in Chester, Pennsylvania, the small, angry industrial town where I came of age in the 1960s, I was scarcely noticeable against a backdrop of gang warfare, street knifings, and murders. I grew up one of the good boys, had perhaps a half-dozen fist fights. In retrospect, my shyness of combat has clear sources.

Many things go into the making of a young thug. One of those things is the consummation of the male romance with the power to intimidate. An infant discovers that random flailings send the baby bottle flying out of the crib and crashing to the floor. Delighted, the joyful babe repeats those motions again and again, seeking to duplicate the feat. Just so, I recall the points at which some of my boyhood friends were finally seduced by the perception of themselves as tough guys. When a mark cowered and surrendered his money without resistance, myth and reality merged—and paid off. It is, after all, only manly to embrace the power to frighten and intimidate. We, as men, are not supposed to give an inch of our lane on the highway; we are to seize the fighter's edge in work and in play and even in love; we are to be valiant in the face of hostile forces.

Unfortunately, poor and powerless young men seem to take all this nonsense literally. As a boy, I saw countless tough guys locked away; I have since buried several, too. They were babies, really—a teenage cousin, a brother of 22, a childhood friend in his mid-twenties—all gone down in episodes of bravado played out in the streets. I came to doubt the virtues of intimidation early on. I chose, perhaps even unconsciously, to remain a shadow—timid, but a survivor.

The fearsomeness mistakenly attributed to me in public places often has a perilous flavor. The most frightening of these confusions occurred in the late 1970s and early 1980s when I worked as a journalist in Chicago. One day, rushing into the office of a magazine I was writing for with a deadline story in hand, I was mistaken for a burglar. The office manager called security and, with an ad hoc posse, pursued me through the labyrinthine halls, nearly to my editor's door. I had no way of proving who I was. I could only move briskly toward the company of someone who knew me.

Another time I was on assignment for a local paper and killing time before an interview. I entered a jewelry store on the city's affluent Near North Side. The proprietor excused herself and returned with an enormous red Doberman pinscher straining at the end of a leash. She stood, the dog extended toward me, silent to my questions, her eyes bulging nearly out of her head. I took a cursory look around, nodded, and bade her good night. Relatively speaking, however, I never fared as badly as another black male journalist. He went to nearby Waukegan, Illinois, a couple of summers ago to work on a story about a murderer who was born there. Mistaking the reporter for the killer, police hauled him from his car at gunpoint and but for his press credentials would probably have tried to book him. Such episodes are not uncommon. Black men trade tales like this all the time.

In "My Negro Problem—And Ours," Podhoretz writes that the hatred he feels for blacks makes itself known to him through a variety of avenues—one being his discomfort with that "special brand of paranoid touchiness" to which he says blacks are prone. No doubt he is speaking here of black men. In time, I learned to smother the rage I felt at so often being taken for a criminal. Not to do so would surely have led to madness—via that special "paranoid touchiness" that so annoyed Podhoretz at the time he wrote the essay.

I began to take precautions to make myself less threatening. I move about with care, particularly late in the evening. I give a wide berth to nervous people on subway platforms during the wee hours, particularly when I have exchanged business clothes for jeans. If I happen to be entering a building behind some people who appear skittish, I may walk by, letting them clear the lobby before I return, so as not to seem to be following them. I have been calm and extremely congenial on those rare occasions when I've been pulled over by the police.

And on late-evening constitutionals along streets less traveled by, I employ what has proved to be an excellent tension-reducing measure: I whistle melodies from Beethoven and Vivaldi and the more popular classical composers. Even steely New Yorkers hunching toward nighttime destinations seem to relax, and occasionally they even join in the tune. Virtually everybody seems to sense that a mugger wouldn't be warbling bright, sunny selections from Vivaldi's *Four Seasons*. It is my equivalent of the cowbell that hikers wear when they know they are in bear country. ♪

SUGGESTIONS FOR WRITING

1. Describe an incident in which you were clearly the outsider, the person who did not belong. What about you enabled others to label you as different? What reactions did your being the outsider provoke? Explore how this experience made you feel.

2. Why did the people in Staples' account react to him in the way that they did? How would you have reacted in a similar situation?

3. When you are in an unfamiliar environment, do you adopt a different set of behaviors? Examine why. If you do not change the way you act, how are you able to maintain your identity?

BLACK/ASIAN CONFLICT:
WHERE DO WE BEGIN?

Vicki Alexander and Grace Lyu-Volckhausen

Sometimes it is easy to make the incorrect assumption that all minority or marginalized groups feel the same way about life in the United States, that they share a common view of in what ways and why they are discriminated against. In a similar fashion, people incorrectly assume all women share the same concerns and face the same set of oppressions. Particularly when a person is a member of the dominant group (white or male or heterosexual and so on), the people who are "different" seem indistinguishable from one another. As is made clear in the conversation between **Grace Lyu-Volckhausen,** *a founder of the Korean YWCA, and* **Vicki Alexander,** *medical director of the Community Family Planning Council, just because some people belong to a group considered to be "different" does not mean that all such groups—or even all members of a single minority group—are the "same."*

VICKI ALEXANDER: I grew up in Los Angeles. My father was U.S. black, Blackfoot Indian, and Irish. Indians often allowed blacks or people escaping disasters like the Irish potato famine to stay on the reservation. We were welcomed there. My mother was a Polish-Russian Jew. My father was a union organizer, and from a very early age I was involved in progressive activities. In the early 1960s I married a college classmate—he was from Korea, a mathematician; he died in 1974 from a brain tumor.

I first was in the movement to free South Africa in the early 1960s, and then the movement for civil rights in this country. I had always wanted to be a doctor, but when I graduated from college I was not accepted by any medical school; after the civil rights movement, I reapplied and was accepted everywhere, with scholarships, and with no change in my record. So the civil rights movement was very important in my becoming a doctor. I decided to become an obgyn because the ones I saw didn't help women.

In that period during the early 1970s, I joined an organization called the Third World Women's Alliance and got involved in the reproductive rights movement. I was organizing to improve health care in Oakland, California, and that brought me into the women's movement, combining my civil rights and women's orientations. In 1978, we decided to allow white people in. It was a very difficult decision. The focus stayed with women of color but broadened—we started to work with lots of different groups. For example, in 1986

NOW asked me to speak at the big rally around abortion in D.C.; I worked with the local NOW chapter and with NARAL, which I see as white women's organizations. But the focus whenever I speak or do something is to make sure people understand how I view things from the perspective of a woman of color.

GRACE LYU-VOLCKHAUSEN: For me, being a feminist is in my genes. My grandmother was one of the earliest Korean feminists; my mom was one of the founders of the Korean Women's Association, and my father was one of the few Korean legislators who sponsored a women's rights bill. So when I came here in 1960 and women were fighting for their rights, I asked, "What is this? We have always been fighting."

I got involved with the women's movement here as a student in the 1960s. At that time, there were about 80 Koreans in New York, mostly students. Within five years, Koreans started to come in. I realized that Korean women were getting jobs in all kinds of labor markets and were getting taken advantage of. So we started the Korean YWCA; I worked with women's groups like Asian Women United. Now I spend most of my time and energy with immigrant women.

In the early days of the New York City Commission on the Status of Women, whenever I brought up immigrant women's labor problems, some women would say, "Oh, my gosh," and then, no response. But my black women fellow commissioners had much more empathy than those corporate white women. We had a common ground right there. Many immigrant Asian women never had jobs in Korea or whatever their native country because women were discouraged from working there. But now they're here, working, keeping house, the whole thing, and my black colleagues are saying, "Look, black women have done that all our lives and we lived through it."

VICKI: Were you a part of the Rainbow Coalition at all?

GRACE: You mean Jesse Jackson's campaign? No. I was working with the state Democratic committee and I was a delegate for Michael Dukakis. But other Asian people were Jesse Jackson delegates. You see, the Korean American community is quite new politically, so whenever these major political events happen we kind of spread out and work with each other. When we had a campaign fund-raiser for Jesse Jackson, every Korean activist was there. Then we had a Dukakis fund-raiser, and we were all there. So everyone supported everyone. I think for the Koreans it was a novelty because at that time in Korea we were so politically oppressed; if you supported the wrong candidate you were thrown in jail or beaten up by cops. But here it is like being a kid in a toy store. Today you go for Jesse Jackson; tomorrow, Dukakis.

VICKI: I was very involved in the Rainbow Coalition. I was elected to the national board of the Rainbow and helped start its women's commission. The Rainbow didn't quite get off the ground.

There was a lot of division among Asian Americans over the Jesse Jackson campaign. But we're definitely in a new period now;

people who were old enemies are no longer enemies. We're getting over that. There are still some people who just will not unite, will not talk, have got to be the right political line. We can't do that anymore.

GRACE: The yearlong boycott of two Korean grocery stores by people in the African American community [on Church Avenue in the Flatbush section of Brooklyn] really soured a lot of things. I think it has soured New York as a whole. During the crisis I was behind the scenes trying to work things out. It was very frustrating.

VICKI: Well, everybody was talking about it. In the group I was in at the time, we were trying to analyze it and ask ourselves, "What's going on here? Should we take a side? Is there a side to take? Is there a middle road?" We tried to understand Korean immigration, because none of the people in the group were Korean.

GRACE: So they just studied the situation.

VICKI: Right. We didn't engage in it. It was so nasty; it was terrible. All these guys, the black leaders, who have become discredited—the Sharptons and the Carsons—really discredited us.

GRACE: I think Koreans wondered, why didn't David Dinkins [New York City's African American mayor] come down to the store? It took him eight months. When the crisis started, we asked him to come out right away—but he vacillated.

Our children remember these things. When they see their parents getting hurt, they remember it. And they have long memories.

VICKI: I think that among the U.S. blacks there is a real hatred of people coming into our community and ripping us off. Once again getting ripped off by people who aren't us. Nationalism in the black community is very high, so blacks can come in and rip us off really badly, and they don't get chastised. The feeling gets fueled by racial incidents. And it's certainly been fueled on a national level by Reagan and Bush.

I feel that there is a longstanding kind of negativism that stems from nationalism; it says if it isn't black, it isn't good. No matter what. I think that's where a lot of the community is coming from. When you look historically at where black people have lived, we have not owned the stores. And on the whole, the money generated through the stores does not get reinvested in the community. So historically, you have a level of oppression not only based on class, but, in the eyes of those blacks and in reality, based on race.

Then come Koreans. Koreans—and Arabs—own stores. But still, they are not black. There is that resentment, but what is clear about Arabs is that they are coming from a poor section of the world. So that's not as antagonistic as the white Jewish store owner. But then, in come Koreans, and nobody knows nothing about Koreans or the struggle in Korea—that's that world over there, Korea, China. The U.S. population is so ignorant, purposely so. But in the eyes of U.S. blacks, that is another body of folks coming over, taking over, and we don't know where they are from. So we must assume there is some money behind them. Maybe they don't have money, but we are assuming that they must have some money to come into our community and build whatever.

When it was just white-black, it wasn't as hard to understand. But when it is black-Asian-Arab, it starts to get very confusing, the class and race stuff starts to overlap. Because of the lack of education in the U.S., it's really a problem. What people need to start is a major education campaign.

GRACE: From the Korean point of view, it doesn't matter what community we come into—black or white. The Koreans come in with a small amount of capital that they borrowed from their friends. They have trouble getting jobs because of discrimination, so they try to make a living by starting businesses that use the least amount of capital; they expend whatever amount of labor is necessary. Where do they go? The places with lowest rents, where there are not that many stores. So they end up going to black neighborhoods, where rent is cheap, where, if you work long hours, you can make profits—they all end up going there. But they don't know who these people are in the communities they go into.

Let me tell you an interesting story, an incredible misunderstanding between blacks and Koreans. Once a former black coworker of mine was furious. He said, "You see that Korean woman there. I am so angry. She is insulting us." I asked, "What did she do?" He said, "Whenever I go there, the woman never puts the change in my hand, she always puts it on the counter." And I said, "Richard, this is because in Korea, a woman does not touch a man's hand. Except her own husband's—in private." He didn't know. It's just a little thing that becomes a big problem. I hear such comments all the time: "That Korean woman never smiles. They are so unfriendly." But in Korea, if you smile that much, they think you are stupid.

VICKI: Also, if you smile at men, it has a prostitution connotation.

GRACE: Absolutely. This cultural gap is so great. Of course, Koreans will say, "These black people, they are always dancing, they are always loud."

VICKI: Or, "They're lazy. They don't work very hard."

GRACE: My only regret in the Church Avenue crisis was that women were not able to get together. Korean women couldn't get together with African American women because we were just so engrossed in our own problems. We were all wringing our hands, "What do we do? What do we do?" And then all these politicians were running away from us. I felt like a pariah when I went to community meetings. People would see me and would not see me. They didn't want to deal with the Koreans because we were a time bomb.

I agonized that we could not pull our women together. Maybe next time there is a crisis we should bring our women together and tell these guys to shut up.

	If I called you because of a black-Korean crisis, would you come out with your friends?
VICKI:	Sure. You have to start building toward it now, at a time of no crisis. You have to establish a relationship with people. And one of the best places to do that is the Medgar Evers College women's center, a black women's center. I think it would be good if the overture came from the Korean women, as people who come from an oppressed state. You were born in South Korea, an oppressed state, and I was born in the U.S., an oppressed state. We're both women oppressed within the oppressed state. There is a real commonality. We are struggling and fighting for our people, but to bridge some of those gaps, we have to start educating now.
GRACE:	The thing is, Asian immigrant women are in a situation where they have to worry about everyday life.
VICKI:	It's the same with black women. We are so worried about food, our kids . . .
GRACE:	The Korean woman doesn't speak the English language. This would be a problem. But their children talk. When there is a crisis in the school the parents will come together.
VICKI:	They'll come together if there is a crisis in the school, but what they will say to me is, "Yo, I've got to put food on the table, to watch my kids—you expect me to come to a meeting? I've got to do the laundry, you can forget it." This is what happens at multiracial women's formations: we start working more on community and working on our families; then it's "Forget it." To expect people to come together might be an illusion. Until some kind of precedent gets set by some people somewhere.
GRACE:	One small thing happened. A church in the black community was having a women's prayer for peace day last March. The Korean YWCA had a mother's chorus. We went to the black church to sing with their choir. It was a great experience. Many of those Korean women had never been to a black church. They were shy; the customs were different. But everyone sang together and was very moved. If we could create a situation like that, we can move on.
VICKI:	Do they have a women's ministry within the church? One of the things the community family planning agencies do is run a mobile clinic and if they have a health fair . . .
GRACE:	We collect abandoned clothing from the Korean Dry Cleaners Association and we give it to a local black church. They have a ministry at the city prison.
VICKI:	We take our mobile clinic to homeless women.
GRACE:	If you need clothing, I will connect you with the Korean dry cleaners.
	We developed a list of 12 things for the Korean merchants to do, which we publicized in the Korean newspapers. We urged them to hire people from the local area. The Korean merchants said they were willing to hire, but needed help from black community groups to recommend people for jobs.

These crises happen, not because the community is down on these merchants, but because there are one or two instigators.

VICKI: That's absolutely true.

GRACE: During the crisis, there were a whole lot of discussions between blacks, Koreans, Jews, and lots of groups. But I was the only Korean woman running around, and I didn't see that many black women either.

VICKI: The sexism within the African American community is really intense. It's almost as though racial injustice issues are mostly the purview of the black male. There are a few exceptions, but racial injustice stuff is the black man's turf.

Before one of the black women activists started a women's center in the community, she was doing a lot of speaking in the black community. She was working with a lot of the black male leaders, trying to get them to understand the issues that are critical to women—sexuality, infant mortality, kids and drugs. She finally decided, I'm getting nowhere with these men who could have some influence.

Even the wife of a prominent black minister only has a certain kind of role to play. She can develop a committee to discuss South Africa, but not for abortion rights or condoms in schools—there are only certain things that women can do.

As a result, women have backed into safe places—health projects, a lot of different agencies that deal with people. But when you talk about issues of social justice and racial justice, women are not in the leadership. Women have been categorized off into women's movements. And it's a contradiction for us. What's more important for us? What is your issue today? Are you going to go march in Bensonhurst or are you going to go march at the clinics getting attacked? It's constantly posed to us that way. It's hard working in the women's movement and the racial justice movement and trying to make the two work together—it just doesn't happen. I tried to do that for 15 years and it's like hitting your head against a brick wall.

GRACE: Asian women aren't even there. For Asian women from immigrant families, we are still in the beginning of a women's movement. It is a major issue. I tell Korean fathers, "Do not treat your daughters as second class." When I speak at colleges, Korean American students say, "My father thinks I can only be a dentist, but my brother can be a doctor." This is a traditional father. I say to the fathers, "If your 5,000-year-old ethic clearly defines women as second-class citizens and wives, why on earth do you send your daughters to college?" They say, "Well, my daughter is very bright." I went to a reception and the leaders of the community—all Mr. Important—were there, and I know their daughters. I say, "How are your daughters doing? They are becoming outstanding lawyers, I am so happy." Their fathers say, "Oh, do you know a young man? I want her to get married." Isn't that something?

I'm not sure we are in the stage where racial injustice has come out as a separate issue. Our young males are still trying to figure things out, but they have their fathers' values. They have that baggage. They think they understand Western values, but they haven't seen anything at home except Mommy doing the domestic work, and many still want to marry a traditional Korean woman. They do feel a certain racism and are trying to work this out. For many young Korean American males the accumulation of frustration will come out.

VICKI: I don't think it's possible to compare a lot of stuff between the two communities. The experiences are totally different. U.S. blacks came out of slavery, were utilized in the labor market as underpaid workers continuously for over 200 years, and for the next 200 years they are on the bottom rung of every parameter—the poorest, least employed, sickest. That's a very conscious control of the labor force. Immigrants are also used at this level, and there is a language barrier. But the Koreans don't let themselves be used that way. They don't assimilate, but they learn how to make a living.

GRACE: The Korean immigration pattern is different from some other Asian groups; it is not starting from zero up. They are a middle-class immigration, with an average of two years' college. In 1980, women's educational background was one year of college; the minimum educational level was high school plus. Even some doctors were working in sweatshops. But they will deal with the racism they feel in the work force and on campus differently from African Americans. They are not organized. Instead of confronting racism directly, they say, "All right, you look down on me; I will show you."

VICKI: Have you ever heard about some reports on Japanese immigrants and youth gangs in California? Apparently, there's a relationship between assimilation and class behavior. The more people get assimilated and disjointed from their cultural heritage, the more vicious their gangs become. Just like black gangs. But still there is this myth that Asians are quiet, hardworking, not complaining. The stereotype of what an Asian kid is, straight A's or whatever, adds to the resentment against Asians.

GRACE: An Asian boy once told me he got a 65 in math and his teacher said, "What's wrong with you, everyone knows Asians aren't supposed to get a 65 in math."

I face stereotypes all the time—people who say to me, "You are not a typical Asian woman!" And then you have to go through what is or is not a typical Asian woman.

VICKI: Maybe I've insulated myself. When I was going through a period of trying to get my own balance in terms of who I was, it was always with women. I did not like being in mixed female-male organizations. When I started feeling more secure, I returned to mixed groups.

But I wouldn't say that a woman running a country makes it fine. That's just like saying, on a nationalist level, that anything black is fine. And I wouldn't say that patriarchy is causing the problem because some men may be just as good as women.

Ten years go, I never would have used the term "patriarchy." Everything that happened to these rich, white, excuse the term, bitches would be assumed to be caused by patriarchy . . . that's were I was at a few years ago. Now, at least, let's talk and not let terminology get in the way.

At this juncture, being in mixed organizations doesn't bother me at all—in fact, I intimidate these men. Now I'm just little ole me trying to engage in some conversation, and they're intimidated.

GRACE: I got that training way back when I was in Korea, in high school. My mother always said, "You have to stand up for your rights." My major battle started in my first year of college. I discovered that every bylaw had "vice-whatever woman"—there was this unspoken assumption that a woman cannot be president. It took us one year to change it.

VICKI: But you had an advantage. You grew up in a family that had strong women as role models. I grew up in a family where women were really in the back. To overcome that was really hard. Today's high school girls are different. They're so outspoken. But they're not so outspoken when it comes to sexuality. Some talk, but they're still very nervous about sex. They giggle and the guys joke. That's their way of handling sexuality.

GRACE: In the Asian community, we do not talk about sex in public.

VICKI: Single-focus issues like reproductive rights are limited. How do we pull women together?

GRACE: Asians won't go in for single issues. We have to bring in everyone: mothers, sisters, lesbian women. There are many Asian lesbians; I know many Korean lesbians who are completely undercover; they don't dare speak openly.

VICKI: Boy, is that a cultural breach.

Look at this U.N. Decade for Women and how women came together in Nairobi, internationally. There are certain things that are important to women—our reproductive capacity and what this means in terms of oppressions. That is a commonality we have that makes us able to interact on all kinds of levels, nonantagonistically. From the beginning, there's a commonness of expectations, of your relationship to the world, to men, whatever. It surfaces and becomes a primary link.

MADRE is a great organization of women talking to women internationally. It started out in Nicaragua and then Central America, but now it is expanding to the Middle East and to North America, with a health focus.

GRACE: There are other common issues that women can work together on, like the family. Every mother wants to protect her children. There's infant mortality, health and medical care, teenage concerns, educating women—and I'm not sure how much we are doing. I agree with the importance of international work. But right now, what I take care of is in New York City.

VICKI: Well, somehow that trust between Korean Americans and African Americans must be built. I don't think it's there right now. What's there is a lack of knowledge, a lack of interaction.

GRACE: If we do things together, we can move on. Step by step. Like what the Korean women's chorus did with the black church; things can build.

VICKI: We have to get together in this country, mourn together, and figure out where we're going to take the movement. People are disoriented. They don't believe in this electoral stuff. Where do we go in this country? I still get a little confused talking about a women's movement because there are so many different kinds. There isn't an anti-racist movement in this country, and the rug was pulled right out from under us during the Gulf War. We are in bad shape. But women can be very important.

GRACE: You and I and other feminist activists can get together and talk. That would be the beginning. 🖋

SUGGESTIONS FOR WRITING

1. You may have experienced the kind of categorizing described by Alexander and Lyu-Volckhausen in their discussion and felt that the assumptions on which people based their opinion of or reaction to you were in error. Describe your experience, focusing not only on how this experience made you feel but also examining the assumptions, the reasons why the other person made them, and why they were in error.

2. Analyze the ways in which the two women in this discussion feel that their two groups differ from each other and the ways in which the two women feel *they* differ from men in their ethnic group because they are women. Then write an essay in which you analyze yourself as a member of your ethnic group. Explore the ways in which you differ from the "norms" associated with that group.

3. Explore the issues of sexism within the two women's communities and see what parallels you can identify between those attitudes and ones in the community in which you grew up.

WOMAN AS AN ATHLETE

Arabella Kenealy, M.D.

The actual biological differences between men and women are far out-
weighed by the physical characteristics and capabilities they share. Certainly
the physical differences have traditionally played a less determining role in
women's lives than have the enormous force of cultural attitudes and mores.
Recent feminist scholarship in the history of medicine has produced the in-
sight that the very origins of modern medicine are thoroughly compromised
by cultural biases regarding gender that have nothing to do with scientific ob-
servation or the experimental method. An example would be the assumption
that women's bodies are too delicate for strenuous physical exercise.

Today we are accustomed to greater attention devoted to women's sports
and women's athletic achievements. We also know that physicians urge both
women and men to pursue some kind of regular exercise. Not so very long
ago, however, medical opinion persisted in limiting women's participation in
athletics. This 1899 article by a female physician was part of a debate spon-
sored by The Nineteenth Century Magazine *on the question of women's*
sports.

"It is wonderful what athletics do for women," a friend observed. "A year ago
Clara could not walk more than two miles without tiring; now she can play
tennis or hockey, or can bicycle all day without feeling it."

That observation fired a train of evidences and examples which had been
accumulating in my mind over a period of years of medical practice.

In what manner have the changes which have recently taken place in the
physique and energies of women been effected?

Have reserves of force, impoverished and abeyant under an older-fashioned
up-bringing, been called into activity and use by new régimes of thought and
training? Were women what they were from lack of opportunity and stress of
circumstance? Are women what they are by virtue of circumstance and gift of
opportunity? Did man's iron heel indeed and grandmotherly tradition result in
the dwarfing and defacement of a sex's powers? Is it faculty heretofore starved
and dwindled, but now reclaimed and added to the complement of human energy—this flood of new activity which fills our illustrated papers with portraits
of feminine prize-winners, and our sporting journals with female "records"? Is
the female Senior Wrangler a bright jewel rescued from the morass of down-
trampled wasted capability which has hitherto but littered the path of progress?

These, and other considerations with which I will not weary the reader, I revolved.

Revolving them I came upon an "if" which seemed to be the crux of the situation. If it could be demonstrated that modern woman possesses all her new
capacities plus those of her older-fashioned sister, then there could be but one
answer to the question.

If Clara from tiring at a two-mile walk had suddenly and simply developed energies which should enable her to bicycle or row or run all day without fatigue, then Clara and the world had plainly benefited—more especially if it should occur to Clara to devote these freshly acquired forces to her fellows' use.

But—and here I stumbled over my crux—if Clara had only acquired these powers at the expense of others, then the case was not at all so clear. If to reclaim abeyant faculties should involve the abeyance of faculties which had previously operated, the question of advantage must rest entirely upon the relative values of the interchanging faculties.

My knowledge of physiology and medicine forbade me to entertain the belief common to the laity that a regimen of habit or diet could result in a material increase of force-production. Change of air, a judicious liver treatment, an efficient blood or nerve tonic will sometimes effect apparent marvels by improving the powers of assimilation and nutrition. But such apparent marvels have their origin in a mere relief of temporary disability, and having nothing to do with so radical a constitutional change as has taken place in Clara and her fellows.

The healthy human body, like a machine, has its fixed standard of force-production, varying according to the individual; and, with trifling variations consequent on temperament and circumstance, every person possesses and finds earlier or later his limitations of energy. According to the powers, and the sensitiveness, any expenditure of force beyond that manufactured by the economy as its daily output is followed by fatigue, irritability, or depression and a general sense of not being up to the mark. Further undue demands upon the resources may result in incapacitation, prostration, or actual illness. These results are modified of course by individual recuperative power and the rate whereat force lost to the system is made up.

Speaking generally, it may be said that an individual generates a certain daily fund of energy, which if he exceed one day he must suffer for the next in impoverished vitality, or meet—but this is a larger question and one which does not belong to the subject—by drawing upon and deteriorating his constitutional capital. Personality varies in the degree of force manufactured, but more especially in the manner in which the force is distributed. Infinite variety is obtained by the combination and association of similar qualities in dissimilar quantity. One of muscle, two of mind, three of emotion: three of muscle, one of mind, two of emotion: one-sixteenth of mind, twelve-sixteenths of muscle, three-sixteenths of emotion. And so *ad infinitum* with the *infinitum* made more endless by still further and more intricate subdivisions of muscular, mental, and emotional attributes. . . .

We come now upon the suggestion that Clara's apparent increase of energy has been an effect merely of altering the relation of her forces in such a manner as to increase the muscle-power at the expense of other qualities—in a word, to destroy a complex, well-planned balance of faculties which had been Nature's scheme when Nature fashioned Clara.

With regard to the value of the newly acquired power I could not but recognise that muscular force, even in its finest developments of skill and endurance, is the most crude and least highly differentiated of all the human powers. It is one which man shares in common with and possesses in a notably less degree than do the lower animals. For strength, mobility, and sinuous grace he cannot aspire to rival the snake—which indeed is lower than the lower animals. For speed and endurance the horse will far outstrip him. For grip and invincible tenacity he is no match for the bull-dog or the ape.

As a matter of fact, it is not mere muscle-power, but the subordination and application of muscle-power to express idea, emotional, intellectual, or moral, which is man's especial forte. In this he is higher than the highest animals. But this has little or no relation with the muscular vigour which makes "strong men" and navvies. Indeed, the athlete is conspicuously lacking in it. He pleases by agility, by the play and achievement of highly trained members. But it may be said that he portrays muscle rather than man.

To tell the truth, we are somewhat in danger to-day of deifying muscle, muscle being properly a mere means to an end, a system of levers whose chief value lies in the purpose they subtend. The levers must be kept in order by due exercise and use for the means for which they are required. But modern feeling is in the direction of amassing muscles which shall enable their possessor to fell oxen or to beat pedestrian and cycling records.

We waste force surely by keeping in condition muscular systems out of all proportion to the needs; the occasions for felling oxen or for supplanting locomotives being virtually nonexistent in civilised communities. One of the advantages indeed of civilisation and one of the means whereby higher faculties are left free to develop is the ability to dispense with such muscular obligations as are indispensable to primitive life—which lives by physical achievement.

It is not wished in any way to discredit the exercise essential to the building up of healthy bodies, and of maintaining the balance mental, emotional, and physical. Only the forced athletics which destroy this balance are condemned. To speak physiologically, the athlete is not a person of fine muscular physique; he is a person whose muscles are hypertrophied, a fact of but little moment were it not a *sine quâ non* that they are hypertrophied at the expense of higher and more valuable factors.

To return, however, to Clara. What are the qualities which Clara and modern woman, of whom she is the prototype, are discarding? And here we come upon a complex question. For the more subtle and fine the essence of human capacity, the more difficult its demonstration. Clara's talents for winning golf matches or for mountain climbing are a power demonstrable and calculable. But Clara's sympathies and Clara's emotionalism and Clara's delicacy and tact, which one can but conclude are the qualities which have gone to feed her augmented sinews, are factors more conspicuous in the breach than in the observance.

Can it be shown then that modern woman is lacking in those which were wont to be considered womanly faculties? Can it be denied? And since the power of a healthy adult can be increased only at the expense of some other power, and since modern woman has inordinately added to her muscle-power, and since muscle-power is the least of human qualities, what is to be deduced but that human capability has lost rather than gained in the exchange?

With Clara at the head of my train of feminine examples, I now set out to determine more exactly what were those qualities she had bartered for a mess of muscle.

That a change indeed had taken place was evident. Clara the athlete was no longer the Clara I remembered two years earlier. She was almost as dissimilar as though she had been another personality. She was as different from herself as their grandmothers were different from the girls of the present day. I drew her portrait as I had first known her. She was then—I had almost written a charming girl—but let me not be betrayed into partisan adjectives, let me portray her as impartially as may be. And to begin with her physical qualifications. She was then—she is now—something more than comely, but her comeliness has altogether changed in character. Where before her beauty was suggestive and elusive, now it is defined. One might have said of her two years since: Her eyes are fine, her features are well modelled, her complexion is sensitive and variable; but, over and beyond these facts, there is a mysterious and nameless something which for the lack of a more definite term I can only describe as "charm;" and it is in this something, which is to her as atmosphere is to landscape, that her chiefest beauty lies.

One would say of her now: Her eyes are fine, her features are well modelled, her complexion is possibly too strong in its contrasting tones, her glance is unwavering and direct; she is a good-looking girl. But the haze, the elusiveness, the subtle suggestion of the face are gone; it is the landscape without atmosphere. Now one could paint her portrait with ease. Formerly only the most ingenious and sympathetic art could have reproduced her subtle and mysterious charm.

There are an added poise and strength about her actions, she inclines to be, and in another year will be, distinctly spare, the mechanism of movement is no longer veiled by a certain mystery of motion which gave her formerly an air of gliding rather than of striding from one place to another. In her evening gown she shows evidence of joints which had been adroitly hidden beneath tissues of soft flesh, and already her modiste has been put to the necessity of puffings and pleatings where Nature had planned the tenderest and most dainty of devices. Her movements are muscular and less womanly. Where they had been quiet and graceful, now they are abrupt and direct. Her voice is louder, her tones are assertive. She says everything—leaves nothing to the imagination.

Exteriorly Clara has distinctly changed. One would suppose that appreciable mental and emotional differences must accompany these marked physical developments. And these, though they cannot so readily be specified, can still be demonstrated.

Curious to relate, Clara's muscle-power has not at all conduced to Clara's usefulness. One might have expected that her new impetus of energy would inspire her to spend it, as had been her wont, in the service of her associates. Strange to tell, the energy but urges her to greater muscular efforts in the pursuit of pleasure, or to her own repute.

In the old days she was one of those invaluable girls who, without being able to point to any very definite achievement at the end of the day, have yet accomplished much. Was there one sick or in trouble, then Clara was the nurse and Clara was the comforter. Had father's ruffled temper to be soothed, or did he need a bright and sympathetic comrade for an expedition; had mother some gift or commission for the great distressed; did brother Tom require assistance in his lessons or a sympathiser with his woes or joys; did Rosy need a ribbon in her hat—Clara's resources had been always at disposal.

Now, however, Clara finds no time for any of these ministrations. Clara is off bicycling upon her own account. "I used to be the idlest person," she will tell you, "finicking all day about the house and getting tired. Now I am splendidly fit. If I feel moped I go for a six-mile spin and come back a new creature!"

When Clara tired with a walk beyond two miles, Clara took flowers and books to her sick or less fortunate friends. Now that she can "manage twenty miles easily," her sick and less fortunate friends miss her. "An out-door life is the only life worth living," Clara announces. "I can't stand knocking about a house—fussing here and fussing there. It's such a shocking waste of time."

And Clara's mother, though she rejoices in her young Amazon's augmented thews and sinews, cannot but sigh for the loss to the home which has resulted from such added vigour as keeps her for ever from it. Still, like her fellows, she misconstrues Clara's muscle capability as evidence of improved health, and, while she sighs for its results, regards it as her maternal duty to be glad.

Now, it is a physiological fact that muscle vigour is no test even of masculine health. A man in training, a man that is at the height of his muscular capacity, is the worst of all subjects for illness. He has little or no resistant power; his recuperative quality is small. Athletes die proverbially young. Lunatics and other diseased persons frequently exhibit muscular strength which seems almost superhuman.

Proofs innumerable might be cited, were it necessary, that muscular vigour, though inseparable from health, is in itself no warranty whatsoever of constitutional integrity. And this, which is true of the sex whose province it is to be muscular, is essentially more true of the sex whose province it is not. So much is this the case indeed that my experience leads me to regard any extreme of muscle-power in a woman as in itself evidence of disease—measuring human and womanly health by another standard than that of mere *motor* capability. As to its place in the world of human beings, there cannot be two opinions but that it is merely subsidiary. *They also work who do but stand and wait.* The power to stand and wait entails as much expenditure of force as does the power to stir and stride.

Clara sitting sewing flowers in Rosy's hat may be using treble the activities she might be employing on a bicycle. She will be exercising in the first place possibly unselfishness, a quality which requires at least as much nerve output as do the movements of mere muscles. She will be exercising the faculties of skill and taste, she will be educating the obedience of hand to eye and mind; and, still further, she will be exerting the delicate muscular force essential to the movements of placing and sewing.

It is true that were she playing golf or bicycling she would be developing such faculties as calculation, self-control, and fortitude, in addition to developing her muscles. And, inasmuch as these are qualities which are less demanded in the trimming of a hat, let her play golf and bicycle. But let her not do these things to the detriment of other valuable faculties. Do not let her fly off at a tangent with the notion that human activity is a thing merely of muscle. As has been said, the employment of muscle in the achievement of some mental or moral idea is the highest possible expression of muscle. The subordination of muscle to mere muscular achievement holds a very inferior place in the scale of doing. The subordination of muscle to womanhood should ever be kept in mind as being an infinitely higher ideal than can ever be the subordination of womanhood to muscle.

The noblest physical potentiality is by no means the power of swift and agile motion any more than the qualities of assertiveness and expression are the highest mental potentiality. As the greatest charm of Clara's face—the charm she has lost in the suspicion of a "bicycle face" (the face of muscular tension)— was incommunicable, a dainty elusive quality which could not be put into words nor reproduced on canvas, so the highest of all attributes are silent, as for example sympathy, that sweetest quality which, without necessity for speech, lays the balm distilled in the crucible of one person's emotions for another's need—lays this balm gently to the wound in that other's nature.

But the power of sympathy is in the inverse ratio of the habit of assertiveness. The further one cultivates assertiveness (that blemish of modern women), the harder the breastplate wherewith the ego is armoured—the less is retained of the power to merge the nature into another's for that other's help and comfort. The more we harden and roughen the hands, made tender by nature to touch the world's wounds, the less do they hold of gentleness and smoothness for those wounds. Use them that they be strong and capable beneath their gentleness. But do not subordinate their higher qualities to mere muscular grip. I have known hands which were healing in their touch—the muscles which moved these moved them to some purpose indeed! All human action, indeed, has a higher end than merely action.

It may be objected that these qualities, the lack whereof I deprecate in Clara, have been well relegated to that morass of submergence whence woman has laboriously emerged—that scorned and scoffed at "sphere" of "influence," of unrecognised and unrewarded labour, that rocking of cradles, that teaching of children prayers, that weaving of laurel wreaths for masculine victors, that embroidering their deeds in tapestry and distilling of unguents for their hurts which occupied woman ere the tide of emancipation set in.

For the reformer has taught her to despise that which, scorn the term as she will and does, must by the nature of things remain her "sphere," instead of teaching her to enlarge and develop and bring to that sphere intelligences which should lift it for ever and before all men from a position of contempt. The whole question of evolution turns indeed on the function of child-bearing. There is no subject occupying the minds of our most eminent politicians, philosophers, or poets, which possesses a tithe of the value belonging to the problem as to the best methods of rearing babies. The philosopher's wisdom is written in sand for every tide to wash away. The Baby is eternal. On his proper nurture devolves the whole question of the race—To be or not to be? Speaking broadly, the tide which made for higher education and more liberty—an undeniable and invaluable impulse when it shall be but rightly directed—was a mere impulse on the part of Nature that the motherhood of her babies should be an intelligent motherhood. It was time instinct should be superseded by intelligence. It was time woman, the mother of men, should be accorded the liberty which belongs to the mothering of freedmen. Nature had no vainglorious ambitions as to a race of female wranglers or golfers; she is not concerned with Amazons, physical or intellectual. She is a one-idea'd, uncompromising old person, and her one idea is the race as embodied in the Baby. . . .

And Nature is groaning for the misinterpretation modern woman is placing upon the slackening of her rein. For Nature knows what are the faculties whence this new muscle-energy is born. She knows it is the birthright of the babies Clara and her sister athletes are squandering. She knows it is the laboriously evolved potentiality of the race they are expending on their muscles.

Nature can but be disgusted with our modern rendering of baby. So sorry a poor creature the baby of this nineteenth century is, indeed, that he cannot assimilate milk. All the resources of the dietist and chemist are taxed to appease the abnormal requirements of his capricious, incompetent stomach. His mother cannot feed him. Those artificial puffings and pads of the modiste are but pitiful insult to his natural needs. And the forces which should have gone to fashion him a stomach capable of digesting the milk of his good wet-nurse Vacca, have been spent in making his mother a muscular system which shall enable her to pay calls or bicycle all day without fatigue.

It is a terrible pity that public opinion sets its face against the discussing of physiological questions in any but medical journals. For physiological questions are of incalculable importance to all persons, seeing that physiology is the science of life. As it is, I dare but hint at a group of important functions, by the physical deterioration and decadence of which the abnormal activities of modern woman are alone possible. Of what consequence, it may be asked, is this to a race which views motherhood with ever-increasing contempt? Of vital consequence, I answer, seeing that, apart absolutely from the incident of motherhood, all the functions of the body—and some in immense degree—influence and modify the mind and character. A woman may be neither wife nor mother, yet is it of immense importance to herself and to the community at large that she retain her womanhood. For womanhood is a beautiful achievement of evolution which it is a crime to deface. With sex are bound up the noblest and fairest aspirations of humanity, and it is at the expense of sex that these abnormal muscle-energies are attained. It is only by approximation to the type masculine—which must be read as a degeneration from the especial excellences Nature planned for the type feminine—that woman is equipping herself with these abnormal sinews.

And it must be understood that such decadence and deterioration show mainly in the loss of the very highest qualities of sex. We do not expect such fine attributes as those of delicacy, tenderness, and virtue from the muscular woman of the brickfields. She can trudge and make bricks all day (as Clara now can bicycle) without undue fatigue, but as such capacity has been attended by a coarsening of body, so the higher evolvements of sex have given place to callousness and lack of modesty. Immodesty is as actual a human degeneration as is indigestion, modesty being, as digestion is, a human function. A brain deteriorated by the rough manual labour of the body to which it belongs loses its more subtle and fine qualities. So an emotional system dwarfed by undue muscular effort loses in its most highly and delicately evolved attributes.

The unsexed female brick-maker may do more than her numerical share in supplying citizens to the State. But of what type are these? It is an unfortunate circumstance that a race may deteriorate pitiably in quality long ere any diminution in quantity occurs.

If Clara were compelled by circumstance to earn her living in a brickfield nobody could question the advantage of such a redistribution of her forces as should enable her to convert higher and more complex—but unremunerative—forces into muscular capability. Belonging to a class, however, which does not live by muscular effort, but, being leisured, is at liberty to develop faculties more complex, such a re-distribution is mere wanton degradation of evolved faculty and a grievous loss to humanity. We might with equal perspicuity uproot the rose bushes and lilies from our gardens and employ them in manuring swede and turnip fields!

The old system for girls of air and exercise inadequate to development and health was wrong, but for my part I am inclined to doubt if it really was so pernicious in its physiological results or so subversive of domestic happiness and the welfare of the race as is the present system which sets our mothers bicycling all day and dancing all night and our grandmothers playing golf.

In her highest development woman is subtle, elusive in that what she suggests is something beyond formulation and fact; a moral and refining influence; as sister, wife, or friend, an inspiration, a comrade and a comforter; as mother, a guardian and guide; as citizen or worker a smoother of life's way, a humaniser, nurse, and teacher.

But none of these her highest attributes are attributes of muscle! And human capability is limited. One cannot possess all the delicately evolved qualities of woman together with the muscular and mental energies of man. And for my part to be a female acrobat or brick-maker appears but a sorry ideal. Modern woman (I speak now of women in the van of the so-called forward movement, and I do not speak of "higher" educated women nor of professional women nor of women trained in any special way, for the wave of "newness" has touched all alike: fashionable woman, fireside woman, all have been splashed by this same wave which, intended to lift them forward in the tide of progress, bids fair to carry them off their feet)—this modern woman, who, instead of serving for a terrible warning, is in danger of proving her sex's example, is restless, is clamorous, is only satisfied when in evidence, is assertive and withal is eminently discontented. She never can get enough, for the reason that the thing she asks is not the thing to satisfy her nature. . . .

In debasing her womanhood, in becoming a neuter, she descends from the standpoint whereat life was interesting. And more and more every year, discarding the duties Nature planned for her employment and delight, she cries out that life is dull and empty.

She no longer preserves and brews. She no longer weaves and fashions. Her children are nursed, fed, clothed, taught, and trained by hirelings; her sick are tended by the professional nurse, her guests are entertained by paid performers.

What truly remain which may be called her duties? What is left to her indeed but boredom? Let me not be regarded as merely bringing a grave indictment against the sex with which I have every sympathy by virtue of belonging to it, and least of all let me be understood to deprecate the right of every woman to be educated and self-supporting. All that I urge is that what she does she shall do in a womanly way, striving against all disability to preserve her womanhood as being the best of her possessions. All that I would warn her against is the error into which she has been temporarily led, the error supposing there is any nobler sphere than that of home, that there is any greater work than that of bearing and training fine types of humanity, seeing that this is the sole business wherewith the mightiest forces of the universe and evolution are concerned. But these things to be wholly worthy must be intelligently done. The reign of mere instinctive motherhood is waning. The era of Intelligent Motherhood approaches. And the first care of Intelligent Motherhood will be to see that none of those powers which belong to her highest development and through her to the highest development of the race shall be impoverished, debased, or misapplied. And in that day she will have ceased from regarding muscle as her worthiest possession. *

Suggestions for Writing

1. Would any of Kenealy's opinions be accepted today? Which ones can *you* accept?

2. Kenealy argues that athletic activity would interfere with women's necessary role in the family. Are there other activities of which that can be or has been argued?

3. What stereotypes about women athletes exist today? What effects do they have on young girls who are interested in sports?

4. What activities are males excluded from because of gender?

TAKING WOMEN STUDENTS SERIOUSLY

Adrienne Rich

*Not so very long ago, many people, men and women alike, rejected the idea
of women's education for other than domestic purposes. During the early
part of the twentieth century, much of women's education took place in
women's academies and colleges. Ever since the Second World War, however, coeducational opportunities for women have expanded. By 1990 more
women than men were enrolled in American colleges and universities. As
has been increasingly noted by persons at all levels of the educational system,
one result of coeducation has been the tendency for instructors to treat female students very differently, often ignoring them or rewarding comparable
accomplishments of male students more extravagantly. To some extent, we
can account for this by realizing that most college professors are men, but evidence of preferential treatment toward men has been found even in classrooms under female supervision. The author of this selection draws upon her
experiences as student and as instructor to call attention to the troubling phenomenon of gender discrimination in the classroom.*

*Adrienne Rich (b. 1929), one of the greatest living American poets,
brings the complexities of her life experience (Southern Protestant/Northeast-
ern Jewish background; marriage and motherhood followed by widowhood
and lesbianism; an invalid's lifelong struggle with severe arthritis) to a diverse
body of work that includes numerous books of poems including* Diving Into
the Wreck, *which won the National Book Award for poetry in 1974. She is
also the author of works of social criticism and theory, including* Of Woman
Born: Motherhood as Experience and Institution *(1976) and the influential essay "Compulsory Heterosexuality and Lesbian Existence" (1978).
She has taught at a number of American colleges and universities.*

I see my function here today as one of trying to create a context, delineate a
background, against which we might talk about women as students and students as women. I would like to speak for a while about this background, and
then I hope that we can have, not so much a question period, as a raising of
concerns, a sharing of questions for which we as yet may have no answers, an
opening of conversations which will go on and on.

When I went to teach at Douglass, a women's college, it was with a particular background which I would like briefly to describe to you. I had graduated
from an all-girls' school in the 1940s, where the head and the majority of the
faculty were independent, unmarried women. One or two held doctorates, but
had been forced by the Depression (and by the fact that they were women) to
take secondary school teaching jobs. These women cared a great deal about the

life of the mind, and they gave a great deal of time and energy—beyond any limit of teaching hours—to those of us who showed special intellectual interest or ability. We were taken to libraries, art museums, lectures at neighboring colleges, set to work on extra research projects, given extra French or Latin reading. Although we sometimes felt "pushed" by them, we held those women in a kind of respect which even then we dimly perceived was not generally accorded to women in the world at large. They were vital individuals, defined not by their relationships but by their personalities; and although under the pressure of the culture we were all certain we wanted to get married, their lives did not appear empty or dreary to us. In a kind of cognitive dissonance, we knew they were "old maids" and therefore supposed to be bitter and lonely; yet we saw them vigorously involved with life. But despite their existence as alternate models of women, the *content* of the education they gave us in no way prepared us to survive as women in a world organized by and for men.

From that school, I went on to Radcliffe, congratulating myself that now I would have great men as my teachers. From 1947 to 1951, when I graduated, I never saw a single woman on a lecture platform, or in front of a class, except when a woman graduate student gave a paper on a special topic. The "great men" talked of other "great men," of the nature of Man, the history of Mankind, the future of Man; and never again was I to experience, from a teacher, the kind of prodding, the insistence that my best could be even better, that I had known in high school. Women students were simply not taken very seriously. Harvard's message to women was an elite mystification: we were, of course, part of Mankind; we were special, achieving women, or we would not have been there; but of course our real goal was to marry—if possible, a Harvard graduate.

In the late sixties, I began teaching at the City College of New York—a crowded, public, urban, multiracial institution as far removed from Harvard as possible. I went there to teach writing in the SEEK[1] Program, which predated Open Admissions and which was then a kind of model for programs designed to open up higher education to poor, black, and Third World students. Although during the next few years we were to see the original concept of SEEK diluted, then violently attacked and betrayed, it was for a short time an extraordinary and intense teaching and learning environment. The characteristics of this environment were a deep commitment on the part of teachers to the minds of their students; a constant, active effort to create or discover the conditions for learning, and to educate ourselves to meet the needs of the new college population; a philosophical attitude based on open discussion of racism, oppression, and the politics of literature and language; and a belief that learning in the classroom could not be isolated from the student's experience as a member of an urban minority group in white America. Here are some of the kinds of questions we, as teachers of writing, found ourselves asking:

---

[1] **SEEK** Search for Education, Elevation, and Knowledge, a program with instruction by college teachers, artists, and writers.

1. What has been the student's experience of education in the inadequate, often abusively racist public school system, which rewards passivity and treats a questioning attitude or independent mind as a behavior problem? What has been her or his experience in a society that consistently undermines the selfhood of the poor and the nonwhite? How can such a student gain that sense of self which is necessary for active participation in education? What does all this mean for us as teachers?
2. How do we go about teaching a canon of literature which has consistently excluded or depreciated nonwhite experience?
3. How can we connect the process of learning to write well with the student's own reality, and not simply teach her/him how to write acceptable lies in standard English?

When I went to teach at Douglass College in 1976, and in teaching women's writing workshops elsewhere, I came to perceive stunning parallels to the questions I had first encountered in teaching the so-called disadvantaged students at City. But in this instance, and against the specific background of the women's movement, the questions framed themselves like this:

1. What has been the student's experience of education in schools which reward female passivity, indoctrinate girls and boys in stereotypic sex roles, and do not take the female mind seriously? How does a woman gain a sense of her *self* in a system—in this case, patriarchal capitalism—which devalues work done by women, denies the importance and uniqueness of female experience, and is physically violent toward women? What does this mean for a woman teacher?
2. How so we, as women, teach women students a canon of literature which has consistently excluded or depreciated female experience, and which often expresses hostility to women and validates violence against us?
3. How can we teach women to move beyond the desire for male approval and getting "good grades" and seek and write their own truths that the culture has distorted or made taboo? (For women, of course, language itself is exclusive: I want to say more about this further on.)

In teaching women, we have two choices: to lend our weight to the forces that indoctrinate women to passivity, self-depreciation, and a sense of powerlessness, in which case the issue of "taking women students seriously" is a moot one; or to consider what we have to work against, as well as with, in ourselves, in our students, in the content of the curriculum, in the structure of the institution, in the society at large. And this means, first of all, taking ourselves seriously: Recognizing that central responsibility of a woman to herself, without which we remain always the Other, the defined, the object, the victim; believing that there is a unique quality of validation, affirmation, challenge, support, that one woman can offer another. Believing in the value and significance of women's experience, traditions, perceptions. Thinking of ourselves seriously, not as one of the boys, not as neuters, or androgynes, but *as women*.

Suppose we were to ask ourselves, simply: What does a woman need to know? Does she not, as a self-conscious, self-defining human being, need a knowledge of her own history, her much-politicized biology, an awareness of the creative work of women of the past, the skills and crafts and techniques and powers exercised by women in different times and cultures, a knowledge of women's rebellions and organized movements against our oppression and how they have been routed or diminished? Without such knowledge women live and have lived without context, vulnerable to the projections of male fantasy, male prescriptions for us, estranged from our own experience because our education has not reflected or echoed it. I would suggest that not biology, but ignorance of our selves, has been the key to our powerlessness.

But the university curriculum, the high-school curriculum, do not provide this kind of knowledge for women, the knowledge of Womankind, whose experience has been so profoundly different from that of Mankind. Only in the precariously budgeted, much-condescended-to area of women's studies is such knowledge available to women students. Only there can they learn about the lives and work of women other than the few select women who are included in the "mainstream" texts, usually misrepresented even when they do appear. Some students, at some institutions, manage to take a majority of courses in women's studies, but the message from on high is that this is self-indulgence, soft-core education: the "real" learning is the study of Mankind.

If there is any misleading concept, it is that of "coeducation": that because women and men are sitting in the same classrooms, hearing the same lectures, reading the same books, performing the same laboratory experiments, they are receiving an equal education. They are not, first because the content of education itself validates men even as it invalidates women. Its very message is that men have been the shapers and thinkers of the world, and that this is only natural. The bias of higher education, including the so-called sciences, is white and male, racist and sexist; and this bias is expressed in both subtle and blatant ways. I have mentioned already the exclusiveness of grammar itself: "The student should test himself on the above questions"; "The poet is representative. He stands among partial men for the complete man." Despite a few halfhearted departures from custom, what the linguist Wendy Martyna has named "He-Man" grammar prevails throughout the culture. The efforts of feminists to reveal the profound ontological implications of sexist grammar are routinely ridiculed by academicians and journalists, including the professedly liberal *Times* columnist Tom Wicker and the professed humanist Jacques Barzun. Sexist grammar burns into the brains of little girls and young women a message that the male is the norm, the standard, the central figure beside which we are the deviants, the marginal, the dependent variables. It lays the foundation for androcentric thinking, and leaves men safe in their solipsistic tunnel-vision.

Women and men do not receive an equal education because outside the classroom women are perceived not as sovereign beings but as prey. The growing incidence of rape on and off the campus may or may not be fed by the proliferations of pornographic magazines and X-rated films available to young males in fraternities and student unions; but it is certainly occurring in a context of widespread images of sexual violence against women, on billboards and in so-called high art. More subtle, more daily than rape is the verbal abuse experienced by the woman student on many campuses—Rutgers for example—where, traversing a street lined with fraternity houses, she must run a gauntlet of male commentary and verbal assault. The undermining of self, of a woman's sense of her right to occupy space and walk freely in the world, is deeply relevant to education. The capacity to think independently, to take intellectual risks, to assert ourselves mentally, is inseparable from our physical way of being in the world, our feelings of personal integrity. If it is dangerous for me to walk home late of an evening from the library, *because I am a woman and can be raped*, how self-possessed, how exuberant can I feel as I sit working in that library? How much of my working energy is drained by the subliminal knowledge that, as a woman, I test my physical right to exist each time I go out alone? Of this knowledge, Susan Griffin[2] has written:

> . . .*more than rape itself, the fear of rape permeates our lives. And what does one do from day to day, with* this *experience, which says, without words and directly to the heart,* your existence, your experience, may end at any moment. *Your experience may end, and the best defense against this is not to be, to deny being in the body, as a self, to . . . avert your gaze, make yourself, as a presence in the world, less felt.*

Finally, rape of the mind. Women students are more and more often now reporting sexual overtures by male professors—one part of our overall growing consciousness of sexual harassment in the workplace. At Yale a legal suit has been brought against the university by a group of women demanding an explicit policy against sexual advances toward female students by male professors. Most young women experience a profound mixture of humiliation and intellectual self-doubt over seductive gestures by men who have the power to award grades, open doors to grants and graduate school, or extend special knowledge and training. Even if turned aside, such gestures constitute mental rape, destructive to a woman's ego. They are acts of domination, as despicable as the molestation of the daughter by the father.

But long before entering college the woman student has experienced her alien identity in a world which misnames her, turns her to its own uses, denying her the resources she needs to become self-affirming, self-defined. The nuclear family teaches her that relationships are more important than selfhood or work; that "whether the phone rings for you, and how often," having the right clothes, doing the dishes, take precedence over study or solitude; that too much intelligence or intensity may make her unmarriageable; that marriage and children—service to others—are, finally, the points on which her life will be judged a success or a failure. In high school, the polarization between feminine attractiveness and independent intelligence comes to an absolute. Meanwhile, the culture resounds with messages. During Solar Energy Week in New York I saw young women wearing "ecology" T-shirts with the legend: CLEAN, CHEAP,

---

[2]**Susan Griffin**   Author of *Rape: The Power of Consciousness.*

AND AVAILABLE; a reminder of the 1960s antiwar button which read: CHICKS SAY YES TO MEN WHO SAY NO. Department store windows feature female mannequins in chains, pinned to the wall with legs spread, smiling in positions of torture. Feminists are depicted in the media as "shrill," "strident," "puritanical," or "humorless," and the lesbian choice—the choice of the woman-identified woman—as pathological or sinister. The young woman sitting in the philosophy classroom, the political science lecture, is already gripped by tensions between her nascent sense of self-worth, and the battering force of messages like these.

Look at a classroom: look at the many kinds of women's faces, postures, expressions. Listen to the women's voices. Listen to the silences, the unasked questions, the blanks. Listen to the small, soft voices, often courageously trying to speak up, voices of women taught early that tones of confidence, challenge, anger, or assertiveness, are strident and unfeminine. Listen to the voices of the women and the voices of the men; observe the space men allow themselves, physically and verbally, the male assumption that people will listen, even when the majority of the group is female. Look at the faces of the silent, and of those who speak. Listen to a woman groping for language in which to express what is on her mind, sensing that the terms of academic discourse are not her language, trying to cut down her thought to the dimensions of a discourse not intended for her (*for it is not fitting that a woman speak in public*); or reading her paper aloud at breakneck speed, throwing her words away, deprecating her own work by a reflex prejudgment: *I do not deserve to take up time and space*.

As women teachers, we can either deny the importance of this context in which women students think, write, read, study, project their own futures; or try to work with it. We can either teach passively, accepting these conditions, or actively, helping our students identify and resist them.

One important thing we can do is *discuss* the context. And this need not happen only in a women's studies course; it can happen anywhere. We can refuse to accept passive, obedient learning and insist upon critical thinking. We can become harder on our women students, giving them the kinds of "cultural prodding" that men receive, but on different terms and in a different style. Most young women need to have their intellectual lives, their work, legitimized against the claims of family, relationships, the old message that a woman is always available for service to others. We need to keep our standards very high, not to accept a woman's preconceived sense of her limitations; we need to be hard to please, while supportive of risk-taking, because self-respect often comes only when exacting standards have been met. At a time when adult literacy is generally low, we need to demand more, not less, of women, both for the sake of their futures as thinking beings, and because historically women have always had to be better than men to do half as well. A romantic sloppiness, an inspired lack of rigor, a self-indulgent incoherence, are symptoms of female self-deprecation. We should help our women students to look very critically at such symptoms, and to understand where they are rooted.

Nor does this mean we should be training women students to "think like men." Men in general think badly: in disjuncture from their personal lives, claiming objectivity where the most irrational passions seethe, losing, as Virginia Woolf observed, their senses in the pursuit of professionalism. It is not easy to think like a woman in a man's world, in the world of the professions; yet the capacity to do that is a strength which we can try to help our students develop. To think like a woman in a man's world means thinking critically, refusing to accept the givens, making connections between facts and ideas which men have left unconnected. It means remembering that every mind resides in a body; remaining accountable to the female bodies in which we live; constantly retesting given hypotheses against lived experience. It means a constant critique of language, for as Wittgenstein[3] (no feminist) observed, "The limits of my language are the limits of my world." And it means that most difficult thing of all: listening and watching in art and literature, in the social sciences, in all the descriptions we are given of the world, for the silences, the absences, the nameless, the unspoken, the encoded—for there we will find the true knowledge of women. And in breaking those silences, naming our selves, uncovering the hidden, making ourselves present, we begin to define a reality which resonates to *us*, which affirms *our* being, which allows the woman teacher and the woman student alike to take ourselves, and each other, seriously: meaning, to begin taking charge of our lives. 🖋

SUGGESTIONS FOR WRITING

1. Have you, as a female student, ever had experiences like the ones Rich recounts? Have you, as a male student, ever observed such incidents? How did you react? Narrate such an experience.

2. How independent of gender bias are the criteria by which we judge academic achievement? In what ways does gender bias play a role in the evaluation of students?

3. What, in your opinion, is the relationship between the classroom atmosphere for women as Rich describes it and the problem of sexual harassment of female students by male professors?

4. How can women students challenge sexist behavior in the classroom?

_____

[3]**Wittgenstein** Ludwig Wittgenstein (1889–1951), philosopher noted for his theories on logic and on language.

LIKE MEXICANS

Gary Soto

At least since the appearance of Shakespeare's Romeo and Juliet, *we have been moved by stories of love between persons of opposite social backgrounds. Many contemporary films derive their appeal from this stock theme. In the following situation, we move beyond mere family differences to potentially vast ethnic and cultural differences. Yet, in some ways, this story points up a truism: When we expect to encounter strong difference, we are surprised by similarities. Sometimes the opposite is true. Nobody claims life is simple.*

Gary Soto (b. 1952), a teacher of Chicano Studies and English at the University of California, Berkeley, is a widely recognized American poet and spokesman for Mexican-Americans. In 1985 he received the American Book Award for his autobiographical work Living Up the Street *(1985). Other books include* California Childhood *(1988),* Who Will Know Us? *(1990), and* Baseball in April *(1990). Soto's poems appear frequently in literary magazines, including* The American Poetry Review.

My grandmother gave me bad advice and good advice when I was in my early teens. For the bad advice, she said that I should become a barber because they made good money and listened to the radio all day. "Honey, they don't work como burros," she would say every time I visited her. She made the sound of donkeys braying. "Like that, honey!" For the good advice, she said that I should marry a Mexican girl. "No Okies, hijo"—she would say—"Look, my son. He marry one and they fight every day about I don't know what and I don't know what." For her, everyone who wasn't Mexican, black, or Asian were Okies. The French were Okies, the Italians in suits were Okies. When I asked about Jews, whom I had read about, she asked for a picture. I rode home on my bicycle and returned with a calendar depicting the important races of the world. "Pues si, son Okies tambien!"[1] she said, nodding her head. She waved the calendar away and we went to the living room where she lectured me on the virtues of the Mexican girl: first, she could cook and, second, she acted like a woman, not a man, in her husband's home. She said she would tell me about a third when I got a little older.

I asked my mother about it—becoming a barber and marrying Mexican. She was in the kitchen. Steam curled from a pot of boiling beans, the radio was on, looking as squat as a loaf of bread. "Well, if you want to be a barber—they say they make good money." She slapped a round steak with a knife, her glasses slipping down with each strike. She stopped and looked up. "If you find a good

---

[1] Well yes, they're Okies too.

Mexican girl, marry her of course." She returned to slapping the meat and I went to the backyard where my brother and David King were sitting on the lawn feeling the inside of their cheeks.

"This is what girls feel like," my brother said, rubbing the inside of his cheek. David put three fingers inside his mouth and scratched. I ignored them and climbed the back fence to see my best friend, Scott, a second-generation Okie. I called him and his mother pointed to the side of the house where his bedroom was, a small aluminum trailer, the kind you gawk at when they're flipped over on the freeway, wheels spinning in the air. I went around to find Scott pitching horseshoes.

I picked up a set of rusty ones and joined him. While we played, we talked about school and friends and record albums. The horseshoes scuffed up dirt, sometimes ringing the iron that threw out a meager shadow like a sundial. After three argued-over games, we pulled two oranges apiece from his tree and started down the alley still talking school and friends and record albums. We pulled more oranges from the alley and talked about who we would marry. "No offense, Scott," I said with an orange slice in my mouth, "but I would never marry an Okie." We walked in step, almost touching, with a sled of shadows dragging behind us. "No offense, Gary," Scott said, "but I would *never* marry a Mexican." I looked at him: a fang of orange slice showed from his munching mouth. I didn't think anything of it. He had his girl and I had mine. But our seventh-grade vision was the same: to marry, get jobs, buy cars and maybe a house if we had money left over.

We talked about our future lives until, to our surprise, we were on the downtown mall, two miles from home. We bought a bag of popcorn at Penneys and sat on a bench near the fountain watching Mexican and Okie girls pass. "That one's mine," I pointed with my chin when a girl with eyebrows arched into black rainbows ambled by. "She's cute," Scott said about a girl with yellow hair and a mouthful of gum. We dreamed aloud, our chins busy pointing out girls. We agreed that we couldn't wait to become men and lift them onto our laps.

But the woman I married was not Mexican but Japanese. It was a surprise to me. For years, I went about wide-eyed in my search for the brown girl in a white dress at a dance. I searched the playground at the baseball diamond. When the girls raced for grounders, their hair bounced like something that couldn't be caught. When they sat together in the lunchroom, heads pressed together, I knew they were talking about us Mexican guys. I saw them and dreamed them. I threw my face into my pillow, making up sentences that were good as in the movies.

But when I was twenty, I fell in love with this other girl who worried my mother, who had my grandmother asking once again to see the calendar of the Important Races of the World. I told her I had thrown it away years before. I took a much-glanced-at snapshot from my wallet. We looked at it together, in silence. Then grandma reclined in her chair, lit a cigarette, and said, "Es pretty." She blew and asked with all her worry pushed up to her forehead: "Chinese?"

I was in love and there was no looking back. She was the one. I told my mother who was slapping hamburger into patties. "Well, sure if you want to marry her," she said. But the more I talked, the more concerned she became.

Later I began to worry. Was it all a mistake? "Marry a Mexican girl," I heard my mother say in my mind. I heard it at breakfast. I heard it over math problems, between Western Civilization and cultural geography. But then one afternoon while I was hitchhiking home from school, it struck me like a baseball in the back: my mother wanted me to marry someone of my own social class—a poor girl. I considered my fiancee, Carolyn, and she didn't look poor, though I knew she came from a family of farm workers and pull-yourself-up-by-your-bootstraps ranchers. I asked my brother, who was marrying Mexican poor that fall, if I should marry a poor girl. He screamed "Yeah" above his terrible guitar playing in his bedroom. I considered my sister who had married Mexican. Cousins were dating Mexican. Uncles were remarrying poor women. I asked Scott, who was still my best friend, and he said, "She's too good for you, so you better not."

I worried about it until Carolyn took me home to meet her parents. We drove in her Plymouth until the houses gave way to farms and ranches and finally her house fifty feet from the highway. When we pulled into the drive, I panicked and begged Carolyn to make a U-turn and go back so we could talk about it over a soda. She pinched my cheek, calling me a "silly boy." I felt better, though, when I got out of the car and saw the house: the chipped paint, a cracked window, boards for a walk to the back door. There were rusting cars near the barn. A tractor with a net of spiderwebs under a mulberry. A field. A bale of barbed wire like children's scribbling leaning against an empty chicken coop. Carolyn took my hand and pulled me to my future mother-in-law who was coming out to greet us.

We had lunch: sandwiches, potato chips, and iced tea. Carolyn and her mother talked mostly about neighbors and the congregation at the Japanese Methodist Church in West Fresno. Her father, who was in khaki work clothes, excused himself with a wave that was almost a salute and went outside. I heard a truck start, a dog bark, and then the truck rattle away.

Carolyn's mother offered another sandwich, but I declined with a shake of my head and a smile. I looked around when I could, when I was not saying over and over that I was a college student, hinting that I could take care of her daughter. I shifted my chair. I saw newspapers piled in corners, dusty cereal boxes and vinegar bottles in corners. The wallpaper was bubbled from rain that had come in from a bad roof. Dust. Dust lay on lamp shades and window sills. These people are just like Mexicans, I thought. Poor people.

Carolyn's mother asked me through Carolyn if I would like a *sushi*. A plate of black and white things were held in front of me. I took one, wide-eyed, and turned it over like a foreign coin. I was biting into one when I saw a kitten crawl up the window screen over the sink. I chewed and the kitten opened its mouth of terror as she crawled higher, wanting in to paw the leftovers from our plates. I looked at Carolyn who said that the cat was just showing off. I looked up in time to see it fall. It crawled up, then fell again.

We talked for an hour and had apple pie and coffee, slowly. Finally, we got up with Carolyn taking my hand. Slightly embarrassed, I tried to pull away but her grip held me. I let her have her way as she led me down the hallway with her mother right behind me. When I opened the door, I was startled by a kitten clinging to the screen door, its mouth screaming "cat food, dog biscuits, *sushi. . . ."* I opened the door and the kitten, still holding on, whined in the language of hungry animals. When I got into Carolyn's car, I looked back: the cat was still clinging. I asked Carolyn if it were possibly hungry, but she said the cat was being silly. She started the car, waved to her mother, and bounced us over the rain-poked drive, patting my thigh for being her lover baby. Carolyn waved again. I looked back, waving, then gawking at a window screen where there were now three kittens clawing and screaming to get in. Like Mexicans, I thought. I remembered the Molinas and how the cats clung to their screens—cats they shot down with squirt guns. On the highway, I felt happy, pleased by it all. I patted Carolyn's thigh. Her people were like Mexicans, only different.

SUGGESTIONS FOR WRITING

1. Perhaps Soto is too quick to minimize the differences between these Mexican-American and Japanese-American families. What difficulties do you think such a couple might encounter?

2. Immigrant families in particular place meals featuring their native cuisine at the center of their family observances. If you are a guest unfamiliar with their dishes or dining customs, you may feel uneasy. Describe a social occasion at which you experienced an "alien" cuisine for the first time.

3. The United States of America is sometimes described as a "melting pot" of diverse immigrant cultures. Reflect on this claim in light of Soto's account.

4. How would you feel about marrying outside your race or ethnic group? How might you react as a parent if your child did so?

THE UNDERDOG

Melvin B. Tolson

In recent years, a recurring political strategy of resurgent minority groups has been to embrace and redefine the pejorative labels historically applied to them. In the following poem, the poet **Melvin B. Tolson** *(1898–1966) catalogues the all-too-familiar arsenal of hateful terms used to designate the only minority group ever brought to these shores in chains, managing paradoxically to end the poem on an affirmative note. Like the well-known cartoon that depicts a vast school of tiny fish about to devour an enormous fish, Tolson's poem suggests a latent power in the status of "underdog."*

Tolson was a black poet, journalist, and educator who was born in Missouri and lived and taught in Texas, Oklahoma, and Alabama. As a weekly columnist for the Washington Tribune, *he championed the literary accomplishments of the Harlem Renaissance, particularly those of the black novelist Richard Wright. Many of these writings were collected and published after Tolson's death as* A Gallery of Harlem Portraits *(1979). His collections of poems include* Rendezvous with America *(1944),* Libretto for the Republic of Liberia *(1953), and* Harlem Gallery: Book I, The Curator *(1965).*

I am the coon, the black bastard,
On the *Queen Mary*,
The United Air Lines,
The Greyhound,
The Twentieth Century Limited.

I am sambo, the shine,
In the St. Regis Iridium,
The Cotton Club,
The Terrace Room of the New Yorker.

I am the nigger, the black son of a bitch,
From the Florida Keys to Caribou, Maine;
From the Golden Gate
To the Statute of Liberty.

I know the deafness of white ears,
The hate of white faces,
The venom of white tongues,
The torture of white hands.

I know the meek
Shall inherit the graves!

In jim crow schools
And jim crow churches,
In the nigger towns
And the Brazos bottoms,

Along Hollywood Boulevard
And Tobacco Road—
My teachers were Vice and Superstition,
Ignorance and Illiteracy . . .
My pals were TB and Syphilis,
Crime and Hunger.

Sambo, nigger, son of a bitch,
I came from the loins
Of the great white masters.

Kikes and bohunks and wops,
Dagos and niggers and crackers . . .
Starved and lousy,
Blind and stinking—
We fought each other,
Killed each other,
Because the great white masters
Played us against each other.

Then a kike said: *Workers of the world, unite!*
And a dago said: *Let us live!*
And a cracker said: *Ours for us!*
And a nigger said: *Walk together, children!*

WE ARE THE UNDERDOGS
ON A HOT TRAIL!

SUGGESTIONS FOR WRITING

1. When the poet turns from epithets about blacks to epithets about other minorities, what role does this transition play?

2. If the poem is *not* about race in American society, what is it about?

3. How do you react to the use of so many racial epithets in the poem? How does your knowledge that the poet was black influence your reading? Why is it acceptable for members of a minority group to use the epithets directed at them ironically among themselves?

EVERYDAY USE

Alice Walker

In this short story from 1973, three members of a family come into conflict over what might seem to be a small matter: a quilt passed down through several generations of women. But the stakes at risk here are quite high. **Alice Walker** *gives both sides an opportunity to express their values, and her story emphasizes the gaps within this vibrant and articulate family.*

Walker (b. 1944) is a novelist, poet, essayist, and literary critic, best known for her novel The Color Purple *(1982). Among her other books are the novels* The Temple of My Familiar *(1989) and* Meridien *(1976); a volume of poetry,* Revolutionary Petunias and Other Poems *(1970); and a collection of her essays,* In Search of Our Mothers' Gardens *(1983).*

for your grandmama

I will wait for her in the yard that Maggie and I made so clean and wavy yesterday afternoon. A yard like this is more comfortable than most people know. It is not just a yard. It is like an extended living room. When the hard clay is swept clean as a floor and the fine sand around the edges lined with tiny, irregular grooves, anyone can come and sit and look up into the elm tree and wait for the breezes that never come inside the house.

Maggie will be nervous until after her sister goes: she will stand hopelessly in corners, homely and ashamed of the burn scars down her arms and legs, eying her sister with a mixture of envy and awe. She thinks her sister has held life always in the palm of one hand, that "no" is a word the world never learned to say to her.

You've no doubt seen those TV shows where the child who has "made it" is confronted, as a surprise, by her own mother and father, tottering in weakly from backstage. (A pleasant surprise, of course: What would they do if parent and child came on the show only to curse out and insult each other?) On TV mother and child embrace and smile into each other's faces. Sometimes the mother and father weep, the child wraps them in her arms and leans across the table to tell how she would not have made it without their help. I have seen these programs.

Sometimes I dream a dream in which Dee and I are suddenly brought together on a TV program of this sort. Out of a dark and soft-seated limousine I am ushered into a bright room filled with many people. There I meet a smiling, gray, sporty man like Johnny Carson who shakes my hand and tells me what a fine girl I have. Then we are on the stage and Dee is embracing me with tears in her eyes. She pins on my dress a large orchid, even though she has told me once that she thinks orchids are tacky flowers.

In real life I am a large, big-boned woman with rough, man-working hands. In the winter I wear flannel nightgowns to bed and overalls during the day. I can kill and clean a hog as mercilessly as a man. My fat keeps me hot in zero weather. I can work outside all day, breaking ice to get water for washing: I can eat pork liver cooked over the open fire minutes after it comes steaming from the hog. One winter I knocked a bull calf straight in the brain between the eyes with a sledge hammer and had the meat hung up to chill before nightfall. But of course all this does not show on television. I am the way my daughter would want me to be: a hundred pounds lighter, my skin like an uncooked barley pancake. My hair glistens in the hot bright lights. Johnny Carson has much to do to keep up with my quick and witty tongue.

But that is a mistake. I know even before I wake up. Who ever knew a Johnson with a quick tongue? Who can even imagine me looking a strange white man in the eye? It seems to me I have talked to them always with one foot raised in flight, with my head turned in whichever way is farthest from them. Dee, though. She would always look anyone in the eye. Hesitation was no part of her nature.

"How do I look, Mama?" Maggie says, showing just enough of her thin body enveloped in pink shirt and red blouse for me to know she's there, almost hidden by the door.

"Come out into the yard," I say.

Have you ever seen a lame animal, perhaps a dog run over by some careless person rich enough to own a car, sidle up to someone who is ignorant enough to be kind to him? That is the way my Maggie walks. She has been like this, chin on chest, eyes on ground, feet in shuffle, ever since the fire that burned the other house to the ground.

Dee is lighter than Maggie, with nicer hair and a fuller figure. She's a woman now, though sometimes I forget. How long ago was it that the other house burned? Ten, twelve years? Sometimes I can still hear the flames and feel Maggie's arms sticking to me, her hair smoking and her dress falling off her in little black papery flakes. Her eyes seemed stretched open, blazed open by the flames reflected in them. And Dee. I see her standing off under the sweet gum tree she used to dig gum out of; a look of concentration on her face as she watched the last dingy gray board of the house fall in toward the red-hot brick chimney. Why don't you do a dance around the ashes? I'd wanted to ask her. She had hated the house that much.

I used to think she hated Maggie, too. But that was before we raised the money, the church and me, to send her to Augusta to school. She used to read to us without pity; forcing words, lies, other folks' habits, whole lives upon us two, sitting trapped and ignorant underneath her voice. She washed us in a river of make-believe, burned us with a lot of knowledge we didn't necessarily need to know. Pressed us to her with the serious way she read, to shove us away at just the moment, like dimwits, we seemed about to understand.

Dee wanted nice things. A yellow organdy dress to wear to her graduation from high school; black pumps to match a green suit she'd made from an old suit somebody gave me. She was determined to stare down any disaster in her efforts. Her eyelids would not flicker for minutes at a time. Often I fought off the temptation to shake her. At sixteen she had a style of her own: and knew what style was.

I never had an education myself. After second grade the school was closed down. Don't ask me why: in 1927 colored asked fewer questions than they do now. Sometimes Maggie reads to me. She stumbles along good-naturedly but can't see well. She knows she is not bright. Like good looks and money, quickness passed her by. She will marry John Thomas (who has mossy teeth in an earnest face) and then I'll be free to sit here and I guess just sing church songs to myself. Although I never was a good singer. Never could carry a tune. I was always better at a man's job. I used to love to milk till I was hooked in the side in '49. Cows are soothing and slow and don't bother you, unless you try to milk them the wrong way.

I have deliberately turned my back on the house. It is three rooms, just like the one that burned, except the roof is tin; they don't make shingle roofs any more. There are no real windows, just some holes cut in the sides, like the portholes in a ship, but not round and not square, with rawhide holding the shutters up on the outside. This house is in a pasture, too, like the other one. No doubt when Dee sees it she will want to tear it down. She wrote me once that no matter where we "choose" to live, she will manage to come see us. But she will never bring her friends. Maggie and I thought about this and Maggie asked me, "Mama, when did Dee ever *have* any friends?"

She had a few. Furtive boys in pink shirts hanging about on washday after school. Nervous girls who never laughed. Impressed with her they worshiped the well-turned phrase, the cute shape, the scalding humor that erupted like bubbles in lye. She read to them.

When she was courting Jimmy T she didn't have much time to pay to us, but turned all her faultfinding power on him. He *flew* to marry a cheap city girl from a family of ignorant flashy people. She hardly had time to recompose herself.

When she comes I will meet—but there they are!

Maggie attempts to make a dash for the house, in her shuffling way, but I stay her with my hand. "Come back here," I say. And she stops and tries to dig a well in the sand with her toe.

It is hard to see them clearly through the strong sun. But even the first glimpse of leg out of the car tells me it is Dee. Her feet were always neat-looking, as if God himself has shaped them with a certain style. From the other side of the car comes a short, stocky man. Hair is all over his head a foot long and hanging from his chin like a kinky mule tail. I hear Maggie suck in her breath. "Uhnnnh," is what it sounds like. Like when you see the wriggling end of a snake just in front of your foot on the road. "Uhnnnh."

Dee next. A dress down to the ground, in this hot weather. A dress so loud it hurts my eyes. There are yellows and oranges enough to throw back the light of the sun. I feel my whole face warming from the heat waves it throws out. Earrings gold, too, and hanging down to her shoulders. Bracelets dangling and making noises when she moves her arm up to shake the folds of the dress out of her armpits. The dress is loose and flows, and as she walks closer, I like it. I hear Maggie go "Uhnnnh" again. It is her sister's hair. It stands straight up like the wool on a sheep. It is black as night and around the edges are two long pigtails that rope about like small lizards disappearing behind her ears.

"Wa-su-zo-Tean-o!" she says, coming on in that gliding way the dress makes her move. The short stocky fellow with the hair to his navel is all grinning and he follows up with "Asalamalakim, my mother and sister!" He moves to hug Maggie but she falls back, right up against the back of my chair. I feel her trembling there and when I look up I see the perspiration falling off her chin.

"Don't get up," says Dee. Since I am stout it takes something of a push. You can see me trying to move a second or two before I make it. She turns, showing white heels through her sandals, and goes back to the car. Out she peeks next with a Polaroid. She stoops down quickly and lines up picture after picture of me sitting there in front of the house with Maggie cowering behind me. She never takes a shot without making sure the house is included. When a cow comes nibbling around the edge of the yard she snaps it and me and Maggie *and* the house. Then she puts the Polaroid in the back seat of the car, and comes up and kisses me on the forehead.

Meanwhile Asalamalakim is going through motions with Maggie's hand. Maggie's hand is as limp as a fish, and probably as cold, despite the sweat, and she keeps trying to pull it back. It looks like Asalamalakim wants to shake hands but wants to do it fancy. Or maybe he don't know how people shake hands. Anyhow, he soon gives up on Maggie.

"Well," I say. "Dee."

"No, Mama," she says. "Not 'Dee.' Wangero Leewanika Kemanjo!"

"What happened to 'Dee'?" I wanted to know.

"She's dead," Wangero said. "I couldn't bear it any longer, being named after the people who oppress me."

"You know as well as me you was named after your aunt Dicie," I said. Dicie is my sister. She named Dee. We called her "Big Dee" after Dee was born.

"But who was *she* named after?" asked Wangero.

"I guess after Grandma Dee," I said.

"And who was she named after?" asked Wangero.

"Her mother," I said, and saw Wangero was getting tired. "That's about as far back as I can trace it," I said. Though, in fact, I probably could have carried it back beyond the Civil War through the branches.

"Well," said Asalamalakim, "there you are."

"Uhnnnh." I heard Maggie say.

"There I was not," I said, "before 'Dicie' cropped up in our family, so why should I try to trace it that far back?"

He just stood there grinning, looking down on me like somebody inspecting a Model A car. Every once in a while he and Wangero sent eye signals over my head.

"How do you pronounce this name?" I asked.

"You don't have to call me by it if you don't want to," said Wangero.

"Why shouldn't I?" I asked. "If that's what you want us to call you, we'll call you."

"I know it might sound awkward at first," said Wangero.

"I'll get used to it," I said. "Ream it out again."

Well, soon we got the name out of the way. Asalamalakim had a name twice as long and three times as hard. After I tripped over it two or three times he told me to just call him Hakim-a-barber. I wanted to ask him was he a barber, but I didn't really think he was, so I didn't ask.

"You must belong to those beef-cattle peoples down the road," I said. They said "Asalamalakim" when they meet you, too, but they didn't shake hands. Always too busy: feeding the cattle, fixing the fences, putting up salt-lick shelters, throwing down hay. When the white folks poisoned some of the herd the men stayed up all night with rifles in their hands. I walked a mile and a half just to see the sight.

Hakim-a-barber said, "I accept some of their doctrines, but farming and raising cattle is not my style." (They didn't tell me, and I didn't ask, whether Wangero [Dee] had really gone and married him.)

We sat down to eat and right away he said he didn't eat collards and pork was unclean. Wangero, though, went on through the chitlins and corn bread, the greens and everything else. She talked a blue streak over the sweet potatoes. Everything delighted her. Even the fact that we still used the benches her daddy made for the table when we couldn't afford to buy chairs.

"Oh, Mama!" she cried. Then turned to Hakim-a-barber. "I never knew how lovely these benches are. You can feel the rump prints," she said, running her hands underneath her and along the bench. Then she gave a sigh and her hand closed over Grandma Dee's butter dish. "That's it!" she said. "I knew there was something I wanted to ask you if I could have." She jumped up from the table and went over in the corner where the churn stood, the milk in it clabber by now. She looked at the churn and looked at it.

"This churn top is what I need," she said. "Didn't Uncle Buddy whittle it out of a tree you all used to have?"

"Yes," I said.

"Uh huh," she said happily. "And I want the dasher, too."

"Uncle Buddy whittle that, too?" asked the barber.

Dee (Wangero) looked up at me.

"Aunt Dee's first husband whittled the dash," said Maggie so low you almost couldn't hear her. "His name was Henry, but they called him Stash."

"Maggie's brain is like an elephant's," Wangero said, laughing. "I can use the churn top as a centerpiece for the alcove table," she said, sliding a plate over the churn, "and I'll think of something artistic to do with the dasher."

When she finished wrapping the dasher the handle stuck out. I took it for a moment in my hands. You didn't even have to look close to see where hands pushing the dasher up and down to make butter had left a kind of sink in the wood. In fact, there were a lot of small sinks; you could see where thumbs and fingers had sunk into the wood. It was beautiful light yellow wood, from a tree that grew in the yard where Big Dee and Stash had lived.

After dinner Dee (Wangero) went to the trunk at the foot of my bed and started rifling through it. Maggie hung back in the kitchen over the dishpan. Out came Wangero with two quilts. They had been pieced by Grandma Dee and then Big Dee and me had hung them on the quilt frames on the front porch and quilted them. One was in the Lone Star pattern. The other was Walk

Around the Mountain. In both of them were scraps of dresses Grandma Dee had worn fifty and more years ago. Bits and pieces of Grandpa Jarrell's Paisley shirts. And one teeny faded blue piece, about the size of a penny matchbox, that was from Great Grandpa Ezra's uniform that he wore in the Civil War.

"Mama," Wangero said sweet as a bird. "Can I have these old quilts?"

I heard something fall in the kitchen, and minute later the kitchen door slammed.

"Why don't you take one or two of the others?" I asked. "These old things was just done by me and Big Dee from some tops your grandma pieced before she died."

"No," said Wangero. "I don't want those. They are stitched around the borders by machine."

"That'll make them last better," I said.

"That's not the point," said Wangero. "These are all pieces of dresses Grandma used to wear. She did all this stitching by hand. Imagine!" She held the quilts securely in her arms, stroking them.

"Some of the pieces, like those lavender ones, come from old clothes her mother handed down to her," I said, moving up to touch the quilts. Dee (Wangero) moved back just enough so that I couldn't reach the quilts. They already belonged to her.

"Imagine!" she breathed again, clutching them closely to her bosom.

"The truth is," I said, "I promised to give them quilts to Maggie, for when she marries John Thomas."

She gasped like a bee had stung her.

"Maggie can't appreciate these quilts!" she said. "She'd probably be backward enough to put them to everyday use."

"I reckon she would," I said. "God knows I been saving 'em for long enough with nobody using 'em. I hope she will!" I didn't want to bring up how I had offered Dee (Wangero) a quilt when she went away to college. Then she had told me they were old-fashioned, out of style.

"But they're *priceless!*" she was saying now, furiously; for she has a temper. "Maggie would put them on the bed and in five years they'd be in rags. Less than that!"

"She can always make some more," I said. "Maggie knows how to quilt."

Dee (Wangero) looked at me with hatred. "You will not understand. The point is these quilts, *these* quilts!"

"Well," I said, stumped. "What would *you* do with them?"

"Hang them," she said. As if that was the only thing you *could* do with quilts.

Maggie by now was standing in the door. I could almost hear the sound her feet made as they scraped over each other.

"She can have them, Mama," she said, like somebody used to never winning anything, or having anything reserved for her. "I can 'member Grandma Dee without the quilts."

I looked at her hard. She had filled her bottom lip with checkerberry snuff and it gave her face a kind of dopey, hangdog look. It was Grandma Dee and Big Dee who taught her how to quilt herself. She stood there with her scarred hands hidden in the folds of her skirt. She looked at her sister with something like fear but she wasn't mad at her. This was Maggie's portion. This was the way she knew God to work.

When I looked at her like that something hit me in the top of my head and ran down to the soles of my feet. Just like when I'm in church and the spirit of God touches me and I get happy and shout. I did something I never had done before: hugged Maggie to me, then dragged her on into the room, snatched the quilts out of Miss Wangero's hands and dumped them into Maggie's lap. Maggie just sat there on my bed with her mouth open.

"Take one or two of the others," I said to Dee.

But she turned without a word and went out to Hakim-a-barber.

"You just don't understand," she said, as Maggie and I came out to the car.

"What don't I understand?" I wanted to know.

"Your heritage," she said. And then she turned to Maggie, kissed her, and said, "You ought to try to make something of yourself, too, Maggie. It's really a new day for us. But from the way you and Mama still live you'd never know it."

She put on some sunglasses that hid everything above the tip of her nose and her chin.

Maggie smiled; maybe at the sunglasses. But a real smile, not scared.

After we watched the car dust settle I asked Maggie to bring me a dip of snuff. And then the two of us sat there just enjoying, until it was time to go in the house and go to bed. ✒

SUGGESTIONS FOR WRITING

1. Which side of the argument does Alice Walker seem to be on? What justifies your opinion?

2. To what extent is the conflict in this story limited to black families? Could similar conflicts occur in other families?

3. What does this story tell us about relationships between mothers and daughters? How much does their social class affect that relationship?

PLAYBOY JOINS THE BATTLE OF THE SEXES

Barbara Ehrenreich

Barbara Ehrenreich (b. 1941), political activist and journalist, has been a contributing editor of Ms. *magazine and has published essays of social criticism in* The Nation, Mother Jones, *and* The New York Times Magazine. *Her books include (with Deirdre English)* For Her Own Good: 150 Years of Experts' Advice to Women *(1978) and* The Hearts of Men: American Dreams and the Flight From Commitment *(1983), from which the following essay on* Playboy *magazine was taken.*

So-called men's magazines accomplish more than the objectification of the female body much commented upon by feminists and others who decry their influence on American men. They also (and in this they share much with literature, films, popular songs, and so forth) portray women as manipulative creatures out to "trap" men into long-term commitments. The best-known such publication is Playboy, *which has significantly influenced American sexual attitudes since 1953.* Playboy, *along with many other publications, reinforces a particular kind of masculine self-image in which the man is a lone outlaw figure intent on casual sex and adventure, suspicious of the supposedly natural feminine impulse toward taming, civilizing, and creating routine and domestic orderliness.* Playboy *is also distinctive in its consumer orientation, seeking to instill in its male readership a taste for the "good life" in which impossibly attractive and alluring women are commodities to be acquired and used along with the expensive stereo equipment, luxury automobiles, and expensive wines the magazine advertises and recommends. Learning to be the tasteful consumer of all such delights, guarding all the while against lasting emotional bonds with the women in question, sums up the much-vaunted "*Playboy *philosophy."*

I don't want my editors marrying anyone and getting a lot of foolish notions in their heads about "togetherness," home, family, and all that jazz.

— Hugh Hefner

The first issue of *Playboy* hit the stands in December 1953. The first centerfold—the famous nude calendar shot of Marilyn Monroe—is already legendary. Less memorable, but no less prophetic of things to come, was the first feature article in the issue. It was a no-holds-barred attack on "the whole concept of alimony," and secondarily, on money-hungry women in general, entitled "Miss Gold-Digger of 1953." From the beginning, *Playboy* loved women—large-breasted, long-legged young women, anyway—and hated wives.

The "Miss Gold-Digger" article made its author a millionaire—not because Hugh Hefner paid him so much but because Hefner could not, at first, afford to pay him at all, at least not in cash. The writer, Burt Zollo (he signed the article "Bob Norman"; even Hefner didn't risk putting his own name in the first issue), had to accept stock in the new magazine in lieu of a fee. The first print run of 70,000 nearly sold out and the magazine passed the one-million mark in 1956, making Hefner and his initial associates millionaires before the end of the decade.

But *Playboy* was more than a publishing phenomenon, it was like the party organ of a diffuse and swelling movement. Writer Myron Brenton called it the "Bible of the beleaguered male."[1] *Playboy* readers taped the centerfolds up in their basements, affixed the rabbit-head insignia to the rear windows of their cars, joined Playboy clubs if they could afford to, and even if they lived more like Babbitts[2] than Bunnies, imagined they were "playboys" at heart. The magazine encouraged the sense of membership in a fraternity of male rebels. After its first reader survey, *Playboy* reported on the marital status of its constituency in the following words: "Approximately half of PLAYBOY'S readers (46.8%) are free men and the other half are free in spirit only."[3]

In the ongoing battle of the sexes, the *Playboy* office in Chicago quickly became the male side's headquarters for war-time propaganda. Unlike the general-audience magazines that dominated fifties' newsstands—*Life, Time,* the *Saturday Evening Post, Look,* etc.—*Playboy* didn't worry about pleasing women readers. The first editorial, penned by Hefner himself, warned:

> *We want to make clear from the very start, we aren't a "family magazine."
> If you're somebody's sister, wife, or mother-in-law and picked us up by
> mistake, please pass us along to the man in your life and get back to your
> Ladies' Home Companion.*

When a Memphis woman wrote in to the second issue protesting the "Miss Gold-Digger" article, she was quickly put in her place. The article, she wrote, was "the most biased piece of tripe I've ever read," and she went on to deliver the classic anti-male rejoinder:

> *Most men are out for just one thing. If they can't get it any other way, some-
> times they consent to marry the girl. Then they think they can brush her off
> in a few months and move on to new pickings. They ought to pay, and pay,
> and pay.*

The editors' printed response was, "Ah, shaddup!"

Hefner laid out the new male strategic initiative in the first issue. Recall that in their losing battle against "female domination," men had been driven

---

[1] Quoted in Joe L. Dubbert, *A Man's Place: Masculinity in Transition* (Englewood Cliffs, N.J.: Prentice-Hall, Inc., 1979), p. 269. [Au.]

[2] George Babbitt, the protagonist of Sinclair Lewis's novel *Babbitt,* is unable to break out of the respectable conventionality of his domestic life. [Ed.]

[3] "Meet the *Playboy* Reader," *Playboy,* April 1958, p. 63. [Au.]

from their living rooms, dens, and even their basement tool shops. Escape seemed to lie only in the great outdoors—the golf course, the fishing hole, or the fantasy world of Westerns. Now Hefner announced his intention to reclaim *the indoors for men.* "Most of today's 'magazines for men' spend all their time out-of-doors—thrashing through thorny thickets or splashing about in fast flowing streams," he observed in the magazine's first editorial. "But we don't mind telling you in advance—we plan spending most of our time inside. WE like our apartment." For therein awaited a new kind of good life for men:

> *We enjoy mixing up cocktails and an* hors d'oeuvre *or two, putting a little mood music on the phonograph, and inviting in a female acquaintance for a quiet discussion on Picasso, Nietzsche, jazz, sex.*

Women would be welcome after men had reconquered the indoors, but only as guests—maybe overnight guests—but not as wives.

In 1953, the notion that the good life consisted of an apartment with mood music rather than a ranch house with barbecue pit was almost subversive. Looking back, Hefner later characterized himself as a pioneer rebel against the gray miasma of conformity that gripped other men. At the time the magazine began, he wrote in 1963, Americans had become "increasingly concerned with security, the safe and the sure, the certain and the known . . . it was unwise to voice an unpopular opinion . . . for it could cost a man his job and his good name."[4] Hefner himself was not a political dissident in any conventional sense; the major intellectual influence in his early life was the Kinsey Report, and he risked his own good name only for the right to publish bare white bosoms. What upset him was the "conformity, togetherness, anonymity, and slow death" men were supposed to endure when the good life, the life which he himself came to represent, was so close at hand.[5]

In fact, it was close at hand, and at the macroeconomic level, nothing could have been more in conformity with the drift of American culture than to advocate a life of pleasurable consumption. The economy, as Riesman, Galbraith,[6] and their colleagues noted, had gotten over the hump of heavy capital accumulation to the happy plateau of the "consumer society." After the privations of the Depression and the war, Americans were supposed to enjoy themselves—held back from total abandon only by the need for Cold War vigilance. Motivational researcher Dr. Ernest Dichter told businessmen:

> *We are now confronted with the problem of permitting the average American to feel moral . . . even when he is spending, even when he is not saving, even when he is taking two vacations a year and buying a second or third*

---

[4]Hugh Hefner, "The Playboy Philosophy," *Playboy*, January 1963, p. 41. [Au.]

[5]Frank Brady, *Hefner* (New York: Macmillan Pub. Co., Inc., 1974), p. 98. [Au.]

[6]Two widely read, influential books of the 1950s were *The Lonely Crowd* by sociologist David Riesman and *The Affluent Society* by economist John Kenneth Galbraith. [Ed.]

car. One of the basic problems of prosperity, then, is to demonstrate that the
hedonistic approach to his life is a moral, not an immoral one.[7]

This was the new consumer ethic, the "fun morality" described by sociologist Martha Wolfenstein, and *Playboy* could not have been better designed to bring the good news to men.

If Hefner was a rebel, it was only because he took the new fun morality seriously. As a guide to life, the new imperative to enjoy was in contradiction with the prescribed discipline of "conformity" and *Playboy*'s daring lay in facing the contradiction head-on. Conformity, or "maturity," as it was more affirmatively labeled by the psychologists, required unstinting effort: developmental "tasks" had to be performed, marriages had to be "worked on," individual whims had to be subordinated to the emotional and financial needs of the family. This was true for both sexes, of course. No one pretended that the adult sex roles—wife/mother and male breadwinner—were "fun." They were presented in the popular culture as achievements, proofs of the informed acquiescence praised as "maturity" or, more rarely, lamented as "slow death." Women would not get public license to have fun on a mass scale for more than a decade, when Helen Gurley Brown took over *Cosmopolitan* and began promoting a tamer, feminine version of sexual and material consumerism. But *Playboy* shed the burdensome aspects of the adult male role at a time when businessmen were still refining the "fun morality" for mass consumption, and the gray flannel rebels were still fumbling for responsible alternatives like Riesman's "autonomy." Even the magazine's name defied the convention of hard-won maturity—*Playboy*.

Playboy's attack on the conventional male role model did not, however, extend to the requirement of earning a living. There were two parts to adult masculinity: One was maintaining a monogamous marriage. The other was working at a socially acceptable job; and *Playboy* had nothing against work. The early issues barely recognized the white-collar blues so fashionable in popular sociology. Instead, there were articles on accoutrements for the rising executive, suggesting that work, too, could be a site of pleasurable consumption. Writing in his "*Playboy* Philosophy" series in 1963, Hefner even credited the magazine with inspiring men to work harder than they might: ". . . *Playboy* exists, in part, as a motivation for men to expend greater effort in their work, develop their capabilities further, and climb higher on the ladder of success." This kind of motivation, he went on, "is obviously desirable in our competitive, free enterprise system," apparently unaware that the average reader was more likely to be a white-collar "organization man" or blue-collar employee rather than a free entrepreneur like himself. Men should throw themselves into their work with "questioning impatience and rebel derring-do." They should overcome their vague, ingrained populism and recognize wealth as an achievement and a means to personal pleasure. Only in one respect did Hefner's philosophy de-

---

[7]Quoted in Douglas T. Miller and Marion Nowak, *The Fifties* (Garden City, N.Y.: Doubleday & Company, Inc., 1977), p. 119. [Au.]

part from the conventional, Dale Carnegie-style credos of male success: *Playboy* believed that men should make money; it did not suggest that they share it.

Playboy charged into the battle of the sexes with a dollar sign on its banner. The issue was money: Men made it; women wanted it. In *Playboy*'s favorite cartoon situation an elderly roué was being taken for a ride by a buxom bubblebrain, and the joke was on him. The message, squeezed between luscious full-color photos and punctuated with female nipples, was simple: You can buy sex on a fee-for-service basis, so don't get caught up in a long-term contract. Phil Silvers quipped in the January 1957 issue:

> *A tip to my fellow men who might be on the brink of disaster: When the little doll says she'll live on your income, she means it all right. But just be sure to get another one for yourself.*[8]

Burt Zollo warned in the June 1953 issue:

> *It is often suggested that woman is more romantic than man. If you'll excuse the ecclesiastical expression—phooey! . . . All woman wants is security. And she's perfectly willing to crush man's adventurous, freedom-loving spirit to get it.*[9]

To stay free, a man had to stay single.

The competition, meanwhile, was still fighting a rearguard battle for patriarchal authority within marriage. In 1956, the editorial director of *True* attributed his magazine's success to the fact that it "stimulates the masculine ego at a time when a man wants to fight back against women's efforts to usurp his traditional role as head of the family."[10] The playboy did not want his "traditional role" back; he just wanted out. Hefner's friend Burt Zollo wrote in one of the early issues:

> *Take a good look at the sorry, regimented husbands trudging down every woman-dominated street in this woman-dominated land. Check what they're doing when you're out on the town with a different dish every night . . . Don't bother asking their advice. Almost to a man, they'll tell you marriage is the greatest. Naturally. Do you expect them to admit they made the biggest mistake of their lives?*[11]

This was strong stuff for the mid-fifties. The suburban migration was in full swing and *Look* had just coined the new noun "togetherness" to bless the isolated, exurban family. Yet here was *Playboy* exhorting its readers to resist marriage and "enjoy the pleasures the female has to offer without becoming emotionally involved"—or, of course, financially involved. Women wrote in

---

[8]Phil Silvers, "Resolution: Never Get Married," *Playboy*, January 1957, p. 77. [Au.]
[9]Burt Zollo, "Open Season on Bachelors," *Playboy*, June 1953, p. 37. [Au.]
[10]Quoted in Myron Brenton, *The American Male* (New York: Coward, McCann, 1966), p. 30. [Au.]
[11]Zollo, loc. cit. [Au.]

with the predictable attacks on immaturity: "It is . . . the weak-minded little idiot boys, not yet grown up, who are afraid of getting 'hooked.' " But the men loved it. One alliterative genius wrote in to thank *Playboy* for exposing those "cunning cuties" with their "suave schemes" for landing a man. And, of course, it was *Playboy*, with its images of cozy concupiscence and extra-marital consumerism, that triumphed while *True* was still "thrashing through the thorny thickets" in the great, womanless outdoors.

One of the most eloquent manifestos of the early male rebellion was a *Playboy* article entitled, "Love, Death, and the Hubby Image," published in 1963. It led off with a mock want ad:

Tired of the Rat Race?
Fed Up with Job Routine?

Well, then . . . how would you like to make $8,000, $20,000—as much as $50,000 and More—working at Home in Your Spare Time? No selling! No commuting! No time clocks to punch!
BE YOUR OWN BOSS!!!
Yes, an Assured Lifetime Income can be yours now in an easy, low-pressure, part-time job that will permit you to spend most of each and every day as you please!—relaxing, watching TV, playing cards, socializing with friends! . . .

"Incredible though it may seem," the article began, "the above offer is completely legitimate. More than 40,000,000 Americans are already so employed. . . ." They were, of course, wives.

According to the writer, William Iversen, husbands were self-sacrificing romantics, toiling ceaselessly to provide their families with "bread, bacon, clothes, furniture, cars, appliances, entertainment, vacations, and country-club memberships." Nor was it enough to meet their daily needs; the heroic male must provide for them even after his own death by building up his savings and life insurance. "Day after day, and week after week the American hubby is thus invited to attend his own funeral." Iversen acknowledged that there were some mutterings of discontent from the distaff side, but he saw no chance of a feminist revival: The role of the housewife "has become much too cushy to be abandoned, even in the teeth of the most crushing boredom." Men, however, had had it with the breadwinner role, and the final paragraph was a stirring incitement to revolt:

The last straw has already been served, and a mere tendency to hemophilia cannot be counted upon to ensure that men will continue to bleed for the plight of the American woman. Neither double eyelashes nor the blindness of night or day can obscure the glaring fact that American marriage can no longer be accepted as an estate in which the sexes shall live half-slave and half-free.[12]

---

[12]William Iversen, "Love, Death and the Hubby Image," *Playboy*, September 1963, p. 92. [Au.]

Playboy had much more to offer the "enslaved" sex than rhetoric: It also proposed an alternative way of life that became ever more concrete and vivid as the years went on. At first there were only the Playmates in the centerfold to suggest what awaited the liberated male, but a wealth of other consumer items soon followed. Throughout the late fifties, the magazine fattened on advertisements for imported liquor, stereo sets, men's colognes, luxury cars, and fine clothes. Manufacturers were beginning to address themselves to the adult male as a consumer in his own right, and they were able to do so, in part, because magazines like *Playboy* (a category which came to include imitators like *Penthouse*, *Gent* and *Chic*) allowed them to effectively "target" the potential sybarites among the great mass of men. New products for men, like toiletries and sports clothes, appeared in the fifties, and familiar products, like liquor, were presented in *Playboy* as accessories to private male pleasures. The new male-centered ensemble of commodities presented in *Playboy* meant that a man could display his status or simply flaunt his earnings without possessing either a house or a wife—and this was, in its own small way, a revolutionary possibility.

Domesticated men had their own commodity ensemble, centered on home appliances and hobby hardware, and for a long time there had seemed to be no alternative. A man expressed his status through the size of his car, the location of his house, and the social and sartorial graces of his wife. The wife and home might be a financial drag on a man, but it was the paraphernalia of family life that established his position in the occupational hierarchy. *Playboy*'s visionary contribution—visionary because it would still be years before a significant mass of men availed themselves of it—was to give the means of status to the single man: not the power lawn mower, but the hi-fi set in mahogany console; not the sedate, four-door Buick, but the racy little Triumph; not the well-groomed wife, but the classy companion who could be rented (for the price of drinks and dinner) one night at a time.

So through its articles, its graphics, and its advertisements *Playboy* presented, by the beginning of the sixties, something approaching a coherent program for the male rebellion: a critique of marriage, a strategy for liberation (reclaiming the indoors as a realm for masculine pleasure), and a utopian vision (defined by its unique commodity ensemble). It may not have been a revolutionary program, but it was most certainly a disruptive one. If even a fraction of *Playboy* readers had acted on it in the late fifties, the "breakdown of the family" would have occurred a full fifteen years before it was eventually announced. Hundreds of thousands of women would have been left without breadwinners or stranded in court fighting for alimony settlements. Yet, for all its potential disruptiveness, *Playboy* was immune to the standard charges leveled against male deviants. You couldn't call it anti-capitalist or un-American, because it was all about making money and spending it. Hefner even told his readers in 1963 that the *Playboy* spirit of acquisitiveness could help "put the United States back in the position of unquestioned world leadership." You *could* call it "immature," but it already called itself that, because maturity was about mortgages and life insurance and *Playboy* was about fun. Finally, it was impervious to the ultimate sanction against male rebellion—the charge of homosexuality. The playboy didn't avoid marriage because he was a little bit "queer," but, on the contrary, because he was so ebulliently, even compulsively heterosexual.

Later in the sixties critics would come up with what seemed to be the ultimately sophisticated charge against *Playboy*: It wasn't really "sexy." There was nothing erotic, *Time* wrote, about the pink-cheeked young Playmates whose every pore and perspiration drop had been air-brushed out of existence. Hefner was "puritanical" after all, and the whole thing was no more mischievous than "a Midwestern Methodist's vision of sin."[13] But the critics misunderstood *Playboy*'s historical role. *Playboy* was not the voice of the sexual revolution, which began, at least overtly, in the sixties, but of the male rebellion, which had begun in the fifties. The real message was not eroticism, but escape—literal escape, from the bondage of breadwinning. For that, the breasts and bottoms were necessary not just to sell the magazine, but to protect it. When, in the first issue, Hefner talked about staying in his apartment, listening to music, and discussing Picasso, there was the Marilyn Monroe centerfold to let you know there was nothing queer about these urbane and indoor pleasures. And when the articles railed against the responsibilities of marriage, there were the nude torsos to reassure you that the alternative was still within the bounds of heterosexuality. Sex—or Hefner's Pepsi-clean version of it—was there to legitimize what was truly subversive about *Playboy*. In every issue, every month, there was a Playmate to prove that a playboy didn't have to be a husband to be a man. ✒

SUGGESTIONS FOR WRITING

1. What do such magazines as *Playboy* teach men about women? What do they *not* reveal about women?

2. Is *Playboy's* message primarily a sexual one? If not, then what is it?

3. Are there magazines that "teach" women about men? What image of men is found in women's magazines?

---

[13]"Think Clean," *Time*, March 3, 1967, p. 76. [Au.]

THE PROBLEM THAT
HAS NO NAME

Betty Friedan

The period of American history from 1945 to 1970 or so, during which the typical occupation for a woman was that of "homemaker," was actually, considering the past two centuries, an atypical period. Women in the nineteenth and early twentieth centuries often worked outside the home. After the Second World War, many American women faced the difficult adjustment of relinquishing wartime jobs to men returning from the service. During the 1950s, as television reruns depict so vividly, one simply assumed that on any given weekday, the housewife-mother could be found at home, managing the household, fending off door-to-door salesmen, and awaiting the return of her children from school and her husband from work.

In her famous book The Feminine Mystique, *from which "The Problem That Has No Name" is taken,* **Betty Friedan** *(b. 1921) was one of the first to call attention to what could be stifling and confining about living exclusively to keep the home fires burning for family members whose lives unfolded in the world beyond. Friedan is the author of numerous books and articles that chart the progress of the recent feminist movement. She was a founding member of the National Organization for Women.*

The problem lay buried, unspoken for many years in the minds of American women. It was a strange stirring, a sense of dissatisfaction, a yearning that women suffered in the middle of the twentieth century in the United States. Each suburban wife struggled with it alone. As she made the beds, shopped for groceries, matched slipcover material, ate peanut butter sandwiches with her children, chauffeured Cub Scouts and Brownies, lay beside her husband at night—she was afraid to ask even of herself the silent question—"Is this all?"

For over fifteen years there was no word of this yearning in the millions of words written about women, for women, in all the columns, books and articles by experts telling women their role was to seek fulfillment as wives and mothers. Over and over women heard in voices of tradition and of Freudian sophistication that they could desire no greater destiny than to glory in their own femininity. . . . They were taught to pity the neurotic, unfeminine, unhappy women who wanted to be poets or physicists or presidents. They learned that truly feminine women do not want careers, higher education, political rights— the independence and the opportunities that the old-fashioned feminists fought for. . . .

By the end of the nineteen-fifties, the average marriage age of women in America dropped to 20, and was still dropping, into the teens. Fourteen million girls were engaged by 17. The proportion of women attending college in com-

THE PROBLEM THAT HAS NO NAME **217**

parison with men dropped from 47 percent in 1920 to 35 percent in 1958. A century earlier, women had fought for higher education; now girls went to college to get a husband. By the mid-fifties, 60 percent dropped out of college to marry, or because they were afraid too much education would be a marriage bar. Colleges built dormitories for "married students," but the students were almost always the husbands. A new degree was instituted for the wives—"Ph.T." (Putting Husband Through).

Then American girls began getting married in high school. And the women's magazines, deploring the unhappy statistics about these young marriages, urged that courses on marriage, and marriage counselors, be installed in the high schools. Girls started going steady at twelve and thirteen, in junior high. Manufacturers put out brassieres with false bosoms of foam rubber for little girls of ten. And an advertisement for a child's dress, sizes 3–6x, in the *New York Times* in the fall of 1960, said: "She Too Can Join the Man-Trap Set." . . .

In a New York hospital, a woman had a nervous breakdown when she found she could not breastfeed her baby. In other hospitals, women dying of cancer refused a drug which research had proved might save their lives: its side effects were said to be unfeminine. "If I have only one life, let me live it as a blonde," a larger-than-life-sized picture of a pretty, vacuous woman proclaimed from newspaper, magazine, and drugstore ads. And across America, three out of every ten women dyed their hair blonde. They ate a chalk called Metrecal, instead of food, to shrink to the size of the thin young models. Department-store buyers reported that American women, since 1939, had become three and four sizes smaller. "Women are out to fit the clothes, instead of vice-versa," one buyer said.

Interior decorators were designing kitchens with mosaic murals and original paintings, for kitchens were once again the center of women's lives. Home sewing became a million-dollar industry. Many women no longer left their homes, except to shop, chauffeur their children, or attend a social engagement with their husbands. Girls were growing up in America without ever having jobs outside the home. In the late fifties, a sociological phenomenon was suddenly remarked: a third of American women now worked, but most were no longer young and very few were pursuing careers. They were married women who held part-time jobs, selling or secretarial, to put their husbands through school, their sons through college, or to help pay the mortgage. Or they were widows supporting families. Fewer and fewer women were entering professional work. The shortages in the nursing, social work, and teaching professions caused crises in almost every American city. Concerned over the Soviet Union's lead in the space race, scientists noted that America's greatest source of unused brain-power was women. But girls would not study physics: it was "unfeminine." . . .

The suburban housewife—she was the dream image of the young American women and the envy, it was said, of women all over the world. The American housewife—freed by science and labor-saving appliances from the drudgery, the dangers of childbirth and the illnesses of her grandmother. She was healthy, beautiful, educated, concerned only about her husband, her children, her home. She had found true feminine fulfillment. As a housewife and mother, she was respected as a full and equal partner to man in his world. She was free to choose automobiles, clothes, appliances, supermarkets; she had everything that women ever dreamed of.

In the fifteen years after World War II, this mystique of feminine fulfillment became the cherished and self-perpetuating core of contemporary American culture. . . .

For over fifteen years, the words written for women, and the words women used when they talked to each other, while their husbands sat on the other side of the room and talked shop or politics or septic tanks, were about problems with their children, or how to keep their husbands happy, or improve their children's school, or cook chicken or make slipcovers. Nobody argued whether women were inferior or superior to men; they were simply different. Words like "emancipation" and "career" sounded strange and embarrassing; no one had used them for years. When a Frenchwoman named Simone de Beauvoir wrote a book called *The Second Sex,* an American critic commented that she obviously "didn't know what life was all about," and besides, she was talking about French women. The "woman problem" in America no longer existed.

If a woman had a problem in the 1950's and 1960's, she knew that something must be wrong with her marriage, or with herself. Other women were satisfied with their lives, she thought. What kind of a woman was she if she did not feel this mysterious fulfillment waxing the kitchen floor? She was so ashamed to admit her dissatisfaction that she never knew how many other women shared it. If she tried to tell her husband, he didn't understand what she was talking about. She did not really understand it herself. For over fifteen years women in America found it harder to talk about this problem than about sex. Even the psychoanalysts had no name for it. When a woman went to a psychiatrist for help, as many women did, she would say, "I'm so ashamed," or "I must be hopelessly neurotic." "I don't know what's wrong with women today," a suburban psychiatrist said uneasily. "I only know something is wrong because most of my patients happen to be women. And their problem isn't sexual." Most women with this problem did not go to see a psychoanalyst, however. "There's nothing wrong really," they kept telling themselves. "There isn't any problem."

But on an April morning in 1959, I heard a mother of four, having coffee with four other mothers in a suburban development fifteen miles from New York, say in a tone of quiet desperation, "the problem." And the others knew, without words, that she was not talking about a problem with her husband, or her children, or her home. Suddenly they realized they all shared the same problem, the problem that has no name. They began, hesitantly, to talk about it. Later, after they had picked up their children at nursery school and taken them home to nap, two of the women cried, in sheer relief, just to know they were not alone. . . .

Just what was this problem that has no name? What were the words women used when they tried to express it? Sometimes a woman would say "I feel empty somehow . . . incomplete." Or she would say, "I feel as if I don't exist." Sometimes she blotted out the feeling with a tranquilizer. Sometimes she thought the problem was with her husband, or her children, or that what she really needed was to redecorate her house, or move to a better neighborhood, or have an affair, or another baby. Sometimes, she went to a doctor with symptoms she could hardly describe: "A tired feeling . . . I get so angry with the children it scares me . . . I feel like crying without any reason." (A Cleveland doctor called it "the housewife's syndrome.") A number of women told me about great bleeding blisters that break out on their hands and arms. "I call it the housewife's blight," said a family doctor in Pennsylvania. "I see it so often lately in these young women with four, five and six children who bury themselves in their dishpans. But it isn't caused by detergent and it isn't cured by cortisone." . . .

A mother of four who left college at nineteen to get married told me:

I've tried everything women are supposed to do—hobbies, gardening, pickling, canning, being very social with my neighbors, joining committees, running PTA teas. I can do it all, and I like it, but it doesn't leave you anything to think about—any feeling of who you are. I never had any career ambitions. All I wanted was to get married and have four children. I love the kids and Bob and my home. There's no problem you can even put a name to. But I'm desperate. I begin to feel I have no personality. I'm a server of food and a putter-on of pants and a bedmaker, somebody who can be called on when you want something. But who am I?

A twenty-three-year-old mother in blue jeans said:

I ask myself why I'm so dissatisfied. I've got my health, fine children, a lovely new home, enough money. My husband has a real future as an electronics engineer. He doesn't have any of these feelings. He says maybe I need a vacation, let's go to New York for a weekend. But that isn't it. I always had this idea we should do everything together. I can't sit down and read a book alone. If the children are napping and I have one hour to myself I just walk through the house waiting for them to wake up. I don't make a move until I know where the rest of the crowd is going. It's as if ever since you were a little girl, there's always been somebody or something that will take care of your life: you parents, or college, or falling in love, or having a child, or moving to a new house. Then you wake up one morning and there's nothing to look forward to.

A young wife in a Long Island development said:

I seem to sleep so much. I don't know why I should be so tired. This house isn't nearly so hard to clean as the cold-water flat we had when I was working. The children are at school all day. It's not the work. I just don't feel alive.

In 1960, the problem that has no name burst like a boil through the image of the happy American housewife. In the television commercials the pretty housewives still beamed over their foaming dishpans and *Time's* cover story on "The Suburban Wife, an American Phenomenon" protested: "Having too good a time . . . to believe that they should be unhappy." But the actual unhappiness of the American housewife was suddenly being reported—from the *New York Times* and *Newsweek* to *Good Housekeeping* and CBS Television ("The Trapped Housewife"), although almost everybody who talked about it found some superficial reason to dismiss it. . . . Some said it was the old problem—education: more and more women had education, which naturally made them unhappy in their role as housewives. "The road from Freud to Frigidaire, from Sophocles to Spock, has turned out to be a bumpy one," reported the *New York Times* (June 28, 1960). . . .

Home economists suggested more realistic preparation for housewives, such as high-school workshops in home appliances. College educators suggested more discussion groups on home management and the family, to prepare women for the adjustment to domestic life. A spate of articles appeared in the mass magazines offering "Fifty-eight Ways to Make Your Marriage More Exciting." No month went by without a new book by a psychiatrist or sexologist offering technical advice on finding greater fulfillment through sex.

A male humorist joked in *Harper's Bazaar* (July, 1960) that the problem could be solved by taking away women's right to vote. ("In the pre-19th Amendment era, the American woman was placid, sheltered and sure of her role in American society. She left all the political decisions to her husband and he, in turn, left all the family decisions to her. Today a woman has to make both the family *and* the political decisions, and it's too much for her.")

A number of educators suggested seriously that women no longer be admitted to the four-year colleges and universities: in the growing college crisis, the education which girls could not use as housewives was more urgently needed than ever by boys to do the work of the atomic age.

The problem was also dismissed with drastic solutions no one could take seriously. (A woman writer proposed in *Harper's* that women be drafted for compulsory service as nurses' aides and baby sitters.) And it was smoothed over with the age-old panaceas: "love is their answer," "the only answer is inner help," "the secret of completeness—children," "a private means of intellectual fulfillment," "to cure this toothache of the spirit—the simple formula of handing one's self and one's will over to God."[1]

The problem was dismissed by telling the housewife she doesn't realize how lucky she is—her own boss, no time clock, no junior executive gunning for her job. . . .

The problem was also, and finally, dismissed by shrugging that there are no solutions: this is what being a woman means, and what is wrong with American women that they can't accept their role gracefully? As *Newsweek* put it (March 7, 1960):

---

[1]See the Seventy-fifth Anniversary Issue of *Good Housekeeping*, May, 1960, "The Gift of Self," a symposium by Margaret Mead, Jessamyn West, *et al.*

She is dissatisfied with a lot that women of other lands can only dream of. Her discontent is deep, pervasive, and impervious to the superficial remedies which are offered at every hand. . . . An army of professional explorers have already charted the major sources of trouble. . . . From the beginning of time, the female cycle has defined and confined woman's role. As Freud was credited with saying: "Anatomy is destiny." Though no group of women has ever pushed these natural restrictions as far as the American wife, it seems that she still cannot accept them with good grace. . . . A young mother with a beautiful family, charm, talent and brains is apt to dismiss her role apologetically. "What do I do?" you hear her say. "Why nothing. I'm just a housewife." A good education, it seems, has given this paragon among women an understanding of the value of everything except her own worth. . . .

The alternative was a choice that few women would contemplate. In the sympathetic words of the *New York Times:* "All admit to being deeply frustrated at times by the lack of privacy, the physical burden, the routine of family life, the confinement of it. However, none would give up her home and family if she had the choice to make again." . . .

The year American women's discontent boiled over, it was also reported *(Look)* that the more than 21,000,000 American women who are single, widowed, or divorced do not cease even after fifty their frenzied, desperate search for a man. And the search begins early—for seventy percent of all American women now marry before they are twenty-four. A pretty twenty-five-year-old secretary took thirty-five different jobs in six months in the futile hope of finding a husband. Women were moving from one political club to another, taking evening courses in accounting or sailing, learning to play golf or ski, joining a number of churches in succession, going to bars alone, in their ceaseless search for a man.

Of the growing thousands of women currently getting psychiatric help in the United States, the married ones were reported dissatisfied with their marriages, the unmarried ones suffering from anxiety and, finally, depression. Strangely, a number of psychiatrists stated that, in their experience, unmarried women patients were happier than married ones. . . .

Even so, most men, and some women, still did not know that this problem was real. But those who had faced it honestly knew that all the superficial remedies, the sympathetic advice, the scolding words and the cheering words were somehow drowning the problem in unreality. A bitter laugh was beginning to be heard from American women. They were admired, envied, pitied, theorized over until they were sick of it, offered drastic solutions or silly choices that no one could take seriously. They got all kinds of advice from the growing armies of marriage and child-guidance counselors, psychotherapists, and armchair psychologists, on how to adjust to their role as housewives. No other road to fulfillment was offered to American women in the middle of the twentieth century. Most adjusted to their role and suffered or ignored the problem that has no name. It can be less painful, for a woman, not to hear the strange, dissatisfied voice stirring within her.

It is no longer possible to ignore that voice, to dismiss the desperation of so many American women. This is not what being a woman means, no matter what the experts say. For human suffering there is a reason; perhaps the reason has not been found because the right questions have not been asked, or pressed far enough. I do not accept the answer that there is no problem because American women have luxuries that women in other times and lands never dreamed of; part of the strange newness of the problem is that it cannot be understood in terms of the age-old material problems of man: poverty, sickness, hunger, cold. The women who suffer this problem have a hunger that food cannot fill. It persists in women whose husbands are struggling interns and law clerks, or prosperous doctors and lawyers; in wives of workers and executives who make $5,000 a year or $50,000. . . .

It is no longer possible today to blame the problem on loss of femininity: to say that education and independence and equality with men have made American women unfeminine. I have heard so many women try to deny this dissatisfied voice within themselves because it does not fit the pretty picture of femininity the experts have given them. I think, in fact, that this is the first clue to the mystery: the problem cannot be understood in the generally accepted terms by which scientists have studied women, doctors have treated them, counselors have advised them, and writers have written about them. . . .

Are the women who finished college, the women who once had dreams beyond housewifery, the ones who suffer the most? According to the experts they are, but listen to these four women:

> My days are all busy, and dull, too. All I ever do is mess around. I get up at eight—I make breakfast, so I do the dishes, have lunch, do some more dishes and some laundry and cleaning in the afternoon. Then it's supper dishes and I get to sit down a few minutes before the children have to be sent to bed. . . . That's all there is to my day. It's just like any other wife's day. Humdrum. The biggest time, I am chasing kids.

> Ye Gods, what do I do with my time? Well, I get up at six. I get my son dressed and then give him breakfast. After that I wash dishes and bathe and feed the baby. Then I get lunch and while the children nap, I sew or mend or iron and do all the other things I can't get done before noon. Then I cook supper for the family and my husband watches TV while I do the dishes. After I get the children to bed, I set my hair and then I go to bed.

> The problem is always being the children's mommy, or the minister's wife and never being myself.

> A film made of any typical morning in my house would look like an old Marx Brothers' comedy. I wash the dishes, rush the older children off to school, dash out in the yard to cultivate the chrysanthemums, run back to make a phone call about a committee meeting, help the youngest child build a blockhouse, spend fifteen minutes skimming the newspapers so I can be well-informed, then scamper down to the washing machines where my thrice-

*weekly laundry includes enough clothes to keep a primitive village going for
an entire year. By noon I'm ready for a padded cell. Very little of what I've
done has been really necessary or important. Outside pressures lash me
through the day. Yet I look upon myself as one of the more relaxed housewives in the neighborhood. Many of my friends are even more frantic. In the
past sixty years we have come full circle and the American housewife is once
again trapped in a squirrel cage. If the cage is now a modern plate-glass-and
broadloom ranch house or a convenient modern apartment, the situation is
no less painful than when her grandmother sat over an embroidery hoop in
her gilt-and-plush parlor and muttered angrily about women's rights.*

The first two women never went to college. They live in developments in
Levittown, New Jersey, and Tacoma, Washington, and were interviewed by a
team of sociologists studying workingmen's wives.[2] The third, a minister's wife,
wrote on the fifteenth reunion questionnaire of her college that she never had
any career ambitions, but wishes now she had.[3] The fourth, who has a Ph.D. in
anthropology, is today a Nebraska housewife with three children.[4] Their words
seem to indicate that housewives of all educational levels suffer the same feeling of desperation.

The fact is that no one today is muttering angrily about "women's rights,"
even though more and more women have gone to college. In a recent study of
all the classes that have graduated from Barnard College,[5] a significant minority of earlier graduates blamed their education for making them want "rights,"
later classes blamed their education for giving them career dreams, but recent
graduates blamed the college for making them feel it was not enough simply to
be a housewife and mother; they did not want to feel guilty if they did not read
books or take part in community activities. But if education is not the cause of
the problem, the fact that education somehow festers in these women may be
a clue.

If the secret of feminine fulfillment is having children, never have so many
women, with the freedom to choose, had so many children, in so few years, so
willingly. If the answer is love, never have women searched for love with such
determination. And yet there is a growing suspicion that the problem may not
be sexual, though it must somehow be related to sex. I have heard from many
doctors evidence of new sexual problems between man and wife—sexual hunger in wives so great their husbands cannot satisfy it. "We have made women

---

[2]Lee Rainwater, Richard P. Coleman, and Gerald Handel, *Workingman's Wife*, New York,
1959.

[3]Betty Friedan, "If One Generation Can Ever Tell Another," *Smith Alumnae Quarterly*,
Northhampton, Mass., Winter, 1961. I first became aware of "the problem that has no name" and
its possible relationship to what I finally called "the feminine mystique" in 1957, when I prepared
an intensive questionnaire and conducted a survey of my own Smith College classmates fifteen
years after graduation. This questionnaire was later used by alumnae classes of Radcliffe and other
women's colleges with similar results.

[4]Than and Juen Robbins, "Why Young Mothers Feel Trapped," *Redbook*, September, 1960.

[5]Marian Freda Poverman, "Alumnae on Parade," *Barnard Alumnae Magazine*, July, 1957.

a sex creature," said a psychiatrist at the Margaret Sanger marriage counseling clinic. . . . Why is there such a market for books and articles offering sexual advice? The kind of sexual orgasm which Kinsey found in statistical plentitude in the recent generations of American women does not seem to make this problem go away.

On the contrary, new neuroses are being seen among women—and problems as yet unnamed as neuroses—which Freud and his followers did not predict, with physical symptoms, anxieties, and defense mechanisms equal to those caused by sexual repression. And strange new problems are being reported in the growing generations of children whose mothers were always there, driving them around, helping them with their homework—an inability to endure pain or discipline or pursue any self-sustained goal of any sort, a devastating boredom with life. . . .

A White House conference was held on the physical and muscular deterioration of American children: were they being over-nurtured? Sociologists noted the astounding organization of suburban children's lives: the lessons, parties, entertainments, play and study groups organized for them. . . .

Can the problem that has no name be somehow related to the domestic routine of the housewife? When a woman tries to put the problem into words, she often merely describes the daily life she leads. What is there in this recital of comfortable domestic detail that could possibly cause such a feeling of desperation? Is she trapped simply by the enormous demands of her role as modern housewife: wife, mistress, mother, nurse, consumer, cook, chauffeur; expert on interior decoration, child care, appliance repair, furniture refinishing, nutrition, and education? . . . She has no time to read books, only magazines; even if she had time, she has lost the power to concentrate. At the end of the day, she is so terribly tired that sometimes her husband has to take over and put the children to bed.

This terrible tiredness took so many women to doctors in the 1950's that one decided to investigate it. He found, surprisingly, that his patients suffering from "housewife's fatigue" slept more than an adult needed to sleep—as much as ten hours a day—and that the actual energy they expended on housework did not tax their capacity. The real problem must be something else, he decided—perhaps a boredom. Some doctors told their women patients they must get out of the house for a day, treat themselves to a movie in town. Others prescribed tranquilizers. Many suburban housewives were taking tranquilizers like cough drops. . . .

It is easy to see the concrete details that trap the suburban housewife, the continual demands on her time. But the chains that bind her in her trap are chains in her own mind and spirit. They are chains made up of mistaken ideas and misinterpreted facts, of incomplete truths and unreal choices. They are not easily seen and not easily shaken off.

How can any woman see the whole truth within the bounds of her own life? How can she believe that voice inside herself, when it denies the conventional, accepted truths by which she has been living? And yet the women I have talked to, who are finally listening to that inner voice, seem in some incredible way to be groping through to a truth that has defied the experts. . . .

I began to see in a strange new light the American return to early marriage and the large families that are causing the population explosion; the recent movement to natural childbirth and breastfeeding, suburban conformity, and the new neuroses, character pathologies and sexual problems being reported by the doctors. I began to see new dimensions to old problems that have long been taken for granted among women: menstrual difficulties, sexual frigidity, promiscuity, pregnancy fears, childbirth depression, the high incidence of emotional breakdown and suicide among women in their twenties and thirties, the menopause crises, the so-called passivity and immaturity of American men, the discrepancy between women's tested intellectual abilities in childhood and their adult achievement, the changing incidence of adult sexual orgasm in American women, and persistent problems in psychotherapy and in women's education.

If I am right, the problem that has no name stirring in the minds of so many American women today is not a matter of loss of femininity or too much education, or the demands of domesticity. It is far more important than anyone recognizes. It is the key to these other new and old problems which have been torturing women and their husbands and children, and puzzling their doctors and educators for years. It may well be the key to our future as a nation and a culture. We can no longer ignore the voice within women that says: "I want something more than my husband and my children and my home." ✒

SUGGESTIONS FOR WRITING

1. Friedan places particular emphasis on the pressures and challenges of motherhood. Argue whether or not motherhood is something every woman should experience.

2. For what kinds of social roles has women's education, then and now, prepared them? Compare the situation Friedan describes what we find today.

3. Do most women still look at their lives and ask themselves silently, "Is this all?" How has the entry of more women into the work force made this response less likely?

4. Must housework and motherhood always produce the response Friedan describes? What can make this role more satisfying? What are the particular cultural values that mothers, by definition, should impart to their families?

NOTES ON CLASS

Paul Fussell

For complex reasons, Americans are strikingly reticent concerning the theme of social class. This, after all, is reputed to be the "land of opportunity," and our fundamental sense of our nationhood is linked to a desire to be distinguished from traditional European societies marked by rigid social hierarchies. At one time, universal public education seemed to hold out the promise that those class distinctions persisting in American society would become increasingly blurred. The author of "Notes on Class" thus goes against the grain of common American sense by insisting that class stratification is a fact of life in the United States. He further argues that the specific classes inhabit highly distinct spheres, guaranteeing little or no knowledge of others' circumstances.

Paul Fussell (b. 1924), was wounded as an infantry officer in World War II. He returned to Harvard University to earn a Ph.D. in English literature. He is a native of California and the product of a wealthy family. For many years he taught at Rutgers University, and then moved to the University of Pennsylvania. He is the author of the books The Great War and Modern Memory *(1975) and* Wartime: Understanding and Behavior in the Second World War *(1989), written to deal with the two world wars using literature and the testimony of front-line troops. In 1983, he published* Class: A Guide Through the American Status System, *a fuller explanation of the themes of this selection, which first appeared in* The Boy Scout Handbook and Other Observations *(1982).*

If the dirty little secret used to be sex, now it is the facts about social class. No subject today is more likely to offend. Over thirty years go Dr. Kinsey generated considerable alarm by disclosing that despite appearance one-quarter of the male population had enjoyed at least one homosexual orgasm. A similar alarm can be occasioned today by asserting that despite the much-discussed mechanism of "social mobility" and the constant redistribution of income in this country, it is virtually impossible to break out of the social class in which one has been nurtured. Bad news for the ambitious as well as the bogus, but there it is.

Defining class is difficult, as sociologists and anthropologists have learned. The more data we feed into the machines, the less likely it is that significant formulations will emerge. What follows here is based not on interviews, questionnaires, or any kind of quantitative technique but on perhaps a more trustworthy method—perception. Theory may inform us that there are three classes in America, high, middle, and low. Perception will tell us that there are at least nine, which I would designate and arrange like this:

Top Out-of-Sight
Upper
Upper Middle

Middle
High-Proletarian
Mid-Proletarian
Low-Proletarian

Destitute
Bottom Out-of-Sight

In addition, there is a floating class with no permanent location in this hierarchy. We can call it Class X. It consists of well-to-do hippies, "artists," "writers" (who write nothing), floating bohemians, politicians out of office, disgraced athletic coaches, residers abroad, rock stars, "celebrities," and the shrewder sort of spies.

The quasi-official division of the population into three economic classes called high-, middle-, and low-income groups rather misses the point, because as a class indicator the amount of money is not as important as the source. Important distinctions at both the top and bottom of the class scale arise less from degree of affluence than from the people or institutions to whom one is beholden for support. For example, the main thing distinguishing the top three classes from each other is the amount of money inherited in relation to the amount currently earned. The Top Out-of-Sight Class (Rockefellers, du Ponts, Mellons, Fords, Whitneys) lives on inherited capital entirely. Its money is like the hats of the Boston ladies who, asked where they got them, answer, "Oh, we *have* our hats." No one whose money, no matter how ample, comes from his own work, like film stars, can be a member of the Top Out-of-Sights, even if the size of his income and the extravagance of his expenditure permit him temporary social access to it.

Since we expect extremes to meet, we are not surprised to find the very lowest class, Bottom Out-of-Sight, similar to the highest in one crucial respect: it is given its money and kept sort of afloat not by its own efforts but by the welfare machinery or the prison system. Members of the Top Out-of-Sight Class sometimes earn some money, as directors or board members of philanthropic or even profitable enterprises, but the amount earned is laughable in relation to the amount already possessed. Membership in the Top Out-of-Sight Class depends on the ability to flourish without working at all, and it is this that suggests a curious brotherhood between those at the top and the bottom of the scale.

It is this also that distinguishes the Upper Class from its betters. It lives on both inherited money and a salary from attractive, if usually slight, work, without which, even if it could survive and even flourish, it would feel bored and a little ashamed. The next class down, the Upper Middle, may possess virtually as much as the two above it. The difference is that it has earned most of it, in law, medicine, oil, real estate, or even the more honorific forms of trade. The Upper Middles are afflicted with a bourgeois sense of shame, a conviction that to live on the earnings of others, even forebears, is not entirely nice.

The Out-of-Sight Classes at top and bottom have something else in common: they are literally all but invisible (hence their name). The façades of Top Out-of-Sight houses are never seen from the street, and such residences (like Rockefeller's upstate New York premises) are often hidden away deep in the hills, safe from envy and its ultimate attendants, confiscatory taxation and finally expropriation. The Bottom Out-of-Sight Class is equally invisible. When not hidden away in institutions or claustrated in monasteries, lamaseries, or communes, it is hiding from creditors, deceived bail-bondsmen, and merchants intent on repossessing cars and furniture. (This class is visible briefly in one place, in the spring on the streets of New York City, but after this ritual yearly show of itself it disappears again.) When you pass a house with a would-be impressive façade addressing the street, you know it is occupied by a mere member of the Upper or Upper Middle Class. The White House is an example. Its residents, even on those occasions when they are Kennedys, can never be classified as Top Out-of-Sight but only Upper Class. The house is simply too conspicuous, and temporary residence there usually constitutes a come-down for most of its occupants. It is a hopelessly Upper- or Upper-Middle-Class place.

Another feature of both Top and Bottom Out-of-Sight Classes is their anxiety to keep their names out of the papers, and this too suggests that socially the President is always rather vulgar. All the classes in between Top and Bottom Out-of-Sight slaver for personal publicity (monograms on shirts, inscribing one's name on lawn-mowers and power tools, etc.), and it is this lust to be known almost as much as income that distinguishes them from their Top and Bottom neighbors. The High- and Mid-Prole Classes can be recognized immediately by their pride in advertising their physical presence, a way of saying, "Look! We pay our bills and have a known place in the community, and you can find us there any time." Thus hypertrophied house-numbers on the front, or house numbers written "Two Hundred Five" ("Two Hundred and Five" is worse) instead of 205, or flamboyant house or family names blazoned on façades, like "The Willows" or "The Polnickis."

(If you go behind the façade into the house itself, you will find a fairly trustworthy class indicator in the kind of wood visible there. The top three classes invariably go in for hardwoods for doors and paneling; the Middle and High-Prole Classes, pine, either plain or "knotty." The knotty-pine "den" is an absolute stigma of the Middle Class, one never to be overcome or disguised by temporarily affected higher usages. Below knotty pine there is plywood.)

Façade study is a badly neglected anthropological field. As we work down from the (largely white-painted) banklike façades of the Upper and Upper Middle Classes, we encounter such Middle and Prole conventions as these, which I rank in order of social status:

Middle

1. A potted tree on either side of the front door, and the more pointy and symmetrical the better.

2. A large rectangular picture-window in a split-level "ranch" house, displaying a table-lamp between two side curtains. The cellophane on the lampshade must be visibly inviolate.
3. Two chairs, usually metal with pipe arms, disposed on the front porch as a "conversation group," in stubborn defiance of the traffic thundering past.

High-Prole

4. Religious shrines in the garden, which if small and understated, are slightly higher class than

Mid-Prole

5. Plaster gnomes and flamingos, and blue or lavender shiny spheres supported by fluted cast-concrete pedestals.

Low-Prole

6. Defunct truck tires painted white and enclosing flower beds. (Auto tires are a grade higher.)
7. Flower-bed designs worked in dead light bulbs or the butts of disused beer bottles.

The Destitute have no façades to decorate, and of course the Bottom Out-of-Sights, being invisible, have none either, although both these classes can occasionally help others decorate theirs—painting tires white on an hourly basis, for example, or even watering and fertilizing the potted trees of the Middle Class. Class X also does not decorate its façades, hoping to stay loose and unidentifiable, ready to relocate and shape-change the moment it sees that its cover has been penetrated.

In this list of façade conventions an important principle emerges. Organic materials have higher status than metal or plastic. We should take warning from Sophie Portnoy's[1] aluminum venetian blinds, which are also lower than wood because the slats are curved, as if "improved," instead of classically flat. The same principle applies, as *The Preppy Handbook* has shown so effectively, to clothing fabrics, which must be cotton or wool, never Dacron or anything of that prole kind. In the same way, yachts with wood hulls, because they must be repaired or replaced (at high cost) more often, are classier than yachts with fiberglass hulls, no matter how shrewdly merchandised. Plastic hulls are cheaper and more practical, which is precisely why they lack class.

As we move down the scale, income of course decreases, but income is less important to class than other seldom-invoked measurements: for example, the

---

[1]**Sophie Portnoy** A character in Philip Roth's novel *Portnoy's Complaint* (1969).

degree to which one's work is supervised by an omnipresent immediate superior. The more free from supervision, the higher the class, which is why a dentist ranks higher than a mechanic working under a foreman in a large auto shop, even if he makes considerably more money than the dentist. The two trades may be thought equally dirty: it is the dentist's freedom from supervision that helps confer class upon him. Likewise, a high-school teacher obliged to file weekly "lesson plans" with a principal or "curriculum co-ordinator" thereby occupies a class position lower than a tenured professor, who reports to no one, even though the high-school teacher may be richer, smarter, and nicer. (Supervisors and Inspectors are titles that go with public schools, post offices, and police departments: the student of class will need to know no more.) It is largely because they must report that even the highest members of the naval and military services lack social status: they all have designated supervisors—even the Chairman of the Joint Chiefs of Staff has to report to the President.

Class is thus defined less by bare income than by constraints and insecurities. It is defined also by habits and attitudes. Take television watching. The Top Out-of-Sight Class doesn't watch at all. It owns the companies and pays others to monitor the thing. It is also entirely devoid of intellectual or even emotional curiosity: it *has* its ideas the way it has its money. The Upper Class does look at television but it prefers Camp offerings, like the films of Jean Harlow or Jon Hall. The Upper Middle Class regards TV as vulgar except for the high-minded emissions of National Educational Television, which it watches avidly, especially when, like the Shakespeare series, they are the most incompetently directed and boring. Upper Middles make a point of forbidding children to watch more than an hour a day and worry a lot about violence in society and sugar in cereal. The Middle Class watches, preferring the more "beautiful" kinds of non-body-contact sports like tennis or gymnastics or figure-skating (the music is a redeeming feature here). With High-, Mid-, and Low-Proles we find heavy viewing of the soaps in the daytime and rugged body-contact sports (football, hockey, boxing) in the evening. The lower one is located in the Prole classes the more likely one is to watch "Bowling for Dollars" and "Wonder Woman" and "The Hulk" and when choosing a game show to prefer "Joker's Wild" to "The Family Feud," whose jokes are sometimes incomprehensible. Destitutes and Bottom Out-of-Sights have in common a problem involving choice. Destitutes usually "own" about three color sets, and the problem is which three programs to run at once. Bottom Out-of-Sights exercise no choice at all, the decisions being made for them by correctional or institutional personnel.

The time when the evening meal is consumed defines class better than, say, the presence or absence on the table of ketchup bottles and ashtrays shaped like little toilets enjoining the diners to "Put Your Butts Here." Destitutes and Bottom Out-of-Sights eat dinner at 5:30, for the Prole staff on which they depend must clean up and be out roller-skating or bowling early in the evening. Thus Proles eat at 6:00 or 6:30. The Middles eat at 7:00, the Upper Middles at 7:30 or, if very ambitious, at 8:00. The Upper and Top Out-of-Sights dine at 8:30 or 9:00 or even later, after nightly protracted "cocktail" sessions lasting usually around two hours. Sometimes they forget to eat at all.

Similarly, the physical appearance of the various classes defines them fairly accurately. Among the top four classes thin is good, and the bottom two classes appear to ape this usage, although down there thin is seldom a matter of choice. It is the three Prole classes that tend to fat, partly as a result of their use of convenience foods and plenty of beer. These are the classes too where anxiety about slipping down a rung causes nervous overeating, resulting in fat that can be rationalized as advertising the security of steady wages and the ability to "eat out" often. Even "Going Out for Breakfast" is not unthinkable for Proles, if we are to believe that they respond to the McDonald's TV ads as they're supposed to. A recent magazine ad for a diet book aimed at Proles stigmatizes a number of erroneous assumptions about body weight, proclaiming with some inelegance that "They're all a crock." Among such vulgar errors is the proposition that "All Social Classes Are Equally Overweight." This the ad rejects by noting quite accurately:

> Your weight is an advertisement of your social standing. A century ago, corpulence was a sign of success. But no more. Today it is the badge of the lower-middle-class, where obesity is four times more prevalent than it is among the upper-middle and middle classes.

It is not just four times more prevalent. It is at least four times more visible, as any observer can testify who has witnessed Prole women perambulating shopping malls in their bright, very tight jersey trousers. Not just obesity but the flaunting of obesity is the Prole sign, as if the object were to give maximum aesthetic offense to the higher classes and thus achieve a form of revenge.

Another physical feature with powerful class meaning is the wearing of plaster casts on legs and ankles by members of the top three classes. These casts, a sort of white badge of honor, betoken stylish mishaps with frivolous but costly toys like horses, skis, snowmobiles, and mopeds. They signify a high level of conspicuous waste in a social world where questions of unpayable medical bills or missed working days do not apply. But in the matter of clothes, the Top Out-of-Sight is different from both Upper and Upper Middle Classes. It prefers to appear in new clothes, whereas the class just below it prefers old clothes. Likewise, all three Prole classes make much of new garments, with the highest possible polyester content. The question does not arise in the same form with Destitutes and Bottom Out-of-Sights. They wear used clothes, the thrift shop and prison supply room serving as their Bonwit's and Korvette's.

This American class system is very hard for foreigners to master, partly because most foreigners imagine that since America was founded by the British it must retain something of British institutions. But our class system is more subtle than the British, more a matter of gradations than of blunt divisions, like the binary distinction between a gentleman and a cad. This seems to lack plausibility here. One seldom encounters in the United States the sort of absolute prohibitions which (half-comically, to be sure) one is asked to believe define the gentleman in England. Like these:

A gentleman never wears brown shoes in the city, or
A gentleman never wears a green suit, or
A gentleman never has soup at lunch, or
A gentleman never uses a comb, or
A gentleman never smells of anything but tar, or
"No gentleman can fail to admire Bellini"

—W. H. Auden.

In America it seems to matter much less the way you present yourself—green, brown, neat, sloppy, scented—than what your backing is—that is, where you money comes from. What the upper orders display here is no special uniform but the kind of psychological security they derive from knowing that others recognize their freedom from petty anxieties and trivial prohibitions.

"Language most shows a man," Ben Jonson used to say. "Speak, that I may see thee." As all acute conservatives like Jonson know, dictional behavior is a powerful signal of a firm class line. Nancy Mitford so indicated in her hilarious essay of 1955, "The English Aristocracy," based in part on Professor Alan S. C. Ross's more sober study "Linguistic Class-Indicators in Present-Day English." Both Mitford and Ross were interested in only one class demarcation, the one dividing the English Upper Class ("U," in their shorthand) from all below it ("non-U"). Their main finding was that euphemism and genteelism are vulgar. People who are socially secure risk nothing by calling a spade a spade, and indicate their top-dog status by doing so as frequently as possible. Thus the U-word is *rich*, the non-U *wealthy*. What U-speakers call *false teeth* non-U's call *dentures*. The same with *wigs* and *hairpieces*, *dying* and *passing away* (or *over*).

For Mitford, linguistic assaults from below are sometimes so shocking that the only kind reaction of a U-person is silence. It is "the only possible U-response," she notes, "to many embarrassing modern situations: the ejaculation of 'cheers' before drinking, for example, or 'It was so nice seeing you' after saying goodbye. In silence, too, one must endure the use of the Christian name by comparative strangers. . . ." In America, although there are more classes distinguishable here, a linguistic polarity is as visible as in England. Here U-speech (or our equivalent of it) characterizes some Top Out-of-Sights, Uppers, Upper Middles, and Class X's. All below is a waste land of genteelism and jargon and pretentious mispronunciation, pathetic evidence of upward social scramble and its hazards. Down below, the ear is bad and no one has been trained to listen. Culture words especially are the downfall of the aspiring. Sometimes it is diphthongs that invite disgrace, as in *be-yóu-ti-ful*. Sometimes the aspirant rushes full-face into disaster by flourishing those secret class indicators, the words *exquisite* and *despicable*, which, like another secret sign, *patina*, he (and of course she as often) stresses on the middle syllable instead of the first. High-class names from cultural history are a frequent cause of betrayal, especially if they are British, like Henry Purcell. In America non-U speakers are fond of usages like "Between he and I." Recalling vaguely that mentioning oneself last, as in "He and I were there," is thought gentlemanly, they apply that principle uniformly, to the entire destruction of the objective case. There's also a problem with *like*. They remember something about the dangers of illiteracy its use invites, and hope to stay out of trouble by always using *as* instead, finally saying things like "He looks as his father." These contortions are common among young (usually insurance or computer) trainees, raised on Leon Uris[2] and *Playboy*, most of them Mid- or High-Proles pounding on the firmly shut doors of the Middle Class. They are the careful, dark-suited first-generation aspirants to American respectability and (hopefully, as they would put it) power. Together with their deployment of the anomalous nominative case on all occasions goes their preference for jargon (you can hear them going at it on airplanes) like *parameters* and *guidelines* and *bottom lines* and *funding, dialogue, interface,* and *lifestyles*. Their world of language is one containing little more than smokescreens and knowing innovations. "Do we gift the Johnsons, dear?" the corporate wife will ask the corporate husband at Christmas time.

Just below these people, down among the Mid- and Low-Proles, the complex sentence gives trouble. It is here that we get sentences beginning with elaborate pseudo-genteel participles like "Being that it was a cold day, the furnace was on." All classes below those peopled by U-speakers find the gerund out of reach and are thus forced to multiply words and say, "The people in front of him at the theater got mad due to the fact that he talked so much" instead of "His talking at the theater annoyed the people in front." (But *people* is not really right: *individuals* is the preferred term with non-U speakers. Grander, somehow.) It is also in the domain of the Mid- and Low-Prole that the double negative comes into its own as well as the superstitious avoidance of *lying* because it may be taken to imply telling untruths. People are thus depicted as always *laying* on the beach, the bed, the grass, the sidewalk, and without the slightest suggestion of their performing sexual exhibitions. A similar unconscious inhibition determines that *set* replace *sit* on all occasions, lest low excremental implications be inferred. The ease with which *sit* can be interchanged with the impolite word is suggested in a Second World War anecdote told by General Matthew Ridgway. Coming upon an unidentifiable head and shoulders peeping out of a ditch near the German border, he shouted, "Put up your hands, you son of a bitch!," to be answered, so he reports, "Aaah, go sit in your hat."

All this is evidence of a sad fact. A deep class gulf opens between two current generations: the older one that had some Latin at school or college and was taught rigorous skeptical "English," complete with the diagramming of sentences; and the younger one taught to read by the optimistic look-say method and encouraged to express itself—as the saying goes—so that its sincerity and well of ideas suffer no violation. This new generation is unable to perceive the number of syllables in a word and cannot spell and is baffled by all questions of etymology (it thinks *chauvinism* has something to do with gender aggressions). It cannot write either, for it has never been subjected to tuition in the sort of English sentence structure which resembles the sonata in being not natural but artificial, not innate but mastered. Because of its misspent, victimized youth,

---

[2]**Leon Uris** Popular American novelist, author of *Exodus* (1958) and *Trinity* (1976).

this generation is already destined to fill permanently the middle-to-low slots in the corporate society without ever quite understanding what devilish mechanism has prevented it from ascending. The disappearance of Latin as an adjunct to the mastery of English can be measured by the rapid replacement of words like *continuing* by solecisms like *ongoing*. A serious moment in cultural history occurred a few years ago when gasoline trucks changed the warning word on the rear from *Inflammable* to *Flammable*. Public education had apparently produced a population which no longer knew *In-* as an intensifier. That this happened at about the moment when every city was rapidly running up a "Cultural Center" might make us laugh, if we don't cry first. In another few generations Latinate words will be found only in learned writing, and the spoken language will have returned to the state it was in before the revival of learning. Words like *intellect* and *curiosity* and *devotion* and *study* will have withered away together with the things they denote.

There's another linguistic class-line, dividing those who persist in honoring the nineteenth-century convention that advertising, if not commerce itself, is reprehensible and not at all to be cooperated with, and those proud to think of themselves not as skeptics but as happy consumers, fulfilled when they can image themselves as functioning members of a system by responding to advertisements. For U-persons a word's succeeding in an ad is a compelling reason never to use it. But possessing no other source of idiom and no extra-local means of criticizing it, the subordinate classes are pleased to appropriate the language of advertising for personal use, dropping brand names all the time and saying things like "They have some lovely fashions in that store." In the same way they embrace all subprofessional euphemisms gladly and employ them proudly, adverting without irony to hair stylists, sanitary engineers, and funeral directors in complicity with the consumer world which cynically casts them as its main victims. They see nothing funny in paying a high price for an article and then, after a solemn pause, receiving part of it back in the form of a "rebate." Trapped in a world wholly defined by the language of consumption and the hype, they harbor restively, defending themselves against actuality by calling habitual drunkards *people with alcohol problems*, madness *mental illness*, drug use *drug abuse*, building lots *homesites*, houses *homes* ("They live in a lovely $250,000 home"), and drinks *beverages*.

Those delighted to employ the vacuous commercial "Have a nice day" and those wouldn't think of saying it belong manifestly to different classes, no matter how we define them, and it is unthinkable that those classes will ever melt. Calvin Coolidge said that the business of America is business. Now apparently the business of America is having a nice day. Tragedy? Don't need it. Irony? Take it away. Have a nice day. Have a nice day. A visiting Englishman of my acquaintance, a U-speaker if there ever was one, has devised the perfect U- response to "Have a nice day": "Thank you," he says, "but I have other plans." The same ultimate divide separate the two classes who say respectively when introduced, "How do you do?" and "Pleased to meet you." There may be comity between those who think *prestigious* a classy word and those who don't, but it won't survive much strain, like relations between those who think *momentarily* means in a moment (airline captain over a loudspeaker: "We'll be taking off momentarily, folks") and those who know it means for a moment. Members of these two classes can sit in adjoining seats on the plane and get along fine (although there's a further division between those who talk to their neighbors in planes and elevators and those who don't), but once the plane has emptied, they will proceed toward different destinations. It's the same with those who conceive that *type* is an adjective ("He's a very classy type person") and those who know it's only a noun or verb.

The pretense that either person can feel at ease in the presence of the other is an essential element of the presiding American fiction. Despite the lowness of the metaphor, the idea of the melting pot is high-minded and noble enough, but empirically it will be found increasingly unconvincing. It is our different language habits as much as anything that makes us, as the title of Richard Polenberg's book puts it, *One Nation Divisible.*

Some people invite constant class trouble because they believe the official American publicity about these matters. The official theory, which experience is constantly disproving, is that one can earn one's way out of his original class. Richard Nixon's behavior indicated dramatically that this is not so. The sign of the Upper Class to which he aspired is total psychological security, expressed in loose carriage, saying what one likes, and imperviousness to what others think. Nixon's vast income from law and politics—his San Clemente property aped the style of the Upper but not the Top Out-of-Sight Class, for everyone knew where it was, and he wanted them to know—could not alleviate his original awkwardness and meanness of soul or his nervousness about the impression he was making, an affliction allied to his instinct for cunning and duplicity. Hammacher Schlemmer might have had him specifically in mind as the consumer of their recently advertised "Champagne Recork": "This unusual stopper keeps 'bubbly' sprightly, sparkling after uncorking ceremony is over. Gold electro-plated." I suspect that it is some of these same characteristics that made Edward Kennedy often seem so inauthentic a member of the Upper Class. (He's not Top Out-of-Sight because he chooses to augment his inheritance by attractive work.)

What, then marks the higher classes? Primarily a desire for privacy, if not invisibility, and a powerful if eccentric desire for freedom. It is this instinct for freedom that may persuade us that inquiring into the American class system this way is an enterprise not entirely facetious. Perhaps after all the whole thing has something, just something, to do with ethics and aesthetics. Perhaps a term like *gentleman* still retains some meanings which are not just sartorial and mannerly. Freedom and grace and independence: it would be nice to believe those words still mean something, and it would be interesting if the reality of the class system—and everyone, after all, hopes to rise—should turn out to be a way we pay those notions a due if unwitting respect.

SUGGESTIONS FOR WRITING

1. To what extent do you think of yourself as a member of a social class? Describe an event that made you aware of the realities of class.

2. If you feel that class divisions are unhealthy in our nation, how should we deal with them?

3. Fussell uses a number of examples to characterize the privileged class. If you were writing an essay on "class," what examples would you cite?

PÂTÉ POVERTY

Katy Butler

We've all heard comments on the "baby boomers," those Americans born between 1946 and 1956 who crowded into schools, overwhelmed the campuses of the late 1960s and early 1970s, and found themselves competing fiercely for jobs and what was left of the "good life." Many baby boomers, as **Katy Butler** *demonstrates, have come to experience the disillusionment of diminishing expectations. The more highly educated ones often find themselves living out the cliche of "champagne tastes with beer pocketbooks."*

This paints a bleak picture, and certainly historians of revolution have argued convincingly that social unrest is commonly sparked by persons experiencing "downward" social mobility. At the same time, Butler detects some healthy aspects of this coming to terms with material expectations that must be renegotiated. The habit of recycling, greater concern with health and nutrition, and the renewed interest in gardening and "sustainable" living are all examples.

This reading was adapted from an article that appeared under a different title in the magazine Mother Jones.

Not long after we married, my husband and I flew to Connecticut to visit my parents. We carried our second-hand suitcases up to what was once my brother's bedroom and dropped them on two beds pushed together to make one. The room was, as it always had been, scrupulously clean and white—but richer than I remembered. The beds had real box springs. A cashmere blanket lay folded at their base; on a nightstand, a red daylily from my mother's garden opened in a carafe of water. Outside the window, rain from a sprinkler fell on a long lawn sloping into the trees. Every room in the house—the spare bedrooms, the basement woodshop, my mother's darkroom, the kitchen smelling of herbs—every room whispered of surplus space and money and time. I took off my shoes and thought, I will never live this way again.

I felt shame, resentment, confusion settling in me. By the standards of their generation, my parents were only comfortably middle-class. Why, then, were they living so much better on one income than Bob and I, who had no children and were nearing 40, were living on two?

I could not blame my parents: They earned what they got. Immigrants from a pinched, postwar Britain, they came to America in the '50s when we were children, with little but my father's education. My mother sewed my clothes; my father worked hard to get his Ph.D. Through the years, things got better. In the '60s, my father traded his secondhand Buick for a new Rambler station wagon. In the '70s, he bought himself a Ford and my mother a Toyota. The $28,000 suburban house they built on a lake in the '60s—my mother tiled the bathroom and taped the Sheetrock herself—was sold in the '70s for a place with three bathrooms, four bedrooms, and a two-car garage. They had enough money to pay for my brother's skiing, my college education, and a fattening retirement fund. I went to college in 1967 with a vague sense that my future would be much the same as my parents' past, only freer. I would marry, write or work in the mornings, and take care of my children in the afternoons.

By the '80s, my parents had raised three children and achieved all the elements of the American Dream on my father's income alone. Yet after 15 years in the full-time work force, I could not afford a child and had never owned a new car.

I couldn't have cared less about a new car. But it was an index of how middle-class life—my family's middle-class life—had changed in the course of a single generation. And nowhere was the change more striking than in what each generation paid for housing and what they got for it. My parents had paid $190 a month—on a 5 percent mortgage—for a four-bedroom house on an acre of land in Connecticut. Bob and I, with a combined income slightly lower than my father's, pay $1,500 a month—on a 9 percent mortgage—for a five-room bungalow slightly larger than my parents' deck. Yet we felt lucky to afford a house at all. For some of our friends, and for younger baby-boomers and those from working-class backgrounds, owning a house was out of the question.

Every night during that visit, I thought bitterly of my downward mobility, not only in money, but in time. Bob and I both worked full time and lived in time-poverty; our house in California was more of a launching pad than a home. We commuted, ate Chinese takeout and microwaved burritos standing up in the kitchen, cleaned the house once in a blue moon, and sometimes went for days without an uninterrupted hour together.

On the last night of our visit to my parents, we all went to the movies. My mother and father, as "senior citizens," paid $2 less than we did.

So it was with a sense of discontent that I returned home, got out of my unreliable but classy-looking old Mercedes, and opened the door to the tiny, cracked stucco house my husband and I bought for a fortune with help from our parents.

I looked at the weeds in the overgrown yard, the ink stain on the couch, the dust in the corners, the mail-order catalogs and sweaters piled on the dining-room table. Our bedroom, I realized, was smaller than anywhere I slept in childhood. On the deck were two Adirondack chairs I ordered because the mail-order catalog said their arms were wide enough to hold a glass of lemonade on hot, lazy, summer afternoons. I hadn't had a single glass of lemonade or a single lazy afternoon all summer; what I had tried to buy was not a chair, but a memory of free time.

In the months after that visit East to what was once my home, I looked at the lives of my friends. With few exceptions, most of their parents were middle to upper-middle class; they had cobbled together some version of the American Dream: kids (the most expensive durable consumer good), education, houses, retirement accounts, and time to enjoy it all. My friends dressed and ate well, but despite our expensive educations, most had only one or two elements of the dream we had all laughed at in our 20s and now could not attain. We had to choose between kids, houses, and time. Those with new cars had no houses; those with houses, no children; those with children, no houses. A few lucky supercouples—a lawyer married to a doctor, say, with an annual combined income of more than $100,000—had everything but time.

There were, of course, some notable improvements over our parents' lives. My women friends had careers and financial independence denied their mothers. But on the whole, I saw a generational dilemma perceived as an individual failure. My friends in the baby-boom generation—so often accused of being conspicuous consumers unable to defer gratification—were deferring things their parents considered basic necessities.

It was the *shame* and pretense of prosperity—in people I'd known since we were all in our 20s and poor—that puzzled me. In the '60s and '70s, we'd all worn jeans and put our money into stereos; now my friends were hiding their downward mobility beneath a veneer of glitz. One of my best friends had fallen in love, moved out of her rent-controlled flat in San Francisco, and taken (with the man she later married) a high-rent house, as nice as my parents', in the wealthy Hills neighborhood of Berkeley. I had gone there for dinner and Molly had met me at the door, tastefully dressed. Her table overlooked thousands of houses sparkling around the bay—like a lord's castle high above his subjects—and I had felt a little envious, almost intimidated.

It was only after she and her husband eventually left town for new jobs—good jobs, paying real money—that Molly told me that she'd been too deep in debt to buy a winter coat, so broke she'd stand in line at the phone company to pay the bill on cut-off day. I was shocked she hadn't trusted me enough to tell me, and something she'd said years before came drifting back, a piece of advice she had heard from her mother: "Never look poor, dear. Americans don't like poor people."

In the same period, my former roommate Nancy—the daughter of a psychiatrist who had earned his diploma on the GI Bill and bought a house with a VA loan—became truly poor. The father of her baby left her without child support, and her work as a technical writer dried up after her computer company lost a major contract. The safety net strung up in the 1930s did not help her: As a contract worker, she didn't qualify for unemployment compensation. Welfare turned her down because her rent was too high.

I lent her a little money with only the vaguest sense of her troubles. Only recently, when she laid it all out for me, did I understand how bad it had been. "I couldn't afford to go to museums but I went for walks. I breast-fed for a long time, and that was a help," she said quietly. "Then I finally got a job and I was even worse off. I couldn't afford food, child care, and transportation to and from work. It makes one ashamed not to be able to buy light bulbs, food, toilet paper."

At the same time, the newspapers were full of stories about yuppies and blackened redfish and the openings of new shopping arcades. The disparity hurt my head. Was I the only one who felt like a failure? Was it only *my* friends who were in trouble? Why was it so hard for me to say to a lunch companion, "Let's go somewhere cheaper?" Acquaintances were wearing $50 haircuts and $75 shoes. A childless couple returned from a student year in Rome, got jobs, furniture, sophisticated clothes, and a nice apartment. They went bicycling in Virginia on vacation that year, staying at bed and breakfast inns. They seemed to be doing just fine.

Recently, Roger explained the secret of their success. They were $18,000 in credit-card debt, thus forcing him to leave his job with a non-profit organization for better-paying but more boring work in the computer industry. "We both had grown-up jobs for the first time, and we thought we should be able to live like grown-ups," he said. "We'd struggled for a long time, and I was sick of this thing the left has about not being desirous, of not wanting money.

"I don't think you have to be unhappy to be on the left," he went on. "I wanted to be able to pick up the tab for 10 people, or take a cab when I wanted. I thought that part of being an adult was being able to go to a restaurant, look at the menu, and go in if you like the food, not because you're looking at the prices. A lot of it was playing grown-up and throwing the old plastic around."

I looked at him across the table, amazed that a friend of mine would link his manhood to shopping or being able to pay the bill at any restaurant. My friends seemed willing to pay almost any price to appear as successful as their parents, even though the rules of the game had changed.

In the months that followed, as I clipped *Wall Street Journal* articles and collected economic reports, I came to see that there was no way most of the baby boom generation could meet the expectations created in the late '40s and '50s, when having both a home and children were attainable goals. Then, the economy was full of predictable middle-class rewards and special subsidies for young families through New Deal and postwar programs like the GI Bill, VA home loans, and subsidized superhighways and schools to serve the suburbs.

In the '70s, as we came of age, the American economy was entering a disguised but deepening decline whose burdens fell disproportionately on the young. The twin pillars of the middle-class dream—affordable housing and enough real income to support children—were crumbling without us knowing it.

Germany and Japan were reaping the fruits of their postwar industrial reconstruction. American products lost their dominance in the world marketplace. Debt from the Vietnam War and a bloated military budget—funded with borrowed money—fueled inflation. American wages (adjusted for inflation) began to fall. Lines formed at gas pumps and OPEC oil shocks hit. Health care costs grew like a cancer on the gross national product without improving adult life expectancy or infant mortality rates. Meat went up, cheese went up, interest rates went up.

When the economy hit the skids, many older people were wearing safety belts. It was the young who went through the windshield. In 1973, 80 percent of those over 35 owned their own homes. But when millions of baby-boomers hit the labor and housing markets soon after, they found starting wages stagnating and their housing costs rising. These changes affected baby boomers of every class, including my friends, who are mostly from college-educated families. Some working-class baby boomers were even harder hit.

When productivity and profits declined, and corporations squeezed unions and exported jobs to cheaper countries, it was younger workers who got the short end of two-tier wage contracts, failed to get good union jobs at all, or were paid minimum wages that did not keep pace with inflation.

When manufacturing declined and service industries grew, it was primarily younger workers who took the lower-paying new jobs. Between 1973 and 1986, the proportion of non-college-educated workers holding the better-paying jobs in manufacturing dropped from one-third to one-quarter.

In our 20s, my friends and I hardly cared. We finished college (paid for primarily by our parents), ate tofu, and hung Indian bedspreads in rented apartments. We were young; it was a lark. We scorned consumerism. But in our 30s, as we married or got sick of having apartments sold out from under us, we wanted to be grown up, we wanted money, we wanted nice things, we wanted houses.

A place of one's own—and children—have been part of ordinary people's conception of the good life ever since most of our ancestors were peasants. In the 1950s and '60s, the dream was attainable even for much of the white American working class. In 1973—the last really good year for the middle-class—the average 30-year-old man could meet mortgage payments on a median-priced home with about a fifth of his income. By 1986, the same home took twice as much of his income.

In the same years, the real median income of all families headed by someone under 30 fell by 26 percent. It was a loss virtually identical to the 27 percent drop in per capita personal income between 1929 and 1933, the deepest year of the Depression.

The Depression created a sense of shared misfortune and national crisis. But the stagflation of the '70s and '80s instilled in its victims a sense of individual failure—and in its survivors, a sort of chumpish pride, as though they'd come up in the world by paying $100,000 for a house that cost their parents a fifth as much.

My friends, who spent much of their 20s marching and organizing on behalf of others, responded to this situation that directly affected their lives not by organizing politically but by making small personal adjustments. If the middle class was going to disappear, they would ape the rich, not the poor. They tried to keep up appearances; they worked harder and got used to less leisure. They spent more on housing and less on charity and savings. They took on more debt and paid it off more slowly. When pushed to the wall, they did with less. They gentrified slums and bought gimcrack condominiums in buildings with pretentious marbled lobbies and paper-thin walls.

Unable to meet the out-of-scale expectations created in the 1950s, they gave up on necessities and comforted themselves with cheap luxuries: fresh-cut flowers, Haagen-Dazs, Cuisinarts, French meals. As poor people often have done, they spent their money on lavish clothes or impressive cars. One elegant woman I know—always beautifully dressed, and partial to $75 shoes—confided recently that she can't figure out how to afford a child; she and her husband don't even own a dresser and keep their clothes in garbage bags. One year I extravagantly gave my father a $200 gift certificate for custom-made shirts, and smiled when he ordered them in a cotton/polyester blend. I couldn't make as much money as he did, but at least, I thought, I knew how to spend it. My friends and I bought clothes of pure cotton and silk with the money our parents had spent on washing machines and baby clothes. The $200 that paid our parents' mortgages would barely cover our car payments; so we made up for it by buying at Lands' End instead of Sears, by learning to call noodles and coffee *fettucine* and *cappuccino*.

Other adaptations involved fundamental changes in our family and personal lives. Women entered the full-time work force and stayed there; now more than half of all women with infants under six months old are working. People delayed marriage into their 30s (men tend not to marry until they earn a breadwinner wage—one of the reasons why marriage rates are so low among young blacks). Others postponed or simply forgot about having children and collected stuffed animals instead.

Although many of my friends cope with their limited economic prospects by keeping up appearances with selective extravagance and credit card debt, others face the truth about the way they live now with some dignity and grace. I recently had dinner with Nancy, my old roommate, in her rent-controlled apartment in San Francisco. She has learned how to do well with nothing; we ate spaghetti and homemade applesauce by candlelight on an old picnic table in a courtyard where daisies grew in olive oil cans. As we talked, her son circled the table on a tricycle. Nancy told me things were much better than they had been when her son was tiny, even though she still rises at four in the morning to get her work done. She still doesn't own a car and she and her son only get out of the city every other month or so. At 34, she owns only a refrigerator, a small Chinese carpet, an antique bench, and her mother's dinner dishes. "I don't feel poor," she said. "I feel as if I actually have luxuries." It turned out she meant taking cabs to work, sending the laundry out, and having the flat cleaned twice a month—tasks done in a previous generation by a wife whose income was not needed.

"You can talk about the economic problems of single mothers," she said earnestly, "but having a child is the most rewarding thing I've ever done. It changed my life for the better. I wouldn't go back. If I didn't have my son to spend my money on, I'd be buying snazzy shoes or yuppified kitchen equipment. Instead, I'm seeing things I'd otherwise miss—I'm standing on the corner with him, waiting for the bus, looking at a seagull standing on top of a flagpole."

I went to dinner with my brother Peter in the flat he shares in the Haight-Ashbury. He is 36, a perpetual student, and lives on about a quarter of what I spend. There's always peace and quiet at his place, a sense of being an expected guest. He knows how to use a pressure cooker and where to find prized items at Goodwill; when he wants to see a show, he works as an usher. When I arrived, the table was set and the lights turned low; there were wine glasses filled with mineral water, cloth napkins folded carefully at each place, and two candle stubs glowing. When it was time, we sat down for homemade lentil soup, warm sourdough rye from the neighborhood bakery, salad, and baked potatoes. I felt so cared for that I ate bread as though it were a rare food, tasting the grains against my palate instead of wolfing it down. There was a sort of Zen luxuriousness about the whole meal: We squeezed maximum enjoyment out of minimum consumption. My deepest needs—warmth, light, quiet, companionship—were satisfied. I didn't miss anything.

I thought of my own life—my constant conversations with myself about wanting a child, a new couch, a weekend cottage, a bigger house on a quieter street—and realized my discontent was cheating me of the life I *had*.

"If it's by choice and it's not overwhelming, having no money can be a way of entering more deeply into your life," my brother said as he served me some more soup.

Not long after that, I bought myself a new raincoat, a year's supply of shampoo, and a pressure cooker. I quit my job as a reporter to become a freelance writer. I wrote to the direct mail association and asked them to take me off the catalog lists. I sold my ancient, infuriating old Mercedes and bought a dull but reliable used Honda. I bought a second-hand copy of *Laurel's Kitchen*, I learned to cook beans, and started using my library card.

I decided that if the economy was going to deprive me of things I deeply wanted, it would not also take my free time.

I began facing the life I *had*, not the life I dreamed of having or thought I deserved to have. I turned off lights. I started to cut the link between consumption and pleasure, between consumption and self-worth. And that paved the way for some unexpected things. I recycled—because it saved money on garbage pickup—and ate less meat and more beans. I walked downtown instead of getting into the car. Having less money forced me to get to know my neighbors and a network of borrowing emerged. My next-door neighbor Mack, a salesman, lost his job and borrowed my computer to type resumes; when my husband's car broke down, Mack lent us his. My husband, Bob, helped Jay, a carpenter, change his clutch; Jay brought us wood scraps for kindling and his wife, Gloria, fed us dinner. One weekend last fall, Bob and I came home from a walk and saw four of our neighbors standing outside Mack's house around a pyramid of sod.

"Found it at the dump," said George, the young contractor who lives down the block. He picked up a roll of sod, laid it out in Mack's front yard, and jumped up and down to set it. "Some landscaper threw away a truckload." Mack's wife, Jan, who works as a flight attendant, laid out another roll, and in half an hour, the patch of dirt in front of their house was transformed into a carpet of green. Jan turned on the sprinkler.

"There's plenty left," said George. "Dig up your yard, and we'll do it too." They all carried their tools around the geraniums that serve as a hedge between our houses. My husband and I raked out wisps of yellow grass. "My grandfather owned this whole block in the '30s," said George over the clatter of rakes. He chopped out a root with his hoe. "There was a dairy farm behind your house, and a vineyard across the street." I cradled a roll of sod against my chest until I smelled like the riverbanks where I skinny-dipped as a child.

Soon our weed patch was covered with a quilt of green, its nap running every which way. Jan knelt down with clippers and snipped along the edge of our walk as though cutting out the armhole of a dress. Mack brought out a six-pack. I squeezed lemons into a jug of iced water and we sat around on the fresh new grass in the falling sunlight with no sense that anything needed to be repaid. I shut my eyes and felt no need to compare our block, held in its growing net of mutual favors and borrowings, with anything else I'd ever known. 🖋

SUGGESTIONS FOR WRITING

1. What is your conception of "the good life"? How do you think you will react if you fail to attain it?

2. In what ways have your expectations of material comfort and rewards influenced your thinking about your education and future?

3. The tone of Butler's essay is not unrelievedly sad. Describe the ways she points to the "silver linings" in these clouds of despair.

4. We seem to enjoy more material conveniences than ever, from videocassette recorders to microwave ovens to telephone answering machines, and yet people (and more people per family) seem to be working harder than ever. What luxuries would you be willing to give up in order to work at a less hectic pace?

Part II
Issues

The categories of gender, race, and class are often the subjects of complex arguments. They are places where conflict can occur, contested turf. It is not easy to say what it means to be a man or a woman, to have a particular racial identity, or to be a member of a certain class. The differences these terms define are hotly contested and tap into deep emotions. Think of the arguments that rage around the issues of women and the priesthood, or around hiring quotas, or taxing the rich. These issues and many others surround the categories of gender, race, and class. In this section you will encounter some complex issues, such as abortion, racism, and violence against women. We have also included a section of writings from around the world, in order to widen our focus and show that these issues are not limited to our American culture.

Some writings in this section recount personal experiences, but many are less personal, more argumentative and more analytical than those in Part 1, Experiences. Many of these writers aren't interested so much in recounting a personal experience as in arguing for a point, trying to convince the reader to take a certain point of view. Similarly, the writing you will be asked to do in this section will force you to take a stand on these issues. You will still be drawing on your own opinions and experiences, but we will ask you to join in the argument, to add your own voice to the conversation. What have you learned about racism? What do you think about abortion or sexual orientation? What do your experiences lead you to believe about the issues raised by gender, race, and class?

4

MAKING A LIVING

In this chapter are accounts and arguments about two of life's inescapable realities—work and money. The selections represent a wide variety of work and economic experiences, from the very rich to the poor. For all of these writers, the work they do and the money they make are very personal matters. Work and income influence how they think about themselves and how they live outside of their employment. For some, work is a source of joy and pride; for others, it is exhausting and degrading. Some have more money than any person can need; others must strive hard just to provide for survival. Experiences also differ in terms of gender. A woman working in a predominantly male environment, for example, does not have the same experience as a woman working among other women. The social differences this book is concerned with all play a part in an individual's experience of work. In each of these readings, though, work and money are powerful forces in and of themselves.

The writing you will be asked to do will focus your attention on work and economic life—on your work experiences, your expectations, and the role money plays in your life. These topics should allow you to understand your position in the social system. If you compare your own experiences and expectations with those of others, you will find interesting similarities and differences that might well be related to your gender, race, and class identity. For example, how do the work experiences of men and women differ? Do members of different racial groups have similar or different economic expectations?

The readings in this chapter show that almost no one goes home from work and simply puts aside their workplace identity. For one thing, the income derived from work determines so many of the details of life—the houses we live in, the cars we drive, the clothes we wear, the food we eat, the medical care we receive, our treatment by the police and courts, our say

in government. The kind of job we have affects how others see us and how we see ourselves.

The readings and writing ideas in this chapter will help you explore this force in your life.

YEAR OF THE BLUE-COLLAR GUY

Steve Olson

This essay was written for Newsweek's *"My Turn" feature, in which non-professional writers get the opportunity to speak from their own experience about an issue that concerns us all.* **Steve Olson,** *a construction worker from Madison, Wisconsin, writes with great conviction about the contribution that "blue-collar guys" make to our society. Clearly he feels these contributions have been overlooked by a society that equates success with having a profession, a "white-collar" job. Olson has a definite point to make, and his brief essay makes it with great energy.*

While the learned are attaching appropriate labels to the 1980s and speculating on what the 1990s will bring, I would like to steal 1989 for my own much maligned group and declare it "the year of the blue-collar guy (BCG)." BCGs have been portrayed as beer-drinking, big-bellied, bigoted rednecks who dress badly. Wearing a suit to a cement-finishing job wouldn't be too bright. Watching my tie go around a motor shaft followed by my neck is not the last thing I want to see in this world. But, more to the point, our necks are too big and our arms and shoulders are too awesome to fit suits well without expensive tailoring. Suits are made for white-collar guys.

But we need big bellies as ballast to stay on the bar stool while we're drinking beer. And our necks are red from the sun and we are somewhat bigoted. But aren't we all? At least our bigotry is open and honest and worn out front like a tattoo. White-collar people are bigoted, too. But it's disguised as the pat on the back that holds you back: "You're not good enough so you need affirmative action." BCGs aren't smart enough to be that cynical. I never met a BCG who didn't respect an honest day's work and a job well done—no matter who did it.

True enough, BCGs aren't perfect. But, I believe this: we are America's last true romantic heroes. When some 21st-century Louis L'Amour writes about this era he won't eulogize the greedy Wall Street insider. He won't commend the narrow-shouldered, wide-hipped lawyers with six-digit unearned incomes doing the same work women can do. His wide-shouldered heroes will be plucked from the ranks of the blue-collar guy. They are the last vestige of the manly world where strength, skill and hard work are still valued.

To some extent our negatives ratings are our own fault. While we were building the world we live in, white-collar types were sitting on their ever-widening butts redefining the values we live by. One symbol of America's opulent wealth is the number of people who can sit and ponder and comment and write without producing a usable product or skill. Hey, get a real job—make something—then talk. These talkers are the guys we drove from the playgrounds into the libraries when we were young and now for 20 years or more we have endured the revenge of the nerds.

BCGs fidgeted our way out of the classroom and into jobs where, it seemed, the only limit to our income was the limit of our physical strength and energy. A co-worker described a BCG as "a guy who is always doing things that end in the letter 'n'—you know—huntin', fishin', workin' . . . " My wise friend is talking energy! I have seen men on the job hand-nail 20 square of shingles (that's 6,480 nails) or more a day, day after day, for weeks. At the same time, they were remodeling their houses, raising children and coaching Little League. I've seen crews frame entire houses in a day—day after day. I've seen guys finish concrete until 11 p.m., go out on a date, then get up at 6 a.m. and do it all over again the next day.

These are amazing feats of strength. There should be stadiums full of screaming fans for these guys. I saw a 40-year-old man neatly fold a 350-pound piece of rubber roofing, put it on his shoulder and, alone, carry it up a ladder and deposit it on a roof. Nobody acknowledged it because the event was too common. One day at noon this same fellow wrestled a 22-year-old college summer worker. In the prime of his life, the college kid was a 6-foot-3, 190-pound bodybuilder and he was out of his league. He was on his back to stay in 90 seconds flat.

GREAT SKILLED WORK FORCE

Mondays are tough on any job. But in our world this pain is eased by stories of weekend adventure. While white-collar types are debating the value of reading over watching TV, BCGs are doing stuff. I have honest to God heard these things on Monday mornings about BCG weekends: "I tore out a wall and added a room," "I built a garage," "I went walleye fishing Saturday and pheasant hunting Sunday," "I played touch football both days"(in January), "I went skydiving," "I went to the sports show and wrestled the bear." Pack a good novel into these weekends.

My purpose is not so much to put down white-collar people as to stress the importance of blue-collar people to this country. Lawyers, politicians and bureaucrats are necessary parts of the process, but this great skilled work force is so taken for granted it is rarely seen as the luxury it truly is. Our plumbing works, our phones work and repairs are made as quickly as humanly possible. I don't think this is true in all parts of the world. But this blue-collar resource is becoming endangered. Being a tradesman is viewed with such disdain these days that most young people I know treat the trades like a temporary summer job. I've seen young guys take minimum-wage jobs just so they can wear suits. It is as if any job without a dress code is a dead-end job. This is partly our own fault. We even tell our own sons, "Don't be like me, get a job people respect." Blue-collar guys ought to brag more, even swagger a little. We should drive our families past the latest job site and say, "That house was a piece of junk, and now it's the best one on the block. I did that." Nobody will respect us if we don't respect ourselves.

Our work is hard, hot, wet, cold and always dirty. It is also often very satisfying. Entailing the use of both brain and body there is a product—a physical result of which to be proud. We have fallen from your roofs, died under heavy equipment and been entombed in your dams. We have done honest, dangerous work. Our skills and energy and strength have transformed lines on paper into physical reality. We are this century's Renaissance men. America could do worse than to honor us. We still do things the old-fashioned way, and we have earned the honor. 🖋

SUGGESTIONS FOR WRITING

1. Describe the audience Olson has in mind for his essay. Is it other "blue-collar guys" or "white-collar" readers? How can you tell?

2. What kind of racial attitudes does Olson express? Agree or disagree with his claim that working-class white people are more honest in their racial attitudes than middle- and upper-class whites.

3. Does society scorn the working-class trades that Olson admires? What attitudes do you have toward carpenters, construction workers, and plumbers?

4. Are you offended by the "macho" attitude that Olson expresses? Why or why not?

ROSIE: PEGGY TERRY

Studs Terkel

*This piece of oral history is part of **Studs Terkel**'s book on World War II,*
The Good War. Terkel reconstructs the experience of this historical event
by having ordinary individuals recount their involvement in the war. Peggy
Terry is an example of the phenomenon that came to be known as "Rosie the
Riveter," a name given to the women who took over "men's work" because
the men were away at war. Women drove trucks, worked in factories, took
on positions of responsibility that they had been denied until the needs of the
war required their effort. In Peggy Terry's case, the job was in a munitions
factory. Her story recounts the complexity of her emotions about her work
and about the war. She also gives a rich description of the new forms of so-
cial life surrounding her work. She was exploring a kind of work experience
few women had known before, and her account puts us in the midst of this
new world.

Studs Terkel (b. 1912) is the author of best-selling works of oral history,
such as Hard Times, Working, *and* The Good War. *He is a long-time col-*
umnist and radio and TV personality in Chicago.

The first work I had after the Depression was at a shell-loading plant in Viola,
Kentucky. It is between Paducah and Mayfield. They were large shells: anti-
aircraft, incendiaries, and tracers. We painted red on the tips of the tracers. My
mother, my sister, and myself worked there. Each of us worked on a different
shift because we had little ones at home. We made the fabulous sum of thirty-
two dollars a week. (Laughs.) To us it was just an absolute miracle. Before that,
we made nothing.

You won't believe how incredibly ignorant I was. I knew vaguely that a war
had started, but I had no idea what it meant.

Didn't you have a radio?

Gosh, no. That was an absolute luxury. We were just moving around, working wherever we could find work. I was eighteen. My husband was nineteen.
We were living day to day. When you are involved in stayin' alive, you don't
think about big things like a war. It didn't occur to us that we were making
these shells to kill people. It never entered my head.

There were no women foremen where we worked. We were just a bunch of
hillbilly women laughin' and talkin'. It was like a social. Now we'd have money
to buy shoes and a dress and pay rent and get some food on the table. We were
just happy to have work.

I worked in building number 11. I pulled a lot of gadgets on a machine. The
shell slid under and powder went into it. Another lever you pulled tamped it

down. Then it moved on a conveyor belt to another building where the detonator was dropped in. You did this over and over.

Tetryl was one of the ingredients and it turned us orange. Just as orange as an orange. Our hair was streaked orange. Our hands, our face, our neck just turned orange, even our eyeballs. We never questioned. None of us ever asked, What is this? Is this harmful? We simply didn't think about it. That was just one of the conditions of the job. The only thing we worried about was other women thinking we had dyed our hair. Back then it was a disgrace if you dyed your hair. We worried what people would say.

We used to laugh about it on the bus. It eventually wore off. But I seem to remember some of the women had breathing problems. The shells were painted a dark gray. When the paint didn't come out smooth, we had to take rags wet with some kind of remover and wash that paint off. The fumes from these rags—it was like breathing cleaning fluid. It burned the nose and throat. Oh, it was difficult to breathe. I remember that.

Nothing ever blew up, but I remember the building where they dropped in the detonator. These detonators are little black things about the size of a thumb. This terrible thunderstorm came and all the lights went out. Somebody knocked a box of detonators off on the floor. Here we were in the pitch dark. Somebody was screaming, "Don't move, anybody!" They were afraid you'd step on the detonator. We were down on our hands and knees crawling out of that building in the storm. (Laughs.) We were in slow motion. If we'd stepped on one. . .

Mamma was what they called terminated—fired. Mamma's mother took sick and died and Mamma asked for time off and they told her no. Mamma said, "Well, I'm gonna be with my mamma. If I have to give up my job, I will just have to." So they terminated Mamma. That's when I started gettin' nasty. I didn't take as much baloney and pushing around as I had taken. I told 'em I was gonna quit, and they told me if I quit they would blacklist me wherever I would go. They had my fingerprints and all that. I guess it was just bluff, because I did get other work.

I think of how little we knew of human rights, union rights. We knew Daddy had been a hell-raiser in the mine workers' union but at that point it hadn't rubbed off on any of us women. Coca Cola and Dr. Pepper were allowed in every building, but not a drop of water. You could only get a drink of water if you went to the cafeteria, which was about two city blocks away. Of course you couldn't leave your machine long enough to go get a drink. I drank Coke and Dr. Pepper and I hated 'em. I hate 'em today. We had to buy it, of course. We couldn't leave to go the bathroom, 'cause it was way the heck over there.

We were awarded the navy E for excellence. We were just so proud of that E. It was like we were a big family, and we hugged and kissed each other. They had the navy band out there celebrating us. We were so proud of ourselves.

First time my mother ever worked at anything except in the fields—first real job Mamma ever had. It was a big break in everybody's life. Once, Mamma woke up in the middle of the night to go to the bathroom and she saw the bus going down. She said, "Oh my goodness, I've overslept." She jerked her clothes on, throwed her lunch in the bag, and was out on the corner, ready to go, when

Boy Blue, our driver, said, "Honey, this is the wrong shift." Mamma wasn't supposed to be there until six in the morning. She never lived that down. She would have enjoyed telling you that.

My world was really very small. When we came from Oklahoma to Paducah, that was like a journey to the center of the earth. It was during the Depression and you did good having bus fare to get across town. That war just widened my world. Especially after I came up to Michigan.

My grandfather went up to Jackson, Michigan, after he retired from the railroad. He wrote back and told us we could make twice as much in the war plants in Jackson. We did. We made ninety dollars a week. We did some kind of testing for airplane radios.

Ohh, I met all those wonderful Polacks. They were the first people I'd ever known that were any different from me. A whole new world just opened up. I learned to drink beer like crazy with 'em. They were all very union-conscious. I learned a lot of things that I didn't even know existed.

We were very patriotic and we understood that the Nazis were someone who would have to be stopped. We didn't know about concentration camps. I don't think anybody I knew did. With the Japanese, that was a whole different thing. We were just ready to wipe them out. They sure as heck didn't look like us. They were yellow little creatures that smiled when they bombed our boys. I remember someone in Paducah got up this idea of burning everything they had that was Japanese. I had this little ceramic cat and I said, "I don't care, I am not burning it." They had this big bonfire and people came and brought what they had that was made in Japan. Threw it on the bonfire. I hid my cat. It's on the shelf in my bathroom right now. (Laughs.)

In all the movies we saw, the Germans were always tall and handsome. There'd be one meanie, a little short dumpy bad Nazi. But the main characters were good-lookin' and they looked like us. The Japanese were all evil. If you can go half your life and not recognize how you're being manipulated, that is sad and kinda scary.

I do remember a nice movie, *The White Cliffs of Dover*. We all sat there with tears pouring down our face. All my life, I hated England, 'cause all my family all my life had wanted England out of Ireland. During the war, all those ill feelings just seemed to go away. It took a war.

I believe the war was the beginning of my seeing things. You just can't stay uninvolved and not knowing when such a momentous thing is happening. It's just little things that start happening and you put one piece with another. Suddenly, a puzzle begins to take shape.

My husband was a paratrooper in the war, in the 101st Airborne Division. He made twenty-six drops in France, North Africa, and Germany. I look back at the war with sadness. I wasn't smart enough to think too deeply then. We had a lotta good times and we had money and we had food on the table and the rent was paid. Which had never happened to us before. But when I look back and think of him. . . .

Until the war he never drank. He never even smoked. When he came back he was an absolute drunkard. And he used to have the most awful nightmares. He'd get up in the middle of the night and start screaming. I'd just sit for hours and hold him while he just shook. We'd go to the movies, and if they'd have films with a lot of shooting in it, he'd just start to shake and have to get up and leave. He started slapping me around and slapped the kids around. He became a brute.

Some fifteen years before, Peggy had recalled her experiences during the Great Depression. She and her young husband were on the road. "We were just kids. I was fifteen and he was sixteen. . . . It was a very nice time, because when you're poor and you stay in one spot, trouble just seems to catch up with you. But when you're moving from town to town, you don't stay there long enough for trouble to catch up with you."[1]

One of the things that bothered him most was his memory of this town he was in. He saw something move by a building and he shot. It was a woman. He never got over that. It seems so obvious to say—wars brutalize people. It brutalized him.

The war gave a lot of people jobs. It led them to expect more than they had before. People's expectations, financially, spiritually, were raised. There was such a beautiful dream. We were gonna reach the end of the rainbow. When the war ended, the rainbow vanished. Almost immediately we went into Korea. There was no peace, which we were promised.

I remember a woman saying on the bus that she hoped the war didn't end until she got her refrigerator paid for. An old man hit her over the head with an umbrella. He said, "How dare you!" (Laughs.)

Ohh, the beautiful celebrations when the war ended. They were selling cigarettes in Paducah. Up until that hour, you couldn't ta bought a pack of cigarettes for love or money. Kirchoff's Bakery was giving away free loaves of bread. Everybody was downtown in the pouring rain and we were dancing. We took off our shoes and put 'em in our purse. We were so happy.

The night my husband came home, we went out with a gang of friends and got drunk. All of us had a tattoo put on. I had a tattoo put up my leg where it wouldn't show. A heart with an arrow through it: Bill and Peggy. When I went to the hospital to have my baby—I got pregnant almost as soon as he came home—I was ashamed of the tattoo. So I put two Band-Aids across it. So the nurse just pulls 'em off, looks at the tattoo, and she says, "Oh, that's exactly in the same spot I got mine." She pulled her uniform up and showed me her tattoo. (Laughs.)

I knew the bomb dropped on Hiroshima was a big terrible thing, but I didn't know it was the horror it was. It was on working people. It wasn't anywhere near the big shots of Japan who started the war in the first place. We didn't drop it on them. Hirohito and his white horse, it never touched him. It was dropped on women and children who had nothing to say about whether their country went to war or not.

---

[1] *Hard Times: An Oral History of the Great Depression* (New York: Pantheon Books, 1970), p. 48. [S.T.]

I was happy my husband would get to come home and wouldn't be sent there from Germany. Every day when the paper came out, there'd be somebody I knew with their picture. An awful lot of kids I knew, went to school and church with, were killed.

No bombs were ever dropped on us. I can't help but believe the cold war started because we were untouched. Except for our boys that went out of the country and were killed, we came out of that war in good shape. People with more money than they'd had in years.

No, I don't think we'd have been satisfied to go back to what we had during the Depression. To be deprived of things we got used to. Materially, we're a thousand times better off. But the war turned me against religion. I was raised in the fundamentalist faith. I was taught that I was nothing. My feeling is if God created me, if God sent his only begotten son to give his life for me, then I am something. My mother died thinking she was nothing. I don't know how chaplains can call themselves men of God and prepare boys to go into battle. If the Bible says, Thou shalt not kill, it doesn't say, Except in time of war. They'll send a man to the electric chair who in a temper killed somebody. But they pin medals on our men. The more people they kill, the more medals they pin on 'em.

I was just so glad when it was over, because I wanted my husband home. I didn't understand any of the implications except that the killing was over and that's a pretty good thing to think about whether you're political or not. (Laughs). The killing be over forever. ✒

SUGGESTIONS FOR WRITING

1. Define Peggy Terry's attitudes toward the war. Do her attitudes change?
2. Describe Terry's feelings about her job. What does it give to her? What does it cost her?
3. How do you feel about the belief that war is good for a weak economy? Would you feel comfortable profiting from a war? Why or why not?
4. Many women are gaining management and professional positions that had been reserved for men until recently. How does their experience compare to Terry's? What are the advantages and disadvantages of these new careers for women?

A PERSONAL HISTORY

Crystal Lee Sutton

*Crystal Lee Sutton (b. 1941) worked for many years in the textile mills of
North Carolina. She is the real-life model for the 1979 film* Norma Rae,
*which tells the story of Sutton's involvement in efforts to unionize workers at
the JP Stevens textile plants. In this oral autobiography, she tells the full
story of her early life, her work in the mills, and her involvement in the
union struggle. Sutton's involvement in the union also raised interesting gender and class questions, as her aggressiveness did not fit with traditional
women's roles. Her union work often brought her into contact with blacks,
in defiance of the segregated social life common in her community. In this
reading, Sutton gives us a portrait of a woman who is actively involved in
gaining control over her own life.*

My first job in the mill was filling batteries. This older woman trained me because she was working her notice. I remember my first day it was so noisy in
there and it was so dusty, that I got to crying because I couldn't hear. And I felt
like I had gotten all stopped up from the lint so we went to the bathroom to eat
our supper. This woman was talking to me and she asked me if I went to school
and I told her where I went to school and what grade I was in. Her name was
Mrs. Johnson and so she said she had a son named Henry who was in the same
grade I was in. And I said, "Yeah, I know Henry. He was my boyfriend when
we first moved to Burlington." She said, "Please don't tell any of the kids at
school that I'm working here 'cause I wouldn't want to embarass him." And I
thought to myself, she had the audacity to say that to me and here I was a teenager working in the mill taking over her job.

But I never said anything to her about it and I never mentioned it at school
either. I felt like if she didn't want me to I wouldn't. Henry was a very smart
boy and I felt like he came from a well-off family. That was just the impression
I got, he never was conceited or anything, but usually the smarter kids came
from the families with a little bit more money than the average textile worker's
kids. The reason I think that is because those parents probably had more
schooling and because they had more money, they had the time to take with
their children instead of working all the time. I always got the feeling when I
was in school that textile work was something to be looked down on because
like the first day of school you had to tell what your mama and daddy did. I
wasn't ashamed of what they did but I would rather not been asked because
there were doctors' children in the room and all. You just got the feeling that
the teacher just didn't want to hear the fact that your parents worked in the
textile mills. I just rather it had been left alone. I didn't think what my parents
did really mattered that much. That was just a feeling I had at a very young age.
The doctors' children were always smarter than the mill children because when

they were called on they knew to answer and the rest of us just wished that we could see through the void. When I went to work in the mill and Mrs. Johnson said what she did to me, I really figured all that out.

Filling batteries was dangerous work with the machines running and the shuttles going very fast. At the time I wore my hair very short, that was just a style I had picked up, and that was good because you come out of there covered with cotton dust and all. At the time I didn't realize how dangerous the work was. I knew that the floors were very oily and you'd see snakes every once in a while, but at the time I just figured that was the way a textile plant was. My wage was probably about a dollar an hour because before I was working for fifty cents an hour at a florist shop and I went to work in the mill because I could make more money. I took distributive education in high school, which meant that I got out of school at 12:30 and went to work in the mill on second shift full time. It was very hard trying to do your homework in the mill, studying Macbeth and all that crap. Where the hell has that done me any good? All I did was memorize enough to pass the test and then forget it. I had this friend that would come down and help me. We would work fast so we could take a break and go up there and get some ice cream so I could study.

Daddy always talked about education. He got real upset because he said that it didn't look like none of his children were going to graduate. So I was the first to graduate in 1959. The only reason I finished school was because of Daddy. I hated every second I went. I even hated study hall and lunch time. I hated it because of the way the teachers treated the working-class kids. I resented that, because I didn't feel like we could help what our parents did and I wasn't ashamed of my parents. I was always proud of them and I didn't think that it was right for the school system to judge us because of where our parents worked. I used to always be secretary or treasurer of something. I remember that first happening to me in the sixth grade. I was voted secretary. And it shocked me. I was in a state of shock the whole year because it always seemed like the higher class kids always got to do stuff like that. And they were always in the play, cheerleaders, majorettes, they definitely dominated the school. I resented that very much. I felt like we needed more attention. There were different classrooms for the different students even back then and we mill kids just couldn't move as fast as the others. It was just impossible to do because we had to work, and we didn't have the help at home. Both my parents only had about an eighth-grade education. So they couldn't very well help a lot. I just hated it.

When I was in the eighth grade I really wanted to quit. I really got this desire to go in the service, and it upset Mama. Now Daddy went along with me because he knew Mama would absolutely refuse to allow it. I finally figured that out when I got a little older, because Mama said only whores went into the army. So I gave up that desire. But I wanted to go into the service to get away from everything, to travel, and to be myself.

I was almost eighteen when I got married. After Mama put a halt to me going into the service, that was all I ever thought about was getting married and getting away from home. I never even thought about getting my own place to myself. I had a job, but I thought I had to get married to get out. I wanted to be a beautician. I really wanted to be a beautician. So I checked around and there was this woman in the neighborhood who had a beauty shop a couple of blocks from us and she told me where to write to for some information. The nearest school was in Raleigh and I just knew that Daddy couldn't afford to send me because I would have to have a place to stay, so I gave up on that idea.

Mark, my son, was three years old when his daddy got killed and I moved back in with Mama and Daddy. No, we were already living with Mama and Daddy when my husband got killed because me and Junior had had a lovers' spat. We were mature in a lot of ways, but we were real jealous, and he liked to take some drinks sometimes. Glenraven Mills where he was working at had a Christmas dinner just for the workers, or that's what Junior told me, and I worked all day long cleaning up that house from top to bottom, I wanted to go to that dinner that night. But he said it was only for the employees. At midnight he still wasn't home and I was fuming. So we had a spat which ended up with him shoving a gun in my face. The bullet didn't hit me, but when the gun went off it broke my nose. So then I went home to Mama and Daddy. We were in the process of getting back together when he got killed in a car accident.

I was about twenty then, and to get my insurance money Daddy had to be my guardian. That was so damn strange, here I was married, widowed, and a mother, and I couldn't even write my own checks. I thought that was stupid. Then Mark was about six months old when I went to work for Southern Life Insurance and I would take him to the babysitter's. After that I went back into the mill and got fired because I refused to check a man that was running. I was pregnant with Jay at the time, and I refused to run behind that man and check him. I tried to tell him, you work at a speed that you can work at five and six days a week. Don't speed up, work at a normal pace. The faster you go the more work they gonna put on you. And I think he got pissed because I had to check him, but that was my job, and I got fired because I finally refused to check him. That was at Glenraven Mills. Then Jay was born in 1962. Jay was six months old when I moved to Roanoke Rapids and I met Cookie Jordan. We married shortly after that. Then Elizabeth was born in 1965. She was probably two when I went to work as a waitress.

I had taken a course on how to be waitress and had gotten a certificate. They were having this teacher over at the Holiday Inn. I went six weeks training to be a waitress. My sister Seretha was working as a waitress at the restaurant and she got me the job. I worked there a pretty good while and I really enjoyed that type of work. But then I wanted to get on at JP Stevens because they paid more money.

I started trying and it took me about two years to get on. What happened was that we moved out to Henry Street and it was a dead end. Two boss men lived on my street and there was a woman who lived behind me that had been at JP Stevens maybe five or six years. She talked for me and Seretha, who was already working at Stevens, talked for me, and then I called both of those boss men. I talked to them personally and finally got hired. So I went to work at JP Stevens in 1972. I was a gift-set operator. You know, like you go to Sears or somewhere and you see these towels fixed in pretty boxes. That was my job, to fold those towels, put pasteboard in them, fold them a certain size and put them in the boxes, put Saran Wrap over them and pack them. I was probably making

$2.25 an hour at that time. That was better than waitressing because I was just making a dollar an hour plus tips. Yeah, that was a lot better. I was also working part-time at Hornes Restaurant.

Then, when Ralph Sizemore opened up a nightclub, he asked me to run it for him. So I worked my notice at the mill, and then when I was going to leave, my boss man told me that if I got over there and didn't like it, he'd give me my job back. So I loved the work at the club and some of my boss men from the mill would even come over, but Cookie bitched about me doing it so much that I finally told James, my boss man, "Reckon you'd give me my job back?" So I went back on the very same shift doing the very same work. Then I worked there until I was terminated in 1973. I was terminated for union activity. I attended my first union meeting on Mother's Day in 1973 and on May 30th I was fired. Less than a month since I attended my first union meeting.

Nobody really approached me about the union. I had been out on sick leave. I had hurt my foot. My sister worked right down from me and she came up and said, "Lee, somebody was handing out union cards but don't you take one 'cause if you do you'll be fired." I said, "Who's handing them out?" She said, "I don't know but don't you take one." Then she went on back there to her job. So I started asking different ones around and nobody would say nothing. So I asked this older woman, "Do you know anything about this union stuff?" And she said, "Lee, all I know is there's a notice about this meeting on the bulletin board." So I took a piece of paper and wrote down the place, it was going to be at a church, and the time. So I started to talk to different ones about if they were going and nobody said nothing, so I asked my friend Liz. I said, "Liz, how about going with me to that union meeting?" She had three little girls. She said, "Lee, I don't have nobody to keep the kids." I said, "Oh, Cookie will keep the children."

I never will forget, I went to Burlington that Saturday on Mother's Day, and Mama got mad with me 'cause I left early to go to that union meeting. She didn't think I ought to go. But I went over to JB Younts, he had been a real close friend, and I knew he knew about unions and all because I remember he tried to get Daddy to join the union at Cone Mills. He told me, "Lee, you do everything you can to try to get that union in." He said, "You get home in time to go to that union meeting." So I did. I never will forget it. Liz and I pulled up at this church—it was a black church—and I had never seen so many blacks in all my life. Liz said, "You sure you want to do this?" and I said, "Well, we're here. We might as well go on in." So we went in and there were maybe four or five other white people there. We went down and sat on the front row 'cause I didn't want to miss out on nothing. After the meeting, I agreed to go into the mill wearing a union button to try to get the union in. We were real strong with the blacks, but we were weak with the whites. So I knew a lot of people I was going to talk with.

Eli Zivkovitch was the organizer. He was from Fairfield, Virginia, an ex-coal miner. He and his family were so poor that at one time they lived in a tent. He was a very handsome man, and I really loved my daddy more than anything in this world, but Eli was like what I wish my daddy had 'a been as far as being more modern, like realizing that women had more worth in this world than just being a sex object. That women had brains and that they should use those brains. It was okay for women to do so-called men's work. The men I had met before had always seemed to be more concerned with a woman's outward appearance. Eli was a good man, a fighter and a survivor. Hours meant nothing to him as far as his work went. He was not a nine-to-five person. He was available when you needed him, and that's the way he taught me to work. Eli said we could talk union and hand out literature on our break time in the canteens. So I got people to join the union real quick like.

Then they started calling me into the office. I had never been called into the office to be talked to about anything. But all of a sudden I couldn't do nothing right. Talking too much, standing in the bathroom too much. Nothing had changed, that was just their agitation trying to get me to quit trying to organize. Eli had give us this book called *What the Company Will Do for You*. It was all blank pages. He told us if they called us in the office for us to write down what they said. Because if they had a right to write us up, we had a right to write them up. I always took my pencil and my little book and I would write down things that was happening. This blew the boss men's mind. They couldn't believe I was doing this.

Then what happened was that the company posted a notice on the bulletin board and it was in effect trying to scare people. It stated something like it was going to be an all black union. Eli said he needed a copy of it to send to the National Labor Relations Board. So different people said they would copy the letter, you know, but whenever they tried they were told they would be fired. So one day, Eli said, "Crystal, I've got to have a copy of that letter." I said, "Okay." So I went up to the bulletin board and I was trying to copy the letter and the boss man came up and said, "You can't copy that, if you do you'll be fired." I went back to Eli that night and said, "Man, they said they'll fire us." He said, "I'm telling you it's your constitutional right," and he said, "I need a copy of that letter." I said, "I'll get a copy of that letter today." So I went on into work and lo and behold they had tables set up with tablecloths on them. They were having a safety dinner for us.

When the company claimed that they had no lost time for accidents they'd give us a little old dinner. But I've actually seen people with an arm in a cast sitting in the office. Prior to the union, we thought they were doing us a favor by letting us come in, sit in the office, and pay us. We didn't know nothing about workmen's compensation.

So I went to the pay phone which the company had conveniently installed to keep us out of the office. They had said we could use it any time we wanted to and I had done so. If there had been a storm, I'd call home to make sure the kids were all right and all. So I called Eli and said, "Look man, I can't copy that letter tonight because we're having a safety supper." Course he had to know what that was, so I quickly explained it to him. So I said, "Anyway, Eli, I'm hungry and I want to eat my supper." But he said, "Look Crystal, you can afford to lose a few pounds and I need that letter." He knew he had made me mad then, so I said, "I'll get that damn letter."

So I started talking around and I came up with this idea. I went over to the ones that were in the union and I said, "Look, Eli needs that letter so I'll tell you what let's do. I'll memorize the first two lines of it and go in the bathroom and write it down. Mary, you memorize the next two" and I told all of them the lines of the paragraph to remember. Well, it got to be a big joke because we were pretending like we were getting water, you know, and trying to read the letter too. But we couldn't remember what we had read by the time we got to the bathroom. So we all got to laughing about it. So I said, "Hell, I got to get that letter." So I said to my sister, she was a service person, I said, "Seretha, I need a clipboard." She said, "What you going to do?" I said, "I'm going to get that letter." We didn't have no set time for a break, they said they would motion for us when it was our turn to go eat. Seretha said, "Oh, God," but she gave me a clipboard.

As soon as they motioned for us, I took the clipboard and went immediately to the bulletin board and started to write. Because of the supper, everyone from management was at this dinner. So they took turns coming up to me telling me that I couldn't copy that letter. If I did, I'd be fired. Then the big man come up and he called me Lee. His name was Mason Lee. I said, "Mr. Lee, I didn't know you knew my name." And he said, "Yeah, I know who you are." He told me that if I didn't leave he was going to call the police to come in there and take me out. I said, "Mr. Lee, sir, you do what you want on your break time, you even get to go out for supper, and we can't even sit on the steps. This is my break time and I'm telling you I'm going to copy this letter. It's my constitutional right." So I continued to write and my knees were shaking like I was going to collapse any minute. I said, "If you do call the cops, you're going to have to call the Chief of Police because my husband is a jealous man and he won't let me ride home with just anybody." I thought to myself I'm going to put him to the test. I'm just going to push him and see what he does do.

So I copied the letter and folded it up and stuck it down my bra figuring well, nobody will get it down there. I went on down there and got me a plate and went to this special canteen that the company had installed within the last month. They no longer let the ones in my department go to the old canteen. As soon as we got into work we had to report to the new canteen. Right there within twenty steps of my job they built this canteen. They went to that much trouble to separate me from the rest of the workers. And I went in there and everybody said, "God, you got more guts, what did they say?" I gave my dinner to some man in there and said, "Well as soon as they blow the whistle, they'll come and get me. Mr. Lee said they were going to fire me and call the police. So y'all can expect anything."

I went back out there when I figured break was about up, put on my lipstick and was acting real cool, calm and collected when we all started back to work. Then here they come. Three of them. "Mr. Lee wants to see you in the office." So I said, "Seretha don't you let nobody mess with my pocketbook, I'll be back shortly." "All right," she said. So they took me up to the door of the main office and pushed a button and the door came open and they took me in there where they were all sitting at a big table and Mason Lee was sitting at the head. He started talking to me and I said, "Mr. Lee, sir," I had me a pencil and a piece of paper, I said, "Before you tell me anything you going to have to tell me all your names and how to spell them." So he started to spell his name and then he stopped and said, "I don't have to do that."

Then he started telling me all the things that I had done wrong. Said I had stayed in the bathroom too long, used the pay phone when I wasn't supposed to, and, you know, all different kinds of reasons. He was talking so much I remember putting my hands on my ears and thinking, here is all these people in here that I have served at the restaurant, a couple of them I'd danced with, and my floorlady who had had me call my husband and get him to bring chicken up to the mill for us. All these people knew he was lying but didn't a one of them have the guts to say so. None of them said, "Mr. Lee you're lying, she used that phone on her break time, she was told she could use it." Nobody said nothing. I said, "I don't have anything to say. There is nobody in here on my side. Y'all are all company people and no matter what I say, y'all are going to be right and I'm going to be wrong." So then he said, "You going to have to leave the plant." And I said, "I don't have no way to go home. I didn't drive the car today, I got a ride with my sister." He said, "You call your husband to come and get you." And I said, "My husband's at work." So he said "You call you a taxi." I said, "I don't have any money. You got to let me go back out there and get my pocketbook." Then he told Tommy Gardner, he said, "You go out there and get her pocketbook." I said, "If anybody touches my pocketbook, I'm going to have a warrant taken out on them for stealing." Finally, he said, "Let her back out there to get her pocketbook."

They went through the door with me and I went on around there and this black woman, Mary Moses, said, "What happened?" I said, "He fired me." Then I said, "Mary, give me your magic marker." So I grabbed it and I took a piece of pasteboard and I wrote the word UNION on it and, for some reason, I don't know why I did it, I climbed on the table and I just slowly turned the sign around. Everybody was in a state of shock and the machines started shutting down and everything got quiet. People started giving me the V sign. Then different ones from management came down there and tried to get me down off the table. Even my sister came down there. She said, "Lee, get down off that table and let me call Cookie to come and get you." Then I said to the boss man, "It's not their break time. Y'all gonna have to fire all of them too." Then sure enough here comes the chief of police. I got off the table and walked over there and he said, "Lee, what's wrong?" I said, "The man fired me and he fired me because I been trying to get the union in." He said, "Come on, let me take you home." I said, "You gonna take me home?" and he said, "Yeah." I said, "I want you to put that in writing." And I handed him a piece of paper and he started to write, and then he balled it up and said, "I don't have to do that." Then he grabbed me and literally forced me out of the gate and I was trying to get back in. I was fighting. It was a damn good thing I didn't know karate or he would have had to shoot me, and would have probably gotten away with it. They forced me in the car and took me to jail and locked me up.

I remembered from watching Perry Mason that they had to allow me to make one phone call. So that's all I'd say. He asked me my name (he knew my name, he lived a block over from me and he was my first cousin's husband) and I'd say, "All I got to say is that you supposed to allow me one phone call. So he did and when he did, I called the union office. Eli wasn't in but the other organizer was and she knew where he was, she'd get in touch with him and they'd be down there just as soon as they could. Well, he took me in there and he's the one that locked me up, shoved me in the cell and locked me up. The women's section of the jail was away from the other part and it was beginning to get dark outside. It was filthy in there. I started crying because I thought nobody really knows where I am. I didn't know whether Eli was going to come or not. I was thinking what effect this was going to have on the kids when the other children found out that their mama had been in jail.

Well, it seemed like forever, but Eli did come. He offered me a cigarette. He squatted down and I was laying on the bed crying. I said, "Eli, you know I don't smoke." Then he walked over and said, "Open this damn door and let her out." Boy, that chief of police put the key in there and he opened that damn door too. The next day Eli went down there with this other organizer from out of town and they met with the city manager and the chief of police and the big people in town and Eli told them that this International would not tolerate such actions, that they were liable to be sued for conspiracy with the companies. And we had no more trouble with them. Prior to that they would circle the hotel where the union office was, watching us, spying on us all the time, but after that, there was not any violence in that campaign whatsoever.

That night Cookie came up to the hotel and Eli explained what happened. Well now, Jay had been born illegitimately and I had always wanted to tell the boys they had different daddies. I wanted my children to know. But Cookie refused to allow me to do so. He had said they didn't have to know things like that. I just knew that when they grew up they would find out and they would hate me for it. If they thought I'd lie to them about that I'd lie to them about anything. So I just told Cookie, I said, "Well nobody will ever have anything to hold over me no more." So I woke the children up and I always kept pictures of their daddy and legal papers in a file box. So I took the pictures out and I told Mark that his real daddy was dead and I told Jay that he had a different daddy. That was the best thing I ever did in my life. I did it because I had been taken to jail and I figured somebody would be cruel enough to get that stuff going with the children in school. And I wanted my children to hear it from me. It set me free, it really did. The children accepted it. They were probably still a little young, but I think it made them even closer to each other. Until this day they're really close. That really set me free because then I had nothing to hide, nothing to be afraid of.

After that I got even more deeper involved with the union campaign. I was fired in 1973 but didn't get reinstated 'til 1978. My case went as high as the second circuit court in New York City. And it took that many years before a decision was made. Joseph Williams was a black man who was fired before me and he was also reinstated three weeks before me. He was also fired for union activity. He still works in the plant in Patterson.

Eli was always coming up with these ideas, like, if he had to go out of town he would ask me to keep the office open because he felt that people should know that somebody was there. We moved from this little room in the hotel to this bigger room. So I kept things going. If people came in with a problem I'd take a statement from them and was always available.

Then he came up with this bright idea. He thought we should have some cheerleaders and I said, "Oh God, Eli, I don't have time to do all this stuff. Cookie's already fussing that I spend too much time at the union office now." But anyway I started talking to the children about it and they were all excited about it. So at one time I had about twenty cheerleaders. I made all the outfits for them. The idea was to get their parents involved with the union. They cheered outside at the meetings and stuff like that. It was very effective.

Then Christmastime came and Eli decided we needed a float for the Christmas parade. That was a hassle because those in charge of the parade didn't want us to have a union float. So we went around to try to find a float and naturally Eli was out of town again. So I got some women and men together and we decided it would be cheaper to rent a float than to try to fix one up. So we went down there and put our name in the pot and then had to go down there and see someone in Roanoke Rapids, some higher-ups, for them to agree to let us be in the parade. I made clown suits and got the cheerleaders and the float ready and none of us mothers had ever been cheerleaders or been on a float. Then what was the most confusing thing was getting them to march, but we got it together. We sang Christmas songs like "Silent Night" and "Santa Claus is Coming to Town," and stuff like that. This was about six months into the union drive. At that time I was on unemployment and they ruled in my favor cause I just explained that I got fired for union activity. The company just did me a favor because that just gave me more time to work for the union. I never will forget all those patterns we cut out for those cheerleader outfits, but we finally got them sewed up in time for Christmas. That was an exciting part of my life because I was doing something I didn't even think I could do.

I worked full-time like that for the union up until Eli resigned. He was mentally and physically worn out. He was there for one year. An organizer's life is hard and can be very lonely. It's twenty-four hours and seven days a week. You deal with the workers but you don't have anybody to talk to about your own problems. Workers tend to forget that organizers are human being also, that we too have families. They forget that we breathe and bleed the same way they do. I really hated to see Eli leave the campaign but I knew that he had done what he said he would do. He had said, "I told y'all the day I came here that I had never lost an election and didn't intend to lose this one. Now I've done all that I can do and the International has sent in other organizers." He needed to be with his family. He probably didn't go home but three or four times and then just for a few days the whole time he was here. He gave his whole self to that campaign. Then when he resigned, I continued talking union and stuff like that, but I wouldn't go to the union office because I felt like the new organizers resented me because Eli and I were so close. And I felt like a lot of them had backstabbed Eli, that they had not supported him like they should have throughout the campaign.

Then I stayed with Cookie until 1976 when he said he had had enough. He didn't want me to get involved with the union from the very beginning and I resented that because there he was at the paper mill making about twelve dollars an hour and he was a shop steward. He said if I got involved I'd get fired. He'd pick me up at work and say, "Well, you made it through one more day."

And I'd say, "Why you keep saying I'm going to get fired? I'm not the only person in the union." And he'd say, "Because I know how you are. When you believe in something you give it all you got." He'd say, "You gonna get fired." And he was right. He wasn't shocked when I got fired. Even though he helped with the cleaning and he learned to iron, he would throw my union work up to me. And I said, "Hell, let the housework go, I'll do it some time. I can do it, I don't need sleep. I can sleep when I'm dead." I just didn't need that kind of crap. So we had an election in 1974 and we won, but we didn't get a contract until October 19, 1980. That's because JP Stevens was found guilty so many times of bargaining unfairly. They had to go through all that in court before they would sit down and bargain for a contract. It took six years to get that contract.

Right after I got fired, Henry Liebframan, a free-lance journalist, heard that a campaign was going on and he came to Roanoke Rapids and talked to Eli. He had been reading about the campaign and heard that textile workers were better off now than they had been in the thirties. He didn't believe that, because he had some family in a plant here, so he wanted to do an article for the *New York Times Magazine*. So Eli said, "You probably want to talk to Crystal because she just got fired." So he interviewed me and he wrote the article for the *New York Times*. It was such a success that the Macmillian Publishing Company asked him to write a book and so he wrote his first book, *Crystal Lee: A Woman of Inheritance*. I agreed to let him do it and Eli was real excited about it because he explained to me about how important it was for union people to learn about unions, doing education work and everything. So I agreed for him to do the book. The book came out in 1975. I'll never forget 'cause one of my first boyfriends, Gilbert Newsome, had a commercial going on the television. He was working at the tire place then, and they were advertising the book *Crystal Lee: A Woman of Inheritance*. I got a big kick out of that. I was proud to have lived long enough to see something I believe in do people good.

It was interesting, too, that a movie was actually made of my life. Mama had always wanted one of us to win the Miss America pageant or something and I thought this was even better than winning a beauty pageant. I felt like my daddy would've been real proud of me. When he first got me the job in Cone Mills, he said, "Now honey, they got a union down there but you don't have nothing to do with it or you'll be fired." And I was brought up to believe in what my daddy said. I never questioned it. I just remember seeing this woman. I found out she was a shop steward, and she was always laughing, carrying on, having a good time. And I said, "What in the world she always going to the office for," and they said she was taking care of union business. And I remember thinking, what in the world could be so bad about having a union when she was having such a good time. But I never asked anybody about it and they never tried to get me to join the union there. I guess they figured that if my parents were anti-union, they figured I probably would be too. What changed my mind about that was living with Cookie Jordan, listening to his meetings and him being a shop steward. He was making more money, had his birthday off, had decent insurance. I thought if he could be in a union, I didn't see why textile workers couldn't have a union too, and make those wages and have some of those benefits.

When I heard about them wanting to make a movie, the author called me about it and I wanted script rights, because you can see sex and violence any-time you cut the TV on. I said it had to be about the union. I said that rinky-dinky stuff wasn't important. So he told them and they said that, naw, they couldn't do that, you know, give me script rights. So I said, "I don't need the publicity to tell them they can't do it." But they did anyway and I didn't make a cent on it.

I understand the political situation now better than I did before. I under-stand the need to be involved with politics. Politics is what makes this world go 'round. It is the ruling factor in why the poor continue to be poor and the rich continue to be rich. This bothers me a lot. Textile workers in North Car-olina are the lowest paid and the least unionized in the South, where the labor struggle is hard and is getting harder every day. I attribute that to people we have in Congress. The Republicans. I understand the importance of history, which I didn't when I was in school. See, the only thing I learned in school about the unions was in economics. I still have my economics book at home and it had three little pages on unions. I remember my teacher when she taught about the unions, she talked about the blacks, the "niggers" as she called them, concentrated on driving big fancy cars and living in shacks. But Cookie Jordan always said I was color blind, that I couldn't tell one color from another. That was another reason he was against me going to that union meeting, because it was going to be in a black church. He was definitely, wholly, against it, but thank God I'm color blind.

Still my kids have only those three pages on unions, about the boycotts and the strikes. There is still a real need for union education in the schools. That's why the struggle is so hard. In my life I haven't seen no difference in the lives of textile workers. 🖋

SUGGESTIONS FOR WRITING

1. How did you respond to Sutton's story? Were you sympathetic or critical? How does your social position affect your reaction to her story?

2. Sutton describes how teachers and schools reacted differently to students, depending on their parents' social standing. Describe an incident in which you observed these reactions in school.

3. Articulate your opinion about labor unions. Does Sutton's story affect your opinion? Is changing people's minds about unions the purpose of her writing?

DEAR MRS. ROOSEVELT

M. W.

This letter is one of many written during the Great Depression in the 1930s by workers complaining about the conditions of their jobs, addressed directly to President Franklin Delano Roosevelt, or in this case, to his wife, Eleanor Roosevelt, in the hope that the government would alleviate their suffering. In this letter a sixty-one-year-old woman who works in a hotel kitchen appeals to Mrs. Roosevelt, who was brought up and lived in the highest possible social class in America, to plead her case with the president. What closes the social gap between the writer and her audience is the fact that they are both women. **M. W.**, *the author of the letter, assumes that Mrs. Roosevelt can understand her situation because she is a woman, and that Mrs. Roosevelt will sympathize with her and change her life.*

This letter is contained in a collection edited by Gerald Markowitz and David Rosner under the title "Slaves of the Depression" (1987). Markowitz and Rosner are historians on the faculty of the City University of New York.

Atlanta, Georgia, February 19, 1937

Dear Mrs. Roosevelt:

Since Congress is in session again, and our wonderful President is also again on the job, I am begging you to help assist the women working in hotels in this country, especially in the South. I have been in the work since I was 32 years of age, and I am near 61 now, and on a hard job in one of our best hotels here in Atlanta, in the salad department.

I leave home at 10:30 A.M. to be on the job at 12 o'clock. I work like fighting fire, until 10 at night, and more than that. We have late people, and very often, it is 10:30 before I leave the department, and I must then dress for the street, get a [trolley] car, and transfer to my home car. I look over the daily paper, then to bed, and it is almost all I can do to get up and do some little things and leave for my work.

Often I go a little ahead of time to get a cup of coffee, and a bite to eat, before 12 o'clock. But it is no use, the waiters call for things, and where is the man in the dept. he has slipped out to smoke a cigarette, and I must leave my dinner, and go on the job. My coffee gets stone cold, and the only dinner and lunch I get is a bite at a time, for I must do all the cleaning behind the 18 year old boy, that they keep at a smaller salary, and help serve the lunch and then get everything ready for the night meal, and most of the time several parties. We had a party of 150 last night, and a good regular run, and some overtime to stay. I grab a cup of coffee, as I am closing up, and swallow a bite of something, as the manager is hurrying to close.

Well. . .what do I get per month for this fast hard work seven days per week and overtime and to 12:30 on Saturday nights. I get $35 per month, and 60 cents out of that on the Old Age Pension. So you see they rate me at $60. I wear some old ragged uniforms that the coffee shop girls have discarded and an average of three per week are run through their house laundry. My top aprons are brought home and put in another laundry at my expense with my caps and so on.

Yesterday. . . I had given to me for lunch a spoon of mashed potato, a little dumpling, made with something, and a spoon of collard greens. I just go ahead and eat a little ice-cream behind the backs of the managers, or I would go hungry, with $25 taken out of my salary, and me eating breakfast at home.

I am an old experienced worker, and fast and clean and give full satisfaction, but that is the life of a Southern hotel woman worker. Young men soon get better pay while the poor women are made the goat on and on. Me and the colored help scrub at night. Me in my dept., and the negros for the cooks and cold meat counters. The men smoke cigarettes and laugh and talk.

Mrs. Roosevelt, is this fair to women in any section of the country, and can you not influence the President to make laws that will stop it. Laws—with six days and 48 hours per week. . . .

We are not fighting for a 30 hour week, we are breaking in health under 10 to 12 hours a day of fast hard work in a hot hot kitchen (will not let cold air in during serving hours) and only beg for 8 hours in a straight watch (not a split watch) and one day to lie in bed, and rest.

If you think I am telling you wrong concerning our work, you will find on looking over the work that I am right, and it is even worse than I am telling you.

I am so old that you cannot do me much good, but for the younger ones it can be a blessing in the coming years. What do I get out of life, and on pay day what do I have, and we all give to Red Cross also.

I am hoping that Dr. Townsend will sometime bring a better pension than we have so far. Capital will not pay us a living wage, so it must come some other route. I am opposed to Coughlin and all those crokers, but I believe that Townsend himself means well.

Thanking you for reading this petition, and hope you may see just what we live under while men are fighting for six hours and more pay. Give the forgotten women in Southern Hotels a chance to eat, and a day to lie in bed and rest from the hard work.

Yes I am in favor of enlarging the Supreme Court, and I know that all that President Roosevelt advocates is right, or he would not advocate it start with, and I know you are extremely proud of such a husband for he is even greater than any that has ever been in our country. We love him, and know that he is for the working man and woman.

M. W. 🖋

Suggestions for Writing

1. What signs in the letter indicate that M. W. is writing to a woman of a higher social class? What is M. W.'s attitude toward Mrs. Roosevelt?

2. What is M. W.'s attitude toward the government in general? Do you believe that the government could help you with problems with your job? If you were having problems on your job, where would you turn for help?

3. Does the letter succeed in getting *your* sympathy? Why or why not?

ECONOMIC INDEPENDENCE AND SOCIAL RESPONSIBILITY: THE WORLD OF UPPER-MIDDLE-CLASS WOMEN

Elizabeth Oakes

Elizabeth Oakes, a cultural anthropologist, interviews Eleanor, an upper-middle-class white woman who has worked on her own in the corporate world and who has been the wife of a corporate executive. The interview covers her work experience, her volunteer efforts, her leisure activities, and her housework. In all of these aspects, her social class plays a determining role. She works with and socializes with other members of her class. In fact, almost every facet of Eleanor's life is a function of the social class she inhabits, the world of the corporate executive. This interview explores the interconnections between the economic facts of this woman's life and her feelings about herself and her position in the world.

INTRODUCTION

For the purpose of understanding the relationship between women and work, I interviewed an upper-middle-class American white woman. What follows are excerpts from those sections of the taped interview in which she speaks of some of the many facets of her life, facets which contribute to a world characterized by economic independence and social responsibility.

Through the words of Eleanor, the world of many upper-middle-class women is explored. It is a world of private girls' school, corporate wifery, suburban life, multiple residences, affluent living conditions as well as work, whether it is running a business, investing in the stock market, or fundraising.

While tempting, it is ill-informed to reduce these elite women to stereotypes of the suburban wife or business executive indistinguishable from her male counterparts. Their lives are as complex as the lives of women from any other class. They, too, have families and households, work and nonwork activities. The fact that they play the stock market or run a business tells us only part of the story; for it is equally important to understand these women's particular sense of social responsibility and their aesthetic sensibility. Each facet of their lives, such as their relationship to their husbands and servants, their homes and hobbies, contributes to a complete picture and reveals the specificity of their experience as upper-middle-class women. Their perception of society is shaped in part by the environment in which they live: a house in the country, traveling to Europe, gardening, etc.

Still, conflict is present in their lives. One such conflict stems from their economic and psychological isolation. This isolation stands in contrast to their deep social involvement with friends and community. They lead isolated lives in private schools, suburbia, and the nuclear family. Yet, at the same time, they develop long-lasting friendships with women of the same class, and they learn social responsibility to their community at an early age. They grow up to perform volunteer work and fundraise. However, their relationship to men—both fathers and husbands—is often distant.

Another conflict exists between their desire to "do for oneself" as opposed to "doing for others." There is tension between the desire to "put oneself first" and the commitment to "do for others"—kin and community.

Finally, this one life history reflects how deeply women of this class yearn for independence, whether it is economic, psychological, or physical.

PERSONAL HISTORY AND BACKGROUND

Eleanor grew up in a family with one sister, one brother, a mother, and a father. She attended a girls' boarding school in Pennsylvania from the ninth grade until senior year. After graduating, she attended college for one year. She then left college and got married. She was nineteen. After ten years of marriage and giving birth to four boys, Eleanor and her professional husband divorced, leaving her as a single mother. She subsequently worked as a real estate broker and an airline executive. She then remarried. Currently, she tends to three residences, fundraises for various organizations, and travels with her husband on business. In the following section, she describes some of the experiences of her boarding school life, her interaction with boys, her first marriage, and life in suburbia.

I went to coed school through eighth grade and the rest of it was female. I was in a private girls' school. There were only a hundred girls—it was small. There were a hundred day students and a hundred boarders. This was outside of Philadelphia, Pennsylvania.

I was a boarder. And the day students (I had a very good friend who was a day student) would come to school with traces of lipstick on from the night before, but we were not allowed to wear lipstick; we had to wear uniforms. They had real natural, normal lives. When they were sixteen they would drive their own car to school and we were so envious we could hardly stand it. And they were outsiders as far as a lot of activities were concerned because being a boarding school, the boarding half had a lot of plays and things that you were involved in, in the evenings, that the day scholars were not part of.

It was unfortunate in many ways culturally. Besides the fact that every student was a girl, the faculty was all female. And the only time that we saw a man was when we went to church on Sunday, which was compulsory—the minister. Or maybe somebody who was working on the grounds or something like that. There was one social activity that they did have—it was kind of horsey country. . .

They had an activity called "beagling." The pack of beagles would go out . . . chasing the smell of rabbits. And they had sort of a Master of the Hounds of the beagles. And the beagles ran and you ran and you ran over fences and you ran and ran and ran. And it all would have been loathsome excepting for the fact that, number one, there was a superb hunt breakfast or tea.

And they're sniffing away and barking and hallooing and there was a lovely hunt tea afterwards and also there were some young men there.

After Boarding School

I went to college for one year and I was married at nineteen and I had my first child when I was twenty-one. I had four children by the time I was twenty-seven. I was the typical housewife. I wouldn't quite say suburban because we raised dogs and were much more apt to live in the country and our life, our times together, were spent with this common hobby of training and showing dogs and hunting. But, ah, so we did spend some time in the suburbs but very briefly. But it was the same kind of life. I mean, I would drive car pools and I was a Boy Scout den mother and I was active in the PTA and that kind of stuff, the usual activities.

Life Now

I'm apt to be in the country three weeks of a month and in the city one week a month. The life is complicated. It's running three places.

One (home) is an apartment in the city. One is a home in the country, and the other is a house in a summer resort area, which is rented out a good bit of the time, but it takes a certain amount of organization. I would say we'd be lucky if we spent thirty days a year there . . . . But it's an oasis for my husband. He really feels he is on an island, and once you get on a ferry, you leave the rest of the country behind. It is very important for him. It's where he relaxes best.

WORK

In the following section Eleanor describes the isolation of housework and suburban nuclear family life. She then goes on to describe the different jobs she has held. In this section the relationship of Eleanor to her work activities becomes evident. From housework to real estate agent, the particularity of "work" to her class position is clear.

One thing that is interesting about being a housewife. I think it's the loneliest job in the world. And there is a certain amount of drinking that is done that I've seen. That, I'm sure, is caused by the loneliness.

And when you take people into an isolated situation, even if it's a two-acre isolation or a quarter-acre isolation, it's very hard. It's also, I think, the job that you have to have the most self-discipline. There's nobody, there's no deadline usually, and there's nobody there, nobody to watch you to see—like at work if you're sitting there with your feet on the desk, everybody sees you doing nothing. It's very easy to do nothing at home. You have to be, I think, extraordinarily well disciplined to make life meaningful.

The first job I got since I had absolutely no training in anything was with a small business that operates corporate aircraft. The corporation owned the aircraft and they hired the company that I worked for to staff it and make sure that the aircraft was kept up and to make all the arrangements for their travel all over the world wherever they were going. And it was a very exciting job because it was the kind of job with a lot of variety of activity for me. I never quite knew when I went to work what I was going to be doing that day.

And I went on trips to Washington to help with my boss to see about helping to get air routes. You had to go. I learned there that the system of government when one has worked in a government agency, whether it be the FAA, CAA, SEC, then you go into private practice and you have a gold mine of a job because you're the person who knows the ins and outs of it. And you never go to a lawyer or a person that has not had training in the government agency in which you wish to get whatever you want. And it was just a big, long learning process. And I found it fascinating.

I learned basically office procedures which I had never been exposed to. I didn't know how to file things. I didn't have to be in charge of the filing, the secretary did that, but I had to know how to find it. And, it was a very, very stimulating and interesting experience. It did not pay an awful lot.

And I started out with very prosaic jobs, keeping records of pilots' flying hours and learning a great deal about aircraft. How fast each airplane flew. How long it would take when the New York office calls and says, "Well, there are two guys who are flying to Detroit and they want to be there; they have to be there for a meeting at eleven. What time do they have to be at the airport?" Learn the times, make arrangements—more housewifery—to make sure that the limousine was waiting for them at the other end, that the motel rooms were ordered, make sure that the schedule fit, that the schedule of the aircraft fit their schedule.

As time went on I found that I was hiring stewardesses. And this was not for the corporate planes but we did also have an aircraft that flew commercially. I would get phone calls from India from the boss saying, "OK, we've arrived safely. What's new? Catch me up."

It was a fun aircraft. The steward spoke seven languages. He was a very handsome, dashing Swiss man and served five-course dinners on the plane flying across the Atlantic with the appropriate wine at each course. Oh, yeah, this particular airplane was the largest and fanciest corporate aircraft in the country. And this aircraft was taken down to Texas . . . where it got the interior . . . it was hard to imagine. It had gold fixtures in the bathroom. And it had a master bed . . . for the CEO, Chief Executive Officer—head of the company. And it had a crew of five, with the pilot, copilot, flight engineer, steward—he always had a steward, would never have a stewardess—and then a maintenance man who would go along. And they would go around the world so they were able to take care of the aircraft wherever they went.

THE CORPORATE WORLD PART I:
THE CORPORATE WIFE

The following section describes the thoughts, feelings, and duties of corporative wives. It details the pushes and pulls on the woman who is forced to put the husband and his job first.

If You Take the Average Corporate Wife . . .

I think one of the reasons why the sacrifices are made to the corporations is 'cause that's where their money comes from—to live the way they want to live. I think that if the wife were financially independent and the income that they had together was enough to make them comfortable, there might be different choices. I think it's a marketplace choice.

The wife had to be a certain part of the functions and I think that I helped him get the job. . . . I had to be interviewed as well as he before he was given the job.

Well, it wasn't a formal interview in that way. I was invited down and the director of the hospital, who was not married at that time, had a dinner party where they had a number of senior-staff members there and their wives and it was a social go-through, I think, mainly, to see if I would be "one of the team."

They pump you about your life and what you are interested in and where you have lived and what you cared about. I think they just wanted to make sure that you didn't eat peas with your knife and things like that. I mean, there was a certain amount of that. That you could pass.

I felt like an IBM wife.

I think the key is, the real key is that the husband's job comes first and that has to be understood. In evaluating the family and the marriage in conjunction with the job, the husband comes first and the job comes first and then after that the family fits in. The IBM stands for "I've Been Moved."

You could never say, "I'm sorry, I like this community. And my children are happy in school. And we won't take the promotion and move." That was the sure path to mediocrity. So I think it doesn't matter what business it is, that is key. And I must say, as a wife, as a marital partner, if the man is not happy in his job I think it's very hard for a marriage to exist because there is nothing that a wife can do to supply the ego feedback the job does.

A good executive works hard and he plays hard too. What I've found is that the competition that is the food that they live on when they are working, they can't turn it off when they come home and it will go into the golf game or the tennis game or whatever it is. They do everything to win. There is no such thing in their lexicon as playing for fun.

But also along with it, I think, is that a good executive is very curious and is always learning and therefore an alive person.

The other thing is that the executive social life is totally arranged by the wife. I mean, she may say, "Do you want to see so-and-so?" But if the wife were not there, there would be no social life. He does not call anyone and say, "Hey, do you want to go out to dinner Saturday night?"

Well, if it's a party that had to do with my husband's business, very often the people who are there, the majority of the men are in the same business and so the reason why we were invited is because of the fact that my husband is who he is in his field. So it is very easy to feel that you are a tagalong. But I have found on the whole that people are very open to talking to you even if you are a "woman not in the field."

. . . it's golf, and it's tennis, and it's bridge, and it's entertaining a great deal in the evenings, but there were people who did—I'm sure—volunteer work which was going on in one way or another.

And certainly in the suburb that I lived in, a lot of people became interior decorators, a lot became real estate brokers. And that was my first exposure because it was a suburb, bedroom community of New York, and everybody was married and two-by-two in New York. Divorce in the sixties was not half as prevalent as it is today. And a single woman was out-of-synch and a single working woman especially was out-of-synch with the rest of the community.

THE CORPORATE WORLD PART II:
THE FEMALE EECUTIVE

In this section Eleanor describes female executives she knows as well as giving her opinions on sexism at the corporate level.

I went to a Board of Directors meeting once in a corporation that I own a few shares of stock. And the question came up, "Why don't you have any women on the Board of Directors?" And this man said, "As soon as there is a woman who is able enough to be on our Board of Directors, I will have her. But I am not going to have a token woman on this Board." And I couldn't agree with him more. I think it is a total disadvantage to any woman or minority member to Peter Principle them into something that they are not able to handle and it is bad for both sides.

Most women who are in my age group who have jobs of responsibility and who have "arrived" have fathers who treated them in the same way that they treated the son if they had sons. Or just treated them as an individual, not as a girl. And this is the way Joan (a friend of mine) was brought up by her father.

She is in the cosmetics world—she's a superb executive. She has a fantastic ability to have people work with her, for her, well. She's very sure of herself. She was, for a period of time, head of a company's international setting-up all over Europe—their cosmetic sales areas. They sent her to Harvard, paid for her to get a quicky MBA, which she did a couple of years ago. I think she's probably about fifty-five now at the most, max. And she is now in charge of their mergers and acquisitions. She is a very able woman. Very warm. Her life is very hectic. There is a vast amount of traveling. There is also a vast amount of what I could consider time spent on trivia which is part of the business. And that is: "how things look," and entertaining, and "are the right people here," and making sure that all of the executives or whoever in whatever country are happy. That would absolutely send me up the wall. It is too much like being a house-wife. I don't want to do it in business.

The woman executive does a great deal more interrelating with people than the man executive does. I think that a man is much more apt to make a deci-sion on his own or discuss things with more people and the woman needs a lit-tle bit more, maybe, a feeling of support before she comes to a decision.

I would like to, also, be a real tough executive. I'd like to have a career goal from the time that I was very young, and devote a great deal of those energies to myself and that goal. Selfish—not selfish, self-centered. Self-confident. Well it isn't necessarily the tough executive, but it's the picture of a life where I really think about myself first. It would be a mind-blowing experience.

INVESTING: TOWARD ECONOMIC INDEPENDENCE

In this section of the interview, Eleanor describes the importance of women's financial independence to the maintenance of their self-respect. She describes how she invests in the stock market, enabling her to keep her independence from her husband. This independence is both psychological and economic.

And it's sad to say, but I think that very often in this world, money is power. It isn't as powerful as ideas, but if you get down below that—it is power—and this is what bugs me so about so many women my age. They say that the stock in the United States is owned at least 52 percent by women, not men, and they're probably a lot of them widows, and they just hand it over to some bank with some conservative policy and those bankers, I think, should go to jail for what they do with people's money. They don't pay any attention to them. They just stash it away in something that's safe and pays very little—and that's what the woman gets—and she pays for that service. It's cruel.

I think that specifically in marriages it's one of the ways that a woman can get out of the domination of a husband. If she has her own money, he can't boss her around in the same way 'cause she can tell him where to head. Whatever her dependency patterns are; I mean sometimes there's somebody who's got plenty of money, I guess, and is still dependent for other reasons. This is why the women in the work force today, I think, have much more of a sense of themselves, plus the power of being independent—and it gets rid of one crutch.

I don't say that I feel powerful. But I feel independent. And I also feel, even though it's slimy, that when one is in a position—if you go into a trust company or something like that—and you have some money—they're gonna treat you with a whole different respect than if you don't. Now it's nothing that—I mean I don't like it—but it's the truth.

When I first had some money after my father died, I could stop working if I wanted to. I knew I had this very good cushion and I knew darn well we were never going to starve and we were going to have a roof over our heads.

A woman friend of mine who—again divorced—went into the financial business world in New York City when she was fifty because there was a need—

the investment companies finally realized that there was a need to have women there as counselors, money consultants, because there were some women who didn't want to talk to a man. She would start off with things like reading the financial pages every day, in the *Times* and the *Wall Street Journal*. Getting certain financial information services. Getting just a feel—doing dry runs, pretends—starting out by being safe—and diversifying and then, as you feel more confidence in yourself, you can grow, put more things in the fields that you believe in, and not have to be so conservative about it. But she was my teacher, and it was very nice of her to take the time.

I spend a considerable amount of time reading and keeping up on things in the financial world, so that I can make a little bit of money on the stock money. I would not be at all happy just handing what I have to somebody else and saying "do it." And if I have a particular goal, or something that I want money for, I'll knock myself out trying to find an option or something else that's gonna make it big.

Now recently I have invested in Kelly Services, the secretarial and other help, and the Reagan administration—what they're doing—and a lot of corporations—what they're doing—is cutting back on regular work force, because they have to pay so many benefits. And so if they have temps, they can pay the temp a little bit more per hour, but they don't have to pay all these extra benefits. So this is good for a temp company.

National Education is a company that specializes in trade schools and reeducation of adults, mostly, and a lot of it is correspondence courses. And with all the layoffs in the steel industry, and so much of the capital areas of the United States, reeducation is necessary to get these people jobs, and I felt that this was really the right thing at the right time. It did very well for a while and it has gone down. . . .

I really am much more apt to invest in a concept and then try and find a company within the concept that I find is doing its best. And I've come through reading *Megatrends*—the market is psychology. Economics, pardon the expression, is not a science, and so I think if one looks towards where you think—either because of demographics or some other reason—there is a need, the person who supplies the need, and supplies it best, is ready to go.

The computer age has made a wonderful thing—because if you have a stock—every stock has a symbol and all you do is punch out the symbol and that will tell you in today's world what it closed, yesterday what it opened, what it is now, and then you can punch other little things which will bring out any late report that the company has sent out on any of its activities—whether it's on dividends or whatever. It's a way you can follow up what the activity of the company is—in between the quarterly reports or the annual reports. And it's marvelous to have that information close by.

I try not to make too many trades because it makes it difficult for my husband's business.

I don't like to borrow money from men. I don't want to be dependent on a man and I don't mind being dependent on a woman.

OUTSIDE INTERESTS

This part of the interview is devoted to elucidation of some of Eleanor's outside interests—gardening and traveling. In this section, she describes the importance of aesthetics in her life.

I like to arrange flowers. It takes a certain amount of creativity. And I'm very sensitive to color. Gardening is creative and a lawn is not creative. It's a totally different thing. We do not have a lawn here other than four little patches of lawn that can be mowed in twenty minutes. The rest of it is in a semiwild state. A lawn isn't a garden. A garden is creating paintings with different colors of things that you put together. And it is a constantly growing thing. It also is a land of friendship. Because if you have perennials, anytime you have a garden, any friend who has a garden and has some perennials, you always have to divide them. So, they share and you share and you look at your garden and you see your friends. It's very personal. I move things around every year. I do a complete map of everything. Really, I'm getting old. I'm doing things that I wouldn't have thought about doing when I was younger. Also there's the time to do it. But there is a map with every perennial that is there in the beds that are drawn to scale and I put a sheet of tissue paper over it every year and show exactly what is where and what color it is and get the idea of how tall it is and then, if I don't like the looks of it this year I will just divide in the spring and put things in different places. It's just such fun.

I love to travel. . . . We started in England and since the four boys were not overly enthusiastic about going to cathedrals and art galleries and things, I tried to make sure that there were athletic things. So we went to Wimbledon, to see the tennis, and then we went over to France and then we spent a few days in Amsterdam and rented a V.W. van, and that was home for the summer, sort of. Then we went to Paris, stayed a few days, and through the Loire—and then we stayed in the south of France, on the Atlantic side, for three weeks, and they went swimming every day, and played tennis, and met French kids—and it took them away from the stress. Then we went to Pamplona to see the running of the bulls—and then went on to Italy—a week in Florence, a week in Rome, and then driving up through northern Italy to Austria and Germany, up through the Rhine, and up through Arles, and took the boat home. But it was fantastic. It exposed them to all kinds of cultures, and different foods and different people. I had wanted to go abroad since I was young, and I knew exactly what I wanted to see, first on my list, in every place. And it was just fabulous.

If I go as a tourist to Europe I'm interested in the history and the culture—and there's much more of it, frankly, there than there is in the Carib [Caribbean], for me. And if you can go with a meaningful purpose and study or be involved in something that's going on in the country—then it would be fascinating—but as a tourist it's very skin deep. I've been back many, many times. I've never been to the Far East which I want to do very badly. I'm either gonna have to do it alone or with a female friend, because my husband doesn't like to be gone out of the country that long—and there's no point in rushing over and rushing back in two weeks—so I won't do that very much. Well, we're going to London next summer, and that's business, but it's usually in this country.

But I love being by myself. And if I don't have a certain amount of time by myself, I get exhausted, drained. So I need recharging battery time. So I can go for a whole day without talking to anybody, just going around doing my thing, and be very happy.

SOCIAL VALUES, SOCIAL RESPONSIBILITY: VOLUNTEER WORK

In this section, Eleanor describes her deep sense of community involvement and social responsibility. She describes the history of women's volunteer work and some of the drawbacks to contemporary forms of this work.

In another life I would like to be some sort of missionary, not a religious missionary. But I would like to have the training and be able to concretely help people.

It's the only kindness that you can do to help people who are, in that particular time, not in a position to help themselves. I wish I could do more. I wish I had the capability to offer more.

I just can't think of anything worse than somebody who is totally self-centered or cares only about themselves and their immediate friends and family. This is a great big world, and I would hate to be such a narrow person. There is always more pleasure in giving than receiving. It is much harder to receive than to give. And if you can do anything to help anybody, it's a double benefit. The old argument, with Freud, whether every "good" deed is selfishly driven, is great politically. Well the dichotomy of life is that you come into life and leave it alone; you're basically in the core. And on the other hand, you're a part of, a brother of everybody else on this earth and the caring has to go out . . . and finding out within your capabilities, your training, and your time is a very hard thing to find. If you find it, you'll find a happy person.

I was brought up by my mother to feel a strong commitment, a debt, to the community that you lived in. And you didn't just take, but within your capabilities you gave what you could.

She was very, very active. We were growing up in Virginia and she was very active with the Community Chest. She was the president of it at different times. She was terribly active in Planned Parenthood which was unheard of practically in the thirties. It was a nondiscussed subject, which did not bother her at all. She was very gung-ho for it. And in those days it was mostly volunteers. They didn't have paid staffs. She would be helping young women and older women. And she told me she was astonished at the number of women who didn't know "where babies came from."

The Junior League was one [volunteer organization] I suppose. The Junior League has changed a great deal from the time that I was a member, when I was first married . . . but it was sort of in . . . My first job was working at a large mental hospital, a state mental hospital outside of Boston, and they thought it might be a good idea for the patients that were able to start a little newspaper and everything in it would be the work of the patients. And you volunteered so many hours a week, and that was what I did.

It [volunteer work] started in the olden days, for ladies to do social work. And, upper-middle-class, middle-class ladies . . . the programs they started— working as gray ladies in the hospitals . . . . There was a great deal more volunteer work in the olden days than there is now . . . . Now, there are very, very few things that volunteers can do. It has become much more professional. And so the volunteer person . . . it pushes them into a fundraising role, which is not really always satisfactory.

I find it awfully hard myself to ask for cash, and I think you have to be terribly sure that the agency that you're asking money for is doing a very fine job in order in get the push. I can be enthusiastic, but to be a good fundraiser you're supposed to say "We would like you to give x number of dollars if you could," and they always put it high, and I just find it distasteful to do that. I don't want to shame somebody into giving money. I want them to give because they want to give. I've had entertaining in the house for fundraising. I've had meals that people come and have music, and in two weeks we're going to have a cellist and a pianist play and have thirty people in the house for after dinner, at eight o'clock. . . .

THE GENDER GAP: RELATIONS WITH WOMEN, NOT WITH MEN

This last section is devoted to Eleanor's views on male-female and female-female relationships. She alludes to the distance women of her position feel toward men and how that is reinforced by society and upbringing. This contrasts starkly with the closeness she feels toward other women.

I had great arguments with my mother when I was a teenager, because—I think, maybe it was later, when I was having children—she always said men were totally different from women and it's just the miracle of the age that you ever get two people as opposite as men and women to live and to coexist in the same space.

I know practically no single men which I think on the whole is because men are very uncomfortable unmarried after a certain age. They're lonely, and they want somebody to come home to. And I think women can handle their loneliness much better than men.

I have found it impossible to be close to a man without having had some sexual feeling somewhere. I haven't had an asexual relationship with a man— there is just something there, there's some chemical something that is just part of the relationship. . . . So I just have never been lucky enough to have had that.

And one of the things that was interesting to me was that I was really quite scared of men. I was working for a company where the only other woman there was the secretary. And I had not been in the company of men all my life. And, ah, learning how to relate to them, making friends, was a new part of my life. And I treasure very dearly two or maybe three couples who would just invite me over to dinner. But almost everybody that I saw in my social life then at that time were women.

Friendship is very, very important to me. I've had certain key women friends in my life that have meant a great deal and I like them. And I particularly like women nowadays when more women are working and doing interesting things. They have more interesting things to say. Some of them are professors; some of them have to do with the field of law; some of them have to do with the field of business; and some are interior decorators in the world of design. And I think that they can be just as fascinating any day as, and sometimes much more so than, talking to a bunch of men.

I feel this very strongly, and it's because tangentially you can touch with every woman in every way—either just because of her sex, or shared experience, or there are any number of ways. You've got any number of togethers there when you need them. ✒

SUGGESTIONS FOR WRITING

1. Analyze Eleanor's feelings about her wealth. Does she show any signs of feeling guilty about it? Is she proud of her position?

2. Eleanor describes her work in the corporate world as "more housewifery." Do the jobs traditionally associated with women in our economy often reflect traditional female roles? Can you give some examples? Does this trend limit the economic potential of women?

3. How much of a woman's life is determined by the occupation of her husband? Is this factor particularly important in the higher social classes, or is it important to all classes of women?

4. How did you react to Eleanor's description of her life? Were you sympathetic to her? Did you think her description of her social environment was accurate? Why or why not?

THE GILDED CAGE

Lewis Lapham

*"The Gilded Cage" is the first chapter from **Lewis Lapham**'s book* Money
and Class in America. *In this reading, Lapham describes the economic anxieties of the rich. The pleasure of Lapham's account for those of us who don't
live in "the gilded cage" is in the details, which show that Lapham is intimately familiar with the class he describes. He knows where the rich live, go
to school, vacation; he knows what they wear, what they eat, how they decorate their houses. Lapham's topic is not only the attitudes of the rich in
America, but the attitudes of all Americans as members of one of the wealthiest societies in the world.*

*Lapham (b. 1935) is a distinguished journalist who has been for many
years the editor of* Harper's *magazine.*

At Yale University in the middle 1950's the man whom I prefer to call George
Amory I knew chiefly by virtue of his reputation for wrecking automobiles. He
was the heir to what was said to be a large Long Island fortune, and I remembered him as a blond and handsome tennis player embodying the ideal of in-
souciant elegance seen in a tailor's window. During the whole of our senior year
I doubt that I spoke to Amory more than once or twice; we would likely have
seen one another in a crowd, probably at a fraternity beer party, and I assume
that we exchanged what we thought were witty observations about the differences between the girls from Vassar and those from Smith. At random intervals
during the 1960's and 1970's I heard rumors of Amory's exploits in the stock
market and the south of France, but I hadn't seen him for almost thirty years
when, shortly after President Reagan's second inaugural in the winter of 1985,
I ran across him in the bar of the Plaza Hotel. He seemed somehow smaller
than I remembered, not as blond or as careless. Ordinarily we would have nodded at one another without a word of recognition, and I remember being
alarmed when Amory carried his drink to my table and abruptly began to recite
what he apparently regarded as the epic poem of his economic defeat. Presumably he chose me as his confessor because we scarcely knew each other, much
less belonged to the same social circles. I wasn't apt to repeat what I heard to
anybody whom he thought important enough to matter.

"I'm nothing," he said. "You understand that, nothing. I earn $250,000 a
year, but it's nothing, and I'm nobody."

Amory at Yale had assumed that the world would entertain him as its guest.
He had little reason to think otherwise. Together with his grandmother's collection of impressionist paintings and the houses in Southampton and Maine,
he looked forward to inheriting a substantial income. Certainly it never had
occurred to him that he might be obliged to suffer the indignity of balancing
his checkbook or looking at a bill.

Things hadn't turned out quite the way he had expected, and in the bar of the Plaza he looked at me with a dazed expression, as if he couldn't believe that he had lost the match. He had three children, but his wife was without substantial means of her own, and somehow he failed to generate enough money to carry him from one week to the next. He explained that most of the paintings had been sold, that he had been forced to rent the house in Southampton for $40,000 during the season, and that the property in Maine had been stolen from him by his sister. He had been busy in the bar making lists of those expenses he deemed inescapable. Handing me a sheet of legal foolscap, he said:

"You figure it out. I can't afford to go to a museum, much less to the theater. I'm lucky if I can take Stephanie to dinner once every six months."

His list of disbursements appears as he gave it to me, the numbers figured on an annual basis in 1985 dollars and annotated to reflect the narrowness of the margin on which Amory was trying to keep up a decent appearance:

Maintenance of a cooperative apartment on Park Avenue: $20,400[1]
Maintenance of the house in Southampton: $10,000
Private school tuitions (one college, one prep school, one grammar school): $30,000
Groceries: $12,000[2]
Interest on a $200,000 loan adjusted to the prime rate: $30,000
Telephone, household repairs and electricity: $12,000
A full-time maid and a part-time laundress: $25,000
Insurance (on art objects, the apartment and his life): $8,000
Lawyers and accountants: $5,000
Club dues and bills: $5,000[3]
Pharmacy (cosmetics, medicine, notions): $5,000
Doctors (primarily for the children): $4,000
Charitable donations: $6,000[4]
Clothes for his wife: $5,000[5]
Clothes for his children: $7,000
Cash expenditures (taxis, newspapers, coffee shops, balloons, etc.): $8,000

---

[1]Given the expense of New York real estate, Amory could count himself lucky to be paying so low a price. He had inherited the apartment, ten rooms at East Seventy-sixth Street, from his mother. By 1985 comparable apartments cost at least $1 million to buy and between $2,000 and $3,000 a month to maintain.

[2]An extremely modest sum, implying the absence of a cook, an inability to give dinner parties and a reliance on canned goods.

[3]Again, a pittance. At his clubs in town Amory could have afforded to do little more than pay his dues and stand his friends to a quarterly round of drinks. At the beach club on Long Island his children would have had to be careful about signing food chits and losing golf balls.

[4]$1,000 to each of his children's schools, the minimum donation acceptable under the rules of what Thorstein Veblen, in *The Theory of the Leisure Class*, defined as "pecuniary decency": $1,000 to Yale University and $2,000 meted out in small denominations to miscellaneous charities dear to Stephanie Amory's friends.

[5]Most of the women in Stephanie Amory's set could draw on an annual clothes allowance of $30,000. Evening dresses designed by Givency or Bill Blass cost between $3,000 and $5,000.

Maintenance of children's expectations (stereo sets, computers, allowances,
   dancing school, books, winter vacations): $30,000
Maintenance of his own expectations: $3,000
Taxes (city, state, federal): $75,000
Total: $300,400

It was no use trying to play the part of a niggling accountant or to suggest
that it might be possible to lead a presentable life on less than $250,000 a year.
Amory was too desperate to fix his attention on small sums. When I remarked
that he might cut back on his children's expectations he said that these were
necessary to allow his children to compete with their peers, to give them a
sense of their proper place in the world. In answer to a question about the club
bills and the charitable donations, Amory pointed out that he allocated nothing for luxury or pleasure, no money for dinner parties, for paintings, for furniture, for a mistress, for psychiatrists, even for a week in Europe.[6]

"As it is," he said, "I live like an animal. I eat tuna fish out of cans and hope
that when the phone rings it isn't somebody dunning me for a bill."

Not knowing what else to do, Amory had resolved to leave New York,
maybe for Old Westbury or Westport, "someplace unimportant," he said,
where he could afford "to stay in the game." He couldn't do for his children
what his parents had done for him, and his feeling of failure showed in his eyes.
He had the look for a man who was being followed by the police.

Seen from a safe distance, Amory's despair seems comic or grotesque, the
stuff of dreaming idiocy that Neil Simon could turn into a commercial farce or
The New York Times editorial page into an occasion for moral outrage. If the
average American family of four earns an annual income of $18,000, by what
ludicrous arithmetic could a man of Amory's means have the effrontery to feel
deprived?

It is a question that on a number of occasions in my life I could as easily have
asked myself. Like Amory, I was born into the ranks of the equestrian class and
educated to the protocols of wealth at prep school and college.[7] Given the circumstances of my childhood in San Francisco, I don't know how I could have
avoided an early acquaintance with the pathologies of wealth. The Lapham
family enjoyed the advantages of social eminence in a city that cared about little else, and most of its members comforted themselves with the telling and re-
telling of tales about the mythical riches of my great-grandfather. He died the
year I was born, by all accounts a very severe but subtle gentlemen who had

---

[6]In May 1987 the fashion tabloid *W* fixed the price of keeping a young mistress in New York
City at $5,000 per month: the sum included rent, clothes, maid and exercise trainer, but not jew-
els, furs or weekends in Mexico.

[7]None of the phrases commonly used to describe the holders of American wealth strike me as
being sufficiently precise. The United States never has managed to put together an "establishment" in the British sense of the word: "plutocracy" is too vague, and "upper class" implies a veneer
of manners that doesn't exist. Borrowed from the Roman usage, equestrian class comprises all those
who can afford to ride rather than walk and who can buy any or all of the baubles that constitute
the proofs of social status. As with the ancient Romans, the rank is for sale.

been one of the partners in the founding of the Texas Oil Company. It was said that he translated poetry from the ancient Greek, played both the organ and the cello, collected shipping companies and oriental jade, and at one point in his life considered the possibility of buying the Monterey Peninsula. That he didn't do so, deciding to acquire instead a less dramatic but more convenient estate in Connecticut, was a source of vast disappointment to his descendants. As a child I occasionally followed my elders around the golf courses at Pebble Beach and Cypress Point, and by listening to their conversation gathered that I had been swindled out of a proprietary view of the Pacific Ocean.

In 1942, during the first autumn of the Second World War, my grandfather was elected mayor of San Francisco. I often rode in municipal limousines, either to Kezar Stadium for the New Year's Day football game or to the Presidio for military ceremonies among returning generals, and somewhere on the journey through streets that I remember as always crowded, I confused the pretensions of family with the imperatives of the public interest. I came to imagine that I was born to ride in triumph and that others, apparently less fortunate and more numerous, were born to stand smiling in the streets and wave their hats.

My self-preoccupation was consistent with the ethos of a city given to believing its own press notices. The citizens of San Francisco dote on a romantic image of themselves, and their provincial narcissism would be difficult to exaggerate. The circumference of the civic interest extends to no more than a hundred miles in three directions, as far as Sonoma County on the north, to Monterey on the south and to Yosemite in the east. In a westerly direction the zone of significance doesn't reach beyond the Golden Gate Bridge. We lived in a fashionable quarter of the city, surrounded by spacious houses belonging to people in similar circumstances, and I attended a private school that nurtured social rather than intellectual pretensions. Everybody went to the same dancing classes, and none of us had any sense of other voices in other parts of town.

The accident of being born into the American equestrian class has obvious advantages, but it also has disadvantages that are not so obvious. Children encouraged to believe themselves either beautiful or rich assume that nothing further will be required of them, and they revert to the condition of aquatic plants drifting in the shallows. The lack of oxygen in the atmosphere makes them giddy with ruinous fantasy.[8] Together with my classmates and peers, I was given to understand that it was sufficient accomplishment merely to have been born. Not that anybody ever said precisely that in so many words, but the assumption was plain enough, and I could confirm it by observing the mechanics of the local society. A man might become a drunkard, a concert pianist or an owner of companies, but none of these occupations would have an important

---

[8]William K. Vanderbilt made the point in a newspaper interview in 1905. "Inherited wealth," he said, "is a big handicap to happiness. It is as certain death to ambition as cocaine is to morality."

bearing on his social rank. If he could pay the club dues, if he could present himself at dinner dressed in the correct clothes for whatever the season of the year, if he could retain the minimum good sense necessary to stay out of jail, then he could command the homage of headwaiters. Headwaiters represented the world's opinion, and their smiling respect confirmed a man in his definition of himself. That definition would be accepted at par value by everyone whom one knew or would be likely to know. A man's morals or achievements would be admired as if they were lawn decorations, with the same cries of mindless approbation that society women bestow on poets and dogs. The gentleman's inadequacies, whether a tendency toward confused sadism or a habit of cheating the customers on the stock exchange, could be excused as unfortunate lapses of judgment or taste. What was important was the appearance of things, and if these could be decently maintained, a man could look forward to a sequence of pleasant invitations. He would be entitled to a view form the box seats.

From the box seats, of course, the world arranges itself into a decorous entertainment conveniently staged for the benefit of the people who can afford the price of admission. The point of view assumes that Australians will play tennis, that Italians will sing or kill one another in Brooklyn, that blacks will dance or riot (always at a seemly distance), and that the holders of a season subscription will live happily ever after, or, if they are very rich, forever.

The comfortable assurance of this point of view implies a corollary refusal to see anything that doesn't appear on the program. Nobody could imagine that they might be dislodged by social upheaval, of no matter what force and velocity, and it was taken for granted that the embarrassments of sex and death would be transformed into the lyrics of a Cole Porter song. The Oedipal drama took place only on stage, in roadshow companies sent out from the darkness of New York, or possibly in certain poor neighborhoods in the Mission District. All manifestations of intelligence remained suspect, as if they were contraband for which a man could be arrested if they were found in his possession. Later in life, if he discovered that he needed the commodity for the conduct of his business, he could hire a Jew.

Similar attitudes of invulnerable privilege were characteristic not only of the students at Hotchkiss and Yale but also of most of the people whom I later came to know in the expensive American professions. Within the labyrinths of the big-time media, in the corridors of Washington law firms and Wall Street brokerage houses, within the honeycombs of most institutions large enough and rich enough to afford their own hermetic models of reality (e.g., the State Department, the Mobil Oil Corporation, Time, Inc.), I found myself in the familiar atmospheres of reverie and dream.

Neither at the Hotchkiss School nor at Yale University did I come across many people who placed their trust in anything other than the authority of wealth. The members of the faculty at both institutions often made fine-sounding speeches about the wonders of the liberal arts—as if they (the liberal arts, not the members of the faculty) were a suite of virgins set upon by Philistine dogs—but the systems of value that governed the workings of the schools were plainly those that prevailed in the better neighborhoods of San Francisco.[9]

Hotchkiss received the majority of its students from the affluent middle class resident in New York City, Connecticut and Long Island. Given the plausible expectations of inheritance among these young men, it was hardly surprising that few of them felt obliged to learn much more than the elementary geography of the civilization in which they would happen to be spending the income. They assumed, as did the faculty, that the mere fact of being present ratified their admission to the ranks of "the best people." A prep school education in the autumn of 1948 was something that one couldn't afford to do without (like dancing school or swimming lessons), but it was not something that deserved much thought or attention. It was a necessary ornament, perhaps, but not the equal of a good shotgun or a trust fund yielding $300,000 a year. Ambition, like leather jackets, was best left to the poor. Everybody who mattered already had arrived at all the places that mattered, and anybody who seemed to be in too much of a hurry to get somewhere else (presumably somewhere he or she didn't belong) must be considered a person of doubtful character or criminal intent. Why would anybody want to strive for anything if all the really important prizes had been handed out in the maternity ward at New York Hospital?[10] Scholarship students might be forgiven the wish to become secretary of state or Chief Justice of the United States, but the heirs of affluence didn't need to think beyond the horizon of their amusements. What was necessary would be given to them; for what they desired over and above those necessities they would pay, grudgingly, the going price.[11]

The faculty did its best to apply a veneer of cultural polish, to impart a sense that somehow it was important to learn at least a few polite phrases of Latin or Greek. Nobody stated the operative principles more succinctly than an English master whom I accompanied on a walk through the countryside in the autumn

---

[9]The attitude doesn't appear to have changed much over the last thirty years; if anything, the emphasis on money has become more pronounced. Tuition at an Ivy League college is now $17,000 a year, and the students apparently worry about preserving the assumptions of ease so expensively maintained by their parents.

In *Campus Life*, a study of undergraduate attitudes published in 1987, Helen Lefkowitz Horowitz remarks on the virulent preoccupation with wealth now afficting students everywhere in the country. She quotes a senior at Duke University, "It seems like all we talk about is money. I try to say that it's not that important. But it's really important to be comfortable, and you can't be comfortable without money."

[10]A variation of this attitude accounted for the more refined Republican opposition to John F. Kennedy's seeking of the presidency in 1960. Politics was an expensive form of social climbing, and the Kennedy's conceivably could be forgiven their vulgarity on the ground that they had no other way of being admitted to the Bath and Tennis Club at Palm Beach.

[11]From the point of view of the *jeunesse dorée* matriculating at the Hotchkiss School in the early 1950's the "bare necessities" would have included property equivalent in value to an apartment on Park Avenue, a house in Southampton or Newport, a seat on the New York Stock Exchange, substantial trust funds (both for oneself and one's eventual wife), memberships in the Racquet, Brook and Piping Rock clubs, miscellaneous paintings and art objects falling due on the deaths of various relatives. Luxuries (i.e., those diversions that had to be ordered à la carte) included such items as a divorce, a racing stable, a third house, political office and an art collection.

of my sophomore year. The walk was compulsory, the result of an offense against the rules, and the few of us who followed the master across the stubbled fields listened with a degree of attentiveness appropriate to the magnitude of our transgressions. I must have been in fairly bad trouble at the time because I can remember the master's reflections on education with unusual clarity. He was a large and untidy man, notable for his constant puffing on a pipe and the holes in the elbows of his tweed jacket. He spoke slowly and obscurely, the words sometimes garbled by the pipe. His thought revealed itself in cryptic episodes, apparently taking him by surprise. He would interrupt himself just as abruptly, subsiding for no discernible reason into a diffident silence that continued for another two or three miles. As follows:

"What we are trying to do here, gentlemen, is to give you an idea of the whole man . . . character, you see, character is what we are interested in. The rest is not very important. Politics and business, I suppose, must get done somehow, and I don't mean to say anything against commerce, of course, but none of it has anything to do with character, you see, with the idea of a gentleman. . . ."

Or again, some miles down the road at the edge of a stream in which the first skein of ice had formed:

"You are the heirs to a great tradition, the magnificent edifice of Western civilization. It's a rich heritage, gentlemen, and we are trying to teach you to find your way around its corridors, its labyrinthine corridors, I might say. . . . "

Or lastly, two hours later, while walking up the hill to the gymnasium, with hearty and reassuring laughter:

"Never read so much that you wear yourselves out in study. Remember the whole man. No poem can take the place of a tramp through the woods in winter . . . know the difference between different orders of things. Most of you have been given a great deal and will be given a great deal more. I think you should learn to respond with informed gratitude."

The guarantee of privilege extended to everybody at Hotchkiss, even to the molelike grinds who hoped only to serve the system that temporarily made fun of their accents and their shoes. Nobody seriously questioned the legitimacy of the regime; nor could anybody conceive of an alternative hierarchy of ideas. A small and dissident minority counted among its members several of the most intelligent boys in school, but they were content to make common cause with the social majority in the elaboration of the manner defined as "casual." The motives of the two factions didn't quite coincide—there is a difference between the ennui of people who own things and the ennui of people who fear the owners—but they shared an equivalent egoism. To be casual at prep school was everything—a manner that implied fluidity, grace, ease, absence of commitment, urbanity, lack of sentiment, indifference to the rules and courage under circumstances always ironic. The style discouraged enthusiasm on the ground that it exposed a person to the risk of failure. Anybody investing time or effort in anything took the appalling risk that the market in his enterprise (i.e., himself) might collapse. Jazz musicians defined the attitude as "cool," and variations of the style later appeared in the 1960's under the rubric of the counterculture. But just as I never met a hippie whom I could have described as a revolutionary, so also I never met a social critic, especially the more eminent among them, whose complaint had more to do with substance than with gesture.

At Yale University in the 1950's the expression of "informed gratitude" meant having the good manners to learn the difference between a Beethoven sonata and a logarithm table. Whitney Griswold, then president of the university, welcomed the members of the freshman class to Woolsey Hall and reminded us in his introductory remarks of the many feats performed on our behalf by the venerable sages whose busts could be seen standing on pedestals along the walls. Griswold's discussion of "the well-rounded man" reiterated the word of advice offered by the Hotchkiss English master. Western civilization had apparently been acquired at some cost, and the class of 1956 had an obligation to maintain it in a decent state of repair.

As an intellectual proposition Yale proved to be a matter of filling out forms. Over a term of four years the representative celebrities of the human soul (Plato, Montaigne, Goethe et al.) put in guest appearances on the academic talk show, and the audience was expected to welcome them with rounds of appreciative applause. Like producers holding up cue cards, the faculty identified those truths deserving of the adjective "great." The students who received the best marks were those who could think of the most flattering explanations for the greatness of the great figures and the great truths.

A few professors made a self-conscious point of taking testimony on all sides of an argument, earnestly considering (pipe thoughtfully in mouth, head inclined diffidently forward and to the left) even the most preposterous hypothesis and keeping an always open mind to the chance of "meaningful dialogue." At the end of the hour or semester, of course, the questions had to be answered in the manner recommended at the beginning. Failure to conform to the presiding truths resulted in second-rate grades and a reputation for being either arrogant or odd.

Before the winter of freshman year the students understood that the politics of a Yale education would have little to do with the university's statements of ennobling purpose. A Yale education was a means of acquiring a cash value. Whatever the faculty said or didn't say, what was important was the diploma, the ticket of admission to Wall Street, the professions, the safe havens of the big money. As an undergraduate I thought this discovery profound; it had a cynical glint to it, in keeping with the novels of Albert Camus and the plays of Bertolt Brecht then in vogue among the apprentice intellectuals who frequented the United Restaurant on Chapel Street. The diner stayed open all night, and one morning at about 3 a.m. I remember telling the cognoscenti about an English professor who had marked one of my papers with an F because I had proposed an unauthorized view of a seventeenth-century divine. In the margin of the paper the professor had written: "I don't care what you think, I'm only interested in knowing that you know what I think." The message pretty much defined the thesis of a Yale education at the time, and the professor was, of course, right. Schools serve the social order and, quite properly, promote the habits of mind necessary to the maintenance of that order.

The education offered at Yale (as at Harvard, Princeton or the University of Michigan) bears comparison to the commercial procedure for stunting caterpillars just prior to the moment of their transformation into butterflies. Silkworms can be made useful, but butterflies blow around in the wind and do nothing to add to the profits of the corporation or the power of the state. Brilliance of mind is all well and good if it leads to some visible improvement (preferably technological) or if it can be translated into a redeeming sum of cash. Otherwise, like the Soviet embassy, it is to be placed under surveillance.[12]

At Yale I was introduced to the perennial American debate that might well be entitled, "What are the humanities, and why do they mean anything to us here in the last decades of the twentieth century?" The debate has been going on for at least thirty years, becoming more agitated and abstract as it steadily loses its meaning. Nobody want to say, at least not for publication, that we live in a society that cares as much about the humanities as it cares about the color of the rain in Tashkent. The study of the liberal arts is one of those appearances that must be kept up, like the belief in the rule of law and the devout observances offered to the doctrines of free enterprise and equal opportunity. By advocating the tepid ideals of "the graceful amateur" and "the well-rounded man" the universities make of humanism a pious and wax-faced thing. Works of art and literature become ornaments preserved, like bank notes or trust funds, in the vaults of an intellectual museum. The society doesn't expect its "best people" (i.e., the Hotchkiss students who grow up to become investment bankers and corporation presidents) to have read William Shakespeare or Dante. Nor does anyone imagine that the secretary of state will know much more history than the rudiments of chronology expounded in a sixth-grade synopsis. If it becomes necessary to display the finery of learning, the corporation can hire a speechwriter or send its chairman to the intellectual haberdashers at the Aspen Institute. Education is a commodity, like Pepsi-Cola or alligator shoes, and freedom is a privilege fully available only to those who can afford it.[13]

The lessons learned at school were confirmed by my experience at different elevations in the choir lofts of the media. After leaving Yale I first found work as a reporter for the *San Francisco Examiner*, a Hearst newspaper known for the artful sensationalism of its headlines. From the *Examiner* I went to the *New York Herald-Tribune* in 1960 and then to various magazines, among them *Life*, *The Saturday Evening Post* and *Harper's*.

---

[12]Much later in life I became a trustee of schools and universities, and I was sorry to see my earlier impressions so resoundingly confirmed. University presidents devoted their principal time and effort to the labor of raising money. Even if they had entered office with a fondness for literature or scholarship (as did A. Bartlett Giamatti at Yale in the late 1970's) they had no choice but to suppress their enthusiasms when flattering the alumni. Giamatti used to say that he couldn't afford to speak plain English. He was obliged to translate his thought into the empty abstraction of a language that he called "the higher institutional."

[13]The humor implicit in the phrase "the best people" is plain enough even to the editors of journals recommending conservative lines of opinion. Apropos the Reagan administration's practice of the arts of chicane, Thomas Fleming, editor of *Chronicles*, observed, in the winter of 1987, "Except in a few rare and fortunate cases, the powers that be, in this and any land, are a remarkably uniform set of real-estate swindlers, market manipulators and well-oiled office seekers." The observation would not have surprised Tom Paine, Ambrose Bierce or Dorothy Parker.

Before I was twenty I thought the pathologies of wealth confined to relatively small numbers of people preserved in the aspic of a specific social class. By the time I was thirty I understood that much of what could be said about the children of the rich also could be said about the nation as a whole and about a society that comforts itself with the dreams of power, innocence and grace.

With the victories over Germany and Japan we learned as Americans to think of ourselves as heirs apparent—not only of the classical and Christian past but also of the earth and all its creation. What was left of Western civilization had passed into the American account, and as the inheritors became increasingly spendthrift (witness over the last forty years the steadily rising curves of inflation, consumption and debt) so also the assumptions of privilege became habitual among larger segments of the population.

In 1905 Edith Wharton published *The House of Mirth*, a novel in which the heroine, a young and beautiful woman named Lily Bart, drifts like a precious ornament on the bright surface of the frivolous, albeit brutal, society summoned into existence by the riches of Twain's Gilded Age. Wharton intended a bitter satire on the self-preoccupation of an ignorant plutocracy. Her heroine declines to sell herself as a commodity, and the novel shows her being inexorably forced out of the soft, well-lighted atmospheres of luxury, "the only climate in which she could breathe," into the deserts of poverty. She cannot live in a world without carriages, engraved invitations, new clothes and the round of frivolous amusements to which she had become accustomed; unable to eat from broken china in a squalid part of town, she prefers to die rather than suffer the "humiliation of dinginess."

The House of Mirth addresses itself to what in 1905 was an irrelevantly small circle of people entranced by their reflections in a tradesman's mirror. In the seventy-odd years since Wharton published the novel the small circle has become considerably larger, and the corollary deformations of character show up in all ranks of American society, among all kinds of people caught up in the perpetual buying of their self-esteem.

The pathologies of wealth usually afflict the inheritors, not the founders, of fortunes, and by the early 1980's the United States supported a *rentier* class of sizable dimensions. In 1859 the country boasted the presence of only three millionaires—John Jacob Astor, William Vanderbilt and August Belmont; it now entertains at least 500,000 millionaires, not counting the innumerable peers of the same financial realm who fail to pay taxes adjusted to their incomes or who derive their wealth from the criminal trades. The real-estate agents on Manhattan's Upper East Side define a millionaire not as an individual who owns assets worth $1 million but as one who earns $1 million a year.

On examining the list of the 400 richest people in America as published last year in *Forbes* magazine, Lester Thurow, the dean of M.I.T's Sloan School of Management and a perceptive economist habitually curious about the arithmetic of social class, discovered that all of the 82 wealthiest families, and 241 of the wealthiest individuals, had inherited all of a major part of their fortunes. He also noticed that the $166 billion in business net worth held by the 482 families and individuals named in *Forbes* provided them with effective control over $2.2 billion in business assets—about 40 percent of all fixed, nonresidential private capital in the United States. The richest 10 percent of the American population (i.e., those families earning more than $218,000 a year) now hold roughly 68 percent of the nation's wealth, and in 1982, for the first time in the nation's history, the money that the American people earned from capital (in rents, dividends and interest) equaled the amount earned in wages. The percentages might seem modest, but when counted as absolute numbers, they translate into a large crowd of eager buyers in the markets in luxury.

Attitudes of entitlement have become as commonplace among the sons of immigrant peddlers as among the daughters of the *haute bourgeoisie*, among the intellectual as well as the merchant classes. Habits of extravagance once plausible only in the children of the rich can be imitated by people with enough money to obtain lines of illusory credit. As larger numbers of people acquire the emblems of wealth, so also they acquire the habits of mind appropriate to the worship and defense of that wealth.[14]

Some weeks after Amory had gone not to Westport but to New Rochelle, I listened to a similar lament from a television producer's wife who no longer could go confidently into department stores. Her husband granted her an allowance of $75,000 a year for clothes and jewelry, but the money wasn't enough, not nearly enough, to maintain her sense of well-being. Unlike Amory, she had been born poor, in a middle-class suburb of Philadelphia, the daughter of a bank examiner. But she had attended Radcliffe on a scholarship in the early 1960's, and together with almost everybody else in her generation she had come to think herself deserving of everything in the world's gift—success, beauty, happiness, fame. The illusion of unlimited means had done the usual damage.

Having been married for some years to the producer, who was successful and often in California, the woman who once had wanted to be a poet had learned to weigh the meaning of her life against the prices paid for clothes, furniture and real estate. She had been unlucky in her assignment of milieu. The producer did business with people who could afford to spend $80,000 for a weekend in Deauville. His wife had learned to value the deference of sales clerks and hotel managers. If somebody else's wife owned a more expensive house in East Hampton, then somebody else's wife obviously had made a better deal with Providence. She no longer could bear to look in department store windows, and if she found herself walking on Fifth Avenue she took care to cross to the opposite side of the street before passing Bergdorf Goodman. Her weariness proceeded from a feeling of humiliation. If she wasn't rich enough to buy whatever she wished to buy, then clearly she was still poor, and what was the point of having any of it? Because she was poor, she was worthless, not fit to be seen in the company of dresses priced at $15,000 or diamond earrings marked down to $33,000 the pair.

In the arenas of academic or philanthropic affairs the complaint has a more decorous and muffled sound. I once heard the correct tone expressed at the

---

[14]The habits of entitlement enjoy the fond endorsement of the federal government, which currently donates $400 billion a year (in Social Security, Medicare, military and Civil Service pensions) to the comfort of the middle and upper classes.

Russell Sage Foundation in New York by a company of prominent scholars and journalists assembled to address the question of energy policy. The discussants had been invited because of their nominally earnest concern about the global distribution of heat and light. Both commodities at the time seemed to be going in disproportionate amounts to the rich and developed nations of the world. It was hoped that the study group might formulate an ethics of energy consumption whereby the less fortunate members of the international polity could find a place closer to the fire. The gentlemen talked in high-sounding abstractions for the whole of a morning and the better part of an afternoon. They worried about the shadow of famine falling across the map of the Third World; they counted the number of people dying of exposure in deserts that none of them had seen. At the end of the day the study director, an admirably complacent professor from Princeton, asked for specific suggestions. He reminded his guests that the foundation had allocated $250,000 for a five-year assessment of the dilemma, and he wanted to know what was the next step toward implementation. For about an hour various members of the group dutifully examined the question but failed to come forward with an idea that everybody hadn't already read in *Newsweek*. At last the delegate from Harvard, sharing George Amory's contempt for the meagerness of $250,000, said the sum was so small that it inhibited the surge of imagination.

"Who can do anything with $250,000?" he said. "The thing to do is to leverage it. Anybody with the right connections in the charity business ought to be able to run it up to $1.5 million before the end of the year. If we had $1.5 million, I'm sure we could come up with an idea."

Everybody applauded this initiative, and the seminar adjourned with the resolution to reconvene when the foundation had raised more cash.

The emphasis on what Wharton would have called "the external finish of life," extends across the whole of the social spectrum and accounts for much of the spending in the public as well as the private sectors of superfluous display. Early in 1985, writing in *The New York Times Magazine*, Claude Brown, a student of the Harlem milieu and author of *Manchild in the Promised Land*, recounted a conversation with a teenage boy convicted of murder who explained that he had wanted "to be somebody," to be able to "rock" (i.e., to wear) a different pair of designer jeans at least twice a week. "Man, it's a bring down," the boy said, "to wear the same pants and the same shirt to school three or four times a week when everybody else is 'showin' fly.' " The same spring *The Washingtonian* published a lead article entitled "Going Broke on $100,000 a Year," in which it was explained that a good many young and ambitious couples in Washington had been ruined by their taste for splendor. By way of illustration the magazine reprinted a number of household budgets as hopelessly out of balance as George Amory's.[15]

---

[15]The nation's consumer debt (i.e., the sum borrowed by indivduals) now stands at $2 trillion, roughly equal to the national debt (another $2 trillion); at least in the opinion of a number of respectable economists, this consumer debt presents a far more dangerous threat to the world's financial stability than the $1 trillion owed by the less developed nations of the Third World.

Two years later, in the spring of 1987, *The New York Times* raised by 200 percent, the cost of pecuniary decency. On the front page of its Sunday Business Section, under the title "Feeling Poor on $600,000 a Year," a correspondent described the misery of the Wall Street novices "just buying their first $1 million co-ops" and beginning to feel intimations of immortality. The paper relied on the authority of Richard Zorn, an investment banker who retained the vestiges of a social and historical perspective.

"They can ape the styles of the rich and famous," Zorn said. "They earn $600,000 and spend $400,000 out-of-pocket. There's the house in Southampton and the nanny and entertaining and art and the wardrobe. But when the Joneses they are keeping up with are the Basses, it comes to the executive jet and the yachts and the sapphires and the million dollar paintings, and it's all over. What it means is that $10 million in liquid capital is not rich."

Talking to the same point, another banker cited in the same dispatch said, "I never knew how poor I was until I had a little money."

The federal government spends a large percentage of its income on the preservation of illusions no less foolish than Lily Bart's. Variations on the theme of dingy humiliation (scored for orchestra and brass band instead of solo flute) echo through the mournful statements of Caspar Weinberger, the former secretary of defense, who wished to enjoy the privilege of conducting simultaneous wars, some nuclear and others merely conventional, on five continents and seven oceans. For this luxury that he perceived as necessity Weinberger asked that the triffling sum of $300 million a day be paid for five years into the Pentagon's account. Let the Congress withhold any part of this allowance, and Weinberger would weep for the loss of Western civilization.[16]

Much the same tone of voice appears in the explanations of U.S. senators who say that they cannot possibly keep up what they regard as a decent appearance on a miserable salary of $89,000 a year. Being accustomed to approving sumptuous military budgets and spending $2,453 for circuit breakers that cost $3 in less refined parts of town, the senators ask their sympathetic retainers in the press how they can be expected to maintain at least two residences and attend, suitably dressed, all the civic occasions to which they owe the favor of their presence. Who will deliver them from the humiliation of having to give lectures in dingy halls? Of dodging like beggars for the coins of a campaign contribution?

Ask an American what money means, and nine times in ten he will say that it is synonymous with freedom, that it opens the doors of feeling and experience, that citizens with enough money can play at being gods and do anything they wish—drive fast cars, charter four-masted sailing vessels, join a peasant rebellion, produce movies, endow museums, campaign for political office, hire an Indian sage, toy with the conglomeration of companies and drink the wine of

---

[16]Few amenities in the modern world cost as much a properly equipped military household. To present a decent naval appearance, the United States maintains a fleet of thirteen aircraft carriers, each of which costs $590,000 a day to operate. Each of the 500,000 American soldiers currently stationed abroad costs $88,000 to outfit in an impressively martial livery.

orgy. No matter what their income, a depressing number of Americans believe that if only they had twice as much, they would inherit the estate of happiness promised them by the Declaration of Independence.

At random intervals over a period of thirty years I have conducted a good many impromptu interviews on this question, asking people of various means to name the combination of numbers that would unlock the vault of paradise. I have put the question to investment bankers and to poets supposedly content with metaphors. The doubling principle holds as firm as the price of emeralds. The man who receives $15,000 a year is sure that he can relieve his sorrow if he had $30,000 a year; the man with $1 million a year knows that all would be well if he had $2 million a year.

All respondents say that if only they could accumulate fortunes of sufficient size and velocity, then they would ascend into the empyrean reflected in the best advertisements; if only they could quit the jobs they loathe, quit pandering to the whim of the company chairman (or the union boss, or the managing editor, or the director of sales); if only they didn't have to keep up appearances, to say what they didn't mean, to lie to themselves and their children; if only they didn't feel so small in the presence of money, then surely they would be free—free of their habitual melancholy, free to act and have, free to rise, like a space vehicle fired straight up from Cape Kennedy, into the thin and intoxicating atmospheres of gratified desire.

It is precisely this belief that crowds them into the corners of envy and rage. Imagining that they can be transformed into gods, they find themselves changed into dwarfs. The United States provides life-support systems for the richest and most expensively educated bourgeoisie in the known history of the world, and yet, despite God knows how many opportunities and no matter how elaborate the communication systems or how often everybody goes to Europe, the equestrian classes remain dissatisfied.

Nobody ever has enough. It is characteristic of the rich, whether the rich man or the rich nation, to think that they never have enough of anything. Not enough love, time, houses, tennis balls, orgasms, dinner invitations, designer clothes, nuclear weapons or appearances on *The Tonight Show*. This has been the urgent news brought to a sympathetic public for the past twenty years by the chorus of sensitive novelists, Norman Mailer as well as Ann Beattie, who publish the continuous chronicle of disappointment. Given the outward circumstances of their lives, their unhappiness sometimes approaches the margin of parody. There they sit, the wonders of the Western world, surrounded by all the toys available to the customer with a credit card, mourning the loss of innocence, the limits of feminism and the death of bumblebees.

Seeking the invisible through the imagery of the visible, the Americans never can get quite all the way to end of the American dream. Even if we achieve what the world is pleased to acknowledge as success, we discover that the seizing of it fails to satisfy the hunger of our spiritual expectation, which is why we so often feel oppressed by the vague melancholy that echoes like a sad blues through the back rooms of so many American stories. The poor little rich girl and the unhappy movie idol, like J. Gatsby, George Amory and the makers of the nation's foreign policy, compose variations on the same lament. Yes, we have everything that anybody can buy in the department store of the free world: the Ferrari, the third husband, the F-16, the villa at Cap d'Antibes, the indoor tennis court, the Jacuzzi and the Strategic Defense Initiative. But no, it isn't enough. We aren't happy. Somehow we deserve more.

As portrayed in Ken Auletta's book, *Greed and Glory on Wall Street: The Fall of the House of Lehman*, the partners in the firm could neither restrain nor appease their appetites for cash. They earned salaries of between $500,000 and $2 million a year, but for reasons that would have been self-evident to George Amory, nothing was ever enough, and everybody always needed more. "Greed was the word that hovered over the troubled partnership. . . . Traders said the bankers were greedy because they were privately angling to sell the firm. Bankers said the traders were greedy to steal their shares and take such fat bonuses." Joan Ganz Cooney, the founder of Children's Television Workshop and the wife of Pete Peterson, one of the principal Lehman partners, explained to Auletta that her husband wanted to sell the firm so "we'd have no money worries." At the time her husband was receiving the equivalent of $5 million a year after taxes—a sum too small to suppress the feelings of anxiety and panic.[17]

Innumerable books by the sons and daughters of the rich remark on a comparable state of deprivation. Gloria Vanderbilt in her autobiography (*Once Upon a Time*, published in 1985) describes her childhood as a vacuum, empty of love or the merest sound of human recognition, as if she were "suspended in a bubble." Sallie Bingham, the reluctant heiress who in 1986 provoked the sale of her family's monopoly interest in the *Louisville Courier Journal*, speaks of being brought up in circumstances similar to those of a political prisoner. She was taught "never to ask the price of anything," but in return for this privilege she was obliged to maintain an attitude of decorous silence—never expressing her thoughts, never presuming to impose "undue stress or criticism" on the men in her family. The historian John A. Garraty noted in his study of *The New Commonwealth* that the unprecedented wealth and comfort of the *alte* nineteenth century in America resulted, paradoxically, in rising levels of exhaustion, anxiety and corruption. He went on to say that "the burgeoning cities of the land expanded the opportunities and fired the imaginations of their inhabitants, yet seemed at the same time to narrow their horizons and reduce them to ciphers."

At college I was struck by the way in which heirs to even modest fortunes fitted their lives into small spaces. They had the resources to travel extensively, to underwrite the acts of the imagination (their own or those of others), to make the acquaintance of their own minds. Instead, they fixed their attention on the tiny distinctions between shirts bought at Tripler's and shirts bought at J. Press, between the inflections of voices in Greenwich, Connecticut, and the

---

[17]The arrest in February 1987 of Martin A. Siegel, a Wall Street *Wunderkind*, provoked his peers and confederates to exclamations of surprise. Siegel at the time was earning upwards of $1 million a year as a notable maker of deals for Kidder, Peabody. When it was discovered that he also was selling confidential tips for suitcases filled with cash, a broker said, "How many yachts can you ski behind at the same time?"

inflections of voices twenty miles north in Armonk. Their preoccupations were those of department store clerks or the editors of *New York* magazine.

Amory, in his senior year, shared a suite of rooms with a prep-school friend, a boy named Wainwright who barely could muster the energy to go to class. The boy had a talent for painting, but his parents had made a mockery of his ambition to study art, and he had learned at St. Paul's to suppress any sudden or suspicious movement of his imagination. He sometimes thought he would like to travel, maybe to India or Greece. But then he thought of the heat and the flies and what he called "the funny-looking people speaking funny-looking languages," and he decided he was better off seeing the world through the eye of an air-conditioned movie theater on Crown Street. His passivity anticipated the passivity of a subsequent generation brought up to sit in front of television screens, and his xenophobia was not too different from that of the foreign policy establishment that thought it could buy off its fear of Communism by staging a war in what it believed to be the air-conditioned movie theater of Vietnam.

Although I have no memory of a specific incident, I know that before I was eight I had begun to suspect that something was wrong with the local presumptions of grace. It was as if a magician at a child's birthday party had made a mistake with the rabbit, thus leaving at least one member of the audience with the awkward suspicion that what was being advertised as paradise might bear a closer resemblance to jail. Possibly it was something about the people waving their hats (not all of whom seemed to be smiling), or perhaps it was a remark overheard in a basement, or a chance encounter with one of Charles Dickens's novels. In San Francisco I had been brought up among people who owned most of what was worth owning in the city; at Yale I had been educated among the heirs to certain affluence; in New York, Los Angeles and Washington I had met many of the people believed to have won all the bets, and yet, despite their ease of manner, hardly anybody seemed to take much pleasure in his or her property. What impressed me was their chronic disappointment and their diminished range of thought and sensibility.

Edith Wharton describes the asylum of wealth as a gilded cage, sumptuous in its decor but stupefying in its vacuity.[18] Lily Bart at least had the wit to know that by making money an end in itself she would be required to give up all but the enameled surface of her humanity. She would become a fly embalmed in expensive amber, meant to be stared at, like the celebrities in tomorrow's papers, by the crowd pressing its collective face against the windows of a Fifth Avenue jeweler.

Unlike widespread poverty, widespread affluence is something new under the sun, and the criminologists recently have begun to discover what was obvious to both Honoré de Balzac and Talleyrand—that is, that the relation between "subjective dissatisfaction and objective deprivation" is a good deal

---

[18]Within a week of being acquitted for the attempted murder of his wife, Claus von Bülow, in an interview with *New York* magazine, observed, "A gilded life may, in many ways, become a gilded cage."

more complicated than anybody at Harvard previously had thought. Apparently it is not poverty that causes crime, but rather the resentment of poverty. This latter condition is as likely to embitter the "subjectively deprived" in a rich society as the "objectively deprived" in a poor society.[19]

In New York the masks of opulence conceal a genuinely terrifying listlessness of spirit. The equestrian classes promenade through the mirrored galleries of the media, their least movements accompanied by a ceaseless murmuring of praise in the fashion magazines as well as in *The New York Times*. Behind the screens of publicity, the mode of feeling is as trivial and cruel as the equivalent modes of feeling prevalent in the ranks of Edith Wharton's plutocracy or F. Scott Fitzgerald's troupe of dancers in the Jazz Age.

SUGGESTIONS FOR WRITING

1. What does Lapham say is the attitude of the very rich toward education? What seems to be *his* attitude toward education? What economic benefits do you expect from your education? What other benefits do you hope to get from your education?

2. How important is money to you? What does Lapham have to say about the desire for money? How much money do you think you have to earn in order to be secure and comfortable?

3. How do you respond to the story of "George Amory"? Why does Lapham use this personal example?

4. Are you convinced by Lapham's argument that we as a country are as spoiled as the rich? Do we all consume too much of the world's resources?

---

[19]The statistical records show that in the United States in the twentieth century the incidence of crime has risen during periods of prosperity (before 1930 and during the 1960's and 1980's) and declined during the Depression, World War II and the decade of the 1970's.

5

VIOLENCE AGAINST WOMEN

How do you feel about walking down a street alone after dark? What is your reaction to horror movies such as Friday the 13th *or* Nightmare on Elm Street? *What is your opinion of magazines such as* Playboy *or* Penthouse?

Perhaps your initial response to the first question would be that you walk wherever and whenever you want to; or perhaps your thought was that walking alone is something you rarely do, particularly after dark. Your response more than likely depends on your gender, for most women do not have the luxury of moving freely. The dark places—strange or familiar—pose a special threat to the woman alone: She is a walking invitation for harassment, no matter her age, style of dress, body language, ethnic background, or class. In the extreme, the woman alone may be beaten, raped, and murdered. On a more regular basis, the woman alone can count on being subjected to taunts, stares, and other types of intimidation. While men may try to understand how these behaviors make women feel, few will experience the same emotions a woman does when she is out alone—or even at home alone. For that matter, neither can women comprehend what makes their abusers act in the way they do.

Two recent events put such male behavior in the spotlight. A young woman, jogging alone in Central Park in New York City, was beaten, brutally raped, and left for dead by a group of young males who were participating in a form of sport they called wilding. *On many college campuses, groups of men walk down sidewalks bumping or shoving oncoming women into the street. While rape is easily labeled as repugnant, the other behavior might be excused as just college fun. Fun for whom? For the women? And what in our culture led both groups of young men to view the women—jogger and pedestrian—as fair game? The* media messages that bombard us daily seem to suggest it is appropriate for men to take what they want, whether it's the advantage on the playing field, the initiative in the dating game, or the woman who is alone.

To be the target of harassment, aggression, or anger—whether expressed in overtly physical violence or covertly in the catcalls and wolf whistles—is something women live with each day. Understanding what seems to be male anger against women is a complicated and perplexing issue. Where do the men who behave violently toward women learn such behaviors? Why don't women act toward men in the same ways? The essays in this section explore these issues at a time when violent crimes against women are increasing at a rate far exceeding other violent crimes and at a time when most American women can at some point in their lives expect to be the victim of assault at the hands of a man.

THE GIRLS IN THEIR
SUMMER DRESSES

Irwin Shaw

Irwin Shaw's story examines at a glance a marriage between a man who likes to look and a woman who feels somehow devalued by his interest in other women. While it could be argued that there's nothing wrong with looking, some women find being the object of a man's gaze an invasion of their privacy. They go on to assert that women generally do not have the same "right" to stare back. In this story Shaw examines how a man's looking at other women affects his marriage.

Shaw (1913–1984) began his career as a playwright. He then wrote short stories for The New Yorker. *For much of his life, Shaw lived abroad, worked as a screenwriter and wrote best-selling novels such as* The Young Lions *(1948) and* Rich Man, Poor Man *(1969).*

Fifth Avenue was shining in the sun when they left the Brevoort. The sun was warm, even though it was February, and everything looked like Sunday morning—the buses and the well-dressed people walking slowly in couples and the quiet buildings with the windows closed.

Michael held Frances's arm tightly as they walked toward Washington Square in the sunlight. They walked lightly, almost smiling, because they had slept late and had a good breakfast and it was Sunday. Michael unbuttoned his coat and let it flap around him in the mild wind.

"Look out," Frances said as they crossed Eighth Street. "You'll break your neck."

Michael laughed and Frances laughed with him.

"She's not so pretty," Frances said. "Anyway, not pretty enough to take a chance of breaking your neck."

Michael laughed again. "How did you know I was looking at her?"

Frances cocked her head to one side and smiled at her husband under the brim of her hat. "Mike, darling." she said.

"O.K.," he said. "Excuse me."

Frances patted his arm lightly and pulled him along a little faster toward Washington Square. "Let's not see anybody all day," she said. "Let's just hang around with each other. You and me. We're always up to our neck in people, drinking their Scotch or drinking our Scotch; we only see each other in bed. I want to go out with my husband all day long. I want him to talk only to me and listen only to me."

"What's to stop us?" Michael asked.

"The Stevensons. They want us to drop by around one o'clock and they'll drive us into the country."

"The cunning Stevensons," Mike said. "Transparent. They can whistle. They can go driving in the country by themselves."

"Is it a date?"

"It's a date."

Frances leaned over and kissed him on the tip of the ear.

"Darling," Michael said, "this is Fifth Avenue."

"Let me arrange a program," Frances said. "A planned Sunday in New York for a young couple with money to throw away."

"Go easy."

"First let's go to the Metropolitan Museum of Art," Frances suggested, because Michael had said during the week he wanted to go. "I haven't been there in three years and there're at least ten pictures I want to see again. Then we can take the bus down to Radio City and watch them skate. And later we'll go down to Cavanaugh's and get a steak as big as a blacksmith's apron, with a bottle of wine, and after that there's a French picture at the Filmarte that everybody says—say, are you listening to me?"

"Sure," he said. He took his eyes off the hatless girl with the dark hair, cut dancer-style like a helmet, who was walking past him.

"That's the program for the day," Frances said flatly. "Or maybe you'd just rather walk up and down Fifth Avenue."

"No," Michael said. "Not at all."

"You always look at other women," Frances said. "Everywhere. Every damned place we go."

"No, darling." Michael said. "I look at everything. God gave me eyes and I look at women and men and subway excavations and moving pictures and the little flowers of the field. I casually inspect the universe."

"You ought to see the look in your eye," Frances said, "as you casually inspect the universe on Fifth Avenue."

"I'm a happily married man." Michael pressed her elbow tenderly. "Example for the whole twentieth century—Mr. and Mrs. Mike Loomis. Hey, let's have a drink," he said, stopping.

"We just had breakfast."

"Now listen, darling," Mike said, choosing his words with care, "it's a nice day and we both felt good and there's no reason why we have to break it up. Let's have a nice Sunday."

"All right. I don't know why I started this. Let's drop it. Let's have a good time."

They joined hands consciously and walked without talking among the baby carriages and the old Italian men in their Sunday clothes and the young women with Scotties in Washington Square Park.

"At least once a year everyone should go the Metropolitan Museum of Art," Frances said after a while, her tone a good imitation of the tone she had used at breakfast and at the beginning of their walk. "And it's nice on Sunday. There're a lot of people looking at the pictures and you get the feeling maybe Art isn't on the decline in New York City, after all—"

"I want to tell you something," Michael said very seriously. "I have not touched another woman. Not once. In all the five years."

"All right," Frances said.

"You believe that, don't you?"

"All right."

They walked between the crowded benches, under the scrubby city-park trees.

"I try not to notice it," Frances said, "but I feel rotten inside, in my stomach, when we pass a woman and you look at her and I see that look in your eye and that's the way you looked at me the first time. In Alice Maxwell's house. Standing there in the living room, next to the radio, with a green hat on and all those people."

"I remember the hat," Michael said.

"The same look," Frances said. "And it makes me feel bad. It makes me feel terrible."

"Sh-h-h, please, darling, sh-h-h."

"I think I would like a drink now," Frances said.

They walked over to a bar on Eighth Street, not saying anything. Michael automatically helping her over curbstones and guiding her past automobiles. They sat near a window in the bar and the sun streamed in and there was a small, cheerful fire in the fireplace. A little Japanese waiter came over and put down some pretzels and smiled happily at them.

"What do you order after breakfast?" Michael asked.

"Brandy, I suppose," Frances said.

"Courvoisier," Michael told the waiter. "Two Courvoisiers."

The waiter came with the glasses and they sat drinking the brandy in the sunlight. Michael finished half his and drank a little water.

"I look at women," he said. "Correct. I don't say it's wrong or right. I look at them. If I pass them on the street and I don't look at them, I'm fooling you, I'm fooling myself."

"You look at them as though you want them," Frances said, playing with her brandy glass. "Every one of them."

"In a way," Michael said, speaking softly and not to his wife, "in a way that's true. I don't do anything about it, but it's true."

"I know it. That's why I feel bad."

"Another brandy," Michael called. "Waiter, two more brandies."

He sighed and closed his eyes and rubbed them gently with his fingertips. "I love the way women look. One of the things I like best about New York is the battalions of women. When I first came to New York from Ohio that was the first thing I noticed, the million wonderful women, all over the city. I walked around with my heart in my throat."

"A kid," Frances said. "That's a kid's feeling."

"Guess again," Michael said. "Guess again. I'm older now. I'm a man getting near middle age, putting on a little fat and I still love to walk along Fifth Avenue at three o'clock on the east side of the street between Fiftieth and Fifty-seventh Streets. They're all out then, shopping, in their furs and their crazy hats, everything all concentrated from all over the world into seven blocks—the best furs, the best clothes, the handsomest women, out to spend money and feeling good about it."

The Japanese waiter put the two drinks down, smiling with great happiness. "Everything is all right?" he asked.

"Everything is wonderful," Michael said.

"If it's just a couple of fur coats," Frances said, "and forty-five-dollar hats—"

It's not the fur coats. Or the hats. That's just the scenery for that particular kind of woman. Understand," he said, "you don't have to listen to this."

"I want to listen."

"I like the girls in the offices. Neat, with their eyeglasses, smart, chipper, knowing what everything is about. I like the girls on Forty-fourth Street at lunchtime, the actresses, all dressed up on nothing a week. I like the salesgirls in the stores, paying attention to you first because you're a man, leaving lady customers waiting. I got all this stuff accumulated in me because I've been thinking about it for ten years and now you've asked for it and here it is."

"Go ahead," Frances said.

"When I think of New York City, I think of all the girls on parade in the city. I don't know whether it's something special with me or whether every man in the city walks around with the same feeling inside him, but I feel as though I'm at a picnic in this city. I like to sit near the women in the theatres, the famous beauties who've taken six hours to get ready and look it. And the young girls at the football games, with the red cheeks, and when the warm weather comes, the girls in their summer dresses." He finished his drink. "That's the story."

Frances finished her drink and swallowed two or three times extra. "You say you love me?"

"I love you."

"I'm pretty, too," Frances said. "As pretty as any of them."

"You're beautiful." Michael said.

"I'm good for you," Frances said, pleading. "I've made a good wife, a good housekeeper, a good friend. I'd do any damn thing for you."

"I know," Michael said. He put his hand out and grasped hers.

"You'd like to be free to—" Frances said.

"Sh-h-h."

"Tell the truth." She took her hand away from under his.

Michael flicked the edge of his glass with his finger. "O.K.," he said gently. "Sometimes I feel I would like to be free."

"Well," Frances said, "any time you say."

"Don't be foolish." Michael swung his chair around to her side of the table and patted her thigh.

She began to cry silently into her handkerchief, bent over just enough so that nobody else in the bar would notice. "Someday," she said, crying, "you're going to make a move."

Michael didn't say anything. He sat watching the bartender slowly peel a lemon.

"Aren't you?" Frances said harshly. "Come on, tell me. Talk. Aren't you?"

"Maybe," Michael said. He moved his chair back again. "How the hell do I know?"

"You know," Frances persisted. "Don't you know?"

"Yes," Michael said after a while, "I know."

Frances stopped crying then. Two or three snuffles into the handkerchief and put it away and her face didn't tell anything to anybody. "At least do me one favor," she said.

"Sure."

"Stop talking about how pretty this woman is or that one. Nice eyes, nice breasts, a pretty figure, good voice." She mimicked his voice. "Keep it to yourself. I'm not interested."

Michael waved to the waiter. "I'll keep it to myself." he said.

Frances flicked the corners of her eyes. "Another brandy," she told the waiter.

"Two," Michael said.

"Yes, Ma'am, yes sir," said the waiter, backing away.

Frances regarded Michael coolly across the table. "Do you want me to call the Stevensons?" she asked. "It'll be nice in the country."

"Sure," Michael said. "Call them."

She got up from the table and walked across the room toward the telephone. Michael watched her walk, thinking what a pretty girl, what nice legs.

SUGGESTIONS FOR WRITING

1. Some men defend "girl watching" by asserting that a woman wouldn't dress provocatively if she did not want to be looked at. Respond to this argument.

2. Examine the balance of power in this marriage. What does the interaction between the husband and wife tell us about their relationship?

3. Perhaps men *are* taught that it is not harmful to look at women in the way that Michael does. There is another form of looking at women that some people say is harmless: pornography. Explore this attitude.

NOTATIONS—THE F TRAIN

Joan Larkin

*It's late at night in a big city, in an unfamiliar part of town. You're alone.
This scenario would cause many people to feel threatened, perhaps only because the "territory" is unknown. A woman by herself late at night can face
intrusions that are particular to her gender. She may be misperceived to be
looking for a man and be harassed; she may be assaulted. From the time they
are small children, most females are taught how to make themselves invisible
so they can pass through unknown territory unharmed. The night is one such
territory, a place many women feel does not belong to them, a place where
they cannot go alone without at least the possibility of trouble.*

*Joan Larkin is a New York writer who expresses these fears in her
poem, Notations—The F Train, in which we listen to a woman's interior
monologue as she waits on the platform for the subway. Larkin is the author
of a book of poetry, Housework (1975), and has published her work in
such magazines as Christopher Street, Aphra, and Amazon Poetry.*

Kool I
Bruce
Head 155
Steam One
Chino
Gonzo 22

What is scrawled on the subway walls
is a certain notion of strength.

> there is also the strength of water
> that flows (around the rock)
> that flows (over the stone)
> that carries with itself
> leaf and leaf and leaf
> the letters of green lives

The station at West 4th Street
smells of smoke; I notice it tonight.

It is 2 o'clock.

There are two women with dyed, worried faces
and hard hair , the color of dolls' wigs
standing together in coats that mimic fur.

They are the only other women
in this night station of men—

men lounging and watching, chewing gum,
reading their Sunday paper,
some with thumbs in their trousers,
with keys, with umbrellas
striding the platform.
One man stands by a post and vomits
and vomits and vomits.

No one seems to be taking
notice of anyone,
except a few whose eyes
let me see that I am alone here.
At this hour, women do not travel.

            water
            travels
            without stopping
            falls, both hitting the stone
            and flowing over the stone
            making the unstopped
            music of water
            its continuous going
            over the earth and through it
            wearing the rock
            the rock the rock
            softening
            everything on earth that is hard
            a certain notion of strength

I may not let my eyes meet
their eyes, on the train to Brooklyn
That is a sort of invitation.

There is a joke the cops in my neighborhood
shared with certain women
during the most recent rape scare.
It was that the victims
had found the rapist desirable
and had asked for it anyway
by being out on the street at night.

Where were you going anyway?
they asked my sister,
who was—and this is a fact—
on her way to a meeting about the survival of earth,
but who, between 9 and 11,
was walked to the park at gunpoint,
raped,
then told to turn her back at the fence

where she clung, waiting
maybe to be murdered,
while the man who had just raped her
ran
into the darkness.

> water
> runs
> it is a certain notion of strength
> a woman has revealed in a film
> which she made by allowing the time
> to look at water
> moving
> to listen to the sound of water
> hour after hour after hour
> keeping her eyes on the water
> and holding it with her camera

They were asking my sister
the tour guide
Where can I find a woman?
My home, so far away.
I have need for a woman.
What are you doing tonight?
I have need, have need, have need.
Where can I find a woman?

On the subway wall, I see the sentence
I doin' it to death!
In a red-yellow rainbow of spray-paint

I,
I,
I,

doin' it,
doin' it,
doin' it,

to death,
to death,
to death.

I am waiting for the F train.
My wombs throbs
when the train thunders
The smoke-stench fills my nostrils.
I am on my way home from the city
late at night, in a station

where there is probably nothing
to be afraid of.

there is a notion of strength
that is without impact

energy that is still like water
energy that keeps going like water
energy that is sustained motion like water

turbulences and falls
flats deeps

and slow dark passages

go down to the water and look

go down to the water and look

go down to the water and look

go down to the water and look

go down to the water and look

SUGGESTIONS FOR WRITING

1. Larkin says that this particular subway station is a place "where there is probably nothing to be afraid of." Why is she afraid?

2. A woman does not have to venture into a large city to face the type of insulting or threatening behaviors that Larkin has described. Men taunt and threaten women in all types of environments. If you have been the victim of or observed someone being subjected to such harassment, describe your responses. How did other people respond to this event?

3. This poem refers to the attitude that women "ask for" the violence and aggressive behavior they receive. Respond to this point of view.

THE USE OF FORCE

William Carlos Williams

Learning to follow social rules is often called acculturation; it can also be interpreted as learning to adapt in order to fit in. At an early age the family, school, and society at large teach the child how to become male or female and offer rewards for fitting into the pattern and punishments for those who don't. Not only do children learn what is expected of them as a female or male, but they also learn what they have a "right" to expect from someone of the opposite gender: domination or submission, courtesy or contempt, and so on.

In "The Use of Force," **William Carlos Williams** *(1883–1963) brings his experiences as a doctor to bear on the events he narrates: the moment when a child learns an important lesson about the balance of power between men and women and between one social class and another. Williams was an American poet, novelist, and short-story writer who, for much of his adult life, worked as a pediatrician in his hometown, Rutherford, New Jersey. It was his work as a physician, Williams asserted, that gave him most important insights into human nature. Although Williams published short fiction, collected in* The Farmer's Daughter *(1961), essays, such as those collected in* In the American Grain *(1925), and plays, he is most highly regarded for his poetry, in particular for his lengthy free-verse work,* Patterson *(1946–58).*

They were new patients to me, all I had was the name, Olson. Please come down as soon as you can, my daughter is very sick.

When I arrived I was met by the mother, a big startled looking woman, very clean and apologetic who merely said, Is this the doctor? and let me in. In the back, she added. You must excuse us, doctor, we have her in the kitchen where it is warm. It is very damp here sometimes.

The child was fully dressed and sitting on her father's lap near the kitchen table. He tried to get up, but I motioned for him not to bother, took off my overcoat and started to look things over. I could see that they were all very nervous, eyeing me up and down distrustfully. As often, in such cases, they weren't telling me more than they had to, it was up to me to tell them; that's why they were spending three dollars on me.

The child was fairly eating me up with her cold, steady eyes, and no expression to her face whatever. She did not move and seemed, inwardly, quiet; an unusually attractive little thing, and as strong as a heifer in appearance. But her face was flushed, she was breathing rapidly, and I realized that she had a high fever. She had magnificent blonde hair, in profusion. One of those picture children often reproduced in advertising leaflets and the photogravure sections of the Sunday papers.

She's had a fever for three days, began the father and we don't know what it comes from. My wife has given her things, you know, like people do, but it don't do no good. And there's been a lot of sickness around. So we tho't you'd better look her over and tell us what is the matter.

As doctors often do I took a trial shot at it as a point of departure. Has she had a sore throat?

Both parents answered me together, No . . . No, she says her throat don't hurt her.

Does your throat hurt you? added the mother to the child. But the little girl's expression didn't change nor did she moved her eyes from my face.

Have you looked?

I tried to, said the mother, but I couldn't see.

As it happens we had been having a number of cases of diphtheria in the school to which the child went during that month and we were all, quite apparently, thinking of that, though no one had as yet spoken of the thing.

Well, I said, suppose we take a look at the throat first. I smiled in my best professional manner and asking for the child's first name I said, come on, Mathilda, open your mouth and let's take a look your throat.

Nothing doing.

Aw, come on, I coaxed, just open your mouth wide and let me take a look. Look, I said opening both hands wide, I haven't anything in my hands. Just open up and let me see.

Such a nice man, put in the mother. Look how kind he is to you. Come on, do what he tells you to. He won't hurt you.

At that I ground my teeth in disgust. If only they wouldn't use the word "hurt" I might be able to get somewhere. But I did not allow myself to be hurried or disturbed but speaking quietly and slowly I approached the child again.

As I moved my chair a little nearer suddenly with one catlike movement both her hands clawed instinctively for my eyes and she almost reached them too. In fact she knocked my glasses flying and they fell, though unbroken, several feet away from me on the kitchen floor.

Both the mother and father almost turned themselves inside out in embarrassment and apology. You bad girl, said the mother, taking her and shaking her by one arm. Look what you've done. The nice man . . .

For heaven's sake, I broke in. Don't call me a nice man to her. I'm here to look at her throat on the chance that she might have diphtheria and possibly die of it. But that's nothing to her. Look here, I said to the child, we're going to look at your throat. You're old enough to understand what I'm saying. Will you open it now by yourself or shall we have to open it for you?

Not a move. Even her expression hadn't changed. Her breaths however were coming faster and faster. Then the battle began. I had to do it. I had to have a throat culture for her own protection. But first I told the parents that it was entirely up to them. I explained the danger but said that I would not insist on a throat examination so long as they would take the responsibility.

If you don't do what the doctor says you'll have to go to the hospital, the mother admonished her severely.

Oh yeah? I had to smile to myself. After all, I had already fallen in love with the savage brat, the parents were contemptible to me. In the ensuing struggle they grew more and more abject, crushed, exhausted while she surely rose to magnificent heights of insane fury of effort bred of her terror of me.

The father tried his best, and he was a big man but the fact that she was his daughter, his shame at her behavior and his dread of hurting her made him release her just at the critical times when I had almost achieved success, till I wanted to kill him. But his dread also that she might have diphtheria made him tell me to go on, go on though he himself was almost fainting, while the mother moved back and forth behind us raising and lowering her hands in an agony of apprehension.

Put her in front of you on your lap, I ordered, and hold both her wrists.

But as soon as he did the child let out a scream. Don't, you're hurting me. Let go of my hands. Let them go I tell you. Then she shrieked terrifyingly, hysterically. Stop it! Stop it! You're killing me!

Do you think she can stand it, doctor! said the mother.

You get out, said the husband to his wife. Do you want her to die of diphtheria?

Come on now, hold her, I said.

Then I grasped the child's head with my left hand and tried to get the wooden tongue depressor between her teeth. She fought, with clenched teeth, desperately! But now I also had grown furious—at a child. I tried to hold myself down but I couldn't. I know how to expose a throat for inspection. And I did my best. When finally I got the wooden spatula behind the last teeth and just the point of it into the mouth cavity, she opened up for an instant but before I could see anything she came down again and gripped the wooden blade between her molars she reduced it to splinters before I could get it out again.

Aren't you ashamed, the mother yelled at her. Aren't you ashamed to act like that in front of the doctor?

Get me a smooth-handled spoon of some sort, I told the mother. We're going through with this. The child's mouth was already bleeding. Her tongue was cut and she was screaming in wild hysterical shrieks. Perhaps I should have desisted and come back in an hour or more. No doubt it would have been better. But I have seen at least two children lying dead in bed of neglect in such cases, and feeling that I must get a diagnosis now or never I went at it again. But the worst of it was that I too had got beyond reason. I could have torn the child apart in my own fury and enjoyed it. It was a pleasure to attack her. My face was burning with it.

The damned little brat must be protected against her own idiocy, one says to one's self at such times. Others must be protected against her. It is a social necessity. And all these things are true. But a blind fury, a feeling of adult shame, bred of a longing for muscular release are the operatives. One goes on to the end.

In the final unreasoning assault I overpowered the child's neck and jaws. I forced the heavy silver spoon back of her teeth and down the throat till she gagged. And there it was—both tonsils covered with membrane. She had fought valiantly to keep me from knowing her secret. She had been hiding that sore throat for three days at least and lying to her parents in order to escape just such an outcome as this.

Now truly she was furious. She had been on the defensive before but now she attacked. Tried to get off her father's lap and fly at me while tears of defeat blinded her eyes. ✒

SUGGESTIONS FOR WRITING

1. Examine the gender roles of the characters in the story: Who is dominant? What privileges does this person assume? Why does the child resist? Does a kind of rape occur?

2. Early in life, girls are taught to submit to the will of men (viewed by some as their oppressors). Pick a childhood experience that demonstrates this phenomenon and explore the lessons that were taught, your reaction to it then, your reactions to it now and your interpretations of it now.

3. Describe an event in your own childhood when you or someone you know broke an important social convention. Explore the results and your reactions.

BAR WARS

Bob Greene

We assume that American law protects people against acts of violence—assault, rape, murder, and so on. Yet many people, especially women, argue that our perception of what constitutes violence needs to be expanded. For example, many women feel they have been assaulted when they are shouted or whistled at as they walk past a group of men. Others are profoundly disturbed by what seems to be the exploitation and merchandising of women in men's magazines. In the following essay, **Bob Greene** *examines an extreme example of the behavior of men and women in a bar that takes things one step beyond men watching and strippers being watched.*

Greene (b. 1947) is a contributing editor for Esquire *and writes the column "American Beat" for that magazine. He is the author of* American Beat *(1983),* Cheeseburgers *(1985), and* Be True to Your School *(1988).*

The continuing evolution of relationships between men and women can take us down a twisting and uncharted highway, with unexpected stops along the way. And so tonight we find ourselves in a bar called B.T.'s, in Dearborn, Michigan. It is nearing 11:00 P.M., and the crowd is getting restless.

There are approximately 150 men packed into the bar. For most of the evening, loud rock music has been playing. Now though, the music has been turned off, and the men are crowding toward the stage in anticipation.

"All right," yells Rick Salas, the bar's night manager, into a microphone. "We're loading up the guns and getting our ammo ready."

Silently, employees of the bar circulate through the crowd, handing black plastic miniature Uzi submachine guns to the men. The miniature Uzis are built not to fire bullets, but to emit hard streams of water.

"Remember," Salas shouts into the mike, "share the guns with the guys at your table."

A woman named Brandy climbs onto the stage. She is wearing a skimpy T-shirt and a bottom that is a cross between a G-string and a pair of bikini underpants.

A heavy-metal song begins to boom through the bar's speaker system. Brandy lifts her arms to cover her face. The men in the bar lean forward, taking aim with their miniature Uzis, and as Brandy stands stark still, they begin to shoot her in the crotch.

The phenomenon started in the Detroit area last summer. Various bars promoted it with various names, but the one that stuck—the one that people used generically when discussing these evenings—was Rambo Wet-Panty Nights.

The concept was simple. The women would take to the stage, the music would start, and the men would aim and shoot between the women's legs. Tonight, seven women have been slated to be shot, one at a time. B.T.'s is a top-less bar, and some of the women who will participate are among the bar's regular dancers. Others are "amateurs," who are here because of cash prizes that are given out for the women who do the best job of being shot at—a hundred dollars for first place, fifty for second, twenty-five for third.

The noise level of the bar rises dramatically as each new women climbs up on the stage and the "open fire" command is given by Rick Salas. The men are whooping and screaming. They are leaning forward, in combat stances, looking down the barrels of the submachine guns and making sure that their aim is true.

From all directions, the streams of water converge on the women's crotches. It is impossible to tell their reactions from a seat in the audience; virtually every one of the women does what Brandy did: covers her face, partly to protect her eyes from errant shots, partly, one suspects, to avoid looking at what is happening out there.

When Rick Salas gives the "cease fire" order after each woman has been shot, the women are directed to dance and to roll around in the slop on the wet stage. Meanwhile, other female employees of the bar are on top of the customers' individual tables, providing more titillation for the already aroused men.

One woman, wearing only a G-string, is crouched atop a table that accommodates four customers. The men are watching the other men shooting at a woman on the stage. The woman crouched on the table takes a piece of ice from one of the customer's drinks and rubs it across her right nipple. At another table another woman is crouched and surrounded by men. The men are hooting as their compatriots fire the guns. One of the men, apparently overcome with excitement, take his glass of beer and puts it on the bare chest of the woman who is crouching on top of his table. Seemingly unfazed, the woman uses both of her hands to massage the sticky liquid into her breasts.

"Come on!" exhorts Rick Salas into the microphone. "Shoot those guns! If you guys were like this in Vietnam, we would have won the war!"

The woman on the stage, her eyes covered with her hands, continues to be assaulted by the shots aimed between her legs. "Born in the U.S.A." is blasting through the speakers.

Out in the audience, a man named Rolf, who identifies himself as a computer-marketing specialist, leans forward and presses on the trigger of his Uzi.

"I got her," he yells above the bedlan. "I got her. She's hot; I know she likes it. She likes it, and she knows that I know she likes it."

A man named Ron, who says that he works for a plastics-manufacturing company, shouts, "You work hard all day, and this is a release. I worked twelve hours today, and this is a way to get some aggression out."

"There's a woman where I work who's about to get married. I keep asking her out, and she keeps saying no, because of the wedding. I know I could nail her, but she won't give me a chance. I think of her being up on that stage, so I could shoot at her."

A man named Dave, who identifies himself as an auto worker, says, "You don't get to do something like this every day. I've shot a .357, a shotgun, a .30-30, and a .44 Magnum. But how many times do you get to shoot a girl in the pussy? This is great."

Waitresses are circulating, saying in calm voices to the men with the guns, "Would anyone like another drink?"

A man named Jonathan, who says he is a batch processor in a chemical factory, says, "This gives you a great feeling of power and authority. The ultimate macho-ism. I'm aiming at her clitoris. She knows I'm shooting at her crotch and she knows it's me and she gets stimulation from it."

A man named Ron, who works at an auto assembly plant, bellows, "It's nice. It's nice. I think that those girls like standing up in front of men and getting shot. Maybe they don't like it at first, but when they get all wet they've got to like it. They've got to like it."

As each woman finishes her turn on the stage, she goes to a dressing room in the back to dry off and change back into street clothes.

A woman named Rio says, "It didn't feel very good. This was the first time that I ever did it. I didn't know what to expect. Men in a place like this, they see tits all the time. But I didn't know what a bunch of animals they were going to turn into when they got guns in their hands."

"I was a little bit scared. Some of the men put their beer and their wine and their drinks into the guns, and that can hurt your eyes if it hits you there. I guess they're just having fun, but I don't know. Maybe I shouldn't be surprised. What can you expect when you put a gun in a person's hand?"

Brandy, the first woman to be shot at, says, "I thought it was great. I had a good time. I think it turns the men on, and that's fine with me. It's kind of a high for me—it really is. I didn't have any bad feelings at all. I just hope the guys who were shooting at me liked it as much as I did. I'll tell you one thing—I'm married, and when I get home tonight my husband and I are going to have a good time."

As woman named Kimberly says, "It was definitely exciting and unusual. I guess the men are being immature in a way, but hey—if their fantasy is shooting a woman, it doesn't bother me. If they want to play, I'll play too."

A woman named Marty says, "They're all with their buddies, and they want to impress their friends. It's a power game. Most of the women cover their faces when they're up there, but I try to look out into the audience and make eye contact with as many of the men with the guns as I can. A lot of times, they'll turn away. If a woman looks them in the eye, they'll turn away.

"They'd rather not think of a woman staring them right back in the eye. And I know what they're thinking—they look up onstage and they think I'm a bitch, and they want to shoot the bitch. But I'm not a bitch, and I won't be intimidated by them. I'm not a bitch."

A woman named Kelly says, "I don't really think about it when I'm up there. I know that there's a lot of guys out there who want to shoot me because it gives them a good time, and they think it's fun. I don't feel as if I'm being used, but I really don't get any satisfaction out of it, either. When I was a little girl, I wanted to grow up to be an actress. I know now that that's never going to happen. That was just a childhood dream. Being up there onstage being shot at—

that may not be acting, but it's entertaining. That's as close as I'll probably ever come."

A woman named Kim, who won the hundred-dollar first prize, says, "How does it feel? It feels degrading. What do I think is going through the men's minds? Frankly, I don't care what's going through their minds. I don't care about them at all. I see them going crazy and banging their heads on the edge of the stage, but I don't think about what they may be thinking. I would never go out with a guy who shoots at me. They may have fantasies, but I don't care what they are. I just block it all out and think of the money I can win. It's healthier."

Now all of the shooting has ended, and Rick Salas has left the microphone and is relaxing in a back office.

"I used to play Army when I was a kid," Salas says. "I dug it. Then Vietnam came around, and everyone was anti-American, antiwar, anti-Army. Even if you liked war games or war movies or war itself, it wasn't something that other people looked up to.

"Sure, there's a little pent-up anger out in our audience. They like shooting at the girls, because the girls are hot and they're good-looking and it's a female body up there. But I really can't tell if they're shooting at the girl's crotch or, say they're shooting at Libya or Nicaragua. It all becomes the same thing."

Alan Markovitz, the owner of B.T.'s, comes in and muses about the other side of the question: not why the men shoot the guns, but why the women go onstage and permit it.

"I ask myself that a lot," he says. "I think a lot of it comes from the fact that many of these girls came from broken homes and got very little attention when they were children. I think that one of the things they're doing onstage—apart from competing for money—is finally getting that attention. Granted, it's a strange way to get attention, but it is attention of one kind."

Rick Salas continues: "We provide a place where guys can get loose and no one has to know about it. I'll admit that some of these guys are frustrated and have to let their frustrations out this way. But that's okay. When the guns are in their hands, they're in control, and they have free rein. They don't have to hold anything in.

"But is there anyone out there who would take a real gun in his hand, and who would shoot it at a real woman? I like to think not."

Out in the main part of the bar, the entertainment has gone back to topless dancing. The Uzis have all been stored until next time, and the remaining men in the bar are looking at the dancers up on the stage.

A visitor to B.T.'s, who has observed all this and has been stunned by it, is preparing to go home. As he is walking through the bar, he finds himself standing next to a dancer named Darlene. Darlene has not been shot at tonight; she will not agree to participate in that particular entertainment. Now, though, she is preparing to go back up onstage for the more conventional topless performance.

"What did you think of tonight?" Darlene asks the visitor.

The visitor says that he cannot quite find words for it. The anger he had seen in the room, the naked hostility in the faces of the men who had been firing the Uzis at the women . . . the visitor says that now I must go back and put it all down on paper, and he is not sure exactly how he will be able to do it.

Think of it as a dream," Darlene says. "That's how I handle it. I see it and I keep telling myself: it's only a dream. . . ." 🖋

SUGGESTIONS FOR WRITING

1. Consider an event when you either observed, participated in, or were the object of male harassment. What precipitated the event? Why did you act, react, or refuse to act the way you did? What cultural messages, norms, and values caused you to behave the way you did? Looking back on this event, what are your reactions, evaluation, and interpretations of what happened?

2. Explore your reactions to the people's attitudes in "Bar Wars"; explain what events, observations, and conditioning influenced or produced your responses.

3. Compare the behaviors of the two groups—women and men—to those of people caught in the behaviors of racial prejudice. In what ways are they similar?

DANGEROUS PARTIES

Paul Keegan

A cultural anthropologist might attend a typical college weekend party and describe it as follows: "The college beer bust (also called kegger or frat party) is a ritualized event displaying activities in which people act out a particular pattern of behaviors in order to accomplish a set of desired goals."

College students often get their introduction to "adult" social life and behaviors at such events, where they learn to drink, mingle, and match up. And why shouldn't they be learning how to do these things? After all, socializing—learning how to play the game—is a large part of a person's college education. But what lessons do these events teach them? What models are the participants attempting to follow? What in their cultural background leads them to assume what they can and cannot do? What happens when things get out of hand? Who is to blame? And how can men know when what they are doing with a woman oversteps the boundaries of what is acceptable behavior and becomes date rape?

Paul Keegan's *article examines a chain of events set in motion by such a gathering. Keegan (b. 1958) is a contributing editor for* Philadelphia Magazine.

I love the University of New Hampshire, its green lawns, its beautiful turn-of-the-century structures, the little paths that snake through the woods to classroom buildings hidden in the trees. I went to college here from 1976 to 1980. It's Everyman's school, ten thousand kids on two hundred acres, cheap and easy to get into for New Hampshire students, expensive and more prestigious for the thirty-nine percent from out of state. Almost everyone can find their niche here, as I eventually did.

But it's the darker side of college life that took me back recently, the side that can emerge at a place like UNH after a night of partying at a bar like the Wildcat. The Wildcat is a pizza-and-beer joint in Durham, a small town that for nine months of the year is overrun by students. Steve Karavasilis, the owner, will pour you a draft beer for a dollar or a pitcher for $3.75. The Wildcat's signature is a wall of windowpanes that creates a huge, moving mosaic of Main Street. That's where the guys sit down with a pitcher to watch girls.

Steve has hung a sign clearly stating that you can't be served unless you are at least twenty-one. But somehow, last February 19, on a cold and clear Thursday night, two twenty-year-old sophomores named Chris and Jon, and a nineteen-year-old sophomore named Gordon, sat here and shared several pitchers of beer with a group of friends. The three were buddies who lived on the fourth floor of UNH's Stoke Hall. They were happy-go-lucky guys with a boyish charm and a bag of fraternity pranks. Jon and Gordon had recently become brothers at Sigma Alpha Epsilon. Jon, from Manchester, New Hampshire, was the character of the bunch, a slick talker who always wore his SAE hat, even when he walked to the shower carrying his soap and shaving cream in a six-pack carton. Gordon was tall and good-looking, a little moody, some thought. He was from Rochester, New York. And Chris, of Lexington, Massachusetts, was not a fraternity brother, but he had lots of friends at SAE.

The boys arrived at the Wildcat that Thursday night sometime between nine-thirty and ten o'clock and drank about six beers apiece. At about twelve-fifteen, they went out into the freezing night and headed back to their dorm, where they encountered an eighteen-year-old freshman named Sara who had been drinking heavily at a fraternity party. One by one, each of the three boys had sex with her. As the incident proceeded, witnesses said, Jon bragged in the hallway that he had a "train" going in his room and then gave his friends high fives, as a football player might do after scoring a touchdown.

Sexual assault, if that is what happened here, goes on at every college in America. About one woman student in eight is raped, according to a government survey. Ninety percent of these are victims of "acquaintance rape," defined as "forced, manipulated, or coerced sexual intercourse by a 'friend' or an acquaintance." Its most repugnant extreme is gang rape. Bernice Sandler of the Association of American Colleges says she has documented evidence of more than seventy incidents of this nationwide in the past four or five years. They usually involve fraternities and drugs or alcohol, she says, and the men nearly always contend that it wasn't rape, that they were merely engaged in group sex with a willing partner.

That was precisely the defense used by the UNH boys when they were arrested five days later. Jon and Chris were charged with aggravated felonious sexual assault, punishable by a maximum of seven and a half to fifteen years in prison, and Gordon with misdemeanor sexual assault. All three pleaded innocent, claiming Sara was a willing and active participant in everything that went on. Sara says she had a lot to drink and does not remember what happened.

Like friends of mine who went to other schools, I remember hearing vague tales about such incidents. What makes this case unique is that everyone on campus soon learned the details of what happened that night, and the turmoil that exploded was unlike anything UNH has experienced since the late sixties.

Four days after *Foster's Daily Democrat*, in nearby Dover, mistakenly reported that the boys had confessed to the crime, three life-sized male effigies were hung from a ledge at UNH's Hamilton Smith Hall along with a huge banner that read BEWARE BOYS, RAPE WILL NOT BE TOLERATED. When the accused were allowed to stay on in Stoke Hall, someone sprayed a graffiti message to UNH President Gordon Haaland on the walkway leading to his office: GORDON, WHY DO YOU ALLOW RAPISTS TO STAY ON CAMPUS? And senior Terry Ollila was barred from taking part in the university's judicial proceedings against the three because she was overhead saying, "I want to see these guys strung up by their balls."

Room 127 of Hamilton Smith Hall, where I struggled through Psychology 401, can feel claustrophobic when all of its 170 seats are full. It was here, in late spring, that the controversy, after simmering for months, began to heat up again. Thanks to a shrewd defense lawyer trying to reverse the tide of opinion running against his clients, the normally private student disciplinary hearings were held in public.

Jon, Chris, Gordon, and eleven other witnesses had their backs to the audience as they testified to the five Judicial Board members facing them across a large table. But they could feel the crowd close behind, hear the shuffling of feet, the coughing, the whispering. For four extraordinary evenings, witnesses nervously described what they had seen and heard, and the hearings soon became the hottest show in town. When sophomore John Prescott described how he had interrupted the alleged assault, he could hear women behind him whispering encouragement: "Yeah, good answer." When the testimony became graphic, the crowd gasped. At one point, when the defense began asking about the alleged victim's previous sex life, Sara's father leapt to his feet shouting.

Finally, in the early morning hours of May 7, the board found all three boys not guilty of sexual assault. Gordon, cleared of all charges, wept with relief. Jon and Chris were suspended for the summer and fall terms for violating a university rule entitled "Respect for Others."

It was at this point that the campus, poised at the precipice for months, went over the edge. Four days later, a hundred people, including Sara, turned out for an "educational forum" that turned into a shouting match and led Dan Garvey, the normally easygoing associate dean of students, to storm out of the room. The next day more than two hundred people showed up at a protest demonstration that was crashed by a group of about twenty fraternity members and boys from the fourth floor of Stoke. "Dykes!" they yelled. "Lesbians! Man-haters!" Then it got much uglier. "Look out, we're gonna rape *you* next!" shouted one. "I had Sara last night!" cried another.

Unrattled, the protesters acted out a satire of a rape trial and read a list of demands: the university should nullify the hearings, make a public apology to Sara, and expel all three boys. As the group began marching to the office of Dean of Student Affairs J. Gregg Sanborn, they encountered Sanborn on the sidewalk. More than a dozen of them surrounded him, linked arms, and said they wouldn't let him go until he promised to respond to their demands.

Sanborn agreed, but in his response he defended the university's handling of the affair. Demonstrators marched to his office, announced they were relieving him of his duties, and hung a HELP WANTED sign from the flagpole. After a weekend of altercations between demonstrators, fraternity members, and other students, campus police arrested eleven protestors for criminal trespass. As the semester ended, a shaken President Haaland wrote an open letter advising everyone to return to UNH next fall "ready to examine our moral behavior."

Until then, I had followed the public agonies of my school from a distance. Incidents like the one in Stoke Hall were rare, I knew, and most nights at UNH were probably filled with the warm times among good friends that I remembered so vividly. Still, each new development also triggered less pleasant memories about college life, until finally I decided that I had to go back and find out exactly what was going on at my old school—or, for that matter, at virtually every school. In truth, though, I suspected I already knew.

When I moved into Stoke Hall as a freshman, in the fall of 1976, the place terrified me. It is a hulking, Y-shaped, eight-story monster, made of brick and concrete, crammed with 680 students. We called it The Zoo. It was named after Harold W. Stoke, president of UNH during the baby-boom years that made high-rise dorms necessary on campuses across America. After a tearful good-bye to my parents, I introduced myself to my roommate, who was stoned, and then I ventured into the hallway to meet my new neighbors. They seemed much older than I, standing in front of their open doors bragging to each other about how much beer they'd drunk last night and how many times they'd gotten laid.

I lasted about two weeks in Stoke, then found an opening in another dorm. My new roommate was Ed, a born-again Christian with a terrible sinus condition who would sit on the edge of his bed and play his guitar, accompanying himself by wheezing through his nose. He was engaged in this favorite hobby the cold January afternoon I returned from the holidays with four friends. My buddies pushed me into the room, laughing and screaming and dancing and tackling each other. Devout Ed looked up from his guitar in disgust and amazement, wheezed, and said, "What happened to *you?*"

What was happening to me, dear Ed, wherever you are, is that I was learning to drink, one of the two major components of a college education. The other, of course, is sex, and soon enough I learned about that, too.

When I returned to Durham last fall, I wasn't surprised to discover that some things don't change. Drinking is still the number one social activity, and beer the beverage of choice. As for sex, you want to try it but you're scared of it, so you usually get drunk before deciding anything. Thus, it's common to get drunk without having sex, but rare to have sex without being drunk.

Drinking remains a surefire way of getting to know someone in a hurry. This is necessary partly because of the tendency of college kids to travel in packs. Everybody goes to parties, not on dates, to get to know people, and at that age, the last thing you want to be is different. There are also practical considerations: hardly anyone has a car. The students' universe is Durham and the campus, for at least the first two years. And on weekends, there isn't anything to do on campus but party.

What has changed dramatically, however, is where the kids party. Today's students were incredulous at my stories about the huge keg blowouts in our dorms. UNH banned kegs from dorms in 1979, my senior year, when New Hampshire raised the drinking age. Then, in 1986, the university stopped serving alcohol at the student union pub when it found itself in the embarrassing position of selling liquor to minors that it couldn't seem to keep out. This leaves just two options for freshmen and sophomores who aren't lucky enough to know an upperclassman with an apartment: they can drink in their rooms with the door shut, or they can go to fraternity parties.

Frats were decidedly uncool in the sixties but began to come back in the mid-seventies. During my visit I couldn't help but notice all the new frat houses that had popped up. Today, UNH has fourteen frats with twelve hundred members. "All the drinking has gone underground," Paul Gowen, chief of the Durham police, told me. "At least bars are controlled environments where they're obligated to cut you off if you have had too much to drink. But wearing a headband and marking it every time you chugalug a sixteen-ounce beer is not exactly what I would call a controlled environment."

Madbury Road, also known as Fraternity Row, looks exactly as you might expect: aristocratic old houses line one side of the street, set back from the road on small hills, with wide lawns stretching in front. Several frat members told me that a spate of bad publicity in the last few years over the usual offenses—alcohol poisonings, vandalism—has made this a period of retrenchment for the Greeks. Parties are now smaller and more exclusive. Posted outside the door are signs that say BROTHERS AND INVITED GUESTS ONLY. "Invited guests" means girls, preferably freshmen. The logic is circular: girls go to frat parties because they're the only place to drink and meet boys, who in turn, joined the frat because that's where the parties are where you drink and meet girls.

Fraternity Row is only a half a block up the hill from Stoke Hall. Forty percent of Stoke's residents last spring were freshman girls—250 of them—which makes the dorm an integral, if unofficial, part of the Greek system. Just out of high school, freshman girls are not yet wise to the ways of fraternity boys. On any Thursday, Friday, or Saturday night on Madbury Road, after about ten o'clock, you'll see clusters of girls marching up from Stoke and the other dorms beyond, toward whichever houses are having parties that night.

There they find the beer, and the boys. Because the fraternity houses stand on private property, police can't go into a frat without probable cause. To protect themselves from the occasional sting operation, most frats now post at the door an enormous boy-man with a thick neck who, with deadly seriousness, asks every girl who enters the same question: "Are you affiliated with or related to anyone affiliated with the liquor commission or any other law enforcement agency?" The girls will either say "No" or "Jeez, you've asked me that *three* times" before he lets them through.

One Friday night last fall I asked a fraternity member to take me to a party, and he agreed on the condition that I not identify him or the fraternity. We met at about eleven o'clock and walked to the frat house for what is known, without a trace of irony, as a Ladies' Tea. We squeezed past about eight guys standing near the door and descended a flight of stairs into the darkness. My first sensation was the overpowering stench of stale beer, and when we reached the bottom, I could see its source. Enormous puddles covered most of the basement floor. Standing in it were a couple of hundred kids jammed into a room the size of a two-car garage, picking up their feet and dropping them into the puddles—dancing—as rock blasted from two enormous speakers. The only illumination came from two flashing lights, one blue, the other yellow.

We pushed our way toward a long wooden bar with a line of frat boys behind it. They stood watching a wave of girls surging toward the corner where the beer was being poured, each girl holding an empty plastic cup in her outstretched hand. Two boys were pouring beer as fast as they could. My guide fetched two beers and told me one hundred tickets to the party were sold to girls, at three dollars apiece. Adding in girlfriends and sorority girls, he said, there were probably between one hundred fifty and two hundred girls in the house. "How many guys?" I shouted. "Oh, probably about seventy."

I asked how many kegs they'd bought tonight, and he led me behind the bar, past the sign that said BROTHERS ONLY BEHIND BAR—NO EXCEPTIONS. In the corner stood a walk-in wooden refrigerator with a "Bud Man" cartoon character painted on the door. Twelve empty kegs were stacked outside it. We opened the refrigerator and found fourteen more fresh kegs of Busch, their blue seals unbroken. Two others were hooked up to hoses that ran out to the bar. My host told me that Anheuser-Busch has student representatives on campus who take the orders, and the local distributor's truck pulls right up to the back door to drop the kegs off. A guy pouring beer said they'd probably go through twenty kegs tonight.

I asked a stocky senior whose shirt was unbuttoned to the middle of a hairless chest whether his frat gets into much trouble. "Oh, once in a while there will be some problems," he said. "You know, if somebody rapes somebody or if there's an alcohol thing." When I asked about the rape controversy he started to get angry.

"Everybody's singling fraternity guys out," he said. "I took a women's studies class last spring because I heard it would be easy. Ha. There were about twenty-five girls and three guys. They started giving me all this shit just because I was in a fraternity. What was I going to say? 'Yes, I think rape is a good thing'? I don't need that shit. So I dropped it and took Introduction to Film," he concluded. "All I had to do for it was sit there and watch movies."

I asked if he thought the rape issue was mostly about girls having sex and then changing their minds the next day. "Absolutely," he said. "I'll bet you guys twenty dollars each I could get laid tonight, no problem. But you know what? If I'm in bed with a girl and she says, 'I'm tired,' and then goes to sleep, you know what I'm thinking? I'm thinking handcuffs."

We walked back into the crowd and I asked where the bathroom was. My guide pointed to a door in a dark corner. When I pushed it open, I was assaulted by the stench of urine, and realized I was standing in a shower. Bits of soap were scattered around. A boy stood peeing on the tile floor. "So this is the urinal," I said, trying not to breath. "Yep," he said, zipping up his pants, "just aim into the drain."

Later, at around one-thirty, I counted five couples on the dance floor making out. "You've Got to Give It to Me" by J. Geils was playing. Just before I left, I noticed a boy dancing with a very attractive girl. They were bathed in yellow light, circling a beer puddle. Her back was to me, but he saw that I was looking at her. They boy smiled broadly at me, knowingly, then looked at the girl, then back at me. It was all he could do to keep from giving me the thumbs-up sign.

That was a typical weekend night; what happened on the traumatic night of February 19, 1987, I pieced together from police records, the testimony of witnesses, and conversations with most of the participants.

On that night, a freshman named Karen decided she was not in the mood to party with the other girls on the fourth floor of Stoke Hall. She was still upset about her grandfather, who had died in the fall. Also, a boy she liked was not treating her well. Karen told the others she'd rather just stay in her room and study. Her friend Sara, however, would have none of it. "Come on," she told Karen. "You never have any fun. What you need is to go out with your friends and have a good time."

This was typical Sara. She was popular, cute, fun-loving, and smart—she'd had a 3.9 grade point average the previous semester. She planned to be a biology major, and her friends marveled at how easily subjects like botany and chemistry came to her. But Sara was also a real partyer. It was not unusual for her to get everybody else on the floor psyched up to go out. And that night, excitement on the fourth floor was running high. There was a Ladies' Tea at Pi Kappa Alpha, a fraternity behind Stoke. The mood was infectious. Finally, Karen smiled and gave in.

Sara was in her room with her best friend, Michele, drinking rum and Cokes and listening to Steve Winwood. By the time they left for the party forty minutes later, Sara had consumed two rum and Cokes, and had finished up with a straight shot. Finally, a little after ten, Karen and two other girls, Noelle and Tracy, were ready, and all five headed out into the cold night. The temperature was hovering around zero as they walked to the three-story frat house they called Pike.

The basement wasn't yet crowded. Sara and Karen squeezed up to the small curved bar. Each grabbed a plastic cup of beer and challenged the other to a chugging contest. Karen won. They laughed and went back for another. As the night wore on, Sara became preoccupied with a Pike brother named Hal who was pouring beer. Michele noticed Sara was drinking fast so she'd have an excuse to return and talk with him. But Hal acted cold, which hurt Sara's feelings.

Within an hour, Michele saw Sara dancing wildly. Later, she saw her leaning against a post, looking very spaced out. When Michele asked her something, Sara didn't seem to hear her. Linda, a freshman who also lived at Stoke, was looking for a friend when she noticed Sara learning against the wall. "Where's Rachel?" Linda shouted. When Sara didn't respond, Linda repeated the question, this time louder. Sara merely stared straight ahead. Finally, Linda shook her and screamed, *"Where is she"* This elicited only a mumble, so Linda gave up.

At about twelve-thirty, Michele, Noelle, and Tracy decided to leave, but Sara said she wanted to stay longer. Karen and Sara agreed there was no reason to leave, since they were both having a good time. They assumed they'd go back together later. At length, Karen staggered upstairs, threw up, and passed out. When she awakened she was lying on the floor near the bathroom. By then, the party was over and Sara was gone.

At about twelve-thirty that night, Jon, Chris, and Gordon were returning to Stoke after their night at the Wildcat. The three sophomores were probably legally intoxicated but not out of control. Chris decided to go up to the fifth floor, while Jon and Gordon went to the fourth, where all three lived. They headed to one of the girls' wings, and on the way, dropped their pants around their ankles and raced down the hall, a favorite prank. They stopped to visit Laura, a dark-haired freshman who used to date Jon, and her roommate, Linda, who tried to talk to Sara at the party. No one was in, so they left a note: "We came to see you in our boxer shorts—Jon and Chris."

On the way back to their wing, the two boys saw a girl in the hallway. She was looking for Scott, she said. Noticing her shirttail sticking out of the zipper of her pants, Gordon tugged on it playfully and said. "What's this?" Both boys laughed.

Before going into his room, Jon asked the girl if he could have a good-night hug, which, he says, she gave him. He then asked for a good-night kiss, and she complied. When the couple backed toward the door, Gordon decided to leave the two of them alone. Without exchanging a word with her, Jon had sex with the girl in his room, where Gordon was already in bed. "I just did it with a girl; she's really horny," Jon told him. Still in his underwear, Gordon decided to check out what was happening. He says he entered Jon's room out of curiosity, without any sexual intentions. But once inside, he changed his mind.

Meanwhile, Jon raced up to the fifth floor to tell his roommate, Chris, what was going on. The two went downstairs to their room. When they reached the door, the boys were surprised to see Linda and Laura, the girls they had left the note for about an hour earlier.

Wordlessly, Chris slipped into the room while Jon, in jeans and T-shirt, stayed outside with the girls, casually discussing the night's partying. The girls saw nothing unusual about Chris going into his own room at one-thirty in the morning, and Jon was being his normal smooth-talking self. But when they drifted near the door, according to the girls' account, Jon said, "Don't go in. Gordy's in their doing bad things with a drunk girl." (Jon denies using the words *bad things* and *drunk*.)

Oh, *really?* the girls said. "We were kidding around with Jon," recalls Laura. "It wasn't like, 'Oh my God, that's awful.' Usually, if your're in someone's room, it's because you want to be." Even though Chris was in the room, too, it's not terribly unusual to go to bed while two people are having sex in the bunk below you. What the girls didn't know was that it was Chris having sex with the girl while Gordon (whose activities with her had not included actual penetration) waited inside for them to leave so he could sneak back to his own room.

Soon Laura and Linda said good-night to Jon. As they passed John Prescott's room, they saw that the sophomore resident assistant was at his desk studying. Laura was a good friend of his, so they stopped in. After some small talk, the girls half-jokingly asked him how he could let such wild stuff go on in his wing and told him about Gordon and the drunk girl.

"It's not my job to monitor people's sex lives," Prescott told them. "But I'll look into it anyway, out of the goodness of my heart."

Prescott, a hotel administration and economics major from Hudson, New Hampshire, went to the room and knocked. When no one answered, he opened the door and saw two figures silhouetted on a bed. (He would later learn it was Jon, having a second round with the girl.) Prescott also saw Chris, sitting on a couch next to the bed, watching. (Chris maintains he was simply getting dressed.) According to Prescott, Chris looked up laughing and whispered, "Get out," waving him away. After telling Chris several times to come out into the hall and being told to go away, Prescott barked. "Get out here *now*." Chris at last obeyed. "I was tense and nervous," Prescott remembers. "You don't confront your friends like that all the time."

Prescott asked if the girl had passed out, and Chris said no. "I want that girl out of the room," Prescott said.

"Oh, come on," Chris replied.

"Is she really drunk?" Prescott asked.

Chris nodded and laughed, Prescott says, although Chris denies this.

"Do you know that what you're doing could be considered rape?" Prescott said.

"No, it's not," Chris answered.

"You guys are going to learn one of these days that someone is going to wake up the next day and think that what happened was wrong, even if she wanted to be in there," Prescott said. "I want that girl out of the room." Chris finally agreed, but said he had to talk to her first.

Despite his role as the enforcer and voice of reason, Prescott nonetheless thought the events on his floor were entertaining—so much so that he went to see two of his friends and told them what had happened. " 'Wow! No way! Unbelievable!' " Prescott remembers them saying. "We were all laughing. It was funny, in a sick kind of way."

As Prescott and his friends went out into the hallway, Jon emerged from the room and walked toward them. When he reached the group, two of the boys said, he gave Prescott's friends high fives. Then he continued past them, slapping the air at knee level, giving low fives to other members of the imaginary team.

Prescott says Jon proceeded to tell the three of them in great detail what he had done with the girl and how he had gone to get Gordon and Chris. All three remember that during this conversation Jon told them he had a "train" going in his room. (Jon denies both the high fives and the train reference.) As the boys were talking, Linda and Laura returned, "not because we were worried about what had happened," Laura remembers. "We were still just hanging out." Then Joe, another freshman on the floor, joined the group. A discussion ensued between the five boys and two girls about whether the boys' behavior was wrong. "Someone said, 'Hey, a drunk girl is fair game,' " Laura recalls, "which made Linda and me a little defensive, obviously." One of the boys suggested that maybe Joe could "get lucky, too." Joe walked toward the door—just to see what was happening, he says.

Inside, Chris was now alone with the girl. She got dressed, and for the first time there was verbal communication: Chris told her a lot of people were in the hallway talking about them and watching the door. He carefully explained how she could avoid them. Just as Joe reached the room, the door opened and the crowd saw a girl walk out, her shirt untucked. Without looking up, she disappeared into the stairwell.

To their astonishment, everyone recognized Sara, the girl who lived on the same floor. They had all assumed it was someone they didn't know, maybe a high school girl. Suddenly the atmosphere in the hallway changed. Linda and Laura were outraged. "You *assholes*!" one of them screamed. "How could you *do* such a thing?" No one was more shocked than Jon: "You mean you *know* her?" It was at that moment that Jon and Chris heard her name for the first time.

By now there were six witnesses, two of them girls who didn't seem to understand the boys' point of view. This was trouble. Chris and Jon decided to talk to Sara to forestall misunderstanding.

When Giselle, Sara's roommate, heard voices calling "Sara, Sara, Sara," she thought she was dreaming. But when she looked up from her bed, she saw two boys bent over her roommate's bed, shaking Sara's shoulder. "What the hell are you doing in here?" she demanded.

"We have to talk to Sara," they said. "It's very important."

Giselle got up. Sara was lying on her side with a nightshirt on. "You okay?" Giselle asked, shaking her gently. Sara nodded. "Do you want to get up?" she asked. Sara shook her head: no. "I don't think she should get up," Giselle said.

But they pleaded with her, so Giselle shrugged and went back to bed. A moment later, she saw Sara standing in the middle of the room, wrapping herself in a blanket. One of the boys held her left arm with his right arm. This must have been, Giselle thought later, to prevent her from falling back into bed.

When the three were out in the hallway, Chris and Jon say, they all agreed on what had happened so there could be no misunderstanding later. Chris then suggested that Jon leave so he could talk to Sara more easily. Alone, they began kissing. They walked a few steps and opened the stairwell door. Then, at some time between three and four in the morning, beneath a window through which a slice of Pi Kappa Alpha was visible, near a heating vent painted the same blue as the walls around them, Chris and Sara got down on the landing and had sex again.

What is most puzzling about the way the kids in Stoke reacted to the incident is that for a least three days, until Sara first spoke with a counselor, no one called it rape. Even Prescott, who had used the term when he talked to Chris outside the room, insists that his main concern was the *perception* that it was rape, not whether it actually was. "These guys were my friends. My concern was *not* for the woman in that room. My concern was for the men. But look where it got me. Now when I see Gordon and say hi, he just gives me a blank look."

Prescott is thin and earnest-looking, with short blond hair and an angular face. Clearly, the incident has taken its toll on him, yet he talks about it willingly. Over the weekend, he told a friend what had happened, setting off the chain reaction of gossip that eventually led to Sara herself; only then did she go to the police. But Prescott's motives, he freely admits, were entirely base. "You know why I told him?" Prescott says today. "I wanted to astonish him."

But why didn't Prescott consider the possibility that the girl in the room was raped? "I just assumed she will willing, since I didn't know any differently," he says. "I saw her walk out of the room. Look, that's how sex happens here. Most scoops happen after parties, and guys go to parties to scoop."

But *three* guys?" "It doesn't surprise me that much," he says. "You hear stories about that kind of thing all the time. I don't expect it to happen, but I'm not ignorant that it goes on. I'm not naive. My fault was in not going to see her *right away*, when she walked back to her room. Then there would be no question. I keep asking myself why I didn't. I don't know. I was like a pendulum swinging back and forth, and finally I just had to try to look at this objectively and make a judgment." He stares into space. "You know, I still can't make one."

Linda, who was one of the witnesses who recognized Sara when she emerged from the room, is transferring to another school. Last spring she took one look at the huge crowds at the Judicial Board hearings and walked away. The next day she was convinced that telling her story was the right thing to do; now she's not so sure. Fraternity members are mad at her, and she's disillusioned about the social life at UNH. "I guess rape happens all the time here," she says, sitting on the bed in her dorm room, wearing shorts and a UNH sweatshirt. "You know, at home, I'd get really drunk and black out and wake up at my boyfriend's house. It wouldn't matter because I was with friends. When I came to school here, people would tell me, 'Linda, don't get so drunk. You're a pretty girl. People may want to take advantage of you.'" She looks down at her hands in her lap and says softly, "I didn't believe that anyone would do something like that. But it's true, they will."

It was a brilliant September day, warm and sunny, when I at last began to feel good about my old school again. President Haaland had called a special convocation to undertake the moral reexamination he had promised in the spring. Sara had transferred to another school; Jon and Chris would soon plead guilty to misdemeanor sexual assault, for which they would each serve two months in prison. The court would also compel them to write a letter of apology to Sara. The misdemeanor charge against Gordon would be dropped altogether.

"Universities have thrived because they are driven by a core set of values," Haaland told the crowd of three thousand. "These shared values are free inquiry, intellectual honesty, personal integrity, and respect for human dignity." Then he announced a series of concrete steps: to make the job of coordinating the sexual-assault program a full-time position; to publicize sexual assault cases; to improve lighting, continue the escort service for women, hire a full-time coordinator for the Greek system, and improve conditions in Stoke Hall, At the end, everybody sang the UNH alma mater: "New Hampshire, alma mater/All hail, all hail to thee!"

At the outdoor reception following the convocation some of the demonstrators who had trapped him on the sidewalk now chatted amiably with Dean Sanborn. "It just floored me that the administration got up there and actually said the word *rape*," said one. "Last year we couldn't even get them to say the word *woman*." The demonstrators, Sanborn told me, "deserve some credit for the change that's occurring."

I wish I could end the story there, when the sky was blue and everything seemed fine again. But then I made one last trip to Durham. Rape crisis programs and well-lit pathways are important, of course, but they don't answer the questions that occurred to me when I met some of this year's freshman class.

Ogre, as his friends call him, is a short, compact freshman whose boxers stick out from beneath his gray football shorts. On the door of his room is a sign that says FISH DEFENSE HQ, and if you ask him about it he'll tell you with a deadpan look that mutant radioactive fish with lungs are attacking us all, that they've already got Peter Tosh[1] and John F. Kennedy. If it weren't for Ogre's regiment, consisting of Opus and Garfield, his stuffed dolls, they'd probably have gotten him, too. Ogre is a funny kid.

While I chatted with Ogre in his room, we were joined by a thin fellow with a blond crewcut, wearing a T-shirt with BUTTHOLE SURFERS silk-screened across three identical images of a bloated African belly with a tiny penis below it. His eyelids drooped: our visitor was zonked. I asked him who the Butthole Surfers were, and he explained they were punk musicians, "not hard-core punk, but definitely influenced by hard-core, for sure." The subject soon turned to acquaintance rape, and the Butthole Surferite said he'd never heard of it. Ogre had. "You know, those notices we've been getting in our mailbox about rape, with the phony scene where she says no and he says yes," Ogre explained. "Oh, yeah," the kid nodded.

Then Ogre summed up what he'd learned from the incident last spring: "You don't shit where you sleep," he said. "You don't have sex with someone in your dorm. It causes too many problems. You've got to face them the next day."

Ogre had been in college only two weeks when he made those remarks, so there's hope that eventually he'll grow up. Perhaps he will even think of other metaphors for making love. For my old school—and, I'd guess, for far too many others—the question is, What will he do in the meantime? ✒

SUGGESTIONS FOR WRITING

1. How does a man know when a women who says no means *no*? What should a boy be taught as he grows up in order to be able to read the signals correctly? What should a girl be taught?

2. Examine the male and female students' reactions to Sara's behavior. Do you agree or disagree with the three men accused of having raped her? Examine the attitudes of the residence hall assistant who did not intervene. What were his reasons for remaining aloof? Do you agree or disagree with his choices? Why or why not?

3. Examine the women students' reactions to the victim, Sara, comparing their responses before they found out it was a person they knew and after they learned her identity. What do these reactions say about how we view the act of rape?

4. Explore your attitudes toward date/acquaintance rape.

---

[1]Jamaican reggae musician and singer who often performed with Bob Marley; Tosh was shot to death in 1987.

TELL THE WOMEN
WE'RE GOING

Raymond Carver

Until recently, rather than being viewed as a crime of violence directed against females, rape achieved a special status by being thought of as a crime for which the victim—the woman—was to blame for her assailant's attack. Some people believed that, once sexually aroused, no man could control himself. In both cases, the responsibility—for arousing the male and for his resulting assault—was attributed to the woman.

The current view of rape interprets it as an act of violence triggered by the attacker's private rage or hatred. The woman is considered the unwitting target for this anger. While the particular sources of this violent rage are as various as the men who commit the crime, rape remains a crime committed by a male against a female.

***Raymond Carver** (1939–1988) examines not only the issue of rape but also explores class rage in the following story. Carver grew up in the Pacific Northwest in a blue-collar family; his experiences of growing up poor, working at menial jobs while trying to make it as a writer, and his battles with alcoholism inform his writings. His characters and themes inhabit a world of middle- and lower-class neighborhoods from which there seems to be no easy escape. Carver published short fiction in collections such as* Will You Please Be Quiet Please *(1976),* What We Talk About When We Talk About Love *(1981), and* Cathedral *(1984). He is also highly regarded as a poet.*

Bill Jamison had always been best friends with Jerry Roberts. The two grew up in the south area, near the old fairgrounds, went through grade school and junior high together, and then on to Eisenhower, where they took as many of the same teachers as they could manage, wore each other's shirts and sweaters and pegged pants, and dated and banged the same girls—whichever came up as a matter of course.

Summers they took jobs together—swamping peaches, picking cherries, stringing hops, anything they could do that paid a little and where there was no boss to get on your ass. And they bought a car together. The summer before their senior year, they chipped in and bought a red '54 Plymouth for $325.

They shared it. It worked out fine.

But Jerry got married before the end of the first semester and dropped out of school to work steady at Robby's Mart.

As for Bill, he'd dated the girl too. Carol was her name, and she went just fine with Jerry, and Bill went over there every chance he got. It made him feel older, having married friends. He'd go over there for lunch or for supper, and they'd listen to Elvis or to Bill Haley and the Comets.

But sometimes Carol and Jerry would start making out right with Bill still there, and he'd have to get up and excuse himself and take a walk to Dezorn's Service Station to get some Coke because there was only the one bed in the apartment, a hide-away that came down in the living room. Or sometimes Jerry and Carol would head off to the bathroom, and Bill would have to move to the kitchen and pretend to be interested in the cupboards and the refrigerator and not trying to listen.

So he stopped going over so much; and then June he graduated, took at job at the Darigold plant, and joined the National Guard. In a year he had a milk route of his own and was going steady with Linda. So Bill and Linda would go over to Jerry and Carol's, drink beer, and listen to records.

Carol and Linda got along fine, and Bill was flattered when Carol said that, confidentially, Linda was "a real person."

Jerry liked Linda too. "She's great," Jerry said.

When Bill and Linda got married, Jerry was best man. The reception, of course, was at the Donnelly Hotel, Jerry and Bill cutting up together and linking arms and tossing off glasses of spiked punch. But once, in the middle of all this happiness, Bill looked at Jerry and thought how much older Jerry looked, a lot older than twenty-two. By then Jerry was the happy father of two kids and had moved up to assistant manager at Robby's, and Carol had one in the oven again.

They saw each other every Saturday and Sunday, sometimes oftener if it was a holiday. If the weather was good, they'd be over at Jerry's to barbecue hot dogs and turn the kids loose in the wading pool Jerry had got for next to nothing, like a lot of other things he got from the Mart.

Jerry had a nice house. It was up on a hill overlooking the Naches. There were other houses around, but not too close. Jerry was doing all right. When Bill and Linda and Jerry and Carol got together, it was always at Jerry's place because Jerry had the barbecue and the records and too many kids to drag around.

It was a Sunday at Jerry's place the time it happened.

The women were in the kitchen straightening up. Jerry's girls were out in the yard throwing a plastic ball into the wading pool yelling, and splashing after it.

Jerry and Bill were sitting in the reclining chairs on the patio, drinking beer and just relaxing.

Bill was doing most of the talking—things about people they knew, about Darigold, about the four-door Pontiac Catalina he was thinking of buying.

Jerry was staring at the clothesline, or at the '68 Chevy hardtop that stood in the garage. Bill was thinking how Jerry was getting to be deep, the way he stared all the time and hardly did any talking at all.

Bill moved in his chair and lighted a cigarette.

He said, "Anything wrong, man? I mean, you know."

Jerry finished his beer and then mashed the can. He shrugged.

"You know," he said.

Bill nodded.

Then Jerry said, "How about a little run?"

"Sounds good to me," Bill said. "I'll tell the women we're going."

They took the Naches River highway out to Gleed, Jerry driving. The day was sunny and warm, and air blew through the car.

"Where we headed?" Bill said.

"Let's shoot a few balls."

"Fine with me," Bill said. He felt a whole lot better just seeing Jerry brighten up.

"Guy's got to get out," Jerry said. He looked at Bill. "You know what I mean?"

Bill understood. He liked to get out with the guys from the plant for the Friday-night bowling league. He liked to stop off twice a week after work to have a few beers with Jack Broderick. He knew a guy's got to get out.

"Still standing," Jerry said, as they pulled up onto the gravel in front of the Rec Center.

They went inside, Bill holding the door for Jerry, Jerry punching Bill lightly in the stomach as he went on by.

"Hey there!"

It was Riley.

"Hey, how you boys keeping?"

It was Riley coming around from behind the counter, grinning. He was a heavy man. He had on a short-sleeved Hawaiian shirt that hung outside his jeans. Riley said, "So how you boys been keeping?"

"Ah, dry up and give up a couple of Olys," Jerry said, winking at Bill. "So how you been, Riley?" Jerry said.

Riley said, "So how you boys doing? Where you been keeping yourselves? You boys getting any on the side? Jerry, the last time I seen you, your old lady was six months gone."

Jerry stood a minute and blinked his eyes.

"So how about the Olys?" Bill said.

They took stools near the window. Jerry said, "What kind of place is this, Riley, that it don't have any girls on a Sunday afternoon?"

Riley laughed. He said, "I guess they're all in church praying for it."

They each had five cans of beer and took two hours to play three racks of rotation and two racks of snooker, Riley sitting on a stool and talking and watching them play, Bill always looking at his watch and then looking at Jerry.

Bill said, "So what do you think, Jerry? I mean, what do you think?" Bill said.

Jerry drained his can, mashed it, then stood for a time turning the can in his hand.

Back on the highway, Jerry opened it up—little jumps of eighty-five and ninety. They'd just passed an old pickup loaded with furniture when they saw the two girls.

"Look at that!" Jerry said, slowing. "I could use some of that."

Jerry drove another mile or so and then pulled off the road. "Let's go back," Jerry said. "Let's try it."

"Jesus," Bill said. "I don't know."

"I could use some," Jerry said.

Bill said, "Yeah, but I don't know."

"For Christ's sake," Jerry said.

Bill glanced at his watch and then looked all around. He said. "You do the talking. I'm rusty."

Jerry hooted as he whipped the car around.

He slowed when he came nearly even with the girls. He pulled the Chevy onto the shoulder across from them. The girls kept on going on their bicycles, but they looked at each other and laughed. The one on the inside was dark-haired, tall, and willowy. The other was light-haired and smaller. They both wore shorts and halters.

"Bitches," Jerry said. He waited for the cars to pass so he could pull a **U**.

"I'll take the brunette," he said. He said, "The little one's yours."

Bill moved his back against the front seat and touched the bridge of his sunglasses. "They're not going to do anything," Bill said.

"They're going to be on your side," Jerry said.

He pulled across the road and drove back. "Get ready," Jerry said.

"Hi," Bill said as the girls bicycled up. "My name's Bill," Bill said.

"That's nice," the brunette said.

"Where are you going?" Bill said.

The girls didn't answer. The little one laughed. They kept bicycling and Jerry kept driving.

"Oh, come on now. Where you going?" Bill said.

"No place," the little one said.

"Where's no place?" Bill said.

"Wouldn't you like to know," the little one said.

"I told you my name," Bill said. "What's yours? My friend's Jerry," Bill said.

The girls looked at each other and laughed.

A car came up from behind. The driver hit his horn.

"Cram it!" Jerry shouted.

He pulled off a little and let the car go around. Then he pulled back up alongside the girls.

Bill said, "We'll give you a lift. We'll take you where you want. That's a promise. You must be tired riding those bicycles. You look tired. Too much exercise isn't good for a person. Especially for girls."

The girls laughed.

"You see?" Bill said. "Now tell us your names."

"I'm Barbara, she's Sharon," the little one said.

"All right!" Jerry said. "Now find out where they're going."

"Where you girls going?" Bill said. "Barb?"

She laughed. "No place," she said. "Just down the road."

"Where down the road?"

"Do you want me to tell them?" she said to the other girl.

"I don't care," the other girl said. "It doesn't make any difference," she said. "I'm not going to go anyplace with anybody anyway," the one named Sharon said.

"Where you going?" Bill said. "Are you going to Picture Rock?"

The girls laughed.

"That's where they're going," Jerry said.

He fed the Chevy gas and pulled up off onto the shoulder so that the girls had to come by on his side.

"Don't be that way," Jerry said. He said, "Come on." He said. "We're all introduced."

The girls just rode on by.

"I won't bite you!" Jerry shouted.

The brunette glanced back. It seemed to Jerry she was looking at him in the right kind of way. But with a girl you could never be sure.

Jerry gunned it back onto the highway, dirt and pebbles flying from under the tires.

"We'll be seeing you!" Bill called as they went speeding by.

"It's in the bag," Jerry said. "You see the look that cunt gave me?"

"I don't know," Bill said. "Maybe we should cut for home."

"We got it made!" Jerry said.

He pulled off the road under some trees. The highway forked here at Picture Rock, one road going on to Yakima, the other heading for Naches, Enumclaw, the Chinook Pass, Seattle.

A hundred yards off the road was a high, sloping, black mound of rock, part of a low range of hills, honeycombed with footpaths and small caves, Indian sign-painting here and there on the cave walls. The cliff side of the rock faced the highway and all over it there were things like this: NACHES 67—GLEED WILDCATS—JESUS SAVES—BEAT YAKIMA—REPENT NOW.

They sat in the car, smoking cigarettes. Mosquitoes came in and tried to get at their hands.

"Wish we had a beer now," Jerry said. "I sure could go for a beer," he said.

Bill said, "Me too," and looked at his watch.

When the girls came into view, Jerry and Bill got out of the car. They leaned against the fender in front.

"Remember," Jerry said, starting away from the car, "the dark one's mine. You got the other one."

The girls dropped their bicycles and started up one of the paths. They disappeared around a bend and then reappeared again, a little higher up. They were standing there and looking down.

"What're you guys following us for?" the brunette called down.

Jerry just started up the path.

The girls turned away and went off again at a trot.

Jerry and Bill kept climbing at a walking pace. Bill was smoking a cigarette, stopping every so often to get a good drag. When the path turned, he looked back and caught a glimpse of the car.

"Move it!" Jerry said.

"I'm coming," Bill said.

They kept climbing. But then Bill had to catch his breath. He couldn't see the car now. He couldn't see the highway, either. To his left and all the way down, he could see a strip of the Naches like a strip of aluminum foil.

Jerry said, "You go right and I'll go straight. We'll cut the cockteasers off."

Bill nodded. He was too winded to speak.

He went higher for a while, and then the path began to drop, turning toward the valley. He looked and saw the girls. He saw them crouched behind an outcrop. Maybe they were smiling.

Bill took out a cigarette. But he could not get it lit. Then Jerry showed up. It did not matter after that.

Bill had just wanted to fuck. Or even to see them naked. On the other hand, it was okay with him if it didn't work out.

He never knew what Jerry wanted. But it started and ended with a rock. Jerry used the same rock on both girls, first on the girl called Sharon and then on the one that was supposed to be Bill's.

SUGGESTIONS FOR WRITING

1. Examine the stereotypes that Carver invokes about the social class of the two men in this story. Agree or disagree that there is some truth in the way that he has depicted these men's attitudes and behaviors.

2. Explore the men's rationales for their actions. Do you accept or reject their reasoning? Why or why not?

3. If women are no longer to be victims of rape, where would you begin changing men's and women's attitudes about men and women? How would you specifically go about it?

OUTRAGE OVER
OMINIPRESENT VIOLENCE:
WHERE TO AIM IT?

Andrea Kannapell

Andrea Kannapell examines a serious problem of concern to women: the threat of a random attack by a man. Given the high crime rate in America in the late twentieth century, men also have good reason to fear for their safety. Yet the fact remains that women, not men, are victimized as a result of their gender far more frequently than are men. In fact, according to some studies, seventy-five percent of the women in America will be the victim of some form of violent assault in their lifetimes. Furthermore, statistics reveal that men commit the vast majority of violent crimes. Kannapell asks us to examine why this is so. She does not provide an answer, but she does point out that more and more women are outraged at the injustices they suffer at the hands of men.

I am angry. Cruelly angry. A drunken man approached me on my doorstep a few days after April's Central Park attack, and I had murder in my heart before I could think.

I am, like the woman beaten and gang-raped in Central Park, 28 years old and white. Like her, I have frequently been in places, perhaps dangerous places, without a man. Without Mace. I am obsessed by that crime.

She could have been me. I've talked to almost every woman I know about it, and I've heard, over and over, the same sentiments. We ask for vengeance, demand public humiliation for the rapists, castration, or, as one woman put it, "something to do with their dicks." This vicious rape broke open the floodgates containing our outrage; we know there are no "safe places"—not the parks, not home, not work. Everywhere we go, women are subject to this kind of violence. When we talk about the Central Park rape, our conversations are litanies of abuse and victimization, of fury and revenge.

What was she doing in Central Park at 10 p.m. that Wednesday? She'd been there before; she had proved to herself that the stories of unfaceable danger were lies, proved it by going back. We're like test pilots sometimes, testing the limits of safety with our lives. But if women didn't push the edges of the envelope, we'd never even get off the ground.

The crime was more sexist than racist, more sexist than classist. Rape laws should be harsher. Ask the woman who sleeps with a bayonet under her bed. Ask the woman who has a baseball bat by her window. Ask *any* woman.

One lovely summer night, I run an all-too-familiar gauntlet. Clusters of men on the streets with nothing better to do than rudely note my passing, trying to outdo one another as they rub their verbal dicks against my female presence.

This is any night, anywhere. Man after man comments on me as I force myself on. "Sssssss, hey, I've got five dollars!" "C'mon with me, girl." "Check out that ass—baby, sit on my face!" All this to me, *me* in my grungy clothes, in my determinedly dull, asexual Chuck Taylor All-Stars. I insist that I will not respond—then a couple of guys in the street bazaar on Second Avenue say, "Oohhhh . . . foxy bitch." I whip around and shoot back. "Will you shut *up-ppppp??????*"—voice rising to a shriek, gaining volume. People are looking. I face the guys, checked and shocked by my own rage. The rule mothers teach daughters is to ignore men's comments, don't give them the gratification of seeing that they've upset you. But what am I gonna do now, ma?

My fury despises the ingrained cautions of the past: Don't get upset, don't take it personally. But caution wins. These two specific guys don't deserve the rage a lifeful of such remarks, "ignored," have engendered. What I need them to know is that it's not okay, not because it might hurt my feelings, but because *I might kill them.* And I don't mean I'm going to "scratch their eyes out": I am a runner, weight lifter, former marathon swimmer; all my family is frighteningly strong. And there are always weapons at hand: the knife in my pocket, my bike pump, broken bottles or lead pipes in the garbage. I mean: *I might kill them.*

So I tell them, "Look. You look like nice guys. But it's not nice to comment on me like I'm just part of the scenery. I'm here for my own purposes. Okay?" One answers. "You know you're just a piece of meat to me, bitch."

Or consider the van that chased me through Greenwich Village, the driver mimicking intercourse, his fist making a cunt and the middle finger of his other hand violently jamming. I jumped my bike to the sidewalk and yelled at him. "Does you *mother* know you're out here doing that?" He screamed at me and gestured viciously till I rode off.

I hoped that by *not* ignoring attentions I don't "ask for" or want or like, by treating them as the attacks they are, by showing my rage, and by evoking a supposedly respected female, I could do some good—get some built-up anger out, and make that man hesitate before he accosted another woman.

But look. Do you notice that I haven't specified race or class? I don't remember race or class. I only remember that it's men.

It was a man who sexually abused my friend's two toddlers. A man who tried to rape me when I was 12. It was another man, a friend's father, who sexually accosted her throughout her teens. I have a friend who's sure the only reason she wasn't molested as a child is because her mother, a pistol-packing incest survivor, swore publicly to kill anyone who touched her daughter. Including her father. It is men.

Why aren't men afraid of our rage?

I depend on the men who respect women, whether they love me or not, to keep me sane, keep me on this side of alienation. Many women do. The happiest example: A woman I know was walking downtown, preoccupied. Suddenly, her heart sinking, she realized she was about to pass a busy construction site. She considered making a long detour, but decided to charge through. The hardhats watched as she squared her shoulders and fixed her eyes on the ground, and skittered past. Silence, until she passed the foreman, who doffed his helmet to her and said, "Good day, ma'am. We don't harass women on this site." I hope that man treasured the astonished joy on her face.

A man's love is no measure of his respect for women, and sometimes women are quiet when they could speak out.

One day in Kentucky, my brother-in-law and I passed a runner as we drove through a park not unlike Central Park. Mark leaned out of the window and yelled. "Oh, honey, pump it! Looking good!" I shook, and drove, and finally pulled over. We talked at length, but he couldn't understand the threatening quality of his attentions. That night, at home, I asked the women of the family to join this discussion. They smiled cautiously at Mark, and said, "It's not so bad, it's rather flattering." But hours later, one by one, my kinswomen came to me privately to say that they understood my outrage.

Fury certainly is the order of the day. After the Central Park attack last April, John Gutfreund, the CEO of Salomon Brothers, called for what sounds like martial law to counter the "reign of terror in the streets." Donald Trump's expensive ads cry out for blood. Wealthy, healthy, educated, English-speaking white America just lost one of our own, and we have the means to shake this country up with our rage.

I say: Keep the rage! This crime was outrageous. Feel it completely, let it force the truth out. But when we call out our big guns, are we aiming at the real target?

It is true that disenfranchisement predisposes a section of the population to commit violent crimes. But women—of all races and all classes and all ages—are subject to this kind of attack from men—of all races and all classes and all ages. Military crackdowns in Harlem will not change that. The liberal (as in *generous*, also as in *white liberal guilt*) application of money and social programs to a particular group of people is not automatically going to make women's lives safer. Understanding how profound and omnipresent violence toward women is, facing that truth—that is a start. 🖋

SUGGESTIONS FOR WRITING

1. In her essay Kannapell asks, "Why aren't men afraid of our rage?" Analyze the situation she has described and answer her question.

2. Examine popular entertainment such as rock videos, popular music, commercials, movies, and print advertising to see to what extent the media promote the attitude that violence against women is acceptable and perhaps to be encouraged. Do these media tell the consumer that abuse is what women want? If so, in what ways?

3. Interview some of your friends, both male and female, in the same way that Kannapell talked with her family to learn their feelings about violence against women. Write an analysis of what you learned and of your feeling about your findings.

4. Are there places in your town or on your campus where you or your friends are reluctant to walk alone? Describe them and talk to others to learn what

places they fear. Try to come up with ways to make the places more safe as well as to educate men and women about how to reclaim their right to walk where and when they wish without fearing for their safety.

6

SEXUAL ORIENTATION

The serious study of human sexuality in its cultural as well as biological manifestations plays an increasingly prominent role in education today. Often, an excellent way to learn how to recognize the historically changing cultural role of sexual orientation is to concentrate on understanding attitudes toward so-called deviant or unorthodox sexualities. Attitudes have been far from fixed throughout our history, so that what is "orthodox" for one era may be relabeled "unorthodox" in another.

Gay people live in ways that make the question of stereotyping by others unavoidable—even though social statistics suggest that at least 10 percent of all Americans are gay. Gay people may be found in all walks of life, and in all occupations and professions. However, anyone who consciously identifies herself or himself as gay will continually be forced into situations where her or his identity is equated with his or her sexual preference. Ever after, others' perceptions typically will be "the gay writer, gay actor, gay musician, gay physician, gay athlete."

You may feel this is understandable, given deeply felt and unshakably held opinions about what is normal or abnormal, or in accordance with human nature. Definitions of "normal" and "abnormal" have been in flux for most of Western history, and only very recently has "identity" come to be equated with sexuality.

Many people are aware that the ancient Greeks tolerated, even actively encouraged, some activities and expressions we might define as "homosexual," a distinction they did not recognize. The development of Christianity brought about an increasing emphasis on the regulation of sexual conduct, but even the Roman Catholic Church stopped short of an absolute ban on homosexuality until the very late Middle Ages. Not until the nineteenth cen-

tury was homosexuality defined as a distinct realm of human experience to be analyzed or regulated. In fact, the word homosexuality was a nineteenth-century coinage. During the last century and a half, the fields of psychiatry, psychology, medicine, and law have all converged to bring about our tendency to speak of a separate "gay community" and to isolate gay people from other social groups. This habit persists even though common sense and experience tell us that gay neighbors, acquaintances, and co-workers are all around us.

If gay persons, as members of a sexual minority, cannot help but be overwhelmingly aware of their sexuality, heterosexual persons often tend to take theirs for granted, assuming a "natural" order from which it has evolved. They may thus fail to notice the determining role sexuality can play in life, and they may not realize the degree to which their heterosexuality provides them with certain basic assumptions and a certain outlook on life. Within the heterosexual framework, women constitute a minority position in terms of social power, and, somewhat like gay persons, must be more alert to the influence of their sexuality on their lives. One fundamental observation concerning heterosexuality is that one rarely sees "heterosexual" used as an adjective to describe a person (for example, "heterosexual politician" or "heterosexual athlete"). As opposed to how gay people are thought of, we as a culture are much more willing to concede that there is more to a "straight" person than his or her sexuality.

The following readings trace the paths of human sexuality through the life cycle. A child is puzzled by the signs of sexual expression exhibited by her divorced parents and their lovers. A young woman worries her mother by taking a struggling musician as her lover. A college professor fears "coming out" as a lesbian to her students. A gay male couple copes with the challenge of living together in a small Southern town. A radical political activist critically examines romantic notions of love and offers a critique of the institution of marriage. A married man coldly calculates his intention to seduce a married woman he does not love and barely desires. A married woman, jolted by her sudden widowhood, becomes confused by *her conflicting reactions. Finally, an aging mother comes to terms with her daughter's lesbianism. Taken together, these selections reinforce one of the most urgent themes of the contemporary study of sexuality: The very word should always be understood as plural.*

DADDY

Jan Clausen

Most state laws make it difficult for gay couples or single parents to raise chil-
dren, and yet, in every state there are gay adults who are determined to be
parents and who work out at times complex arrangements to do so. Occa-
sionally gay couples adopt children together, and some lesbians bear children
themselves. A gay man and a gay woman may even serve together as a
child's adoptive parents. What effects could such parenting have on the child?
As a society whose studies and theories of child development largely assume
the presence of two heterosexual parents, we are ill equipped to say.
"Daddy" is presented to us from the point of view of a little girl whose time is
divided between her divorced parents' households.

Jan Clausen (b. 1950), originally from Oregon, lives in New York,
where she is active in a number of feminist and lesbian political groups. She
founded the magazine Conditions *in 1977 and was its editor for five years.*
She has written poetry, fiction, and criticism. Her books include Waking at
the Bottom of the Dark *(1979),* Mother, Sister, Daughter, Lover
(1980), and Sinking Stealing *(1985).*

I like my Daddy's best. It has more rooms. Mommy just has an apartment and
you have to go upstairs. The bathroom is in my room. Daddy has two bath-
rooms. He owns the whole house. Mommy used to live there when I was a little
baby. Before they got divorced. That means not married anymore. You get married when you love each other.

Mommy loves me. Daddy says I'm his favorite girl in the whole world, sugar.
He always calls me sugar. We like to go to a restaurant for breakfast. Sometimes
we go there for dinner if he has to work in the city. I went to his office lots of
times. He has books there. You go way up in the elevator. Sometimes I feel like
I'm going to throw up. But I don't. Then you see the river. There's no one there
except Daddy and me. Sometimes Ellen comes.

My Mommy works. She goes to meetings. First I have to go to school and
then daycare. You can make noise at daycare. At school you have to be quiet
or you get punished. But I didn't ever get punished. Mommy helps me with my
homework. Sometimes we read a book together. Daddy asks me add and take
away. He says sugar you're so smart you can be anything you want to be when
you grow up. A doctor or lawyer or a professor or anything. My Daddy's a lawyer. I don't know if I'll get married.

Daddy said maybe next year I can go to a different school where they
have lots of things to play with. You can paint and go on trips and they
have nice books. The kids make so much noise in my class. Some of
them talk Spanish and the boys are bad. I got a star for doing my homework right.

My Daddy takes me on Sunday. Sometimes I sleep there if Mommy goes away. I have to be good. Daddy says he'll get me something when we go shopping if I behave. I have to take a bath before I go and brush my hair. Daddy says he likes little girls that smell nice and clean. Sometimes Ellen lets me try her perfume. Once she let me put some powder on my face and some blue stuff on my eyes. That's eye shadow. But I had to wash my face before I went home. Mommy doesn't wear makeup. Or Carolyn. They said it looks silly.

Once in the summer I stayed at my Daddy's for a whole week. Ellen was there. She helped take care of me. You're so helpless David she said. She laughed. We all laughed. I had fun. We went to Coney Island. During the week I just call my Daddy two times because he works hard. Sometimes if he goes on a trip he can't see me. Daddy and Ellen went on a trip to Florida. They had to fly in an airplane. They sent me a postcard every day. You could go swimming in the winter there. Mommy and me went to the country but the car broke.

Sometimes Carolyn stays overnight. We only have two beds. She has to sleep in the same bed with Mommy. When I wake up I get in bed with them. We all hug each other. Carolyn and Mommy kiss each other all the time. But they aren't married. Only a man and a woman can get married. When they want to have a baby the man's penis gets bigger and he puts it in the woman's vagina. It feels good to touch your vagina. Me and Veronica did it in the bathtub. When the baby comes out the doctor has to cut the Mommy's vagina with some scissors. Mommy showed me a picture in her book.

I saw Daddy's penis before. Mommy has hair on her vagina. She has hair on her legs and Carolyn has lots of hair on her legs like a man. Ellen doesn't. Mommy said maybe Ellen does have hair on her legs but she shaves it. Sometimes I forget and call Carolyn Ellen. She gets mad. Sometimes I forget and call Mommy Daddy. I have a cat called Meatball at Mommy's but sometimes I forget and call Meatball Max instead. That's Daddy's dog.

Daddy is all Jewish. So is Ellen. Mommy is only part Jewish. But Daddy said I could be Jewish if I want. You can't have Christmas if you're Jewish. Mommy and me had a little Christmas tree. Carolyn came. We made cookies. I had Chanukah at my Daddy's. He gave me a doll named Samantha that talks and a skateboard and green pants and a yellow top. He says when I learn to tell time he'll get me a watch.

I wish Mommy would get me a TV. I just have a little one. Sometimes it gets broken. Daddy has a color TV at his house. It has a thing with buttons you push to change the program. Mommy said I watch too much TV. I said if you get me a new TV I promise I'll only watch two programs every day. Mommy said we're not going to just throw things away and get a new one every year. I told her Andrea has a color TV in her house and Veronica has a nice big TV in her room that you can see good. Mommy said I'm not getting a TV and that's all. Mommy made me feel bad. I started crying. Mommy said go to your room you're spoiling my dinner. I said *asshole* to Mommy. That's a curse. Sometimes my Mommy says a curse to me. I cried and cried.

Mommy said get in your room. She spanked me and said now get in your room. I ran in my room and closed the door. Mommy hurts my feelings. She won't let me watch TV. She always goes to a meeting and I have to stay with the baby sitter. I don't say a curse to my Daddy. My Daddy isn't mean to me. I screamed and screamed for my Daddy and Mrs. Taylor next door got mad and banged on the wall.

Mommy said go in the other room and call him then. Daddy said you sound like you've been crying. What's the matter, sugar. Nothing I said. Daddy doesn't like me to cry. He says crying is for little babies. I can't stand to see a woman cry, sugar, he says. Then I laugh and he tells me blow my nose. What are we going to do on Sunday I said. Oh that's a surprise Daddy said. Is it going somewhere I said. Yes we're going somewhere but that's not the real surprise Daddy said. Is it a present I said. Daddy said just wait and see, what did you do in school today. Daddy always asks what did I do in school. I told him the teacher had to punish Carlos. Daddy said listen isn't it about your bedtime. I have work to do. Ellen says hi. Blow me a goodnight kiss.

I hugged my Mommy. She hugged me back. She said she was sorry she got mad. But don't beg for things. A new TV is expensive. We don't need it. Mommy always says it's too expensive. I said I wish you were married to the President. Then we could live in the White House. I saw a picture in school. You could have anything you want. They don't have cockroaches.

The President is a good man. He helps people. George Washington was the President. Veronica gave me a doll of his wife at my birthday. It has a long dress. Mommy said he was mean to Indians and Black people. But we studied about him in school and he wasn't. They had voted once. You could vote for Ford or Carter. My Daddy voted for Carter. I'm glad my Daddy voted for who won. My Mommy didn't vote.

Mommy doesn't like things. She doesn't like the President and she doesn't like Mary Hartman like my Daddy. I told her to get Charmin toilet paper like they have on TV because it's so soft to squeeze. She said that's a rip-off. She only takes me to McDonald's once every month. I got a Ronald McDonald cup to drink my milk. She said that's a gimmick. I like milk. Milk is a natural. I told Mommy that and she got mad. I said you don't like anything Mommy. She said I like lots of things. I like plants. I like to play basketball. I like sleeping late on Sunday mornings. I like to eat. I like books. I like women. I like you.

Do you like men I said. I don't like most men very much Mommy said. Some men are okay. My Daddy likes women I said. Does he Mommy said.

I asked my Daddy does he like women. He said extremely. Some of my favorite people are woman he said. Like you. And Ellen. Why do you ask. I said I don't know, Daddy said do you like men. I love you Daddy I said. I bet she gets that you know where Ellen said.

On Sunday we had breakfast at my Daddy's house. We had pancakes. Daddy makes them. He puts on his cook's hat. Then we went shopping. Then we went to a movie of Cinderella. Ellen came too. Then we went to a restaurant. I had ice cream with chocolate. Ellen and Daddy held each other's hand. Daddy said now I'm going to tell you the surprise. Ellen and I are getting married. How does that sound, sugar. Ellen said for god's sake David give her a little time to react.

Daddy said I can be in the wedding. He said Ellen will wear a pretty dress and he will break a glass. He did that when he and Mommy got married too.

Then Ellen will have the same name as Mommy and Daddy and me and I can call her Mommy too if I want. I won't have to see my Daddy just on Sunday because Ellen will be there to help take care of me. She only works in the morning. It will be like a real family with a Mommy and Daddy and a kid. But I can't say that part because Daddy said it's supposed to still be a secret.

I didn't feel good when Daddy brought me home. I felt like I had to throw up. Mommy held my hand. I lay down on the bed and she brought Meatball to play with me. She asked what did I do with Daddy today. She always asks me that. I told her we saw Cinderella. It was okay. She rode in a pumpkin. Some parts were boring. The Prince loved her. Daddy and Ellen are going to get married.

I started crying. I cried hard. Then I had to throw up. It got on the rug. Mommy got the washcloth. She brought my pajamas. She hugged me. She said I love you. She said it won't be so different when Daddy and Ellen are married. You like Ellen don't you.

I love you Mommy, I love you, I love you I said. Why don't you like my Daddy. I love my Daddy.

I don't dislike your father Mommy said. We don't have much in common that's all. I'm happy living here just with you. You're special to me and you're special to your Daddy. You see him every week.

I cried and cried. I love you Mommy. I love you and Daddy both the same. And I love Ellen because she's going to be my Mommy too. I'll miss you. I'll miss you so much when I live there. I'll cry. I'm going to have a big sunny room and Daddy said he'll paint it and I can pick a color. I'm going to have a new kitty so I won't miss Meatball. Next year I can go to that nice school and Ellen might have a baby. It would be a brother or a sister. Daddy's going to get me a bicycle. I can take anything there I want. I'll just leave a few toys here for when I come to visit you on Sunday. 🖋

SUGGESTIONS FOR WRITING

1. Whose parental care does the child prefer? What are the reasons for this?

2. Her parents' divorce was very unsettling. Consider the reasons for her anxieties, as you see them. What are the reasons for the child's confusion?

3. The child has noticed different aspects in the personal appearance of her lesbian mother and her father's fiancée. What kinds of conclusions do we draw about people from their appearance or dress?

4. Some child psychologists argue that young children understand much more about adult sexuality than they appear to. Using Clausen's "Daddy" as an example, what do you think?

OUTSIDER AND OUTCAST IN SMALLTOWN AMERICA

Louie Crew

For centuries, persons who live unconventional lives have gravitated toward urban areas, which are more tolerant because of the greater anonymity that comes with city life. But it is not always possible for non-conformists to live in cities, and many of them prefer small-town life, for all its drawbacks. In small towns, one's behavior is much more subject to the scrutiny and judgment of one's neighbors. **Louie Crew** *describes his life as a gay white man, living with his black lover in what may seem to be the unlikeliest region of all: the rural South. Here, Bible-belt attitudes produce a strict view of acceptable sexual behavior, and the lingering effects of institutional racism dictate an uneasy truce between the races. Of course, whatever the region, a gay person observing the social rites of heterosexuals always has the sense of being an outsider.*

Crew (b. 1936) grew up in Alabama, attended Baylor University in Texas, and returned to Alabama to receive advanced degrees from Auburn University and the University of Alabama. He has taught at colleges and universities in the United States and in China. He has been active in the gay rights movement, particularly within the Episcopal Church, for whose gay members he founded a national organization called Integrity.

From 1973 to 1979, my spouse and I lived in Fort Valley, a town of 12,000 people, the seat of Peach County, sixty miles northeast of Plains, right in the geographic center of Georgia. I taught English at a local black college and my spouse was variously a nurse, hairdresser, choreographer for the college majorettes, caterer, and fashion designer.

The two of us have often been asked how we survived as a gay, racially integrated couple living openly in that small town. We are still perhaps too close to the Georgia experience and very much caught up in our similar struggles in central Wisconsin to offer a definite explanation, but our tentative conjectures should interest anyone who values the role of the dissident in our democracy.

Survive we did. We even throve before our departure. Professionally, my colleagues and the Regents of the University System of Georgia awarded me tenure, and the Chamber of Commerce awarded my spouse a career medal in cosmetology. Socially, we had friends from the full range of the economic classes in the community. We had attended six farewell parties in our honor before we called a halt to further fetes, especially several planned at too great a sacrifice by some of the poorest folks in the town. Furthermore, I had been away only four months when the college brought me back to address an assembly of Georgia judges, mayors, police chiefs, and wardens. We are still called two to three times a week by scores of people seeking my spouse's advice on fashion, cooking, or the like.

It was not always so. In 1974 my spouse and I were denied housing which we had "secured" earlier before the realtor saw my spouse's color. HUD documented that the realtor thought that "the black man looked like a criminal." Once, the town was up in arms when a bishop accused the two of us of causing a tornado which had hit the town early in 1975, an accusation which appeared on the front page of the newspaper. "This is the voice of God. The town of Fort Valley is harboring Sodomists. Would one expect God to keep silent when homosexuals are tolerated? We remember what He did to Sodom and Gomorrah" (*The Macon Herald*, March 20, 1975: I). A year later my Episcopal vestry asked me to leave the parish, and my own bishop summoned me for discipline for releasing to the national press correspondence related to the vestry's back-room maneuvers. Prompted in part by such officials, the local citizens for years routinely heckled us in public, sometimes threw rocks at our apartment, trained their children to spit on us from their bicycles if we dared to jog, and badgered us with hate calls on an average of six to eight times a week.

One such episode offers a partial clue to the cause of our survival. It was late summer, 1975 or 1976. I was on my motorcycle to post mail at the street-side box just before the one daily pickup at 6:00 P.M. About fifty yards away, fully audible to about seventy pedestrians milling about the court house and other public buildings, a group of police officers, all men, began shouting at me from the steps of their headquarters: "Louise! Faggot! Queer!"

Anyone who has ever tried to ease a motorcycle from a still position without revving the engine knows that the feat is impossible: try as I did to avoid the suggestion, I sounded as if I were riding off in a huff. About half-way up the street, I thought to myself, "I'd rather rot in jail than feel the way I do now." I turned around, drove back—the policemen still shouting and laughing—and parked in the lot of the station. When I walked to the steps, only the lone black policeman remained.

"Did you speak to me?" I asked him.

"No, sir," he replied emphatically.

Inside I badgered the desk sergeant to tell her chief to call me as soon as she could locate him, and I indicated that I would press charges if necessary to prevent a recurrence. I explained that the police misconduct was an open invitation to more violent hoodlums to act out the officers' fantasies with impunity in the dark. Later, I persuaded a black city commissioner and a white one, the latter our grocer and the former our mortician, to threaten the culprits with suspension if ever such misconduct occurred again.

Over a year later, late one Friday after his payday, a black friend of my spouse knocked at our door to offer a share of his Scotch to celebrate his raise—or so he said. Thus primed, he asked me. "You don't recognize me, do you?"

"No," I admitted.

"I'm the lone black policeman that day you were heckled. I came by really because I thought you two might want to know what happened inside when Louie stormed up to the sergeant."

"Yes," we said.

"Well, all the guys were crouching behind the partition to keep you from seeing that they were listening. Their eyes bulged when you threatened to bring in the F.B.I. and such. Then when you left, one spoke for all when he said, 'But sissies aren't supposed to do things like that!' "

Ironically, I believe that a major reason for our thriving on our own terms of candor about our relationship has been our commitment to resist the intimidation heaped upon us. For too long lesbians and gay males have unwillingly encouraged abuses against ourselves by serving advance notice to any bullies, be they the barnyard-playground variety, or the Bible-wielding pulpiteers, that we would whimper or run into hiding when confronted with even the threat of exposure. It is easy to confuse sensible nonviolence with cowardly nonresistance.

In my view, violent resistance would be counter-productive, especially for lesbians and gays who are outnumbered 10 to 1 by heterosexuals, according to Kinsey's statistics. Yet our personal experience suggests that special kinds of creative nonviolent resistance are a major source of hope if lesbians and gay males are going to reverse the physical and mental intimidation which is our daily portion in this culture.

Resistance to oppression can be random and spontaneous, as in part was my decision to return to confront the police hecklers, or organized and sustained, as more typically has been the resistance by which my spouse and I have survived. I believe that only organized and sustained resistance offers much hope for long-range change in any community. The random act is too soon forgotten or too easily romanticized.

Once we had committed ourselves to one another, my spouse and I never gave much thought for ourselves to the traditional device most gays have used for survival, the notorious "closet" in which one hides one's identity from all but a select group of friends. In the first place, a black man and a white man integrating a Georgia small town simply cannot be inconspicuous. More importantly, the joint checking account and other equitable economics fundamental to the quality of our marriage are public, not private acts. Our denial of the obvious would have secured closet space only for our suffocation; we would have lied, "We are ashamed and live in secret."

All of our resistance stems from our sense of our own worth, our conviction that we and our kind do not deserve the suffering which heterosexuals continue to encourage or condone for sexual outcasts. Dr. Martin Luther King used to say, "Those who go to the back of the bus, deserve the back of the bus."

Our survival on our own terms has depended very much on our knowing and respecting many of the rules of the system which we resist. We are not simply dissenters, but conscientious ones.

For example, we are both very hard workers. As a controversial person, I know that my professionalism comes under far more scrutiny than that of others. I learned early in my career that I would secure space for my differences by handling routine matters carefully. If one stays on good terms with secretaries, meets all deadlines, and willingly does one's fair share of the busy work of institutions, one is usually already well on the way towards earning collegial space, if not collegial support. In Georgia, I routinely volunteered to be secretary for most committees on which I served, thereby having enormous influence on the final form of the groups' deliberations without monopolizing the forum as most other molders of policy do. My spouse's many talents and sensibilities made him an invaluable advisor and confidante to scores of people in the community. Of course, living as we did in a hairdresser's salon, we knew a great deal more about the rest of the public than that public knew about us.

My spouse and I are fortunate in the fact that we like the enormous amount of work which we do. We are not mere opportunists working hard only as a gimmick to exploit the public for lesbian and gay issues. Both of us worked intensely at our professional assignment long before we were acknowledged dissidents with new excessive pressures to excel. We feel that now we must, however unfairly, be twice as effective as our competitors just to remain employed at all.

Our survival has also depended very much on our thorough knowledge of the system, often knowledge more thorough than that of those who would use the system against us. For example, when my bishop summoned me for discipline, I was able to show him that his own canons give him no authority to discipline a lay person except by ex-communication. In fact, so hierarchical have the canons of his diocese become, that the only laity who exist worthy of their mention are the few lay persons on vestries.

Especially helpful has been our knowledge of communication procedures. For example, when an area minister attacked lesbians and gays on a TV talk show, I requested equal time; so well received was my response that for two more years I was a regular panelist on the talk show, thereby reaching most residents of the entire middle Georgia area as a known gay person, yet one speaking not just to sexual issues, but to a full range of religious and social topics.

When I was occasionally denied access to media, as in the parish or diocese or as on campus when gossip flared, I knew the value of candid explanations thoughtfully prepared, xeroxed, and circulated to enough folks to assure that the gossips would have access to the truthful version. For example, the vestry, which acted in secret, was caught by surprise when I sent copies of their hateful letter to most other parishioners, together with a copy of a psalm which I wrote protesting their turning the House of Prayer into a Court House. I also was able to explain that I continued to attend, not in defiance of their withdrawn invitation, but in obedience to the much higher invitation issued to us all by the real head of the Church. In January, 1979, in the first open meeting of the parish since the vestry's letter of unwelcome three years earlier, the entire parish voted to censure the vestry for that action and to extend to me the full welcome which the vestry had tried to deny. Only three voted against censure, all three of them a minority of the vestry being censured.

My spouse and I have been very conscious of the risks of our convictions. We have viewed our credentials—my doctorate and his professional licenses—not as badges of comfortable respectability, but as assets to be invested in social change. Dr. King did not sit crying in the Albany jail, "Why don't these folks respect me? How did this happen? What am I doing here?" When my spouse and I have been denied jobs for which we were the most qualified applicants, we have not naively asked how such things could be, nor have we dwelt overly long on self-pity, for we have known in advance the prices we might have to pay, even if to lose our lives. Our realism about danger and risk has helped us to preserve our sanity when everyone about us has seemed insane. I remember the joy which my spouse shared with me over the fact that he had just been fired for his efforts to organize other black nurses to protest their being treated as orderlies by the white managers of a local hospital.

Never, however, have we affirmed the injustices. Finally, we simply cannot be surprised by any evil and are thus less likely to be intimidated by it. Hence, we find ourselves heirs to a special hybrid of courage, a form of courage too often ignored by the heterosexual majority, but widely manifest among sexual outcasts, not the courage of bravado on battlegrounds or sportsfields, but the delicate courage of the lone person who patiently waits out the stupidity of the herd, the cagey courage that has operated many an underground railway station.

Our survival in smalltown America has been helped least, I suspect, by our annoying insistence that potential friends receive us not only in our own right, but also as members of the larger lesbian/gay and black communities of which we are a part. Too many whites and heterosexuals are prepared to single us out as "good queers" or "good niggers," offering us thereby the "rewards" of their friendship only at too great a cost to our integrity. My priest did not whip up the vestry against me the first year we lived openly together. He was perfectly happy to have one of his "clever queers" to dress his wife's hair and the other to help him write his annual report. We became scandalous only when the two of us began to organize the national group of lesbian and gay-male Episcopalians, known as INTEGRITY; then we were no longer just quaint. We threatened his image of himself as the arbiter of community morality, especially as he faced scores of queries from brother priests elsewhere.

Many lesbians and gay males are tamed by dependencies upon carefully selected heterosexual friends with whom they have shared their secret, often never realizing that in themselves alone, they could provide far more affirmation and discover far more strength than is being cultivated by the terms of these "friendships." Lesbians and gay males have always been taught to survive on the heterosexuals' terms, rarely on one's own terms, and almost never on the terms of a community shared with other lesbians and gay males.

Heterosexuals are often thus the losers. The heterosexual acquaintances close to us early on when we were less visible who dropped us later as our notoriety spread were in most cases folks of demonstrably much less character strength than those heterosexuals who remained our friends even as we asserted our difference with thoughtful independence.

My spouse and I have never been exclusive nor aspired to move to any ghetto. In December, 1978, on the night the Macon rabbi and I had successfully organized the area's Jews and gays to protest a concert by Anita Bryant, I returned home to watch the videotape of the march on the late news in the company of eight house guests invited by my spouse for a surprise party, not one of them gay (for some strange reason nine out of ten folks are not), not one of them obligated to be at the earlier march, and not one of them uneasy, as most of our acquaintances would have been a few years earlier before we had undertaken this reeducation together.

Folks who work for social change need to be very careful to allow room for it to happen, not to allow realistic appraisals of risks to prevent their cultivation of the very change which they germinate.

Our survival has been helped in no small way by our candor and clarity in response to rumor and gossip, which are among our biggest enemies. On my campus in Georgia, I voluntarily spoke about sexual issues to an average of 50 classes per year outside my discipline. Initially, those encounters sharpened my wits for tougher national forums, but long after I no longer needed these occasions personally for rehearsal, I continued to accept the invitations, thereby reaching a vast majority of the citizens of the small town where we continued to live. I used to enjoy the humor of sharing with such groups facts which would make my day-to-day life more pleasant. For example, I routinely noted that when a male student is shocked at my simple public, "Hello," he would look both ways to see who might have seen him being friendly with the gay professor. By doing this he is telling me and all other knowledgeable folks far more new information about his own body chemistry that he is finding out about mine. More informed male students would reply, "Hello" when greeted. With this method I disarmed the hatefulness of one of their more debilitating weapons of ostracism.

All personal references in public discussions inevitably invade one's privacy, but I have usually found the invasion a small price to pay for the opportunity to educate the public to the fact that the issues which most concern sexual outcasts are not genital, as the casters-out have so lewdly imagined, but issues of justice and simple fairness.

Resistance is ultimately an art which no one masters to perfection. Early in my struggles, I said to a gay colleague living openly in rural Nebraska, "We must stamp on every snake." Wisely he counseled, "Only if you want to get foot poisoning." I often wish I had more of the wisdom mentioned in *Ecclesiastes*, the ability to judge accurately, "The time to speak and the time to refrain from speaking." Much of the time I think it wise to pass public hecklers without acknowledging their taunts, especially when they are cowardly hiding in a crowd. When I faced bullies head-on, I have tried to do so patiently, disarming them by my own control of the situation. Of course, I am not guaranteed that their violence can thus be aborted every time.

Two major sources of our survival are essentially very private—one, the intense care and love my spouse and I share, and the other, our strong faith in God as Unbounding Love. To these we prefer to make our secular witness, more by what we do than by what we say.

I am not a masochist. I would never choose the hard lot of the sexual outcast in smalltown America. Had I the choice to change myself but not the world, I would return as a white male heterosexual city-slicker millionaire, not because whites, males, heterosexuals, city-slickers, and millionaires are better, but because they have it easier.

Yet everyone faces a different choice: accept the world the way you find it, or change it. For year after year I dissented, right in my own neighborhood.

America preserves an ideal of freedom, although it denies freedom in scores of instances. My eighth-grade civics teacher in Alabama did not mention the price I would have pay for the freedom of speech she taught me to value. I know now that the docile and ignorant dislike you fiercely when you speak truth they prefer not to hear. But I had a good civics class, one that showed me how to change our government. I rejoice.

Sometimes I think a society's critics must appreciate the society far more than others, for the critics typically take very seriously the society's idle promises and forgotten dreams. When I occasionally see them, I certainly don't find many of my heterosexual eighth-grade classmates probing much farther than the issues of our common Form 1040 headaches and the issues as delivered by the evening news. Their lives seem often far duller than ours and the main adventures in pioneering they experience come vicariously, through television, the movies, and for a few, through books. In defining me as a criminal, my society may well have hidden a major blessing in its curse by forcing me out of lethargy into an on-going, rigorous questioning of the entire process. Not only do I teach *The Adventures of Huckleberry Finn*, my spouse and I have in an important sense had the chance to be Huck and Jim fleeing a different form of slavery and injustice in a very real present. 🖋

SUGGESTIONS FOR WRITING

1. The disapproval Crew and his lover encountered may not be surprising, but what is your response to his discussion of the acceptance and friendship they discovered?

2. Like the author, have you ever been in a situation where you generally faced strong disapproval, yet found some persons willing to extend the hand of friendship? Describe what this was like.

3. Why, in referring to his career, does Crew say, "I know that my professionalism comes under far more scrutiny than that of others?"

4. What does the author mean, in the last paragraph, about society's critics' having a greater appreciation of the society?

TELL MARTHA NOT TO MOAN

Sherley Anne Williams

We are abundantly aware of cultural stereotypes about single mothers or about women (the "double standard") who sleep around. The author of this story confronts these stereotypes in ways that suggest there is more to such women as Martha than meets the eye. Mamma, falling back upon another cultural stereotype, despairs over the fact that the man in Martha's life is a musician. Popular music, after all, is filled with references concerning traveling musicians moving from one "one-night stand" to another. Not surprisingly, parents are not often thrilled to learn that their daughters have taken up with musicians.

Sherley Anne Williams (b. 1944) is a professor of literature at the University of California, San Diego. She has been a regular contributor of stories and poems to The Massachusetts Review *(where this story first appeared) and to other distinguished literary periodicals. She won the 1976 National Book Award for Poetry for* The Peacock Poems. *Her other books include the collection of poems* Some One Sweet Angel Chile *(1982) and a volume of literary criticism on black writers called* Give Birth to Brightness *(1972).*

My mamma is a big woman, tall and stout, and men like her cause she soft and fluffy-looking. When she round them it all smiles and dimples and her mouth be looking like it couldn't never be fixed to say nothing but darling and honey.

They see her now, they sho see something different. I should not even come today. Since I had Larry things ain't been too good between us. But—that's my mamma and I know she gon be there when I need her. And sometime when I come, it okay. But this ain't gon be one a them times. Her eyes looking all ove me and I know it coming. She snort cause she want to say god damn but she don't cuss. "When it due, Martha?"

First I start to say, what. But I know it ain't no use. You can't fool old folks bout something like that, so I tell her.

"Last part of November."

"Who the daddy?"

"Time."

"That man what play piano at the Legion?"

"Yeah."

"What he gon do bout it?"

"Mamma, it ain't too much he can do, now is it? The baby on its way."

She don't say nothing for a long time. She sit looking at her hands. They all wet from where she been washing dishes and they all wrinkled like yo hand be when they been in water too long. She get up and get a dish cloth and dry em, then sit down at the table. "Where he at now?"

"Gone."

"Gone? Gone where?" I don't say nothing and she start cussing then. I get kinda scared cause mamma got be real mad foe she cuss and I don't know who she cussing—me or Time. Then she start talking to me. "Martha, you just a fool. I told you that man wan't no good first time I seed him. A musician the worst kind of men you can get mixed up with. Look at you. You ain't even eighteen years old yet, Larry just barely two, and here you is pregnant again." She go on like that for a while and I don't say nothing. Couldn't no way. By the time I get my mouth fixed to say something, she done raced on so far ahead that what I got to say don't have nothing to do with what she saying right then. Finally she stop and ask, "What you gon do now? You want to come back here?" She ain't never liked me living with Orine and when I say no, she ask, "Why not? It be easier for you."

I shake my head again. "If I here, Time won't know where to find me, and Time coming; he be back. He gon to make a place for us, you a see."

"Hump, you just played the fool again, Martha."

"No Mamma, that not it at all; Time want me."

"Is that what he say when he left?"

"No, but . . . "

Well, like the first night we met, he come over to me like he knowed me for a long time and like I been his for awmost that long. Yeah, I think that how it was. Cause I didn't even see him when we come in the Legion that first night.

Me and Orine, we just got our checks that day. We went downtown and Orine bought her some new dresses. But the dress she want to wear that night don't look right so we go racing back to town and change it. Then we had to hurry home and get dressed. It Friday night and the Legion crowded. You got to get there early on the weekend if you want a seat. And Orine don't want just any seat; she want one right up front. "Who gon see you way back there? Nobody. You don't dance, how you gon meet people? You don't meet people, what you doing out?" So we sit up front. Whole lots a people there that night. You can't even see the bandstand cross the dance floor. We sharing the table with some more people and Orine keep jabbing me, telling me to sit cool. And I try cause Orine say it a good thing to be cool.

The set end and people start leaving the dance floor. That when I see Time. He just getting up from the piano. I like him right off cause I like men what look like him. He kind of tall and slim. First time I ever seed a man wear his hair so long and nappy—he tell me once it an African Bush—but he look good anyway and he know it. He look round all cool. He step down from the bandstand and start walking toward me. He come over to the table and just look. "You," he say, "you my Black queen." And he bow down most to the floor.

Ah shit! I mad cause I think he just trying to run a game. "What you trying to prove, fool?" I ask him.

"Ah man," he say and it like I cut him. That the way he say it. "Ah man. I call this woman my Black queen—tell her she can rule my life and she call me a fool."

"And sides what, nigga," I tell him then, "I ain't black." And I ain't, I don't care what Time say. I just a dark woman.

"What's the matter, you shamed of being Black? Ain't nobody told you Black is pretty?" He talk all loud and people start gathering round. Somebody say, "Yeah, you tell her bout it, soul." I embarrassed and I look over at Orine. But she just grinning, not saying nothing. I guess he waiting to see what I gon do so I stand up.

"Well if I is black, I is a fine black." And I walk over to the bar. I walk just like I don't know they watching my ass, and I hold my head up. Time follow me right on over to the bar and put his arm round my shoulder.

"You want a drink?" I start to say no cause I scared. Man not supposed to make you feel like he make me feel. Not just like doing it—but, oh, like it right for him to be there with me, touching me. So I say yes. "What's your name?" he ask then.

I smile and say, "They call me the player." Orine told a man that once in Berkeley and he didn't know what to say. Orine a smart woman.

"Well they call me Time and I know yo mamma done told you Time ain't nothing to play with." His smile cooler than mine. We don't say nothing for a long while. He just stand there with his arm round my shoulder looking at us in the mirror behind the bar. Finally he say, "Yeah, you gon be my Black queen." And he look down at me and laugh. I don't know what to do, don't know what to say neither, so I just smile.

"You gon tell me your name or not?"

"Martha."

He laugh. "That a good name for you."

"My mamma name me that so I be good. She name all us kids from the Bible," I tell him laughing.

"And is you good?"

I nod yes and no all at the same time and kind of mumble cause I don't know what to say. Mamma really did name all us kids from the Bible. She always saying, "My mamma name me Veronica after the woman in the Bible and I a better woman for it. That why I name all my kids from the Bible. They got something to look up to." But mamma don't think I'm good, specially since I got Larry. Maybe Time ain't gon think I good neither. So I don't answer, just smile and move on back to the table. I hear him singing soft-like. "Oh Mary don't you weep, tell yo sister Martha not to moan." And I kind of glad cause most people don't even think bout that when I tell em my name. That make me know he really smart.

We went out for breakfast after the Legion close. Him and me and Orine and German, the drummer. Only places open is on the other side of town and at first Time don't want to go. But we finally swade him.

Time got funny eyes, you can't hardly see into em. You look and you look and you can't tell nothing from em. It make me feel funny when he look at me. I finally get used to it, but that night he just sit there looking and don't say nothing for a long time after we order.

"So you don't like Black?" he finally say.

"Do you?" I ask. I think I just ask him questions, then I don't have to talk so much. But I don't want him to talk bout that right then, so I smile and say. "Let's talk bout you."

"I am not what I am." He smiling and I smile back, but I feel funny cause I think I supposed to know what he mean.

"What kind of game you trying to run?" Orine ask. Then she laugh. "Just cause we from the country don't mean we ain't hip to niggas trying to be big-time. Ain't that right, Martha?"

I don't know what to say, but I know Time don't like that. I think he was going to cuss Orine out, but German put his around round Orine and he laugh. "He just mean he ain't what he want to be. Don't pay no mind to that cat. He always trying to blow some shit." And he start talking that talk, rapping to Orine.

I look at Time. "That what you mean?"

He all lounged back in the seat, his legs stretched way out under the table. He pour salt in a napkin and mix it up with his finger. "Yeah, that's what I mean. That's all about me. Black is pretty, Martha." He touch my face with one finger. "You let white people make you believe you ugly. I bet you don't even dream."

"I do too."

"What do you dream?"

"Huh?" I don't know what he talking bout. I kind of smile and look at him out the corner of my eye. "I dreams bout a man like you. Why, just last night, I dream—"

He start laughing. "That's all right. That's all right."

The food come then and we all start eating. Time act like he forgot all bout dreams. I never figure out how he think I can just sit there and tell him the dreams I have at night, just like that. It don't seem like what I dream bout at night mean as much as what I think bout during the day.

We leaving when Time trip over this white man's feet. That man's feet all out in the aisle but Time don't never be watching where he going no way. "Excuse me," he say kind of mean.

"Say, watch it buddy." That white man talk most as nasty as Time. He kind of old and maybe he drunk or an Okie.

"Man, I said excuse me. You the one got your feet in the aisle."

"You," that man say, starting to get up, "you better watch yourself boy."

And what he want to say that for? Time step back and say real quiet, "No, motherfucker. You the one. You better watch yourself and your daughter too. See how many babies she gon have by boys like me." That man get all red in the face, but the woman in the booth with him finally start pulling at him, telling him to sit down, shut up. Cause Time set to kill that man.

I touch Time's arm first, then put my arm round his waist. "Ain't no use getting messed behind somebody like that."

Time and that man just looking at each other, not wanting to back down. People was gon start wondering what going on in a few minutes. I tell him, "Got something for you, baby," and he look down at me and grin. Orine pick it up. We go out that place singing, "Good loving, good, good loving, make you feel so clean."

"You like to hear me play?" he ask when we in the car.

"This is the first time they ever have anybody here that sound that good."

"Yeah," Orine say. "How come you all staying round a little jive-ass town like Ashley?"

"We going to New York pretty soon," Time say kind of snappy.

"Well, shit, baby, you—"

"When you going to New York?" I ask real quick. When Orine in a bad mood, can't nobody say nothing right.

"Couple of months." He lean back and put his arm round me. "They doing so many things with music back there. Up in the City, they doing one maybe two things. In L.A. they doing another one, two things. But, man, in New York, they doing everything. Person couldn't never get stuck in one groove there. So many things going on, you got to be hip, real hip to keep up. You always growing there. Shit, if you 'live and playing, you can't help but grow. Say, man," he reach and tap German on the shoulder, "let's leave right now."

We all crack up. Then I say, "I sorry but I can't go, got to take care of my baby."

He laugh, "Sugar, you got yo baby right here."

"Well, I must got two babies then."

We pull in front of the partment house then but don't no one move. Finally Time reach over and touch my hair. "You gon by my Black queen?"

I look straight ahead at the night. "Yeah," I say. "Yeah."

We go in and I check first on Larry cause sometimes that girl don't watch him good. When I come in some nights, he be all out the cover and shivering but too sleepy to get back under em. Time come in when I'm pulling the cover up on Orine two kids.

"Which one yours," he ask.

I go over to Larry bed. "This my baby," I tell him.

"What's his name?"

"Larry."

"Oh, I suppose you name him after his daddy?"

I don't like the way he say that, like I was wrong to name him after his daddy. "Who else I gon name him after?" He don't say nothing and I leave him standing there. I mad now and I go in the bedroom and start pulling off my clothes. I think, That nigga can stand up in the living room all night, for all I care; let Orine talk to German and him, too. But Time come in the bedroom and put his arms round me. He touch my hair and my face and my tittie, and it scare me. I try to pull away but he hold me too close. "Martha," he say, "Black Martha." Then he just stand there holding me, not saying nothing, with his hand covering one side on my face. I stand there trembling but he don't notice. I know a woman not supposed to feel the way I feel bout Time, not right way. But I do.

He tell me things nobody ever say to me before. And I want to tell him that I ain't never like no man much as I like him. But sometime you tell a man that and he go cause he think you liking him a whole lot gon hang him up.

"You and me," he say after we in bed, "we can make it together real good." He laugh. "I used to think all I needed was that music, but it take a woman to make that music sing, I think. So now stead of the music and me, it be the music and me and you."

"You left out Larry," I tell him. I don't think he want to hear that. But Larry my baby.

"How come you couldn't be free," he say real low. Then, "How you going when I go if you got a baby?"

"When you going?"

He turn his back to me. "Oh, I don't know. You know what the song say. 'When a woman take the blues, She tuck her head and cry. But when a man catch the blues, he grab his shoes and slide.' Next time I get the blues," he laugh a little, "next time the man get too much for me, I leave here and go someplace else. He always chasing me. The god damn white man." He turn over and reach for me. "You feel good. He chasing me and I chasing dreams. You think I'm crazy, huh? But I'm not. I just got so many, many things going on inside me I don't know which one to let out first. They all want out so bad. When I play—I got to be better, Martha. You gon help me?"

"Yes, Time, I help you."

"You see," and reach over and turn on the light and look down at me, "I'm not what I am. I up tight on the inside but I can't get it to show on the outside. I don't know how to make it come out. You ever hear Coltrane blow? That man is together. He showing on the outside what he got on the inside. When I can do that, then I be somewhere. But I can't go by myself. I need a woman. A Black woman. Them other women steal your soul and don't leave nothing. But a Black woman—" He laugh and pull me close. He want me and that all I care bout.

Mamma come over the next morning and come right on in the bedroom, just like she always do. I kind of shamed for her to see me like that, with a man and all, but she don't say nothing cept scuse me, then turn away. "I come to get Larry."

"He in the other bedroom," I say, starting to get up.

"That's okay; I get him." And she go out and close the door.

I start to get out the bed anyway. Time reach for his cigarettes and light one. "Your mamma don't believe in knocking, do she?"

I start to tell him not to talk so loud cause Mamma a hear him, but that might make him mad. "Well, it ain't usually nobody in here with me for her to walk in on." I standing by the bed buttoning my house coat and Time reach out and pull my arm, smiling.

"I know you ain't no tramp, Martha. Come on, get back in bed."

I pull my arm way and start out the door. "I got to get Larry's clothes together," I tell him. I do got to get them clothes together cause when Mamma come for Larry like that on Sadday morning, she want to keep him for the rest of the weekend. But—I don't know. It just don't seem right for me to be in the bed with a man and my mamma in the next room.

I think Orine and German still in the other bedroom. But I don't know; Orine don't too much like for her mens to stay all night. She say it make a bad impression on her kids. I glad the door close anyway. If Mamma gon start talking that "why don't you come home" talk the way she usually do, it best for Orine not to hear it.

Orine's two kids still sleep but Mamma got Larry on his bed tickling him and playing with him. He like that. "Boy, you sho happy for it to be so early in the morning," I tell him.

Mamma stop tickling him and he lay there breathing hard for a minute. "Big Mamma," he say laughing and pointing at her. I just laugh at him and go get his clothes.

"You gon marry this one?" Every man I been with since I had Larry, she ask that about.

"You think marrying gon save my soul, Mamma?" I sorry right away cause Mamma don't like me to make fun of God. But I swear I gets tired of all that. What I want to marry for anyway? Get somebody like Daddy always coming and going and every time he go leave a baby behind. Or get a man what stay round and beat me all the time and have my kids thinking they big shit just cause they got a daddy what stay with them, like them saddity kids at school. Shit, married or single they still doing the same thing when they goes to bed.

Mamma don't say nothing else bout it. She ask where he work. I tell her and then take Larry in the bathroom and wash him up.

"The older you get, the more foolish you get. Martha. Them musicians ain't got nothing for a woman. Lots sweet talk and babies, that's all. Welfare don't even want to give you nothing for the one you got now, how you gon—" I sorry but I just stop listening. Mamma run her mouth like a clatterbone on a goose ass sometime. I just go and give her the baby and get the rest of his things ready.

"So your mamma don't like musicians, huh?" Time say when I get back in the bedroom. "Square-ass people. Everything they don't know about, they hate. Lord deliver me from a square-ass town with square-ass people." He turn over.

"You wasn't calling me square last night."

"I'm not calling you square now, Martha."

I get back in the bed then and he put his arm round me. "But they say what they want to say. Long as they don't mess with me things be okay. But that's impossible. Somebody always got to have their little say about your life. They want to tell you where to go, how to play, what to play, where to play it—shit, even who to fuck and how to fuck em. But when I get to New York—"

"Time, let's don't talk now."

He laugh then. "Martha, you so Black." I don't know what I should say so I don't say nothing, just get closer and we don't talk.

That how it is lots a time with me and him. It seem like all I got is lots little pitchers in my mind and can't tell nobody what they look like. Once I try to tell him bout that, bout the pitchers, and he just laugh. "Least your head ain't empty. Maybe now you got some pictures, you get some thoughts." That make me mad and I start cussing, but he laugh and kiss me and hold me. And that time, when we doing it, it all—all angry and like he want to hurt me. And I think bout that song he sing that first night bout having the blues. But that the only time he mean like that.

Time and German brung the piano a couple days after that. The piano small and all shiny black wood. Time cussed German when German knocked it against the front door getting it in the house. Time went to put it in the bed-room but I want him to be thinking bout me, not some damn piano when he in there. I tell him he put it in the living room or it don't come in the house. Orine don't want it in the house period, say it too damn noisy—that's what she tell me. She don't say nothing to Time. I think she halfway scared of him. He pretty good bout playing it though. He don't never play it when the babies is sleep or at least he don't play loud as he can. But all he thinking bout when he playing is that piano. You talk to him, he don't answer; you touch him, he don't look up. One time I say to him, "Pay me some tention," but he don't even hear. I hit his hand, not hard, just playing. He look at me but he don't stop playing. "Get out of here, Martha." First I start to tell him he can't tell me what to do in my own self's house, but he just looking at me. Looking at me and playing and not saying nothing. I leave.

His friends come over most evenings when he home, not playing. It like Time is the leader. Whatever he say go. They always telling him how good he is. "Out of sight, man, the way you play." "You ought to get out of this little town so somebody can hear you play." Most times, he just smile and don't say nothing, or he just say thanks. But I wonder if he really believe em. I tell him, sometime, that he sound better than lots a them men on records. He give me his little cool smile. But I feel he glad I tell him that.

When his friends come over, we sit round laughing and talking and drinking. Orine like that cause she be playing up to em all and they be telling her what a fine ass she got. They don't tell me nothing like that cause Time be sitting right there, but long as Time telling me, I don' care. It like when we go to the Legion, after Time and German started being with us. We all the time get in free and then get to sit at one a the big front tables. And Orine like that cause it make her think she big-time. But she still her same old picky self; all the time telling me to "sit cool, Martha," and "be cool, girl." Acting like cool the most important thing in the world. I finally just tell her. "Time like me just the way I am, cool or not." And it true; Time always saying that I be myself and I be fine.

Time and his friends, they talk mostly bout music, music and New York City and white people. Sometime I get so sick a listening to em. Always talking bout how they gon put something over on the white man, gon take something way from him, gon to this, gon do that. Ah shit! I tell em. But they don't pay me no mind.

German say, one night, "Man, this white man come asking if I want to play at his house for—"

"What you tell him, man, 'Put money in my purse'?" Time ask. They all crack up. Me and Orine sit there quiet. Orine all swole up cause Time and them running some kind of game and she don't know what going down.

"Hey, man, yo all member that time up in Frisco when we got fired from that gig and wan't none of our old ladies working?" That Brown, he play bass with em.

"Man," Time say, "all I remember is that I stayed high most of the time. But how'd I stay high if ain't nobody had no bread? Somebody was putting something in somebody's purse." He lean back laughing a little. "Verna's mamma must have been sending her money till she got a job. Yeah, yeah man, that was it. You remember the first time her mamma sent that money and she gave it all to me to hold?"

"And what she wanna do that for? You went out and gambled half a it away and bought pot with most of the rest." German not laughing much as Time and Brown.

"Man, I was scared to tell her, cause you remember how easy it was for her to get her jaws tight. But she was cool, didn't say nothing. I told her I was going to get food with the rest of the money and asked her what she wanted, and—"

"And she say cigarettes," Brown break in laughing, "and this cat, man, this cat tell her, 'Woman, we ain't wasting this bread on no nonessentials!'" He doubled over laughing. They all laughing. But I don't think it that funny. Any woman can give a man money.

"I thought the babe was gon kill me, her jaws was so tight. But even with her jaws tight, Verna was still cool. She just say, 'Baby, you done fucked up fifty dollars on nonessentials; let me try thirty cents.'"

That really funny to em. They all cracking up but me. Time sit there smiling just a little and shaking his head. Then, he reach out and squeeze my knee and smile at me. And I know it like I say; any woman can give a man money.

German been twitching round in his chair and finally he say, "Yeah, man, this fay dude want me to play at his house for fifty cent." That German always got to hear hisself talk. "I tell him take his fifty cent and shove it up his ass—oh scuse me. I forgot that baby was here—but I told him what to do with it. When I play for honkies, I tell him, I don't play for less than two hundred dollars and he so foolish he gon pay it." They all laugh, but I know German lying. Anybody offer him ten cent let lone fifty, he gon play.

"It ain't the money, man," Time say. "They just don't know what the fuck going on." I tell him Larry sitting right there. I know he ain't gon pay me no mind, but I feel if German can respect my baby, Time can too. "Man they go out to some little school, learn a few chords, and they think they know it all. Then, if you working for a white man, he fire you and hire him. No, man, I can't tie shit from no white man."

"That where you wrong," I tell him. "Somebody you don't like, you supposed to take em for everything they got. Take em and tell em to kiss yo butt."

"That another one of your pictures, I guess," Time say. And they all laugh cause he told em bout that, too, one time when he was mad with me.

"No, no," I say. "Listen, one day I walking downtown and this white man offer me a ride. I say okay and get in the car. He start talking and hinting round and finally he come on out and say it. I give you twenty dollars, he say. I say okay. We in Chinatown by then and at the next stop light he get out his wallet and give me a twenty-dollar bill. 'That what I like bout you colored women,' he say easing all back in his seat just like he already done got some and waiting to get some more. 'Yeah,' he say, 'you all so easy to get.' I put that money in my purse, open the door and tell him, 'Motherfucker, you ain't got shit here,' and slam the door."

"Watch your mouth," Time say, "Larry sitting here." We all crack up.

"What he do then?" Orine ask.

"What could he do? We in Chinatown and all them colored folks walking round. You know they ain't gon let no white man do nothing to me."

Time tell me after we go to bed that night that he kill me if he ever see me with a white man.

I laugh and kiss him. "What I want with a white man when I got you?" We both laugh and get in the bed. I lay stretched out waiting for him to reach for me. It funny, I think, how colored men don't never want no colored women messing with no white mens but the first chance he get, that colored man gon be right there in that white woman's bed. Yeah, colored men sho give colored womens a hard way to go. But I know if Time got to give a hard way to go, it ain't gon be for scaggy fay babe, and I kinda smile to myself.

"Martha—"

"Yeah, Time," I say turning to him.

"How old you—eighteen? What you want to do in life? What you want to be?" What he mean? "I want to be with you," I tell him.

"No, I mean really. What you want?" Why he want to know, I wonder. Everytime he start talking serious-like, I think he must be hearing his sliding song.

"I don't want to have to ask nobody for nothing. I want to be able to take care of my own self." I won't be no weight on you, Time, I want to tell him. I won't be no trouble to you.

"Then what are you doing on the Welfare?"

"What else I gon do? Go out and scrub somebody else's toilets like my mamma did so Larry can run wild like I did? No. I stay on Welfare awhile, thank you."

"You see what the white man have done to us, is doing to us?"

"White man my ass," I tell him. "That was my no good daddy. If he'd gone out and worked, we woulda been better off."

"How he gon work if the man won't let him?"

"You just let the man turn you out. Yeah, that man got yo mind."

"What you mean?" he ask real quiet. But I don't pay no tention to him.

"You always talking bout music and New York City, New York City and the white man. Why don't you forget all that shit and get a job like other men? I hate that damn piano."

He grab my shoulder real tight. "What you mean, 'got my mind?' What you mean?" And he start shaking me. But I crying and thinking bout he gon leave.

"You laugh cause I say all I got in my mind is pitchers but least they better some old music. That all you ever think about, Time."

"What you mean? What you mean?"

Finally I scream. "You ain't gon no damn New York City and it ain't the white man what gon keep you. You just using him for a scuse cause you scared. Maybe you can't play." That the only time he ever hit me. And I cry cause I know he gon leave for sho. He hold me and say don't cry, say he sorry, but I can't stop. Orine bamming on the door and Time yelling at her to leave us lone and the babies crying and finally he start to pull away. I say, "Time . . ." He still for a long time, then he say, "Okay, Okay, Martha."

No, it not like he don't want me no more, he—

"Martha. Martha. You ain't been listening to a word I say."

"Mamma." I say it soft cause I don't want to hurt her. "Please leave me lone. You and Orine—and Time too, sometime—yo all treat me like I don't know nothing. But just cause it don't seem like to you that I know what I'm doing, that don't mean nothing. You can't see into my life."

"I see enough to know you just get into one mess after another." She shake her head and her voice come kinda slow. "Martha, I named you after that woman in the Bible cause I want you to be like her. Be good in the same way she is. Martha, that woman ain't never stopped believing. She humble and patient and the Lord make a place for her." She lean her hands on the table. Been in them dishes again, hands all wrinkled and shiny wet. "But that was the Bible. You ain't got the time to be patient, to be waiting for Time or no one else to make no place for you. That man ain't no good. I told you—"

Words coming faster and faster. She got the cow by the tail and gon on down shit creek. It don't matter though. She talk and I sit here thinking bout Time. "You feel good . . . You gon be my Black queen? . . . We can make it together . . . You feel good . . ." He be back. ✒

SUGGESTIONS FOR WRITING

1. Narrate this same story from Mamma's point of view.

2. In what ways has Martha defined herself in relation to her lover? In what ways does she remain an independent woman? How does she know that Time will return to her?

3. Does Williams present any one of the characters more sympathetically than the others? Which one? How would you view the same situation in your own family?

CONFESSIONS OF A
CLOSET BAPTIST

Mab Segrest

Being a teacher places one in a conspicuous position: Like it or not, teachers
serve as role models for their students. Since they are products of a society
that assumes heterosexuality as the norm, students tend to assume that their
teachers are heterosexual. But what if the teacher is gay? Furthermore, what
if she is employed by a conservative church-related private college whose affil-
iated denomination staunchly opposes homosexuality? Most demographers
agree that roughly 10 percent of the population is gay, so it only stands to
reason that gay people will be found in any social setting, including member-
ship in the faculty of such a college. Segrest describes the dilemma that occurs
when a homosexual professor at a small conservative college is confronted by
her students' pronounced homophobia. Even if she keeps a low profile, how
does she react if the subject of homosexuality comes up in her classroom?
Moreover, does she dare to reach out to a student she recognizes as "coming
out" to her?

Mab Segrest (b. 1949) grew up white in a largely black county in rural
Alabama. She participated in the civil rights movement, and eventually at-
tended Duke University, where she earned her Ph.D in American literature.
She taught for a number of years at a small church-related college in North
Carolina, which provided the experiences she writes about in "Confessions of
A Closet Baptist." During the late 1970s she was a founding member of the
lesbian journal Feminary, *where her first publications appeared. In 1985,*
she published My Mama's Dead Squirrel: Lesbian Essays on Southern
Culture, *which included this essay. During the 1980s, Segrest served as di-*
rector of North Carolinians Against Racist and Religious Violence. In this
capacity she monitored the activity of Ku Klux Klan and neo-Nazi groups in
North Carolina. She has written extensively about the 1979 Greensboro
Klan murders and the ensuing trials, as well as other trials involving North
Carolina white supremacists.

I lead a double life. By day I'm a relatively mild-mannered English teacher at a
Southern Baptist college. By night—and on Tuesdays and Thursdays and
weekends—I am a lesbian writer and editor, a collective member of *Feminary*,
a lesbian-feminist journal for the South. My employers do not know about my
other life. When they find out, I assume I will be fired, maybe prayed to death.
For the past four years my life has moved rapidly in opposite directions.

When I started teaching English at my present school five years ago, I knew
I was a lesbian. I was living with P, my first woman lover. But I wasn't out politically. I had not yet discovered the lesbian culture and lesbian community

that is now such an important part of my life. The first time I had let myself realize I was in love with P, I sat under a willow tree by the lake at the Girl Scout camp where we both worked and said aloud to myself in the New York darkness: "I am a lesbian." I had to see how it sounded, and after I'd said that, gradually, I felt I could say anything. When, three years ago, P left to live with a man, I knew my life had changed. I read lesbian books and journals with great excitement. I joined the collective of *Feminary*, then a local feminist journal, and helped turn it into a journal for Southern lesbians. I started writing. I did all this while working for the Baptists, feeling myself making decisions that were somehow as frightening as they were inevitable. Early issues of *Feminary* record the process. First there is a poem by "Mabel." Then an article by "Mab." Then the whole leap: "Mab Segrest." I knew if I could not write my name, I couldn't write anything. I also knew: if I can't be myself and teach, I won't teach.

It is fall as I write this, and September brings back memories of new, plaid cotton dresses, clean notebooks, pencils sharpened to fine points, and especially a stack of unopened books full of things I didn't yet know. Since my junior year in college, over a decade ago, I have wanted to be a teacher. For a long time—before P and I both made the brave, reckless leap that a woman makes when she loves another woman for the first time—teaching was the most important thing in my life. I have always liked school. And I always—always!—loved to read. During my childhood I spent many hours with books on the front porch swing or in my father's chair by the gas heater. I pondered things in long conversations with myself walking home from school, my hands waving slightly as I held forth to some invisible audience. Now in my classes I love the challenge of looking out over a sea of consciousness, watching eyes focus and unfocus, as words register or float out the back window—every period the necessity to generate interest, every hour a hundred tiny failures and successes. Teaching is the work I love best. I can bring much of myself to it and much of it into myself. But as a lesbian teacher in a society that hates homosexuals—especially homosexual teachers—I have learned a caution toward my students and my school that saddens me. The things my life has taught me best I cannot teach directly. I do not believe that I am the only one who suffers.

The first time homosexuality came up in my classroom it was a shock to my system. It was in freshman composition, and I was letting a class choose debate topics. They picked gay rights, but nobody wanted to argue the gay side. Finally, three of my more vociferous students volunteered. I went home shaken. I dreamed that night I was in class, my back to my students, writing on the board (I always feel most vulnerable then), and students were taunting me from the desks—"lesbian! queer!"

The day of the debate I took a seat in the back row, afraid that if I stood up front *IT* would show. I would give myself away: develop a tic, tremble, stutter, throw up, then faint dead away. I kept quiet as my three pro-students held off the Bible with the Bill of Rights, to everyone's amazement, including my own. (I certainly knew it could be done; I just hadn't expected them to do it. No one else in the class had figured any legitimate arguments were possible.) Then the anti-gay side rallied and hit on a winning tactic. They implied that if the opponents really believed their own arguments, they were pretty "funny." I called an end to the debate, and the pro-gay side quickly explained how they didn't mean anything they had said. Then one of my female students wanted to discuss how Christians should love people even when they were sick and sinful. I said the discussion was over and dismissed the class. The only time I had spoken during the entire debate was in response to a male student behind me who had reacted defensively to a mention of homosexuality in the army with, "Yes, and where *my* father works, they castrate people like that." I turned to him with quiet fury. "Are you advocating it?" All in all I survived the day, but without much self-respect.

The next year, on a theme, a freshwoman explained to me how you could tell gay people "by the bandannas they wear in their pockets and around their necks." She concluded, "I think homosexuals are a menace to society. *What do you think?*" A pregnant question, indeed. I pondered for a while, then wrote back in the margin, "I think society is a menace to homosexuals." I resisted wearing a red bandanna the day I handed back the papers.

Sometimes friends ask me why I stay. I often ask myself, and I'm still not sure. A Southern Baptist school is not the most comfortable place for a gay teacher to be—sitting on the buckle of the Bible Belt. The Southern Baptist Convention even appointed Anita Bryant a vice-president in her queer-hunting days. I guess I stay partly because teaching jobs are hard to come by around here, and I'm committed to working on *Feminary*. I have begun to apply for other jobs, but so far without success. I wonder how different it would be in other places where bigotry might be more subtle, dangers more carefully concealed. Mostly I stay because I like my students. They remind me, many of them, of myself at their age: making new and scary breaks from hometown values, at first not straying very far and needing to be told, "There's a bigger world. Go for it." Teaching them is like being a missionary, an analogy many of them would understand.

Two years ago I came out for the first time to a student. I had resolved that if any student ever asked me to identify myself, I would. So when Fred came up to my desk before Christmas vacation, sporting one new earring and wanting to talk about bars in Washington, I knew it was coming.

"Where do *you* go to dance?" he asked. (At the time, there was one gay disco in the vicinity.)

"Oh," I evaded, "you probably wouldn't know it. What about you?"

"Oh, you wouldn't know it either." Then, quickly, "It's between Chapel Hill and Durham."

Me: "I think I do. It starts with a C?"

Him: "Yes. *You* go there?" His eyes lit up.

Me: "Yep."

Him: Politely, giving me an out, "You probably just went one time and got disgusted?"

Me: "Nope."

By this time the class was filling with students, milling around my desk and the blackboard behind us. I suggested to Fred that we finish the conversation after class. We did—in the middle of the campus on a bench which we could see anyone coming for at least half a mile. I felt a sudden sympathy for the CIA.

He asked me if he could tell his friends. I took a deep breath and said yes. But they never came to see me. I still don't know how far word has spread; every now and then I have the feeling I exchange meaningful glances with certain students. I would like for gay students to know I am there if they need me—or maybe just to know I am there—but I do not take the initiative to spread the word around. I have made the decision to be *out* in what I write and *in* where I teach, not wanting to risk a job I enjoy or financial security; but it is not a decision I always feel good about.

I see the unease of most college students over sexuality—whether they express it in swaggering and hollow laughter over queer jokes, or in timidity, or in the half-proud confession of a preacher at how he knocked his wife's teeth out—and I know that it is part of a larger disease with sexuality and the definitions of *men* and *women* in this society. I see how they, and most of us, have been taught to fear all of our feelings. And I understand all too well when I realize I am afraid to write—to even know—what I think and feel for fear of losing my job; how money buys conformity; how subtly we are terrorized into staying in line.

The closest I ever came to saying what I wanted to was in an American literature class last year. Gay rights came up again—I think I may have even steered the discussion in that direction. And a student finally said to me, "But what about teachers? We can't have homosexuals teaching students!" I resisted leaping up on the podium and flashing the big *L* emblazoned on a leotard beneath my blouse. Instead, I took a deep breath and began slowly. "Well, in my opinion, you don't learn sexual preference in the classroom. I mean, that's not what we are doing here. *If* you had a gay or lesbian teacher, he or she would not teach you about sexual preference." I paused to catch my breath. They were all listening. "What he or she would say, *if you had* a gay teacher, is this . . . " (by now I was lightly beating on the podium) " '. . . don't let them make you afraid to be who you are. To know who you are.' She would tell you, 'Don't let them get you. Don't let them make you afraid.' " I stopped abruptly and in the silence turned to think of something to write on the board.

If they ever *do* have a lesbian teacher, that is exactly what she will say. ✒

SUGGESTIONS FOR WRITING

1. What do you do when friends or acquaintances denounce homosexuals? Describe such an incident.

2. If you found yourself in Segrest's situation, what would you do? How would you have handled the conversation she describes with the gay male student?

3. How would you react to the discovery that your professor was gay? Would your reaction be the same if you realized she hadn't intended to make that knowledge public as it would be if she proudly proclaimed the fact? Explain the reasons for any difference in your reactions.

MARRIAGE AND LOVE

Emma Goldman

*Most of us have a "romantic" streak. Our popular culture abounds with references to "love." **Emma Goldman,** author of this essay, became profoundly disillusioned with marriage and "love," but she insisted that women had a right to demand sexual freedom, which she defended as necessarily distinct from idealized notions of romantic love.*

Goldman (1869–1940) was one of the most influential American feminists and radical activists. She was born in Lithuania and emigrated to the Unites States in 1886. She soon became involved in the labor movement and eventually developed an anarchist philosophy. Like many radicals, she was a victim of the Red Scare, which convulsed the United States near the end of the First World War and for several years thereafter. She was sentenced to federal prison in 1917 for her opposition to the military draft. After serving two years, she was deported to the Soviet Union. She was not long in becoming disillusioned with the Bolshevik leadership of the revolution. She spent her remaining years in Britian, Canada, and, on a 1936 lecture tour, the United States. In 1934 her autobiography, Living My Life, was published.

A tireless activist on behalf of anarchist and feminist causes, and not without a sense of humor, Goldman always kept a bag packed and ready for her several trips to prison. She contributed the memorable statement "If I can't dance, I don't want to be part of your revolution," inspired by what she saw as the grim determination and asceticism of the Russian Bolsheviks. She was considered scandalous in her day for her vigorous demand for universal access to contraception. Like many radical feminists, she considered women's lot of childbearing to be a means of enslavement. Unlike most American feminists, she opposed women's suffrage because of her anarchism. For her, the point was not to gain greater participation in the state but to work for its abolition.

The popular notion about marriage and love is that they are synonymous, that they spring from the same motives, and cover the same human needs. Like most popular notions this also rests not on actual facts, but on superstition.

Marriage and love have nothing in common; they are as far apart as the poles; are, in fact, antagonistic to each other. No doubt some marriages have been the result of love. Not, however, because love could assert itself only in marriage; much rather is it because few people can completely outgrow a convention. There are today large numbers of men and women to whom marriage is naught but a farce, but who submit to it for the sake of public opinion. At any rate, while it is true that some marriages are based on love, and while it is equally true that in some cases love continues in married life, I maintain that it does so regardless of marriage, and not because of it.

On the other hand, it is utterly false that love results from marriage. On rare occasions one does hear of a miraculous case of a married couple falling in love after marriage, but on close examination it will be found that it is a mere adjustment to the inevitable. Certainly the growing-used to each other is far away from the spontaneity, the intensity, and beauty of love, without which the intimacy of marriage must prove degrading to both the woman and the man.

Marriage is primarily an economic arrangement, an insurance pact. It differs from the ordinary life insurance agreement only in that it is more binding, more exacting. Its returns are insignificantly small compared with the investments. In taking out an insurance policy one pays for it in dollars and cents, always at liberty to discontinue payments. If, however, woman's premium is a husband, she pays for it with her name, her privacy, her self-respect, her very life "until death doth part." Moreover, the marriage insurance condemns her to life-long dependency, to parasitism, to complete uselessness, individual as well as social. Man, too, pays his toll, but as his sphere is wider, marriage does not limit him as much as woman. He feels his chains more in an economic sense.

Thus Dante's motto over Inferno applies with equal force to marriage: "Ye who enter here leave all hope behind."

That marriage is a failure none but the very stupid will deny. One has but to glance over the statistics of divorce to realize how bitter a failure marriage really is. Nor will the stereotyped Philistine argument that the laxity of divorce laws and the growing looseness of women account for the fact that: first, every twelfth marriage ends in divorce; second, that since 1870 divorces have increased from 28 to 73 for every hundred thousand population; third, that adultery, since 1867, as ground for divorce, has increased 270.8 per cent.; fourth, that desertion increased 369.8 per cent.

Added to these starling figures is a vast amount of material, dramatic and literary, further elucidating this subject. Robert Herrick, in *Together*; Pinero, in *Mid-Channel*; Eugene Walker, in *Paid in Full*, and scores of other writers are discussing the barrenness, the monotony, the sordidness, the inadequacy of marriage as a factor for harmony and understanding.

The thoughtful social student will not content himself with the popular superficial excuse for this phenomenon. He will have to dig down deeper into the very life of the sexes to know why marriage proves so disastrous.

Edward Carpenter says that behind every marriage stands the life-long environment of the two sexes; an environment so different from each other that man and woman must remain strangers. Separated by an insurmountable wall of superstition, custom, and habit, marriage has not the potentiality of developing knowledge of, and respect for, each other, without which every union is doomed to failure.

Henrik Ibsen, the hater of all social shams, was probably the first to realize this great truth. Nora leaves her husband, not—as the stupid critic would have it—because she is tired of her responsibilities or feels the need of woman's rights, but because she has come to know that for eight years she had lived with a stranger and borne him children. Can there by anything more humiliating, more degrading than a life-long proximity between two strangers? No need for the woman to know anything of the man, save his income. As to the knowledge of the woman—what is there to know except the she has a pleasing appearance? We have not yet outgrown the theologic myth that woman has no soul, that she is a mere appendix to man, made out of his rib just for the convenience of the gentleman who was so strong that he was afraid of his own shadow.

Perchance the poor quality of the material whence woman comes is responsible for her inferiority. At any rate, woman has no soul—what is there to know about her? Besides, the less soul a woman has the greater her asset as a wife, the more readily will she absorb herself in her husband. It is this slavish acquiescence to man's superiority that has kept the marriage institution seemingly intact for so long a period. Now that woman is coming into her own, now that she is actually growing aware of herself as a being outside of the master's grace, the sacred institution of marriage is gradually being undermined, and no amount of sentimental lamentation can stay it.

From infancy, almost the average girl is told that marriage is her ultimate goal; therefore her training and education must be directed toward that end. Like the mute beast fattened for slaughter, she is prepared for that. Yet, strange to say, she is allowed to know much less about her function as wife and mother than the ordinary artisan of his trade. It is indecent and filthy for a respectable girl to know anything of the marital relation. Oh, for the inconsistency of respectability, that needs the marriage vow to turn something which is filthy into the purest and most sacred arrangement that none dare question or criticize. Yet that is exactly the attitude of the average upholder of marriage. The prospective wife and mother is kept in complete ignorance of her only asset in the competitive field—sex. Thus she enters into life-long relations with a man only to find herself shocked, repelled, outraged beyond measure by the most natural and healthy instinct, sex. It is safe to say that a large percentage of the unhappiness, misery, distress, and physical suffering of matrimony is due to the criminal ignorance in sex matters that is being extolled as a great virtue. Nor is it at all an exaggeration when I say that more than one home has been broken up because of this deplorable fact.

If, however, woman is free and big enough to learn the mystery of sex without the sanction of State or Church, she will stand condemned as utterly unfit to become the wife of a "good" man, his goodness consisting of an empty head and plenty of money. Can there by anything more outrageous than the idea that a healthy, grown woman, full of life and passion, must deny nature's demand, must subdue her most intense craving, undermine her health and break her spirit, must stunt her vision, abstain from the depth and glory of sex experience until a "good" man comes along to take her unto himself as a wife? That is precisely what marriage means. How can such an arrangement end except in failure? This is one, though not the least important, factor of marriage, which differentiates it from love.

Ours is a practical age. The time when Romeo and Juliet risked the wrath of their fathers for love, when Gretchen exposed herself to gossip of her neighbors for love, is no more. If, on rare occasions, young people allow themselves the luxury of romance, they are taken in care by the elders, drilled and pounded until they become "sensible."

The moral lesson instilled in the girl is not whether the man has aroused her love, but rather is it, "How much?" The important and only God of practical American life: Can the man make a living? Can he support a wife? That is the only thing that justifies marriage. Gradually this saturates every thought of the girl; her dreams are not of moonlight and kisses, of laughter and tears; she dreams of shopping tours and bargain counters. This soul-poverty and sordidness are the elements inherent in the marriage institution. The State and the Church approve of no other ideal, simply because it is the one that necessitates the State and Church control of men and women.

Doubtless there are people who continue to consider love above dollars and cents. Particularly is this true of that class whom economic necessity has forced to become self-supporting. The tremendous change in woman's position, wrought by that mighty factor, is indeed phenomenal when we reflect that it is but a short time since she has entered the industrial arena. Six million women wage-earners; six million women, who have the equal right with men to be exploited, to be robbed, to go on strike; aye, to starve even. Anything more, my lord? Yes, six million wage-workers in every walk of life, from the highest brain work to the most difficult menial labor in the mines and on the railroad tracks; yes, even detectives and policemen. Surely the emancipation is complete.

Yet with all that, but a very small number of the vast army of women wage-workers look upon work as a permanent issue, in the same light as does man. No matter how decrepit the latter, he has been taught to be independent, self-supporting. Oh, I know that no one is really independent in our economic treadmill; still, the poorest specimen of a man hates to be a parasite; to be known as such, at any rate.

The woman considers her position as worker transitory, to be thrown aside for the first bidder. That is why it is infinitely harder to organize women than men. "Why should I join a union? I am going to get married, to have a home." Has she not been taught from infancy to look upon that as her ultimate calling? She learns soon enough that the home, though not so large a prison as the factory, has more solid doors and bars. It has a keeper so faithful that naught can escape him. The most tragic part, however, is that the home no longer frees her from wage-slavery; it only increases her task.

According to the latest statistics submitted before a Committee "on labor and wages, and congestion of population," ten per cent of the wage workers in New York City alone are married, yet they must continue to work at the most poorly paid labor in the world. Add to this horrible aspect the drudgery of housework, and what remains of the protection and glory of the home? As a matter of fact, even the middle-class girl in marriage can not speak of her home, since it is the man who creates her sphere. It is not important whether the husband is a brute or a darling. What I wish to prove is that marriage guarantees woman a home only by the grace of her husband. There she moves about in *his* home, year after year, until her aspect of life and human affairs becomes as flat, narrow, and drab as her surroundings. Small wonder if she becomes a nag, petty, quarrelsome, gossipy, unbearable, thus driving the man from the house. She could not go, if she wanted to; there is no place to go. Besides, a short period of married life, of complete surrender of all faculties, absolutely incapacitates the average woman for the outside world. She becomes reckless in appearance, clumsy in her movements, dependent in her decisions, cowardly in her judgment, a weight and a bore, which most men grow to hate and despise. Wonderfully inspiring atmosphere for the bearing of life, is it not?

But the child, how is it be protected, if not for marriage? After all, is not that the most important consideration? The sham, the hypocrisy of it! Marriage protecting the child, yet thousands of children destitute and homeless. Marriage protecting the child, yet orphan asylums and reformatories overcrowded, the Society for the Prevention of Cruelty to Children keeping busy in rescuing the little victims from "loving parents," to place them under more loving care, the Gerry Society. Oh, the mockery of it!

Marriage may have the power to "bring the horse to water," but has it ever made him drink? The law will place the father under arrest, and put him in convict's clothes; but has that ever stilled the hunger of the child? If the parent has no work, or if he hides his identity, what does marriage do then? It invokes the law to bring the man to "justice," to put him safely behind closed doors; his labor, however, goes not to the child, but to the State. The child receives but a blighted memory of its father's stripes.

As to the protection of the woman,—therein lies the curse of marriage. Not that it really protects her, but the very idea is so revolting, such an outrage and insult on life, so degrading to human dignity, as to forever condemn this parasitic institution.

It is like that other parental arrangement—capitalism. It robs man of his birthright, stunts his growth, poisons his body, keeps him in ignorance, in poverty and dependence, and then institutes charities that thrive on the last vestige of man's self-respect.

The institution of marriage makes a parasite of woman, an absolute dependent. It incapacitates her for life's struggle, annihilates her social consciousness, paralyzes her imagination, and then imposes its gracious protection, which is in reality a snare, a travesty on human character.

If motherhood is the highest fulfillment of woman's nature, what other protection does it need save love and freedom? Marriage but defiles, outrages and corrupts her fulfillment. Does it not say to woman, Only when you follow me shall you bring forth life? Does it not condemn her to the block, does it not degrade and shame her if she refuses to buy her right to motherhood by selling herself? Does not marriage only sanction motherhood, even though conceived in hatred, in compulsion? Yet, if motherhood be of free choice, of love, of ecstasy, of defiant passion, does it not place a crown of thorns upon an innocent head and carve in letters or blood the hideous epithet, Bastard? Were marriage to contain all the virtues claimed for it, its crimes against motherhood would exclude it forever from the realm of love.

Love, the strongest and deepest element in life, the harbinger of hope, of joy, of ecstasy; love, the defier of all laws, of all conventions; love, the freest, the most powerful moulder of human destiny; how can such an all-compelling force be synonymous with that poor little State and Church-begotten weed, marriage?

Free love? As if love is anything but free! Man has bought brains, but all the millions in the world have failed to buy love. Man has subdued bodies, but all the power on earth has been unable to subdue love. Man has conquered whole nations, but all his armies could not conquer love. Man has chained and fettered the spirit, but he has been utterly helpless before love. High on a throne, with all the splendor and pomp his gold can command, man is yet poor and desolate, if love passes him by. And if it stays, the poorest hovel is radiant with warmth, with life and color. Thus love has the magic power to make of a beggar a king. Yes, love is free; it can dwell in no other atmosphere. In freedom it gives itself unreservedly, abundantly, completely. All the laws on the statutes, all the courts in the universe, cannot tear it from the soil, once love has taken root. If, however, the soil is sterile, how can marriage make it bear fruit? It is like the last desperate struggle of fleeting life against death.

Love needs no protection; it is its own protection. So long as love begets life no child is deserted, or hungry, or famished for the want of affection. I know this to be true. I know women who became mothers in freedom by the men they loved. Few children in wedlock enjoy the care, the protection, the devotion free motherhood is capable of bestowing.

The defenders of authority dread the advent of a free motherhood, lest it will rob them of their prey. Who would fight wars? Who would create wealth? Who would make the policeman, the jailer, if woman were to refuse the indiscriminate breeding of children? The race, the race! shouts the king, the president, the capitalist, the priest. The race must be preserved, though woman be degraded to a mere machine,—and the marriage institution is our only safety valve against the pernicious sex-awakening of woman. But in vain these frantic efforts to maintain a state of bondage. In vain, too, the edicts of the Church, the mad attacks of rulers, in vain even the arm of the law. Woman no longer wants to be a party to the production of a race of sickly, feeble, decrepit, wretched human beings, who have neither the strength nor moral courage to throw off the yoke of poverty and slavery. Instead she desires fewer and better children, begotten and reared in love and through free choice; not by compulsion, as marriage imposes. Our pseudo-moralists have yet to learn the deep sense of responsibility toward the child, that love in freedom has awakened in the breast of woman. Rather would she forego forever the glory of motherhood than bring forth life in an atmosphere that breathes only destruction and death. And if she does become a mother, it is to give to the child the deepest and best her being can yield. To grow with the child is her motto; she knows that in that manner alone can she help build true manhood and womanhood.

Ibsen must have had a vision of free mother, when, with a master stroke, he portrayed Mrs. Alving. She was the ideal mother because she had outgrown marriage and all its horrors, because she had broken her chains, and set her spirit free to soar until it returned a personality, regenerated and strong. Alas, it was too late to rescue her life's joy, her Oswald; but not too late to realize that love in freedom is the only condition of a beautiful life. Those who, like Mrs.

Alving, have paid with blood and tears for their spiritual awakening, repudiate marriage as an imposition, a shallow, empty mockery. They know, whether love last but one brief span of time or for eternity, it is the only creative, inspiring, elevating basis for a new race, a new world.

In our present pygmy state love is indeed a stranger to most people. Misunderstood and shunned, it rarely takes root; or if it does, it soon withers and dies. Its delicate fiber can not endure the stress and strain of the daily grind. Its soul is too complex to adjust itself to the slimy woof of our social fabric. It weeps and moans and suffers with those who have need of it, yet lack the capacity to rise to love's summit.

Some day, some day men and women will rise, they will reach the mountain peak, they will meet big and strong and free, ready to receive, to partake, and to bask in the golden rays of love. What fancy, what imagination, what poetic genius can foresee even approximately the potentialities of such a force in the life of men and women. If the world is ever to give birth to true companionship and oneness, not marriage, but love will be the parent. 🖋

Suggestions for Writing

1. Do Goldman's demands seem less radical today? In what ways do contemporary attitudes toward marriage and love conform to what she envisioned?

2. Who would find these views more threatening, men or women? Why?

3. Do you believe you need to be married in order to have a satisfying life?

ONE OFF THE SHORT LIST

Doris Lessing

Uneasy relations between men and women are nothing new in fiction. Feminism, however, casts this age-old theme in a new light. Perhaps the most disturbing insight of feminist thought is the link between sex and violence, with rape being only the most extreme expression of a violent attitude toward women. "One off the Short List" paints a particularly bleak picture of adult sexuality, giving us a male character who coldly plots to add a woman he finds attractive to his list of sexual conquests.

Doris Lessing (b. 1919) has become, partly through the attention encouraged by recent feminist scholarship, one of the most highly regarded of contemporary writers. She is prolific, and her writings are varied. In contrast to her earlier novels and short stories, of which "One Off the Short List" is an example, her recent books would be classified as science fiction. She remains best known for her series of novels called Children of Violence *(1952–1965),* The Golden Notebook *(1962), and* The Summer Before the Dark *(1973). Born in what is now Iran, Lessing has lived in Rhodesia (now Zimbabwe) and England.*

When he had first seen Barbara Coles, some years before, he only noticed her because someone said: "That's Johnson's new girl." He certainly had not used of her the private erotic formula: *Yes, that one.* He even wondered what Johnson saw in her. "She won't last long," he remembered thinking, as he watched Johnson, a handsome man, but rather flushed with drink, flirting with some unknown girl while Barbara stood by a wall looking on. He thought she had a sullen expression.

She was a pale girl, not slim, for her frame was generous, but her figure could pass as good. Her straight yellow hair was parted on one side in a way that struck him as gauche. He did not notice what she wore. But her eyes were all right, he remembered: large, and solidly green, square looking because of some trick of the flesh at their corners. Emeraldlike eyes in the face of a schoolgirl, or young schoolmistress who was watching her lover flirt and would later sulk about it.

Her name sometimes cropped up in the papers. She was a stage decorator, a designer, something on those lines.

Then a Sunday newspaper had a competition for stage design and she won it. Barbara Coles was one of the "names" in the theatre, and her photograph was seen about. It was always serious. He remembered having thought her sullen.

One night he saw her across the room at a party. She was talking with a well-known actor. Her yellow hair was still done on one side, but now it looked sophisticated. She wore an emerald ring on her right hand that seemed deliberately to invite comparison with her eyes. He walked over and said: "We have met before, Graham Spence." He noted, with discomfort, that he sounded abrupt. "I'm sorry, I don't remember, but how do you do?" she said, smiling. And continued her conversation.

He hung around a bit, but soon she went off with a group of people she was inviting to her home for a drink. She did not invite Graham. There was about her an assurance, a carelessness, that he recognised as the signature of success. It was then, watching her laugh as she went off with her friends, that he used the formula: "*Yes, that one.*" And he went home to his wife with enjoyable expectation, as if his date with Barbara Coles were already arranged.

His marriage was twenty years old. At first it had been stormy, painful, tragic— full of partings, betrayals and sweet reconciliations. It had taken him at least a decade to realize that there was nothing remarkable about this marriage that he had lived through with such surprise of the mind and the senses. On the contrary, the marriages of most of the people he knew, whether they were first, second or third attempts, were just the same. His had run true to form even to the serious love affair with the young girl for whose sake he had *almost* divorced his wife—yet at the last moment had changed his mind, letting the girl down so that he must have her for always (not unpleasurably) on his conscience. It was with humiliation that he had understood that this drama was not at all the unique thing he had imagined. It was nothing more than the experience of everyone in his circle. And presumably in everybody else's circle too?

Anyway, round about the tenth year of his marriage he had seen a good many things clearly, a certain kind of emotional adventure went from his life, and the marriage itself changed.

His wife had married a poor youth with a great future as a writer. Sacrifices had been made, chiefly by her, for that future. He was neither unaware of them, nor ungrateful; in fact he felt permanently guilty about it. He at last published a decently successful book, then a second which now, thank God, no one remembered. He had drifted into radio, television, book reviewing.

He understood he was not going to make it; that he had become—not a hack, no one could call him that—but a member of that army of people who live by their wits on the fringes of the arts. The moment of realisation was when he was in a pub one lunchtime near the B.B.C. where he often dropped in to meet others like himself: he understood that was why he went there— they *were* like him. Just as that melodramatic marriage had turned out to be like everyone else's—except that it had been shared with one woman instead of with two or three—so it had turned out that his unique talent, his struggles as a writer had led him here, to this pub and the half dozen pubs like it, where all the men in sight had the same history. They all had their novel, their play, their book of poems, a moment of fame, to their credit. Yet here they were, running television programmes about which they were cynical (to each other or to their wives) or writing reviews about other people's books. Yes, that's what he had become, an impresario of other people's talent. These two moments of clarity, about his marriage and about his talent, had roughly coincided: and (perhaps not by chance) had coincided with his wife's decision to leave him for a man younger than himself who had a future, she said, as a playwright. Well, he had talked her out of it. For her part she had to understand he was not going to be the T. S. Eliot or Graham Greene of our time—but after all, how many were? She must finally understand this, for he could no longer bear her awful bitterness. For his part he must stop coming home drunk at five in the morning, and starting a new romantic affair every six months which he took so seriously that he made her miserable because of her implied deficiencies. In short he was to be a good husband. (He had always been a dutiful father.) And she a good wife. And so it was: the marriage became stable, as they say.

The formula: *Yes, that one* no longer implied a necessarily sexual relationship. In its more mature form, it was far from being something he was ashamed of. On the contrary, it expressed a humorous respect for what he was, for his real talents and flair, which had turned out to be not artistic after all, but to do with emotional life, hard-earned experience. It expressed an ironical dignity, a proving to himself not only: I can be honest about myself, but also: I have earned the best in *that* field whenever I want it.

He watched the field for the women who were well known in the arts, or in politics; looked out for photographs, listened for bits of gossip. He made a point of going to see them act, or dance, or orate. He built up a not unshrewed picture of them. He would either quietly pull strings to meet her or—more often, for there was a gambler's pleasure in waiting—bide his time until he met her in the natural course of events, which was bound to happen sooner or later. He would be seen out with her a few times in public, which was in order, since his work meant he had to entertain well-known people, male and female. His wife always knew, he told her. He might have a brief affair with this woman, but more often than not it was the appearance of an affair. Not that he didn't get pleasure from other people envying him—he would make a point, for instance, of taking this woman into the pubs where his male colleagues went. It was that his real pleasure came when he saw her surprise at how well she was understood by him. He enjoyed the atmosphere he was able to set up between an intelligent woman and himself: a humorous complicity which had in it much that was unspoken, and which almost made sex irrelevant.

Onto the list of women with whom he planned to have this relationship went Barbara Coles. There was no hurry. Next week, next month, next year, they would meet at a party. The world of well-known people in London is a small one. Big and little fishes, they drift around, nose each other, flirt their fins, wriggle off again. When he bumped into Barbara Coles, it would be time to decide whether or not to sleep with her.

Meanwhile he listened. But he didn't discover much. She had a husband and children, but the husband seemed to be in the background. The children were charming and well brought up, like everyone else's children. She had affairs, they said; but while several men he met sounded familiar with her, it was hard to determine whether they had slept with her, because none directly boasted of her. She was spoken of in terms of her friends, her work, her house, a party she had given, a job she had found someone. She was liked, she was respected, and Graham Spence's self-esteem was flattered because he had chosen her. He looked forward to saying in just the same tone: "Barbara Coles asked me what I thought about the set and I told her quite frankly. . . ."

Then by chance he met a young man who did boast about Barbara Coles: he claimed to have had the great love affair with her, and recently at that: and he spoke of it as something generally known. Graham realised how much he had already become involved with her in his imagination because of how perturbed he was now, on account of the character of this youth, Jack Kennaway. He had recently become successful as a magazine editor—one of those young men who, not as rare as one might suppose in the big cities, are successful from sheer impertinence, effrontery. Without much talent or taste, yet he had the charm of his effrontery. "Yes, I'm going to succeed, because I've decided to; yes, I may be stupid, but not so stupid that I don't know my deficiencies. Yes, I'm going to be successful because you people with integrity, etc., etc., simply don't believe in the possibility of people like me. You are too cowardly to stop me. Yes, I've taken your measure and I'm going to succeed because I've got the courage, not only to be unscrupulous, but to be quite frank about it. And besides, you admire me, you must, or otherwise you'd stop me. . . ." Well, that was young Jack Kennaway, and he shocked Graham. He was a tall, languishing young man, handsome in a dark melting way, and, it was quite clear, he was either asexual or homosexual. And this youth boasted of the favours of Barbara Coles; boasted, indeed, of her love. Either she was a raving neurotic with a taste for neurotics; or Jack Kennaway was a most accomplished liar; or she slept with anyone. Graham was intrigued. He took Jack Kennaway out to dinner in order to hear him talk about Barbara Coles. There was no doubt the two were pretty close—all those dinners, theatres, weekends in the county—Graham Spence felt he had put his finger on the secret pulse of Barbara Coles; and it was intolerable that he must wait to meet her; he decided to arrange it.

It became unnecessary. She was in the news again, with a run of luck. She had done a successful historical play, and immediately afterwards a modern play, and then a hit musical. In all three, the sets were remarked on. Graham saw some interviews in newspapers and on television. These all centered around the theme of her being able to deal easily with so many different styles of theatre; but the real point was, of course, that she was a woman, which naturally added piquancy to the thing. And now Graham Spence was asked to do a half-hour radio interview with her. He planned the questions he would ask her with care, drawing on what people had said of her, but above all on his instinct and experience with women. The interview was to be at nine-thirty at night; he was to pick her up at six from the theatre where she was currently at work, so that there would be time, as the letter from the B.B.C. had put it, "for you and Miss Coles to get to know each other."

At six he was at the stage door, but a message from Miss Coles said she was not quite ready, could he wait a little. He hung about, then went to the pub opposite for a quick one, but still no Miss Coles. So he made his way backstage, directed by voices, hammering, laughter. It was badly lit, and the group of people at work did not see him. The director, James Poynter, had his arm around Barbara's shoulders. He was newly well-known, a carelessly good-looking young man reputed to be intelligent. Barbara Coles wore a dark blue overall, and her flat hair fell over her face so that she kept pushing it back with the hand that had the emerald on it. These two stood close, side by side. Three young men, stagehands, were on the other side of a trestle which had sketches and drawings on it. They were studying some sketches. Barbara said in a voice warm with energy: "Well, so I thought if we did *this*—do you see, James? What do you think, Steven?" "Well, love," said the young man she called Steven, "I see your idea, but I wonder if . . . " "I think you're right, Babs," said the director. "Look," said Barbara, holding one of the sketches toward Steven, "look, let me show you." They all leaned forward, the five of them, absorbed in the business.

Suddenly Graham couldn't stand it. He understood he was shaken to his depths. He went off stage, and stood with his back against a wall in the dingy passage that led to the dressing room. His eyes were filled with tears. He was seeing what a long way he had come from the crude, uncompromising, admirable young egomaniac he had been when he was twenty. That group of people there—working, joking, arguing, yes, that's what he hadn't known for years. What bound them was the democracy of respect for each other's work, a confidence in themselves and in each other. They looked like people banded together against a world which they—no, not despised, but which they measured, understood, would fight to the death, out of respect for what *they* stood for, for what *it* stood for. It was a long time since he felt part of that balance. And he understood that he had seen Barbara Coles when she was most herself, at ease with a group of people she worked with. It was then, with the tears drying on his eyelids, which felt old and ironic, that he decided he would sleep with Barbara Coles. It was a necessity for him. He went back through the door onto the stage, burning with this single determination.

The five were still together. Barbara had a length of blue gleaming stuff which she was draping over the shoulder of Steven, the stagehand. He was showing it off, and the others watched. "What do you think, James?" she asked the director. "We've got that sort of dirty green, and I thought . . . " "Well," said James, not sure at all, "well, Babs, well . . . "

Now Graham went forward so that he stood beside Barbara, and said: "I'm Graham Spence, we've met before." For the second time she smiled socially and said: "Oh, I'm sorry, I don't remember." Graham nodded at James, whom he had known, or at least had met off and on, for years. But it was obvious James didn't remember him either.

"From the B.B.C.," said Graham to Barbara, again sounding abrupt, against his will. "Oh, I'm sorry, I'm sorry, I forgot all about it. I've got to be interviewed," she said to the group. "Mr. Spence is a journalist." Graham allowed himself a small smile ironical of the word journalist, but she was not looking at him. She was going on with her work. "We should decide tonight," she said. "Steven's right." "Yes, I am right," said the stagehand. "She's right, James, we need that blue with that sludge-green everywhere." "James," said Barbara, "James, what's wrong with it? You haven't said." She moved forward to James, passing Graham. Remembering him again, she became contrite. "I'm sorry," she said, "we can none of us agree. Well, look"—she turned to Graham—"you advise us, we've got so involved with it that . . . " At which James laughed, and so did the stagehands. "No, Babs," said James, "of course Mr. Spence can't advise. He's just this moment come in. We've got to decide. Well I'll give you till tomorrow morning. Time to go home, it must be six by now."

"It's nearly seven," said Graham, taking command.

"It isn't!" said Barbara, dramatic. "My God, how terrible, how appalling, how could I have done such a thing. . . . " She was laughing at herself. "Well, you'll have to forgive me, Mr. Spence, because you haven't got any alternative."

They began laughing again: this was clearly a group joke. And now Graham took his chance. He said firmly, as if he were her director, in fact copying James Poynter's manner with her: "No, Miss Coles. I won't forgive you. I've been kicking my heels for nearly an hour." She grimaced, then laughed and accepted it. James said: "There, Babs, that's how you ought to be treated. We spoil you." He kissed her on the cheek, she kissed him on both his, the stagehands moved off. "Have a good evening, Babs," said James, going, and nodding to Graham, who stood concealing his pleasure with difficulty. He knew, because he had had the courage to be firm, indeed, peremptory, with Barbara, that he had saved himself hours of maneuvering. Several drinks, a dinner—perhaps two or three evenings of drinks and dinners—had been saved because he was now on this footing with Barbara Coles, a man who could say: "No, I won't forgive you, you've kept me waiting."

She said: "I've just got to . . . " and went ahead of him. In the passage she hung her overall on a peg. She was thinking, it seemed, of something else, but seeing him watching her, she smiled at him companionably: he realised with triumph it was the sort of smile she would offer one of the stagehands, or even James. She said again: "Just one second . . . "and went to the stage-door office. She and the stage doorman conferred. There was some problem. Graham said, taking another chance: "What's the trouble, can I help?"as if he could help, as if he expected to be able to. "Well . . ." she said, frowning. Then, to the man: "No, it'll be all right. Goodnight." She came to Graham. "We've got ourselves into a bit of a fuss because half the set's in Liverpool and half's here and—but it will sort itself out." She stood, at ease, chatting to him, one colleague to another. All this was admirable, he felt; but there would be a bad moment when they emerged from the special atmosphere of the theatre into the street. He took another decision, grasped her arm firmly, and said: "We're going to have a drink before we do anything at all, it's a terrible evening out." Her arm felt resistant, but remained within his. It was raining outside luckily. He directed her, authoritative: "No, not that pub, there's a nicer one around the corner." "Oh, but I like this pub," said Barbara, "we always use it."

"Of course you do," he said to himself. But in that pub there would be the stagehands, and probably James, and he'd lose contact with her. He'd become a *journalist* again. He took her firmly out of danger around two corners, into a pub he picked at random. A quick look around—no, they weren't there. At least, if there were people from the theatre, she showed no sign. She asked for a beer. He ordered her a double Scotch, which she accepted. Then, having won a dozen preliminary rounds already, he took time to think. Something was bothering him—what? Yes, it was what he had observed backstage, Barbara and James Poynter. Was she having an affair with him? Because if so, it would all be much more difficult. He made himself see the two of them together, and thought with a jealousy surprisingly strong: *Yes, that's it.* Meantime he sat looking at her, seeing himself look at her, *a man gazing in calm appreciation at a woman*: waiting for her to feel it and respond. She was examining the pub. Her white woollen suit was belted, and had a not unprovocative suggestion of being a uniform. Her flat yellow hair, hastily pushed back after work, was untidy. Her clear white skin, without any colour, made her look tired. Not very exciting, at the moment, thought Graham, but maintaining his appreciative pose for when she would turn and see it. He knew what she would see: he was relying not only on the "warm kindly" beam of his gaze, for this was merely a reinforcement of the impression he knew he made. He had black hair, a little greyed. His clothes were loose and bulky—masculine. His eyes were humorous and appreciative. He was not, never had been, concerned to lessen the impression of being settled, dependable: the husband and father. On the contrary, he knew women found it reassuring.

When she at last turned she said, almost apologetic: "Would you mind if we sat down? I've been lugging great things around all day." She had spotted two empty chairs in a corner. So had he, but rejected them, because there were other people at the table. "But my dear, of course!" They took the chairs, and then Barbara said: "If you'll excuse me a moment." She had remembered she needed make-up. He watched her go off, annoyed with himself. She was tired; and he could have understood, protected, sheltered. He realised that in the other pub, with the people she had worked with all day, she would not have thought: "I must make myself up, I must be on show." That was for outsiders. She had not, until now, considered Graham an outsider, because of his taking his chance to seem one of the working group in the theatre; but now he had thrown his opportunity away. She returned armoured. Her hair was sleek, no longer defenseless. And she had made up her eyes. Her eyebrows were untouched, pale gold streaks above the brilliant green eyes whose lashes were blackened. Rather good, he thought, the contrast. Yes, but the moment had gone when he could say: Did you know you had a smudge on your cheek? Or— my dear girl!—pushing her hair back with the edge of a brotherly hand. In fact, unless he was careful, he'd be back at starting point.

He remarked: "That emerald is very cunning"—smiling into her eyes.

She smiled politely, and said: "It's not cunning, it's an accident, it was my grandmother's." She flirted her hand lightly by her face, though, smiling. But that was something she had done before, to a compliment she had had before, and often. It was all social, she had become social entirely. She remarked: "Didn't you say it was half past nine we had to record?"

"My dear Barbara, we've got two hours. We'll have another drink or two, then I'll ask you a couple of questions, then we'll drop down to the studio and get it over, and then we'll have a comfortable supper."

"I'd rather eat now, if you don't mind. I had no lunch, and I'm really hungry."

"But my dear, of course." He was angry. Just as he had been surprised by his real jealousy over James, so now he was thrown off balance by his anger: he had been counting on the long quiet dinner afterwards to establish intimacy. "Finish your drink and I'll take you to Nott's." Nott's was expensive. He glanced at her assessingly as he mentioned it. She said: "I wonder if you know Butler's? It's good and it's rather close." Butler's was good, and it was cheap, and he gave her a good mark for liking it. But Nott's it was going to be. "My dear, we'll get into a taxi and be at Nott's in a moment, don't worry."

She obediently got to her feet: the way she did it made him understand how badly he had slipped. She was saying to herself: Very well, he's like that, then all right, I'll do what he wants and get it over with. . . .

Swallowing his own drink he followed her, and took her arm in the pub doorway. It was polite within his. Outside it drizzled. No taxi. He was having bad luck now. They walked in silence to the end of the street. There Barbara glanced into a side street where a sign said: BUTLER'S. Not to remind him of it, on the contrary, she concealed the glance. And here she was, entirely at his disposal, they might never have shared the comradely moment in the theatre.

They walked half a mile to Nott's. No taxis. She made conversation: this was, he saw, to cover any embarrassment he might feel because of a half-mile walk through the rain when she was tired. She was talking about some theory to do with the theatre, with designs for theatre building. He heard himself saying, and repeatedly: Yes, yes, yes. He thought about Nott's, how to get things right when they reached Nott's There he took the headwaiter aside, gave him a pound, and instructions. They were put in a corner. Large Scotches appeared. The menus were spread. "And now, my dear," he said, "I apologise for dragging you here, but I hope you'll think it's worth it."

"Oh, it's charming. I've always liked it. It's just that . . . " She stopped herself saying: it's such a long way. She smiled at him, rasing her glass, and said: "It's one of my very favorite places, and I'm glad you dragged me here." Her voice was flat with tiredness. All this was appalling; he knew it; and he sat thinking how to retrieve his position. Meanwhile she fingered the menu. The headwaiter took the order, but Graham made a gesture which said: Wait a moment. He wanted the Scotch to take effect before she ate. But she saw his silent order; and without annoyance or reproach, leaned forward to say, sounding patient: "Graham, please, I've got to eat, you don't want me drunk when you interview me, do you?"

"They are bringing it as fast as they can," he said, making it sound as if she were greedy. He looked neither at the headwaiter nor at Barbara. He noted in himself, as he slipped further and further away from contact with her, a cold determination growing in him; one apart from, apparently, any conscious act of will, that come what may, if it took all night, he'd be in her bed before morning. And now, seeing the small pale face, with the enormous green eyes, it was for the first time that he imagined her in his arms. Although he had said: *Yes, that one*, weeks ago, it was only now that he imagined her as a sensual experience. Now he did, so strongly that he could only glance at her, and then away towards the waiters who were bringing food.

"Thank the Lord," said Barbara, and all at once her voice was gay and intimate. "Thank heavens. Thank every power that is. . . ." She was making fun of her own exaggeration; and, as he saw, because she wanted to put him at his ease after his boorishness over delaying the food. (She hadn't been taken in, he saw, humiliated, disliking her.) "Thank all the gods of Nott's," she went on, "because if I hadn't eaten inside five minutes I'd have died, I tell you." With which she picked up her knife and fork and began on her steak. He poured wine, smiling with her, thinking that *this* moment of closeness he would not throw away. He watched her frank hunger as she ate, and thought: Sensual—it's strange I hadn't wondered whether she would be or not.

"Now," she said, sitting back, having taken the edge off her hunger: "Let's get to work."

He said: "I've thought it over very carefully—how to present you. The first thing seems to me, we must get away from that old chestnut: Miss Coles, how extraordinary for a woman to be so versatile in her work . . . I hope you agree?" This was his trump card. He had noted, when he had seen her on television, her polite smile when this note was struck. (The smile he had seen so often tonight.) This smile said: All right, if you *have* to be stupid, what can I do?

Now she laughed and said: "What a relief. I was afraid you were going to do the same thing."

"Good, now you eat and I'll talk."

In his carefully prepared monologue he spoke of the different styles of theatre she had shown herself mistress of, but not directly: he was flattering her on the breadth of her experience; the complexity of her character, as shown in her work. She ate, steadily, her face showing nothing. At last she asked: "And how did you plan to introduce this?"

He had meant to spring that on her as a surprise, something like: Miss Coles, a surprisingly young woman for what she has accomplished (she was thirty? thirty-two?) and a very attractive one. . . . "Perhaps I can give you an idea of what she's like if I say she could be taken for the film star Marie Carletta. . . ." The Carletta was a strong earthy blonde, known to be intellectual. He now saw he could not possibly say this: he could imagine her cool look if he did. She said: "Do you mind if we get away from all that—my manifold talents, et cetera. . . ." He felt himself stiffen with annoyance; particularly because this was not an accusation, he saw she did not think him worth one. She had assessed him: This is the kind of man who uses this kind of flattery and therefore. . . . It made him angrier that she did not even trouble to say: Why did you do exactly what you promised you wouldn't? She was being invincibly polite, tying to conceal her patience with his stupidity.

"After all," she was saying, "it is a stage designer's job to design what comes up. Would anyone take, let's say Johnnie Cranmore" (another stage designer) "onto the air or television and say: How very versatile you are because you did that musical about Java last month and a modern play about Irish labourers this?"

He battened down his anger. "My dear Barbara. I'm sorry. I didn't realise that what I said would sound just like the mixture as before. So what shall we talk about?"

"What I was saying as we walked to the restaurant: can we get away from the personal stuff?"

Now he almost panicked. Then, thank God, he laughed from nervousness, for she laughed and said: "You didn't hear one word I said."

"No, I didn't. I was frightened you were going to be furious because I made you walk so far when you were tired."

They laughed together, back to where they had been in the theatre. He leaned over, took her hand, kissed it. He said: "Tell me again." he thought: Damn, now she's going to be earnest and intellectual.

But he understood he had been stupid. He had forgotten himself at twenty—or, for that matter, at thirty; forgotten one could live inside an idea, a set of ideas, with enthusiasm. For in talking about her ideas (also the ideas of the people she worked with) for a new theatre, a new style of theatre, she was as she had been with her colleagues over the sketches or the blue material. She was easy, informal, almost chattering. This was how, he remembered, one talked about ideas that were a breath of life. The ideas, he thought, were intelligent enough; and he would agree with them, with her, if he believed it mattered a damn one way or another, if any of these enthusiasms mattered a damn. But at least he now had the key, he knew what to do. At the end of not more than half an hour, they were again two professionals, talking about ideas they shared, for he remembered caring about all this himself once. *When? How many years ago was it that he had been able to care?*

At last he said: "My dear Barbara, do you realise the impossible position you're putting me in? Margaret Ruyen who runs this programme is determined to do you personally, the poor woman hasn't got a serious thought in her head."

Barbara frowned. He put his hand on hers, teasing her for the frown: "No, wait, trust me, we'll circumvent her." She smiled. In fact Margaret Ruyen had left it all to him, had said nothing about Miss Coles.

"They aren't very bright—the brass," he said. "Well, never mind: we'll work out what we want, do it, and it'll be a *fait accompli*."

"Thank you, what a relief. How lucky I was to be given you to interview me." She was relaxed now, because of the whisky, the food, the wine, above all because of this new complicity against Margaret Ruyen. It would all be easy. They worked out five or six questions, over coffee, and took a taxi through rain to the studios. He noted that the cold necessity to have her, to make her, to beat her down, had left him. He was even seeing himself, as the evening ended, kissing her on the cheek and going home to his wife. This comradeship was extraordinarily pleasant. It was balm to the wound he had not known he carried until that evening, when he had had to accept the justice of the word *journalist*. He felt he could talk forever about the state of the theatre, its finances, the stupidity of the government, the philistinism of . . .

At the studios he was careful to make a joke so that they walked in on the laugh. He was careful that the interview began at once, without conversation with Margaret Ruyen; and that from the moment the green light went on, his voice lost its easy familiarity. He made sure that not one personal note was struck during the interview. Afterwards, Margaret Ruyen, who was pleased, came forward to say so; but he took her aside to say that Miss Coles was tired and needed to be taken home at once: for he knew this must look to Barbara as if he was squaring a producer who had been expecting a different interview. He led Barbara off, her hand held tight in his against his side. "Well," he said, "we've done it, and I don't think she knows what hit her."

"Thank you," she said, "it really was pleasant to talk about something sensible for once."

He kissed her lightly on the mouth. She returned it, smiling. By now he felt sure that the mood need not slip again, he could hold it.

"There are two things we can do," he said. "You can come to my club and have a drink. Or I can drive you home and you can give me a drink. I have to go past you."

"Where do you live?"

"Wimbledon." He lived, in fact, at Highgate; but she lived in Fulham. He was taking another chance, but by the time she found out, they would be in a position to laugh over his ruse.

"Good," she said. "You can drop me home then. I have to get up early." He made no comment. In the taxi he took her hand; it was heavy in his, and he asked: "Does James slave-drive you?"

"I didn't realize you knew him—no, he doesn't."

"Well I don't know him intimately. What's he like to work with?"

"Wonderful," she said at once. "There's no one I enjoy working with more."

Jealousy spurted in him. He could not help himself: "Are you having an affair with him?"

She looked: what's it to do with you? but said: "No, I'm not."

"He's very attractive," he said, with a chuckle of worldly complicity. She said nothing, and he insisted: "If I were a woman I'd have an affair with James."

It seemed she might very well say nothing. But she remarked: "He's married."

His spirits rose in a swoop. It was the first stupid remark she had made. It was a remark of such staggering stupidity that . . . he let out a humoring snort of laughter, put his arm around her, kissed her, said: "My dear little Babs."

She said: "Why Babs?"

"Is that the prerogative of James. And of the stagehands?" he could not prevent himself adding.

"I'm only called that at work." She was stiff inside his arm.

"My dear Barbara, then . . . " He waited for her to enlighten and explain, but she said nothing. Soon she moved out of his arm, on the pretext of lighting a cigarette. He lit it for her. He noted that his determination to lay her and at all costs, had come back. They were outside her house. He said quickly: "And now, Barbara, you can make me a cup of coffee and give me a brandy." She hesitated; but he was out the taxi, paying, opening the door for her. The house had no lights on, he noted. He said: "We'll be very quiet so as not to wake the children."

She turned her head slowly to look at him. She said, flat, replying to his real question: "My husband is away. As for the children, they are visiting friends tonight." She now went ahead of him to the door of the house. It was a small house, in a terrace of small and not very pretty houses. Inside a little, bright, intimate hall, she said: "I'll go and make some coffee. Then, my friend, you must go home because I'm very tired."

The *my friend* struck him deep, because he had become vulnerable during their comradeship. He said gabbing: "You're annoyed with me—oh, please don't, I'm sorry."

She smiled, from a cool distance. He saw, in the small light from the ceiling, her extraordinary eyes. "Green" eyes are hazel, are brown with green flecks, are even blue. Eyes are chequered, flawed, changing. Hers were solid green, but really, he had never seen anything like them before. They were like very deep water. They were like—well, emeralds; or the absolute clarity of green in the depths of a tree in summer. And now, as she smiled almost perpendicularly up at him, he saw a darkness come over them. Darkness swallowed the clear green. She said: "I'm not in the least annoyed." It was as if she had yawned with boredom. "And now I'll get the things . . . in there." She nodded at a white door and left him. He went into a long, very tidy white room, that had a narrow bed in one corner, a table covered with drawings, sketches, pencils. Two small chairs stood near a low round table: an area of comfort in the working room. He was thinking: I wouldn't like it if my wife had a room like this. I wonder what Barbara's husband . . . ? He had not thought of her till now in relation to her husband, or to her children. Hard to imagine her with a frying pan in her hand, or for that matter, cosy in the double bed.

A noise outside: he hastily arranged himself, leaning with one arm on the mantelpiece. She came in with a small tray that had cups, glasses, brandy, coffeepot. She looked abstracted. Graham was on the whole flattered by this: it probably meant she was at ease in his presence. He realised he was a little tight and rather tired. Of course, she was tired too, that was why she was vague. He remembered that earlier that evening he had lost a chance by not using her tiredness. Well now, if he were intelligent . . . She was about to pour coffee. He firmly took the coffeepot out of her hand, and nodded at a chair. Smiling, she obeyed him. "That's better," he said. He poured coffee, poured brandy, and pulled the table towards her. She watched him. Then he took her hand, kissed it, patted it, laid it down gently. Yes, he thought, I did that well.

Now, a problem. He wanted to be closer to her, but she was fitted into a damned silly little chair that had arms. If he were to sit by her on the floor . . .? But no, for him, the big bulky reassuring man, there could be no casual gestures, no informal postures. Suppose I scoop her out of the chair onto the bed? He drank his coffee as he plotted. Yes, he'd carry her to the bed, but not yet.

"Graham," she said, setting down her cup. She was, he saw with annoyance, looking tolerant. "Graham, in about half an hour I want to be in bed and asleep."

As she said this, she offered him a smile of amusement at this situation— man and woman maneuvering, the great comic situation. And with part of himself he could have shared it. Almost, he smiled with her, laughed. (Not till days later he exclaimed to himself: Lord what a mistake I made, not to share the joke with her then: that was where I went seriously wrong.) But he could not smile. His face was frozen, with a stiff pride. Not because she had been watching him plot; the amusement she now offered him took the sting out of that; but because of his revived determination that he was going to have his own way, he was going to have her. He was not going home. But he felt that he held a bunch of keys, and did not know which one to choose.

He lifted the second small chair opposite to Barbara, moving aside the coffee table for this purpose. He sat in this chair, leaned forward, took her two hands, and said: "My dear, don't make me go home yet, don't, I beg you." The trouble was, nothing had happened all evening that could be felt to lead up to these words and his tone—simple, dignified, human being pleading with human being for surcease. He saw himself leaning forward, his big hands swallowing her small ones; he saw his face, warm with the appeal. And he realised he had meant the words he used. They were nothing more than what he felt. He wanted to stay with her because she wanted him to, because he was her colleague, a fellow worker in the arts. He needed this desperately. But she was examining him, curious rather than surprised, and from a critical distance. He heard himself saying: "If James were here, I wonder what you'd do?" His voice was aggrieved; he saw the sudden dark descend over her eyes, and she said: "Graham, would you like some more coffee before you go?"

He said: "I've been wanting to meet you for years. I know a good many people who know you."

She leaned forward, poured herself a little more brandy, sat back, holding the glass between her two palms on her chest. An odd gesture: Graham felt that this vessel she was cherishing between her hands was herself. A patient, long-suffering gesture. He thought of various men who had mentioned her. He thought of Jack Kennaway, wavered, panicked, said: "For instance, Jack Kennaway."

And now, at the name, an emotion lit her eyes—what was it? He went on, deliberately testing this emotion, adding to it: "I had dinner with him last week—oh, quite by chance!—and he was talking about you."

"Was he?"

He remembered he had thought her sullen, all those years ago. Now she seemed defensive, and she frowned. He said: "In fact he spent most of the evening talking about you."

She said in short, breathless sentences, which he realised were due to anger: "I can very well imagine what he says. But surely you can't think I enjoy being reminded that . . . " She broke off, resenting him, he saw, because he forced her down onto a level she despised. But it was not his level either: it was all her fault, all hers! He couldn't remember not being in control of a situation with a woman for years. Again he felt like a man teetering on a tightrope. He said, trying to make good use of Jack Kennaway, even at this late hour: "Of course, he's a charming boy, but not a man at all."

She looked at him, silent, guarding her brandy glass against her breasts.

"Unless appearances are totally deceptive, of course." He could not resist probing, even though he knew it was fatal.

She said nothing.

"Do you know you are supposed to have had the great affair with Jack Kennaway?" he exclaimed, making this an amused expostulation against the fools who could believe it.

"So I am told." She set down her glass. "And now," she said, standing up, dismissing him. He lost his head, took a step forward, grabbed her in his arms, and groaned: "Barbara!"

She turned her face this way and that under his kisses. He snatched a diagnostic look at her expression—it was still patient. He placed his lips against her neck, groaned "Barbara" again, and waited. She would have to do something. Fight free, respond, something. She did nothing at all. At last she said: "For the Lord's sake, Graham!" She sounded amused: he was again being offered amusement. But if he shared it with her, it would be the end of his chance to have her. He clamped his mouth over hers, silencing her. She did not fight him off so much as blow him off. Her mouth treated his attacking mouth as a woman blows and laughs in water, puffing off waves or spray with a laugh, turning aside her head. It was a gesture half annoyance, half humour. He continued to kiss her while she moved her head and face about under the kisses as if they were small attacking waves.

And so began what, when he looked back on it afterwards, was the most embarrassing experience of his life. Even at the time he hated her for his ineptitude. For he held her there for what must have been nearly half an hour. She was much shorter than he, he had to bend, and his neck ached. He held her rigid, his thighs on either side of hers, her arms clamped to her side in a bear's hug. She was unable to move, except for her head. When his mouth ground hers open and his tongue moved and writhed inside it, she still remained passive. And he could not stop himself. While with his intelligence he watched this ridiculous scene, he was determined to go on, because sooner or later her body must soften in wanting his. And he could not stop because he could not face the horror of the moment when he set her free and she looked at him. And he hated her more, every moment. Catching glimpses of her great green eyes, open and dismal beneath his, he knew he had never disliked anything more than those "jewelled" eyes. They were repulsive to him. It occurred to him at last that even if by now she wanted him, he wouldn't know it, because she was not able to move at all. He cautiously loosened his hold so that she had an inch or so leeway. She remained quite passive. As if, he thought derisively, she had read or been told that the way to incite men maddened by lust was to fight them. He found he was thinking: Stupid cow, so you imagine I find you attractive, do you? You've got the conceit to think that!

The sheer, raving insanity of this thought hit him, opened his arms, his thighs, and lifted his tongue out of her mouth. She stepped back, wiping her mouth with the back of her hand, and stood dazed with incredulity. The embarrassment that lay in wait for him nearly engulfed him, but he let anger postpone it. She said positively apologetic, even, at this moment, humorous: "You're crazy, Graham. What's the matter, are you drunk? You don't seem drunk. You don't even find me attractive."

The blood of hatred went to his head and he gripped her again. Now she had got her face firmly twisted away so that he could not reach her mouth, and she repeated steadily as he kissed the parts of her cheeks and neck that were available to him: "Graham, let me go, do let me go, Graham." She went on saying this; he went on squeezing, grinding, kissing and licking. It might go on all

ONE OFF THE SHORT LIST **393**

night: it was a sheer contest of wills, nothing else. He thought: It's only a really masculine woman who wouldn't have given in by now of sheer decency of the flesh! One thing he knew, however: that she would be in that bed, in his arms, and very soon. He let her go, but said: "I'm going to sleep with you tonight, you know that, don't you?"

She leaned with hand on the mantelpiece to steady herself. Her face was colourless, since he had licked all the makeup off. She seemed quite different: small and defenseless with her large mouth pale now, her smudged green eyes fringed with gold. And now, for the first time, he felt what it might have been supposed (certainly by her) he felt hours ago. Seeing the small damp flesh of her face, he felt kinship, intimacy with her, he felt intimacy of the flesh, the affection and good humour of sensuality. He felt she was flesh of his flesh, his sister in the flesh. He felt desire for her, instead of the will to have her; and because of this, was ashamed of the farce he had been playing. Now he desired simply to take her into bed in the affection of his senses.

She said: "What on earth am I supposed to do? Telephone for the police, or what?" He was hurt that she still addressed the man who had ground her into sulky apathy; she was not addressing *him* at all.

She said: "Or scream for the neighbours, is that what you want?"

The gold-fringed eyes were almost black, because of the depth of the shadow of boredom over them. She was bored and weary to the point of falling to the floor, he could see that.

He said: "I'm going to sleep with you."

"But how can you possibly want to?"—a reasonable, a civilised demand addressed to a man who (he could see) she believed would respond to it. She said: "You know I don't want to, and I know you don't really give a damn one way or the other."

He was stung back into being the boor because she had not the intelligence to see that the boor no longer existed; because she could not see that this was a man who wanted her in a way which she must respond to.

There she stood, supporting herself with one hand, looking small and white and exhausted, and utterly incredulous. She was going to turn and walk off out of simple incredulity, he could see that. "Do you think I don't mean it?" he demanded, grinding this out between his teeth. She made a movement—she was on the point of going away. His hand shot out on its own volition and grasped her wrist. She frowned. His other hand grasped her other wrist. His body hove up against hers to start the pressure of a new embrace. Before it could, she said: "Oh Lord, no. I'm not going through all that again. Right, then."

"What do you mean—right, then?" he demanded.

She said: "You're going to sleep with me. O.K. Anything rather than go through that again. Shall we get it over with?"

He grinned, saying in silence: "No darling, oh no you don't. I don't care what words you use. I'm going to have you now and that's all there is to it."

She shrugged. The contempt, the weariness of it, had no effect on him, because he was now again hating her so much that wanting her was like needing to kill something or someone.

She took her clothes off, as if she were going to bed by herself: her jacket, skirt, petticoat. She stood in white bra and panties, a rather solid girl, brown-skinned still from the summer. He felt a flash of affection for the brown girl with her loose yellow hair as she stood naked. She got into bed and lay there, while the green eyes looked at him in civilised appeal: Are you really going through with this? Do you have to? Yes, his eyes said back: I do have to. She shifted her gaze aside, to the wall, saying silently: Well, if you want to take me without any desire at all on my part, then go ahead, if you're not ashamed. He was not ashamed, because he was maintaining the flame of hate for her which he knew quite well was all that stood between him and shame. He took off his clothes, and got into bed beside her. As he did so, knowing he was putting himself in the position of raping a woman who was making it elaborately clear he bored her, his flesh subsided completely, sad, and full of reproach because a few moments ago it was reaching out for his sister whom he could have made happy. He lay on his side by her, secretly at work on himself, while he supported himself across her body on his elbow, using the free hand to manipulate her breasts. He saw that she gritted her teeth against his touch. At least she could not know that after all this fuss he was not potent.

In order to incite himself, he clasped her again. She felt his smallness, writhed free of him, said: "Lie down."

While she had been lying there, she had been thinking: The only way to get this over with is to make him big again, otherwise I've got to put up with him all night. His hatred of her was giving him a clairvoyance: he knew very well what went on through her mind. She had switched on, with the determination to *get it all over with*, a sensual good humour, a patience. He lay down. She squatted beside him, the light from the ceiling blooming on her brown shoulders, her flat fair hair falling over her face. But she would not look at his face. Like a bored, skilled wife, she was: or like a prostitute. She administered to him, she was setting herself to please him. Yes, he thought, she's sensual, or she could be. Meanwhile she was succeeding in defeating the reluctance of his flesh, which was the tender token of a possible desire for her, by using a cold skill that was the result of her contempt for him. Just as he decided: Right, it's enough, now I shall have her properly, she made him come. It was not a trick, to hurry or cheat him, what defeated him was her transparent thought: Yes, that's what he's worth.

Then, having succeeded, and waited for a moment or two, she stood up, naked, the fringes of gold at her loins and in her armpits speaking to him in a language quite different from that of her green, bored eyes. She looked at him and thought, showing it plainly: What sort of a man is it who . . .? He watched the slight movement of her shoulders: a just-checked shrug. She went out of the room: then the sound of running water. Soon she came back in a white dressing gown, carrying a yellow towel. She handed him the towel, looking away in politeness as he used it. "Are you going home now?" she enquired hopefully, at this point.

"No, I'm not." He believed that now he would have to start fighting her again, but she lay down beside him, not touching him (he could feel the distaste of her flesh for his) and he thought: Very well, my dear, but there's a lot

of the night left yet. He said aloud: "I'm going to have you properly tonight."
She said nothing, lay silent, yawned. Then she remarked consolingly, and he
could have laughed outright from sheer surprise: "Those were hardly conducive
circumstances for making love." She was *consoling* him. He hated her for it. A
proper little slut: I force her into bed, she doesn't want me, but she still has to
make me feel good, like a prostitute. But even while he hated her he responded
in kind, from the habit of sexual generosity. "It's because of my admiration for you,
because . . . after all, I was holding in my arms one of the thousand women."

A pause. "The thousand?" she enquired, carefully.

"The thousand especial women."

"In Britain or in the world? You choose them for their brains, their beauty—
what?"

"Whatever it is that makes them outstanding," he said, offering her a compliment.

"Well," she remarked at last, inciting him to be amused again: "I hope that
at least there's a short list you can say I am on, for politeness' sake."

He did not reply for he understood he was sleepy. He was still telling himself
that he must stay awake when he was slowly waking and it was morning. It was
about eight. Barbara was not there. He thought: My God! What on earth shall
I tell my wife? Where was Barbara? He remembered the ridiculous scenes of last
night and nearly succumbed to shame. Then he thought, reviving anger: If she
didn't sleep beside me here I'll never forgive her . . . He sat up, quietly, determined to go through the house until he found her and, having found her, to
possess her, when the door opened and she came in. She was fully dressed in a
green suit, her hair done, her eyes made up. She carried a tray of coffee, which
she set down beside the bed. He was conscious of his big loose hairy body, half
uncovered. He said to himself that he was not going to lie in bed, naked, while
she was dressed. He said: "Have you got a gown of some kind?" She handed
him, without speaking, a towel, and said: "The bathroom's second on the left."
She went out. He followed, the towel around him. Everything in the house was
gay, intimate—not at all like her efficient working room. He wanted to find
out where she had slept, and opened the first door. It was the kitchen, and she
was in it, putting a brown earthenware dish into the oven. "The next door,"
said Barbara. He went hastily past the second door, and opened (he hoped
quietly) the third. It was a cupboard full of linen. "This door," said Barbara,
behind him.

"So all right then, where did you sleep?"

"What's it to do with you? Upstairs, in my own bed. Now, if you have everything, I'll say goodbye, I want to get to the theatre."

"I'll take you," he said at once.

He saw again the movement of her eyes, the dark swallowing the light in
deadly boredom. "I'll take you," he insisted.

"I'd prefer to go by myself," she remarked. Then she smiled: "However,
you'll take me. Then you'll make a point of coming right in, so that James and
everyone can see—that's what you want to take me for, isn't it?"

He hated her, finally, and quite simply, for her intelligence; that not once
had he got away with anything, that she had been watching, since they had

met yesterday, every movement of his campaign for her. However, some fate or inner urge over which he had no control made him say sentimentally: "My dear, you must see that I'd like at least to take you to your work."

"Not at all, have it on me," she said, giving him the lie direct. She went past him to the room he had slept in. "I shall be leaving in ten minutes," she said.

He took a shower, fast. When he returned, the workroom was already tidied, the bed made, all signs of the night gone. Also, there were no signs of the coffee she had brought in for him. He did not like to ask for it, for fear of an outright refusal. Besides, she was ready, her coat on, her handbag under her arm. He went, without a word, to the front door, and she came after him, silent.

He could see that every fibre of her body signalled a simple message: Oh God, for the moment when I can be rid of this boor! She was nothing but a slut, he thought.

A taxi came. In it she sat as far away from him as she could. He thought of what he should say to his wife.

Outside the theatre she remarked: "You could drop me here, if you liked." It was not a plea, she was too proud for that. "I'll take you in," he said, and saw her thinking: Very well, I'll go through with it to shame him. He was determined to take her in and hand her over to her colleagues, he was afraid she would give him the slip. But far from playing it down, she seemed determined to play it his way. At the stage door, she said to the doorman: "This is Mr. Spence, Tom—do you remember, Mr. Spence from last night?" "Good morning Babs," said the man, examining Graham, politely, as he had been ordered to do.

Barbara went to the door to the stage, opened it, held it open for him. He went in first, then held it open for her. Together they walked into the cavernous, littered, badly lit place and she called out: "James, James!" A man's voice called out from the front of the house: "Here, Babs, why are you so late?"

The auditorium opened before them, darkish, silent, save for an early-morning busyness of charwomen. A vacuum cleaner roared, smally, somewhere close. A couple of stagehands stood looking up at a drop which had a design of blue and green spirals. James stood with his back to the auditorium, smoking. "You're late, Babs," he said again. He saw Graham behind her, and nodded. Barbara and James kissed. Barbara said, giving allowance to every syllable: "You remember Mr. Spence from last night?" James nodded: How do you do? Barbara stood beside him, and they looked together up at the blue-and-green backdrop. Then Barbara looked again at Graham asking silently: All right now, isn't that enough? He could see her eyes, sullen with boredom.

He said: "Bye, Babs. Bye, James. I'll ring you, Babs." No response, she ignored him. He walked off slowly, listening for what might be said. For instance: "Babs, for God's sake, what are you doing with him?" Or she might say: "Are you wondering about Graham Spence? Let me explain."

Graham passed the stagehands who, he could have sworn, didn't recognise him. Then at last he heard James's voice to Barbara: "It's no good, Babs, I know you're enamored of that particular shade of blue, but do have another look at it, there's a good girl. . . ." Graham left the stage, went past the office where the stage doorman sat reading a newspaper. He looked up, nodded, went back to his paper. Graham went to find a taxi, thinking: I'd better think up something convincing, then I'll telephone my wife.

Luckily he had an excuse not to be at home that day, for this evening he had to interview a young man (for television) about his new novel. ✐

SUGGESTIONS FOR WRITING

1. Describe your feelings as you read this story. How typical is this man's behavior? Explain.

2. What are your thoughts about Barbara's behavior during the joyless one-night stand? Why does she behave as she does?

3. If you have ever observed men talking about women as sexual conquests, referring to them as if they were points scored in a basketball game, describe how you felt about such conversations. How did you react?

4. Analyze the relationship between the interviewer's designs on Barbara and his homophobic comments about her male co-workers.

THE STORY OF AN HOUR

Kate Chopin

In traditional societies, women were subservient to their fathers until they married, at which time religion, law, and custom dictated they owed allegiance to their husbands. As a result, when widowhood came, women's grief could well be tempered by the growing realization that they could now do more or less as they pleased. Of course, certain other conditions had to be met, such as the assurance of a sufficient legacy from one's late husband. In the earliest civilizations, enormous pressure would be brought to bear on a widow to remarry. Typically, the pressure would be exerted by her late husband's relatives, since her husband's property would revert to them in such a case. Ancient Chinese widows were known to disfigure their own faces to render themselves so unattractive to prospective suitors that they could remain as widows with their material comfort assured. But we do not have to journey all the way back to ancient times to find cultures that forced wives to submit to the will of their husbands. Set in the late nineteenth century in the United States, "The Story of an Hour" delves into some of the painfully contradictory aspects of widowhood.

Kate Chopin *(1850–1904) is a leading example of a writer rediscovered and brought to a long-overdue recognition by recent feminist scholarship. Chopin, who lived in New Orleans, did most of her writing as a widow with six children. Her 1899 novel,* The Awakening, *now circulates widely, and a selection from her collected works,* The Storm and Other Stories, *appeared in 1974.*

Knowing that Mrs. Mallard was afflicted with a heart trouble, great care was taken to break to her as gently as possible the news of her husband's death.

It was her sister Josephine who told her, in broken sentences; veiled hints that revealed in half concealing. Her husband's friend Richards was there, too, near her. It was he who had been in the newspaper office when intelligence of the railroad disaster was received, with Brently Mallard's name leading the list of "killed." He had only taken the time to assure himself of its truth by a second telegram, and had hastened to forestall any less careful, less tender friend in bearing the sad message.

She did not hear the story as many women have heard the same, with a paralyzed inability to accept its significance. She wept at once, with sudden, wild abandonment, in her sister's arms. When the storm of grief had spent itself she went away to her room alone. She would have no one follow her.

There stood, facing the open window, a comfortable, roomy armchair. Into this she sank, pressed down by a physical exhaustion that haunted her body and seemed to reach into her soul.

She could see in the open square before her house the tops of trees that were all aquiver with the new spring life. The delicious breath of rain was in the air. In the street below a peddler was crying his wares. The notes of a distant song which some one was singing reached her faintly, and countless sparrows were twittering in the eaves.

There were patches of blue sky showing here and there through the clouds that had met and piled one above the other in the west facing her window.

She sat with her head thrown back upon the cushion of the chair, quite motionless, except when a sob came up into her throat and shook her, as a child who has cried itself to sleep continues to sob in its dreams.

She was young, with a fair, calm face, whose lines bespoke repression and even a certain strength. But now there was a dull stare in her eyes, whose gaze was fixed away off yonder on one of those patches of blue sky. It was not a glance of reflection, but rather indicated a suspension of intelligent thought.

There was something coming to her and she was waiting for it, fearfully. What was it? She did not know; it was too subtle and elusive to name. But she felt it, creeping out of the sky, reaching toward her through the sounds, the scents, the color that filled the air.

Now her bosom rose and fell tumultuously. She was beginning to recognize this thing that was approaching to possess her, and she was striving to beat it back with her will—as powerless as her two white slender hands would have been.

When she abandoned herself a little whispered word escaped her slightly parted lips. She said it over and over and under her breath: "free, free, free!" The vacant stare and the look of terror that had followed it went from her eyes. They stayed keen and bright. Her pulses beat fast, and the coursing blood warmed and relaxed every inch of her body.

She did not stop to ask if it were or were not a monstrous joy that held her. A clear and exalted perception enabled her to dismiss the suggestion as trivial.

She knew that she would weep again when she saw the kind, tender hands folded in death; the face that had never looked save with love upon her, fixed and gray and dead. But she saw beyond that bitter moment a long procession of years to come that would belong to her absolutely. And she opened and spread her arms out to them in welcome.

There would be no one to live for her during those coming years; she would live for herself. There would be no powerful will bending hers in that blind persistence with which men and women believe they have a right to impose a private will upon a fellow-creature. A kind intention or a cruel intention made the act seem no less a crime as she looked upon it in that brief moment of illumination.

And yet she had loved him—sometimes. Often she had not. What did it matter! What could love, the unsolved mystery, count for in face of this possession of self-assertion which she suddenly recognized as the strongest impulse of her being!

"Free! Body and soul free!" she kept whispering.

Josephine was kneeling before the closed door with her lips to the keyhole, imploring for admission. "Louise, open the door! I beg; open the door—you will make yourself ill. What are you doing, Louise? For heaven's sake open the door."

"Go away. I am not making myself ill." No; she was drinking in a very elixir of life through that open window.

Her fancy was running riot along those days ahead of her. Spring days, and summer days, and all sorts of days that would be her own. She breathed a quick prayer that life might be long. It was only yesterday she had thought with a shudder that life might be long.

She rose at length and opened the door to her sister's importunities. There was a feverish triumph in her eyes, and she carried herself unwittingly like a goddess of Victory. She clasped her sister's waist, and together they descended the stairs. Richards stood waiting for them at the bottom.

Some one was opening the front door with a latchkey. It was Brently Mallard who entered, a little travel-stained, composedly carrying his grip-sack and umbrella. He had been far from the scene of the accident, and did not even know there had been one. He stood amazed at Josephine's piercing cry; at Richard's quick motion to screen him from the view of his wife.

But Richards was too late.

When the doctors came they said she had died of heart disease—of joy that kills.

SUGGESTIONS FOR WRITING

1. Consider the impact of this story in terms of its length. To what extent does the brief nature of the tale heighten its power?

2. One never really knows how one will respond to extreme situations until they arise. How do you think you would behave if you received the kinds of reports, in succession, that Mrs. Mallard did?

3. Discuss this story in light of Emma Goldman's essay on marriage.

AN OPEN LETTER TO MOTHERS WHOSE DAUGHTERS HAPPEN TO BE LESBIANS

D. Clarke

When parents imagine their children's futures, they typically project aspects of their own lives onto the prospects of their sons or daughters. Learning that a son or daughter is gay may cause extreme confusion, not the least of which is the disappointment over expectations suddenly canceled out. Confronted with such a situation, a mother may ask herself, "What did I do, or fail to do?" Despite the myriad attempts by psychologists and others to determine what "causes" homosexuality, the answer to that anguished question may indeed by "nothing." For that matter, gay theorists and activists would want to turn the question around, so that it becomes a question about what "causes" heterosexuality.

The anonymous author of this open letter, which appeared in a collection edited by Louise Rafkin called Different Daughters: A Book by Mothers of Lesbians *(1987), acknowledges her disappointment over abandoned hope for the grandchildren she had expected, but she urges other mothers of lesbians to put aside their self-reproach and to keep the lines of communication with their daughters open.*

The title of this letter was chosen with care. Being a lesbian is only one factor of a personality and it is something that one is or one is not. The only option for a parent is to accept the fact with courage, first to oneself, and then, with more courage, to one's friends, associates, and parents. That it is commonly in that order is, itself, a sad commentary.

I have one child, a daughter. She is twenty-six years old and since the day she was born she has been the light of my life. There has never been a day in that time that I have been anything other than proud of her. She is bright, literate, attractive, competent, multitalented, has more compassion for people in her little finger than I have in my whole body, and is stubborn, lesbian, and gets bad head colds when her feet get wet.

I suspect that self-acknowledgment of her lesbianism came early on in her life; the announcement to me came only a few years ago, and it came with no great surprise. I probably had much subliminal input along the way, although deliberate speculation on this aspect of my child's life would have seemed as gross an invasion of privacy to me as reading her diary. My reaction was anticlimactic, along the lines of: "Really? Now where would you like to go for dinner?" The surprise was my realization, very slowly, of the effort it had taken her to make this announcement, and her honesty in telling me. Quite frankly, I felt it was none of my business.

There was a fleeting sadness on two counts. First, as a free-thinker myself, I have a clear understanding of the unhappiness which can come from standing opposed to culturally imposed mores. A little deeper analysis told me, however, that this is nothing as compared to the unhappiness of living a lie, particularly to a truth-seeker and lover of justice such as my child has been all her life. The first is a social penalty; the second is mentally destructive.

The second basis for regret was, of course, grandchildren! But even less consideration was necessary to show me how irrational this was. Firstly, lesbianism is an assertion of womanhood, not a denial, and nothing about it precludes motherhood. Secondly, my mother spoke to me wistfully of "nice little families" and the penalties of being an only child, and my mother-in-law was determined that I would have four children, and indeed wrote in her will in that determined belief, thereby fouling up the question of my daughter's inheritance for years to come. Each of them in her own way brought as much pressure to bear on me as they considered safe, but in spite of this I, and I alone, decided on one child. I am ashamed that for even a split second I had the arrogance to presume my daughter should have children to please me. My pleasure in grandchildren would probably be transient, and certainly intermittent. Heavens above, I might not even like them! We are talking about people here, not Cabbage Patch kids.

After my reactions to her statement established me as a fairly civilized and decent person, I began to be admitted to her circle of friends, lovers and activities, and be a party to general discussions. I began to realize why she felt compelled to inform me of her lifestyle, and why it was such an effort, because I began to hear the horror stories. Without exaggeration, that is what they truly are.

I heard of children who were, at best, persuaded to undergo psychiatric treatment and, at the worst, incarcerated in institutions for treatment of insanity. I heard of children who, as a reward for honesty were a) disowned, with the possibility of being accepted when they returned to "normality," or b) disowned by those they loved and trusted most without chance of redemption. I heard of children who were blackmailed by withdrawal of financial support, threatened with heart attacks and nervous breakdowns, all as attempts to make them live their lives by other people's rules.

Bigotry, disapproval, or holier-than-thou patronage from neighbors who might not even be neighbors within a year, or from associates in the work place, is apparently more important than the appeal for understanding and support from a being for whose existence you are entirely responsible. My child apparently feared these reactions, and that hurt, until I realized that it was a result of hearing the experiences of others.

To withdraw financial and emotional support from a child just trying to make that final step into total independence, to apply pressure by threatening illness, to induce self-doubt and imply mental instability at an age when introspection and lack of experience lends credence to the charge; all this add up to psychological abuse, whichever way you choose to look at it. Am I reaching any of you out there? I am a mother of an only daughter, married to the same man for thirty years, in other words a card-carrying member of your own union, and I am telling to that this behavior is inexcusable, and it is ugly. Sometimes an attempt is made to justify these reactions on the basis of concern for the child's future and happiness. It is very hard to see how such behavior translates into concern for the happiness of a child who is taking her courage in both hands and asking for love and support.

Take a look at your lesbian child on this basis: you can lie to your child, your neighbors, or your psychiatrist, but you cannot successfully lie to yourself. What is so lacking in your life that you need to achieve total control of another person to feel fulfilled? Or, why is your ego so frail that only total control and obedience can assure you that you have any value? Or, whence springs an insecurity which can only be assuaged by the knowledge the whole world is marching in lockstep to your drum? These are good questions to start with. The dominant question is, however: When did society's opinion or approval become more important to you than the chance for happiness for your own child? Listen to her and believe, however hard it may be for you, that she knows better than you do what makes her happy or unhappy. As a person she has a right to make her own decisions, and as your child she has the right to expect your support. ✒

SUGGESTIONS FOR WRITING

1. Contrast the likely reactions of a mother who learns her daughter is a lesbian to those of a father who learns his son is gay.

2. React to the author's statement "Being a lesbian is only one factor of a personality and it is something that one is or one is not."

3. Is this mother's attitude surprising? What kind of attitude would you describe as typical in this situation?

4. What arguments does Clarke make to mothers that could persuade them to accept their daughters' lesbianism?

7

ABORTION

You may recall seeing news reports of anti-abortion groups picketing women's clinics, ha-rassing women visiting the clinic for advice or an abortion. In some cases, right-to-life advo-cates have been responsible for bombing abortion clinics. With public sentiment increasingly against "abortion on demand," both right-to-life and pro-choice advocates have made abor-tion a key issue in both national and local elections. Pro-choice people argue that a woman's reproductive rights are hers to control as she sees fit, including the right to terminate an un-wanted pregnancy. They assert that only the woman should make this most difficult of de-cisions, not the state, not her parents, not her husband, lover, or boyfriend. Moderate supporters of the right-to-life point of view counter that only the victims of rape or incest and women whose lives would be endangered by carrying the pregnancy to term should be al-lowed to have abortions. Strict proponents of the pro-life movement, on the other hand, are adamant in denying rights to legal abortions, even to victims of incest and rape.

Prior to the 1973 Supreme Court Roe v. Wade decision legalizing abortion, many women seeking abortions wound up dead at the hands of unscrupulous people who masquer-aded as qualified care-givers. Because abortions were illegal, women could rely on no one to help them if they suffered complications as a result of the abortionist's mistakes. Not only did women risk their lives, but they also often suffered indignities, physical abuse, disfigure-ment, and sterility, assuming they could find someone to perform the procedure . . . and as-suming they had the large sum of money needed to pay for the illegal operation.

In an effort the protect the "sanctity of human life," President Ronald Reagan and many conservative lawmakers worked to make abortion once again illegal except when the mother's life was at risk. In 1989, the Supreme Court upheld Webster v. Reproductive

Health Services, *a Missouri case permitting public hospitals to perform abortions only if the mother's life is in danger. With this decision, the Supreme Court drew closer than any time since 1973 to repealing—or at least severely limiting abortion rights, and it continues to hear further challenges to the* Roe v. Wade *decision.*

Critics of this drive to repeal Roe v. Wade *point out that no matter what lawmakers decide, women wanting to end a pregnancy will do so. And, they point out, women with money—women from the more privileged classes—will still be able to obtain safe abortions. Pro-choice advocates feel that poor women will suffer in disproportionate numbers because they will be unable to pay the price of a safe abortion.*

THE STORY OF SADIE SACHS

Margaret Sanger

*Margaret Higgins Sanger (1880–1966) fought tirelessly for women's re-
productive rights in America. A child of a family of eleven whose mother
died at forty-eight and whose father was a poor provider at best, Sanger
knew the hardships of having too many children too close together. After her
own three children were in school, Sanger worked as a trained public health
nurse in the New York slums. Her experience with desperate mothers of
large families who begged for her help motivated her to devote her life to seeing that women had access to information about birth control, a phrase she
coined.*

*In the 1920s it become legal for physicians to give married women who
might suffer serious birth-related health problems the birth-control information that they needed in order to prevent additional pregnancies. And it was
not until 1937 that American doctors could legally provide any woman who
asked with information about birth control. In the following selection, Sanger
describes the plight of one woman who could not obtain help to prevent an
additional pregnancy.*

During these years in New York trained nurses were in great demand. Few
people wanted to enter hospitals; they were afraid they might be "practiced"
upon, and consented to go only in desperate emergencies. Sentiment was
especially vehement in the matter of having babies. A woman's own bedroom, no matter how inconveniently arranged, was the usual place for her
lying-in. I was not sufficiently free from domestic duties to be a general
nurse, but I could ordinarily manage obstetrical cases because I was notified
far enough ahead to plan my schedule. And after serving my two weeks I
could get home again.

Sometimes I was summoned to small apartments occupied by young clerks,
insurance salesmen, or lawyers, just starting out, most of them under thirty and
whose wives were having their first or second baby. They were always eager to
know the best and latest method in infant care and feeding. In particular, Jewish patients, whose lives centered around the family, welcomed advice and followed it implicitly.

But more and more my calls began to come from the Lower East Side, as
though I were being magnetically drawn there by some force outside my control. I hated the wretchedness and hopelessness of the poor, and never experienced that satisfaction in working among them that so many noble women
have found. My concern for my patients was now quite different from my earlier hospital attitude. I could see that much was wrong with them which did not
appear in the physiological or medical diagnosis. A woman in childbirth was
not merely a woman in childbirth. My expanded outlook included a view of her

background, her potentialities as a human being, the kind of children she was bearing, and what was going to happen to them.

The wives of small shopkeepers were my most frequent cases, but I had carpenters, truck drivers, dishwashers, and pushcart vendors. I admired intensely the consideration most of these people had for their own. Money to pay doctor and nurse had been carefully saved months in advance—parents-in-law, grandfathers, grandmothers, all contributing.

As soon as the neighbors learned that a nurse was in the building they came in a friendly way to visit, often carrying fruit, jellies, or gefüllter fish made after a cherished recipe. It was infinitely pathetic to me that they, so poor themselves, should bring me food. Later they drifted in again with the excuse of getting the plate, and sat down for a nice talk; there was no hurry. Always back of the little gift was the question, "I am pregnant (or my daughter, or my sister is). Tell me something to keep from having another baby. We cannot afford another yet."

I tried to explain the only two methods I had ever heard of among the middle classes, both of which were invariably brushed aside as unacceptable. They were of no certain avail to the wife because they placed the burden of responsibility solely upon the husband—a burden which he seldom assumed. What she was seeking was self-protection she could herself use, and there was none.

Below this stratum of society was one in truly desperate circumstances. The men were sullen and unskilled, picking up odd jobs now and then, but more often unemployed, lounging in and out of the house at all hours of the day and night. The women seemed to slink on their way to market and were without neighborliness.

These submerged, untouched classes were beyond the scope of organized charity or religion. No labor union, no church, not even the Salvation Army reached them. They were apprehensive of everyone and rejected help of any kind, ordering all intruders to keep out; both birth and death they considered their own business. Social agents, who were just beginning to appear, were profoundly mistrusted because they pried into homes and lives, asking questions about wages, how many were in the family, had any of them ever been in jail. Often two or three had been there or were now under suspicion of prostitution, shoplifting, purse snatching, petty thievery, and, in consequence, passed furtively by the big blue uniforms on the corner.

The utmost depression came over me as I approached this surreptitious region. Below Fourteenth Street I seemed to be breathing a different air, to be in another world and country where the people had habits and customs alien to anything I had ever heard about.

There were then approximately ten thousand apartments in New York into which no sun ray penetrated directly; such windows as they had opened only on a narrow court from which rose fetid odors. It was seldom cleaned, though garbage and refuse often went down into it. All these dwellings were pervaded by the foul breath of poverty, that moldy, indefinable, indescribable smell which cannot be fumigated out, sickening to me but apparently unnoticed by those who lived there. When I set to work with antiseptics, their pungent sting, at least temporarily, obscured the stench.

I remember one confinement case to which I was called by the doctor of an insurance company. I climbed up the five flights and entered the airless rooms, but the baby had come with too great speed. A boy of ten had been the only assistant. Five flights was a long way; he had wrapped the placenta in a piece of newspaper and dropped it out the window into the court.

Many families took in "boarders," as they were termed, whose small contributions paid the rent. These derelicts, wanders, alternately working and drinking, were crowded in with the children; a single room sometimes held as many as six sleepers. Little girls were accustomed to dressing and undressing in front of the men, and were often violated, occasionally by their own fathers or brothers, before they reached the age of puberty.

Pregnancy was a chronic condition among the women of this class. Suggestions as to what to do for a girl who was "in trouble" or a married woman who was "caught" passed from mouth to mouth—herb teas, turpentine, steaming, rolling downstairs, inserting slippery elm, knitting needles, shoe-hooks. When they had word of a new remedy they hurried to the drugstore, and if the clerk were inclined to be friendly he might say, "Oh, that won't help you, but here's something that may." The younger druggists usually refused to give advice because, if it were to be known, they would come under the law; midwives were even more fearful. The doomed women implored me to reveal the "secret" rich people had, offering to pay me extra to tell them; many really believed I was holding back information for money. They asked everybody and tried anything, but nothing did them any good. On Saturday nights I have seen groups of from fifty to one hundred with their shawls over their heads waiting outside the office of a five-dollar abortionist.

Each time I returned to this district, which was becoming a recurrent nightmare, I used to hear that Mrs. Cohen "had been carried to a hospital, but had never come back," or that Mrs. Kelly "had sent the children to a neighbor and had put her head into the gas oven." Day after day such tales were poured into my ears—a baby born dead, great relief—the death of an older child, sorrow but again relief of a sort—the story told a thousand times of death from abortion and children going into institutions. I shuddered with horror as I listened to the details and studied the reasons back of them—destitution linked with excessive childbearing. The waste of life seemed utterly senseless. One by one worried, sad, pensive, and aging faces marshaled themselves before me in my dreams, sometimes appealingly, sometimes accusingly.

These were not merely "unfortunate conditions among the poor" such as we read about. I knew the women personally. They were living, breathing, human beings, with hopes, fears, and aspirations like my own, yet their weary, misshapen bodies, "always ailing, never failing," were destined to be thrown on the scrap heap before they were thirty-five. I could not escape from the facts of their wretchedness; neither was I able to see any way out. My own cozy and comfortable family existence was becoming a reproach to me.

Then one stifling mid-July day of 1912 I was summoned to a Grand Street tenement. My patient was a small, slight Russian Jewess, about twenty-eight years old, of the special cast of feature to which suffering lends a madonna-like expression. The cramped three-room apartment was in a sorry state of turmoil.

Jake Sachs, a truck driver scarcely older than his wife, had come home to find the three children crying and her unconscious from the effects of a self-induced abortion. He had called the nearest doctor, who in turn had sent for me. Jake's earnings were trifling, and most of them had gone to keep the none-too-strong children clean and properly fed. But his wife's ingenuity had helped them to save a little, and this he was glad to spend on a nurse rather than have her go to a hospital.

The doctor and I settled ourselves to the task of fighting the septicemia. Never had I worked so fast, never so concentratedly. The sultry days and nights were melted into a torpid inferno. It did not seem possible there could be such heat, and every bit of food, ice, and drugs had to be carried up three flights of stairs.

Jake was more kind and thoughtful than many of the husbands I had encountered. He loved his children, and had always helped his wife wash and dress them. He had brought water up and carried garbage down before he left in the morning, and did as much as he could for me while he anxiously watched her progress.

After a fortnight Mrs. Sachs' recovery was in sight. Neighbors, ordinarily fatalistic as to the results of abortion, were genuinely pleased that she had survived. She smiled wanly at all who came to see her and thanked them gently, but she could not respond to their hearty congratulations. She appeared to be more despondent and anxious than she should have been, and spent too much time in meditation.

At the end of three weeks, as I was preparing to leave the fragile patient to take up her difficult life once more, she finally voiced her fears, "Another baby will finish me, I suppose?"

"It's too early to talk about that," I temporized.

But when the doctor came to make his last call, I drew him aside. "Mrs. Sachs is terribly worried about having another baby."

"She well may be," replied the doctor, and then he stood before her and said, "Any more such capers, young woman, and there'll be no need to send for me."

"I know, doctor," she replied timidly, "but," and she hesitated as though it took all her courage to say it, "what can I do to prevent it?"

The doctor was a kindly man, and he had worked hard to save her, but such incidents had become so familiar to him that he had long since lost whatever delicacy he might once have had. He laughed good-naturedly. "You want to have your cake and eat it too, do you? Well, it can't done."

Then picking up his hat and bag to depart he said. "Tell Jake to sleep on the roof."

I glanced quickly at Mrs. Sachs. Even through my sudden tears I could see stamped on her face an expression of absolute despair. We simply looked at each other, saying no word until the door had closed behind the doctor. Then she lifted her thin, blue-veined hands and clasped them beseechingly. "He can't understand. He's only a man. But you do, don't you? Please tell me the secret, and I'll never breathe it to a soul. *Please!*"

What was I to do? I could not speak the conventionally comforting phrases which would be of no comfort. Instead, I made her as physically easy as I could and promised to come back in a few days to talk with her again. A little later, when she slept, I tiptoed away.

Night after night the wistful image of Mrs. Sachs appeared before me. I made all sorts of excuses to myself for not going back. I was busy on other cases; I really did not know what to say to her or how to convince her of my own ignorance; I was helpless to avert such monstrous atrocities. Time rolled by and I did nothing.

The telephone rang one evening three months later, and Jake Sachs' agitated voice begged me to come at once; his wife was sick again and from the same cause. For a wild moment I thought of sending someone else, but actually, of course, I hurried into my uniform, caught up my bag, and started out. All the way I longed for a subway wreck, an explosion, anything to keep me from having to enter that home again. But nothing happened, even to delay me. I turned into the dingy doorway and climbed the familiar stairs once more. The children were there, young little things.

Mrs. Sachs was in a coma and died within ten minutes. I folded her still hands across her breast, remembering how they had pleaded with me, begging so humbly for the knowledge which was her right. I drew a sheet over her pallid face. Jake was sobbing, running his hands through his hair and pulling it out like an insane person. Over and over again he wailed, "My God! My God! My God!"

I left him pacing desperately back and forth, and for hours I myself walked and walked and walked through the hushed streets. When I finally arrived home and let myself quietly in, all the household was sleeping. I looked out my window and down upon the dimly lighted city. Its pains and griefs crowded in upon me, a moving picture rolled before my eyes with photographic clearness: women writhing in travail to bring forth little babies; the babies themselves naked and hungry, wrapped in newspapers to keep them from the cold; six-year-old children with pinched, pale, wrinkled faces, old in concentrated wretchedness, pushed into gray and fetid cellars, crouching on stone floors, their small scrawny hands scuttling through rags, making lamp shades, artificial flowers; white coffins, black coffins, coffins, coffins interminably passing in never-ending succession. The scenes piled one upon another on another. I could bear it no longer.

As I stood there the darkness faded. The sun came up and threw its reflection over the house tops. It was the dawn of a new day in my life also. The doubt and questioning, the experimenting and trying, were now to be put behind me. I knew I could not go back merely to keeping people alive.

I went to bed, knowing that no matter what it might cost, I was finished with palliatives and superficial cures; I was resolved to seek out the root of evil, to do something to change the destiny of mothers whose miseries were vast as the sky. 🖋

SUGGESTIONS FOR WRITING

1. Discuss whether birth-control information should be made available to teenagers under the age of eighteen without their parents' consent.

2. Examine expectations regarding who takes responsibility for birth control. Suggest ways that both women and men learn to share the responsibility for preventing conception.

3. Federal money is being withdrawn from projects that provide birth-control information and products to low-income individuals. Examine whether or not this is a wise choice and explore whether or not people are being punished simply for being poor.

4. A recent French television commercial shows a teenage boy on his sixteenth birthday receiving a box of condoms from his parents as they sit around the dinner table preparing to eat his birthday cake. Compare the attitudes in your family or in our culture to those implicit in this ad.

DR. SPENCER IS JUST DOWN THE STREET

Anonymous

*Since the Supreme Court's Roe v. Wade decision in 1973 made it possible
for women to obtain legal abortions, there has been little talk about the abortion underground network of earlier times. Despite the anguish a woman can
suffer when she decides to terminate a pregnancy, the choice to do so is, in
most instances, now hers. Women who do seek an abortion can be assured
that the medical care they receive will be competent and that the cost of the
procedure will be reasonable. These expectations were not always the case
for the generations of women for whom abortion was not a legal option.*

*The following is an anonymous article first published in 1969, four years
before abortions were made legal in the United States.*

I didn't read Dr. Spencer's obit over the breakfast table, as did untold thousands
of his other ex-patients. My husband brings the newspaper home from the university, so I'm always several hours behind the rest of America. When he
pointed out the item, I let out an involuntary, "Oh, no!"

"Why are you so sad, Mommy!" asked my five-year-old.

"Because a good man died," I answered. "A very good man indeed."

"Was he old?"

I nodded, feeling teary and uncomposed.

"Then you shouldn't be sad. Just like you told me with Grandma, old people
die when their lives end. Right?"

"Yes, honey, that's true. But he was a very special man. I'll tell you about
him someday."

I thought of all the bowed heads out there that day. Maybe even some rosary
masses and some sitting of Shivahs. And I thought about the middle-aged, middle-class ladies of my generation who read the same obit and who made appropriately liberal comments about how interesting it was that one man had
performed so many abortions and how necessary it is to liberalize the abortion
laws, whereupon their middle-aged, middle-class husbands nodded assent,
never for a second dreaming that their very own wives might have journeyed
to Ashland, Pennsylvania, in the days of their defiant youth.

But, unlike too many of my peers who choose to forget, I remember what it
was like for those of us of the pre-pill diaphragm generation during the early fifties. Dr. Spencer was our guru.

We made love, those of us who identified with Kerouac and Ginsberg (little
did we know that they were not interested), who patronized art movies (the
summer festival at the Thalia in New York was big time), who hated Joe Mc-
Carthy, who loved James Agee, who dug sounds of Charlie Parker and Billie

Holliday. We learned in our anthropology courses about cultural relativism and in our literature courses about those seventeenth-century swingers, and we added it up as an ode to sexual freedom. Freedom also to leave our Margaret Sanger diaphragms around in bureau drawers so that our fathers would spend the whole night throwing up and questioning what went wrong.

In a *Realist* interview, Dr. Spencer talked about the poor souls who came to him after having been raped by psychiatrists, D.A.s, and even priests. It wasn't like that for us—no rapes, no incest, no fears of German measles maiming our unborn children. Our generation was called "Silent" and "Beat," but some of us did manage to express ourselves in bed.

Dr. Spencer didn't ask personal questions, and he didn't moralize. He was just there, out there in Ashland, like Mecca and Jerusalem and Lourdes and all of the other shrines to which people are drawn in times of need.

I visited Ashland several times between 1953 and 1955, once for my own pregnancy and later as an accompanist for friends. Dr. Spencer always specified on the telephone that the patient bring a girl friend. I never asked him the reason, but I suspect he thought that the presence of men, especially in the hotel, might rile the townspeople. He was probably right.

Sleepy-eyed and dreary—that describes Ashland. Four or five thousand people (*The New York Times* said twelve thousand, but I don't believe it) housed in winding tiers above the main street. The heyday of coal mining was over; and despite what people might have said publicly about Dr. Spencer (it's always fashionable to condemn crime), he was obviously good business for the town. At a gas station, we were told, without asking, "Dr. Spencer is just down the street." The druggist said cheerfully, "I suppose you want the Sunday *Times*. I always get a pile of 'em for you girls," and the hotel clerk commented matter-of-factly, "You'll just be here for tonight." No question mark.

My first trip, my *own* trip, took place on Easter weekend. Dr. Spencer was a pathologist, a general practitioner, and a specialist in chest diseases. And even on a Saturday afternoon—which must have been his busiest day for the working girls and students and, yes, mothers (a frail, very young girl, a mother of four, told me that she had wanted to come during the week to "avoid the crowd" but that her husband couldn't get off work to babysit)—the waiting room of his eleven-room clinic was lined with several "legitimate" patients. On the walls there were displayed the usual diplomas (his medical degree was from the University of Pennsylvania in 1916), plus several eerie hair wreaths, those framed Victorian ornaments containing bits of hair from now-deceased relatives. But on the operating walls and on those of the numerous recovery rooms (each of which had a bed as well as a chair for the faithful companion) were hundreds, maybe thousands, of small wooden plaques from souvenir shops painted with homespun philosophy and witticisms, all diabolically appropriate. As I emerged from anesthesia, I saw one that read, "Today Is the Tomorrow You Dreaded So Much Yesterday." Another one that etched itself in my memory was, "If You're Out Driving, Don't Park. That's How Accidents Happen."

My initial interview with Dr. Spencer couldn't have been more relaxing or more reassuring. He was small, almost frail, with wispy white hair; I thought he was at least eighty then and was startled to learn that he died at seventy-nine, some sixteen years later. After asking a couple of questions to establish the onset of pregnancy, he began a soft-spoken but passionate diatribe about the need for better abortion laws. He spoke of Thomas Paine and Charles Darwin and especially of Abraham Lincoln, who, he said, "consciously broke bad laws." Then, after producing from the bowels of his cluttered desk a hand-printed document, protected by torn cellophane—which outlined his philosophy and his justification for his "crime," he asked me to sign a strangely worded and obviously meaningless paper, agreeing to assume half of the court costs in case of his arrest. When I returned with a friend a few months later, he had abandoned that part of the ritual, muttering, "My files were getting too full anyway."

The injection that he gave me on that afternoon was something he called his own secret. "I can't tell you what's in it, but I promise it won't hurt, and it'll start things up just enough so I can finish tomorrow morning."

I spent the evening watching a dreadful double bill at the local movie house (I remember distinctly having suffered through Hopalong Cassidy, but it couldn't have been, not in 1953), slept well, and arrived at his office the next morning just as the church bells were tolling the joys of Easter. My friend reported that, as he was about to begin the curettage (a process that took, from the time he administered the sodium pentothal [an anesthetic] until I woke up, about half an hour), a farmer appeared at the operating room door and asked him to go fishing. "Nope, I've got a busy day. Gotta get these girls started home before the heavy traffic," he replied.

Later, as I lay serenely in the comfort of the white-sheeted bed, the church bells were still ringing and I was convinced that the man that Christianity was heralding that day was Dr. Spencer. I could not have felt more exultation than I did as Dr. Spencer patted my hand. "Diaphragms don't work in the medicine chest," he said, after establishing the fact that I owned one, "and I don't like to see any patient more than once."

He presented me with a pile of envelopes, each containing enough medication to supply several post-abortion patients. One was labeled ambiguously "T.P.M." "That one means 'to prevent milk,' " he chuckled. "I don't want any nosey mothers to get upset."

When I paid him the forty dollars, I kissed his cheek. And note well: no mention of payment was made until after the operation. I heard that he willingly skipped the fee for hardship cases; even when he was involved in court cases, he never charged more than one hundred dollars.

"Go get yourself a good meal at the hotel before you start back," he advised. "You'll probably see a few of the other girls there too, but listen, don't act like you recognize them, okay?"

So there we were, eating a traditional ham and sweet potatoes Easter dinner in a daffodil-decorated dining room, empty except for four other Spencer "couples." What a fitting close to the only meaningful Easter of my life—it was I was had risen and I who had been given a new life. I wanted to sing and dance.

I telephoned my parents en route back to campus, pretending, of course, that I'd spent a quiet day in the library; and when my mother asked timidly (she was accustomed to angry denunciation of all those holidays to which I'd been subjected as a child) if I'd had "anything special to eat," I gleefully described the entire menu, beginning with the daffodils and ending with the lemon pie. I think I might have even thrown in something about the jubilant sound of the bells. It was a good Easter for her, too.

For the next few years, I was besieged with requests for particulars about Dr. Spencer. For reasons unclear to me, many of his patients were reluctant to pass on information. I became known as "the source," and I was approached by nervous boys and swollen-eyed girls, all of whom talked about their "friend in trouble." Once there was a midnight call from the West Coast. The caller refused to say how she had been told about me, but I was a pushover for anyone's "friend in trouble." To withhold information about the Saint of Ashland was, to me, equivalent to being an accessory to a crime, for I, too, believed that bad laws should be broken. Maybe I saw myself as Mrs. Lincoln or Mrs. Paine—who knows? In any case, I was proud to steer the needy toward Ashland.

The experiences of those who visited other abortionists were grim indeed. One girl, in the clutches of a demented old lady wielding a germ-infested catheter ("I insert it, dearie, and tomorrow you have a few pains, that's all") was forced to describe in detail the extent of her "sin." She spent three weeks in the hospital with a serious infection that rendered her permanently sterile.

Then there was my friend whose boyfriend's parents were footing the abortion bill. They wouldn't allow her to go to Dr. Spencer, feeling, in the great tradition of those who believe "you get what you pay for," that forty dollars wasn't enough to guarantee a competent job. She was met in a hotel room by two men who stuffed a towel in her mouth so she wouldn't yell. No anesthesia, of course, because, "We want you to remember this and not mess around anymore." She passed out at one point, and they dutifully waited until she revived before continuing the massacre, while, at the same time, the boyfriend's parents were bragging to their suburban friends how they'd paid eight hundred dollars for "two of the best doctors in New York."

So, those of us who had experienced the warmth and kindness of Dr. Spencer were doubly grateful. I couldn't bring myself to buy any of those corny plaques for him, but I had friends who did; and I remember one girl who sent him a hand-woven smoking jacket. A sentimental thank-you note and a birth announcement when my first child was born were all I ever managed. I sometimes speculated if he recognized my name when it cropped up so often as a "referral."

During my early years as a faculty wife, I suggested Dr. Spencer to a few students. It was often difficult to contact him because he kept trying to retire. At that time he sent out mimeographed instructions on contacting other doctors in Cuba—until Castro denounced both prostitution and abortion as equivalent vices—and in Puerto Rico. (Several years ago, The Realist solicited contributions for an around-the-world trip for him and his wife, which they took.) And in recent years, nothing—but then, students with whom I'm in contact now have a whole different bag.

Dr. Spencer's coterie spoke of him as mad and crazy and eccentric, and we meant these labels as adulatory. He once asked two friends, one white and one black, if they were sisters. They laughed, undoubtedly with some embarrassment, and he said, as he looked at them for the first time, "Oh, golly, excuse me. But you know, Lincoln wouldn't have noticed either."

He was wrong, of course, about Lincoln. Dr. Spencer misunderstood a lot of history. When I heard that he sported a Goldwater button before the 1962 election, I was stunned. Then I realized that it figured—that is, it figured for him. The individual rebel, the individual act, the individual protest—all of this he identified correctly with the best of the conservatives but wrongly with the current batch for whom their emasculated creed is thinly masked bigotry and cold-warrior aggressiveness. Dr. Spencer was a conservative who was an ardent atheist, a conservative who disapproved of gun registration, a conservative who won the support of the United Mine Workers Union because of his willingness to go down into the mines to aid injured miners, a conservative who maintained that outlawing premarital sex wouldn't work any better than Prohibition. You see, it figures.

When I left Ashland, I felt cleansed, grateful, and free, and my experience was repeated many thousand times. In destroying a life (and I never deceived myself about that: I wept bitterly a few weeks later when I found in a biology book a life-size drawing of an eight-week embryo), he saved mine. He saved me from a life with a man I didn't love, and he freed me for the life I have now with a superb husband and two magnificent daughters.

When this—what should I call it: testimonial? eulogy? chronicle?—is published, I'll save it to show my daughters, hoping that by the time they read it, they'll be appalled at my having published it anonymously, but that they'll understand enough about me to forgive the cowardice of a mother for whom the world is not all that she wants it to be. 🖋

SUGGESTIONS FOR WRITING

1. Argue for your point of view concerning state laws requiring that the parents of a woman under the age of 18 be notified that their child is seeking an abortion.

2. In light of the controversy over legalized abortion, determine what point the author of this article is trying to make. How does she persuade the reader to see her point of view?

3. What are Dr. Spencer's attitudes toward the women he treats?

4. Examine the narrator's attitudes about being sexually active and single; have college students' attitudes changed since then? Compare the two sets of values.

WE DO ABORTIONS HERE:
A NURSE'S STORY

Sallie Tisdale

*In the controversy surrounding the issue of abortion, attention generally fo-
cuses on the women seeking the abortion and the doctors who perform the
procedure. Yet of equal importance are the nurses who attend the doctors
and their patients. They provide information, support, and care to the
women facing a decision that can affect the rest of their lives.*

At the time she wrote this essay, **Sallie Tisdale** *was a nurse in an abortion clinic. Not only does her essay reflect the realities of the abortion clinic,
but it also examines the attitudes of and about the women who go there. Tisdale
shares her ambivalence and leaves her readers to sort out their own feelings.*

Tisdale (b. 1957) has written three books on the nursing profession: The
Sorcerer's Apprentice: Medical Miracles and Other Disasters *(1986),*
Harvest Moon: Portrait of a Nursing Home *(1987), and* Lot's Wife:
Salt and the Human Condition *(1988). She also is a frequent contributor
on health issues to such magazines as* Harpers, The New Yorker, *and*
Whole Earth Review.

We do abortions here; that is all we do. There are weary, grim moments when
I think I cannot bear another basin of bloody remains, utter another kind
phrase of reassurance. So I leave the procedure room in the back and reach for
a new chart. Soon I am talking to an eighteen-year-old woman pregnant for
the fourth time. I push up her sleeve to check her blood pressure and find row
upon row of needle marks, neat and parallel and discolored. She has been so
hungry for her drug for so long that she has taken to using the loose skin of her
upper arms; her elbows are already a permanent ruin of bruises. She is surprised
to find herself nearly four months pregnant. I suspect she is often surprised, in
a mild way, by the blows she is dealt. I prepare myself for another basin, another
brief and chafing loss.

"How can you stand it?" Even the clients ask. They see the machine, the
strange instruments, the blood, the final stroke that wipes away the promise of
pregnancy. Sometimes I see that too: I watch a woman's swollen abdomen sink
to softness in a few stuttering moments and my own belly flip-flops with sorrow.
But all it takes for me to catch my breath is another interview, one more story
that sounds so much like the last one. There is a numbing sameness lurking in
this job: the same questions, the same answers, even the same trembling tone
in the voices. The worst is the sameness of human failure, of inadequacy in the
face of each day's dull demands.

In describing this work, I find it difficult to explain how much I enjoy it
most of the time. We laugh a lot here, as friends and as professional peers. It's

nice to be with women all day. I like the sudden, transient bonds I forge with some clients: moments when I am in my strength, remembering weakness, and a woman in weakness reaches out for my strength. What I offer is not power, but solidness, offered almost eagerly. Certain clients waken in me every tender urge I have—others make me wince and bite my tongue. Both challenge me to find a balance. It is a sweet brutality we practice here, a stark and loving dispassion.

I look at abortion as if I am standing on a cliff with a telescope, gazing at some great vista. I can sweep the horizon with both eyes, survey the scene in all its distance and size. Or I can put my eye to the lens and focus on the small details, suddenly so close. In abortion the absolute must always be tempered by the contextual, because both are real, both valid, both hard. How can we do this? How can we refuse? Each abortion is a measure of our failure to protect, to nourish our own. Each basin I empty is a promise—but a promise broken a long time ago.

I grew up on the great promise of birth control. Like many women my age, I took the pill as soon as I was sexually active. To risk pregnancy when it was so easy to avoid seemed stupid, and my contraceptive success, as it were, was part of the promise of social enlightenment. But birth control fails, far more frequently than laboratory trials predict. Many of our clients take the pill; its failure to protect them is a shocking realization. We have clients who have been sterilized, whose husbands have had vasectomies; each one is a statistical misfit, fine print come to life. The anger and shame of these women I hold in one hand, and the basin in the other. The distance between the two, the length I pace and try to measure, is the size of an abortion.

The procedure is disarmingly simple. Women are surprised, as though the mystery of conception, a dark and hidden genesis, requires an elaborate finale. In the first trimester of pregnancy, it's a mere few minutes of vacuuming, a neat tidying up. I give a woman a small yellow Valium, and when it has begun to relax her, I lead her into the back, into bareness, the stirrups. The doctor reaches in her, opening the narrow tunnel to the uterus with a succession of slim, smooth bars of steel. He inserts a plastic tube and hooks it to a hose on the machine. The woman is framed against white paper that crackles as she moves, the light bright in her eyes. Then the machine rumbles low and loud in the small windowless room; the doctor moves the tube back and forth with an efficient rhythm, and the long tail of it fills with blood that spurts and stumbles along into a jar. He is usually finished in a few minutes. They are long minutes for the woman; her uterus frequently reacts to its abrupt emptying with a powerful, unceasing cramp, which cuts off the blood vessels and enfolds the irritated, bleeding tissue.

I am learning to recognize the shadows that cross the faces of the women I hold. While the doctor works between her spread legs, the paper drape hiding his intent expression, I stand beside the table. I hold the woman's hands in mine, resting them just below her ribs. I watch her eyes, finger her necklace, stroke her hair. I ask about her job, her family; in a haze she answers me; we chatter, faces close, eyes meeting and sliding apart.

I watch the shadows that creep up unnoticed and suddenly darken her face as she screws up her features and pushes a tear out each side to slide down her cheeks. I have learned to anticipate the quiver of chin, the rapid intake of breath and the surprising sobs that rise soon after the machine starts to drum. I know this is when the cramp deepens, and the tears are partly the tears that follow pain—the sharp, childish crying when one bumps one's head on a cabinet door. But a well of woe seems to open beneath many women when they hear that thumping sound. The anticipation of the moment has finally come to fruit; the moment has arrived when the loss is no longer an imagined one. It has come true.

I am struck by the sameness and I am struck every day by the variety here—how this commonplace dilemma can so display the differences of women. A twenty-one-year-old woman, unemployed, uneducated, without family, in the fifth month of her fifth pregnancy. A forty-two-year-old mother of teenagers, shocked by her condition, refusing to tell her husband. A twenty-three-year-old mother of two having her seventh abortion, and many women in their thirties having their first. Some are stoic, some hysterical, a few giggle uncontrollably, many cry.

I talk to a sixteen-year-old uneducated girl who was raped. She has gonorrhea. She describes blinding headaches, attacks of breathlessness, nausea. "Sometimes I feel like two different people," she tells me with a calm smile, "and I talk to myself."

I pull out my plastic models. She listens patiently for a time, and then holds her hands wide in front of her stomach.

"When's the baby going to go up into my stomach?" she asks.

I blink. "What do you mean?"

"Well," she says, still smiling, "when women get so big, isn't the baby in your stomach? Doesn't it hatch out of an egg there?"

My first question in an interview is always the same. As I walk down the hall with the woman, as we get settled in chairs and I glance through her files, I am trying to gauge her, to get a sense of the words, and the tone, I should use. With some I joke, with others I chat, sometimes I fall into a brisk, business-like patter. But I ask every woman, "Are you sure you want to have an abortion?" Most nod with grim knowing smiles. "Oh, yes," they sigh. Some seek forgiveness, offer excuses. Occasionally a woman will flinch and say, "Please don't use that word."

Later I describe the procedure to come, using care with my language. I don't say "pain" any more than I would say "baby." So many are afraid to ask how much it will hurt. "My sister told me—" I hear. "A friend of mine said—" and the dire expectations unravel. I prick the index finger of a woman for a drop of blood to test, and as the tiny lancet approaches the skin she averts her eyes, holding her trembling hand out to me and jumping at my touch.

It is when I am holding a plastic uterus in one hand, a suction tube in the other, moving them together in imitation of the scrubbing to come, that women ask the most secret question. I am speaking in a matter-of-fact voice about "the tissue" and "the contents" when the woman suddenly catches my eye and asks, "How big is the baby now?" These words suggest a quiet need for a definition of the boundaries being drawn. It isn't so odd, after all, that she feels relief when I describe the growing bud's bulbous shape, its miniature nature. Again I gauge, and sometimes lie a little, weaseling around its infantile features until its clinging power slackens.

But when I look in the basin, among the curdlike blood clots, I see an elfin thorax, attenuated, its pencilline ribs all in parallel rows with tiny knobs of spine rounding upwards. A translucent arm and hand swim beside.

A sleepy-eyed girl, just fourteen, watched me with a slight and goofy smile all through her abortion. "Does it have little feet and little fingers and all?" she'd asked earlier. When the suction was over she sat up woozily at the end of the table and murmured, "Can I see it?" I shook my head firmly.

"It's not allowed," I told her sternly, because I knew she didn't really want to see what was left. She accepted this statement of authority, and a shadow of confused relief crossed her plain, pale face.

Privately, even grudgingly, my colleagues might admit the power of abortion to provoke emotion. But they seem to prefer the broad view and disdain the telescope. Abortion is a matter of choice, privacy, control. Its uncertainty lies in specific cases: retarded women and girls too young to give consent for surgery, women who are ill or hostile or psychotic. Such common dilemmas are met with both compassion and impatience: they slow things down. We are too busy to chew over ethics. One person might discuss certain concerns, behind closed doors, or describe a particularly disturbing dream. But generally there is to be no ambivalence.

Every day I take calls from women who are annoyed that we cannot see them, cannot do their abortion today, this morning, now. They argue the price, demand that we stay after hours to accommodate their job or class schedule. Abortion is so routine that one expects it to be like a manicure: quick, cheap, and painless.

Still, I've cultivated a certain disregard. It isn't negligence, but I don't always pay attention. I couldn't be here if I tried to judge each case on its merits; after all, we do over a hundred abortions a week. At some point each individual in this line of work draws a boundary and adheres to it. For one physician the boundary is a particular week of gestation; for another, it is a certain number of repeated abortions. But these boundaries can be fluid too: one physician overruled his own limit to abort a mature but severely malformed fetus. For me, the limit is allowing my clients to carry their own burden, shoulder the responsibility themselves. I shoulder the burden of trying not to judge them.

This city has several "crisis pregnancy centers" advertised in the Yellow Pages. They are small offices staffed by volunteers, and they offer free pregnancy testing, glossy photos of dead fetuses, and movies. I had a client recently whose mother is active in the anti-abortion movement. The young woman went to the local crisis center and was told that the doctor would make her touch her dismembered baby, that the pain would be the most horrible she could imagine, and that she might, after an abortion, never to able to have children. All lies. They called her at home and at work, over and over and over, but she had been wise enough to give a false name. She came to us a fugitive. We who do abortions are marked, by some, as impure. It's dirty work.

When a deliveryman comes to the sliding glass window by the reception desk and tilts a box toward me, I hesitate. I read the packing slip, assess the shape and weight of the box in light of its supposed contents. We request familiar faces. The doors are carefully locked; I have learned to half glance around at bags and boxes, looking for a telltale sign. I register with security when I arrive, and I am careful not to bang a door. We are all a little on edge here.

Concern about size and shape seem to be natural, and so is the relief that follows. We make the powerful assumption that the fetus is different from us, and even when we admit the similarities, it is too simplistic to be seduced by form alone. But the form is enormously potent—humanoid, powerless, palm-sized, and pure, it evokes an almost fierce tenderness when viewed simply as what it appears to be. But appearance, and even potential, aren't enough. The fetus, in becoming itself, can ruin others; it utter dependence has a sinister side. When I am struck in the moment by the contents in the basin, I am careful to remember the context, to note the tearful teenager and the woman sighing with something more than relief. One kind of question, though, I find considerably trickier.

"Can you tell what it is?" I am asked, and this means gender. This question is asked by couples, not women alone. Always couples would abort a girl and keep a boy. I have been asked about twins, and even if I could tell what race the father was.

An eighteen-year-old woman with three daughters brought her husband to the interview. He glared first at me, then at his wife, as he sank lower and lower in his chair, picking his teeth with a toothpick. He interrupted a conversation with his wife to ask if I could tell whether the baby would be a boy or a girl. I told him I could not.

"Good," he replied in a slow and strangely malevolent voice, " 'cause if it was a boy I'd wring her neck."

In a literal sense, abortion exists because we are able to ask such questions, able to assign a value to the fetus which can shift with changing circumstances. If the human bond to a child were as primitive and unflinchingly narrow as that of other animals, there would be no abortion. There would be no abortion because there would be nothing more important than caring for the young and perpetuating the species, no reason for sex but to make babies. I sense this sometimes, this wordless organic duty, when I do ultrasounds.

We do ultrasound, a sound-wave test that paints a faint, gray picture of the fetus, whenever we're uncertain of gestation. Age is measured by the width of the skull and confirmed by the length of the femur or thighbone; we speak of a pregnancy as being a certain "femur length" in weeks. The usual concern is whether a pregnancy is within the legal limit for an abortion. Women this far along have bellies which swell out round and tight like trim muscles. When they lie flat, the mound rises softly above the hips, pressing the umbilicus upward.

It takes practice to read an ultrasound picture, which is grainy and etched as though in strokes of charcoal. But suddenly a rapid rhythmic motion appears—the beating heart. Nearby is a soft oval, scratched with lines—the skull.

The leg is harder to find, and then suddenly the fetus moves, bobbing in the surf. The skull turns away, an arm slides across the screen, the torso rolls. I know the weight of a baby's head on my shoulder, the whisper of lips on ears, the delicate curve of a fragile spine in my hand. I know how heavy and correct a newborn cradled feels. The creature I watch in secret requires nothing from me but to be left alone, and that is precisely what won't be done.

These inadvertently made beings are caught in a twisting web of motive and desire. They are at least inconvenient, sometimes quite literally dangerous in the womb, but most often they fall somewhere in between—consequences never quite believed in come to roost. Their virtue rises and falls outside their own nature: they become only what we make them. A fetus created by accident is the most absolute kind of surprise. Whether the blame lies in a failed IUD, a slipped condom, or a false impression of safety, that fetus is a thing whose creation has been actively worked against. Its existence is an error. I think this is why so few women, even late in a pregnancy, will consider giving a baby up for adoption. To do so means making the fetus real—imagining it as something whole and outside oneself. The decision to terminate a pregnancy is sometimes so difficult and confounding that it creates an enormous demand for immediate action. The decision is a rejection; the pregnancy has become something to be rid of, a condition to be ended. It is a burden, a weight, a thing separate.

Women have abortions because they are too old, and too young, too poor, and too rich, too stupid, and too smart. I see women who berate themselves with violent emotions for their first and only abortion, and others who return three times, five times, hauling two or three children, who cannot remember to take a pill or where they put the diaphragm. We talk glibly about choice. But the choice for what? I see all the broken promises in lives lived like a series of impromptu obstacles. There are the sweet, light promises of love and intimacy, the glittering promise of education and progress, the warm promise of safe families, long years of innocence and community. And there is the promise of freedom: freedom from failure, from faithlessness. Freedom from biology. The early feminist defense of abortion asked many questions, but the one I remember is this: Is biology destiny? And the answer is yes, sometimes it is. Women who have the fewest choices of all exercise their right to abortion the most.

Oh, the ignorance. I take a woman to the back room and ask her to undress; a few minutes later I return and find her positioned discreetly behind a drape, still wearing underpants. "Do I have to take these off too?" she asks, a little shocked. Some swear they have not had sex, many do not know what a uterus is, how sperm and egg meet, how sex makes babies. Some late seekers do not believe themselves pregnant; they believe themselves *impregnable*. I was chastised when I began this job for referring to some clients as girls: it is a feminist heresy. They come so young, snapping gum, sockless and sneakered, and their shakily applied eyeliner smears when they cry. I call them girls with maternal benignity. I cannot image them as mothers.

The doctor seats himself between the woman's thighs and reaches into the dilated opening of a five-month pregnant uterus. Quickly he grabs and crushes the fetus in several places, and the room is filled with a low clatter and snap of forceps, the click of the tanaculum, and a pulling, sucking sound. The paper crinkles as the drugged and sleepy woman shifts, the nurse's low, honey-brown voice explains each step in delicate words.

I have fetus dreams, we all do here: dreams of abortions one after the other; of buckets of blood splashed on the walls; trees full of crawling fetuses. I dreamed that two men grabbed me and began to drag me away. "Let's do an abortion," they said with a sickening leer, and I began to scream, plunged into a vision of sucking, scraping pain, of being spread and torn by impartial instruments that do only what they are bidden. I woke from this dream barely able to breathe and thought of kitchen tables and coat hangers, knitting needles striped with blood, and women all alone clutching a pillow in their teeth to keep the screams from piercing the apartment-house walls. Abortion is the narrowest edge between kindness and cruelty. Done as well as it can be, it is still violence—merciful violence, like putting a suffering animal to death.

Maggie, one of the nurses, received a call at midnight not long ago. It was a woman in her twentieth week of pregnancy; the necessarily gradual process of cervical dilation begun the day before had stimulated labor, as it sometimes does. Maggie and one of the doctors met the woman at the office in the night. Maggie helped her onto the table, and as she lay down the fetus was delivered into Maggie's hands. When Maggie told me about it the next day, she cupped her hands into a small bowl—"It was just like a little kitten," she said softly, wonderingly. "Everything was still attached."

At the end of the day I clean out the suction jars, pouring blood into the sink, splashing the sides with flecks of tissue. From the sink rises a rich and humid smell, hot, earthy and moldering; it is the smell of something recently alive beginning to decay. I take care of the plastic tub on the floor, filled with pieces too big to be trusted to the trash. The law defines the contents of the bucket I hold protectively against my chest as "tissue." Some would say my complicity in filling that bucket gives me no right to call it anything else. I slip the tissue gently into a bag and place it in the freezer, to be burned at another time. Abortion requires of me an entirely new set of assumptions. It requires a willingness to live with conflict, fearlessness, and grief. As I close the freezer door, I imagine a world where this won't be necessary, and then return to the world where it it. ✒

SUGGESTIONS FOR WRITING

1. Analyze Tisdale's attitude toward abortion and discuss the ways in which she makes her feelings clear. In what ways is she torn by what she sees and what she does?

2. Tisdale's article uses graphic descriptions. Examine your reactions to them. Why do you think she included them in her essay? What effect did they have on you and your attitude toward abortion?

3. What attitudes does Tisdale exhibit toward the women who come to the clinic for help?

4. How does the fact that the author is a woman increase the article's impact? Is there a conflict between Tisdale's feelings as a nurse or as a woman and what she does for a living?

MY ABORTION

Deborah Salazar

*The decision to have an abortion is not an easy one, and the reasons for ter-minating a pregnancy are as varied as the women who do so. Pro-life advo-cates are convinced that abortion is murder. **Deborah Salazar's** essay describes her experience at an abortion clinic that was being picketed by pro-life demonstrators. Salazar is a poet who lives in Baton Rouge, Louisiana.*

The procedure itself was the easiest part. A friend had told me to close my eyes and think about anything, think about Donald Duck—sweet and useless ad-vice, I thought at the time—but when I heard the machine come on and the doctor say, "The cervix is slanted at a right angle, this could be a problem; okay, honey, *relax*," I thought, Donald Duck, Donald Duck, Donald Duck, Donald Duck. I will never be able to watch another Donald Duck cartoon without thinking about my abortion, but I went through the experience feeling pretty calm and entitled. Twenty-seven years old and pregnant for the first time in my life. God bless America, I thought, I sure as hell want a cheap, legal, safe abortion.

After I learned that I was pregnant, I started practicing a necessary detach-ment. The Supreme Court was due to hand down its *Webster* decision any day, and the usual mobs of protesters around women's clinics were doubling in size. I got up before dawn on the fifteenth of June and packed a paper bag with a sweater and socks (because the receptionist said it would be cold inside the clinic) and maxi pads. I wanted to get there as soon as the doors opened, before most of the cross-waving, sign-carrying, chanting, singing protesters showed up. When I pulled into the clinic parking lot with my friend Beth, I saw only two people standing on the curb: a woman, dressed all in black, and a man. As we got closer, I saw that the woman was about my age, with straight black hair and pale eyes turned skyward. She was moaning the words, "Don't kill me, Mommy, don't kill me."

The man and the woman followed our car until it stopped at the door. I stepped out, and the man stood in front of me. He was tall, wearing a suit and tie and singing, "Jesus loves the little children." I laughed in his face. Strange. Three years ago I had worked as a volunteer escort at this very clinic, and I'd always been so solemn with these people. I never would've expected to laugh today. The man obviously hadn't expected me to laugh either. He got angry. "Lesbian!" he called after me as I walked into the clinic. "You're a lesbian. That's why you hate babies!" A tall young man wearing an official clinic-escort T-shirt was standing at the threshold. "Sorry about this," he muttered as I passed by. I was still laughing. "I wish I were a lesbian," I said a little hysteri-cally. "I wouldn't be pregnant." And then I was inside the clinic.

I knew the routine. I took my forms and my plastic cup. I went directly to the bathroom. I could hear the protesters while I was in the bathroom. I could hear them the whole time I was in the clinic. The chanting was discontinuous, but it was louder every time it started up. "Murderers! Murderers!" I could hear them in the dressing room, in the weigh-in room, in counseling, in recovery, although I don't remember if I heard them in the procedure room itself. I was told later that my encounter with the protesters had been relatively un-dramatic; one escort said that these days he was seeing protesters trying to hold car doors shut while women fought to get out.

After I turned in my urine cup, I sat back in the waiting room and started filling out forms. One of them was a personal questionnaire that included the question, "What method of birth control were you using at the time you got pregnant?" I thought about lying for a second before I checked the box beside "none." One of the protestors outside had started playing a tape of a baby cry-ing. I signed my name over and over. Yes, I understand the risks involved, yes, I understand that the alternatives to abortion are birth and adoption. I wanted to do more—I wanted to fill out a page or so explaining why I had chosen to do this. I wanted to explain to someone that I was a responsible person; you see, ladies and gentlemen, I never had sex without condoms unless I was having my period; I got pregnant during my period, isn't there something I could sign swearing to that? I had a three-day affair with a friend, I'm broke and unem-ployed, I can't give up a baby for adoption, I can't afford to be pregnant while I look for a job.

In counseling, I was asked why I'd gone off the pill, and I didn't hesitate to respond, "I can get rid of an accidental pregnancy. I can't get rid of cancer." In the lounge room where I sat in my dressing gown before going in to see the doc-tor, there was a tiny television (Pee-wee Herman was on) and a table with mag-azines (Cosmopolitan, Vogue, American Baby). The room was already filled to capacity, all twelve chairs taken, when the little bowhead came in. She couldn't have been more than seventeen, wearing only her gown and a very big white satin bow in her hair. She was a beauty. She looked like she belonged on a homecoming float. She had been crying. "I hate them," she announced, drop-ping her shopping bag of clothes on the floor. "They don't have to say the things they say. Makes me want to go out there and shoot them with a gun."

"You can't hear them that well in here, honey," one of the older women said. "You can watch the cartoons."

"You know what one of them called my mama?" the beauty said. "Called her a slut, an unchristian woman. My mama yelled back that I got raped by a priest, that's how come I'm here." Stares. The bowhead picked up her shopping bag and leaned against the wall. She spoke again in a quieter voice. "I didn't really get raped by a priest. My mama just said that."

The doctor was late that morning. Outside, the chants were getting louder, competing with Pee-wee Herman, who was on full blast. The protesters were singing a hymn when my name was called. I walked down a short hallway in my bare feet, and then liquid Valium injected directly into my left arm made everything after that feel like it was taking place on another planet. I remember that the doctor was wearing a dark red surgical outfit and that it looked pretty gruesome—I wished he'd worn the traditional pale blue or green. I remember that the Valium made me want to laugh and I didn't want to laugh because I was afraid I'd wiggle, and I'd been warned *not* to wiggle unless I wanted my uterus perforated. I'd been at the clinic six hours already, preparing for this little operation that would take only five minutes. I remember that after the machine came on, it seemed like less than five minutes. I remember that it hurt and that I was amazed at how empty, relieved, and not pregnant I felt as soon as it was over. The cramps that followed were painful but not terribly so; I could feel my uterus contracting, trying to collapse back to its former size. I was led by a nurse into a dark room, where I sat on a soft mat in a soft chair and bled for a while. I closed my eyes. The woman in the next seat was sobbing softly. I knew it was the blond with the white bow in her hair. I reached over and took her hand in mine. The Valium made me feel as though we were both wearing gloves. Her hand was so still I wondered if she knew I was there, but the sobbing grew softer and softer and eventually it just stopped. 🖋

SUGGESTIONS FOR WRITING

1. Analyze your responses to Salazar's article.

2. Although Salazar makes it clear that she is taking the responsibility for the results of her sexual activity when she says that she chose an abortion over the pill, she makes no mention of the man's responsibility who impregnated her. Discuss men's responsibility for preventing conception.

3. In what ways did the demonstrators attempt to influence the women coming to the clinic for their abortions? Explore your responses to their methods; do you agree with the tactics they used? Why?

ABORTION, LIES AND VIDEOTAPE

Thomas H. Stahel

In America, the debate over a woman's right to have an abortion continues to grow more heated as the Supreme Court hears and rules on relevant cases. One activist anti-abortion group, Operation Rescue, founded by Randall Terry, does more than simply lobby for changes in the law that would make abortion once again illegal in this country. This organization attempts, through propaganda, picketing and other forms of civil disobedience, to prevent women seeking abortions as well as doctors and staff from entering clinics where this procedure is performed.

Thomas H. Stahel (b. 1938) is a Jesuit Roman Catholic priest who, in the following essay, examines his responses to a meeting of Operation Rescue that he attended in New York City.

On the Sunday morning after Gov. Bob Martinez failed to get more restrictive abortion laws in Florida, I watched him with admiration on CNN's Newsmaker program. The Governor said the struggle would go on because it is a matter of conscience, not political expediency. One of two political consultants invited by Newsmaker to comment on the Florida story said the pro-life movement was going down to defeat because pro-lifers have used "thug tactics" and "have intimidated and harmed people." This kind of language, inaccurate as commentary on a Governor's legitimate actions, is equally untruthful when applied to the members of Operation Rescue, presumably the "things" who block doorways of abortion clinics as a nonviolent form of resistance to the killing going on inside.

The night before this Newsmaker program I attended an Operation Rescue rally in the Glad Tidings Tabernacle, on Manhattan's West 33rd Street, where the emphasis was on prayer, nonviolence and conversion rather than pushing people around. In fact, the only noticeable commotion, as my friends and I approached the pink neon cross over the church entrance, was in a group of pro-abortionists behind police barricades who were shouting: "Two, four, six, eight, separate the church and state."

Within the Evangelical setting of the tabernacle, the evening's most memorable speaker was Father Benedict F. Groeschel, a Franciscan, whose accent was pure New York and whose message was pure St. Francis. It was not the movement's task to judge or condemn, he said, but to pray, persuade and convert, all of which would be impossible apart from "our divine Saviour"—in that setting, could any other expression have sounded more Catholic? According to Luke's Gospel, Father Groeschel reminded the rally, the Lord had said at the time of His execution, "Father, forgive them for they know not what they do," and those words ought to be the watchword of any rescue.

Randall Terry, the founder of Operation Rescue, was supposed to be on hand, but he is in an Atlanta jail. So, on a large-screen television in the main aisle of the church, the rally watched a videotape that Mr. Terry had made in anticipation of his being unavailable. In preaching style, Mr. Terry is as different from Father Groeschel as Revelation is from Luke. Apocalyptic and sectarian, he begins with a shrewd question, "Who in the United States would have thought, just 35 years ago, in the time of Eisenhower, that by 1989 we would have killed 25 million babies?" and he ends with a speculation: "My friends, 35 years from now, unless we wake up, we may be living in a secularist state that put Christians in concentration camps." I balk here and at other places in his sermon. Still, I recognize that Randall Terry is on to a frightening truth, better expressed by a friend who participated in a rescue last year—"If people can accept abortion, they can accept anything"—and I recognize I have more in common with Mr. Terry in this matter than with those who regard him as a laughable throwback to an age that thought abortion sinful.

Yet, when another preacher asks those who are going on the rescue to stand up, I remain seated. I admire those who stand—family men and women, nuns, Franciscans, some men who I bet are priests in mufti (like me)—and I am grateful for both their conviction and their dedication to nonviolent persuasion. But I do not think it is "saving babies," as they say, because the woman who wants an abortion will simply come back the next day or go to another clinic. I know that if the rescue persuades even one woman to rethink her abortion decision, that is significant, not just for her, but especially for the baby. But if I had a sister or niece or friend who was determined to get an abortion, despite my plea, would I physically block her entry into the clinic? Would I want a stranger to?

If I hesitate to sit in clinic doorways, I can at least block—I decide in the Glad Tidings Tabernacle—as much of the phony pro-abortion rhetoric as possible. The pro-abortion people can seize the moral high ground, as they are constantly attempting to do, only by covering up reality with euphemisms. Abortion (killing) becomes "choice," etc. Just now Broadway audiences are laughing at Larry Gelbart's new show "Mastergate," a satire on the Iran/Contra hearings, whose bite comes from disgust with political and moral doubletalk. This corruption of language would be funny in the real world, too, if it were not so deadly—which is, of course, Larry Gelbart's witty point.

Here are some of the euphemisms that need to be unmasked. They were rehearsed yet again during the week of the Florida story as if they were unanswerable arguments, and that is what is unacceptable.

"A woman has a right to control her reproductive destiny." Indeed she has. The question is, always has been, whether the means used to this end are moral. Killing what is in the womb (fetus, child, baby, in any case a human being in development) is not normally a legitimate means. There are other ways that people can control their destiny.

"It must be the woman's choice." Of course. The woman who does *not* get an abortion also chooses. The question is, what does she choose? The infinitive "to choose" makes no sense here without knowing the object of the choice—

either bearing or aborting the child. In fact, what pro-abortionists choose is an act of violence. But since "violence" is not a good word in our society, they prefer to speak merely of "choice," as if it were undifferentiated, made no difference. It makes a difference to the developing human being in the womb. Calling these people "pro-choice" may be polite, but it is not the accurate description of their preference, which is "pro-abortion."

"This is a private choice in which government has no right to intrude." Well, I should have thought that a choice to end the life of a distinct and developing human being was the opposite of "private." After all, government now regulates other lesser and apparently private choices that involve the lives of others—smoking, for example. But the pro-abortionists who urge their eccentric view of "privacy" are not consistent. They want government to keep out, but they also want government to pay for abortions. I say, if the Faye Wattletons and Kate Michelmans of this world, along with rich and powerful people like the editorial writers of *The New York Times* think that killing the black and brown babies of the poor is a good idea, then let them pay for it. They can afford it. Let's not enlist government, which is supposed to represent all of us, in this ghastly and racist project.

Just as the Operation Rescue rally at the Glad Tidings Tabernacle was ending, a Catholic participant got up and said he would not be satisfied until Cardinal John O'Connor got arrested along with him and his friends at a rescue. Which leads me to end these remarks on rhetoric with a word of advice to my friends in the movement and to the Cardinal himself (who suggested in a homily on Respect Life Sunday that he had considered such a possibility): It's a bad idea. First, because there are many Catholics and other Christians who are opposed to abortion but doubtful about rescues as the best means to oppose it. Second, because there is already too much confused rhetoric suggesting that opposition to abortion is a religious choice and nothing more. Pro-abortionists would like to foster this idea because it enables them to sidestep questions of morality that may be influenced by religious belief but that must be faced whether one is religious or not. If the Cardinal were to be involved in a rescue, the confusion would only be compounded. I thank the friends who took me to this rally, and other friends who also have participated in a rescue, and I say to them: I hope this article helps. 🖋

SUGGESTIONS FOR WRITING

1. Stahel explores his personal conflict regarding the behavior of Operation Rescue when he asks," . . . if I had a sister or niece or friend who was determined to get an abortion, despite my plea, would I physically block her entry into the clinic? Would I want a stranger to?" For him, when the political becomes the personal, right and wrong grow fuzzy. Explore his dilemma and your reactions to it.

2. In the latter section of this essay, Stahel discusses how language can hide what an issue is really about when he discusses euphemisms. React to these

ideas either as they relate to the abortion question or to another issue that is important to you such as racial prejudice or sexual discrimination.

3. Civil disobedience, breaking the law for a higher moral or ethical purpose, is an American tradition. Respond to this phenomenon with regard to the activities of Operation Rescue.

8

AIDS

In 1981, strange illnesses began showing up in America among gay men. At first, no one was certain how these diseases were being spread nor precisely what group of people was at risk. These deadly diseases have come to be known as acquired immune deficiency syndrome, or AIDS.

In the early 1980s, when AIDS first appeared among the gay male population, the gay liberation movement in America had gained great momentum; many men and women were living openly gay lives and forming productive communities. Such openness offended people who consider homosexuality to be depraved, and, to them, the AIDS epidemic appeared to be a just punishment. AIDS was looked upon as "gay man's cancer"; it couldn't happen to straight people. That the epidemic next struck intravenous drug users, prostitutes, and members of minority groups seemed to reinforce that attitude. Yet in Africa, where scientists now believe the disease originated, AIDS is primarily a heterosexual disease that, by some estimations, threatens to destroy whole populations within the next decade or two.

Those who have been affected by AIDS assert that the United States government was very slow to react to the epidemic. When the Centers for Disease Control began reporting early incidences of AIDS, little was done to investigate the origins of the disease. Yet in 1982, when seven people died from cyanide-laced Tylenol capsules, public officials worked relentlessly to track down the cause of the poisoning, and the public outcry and media attention were vigorous. That was not the case for AIDS; the media apparently were reluctant to follow up on a story that dealt with the deaths of gays. Not until movie star Rock Hudson died from AIDS in 1985 did the media begin giving the epidemic wide coverage. Although the Reagan administration had planned to cut allocations for AIDS research in 1985, after Hudson died, they significantly increased AIDS-related spending.

In 1986, Surgeon General C. Everett Koop released his "Report on Acquired Immune Deficiency." Koop, well aware of the dangers AIDS posed to the "average" American, outlined a wide-ranging campaign to educate citizens about how AIDS is transmitted and how to avoid contracting it; in short, he talked about "safe sex." But his advice was not what many people wanted to hear; they preferred to think AIDS was a nasty disease that only nasty people caught. In May 1988, the U.S. Public Health Service distributed an AIDS awareness guide to every household in America. Today, public service announcements are broadcast regularly on radio and TV, and in many parts of the country the information campaign extends to billboards, posters in public schools, and work by volunteers. And basketball star Magic Johnson's 1991 public disclosure of his HIV-positive status brought AIDS to the attention of most Americans.

A 1988 report of the World Health Organization estimated the number of persons suffering from AIDS worldwide to be 250,000; just a year later, more than 100,000 Americans alone had full-blown AIDS. By the end of 1990, 100,000 Americans had died of AIDS, 31,000 in that single year. In light of these numbers, some people are calling for mandatory testing of at-risk populations. In California, for example, a 1986 initiative called for quarantining of and discrimination against AIDS patients; voters defeated it two to one. The epidemic poses potential problems for health-care facilities, many of which will not treat people who cannot pay for their care. Insurance companies make getting, and sometimes maintaining, health insurance difficult for persons diagnosed as having the human immunodeficiency virus, or HIV, even though these persons show no signs of full-blown AIDS. Thousands of HIV-positive babies face only a short life; many people—children and adults who are in the terminal stages of their illness—have nowhere to go. Often abandoned *by their families, these people are feared not only by those who formerly loved them but by the doctors and other health-care professionals who care for them as they die.*

AIDS is not a pretty disease; it disfigures the body and can destroy the mind. Because of the early association with homosexuality and drug abuse, AIDS has earned a special distinction for its victims: They are blamed for their illness, much in the same way that a rape victim is blamed for being assaulted. The essays in this section offer a variety of responses to AIDS.

I Remember

John Doe

The following piece by an anonymous contributor to the Village Voice, *a liberal New York weekly newspaper, reflects the growing public awareness of the AIDS epidemic and people's changing attitudes as they began to realize that AIDS would be something more than a local epidemic.*

I remember when people called it "gay" cancer.

I remember when everyone thought you got it from poppers.

I remember dinner with a friend whose doctor had told him "tops" don't have to worry.

I remember when the acronym hadn't yet been coined.

I remember when a friend whose father ran a government health agency had appendicitis and how his father wouldn't let the doctors transfuse him, and wondering what he knew that no one else did.

I remember when some of the early ones got sick all the time and made jokes about being rundown, then died without knowing what hit them.

I remember wondering, much later, whether they'd been better off.

I remember seeing R. in a restaurant after he was diagnosed and being amazed at his healthy complexion.

I remember hearing that R. had enrolled in a drug test that involved a placebo.

I remember hearing that a week after the protocol ended R. came down with pneumocystis.

I remember keeping up with each generation of acronyms: GRID, AIDS, SIDA, HIV.

I remember running into B. one year on the subway, and hearing his story about taking time off to help an ex-boyfriend die.

I remember running into R. another year at the Palladium and listening to his story about taking time off to help his brother die.

I remember wild rumors about guys who went crazy when they found out, and had sex with anyone they could pick up.

I remember thinking those stories were untrue.

I remember attending a GMHC buddy meeting and feeling angry when the buddies criticized "clients" who went on having sex.

I remember when I stopped having sex.

I remember when I started censoring fantasies that involved unsafe practices.

I remember when I made a list of all my sex partners and tried to calculate the odds.

I remember thinking I was lucky they all fit on a list.

I remember realizing that it was much more of a crapshoot than I could figure.

I remember the first year the subject came up once in every conversation.

I remember the first year the occasional *Times* obit became one and then more and then too many a day.

I remember when the obits began to mention unrelated survivors as life partners or longtime companions.

I remember how it incensed me when journalists reported that the disease hadn't yet spread to the "general population."

I remember my ignorant surprise when women began to get it, even women who didn't use drugs.

I remembering wondering what happened to the Haitians (and to Haitian jokes).

I remember the syphilis theory, the swine fever theory, the germ warfare theory, and that crazy guy who postered the city with paranoid screeds about the CIA.

I remember how relieved F. was when the thing on his face turned out to be an ordinary melanoma.

I remember how friends would casually palpate their glands while we talked.

I remember when N.'s shrink forbade him to do that.

I remember D. getting sick and his best friend saying it was all his boyfriend's fault. "I blame him," she told me. "He was the promiscuous one."

I remember trying to remember that no matter what you thought you knew about people, you never truly knew what they did for sex.

I remember thinking that I'd have to start considering junkies as human beings.

I remember when my AA friend began to report that it was "sweeping the rooms."

I remember when my former-drug-abuser friend told me she thought she was "ARC-ing."

I remember the whole year my officemate spent shouting at doctors on the phone while his life partner was dying.

I remember everyone around him pretending not to hear.

I remember the horror stories, the miracle cures, the crystal cures, the religious conversions, the radical diets.

I remember when I finally took the test, carrying a vial of my blood to Bellevue on the Second Avenue bus.

I remember my doctor's failure to warn me that using a fake name (like the one I'm using here) was best when you were tested for HIV.

I remember not being able to get life insurance later on.

I remember my doctor's chipper attitude when he said I'd make a good candidate for AZT.

I remember bigots at the Washington march shouting "AIDS is the cure."

I remember calling it "Large A" or "the A-word."

I remember the first time I recognized a KS lesion.

I remember catching myself saying "victims" sometimes.

I remember thinking you were safe after five years, then seven, then 10, and then reading in the *Times* that the virus could escape detection in another set of cells.

I remember dealing with that.

SUGGESTIONS FOR WRITING

1. Try to recall your introduction to the AIDS epidemic. Did you learn of it first as a disease affecting only gay men? If so, what was your reaction and that of your friends, teachers, and family? If not, what group or groups of people did you perceive as threatened by the disease? How did that awareness affect you? Your friends?

2. Examine the attitude behind the statement "AIDS is the cure," which Doe mentions toward the conclusion of this piece. Examine your reactions to that statement.

3. Public health experts predict that college students will be the next group to develop widespread AIDS. Respond to this prediction.

4. In what ways does Doe let you know that concern about AIDS pervades our culture? What key issues do you see relating to AIDS in the 1990s?

TALKING AIDS TO DEATH

Randy Shilts

Public reaction to the AIDS epidemic in this country has changed over time. At first people willingly believed that having AIDS or ARC (AIDS-related complex), or testing positive for the human immunodeficiency virus (HIV), was an issue of concern only to gay males. As time passed and other groups were also found to be at risk, people have become more aware that AIDS might someday directly affect their own lives. Now that people know AIDS can be contracted as the result of one casual sexual encounter, many people feel more compassion for AIDS patients. Others continue to resist a more extensive effort to develop new treatments and a vaccine.

*Randy Shilts (b. 1951), a national correspondent for the San Fran-*cisco Chronicle, *was the first openly gay mainstream journalist in California. Shilts writes frequently on gay issues and on the AIDS epidemic. His book* The Mayor of Castro Street: The Life and Times of Harvey Milk *(1982) not only provides a biography of assassinated San Francisco supervisor Harvey Milk, but it also chronicles the homosexual movement in San Francisco. In 1987, Shilts published the definitive history of the AIDS crisis in the United States:* And the Band Played On: Politics, People, and the AIDS Epidemic.

I'm talking to my friend Kit Herman when I notice a barely perceptible spot on the left side of his face. Slowly, it grows up his cheekbone, down to his chin, and forward to his mouth. He talks on cheerfully, as if nothing is wrong, and I'm amazed that I'm able to smile and chat on, too, as if nothing were there. His eyes become sunken; his hair turns gray; his ear is turning purple now, swelling into a carcinomatous cauliflower, and still we talk on. He's dying in front of me. He'll be dead soon, if nothing is done.

Dead soon, if nothing is done.

"Excuse me, Mr. Shilts, I asked if you are absolutely sure, if you can categorically state that you definitely cannot get AIDS from a mosquito."

I forget the early-morning nightmare and shift into my canned response. All my responses are canned now. I'm an AIDS talk-show jukebox. Press the button, any button on the AIDS question list, and I have my canned answer ready. Is this Chicago or Detroit?

"Of course you can get AIDS from a mosquito," I begin.

Here, I pause for dramatic effect. In that brief moment, I can almost hear the caller murmur, "I *knew* it."

"If you have unprotected anal intercourse with an infected mosquito, you'll get AIDS," I continue. "Anything short of that and you won't."

The talk-show host likes the answer. All the talk-show hosts like my answers because they're short, punchy, and to the point. Not like those boring doctors with long recitations of scientific studies so overwritten with maybes and qualifiers that they frighten more than they reassure an AIDS-hysteric public. I give good interview, talk-show producers agree. It's amazing, they say, how I always stay so cool and never lose my temper.

"Mr. Shilts, has there ever been a case of anyone getting AIDS from a gay waiter?"

"In San Francisco, I don't think they allow heterosexuals to be waiters. This fact proves absolutely that if you could get AIDS from a gay waiter, all northern California would be dead by now."

I gave that same answer once on a Bay Area talk show, and my caller, by the sound of her a little old lady, quickly rejoined: "What if that gay waiter took my salad back into the kitchen and ejaculated into my salad dressing? Couldn't I get AIDS then?"

I didn't have a pat answer for that one, and I still wonder at what this elderly caller thought went on in the kitchens of San Francisco restaurants. Fortunately, this morning's phone-in—in Chicago, it turned out—is not as imaginative.

"You know, your question reminds me of a joke we had in California a couple of years back," I told the caller. "How many heterosexual waiters in San Francisco does it take to screw in a light bulb? The answer is both of them."

The host laughs, the caller is silent. Next comes the obligatory question about whether AIDS can be spread through coughing.

I had written a book to change the world, and here I was on talk shows throughout America, answering questions about mosquitoes and gay waiters.

This wasn't exactly what I had envisioned when I began writing *And the Band Played On*. I had hoped to effect some fundamental changes. I really believed I could alter the performance on the institutions that had allowed AIDS to sweep through America unchecked.

AIDS had spread, my book attested, because politicians, particularly those in charge of federal-level response, had viewed the disease as a political issue, not an issue of public health—they deprived researchers of anything near the resources that were needed to fight it. AIDS had spread because government health officials consistently lied to the American people about the need for more funds, being more concerned with satisfying their political bosses and protecting their own jobs than with telling the truth and protecting the public health. And AIDS had spread because indolent news organizations shunned their responsibility to provide tough, adversarial reportage, instead basing stories largely on the Official Truth of government press releases. The response to AIDS was never even remotely commensurate with the scope of the problem.

I figured the federal government, finally exposed, would stumble over itself to accelerate the pace of AIDS research and put AIDS-prevention programs on an emergency footing. Once publicly embarrassed by the revelations of its years of shameful neglect, the media would launch serious investigative reporting on the epidemic. Health officials would step forward and finally lay bare the truth about how official disregard had cost this country hundreds of thousands of lives. And it would never happen again.

I was stunned by the "success" of my book. I quickly acquired all the trappings of bestsellerdom: 60 *Minutes* coverage of my "startling" revelations, a Book of the Month Club contract, a miniseries deal with NBC, translation into six languages, book tours on three continents, featured roles in move-star-studded AIDS fundraisers, regular appearances on network news shows, and hefty fees on the college lecture circuit. A central figure in my book became one of *People* magazines "25 Most Intriguing People of 1987," even though he had been dead for nearly four years, and the *Los Angeles Herald Examiner* pronounced me one of the "in" authors of 1988. The mayor of San Francisco even proclaimed my birthday last year "Randy Shilts Day."

And one warm summer day as I was sunning at a gay resort in the redwoods north of San Francisco, a well-toned, perfectly tanned young man slid into a chaise next to me and offered the ultimate testimony to my fifteen minutes of fame. His dark eyelashes rising and falling shyly, he whispered, "When I saw you on *Good Morning America* a couple weeks ago, I wondered what it would be like to go to bed with you."

"You're the world's first AIDS celebrity," enthused a friend at the World Health Organization, after hearing one of WHO's most eminent AIDS authorities say he would grant me an interview on one condition—that I autograph his copy of my book. "It must be great," he said.

It's not so great.

The bitter irony is, my role as an AIDS celebrity just gives me a more elevated promontory from which to watch the world make the same mistakes in the handling of the AIDS epidemic that I had hoped my work would help to change. When I return from network tapings and celebrity glad-handing, I come back to my home in San Francisco's gay community and see friends dying. The lesions spread from their cheeks to cover their faces, their hair falls out, they die slowly, horribly, and sometimes, suddenly, before anybody has a chance to know they're sick. They die in my arms and in my dreams, and nothing at all has changed.

Never before have I succeeded so well; never before have I failed so miserably.

I gave my first speech on the college lecture circuit at the University of California Los Angeles in January 1988. I told the audience that there were 50,000 diagnosed AIDS cases in the United States as of that week and that within a few months there would be more people suffering from this deadly disease in the U.S. than there were Americans killed during the Vietnam War. There were audible gasps. During the question-and-answer session, several students explained that they had heard that the number of AIDS cases in America was leveling off.

In the next speech, at the University of Tennessee, I decided to correct such misapprehension by adding the federal government's projections—the 270,000 expected to be dead or dying from AIDS in 1991, when the disease would kill more people than any single form of cancer, more than car accidents. When I spoke at St. Cloud State University in Minnesota three months later, I noted that the number of American AIDS cases had that week surpassed the Vietnam benchmark. The reaction was more a troubled murmur than a gasp.

By the time I spoke at New York City's New School for Social Research in June and there were 65,000 AIDS cases nationally, the numbers were changing so fast that the constant editing made my notes difficult to read. By then as many as 1,000 Americans a week were learning that they, too, had AIDS, or on the average, about one every fourteen minutes. There were new government projections to report, too: By 1993, some 450,000 Americans would be diagnosed with AIDS. In that year, one American will be diagnosed with the disease every thirty-six seconds. Again, I heard the gasps.

For my talk at a hospital administrators' conference in Washington in August, I started using little yellow stick-ons to update the numbers on my outline. That made it easier to read; there were now 72,000 AIDS cases. Probably this month, or next, I'll tell another college audience that the nation's AIDS case load has topped 100,000, and there will be gasps again.

The gasps always amaze me. Why are they surprised? In epidemics, people get sick and die. That's what epidemics do to people and that's why epidemics are bad.

When Kit Herman was diagnosed with AIDS on May 13, 1986, his doctor leaned over his hospital bed, took his hand, and assured him, "Don't worry, you're in time for AZT." The drug worked so well that all Kit's friends let themselves think he might make it. And we were bolstered by the National Institutes of Health's assurance that AZT was only the first generation of AIDS drugs, and that the hundreds of millions of federal dollars going into AIDS treatment research meant there would soon be a second and third generation of treatments to sustain life beyond AZT's effectiveness. Surely nothing was more important, considering the federal government's own estimates that between 1 and 1.5 million Americans were infected with the Human Immunodeficiency Virus (HIV), and virtually all would die within the next decade if nothing was done. The new drugs, the NIH assured everyone, were "in the pipeline," and government scientists were working as fast as they possibly could.

Despite my nagging, not one of dozens of public-affairs-show producers chose to look seriously into the development of those long-sought second and third generations of AIDS drugs. In fact, clinical trials of AIDS drugs were hopelessly stalled in the morass of bureaucracy at the NIH, but this story tip never seemed to cut it with producers. Clinical trials were not sexy. Clinical trials were boring.

I made my third Nightline appearance in January 1988 because new estimates had been released revealing that one in sixty-one babies born in New York City carried antibodies to the AIDS virus. And the link between those babies and the disease was intravenous drug use by one or both parents. Suddenly, junkies had become the group most likely to catch and spread AIDS through the heterosexual community. Free needles to junkies—now there was a sizzling television topic. I told the show's producers I'd talk about that, but that I was much more interested in the issue of AIDS treatments—which seemed most relevant to the night's program, since Ted Koppel's other guest was Dr. Anthony Fauci, associate NIH director for AIDS, and the Reagan administration's most visible AIDS official.

After fifteen minutes of talk on the ins and outs and pros and cons of free needles for intravenous drug users, I raised the subject of the pressing need for AIDS treatments. Koppel asked Fauci what was happening. The doctor launched into a discussion of treatments "in the pipeline" and how government scientists were working as fast as they possibly could.

I'd heard the same words from NIH officials for three years: drugs were in the pipeline. Maybe it was true, but when were they going to come out of their goddamn pipeline? Before I could formulate a polite retort to Fauci's stall, however, the segment was over, Ted was thanking us, and the red light on the camera had blipped off. Everyone seemed satisfied that the government was doing everything it possibly could to develop AIDS treatments.

Three months later, I was reading a week-old *New York Times* in Kit's room in the AIDS ward at San Francisco General Hospital. It was April, nearly two years after my friend's AIDS diagnosis. AZT had given him two years of nearly perfect health, but now its effect was wearing off and Kit had suffered his first major AIDS-related infection since his original bout with pneumonia—cryptococcal meningitis. The meningitis could be treated, we all knew, but the discovery of this insidious brain infection meant more diseases were likely to follow. And the long-promised second and third generations of AIDS drugs were still nowhere on the horizon.

While perusing the worn copy of the *Times*, I saw a story about Dr. Fauci's testimony at a congressional hearing. After making Fauci swear an oath to tell the truth, a subcommittee headed by Representative Ted Weiss of New York City asked why it was taking so long to get new AIDS treatments into testing at a time when Congress was putting hundreds of millions of dollars into NIH budgets for just such purposes. At first Fauci talked about unavoidable delays. He claimed government scientists were working as fast as they could. Pressed harder, he finally admitted that the problem stemmed "almost exclusively" from the lack of staffing in his agency. Congress had allocated funds, it was true, but the Reagan administration had gotten around spending the money by stingily refusing to let Fauci hire anybody. Fauci had requested 127 positions to speed the development of AIDS treatments; the administration had granted him eleven. And for a year, he had not told anyone. For a year, this spokesman for the public health answered reporters that AIDS drugs were in the pipeline and that government scientists had all the money they needed. It seemed that only when faced with the penalty of perjury would one of the administration's top AIDS officials tell the truth. That was the real story, I thought, but for some reason nobody else had picked up on it.

At the international AIDS conference in Stockholm two months later, the other reporters in "the AIDS pack" congratulated me on my success and asked what I was working on now. I admitted that I was too busy promoting the British and German release of my book to do much writing myself, and next month I had the Australian tour. But if I *were* reporting, I added with a vaguely conspiratorial tone, I'd look at the *scandal* in the NIH. Nobody had picked up that

New York Times story from a few months ago about staffing shortages on AIDS clinical trials. The lives of 1.5 million HIV-infected Americans hung in the balance, and the only way you could get a straight answer out of an administration AIDS official was to put him under oath and make him face the charge of perjury. Where I went to journalism school, *that* was a news story.

One reporter responded to my tip with the question: "But who's going to play *you* in the miniseries?"

A few minutes later, when Dr. Fauci came into the press room, the world's leading AIDS journalists got back to the serious business of transcribing his remarks. Nobody asked him if he was actually telling the truth, or whether they should put him under oath to ensure a candid response to questions about when we'd get AIDS treatments. Most of the subsequent news accounts of Dr. Fauci's comments faithfully reported that many AIDS treatments were in the pipeline. Government scientists, he said once more, were doing all they possibly could.

The producer assured my publisher that Morton Downey Jr. would be "serious" about AIDS. "He's not going to play games on this issue," the producer said, adding solemnly: "His brother has AIDS. He understands the need for compassion." The abundance of Mr. Downey's compassion was implicit in the night's call-in poll question: "Should all people with AIDS be quarantined?"

Downey's first question to me was, "You *are* a homosexual, aren't you?"

He wasn't ready for my canned answer: "Why do you ask? Do you want a date or something?"

The show shifted into an earnest discussion of quarantine. In his television studio, Clearasil-addled high school students from suburban New Jersey held up MORTON DOWNEY FAN CLUB signs and cheered aggressively when the truculent, chain-smoking host appeared to favor a kind of homespun AIDS Auschwitz. The youths shouted down any audience member who stepped forward to defend the rights of AIDS sufferers, their howls growing particularly vitriolic if the speakers were gay. These kids were the ilk from which Hitler drew his Nazi youth. In the first commercial break, the other guest, an AIDS activist, and I told Downey we would walk off the show if he didn't tone down his gay-baiting rhetoric. Smiling amiably, Downey took a long drag on his cigarette and assured us, "Don't worry, I have a fallback position."

That comment provided one of the most lucid moments in my year as an AIDS celebrity. Downey's "fallback position," it was clear, was the opposite of what he was promoting on the air. Of course, he didn't *really* believe that people with AIDS, people like his brother, should all be locked up. This was merely a deliciously provocative posture to exploit the working-class resentments of people who needed someone to hate. AIDS sufferers and gays would do for this week. Next week, if viewership dropped and Downey needed a new whipping boy, maybe he'd move on to Arabs, maybe Jews. It didn't seem to matter much to him, since he didn't believe what he was saying anyway. For Morton Downey Jr., talking about AIDS was not an act of conscience; it was a ratings ploy. He knew it, he let his guests know it, his producers certainly knew it, and his television station knew it. The only people left out of the joke were his audience.

The organizers of the Desert AIDS Project had enlisted actor Kirk Douglas and CBS morning anchor Kathleen Sullivan to be honorary co-chairs of the Palm Springs fundraiser. The main events would include a celebrity tennis match pitting Douglas against Mayor Sonny Bono, and a $1,500-a-head dinner at which I would receive a Lucite plaque for my contributions to the fight against AIDS. The next morning I would fly to L.A. to speak at still another event, this one with Shirley MacLaine, Valerie Harper, and Susan Dey of *L.A. Law*.

The desert night was exquisite. There were 130 dinner guests, the personification of elegance and confidence, who gathered on a magnificent patio of chocolate-brown Arizona flagstone at the home of one of Palm Spring's most celebrated interior designers. A lot of people had come simply to see what was regarded as one of the most sumptuous dwellings in this sumptuous town.

When I was called to accept my reward, I began with the same lineup of jokes I use on talk shows and on the college lecture circuit. They work every time.

I told the crowd about how you get AIDS from a mosquito.

Kirk Douglas laughed; everybody laughed.

Next, I did the how-many-gay-waiters joke.

Kirk Douglas laughed; everybody laughed.

Then I mentioned the woman who asked whether she could get AIDS from a waiter ejaculating in her salad dressing.

That one always has my college audiences rolling in the aisles, so I paused for the expected hilarity.

But in the utter stillness of the desert night air, all that could be heard was the sound of Kirk Douglas's steel jaw dropping to the magnificent patio of chocolate-brown Arizona flagstone. The rest was silence.

"You've got to remember that most of these people came because they're my clients," the host confided later. "You said that, and all I could think was how I'd have to go back to stitching slipcovers when this was done."

It turned out that there was more to my lead-balloon remark than a misjudged audience. Local AIDS organizers told me that a year earlier, a rumor that one of Palm Springs's most popular restaurants was owned by a homosexual, and that most of its waiters were gay, had terrified the elite community. Patronage at the eatery quickly plummeted, and it had nearly gone out of business. Fears that I dismissed as laughable were the genuine concerns of my audience, I realized. My San Francisco joke was a Palm Springs fable.

As I watched the busboys clear the tables later that night, I made a mental note not to tell that joke before dinner again. Never had I seen so many uneaten salads, so much wasted iceberg lettuce.

A friend had just tested antibody positive, and I was doing my best to cheer him up as we ambled down the sidewalk toward a Castro Street restaurant a few blocks from where I live in San Francisco. It seems most of my conversations now have to do with who has tested positive or lucked out and turned up negative, or who is too afraid to be tested. We had parked our car near Coming Home, the local hospice for AIDS patients and others suffering from terminal illnesses, and as we stepped around a nondescript, powder-blue van that blocked our path, two men in white uniforms emerged from the hospice's side door. They carried a stretcher, and on the stretcher was a corpse, neatly wrapped with navy-blue straps. My friend and I stopped walking. The men quickly guided the stretcher into the back of the van, climbed in the front doors, and drove away. We continued our walk but didn't say anything.

I wondered if the corpse was someone I had known. I'd find out Thursday when the weekly gay paper came out. Every week there are at least two pages filled with obituaries of the previous week's departed. Each week, when I turn to those pages, I hold my breath, wondering whose picture I'll see. It's the only way to keep track, what with so many people dying.

Sometimes I wonder if an aberrant mother or two going to mass at the Most Holy Redeemer Church across the street from Coming Home Hospice has ever warned a child, "That's where you'll end up if you don't obey God's law." Or whether some youngster, feeling that first awareness of a different sexuality, has looked at the doorway of this modern charnel house with an awesome, gnawing dread of annihilation.

"Is the limousine here? Where are the dancers?"

The room fell silent. Blake Rothaus had sounded coherent until that moment, but he was near death now and his brain was going. We were gathered around his bed in a small frame house on a dusty street in Oklahoma City. The twenty-four-year-old was frail and connected to life through a web of clear plastic tubing. He stared up at us and seemed to recognize from our looks that he had lapsed into dementia. A friend broke the uncomfortable silence.

"Of course, we all brought our dancing shoes," he said. "Nice fashionable pumps at that. I wouldn't go out without them."

Everyone laughed and Blake Rothaus was lucid again.

Blake had gone to high school in a San Francisco suburb. When he was a sophomore, he told us, he and his best friend sometimes skipped school, sneaking to the city to spend their afternoons in the gay neighborhood around Castro Street.

It's a common sight, suburban teenagers playing hooky on Castro Street. I could easily imagine him standing on a corner not far from my house. But back in 1982, when he was eighteen, I was already writing about a mysterious, unnamed disease that had claimed 330 victims in the United States.

Blake moved back to Oklahoma City with his family after he graduated from high school. When he fell ill with AIDS, he didn't mope. Instead, he started pestering Oklahoma health officials with demands to educate people about this disease and to provide services for the sick. The state health department didn't recoil. At the age of twenty-two, Blake Rothaus had become the one-man nucleus for Oklahoma's first AIDS-patient services. He was the hero of the Sooner State's AIDS movement and something of a local legend.

Though the state had reported only 250 AIDS cases, Oklahoma City had a well-coordinated network of religious leaders, social workers, health-care providers, gay-rights advocates, state legislators, and businessmen, all committed to providing a sane and humane response to this frightening new disease.

"I think it's the old Dust Bowl mentality," suggested one AIDS organizer. "When the hard times come, people pull together."

My past year's travels to twenty-nine states and talks with literally thousands of people have convinced me of one thing about this country and AIDS: most Americans want to do the right thing about this epidemic. Some might worry about mosquitoes and a few may be suspicious of their salad dressing. But beyond these fears is a reservoir of compassion and concern that goes vastly underreported by a media that needs conflict and heartlessness to fashion a good news hook.

In Kalamazoo, Michigan, when I visited my stepmother, I was buttonholed by a dozen middle-aged women who wondered anxiously whether we were any closer to a vaccine or a long-term treatment. One mentioned a hemophiliac nephew. Another had a gay brother in Chicago. A third went to a gay hairdresser who, she quickly added, was one of the finest people you'd ever meet. When I returned to my conservative hometown of Aurora, Illinois, nestled among endless fields of corn and soy, the local health department told me they receive more calls than they know what to do with from women's groups, parishes, and community organizations that want to do something to help. In New Orleans, the archconservative, pronuke, antigay bishop had taken up the founding of an AIDS hospice as a personal mission because, he said, when people are sick, you've got to help them out.

Scientists, reporters, and politicians privately tell me that of course *they* want to do more about AIDS, but they have to think about the Morton Downeys of the world, who argue that too much research or too much news space or too much official sympathy is being meted out to a bunch of miscreants. They do as much as they can, they insist; more would rile the resentments of the masses. So the institutions fumble along, convinced they must pander to the lowest common denominator, while the women and men of America's heartland pull me aside to fret about a dying cousin or co-worker and to plead, "When will there be a cure? When will this be over?"

"I think I'll make it through this time," Kit said to me, "but I don't have it in me to go through it again."

We were in room 3 in San Francisco General Hospital's ward 5A, the AIDS ward. The poplar trees outside Kit's window were losing their leaves, and the first winter's chill was settling over the city. I was preparing to leave for my fourth and, I hoped, final media tour, this time for release of the book in paperback and on audiocassette; Kit was preparing to die.

The seizures had started a week earlier, indicating he was suffering either from toxoplasmosis, caused by a gluttonous protozoa that sets up housekeeping in the brain; or perhaps it was a relapse of cryptococcal meningitis; or, another specialist guessed, it could be one of those other nasty brain infections that nobody had seen much of until the past year. Now that AIDS patients were living longer, they fell victim to even more exotic infections than in the early days. But the seizures were only part of it. Kit had slowly been losing the sight in his left eye to a herpes infection. And the Kaposi's sarcoma lesions that had scarred his face were beginning to coat the inside of his lungs. When Kit mentioned he'd like to live until Christmas, the doctors said he might want to consider having an early celebration this year, because he wasn't going to be alive in December.

"I can't take another infection," Kit said.

"What does that mean?"

"Morphine," Kit answered, adding mischievously, "lots of it."

We talked briefly about the mechanics of suicide. We both knew people who'd made a mess of it, and people who had done it right. It was hardly the first time the subject had come up in conversation for either of us. Gay men facing AIDS now exchange formulas for suicide as casually as housewives swap recipes for chocolate-chip cookies.

Kit was released from the hospital a few days later. He had decided to take his life on a Tuesday morning. I had to give my first round of interviews in Los Angeles that day, so I stopped on the way to the airport to say goodbye on Monday. All day Tuesday, while I gave my perfectly formed sound bites in a round of network radio appearances, I wondered: Is this the moment he's slipping out of consciousness and into that perfect darkness? When I called that night, it turned out he'd delayed his suicide until Thursday to talk to a few more relatives. I had to give a speech in Portland that day, so on the way to the airport I stopped again. He showed me the amber-brown bottle with the bubble-gum-pink morphine syrup, and we said another goodbye.

The next morning, Kit drank his morphine and fell into a deep sleep. That afternoon, he awoke and drowsily asked what time it was. When told it was five hours later, he murmured, "That's amazing. I should have been dead hours ago."

And then he went back to sleep.

That night, Kit woke up again.

"You know what they say about near-death experiences?" he asked. "Going toward the light?"

Shaking his head, he sighed, "No light. Nothing."

His suicide attempt a failure, Kit decided the timing of his death would now be up to God. I kept up on the bizarre sequence of events by phone and called as soon as I got back to San Francisco. I was going to tell Kit that his theme song should be "Never Can Say Goodbye," but then the person on the other end of the phone told me that Kit had lapsed into a coma.

The next morning, he died.

Kit's death was like everything about AIDS—anticlimactic. By the time he actually did die, I was almost beyond feeling.

The next day, I flew to Boston for the start of the paperback tour, my heart torn between rage and sorrow. All week, as I was chauffeured to my appearances on *Good Morning America*, *Larry King Live*, and various CNN shows, I kept thinking, it's all going to break. I'm going to be on a TV show with some officious government health spokesman lying to protect his job, and I'm going to start shouting, "You lying son of a bitch. Don't you know there are people, real people, people I love out there dying?" Or I'll be on a call-in show and another mother will phone about her thirty-seven-year-old son who just died and it will hit me at once, and I'll start weeping.

But day after day as the tour went on, no matter how many official lies I heard and how many grieving mothers I talked to, the crack-up never occurred. All my answers came out rationally in tight little sound bites about institutional barriers to AIDS treatments and projections about 1993 case loads.

By the last day of the tour, when a limousine picked me up at my Beverly Hills hotel for my last round of satellite TV interviews, I knew I had to stop. In a few weeks I'd return to being national correspondent for the *Chronicle*, and it was time to get off the AIDS celebrity circuit, end the interviews and decline the invitations to the star-studded fundraisers, and get back to work as a newspaper reporter. That afternoon, there was just one last radio interview to a call-in show in the San Fernando Valley, and then it would be over.

The first caller asked why his tax money should go toward funding an AIDS cure when people got the disease through their own misdeeds.

I used my standard jukebox answer about how most cancer cases are linked to people's behavior but that nobody ever suggested we stop trying to find a cure for cancer.

A second caller phoned to ask why her tax money should go to finding an AIDS cure when these people clearly deserved what they got.

I calmly put a new spin on the same answer, saying in America you usually don't sentence people to die for having a different lifestyle from yours.

Then a third caller phoned in to say that he didn't care if all those queers and junkies died, as did a fourth and fifth and sixth caller. By then I was shouting, "You stupid bigot. You just want to kill off everybody you don't like. You goddamn Nazi."

The talk-show host sat in stunned silence. She'd heard I was so *reasonable*. My anger baited the audience further, and the seventh and eight callers began talking about "you guys," as if only a faggot like myself could give a shit about whether AIDS patients all dropped dead tomorrow.

In their voices, I heard the reporters asking polite questions of NIH officials. Of course, they had to be polite to the government doctors; dying queers weren't anything to lose your temper over. I heard the dissembling NIH researchers go home to their wives at night, complain about the lack of personnel, and shrug; this was just how it was going to have to be for a while. They'd excuse their inaction by telling themselves that if they went public and lost their jobs, worse people would replace them. It was best to go along. But how would they feel if *their* friends, *their* daughters were dying of this disease? Would they be silent—or would they shout? Maybe they'll forgive me for suspecting they believed that ultimately a bunch of fags weren't worth losing a job over. And when I got home, I was going to have to watch my friends get shoved into powder-blue vans, and it wasn't going to change.

The history of the AIDS epidemic, of yesterday and of today, was echoing in the voices of those callers. And I was screaming at them, and the show host just sat there stunned, and I realized I had rendered myself utterly and completely inarticulate.

I stopped, took a deep breath, and returned to compound-complex sentences about the American tradition of compassion and the overriding need to overcome institutional barriers to AIDS treatments.

When I got home to San Francisco that night, I looked over some notes I had taken from a conversation I'd had with Kit during his last stay in the hospital. I was carping about how frustrated I was at the prospect of returning to my reporting job. If an internationally acclaimed best seller hadn't done shit to change the world, what good would mere newspaper stories do?

"The limits of information," Kit said. "There's been a lot written on it."

"Oh," I said.

Kit closed his eyes briefly and faded into sleep while plastic tubes fed him a cornucopia of antibiotics. After five minutes, he stirred, looked up, and added, as if we had never stopped talking, "But you don't really have a choice. You've got to keep on doing it. What else are you going to do?"

SUGGESTIONS FOR WRITING

1. Respond to Shilts' comment that "in America you usually don't sentence people to die for having a different lifestyle from yours."

2. Examine Shilts' anger over the public's seemingly callous attitude to the AIDS crisis. Why, in the last section of the essay, does his behavior shock the call-in show hostess who had "heard [he] was so *reasonable?*"

3. What mistakes does Shilts see that the "world" is making in handling the AIDS crisis? Do you agree or disagree with his interpretation of the events he describes? Support your points. You may wish to consider the title of the essay in your discussion.

4. Describe and analyze your reactions to Shilts' description of Kit Herman. Why did Shilts include his story in his article? Is it effective? Explain why or why not.

BEING POSITIVE IS POSITIVE

Elisabeth

*In the early years of the AIDS epidemic people who did not consider them-
selves to be members of an at-risk group paid little attention to what was happening to those who were. When the crisis began affecting a wider segment of
the population, however, attitudes changed. In its issue of August 10, 1987,
Newsweek, for example, ran a cover story featuring pictures and brief biog-
raphies of more than 300 American men, women, and children who had
died of the disease in the past year; many of them were neither gay nor drug
users. Stories of "ordinary" people dealing with AIDS became commonplace
in the media; Ryan White, a hemophiliac child in Indiana who had been
banned from school because he had contracted AIDS from a blood transfu-
sion, became a national figure. AIDS no longer was limited to groups whose
infection could be blamed on their way of life. AIDS had come into the home
next door, perhaps into your home.*

*It is estimated that by the year 2000 every American will either be or will
know at least one person who is HIV-positive or who suffers from or who
has died from AIDS or ARC (AIDS-related complex). According to recent
projections, the next at-risk population is college students; studies now indicate that one out of 500 students already carries the AIDS virus.*

*Although AIDS remains incurable, many AIDS patients demonstrate
great strength.* **Elisabeth,** *a German woman interviewed by Ines Rieder
and Patricia Ruppelt for their book* AIDS: The Women *(1988), speaks
with dignity about her disease and the ways it has affected her life.*

If I was the heroine of a nineteenth-century romantic novel, the day that dramatically changed my life would have been dark, with an oppressive atmosphere and a thunderstorm approaching. But, since I am a quite unheroic
woman of twenty-nine, living in modern Berlin, it was a beautiful, sunny April
day in 1986 when my boyfriend Jan rushed into my apartment, collapsed on a
chair and said, "I am positive." He had had these strangely swollen lymph
nodes for more than a year, and because no doctor had been able to find the
reason for this phenomenon, we finally thought of sending him for an AIDS
test—just to make sure it was not AIDS. The idea that he could be infected was
removed and unrealistic. This was the disease of homosexuals and drug addicts,
not people like us who had just a few same sex experiences. Imagine how
shocked and unprepared we were when all of a sudden AIDS was there: in my
apartment, in my boyfriend . . . and in me?

In those days, the general belief was that only 5 to 20 percent of those infected would eventually develop the disease, and I tried to console Jan by telling him that chances were limited that he'd ever get the disease. Apart from
that, all we had to do, was to use rubbers, which we had been doing anyway dur-

ing the "dangerous days," so we'd be able to handle that. It took me hours, days, and weeks to understand the full range of consequences—the first being that very likely I would also be infected.

A letter I wrote to a very close friend during the days when I was waiting for my test result shows how I felt then:

> The threat of being infected has been poisoning my life for the past three weeks. I am more or less resigned to the fact that I have been infected, as we have often slept together while I was menstruating.Whenever I don't have to concentrate on something else, my thoughts revolve around this problem. It means that my sexual life will become much more complicated and inhibited, that intercourse will only be possible with a condom and that oral sex and deep kissing will be dangerous as well. It means that I'll be carrying the stigma of the infected, and that I have to tell every future sexual partner about it. But those are only minor problems compared with confronting the facts that I may never be able to have children and that I may die much younger than I had imagined.
>
> Over the past days I've handled this problem as if the positive result has already been verified, and it will be a relief to know for sure. There is nothing worse than this state between fear and hope. I trust myself to be capable of handling the situation and dealing with all the consequences, maybe even turning it into something positive. Right now there is a deep sadness in me and I am writing this with tears in my eyes.
>
> I spent the whole day yesterday wondering what it means to me that I may die during the next five years. On the one hand this is a very abstract thought, and on the other it is a question that touches my deepest emotions and instincts. It makes me look back on how I have lived so far, and I realize that I have been content with my life. I don't think I've missed anything essential or that I could have gotten further in my personal development if I'd done things differently. That's a very consoling thought.

I thought I was prepared for the result being positive, but when I actually heard it, I felt as if the rug had been pulled out from under my feet. I cried the whole afternoon, night and the next morning. Then I tried to pull myself together because my mother was coming to visit me. More than anything, I didn't want her to know. I am still convinced that she'd worry herself to death.

Before, when I would have occasional nightmares, I'd wake up and be relieved that it was just a dream. Now, after receiving my test results, it was the other way around. My life became a nightmare from which I could escape only be sleeping and having nice dreams, only to wake to the horrors of reality. I felt doomed; I saw my life like a play on a stage with a background that had always been bright but now had turned to gray. I've always loved to dance; dancing for me is an expression of life and joy. But after finding out that I was infected with AIDS, I couldn't dance for months, since I felt much closer to death and sadness than to the joy of life.

I felt like a prisoner, whom the infection had deprived of the freedom to develop in any direction she'd choose. I had to stop smoking and lounging for hours in the sun. My sexual life became very restricted at a point in my life when I had finally come to enjoy sex after years of fears, inhibitions and dissatisfaction. And I felt that the infection forced me to commit myself to my relationship with Jan, because no healthy man would ever run the risk of being with me. It seemed that the only alternative to staying in this often difficult relationship was to be on my own, and this didn't appeal to me.

I had to realize that the free will that we human beings are so proud of is very limited, with the final limitation being death itself. Apparently it wasn't for me to decide when and how I would die. To preserve an illusion of freedom of will, I fled into thoughts of suicide: If worse came to worst, I could still decide myself when I'd die, instead of leaving it up to this malicious virus.

Confronting dying and death is probably the most difficult part of dealing with AIDS. In the summer of 1986, a study by AIDS specialists in Frankfurt was published, stating for the first time that probably 100 percent of the HIV-infected would develop full-blown AIDS. One of my friends, who is a doctor, and someone from the Berlin Aids-Hilfe (AIDS Assistance) confirmed this information. That's when I entered the worst phase of my depression.

Now I no longer believe in statistics. I am very angry that HIV-positive people, whose health is fragile, are deprived of any hope. This attitude might really kill them. Instead of telling people to prepare for their deaths, they should be encouraged to activate the incredible self-healing energies that each of us possesses. This is only possible if there is hope and a strong will to live.

Many cancer patients as well as AIDS patients have far outlived prognoses that were made on the basis of statistics. And even if our modern medical science hasn't come up with a treatment for certain diseases yet, it doesn't mean that nobody can be cured from such a disease. Experience has proven that there is no disease that kills 100 percent of the people who have ever gotten it. There are always exceptions. And why shouldn't everybody try to be an exception? A book by Bernie S. Siegel, *Love, Medicine and Miracles*, has encouraged me to develop this perspective.

Dealing with the question of death, I have found books by Elisabeth Kübler-Ross very helpful. She describes death as a mostly beautiful transformation from one state of existence into another. In our society, death is a taboo subject because it is seen as the end of the one precious life that one has. To me the Buddhist and Hindu idea of reincarnation and karma makes more sense than the notion of this being the one and only life and death we have. Not that I am especially happy about the idea of having to go through all of the problems and suffering of life again, but it puts things into a different perspective. Modern science has now started to reconfirm theories of reincarnation by studies of death and dying, or experiences of former lives, under hypnosis. Still, I am aware that this is a question of belief which many people might not share with me. All I know is that it has helped me in developing a sense of inner peace and calm in coping with the fact that I am HIV-positive.

I have also thought and read about the different aspects and interpretations of "disease." In modern society, disease is an unpleasant malfunctioning of the body which has to be overcome as soon as possible. Indeed, we may harm our bodies on the physical level by not getting enough rest, or by not nurturing them in the right way. But disease can also be seen as the materialization of a conflict or problem in our emotional, intellectual or spiritual "body" which we fail to recognize and treat and which later shifts to the physical level. Once we get sick, we immediately pay a lot of attention to the well-being of our bodies, and we might start wondering why we got sick in the first place. I think a disease, or the threat of becoming sick in the case of HIV-infected people, can also be seen as a great chance to reflect on our way of life, to ask whether we feel content and balanced in the important aspects of our lives or whether we would rather change something to live more happily.

I have often wondered what I may have done wrong so that my body has had to warn me by threatening to become seriously sick. I haven't come up with any clear answers. I enjoy the process of becoming more aware of what I am doing and how I am doing it, though. On the whole, I have become much more conscious of my way of life instead of just drifting along. And I have begun to recognize ways in which I didn't do what was best for me, but rather did what people expected from me. For instance, I slept with many men without really enjoying it, just because they wanted to and I didn't have the courage to say no. (Siegel's book explains that typical cancer patients are those really "nice" people who put all of their energies into pleasing others instead of listening to their own needs and desires to be nice to themselves.)

I've also realized, while wondering why I've gotten this infection, that intellectually I've perceived the world in a very negative way, although I am a good-humored person who loves to laugh. I have been politically active for years, and by dealing with starvation in the so-called third world or torture under fascist regimes, I just didn't maintain an optimistic outlook on life and the world. I am still very aware of the horror and misery that has to be overcome, but at the same time I want to enjoy the beauty of the world. AIDS put me on this new track. As paradoxical as this may seem, knowing that I am positive, I have learned to be more positive.

The change came about last September, when I was in my most depressed phase, facing death and feeling like I had been sucked into a black hole. The telephone rang and a friend of mine told me very excitedly about a shaman who had healed a friend of hers who had cancer. This shaman would come to West Germany in November, and she urged me to go for a healing. It sounded pretty weird to me and for weeks I couldn't decide, but finally I went. Psychically and emotionally I was really worn out, and I still had my doubts.

The healing didn't change my being HIV-positive, but it changed my attitude towards life, and slowly I started feeling better. The rites, ceremonies and meditations out in nature made me feel happier, more peaceful and connected to the world around me. I felt that I was part of a larger organism. During the workshop, the shaman taught us to perceive the beauty of nature. Since then I have very consciously enjoyed the changing seasons, the color of leaves, the smell of flowers, and all this has enriched my life. I have also become aware of how much friendship and love I am given. "You have the choice: You can concentrate on the negative aspects of life and be desperate, or you can concentrate on the positive aspects of life and be happy." This message sounds very simple, but I had a very hard time getting it. I still doubt it at times. However,

I think for a HIV-positive person it is a matter of survival. If we don't fill ourselves with positive energy, our immune system will lose its strength to fight the virus.

There have been all sorts of puns with the word AIDS, two of which I like. A friend once said, "Maybe AIDS means for you that it is an aid to find your way on what might be a more spiritual path." The other is, "AIDS means Accelerated Inner Development."

What does being infected mean to me after one and a half years? It means that being positive has become completely a part of me and even my dreams take account of it.

It means that I am no longer afraid of death and that by overcoming this fundamental fear, I have become less fearful in general. Once the fear of death has lost its importance, all of the other horrors seem minor. However, I am still afraid of dying miserably and with a lot of physical pain, just as I have always been terrified of torture.

It means that being positive has become a crucial and dominating issue in my relationships. In spite of my worries that I'd have to stay alone because no HIV-negative man would want to be with a dangerous monster, an untouchable, I separated from Jan. In many ways I had come to perceive this relationship as destructive, the infection being just one part of that. The separation proved to me that AIDS couldn't control my life so thoroughly that it could force me to stay in an unhappy relationship. This was a very liberating experience.

I met a man who is not at all afraid of getting infected, who reacted very calmly to my being positive and transformed me from a dangerous beast into a human being again. I have been together with him for nearly a year now. Still, the fear of transmitting the disease is there, and if my partner isn't concerned, I sometimes am.

Being positive means that my sexual life has become more difficult, restricted, inhibited, controlled. I don't mind condoms at all, but not being allowed to do other practices has made my sexual life a lot poorer and altogether less enjoyable. Telling a new partner that I am positive is very difficult for me too, since I always have to prepare myself for rejection. Learning how to handle these sexual problems has sometimes made me feel like a thirteen-year-old girl facing her first sexual experience.

The fear of being rejected, to have people get panicky and turn away from me (even if it's just a little thing like refusing to drink from my glass), has made me very selective in choosing whom to tell. This has divided my friends into two groups—those who know and those who don't. Similarly, there are two versions of my life, and often I have to make up stories so as not to betray my infection.

Finally, being positive means that I belong to a discriminated minority. This really upset me in the beginning, since I have always been integrated into society. All of a sudden I was an outcast. If it becomes known that someone is HIV-positive, this person may have problems getting an apartment, a job, insurance, medical treatment. This discrimination can destroy the roots of one's existence, which is a frightening prospect.

In West Germany, some people have already lost their jobs because of being infected, although this is illegal. And last but not least, there is a tradition in West Germany about how to deal with unwanted elements of society. Bavaria was the first, and so far the only, West German federal state to introduce discriminatory laws to control groups that are considered primarily threatened by AIDS: homosexuals, drug addicts and prostitutes. These laws were initiated by the Bavarian Minister of Domestic Affairs, Peter Gauweiler—the son of one of the administrators of the Warsaw ghetto. I don't mean to say that this country is becoming a fascist state again; it's still far from that. But we have to be careful and attentive.

After about six months of trying to cope with the infection myself, I got involved with the Berlin Aids-Hilfe and helped to start a women's group. In this group we share our experiences, support each other, look for ways to handle the situation together. All of us have found that after the initial shock and desperation, the infection has had a very positive effect on our personal development. By sharing this experience with newcomers, I hope that we can show them that life can be joyful and fulfilled despite the infection, and maybe even more so. As a woman in the group once said, "Being positive is positive!"

Through the infection and the questions I have had to confront as a result of it, I have come to a deeper and fuller understanding of life, and I will continue on this track. The dark background of this stage of my life has disappeared, and I love to dance again—consciously enjoying that I am alive and happy. ✒

SUGGESTIONS FOR WRITING

1. Elisabeth articulates compelling reasons for being angry that she has AIDS. Analyze her feelings and compare them to what yours might be if you faced what lies ahead of her.

2. How was Elisabeth able to develop a positive attitude about her illness? Explore your feelings about what she has to say.

3. One of Elisabeth's friends tells her that AIDS stands for "Accelerated Inner Development," and from what many people say about knowing persons with a terminal illness, this is often the case. Describe the kind of person Elisabeth is; from what does she derive her strength? What did her friend mean by Accelerated Inner Development, and how can an illness such as AIDS bring about these changes?

4. Elisabeth says her illness has made her a member of a "discriminated minority." What does she mean by this? In what ways are HIV-positive, ARC, and AIDS patients subjected to discrimination? Do you agree with the ways in which they are treated? Why or why not?

IDENTIFY ALL CARRIERS

William F. Buckley, Jr.

In the interests of public health, many people feel that it is essential to iden-
tify persons infected with the AIDS virus, even persons who test HIV-posi-
tive but who exhibit none of the symptoms of the actual disease. **William F.**
Buckley, Jr., *believes that civil rights advocates have gone too far in trying*
to protect people who have AIDS. He offers some blunt suggestions for deal-
ing with the AIDS epidemic, now that it has killed more than 250,000
Americans.

An outspoken conservative, Buckley (b.1925) is a syndicated columnist,
the editor of the National Review, *and the author of numerous scholarly*
books as well as series of espionage novels revolving around a character
named Blackford Oakes. Known for his ascerbic interviewing style, Buckley
has been the host of the Emmy Award-winning Firing Line *since 1966.*

I have read and listened, and I think now that I can convincingly crystallize the
thoughts chasing about in the minds of, first, those whose concern with AIDS
victims is based primarily on a concern for them and for the maintenance of
the most rigid standards of civil liberties and personal privacy, and, second,
those whose anxiety to protect the public impels them to give subordinate attention to the civil amenities of those who suffer from AIDS and primary attention to the safety of those who do not.

Arguments used by both sides are sometimes utilitarian, sometimes moral,
sometimes a little of each—and almost always a little elusive. Most readers will
locate their own inclinations and priorities somewhere other than in the polar
positions here put forward by design.

School A suspects, in the array of arguments of School B, a venture in ethical opportunism. Look, they say, we have made enormous headway in the matter of civil rights for all, dislodging the straight-laced from mummified
positions they inherited through eclectic superstitions ranging from the Bible's
to Freud's. A generation ago, homosexuals lived mostly in the closet. Nowadays they take over cities and parade on Halloween and demand equal rights
for themselves qua homosexuals, not merely as apparently disinterested civil
libertarians.

Along comes AIDS, School A continues, and even though it is well known
that the virus can be communicated by infected needles, known also that heterosexuals can transmit the virus, still it is both a fact and the popular perception that AIDS is the special curse of the homosexual, transmitted through
anal sex between males. And if you look hard, you will discern that little smirk
on the face of the man oh-so-concerned about public health. He is looking for
ways to safeguard the public, sure, but he is by no means reluctant, in the course
of doing so, to sound an invidious tocsin whose clamor is a call to undo all the

understanding so painfully cultivated over a generation by those who have fought for the privacy of their bedroom. What School B is really complaining about is the extension of civil rights to homosexuals.

School A will not say all that in words quite so jut-jawed, but it plainly feels that no laws or regulations should be passed that have the effect of identifying the AIDS carrier. It isn't, School A concedes, as if AIDS were transmitted via public drinking fountains. But any attempt to segregate the AIDS carrier is primarily an act of moral ostracism.

School B does in fact tend to disapprove forcefully of homosexuality, but tends to approach the problem of AIDS empirically. It argues that acquired immune deficiency syndrome is potentially the most serious epidemic to have shown its face in this century. Summarizing currently accepted statistics, *The Economist* recently raised the possibility "that the AIDS virus will have killed more than 250,000 Americans in eight years' time." Moreover, if the epidemic extended to that point, it would burst through existing boundaries. There would then be "no guarantee that the disease will remain largely confined to groups at special risk, such as homosexuals, hemophiliacs and people who inject drugs intravenously. If AIDS were to spread through the general population, it would become a catastrophe." Accordingly, School B says, we face a uilitarian imperative, and this requires absolutely nothing less than the identification of the million-odd people, who, the doctors estimate, are carriers.

How?

Well, the military has taken the first concrete step. Two million solders will be given the blood test, and those who have AIDS will be discreetly discharged.

Discreetly, you say!

Hold on. I'm coming to that. You have the military making the first massive move designed to identify AIDS sufferers—and, bear in mind, an AIDS carrier today is an AIDS carrier on the day of his death, which day, depending on the viral strain, will be two years from now or when he is threescore and 10. The next logical step would be to require of anyone who seeks a marriage license that he present himself not only with a Wassermann test but also an AIDS test.

But if he has AIDS, should he then be free to marry?

Only after the intended spouse is advised that her intended husband has AIDS, and agrees to sterilization. We know already of children born with the disease, transmitted by the mother, who contracted it from the father.

What then would School B suggest for those who are not in the military and who do not set out to get a marriage license? Universal testing?

Yes, in stages. But in rapid stages. The next logical enforcer is the insurance company. Blue Cross, for instance, can reasonably require of those who wish to join it a physical examination that requires tests. Almost every American, making his way from infancy to maturity, needs to pass by one or another institutional turnstile. Here the lady will spring out, her right hand on a needle, her left on a computer, to capture a blood specimen.

Is it then proposed by School B that AIDS carriers should be publicly identified as such?

The evidence is not completely in as to the communicability of the disease. But while much has been said that is reassuring, the moment has not yet come when men and women of science are unanimously agreed that AIDS cannot be casually communicated. Let us be patient on that score, pending any tilt in the evidence: If the news is progressively reassuring, public identification would not be necessary. If it turns in the other direction and AIDS develops among, say, children who have merely rough-housed with other children who suffer from AIDS, then more drastic segregation measures would be called for.

But if the time has not come, and may never come, for public identification, what then of private identification?

Everyone detected with AIDS should be tattooed in the upper forearm, to protect common-needle users, and on the buttocks, to prevent the victimization of other homosexuals.

You have got to be kidding! That's exactly what we suspected all along! You are calling for the return of the Scarlet Letter, but only for homosexuals!

Answer: The Scarlet Letter was designed to stimulate public obloquy. The AIDS tattoo is designed for private protection. And the whole point of this is that we are not talking about a kidding matter. Our society is generally threatened, and in order to fight AIDS, we need the civil equivalent of universal military training. *

SUGGESTIONS FOR WRITING

1. Respond to Buckley's suggestion that "everyone detected with AIDS should be tattooed." If you agree with his suggestion, give reasons why you support his point of view; if you disagree, what concrete alternatives would you suggest?

2. Do you agree with Buckley's call for universal testing and identification of AIDS carriers? Why or why not?

3. If, as Buckley says, our society is "generally threatened" by the AIDS epidemic, explore the ways in which this threat can be handled.

AIDS AND CIVIL RIGHTS

Cindy Patton

*In this section, authors William F. Buckley, Jr., and David R. Carlin, Jr.,
discuss the public's right to know who is an AIDS carrier.* **Cindy Patton,**
*on the other hand, makes it clear that persons suffering from the AIDS virus
face a difficult time getting help in dealing with their illness. Former United
States Surgeon General C. Everett Koop astutely compared the current
AIDS epidemic to the Black Death (bubonic plague), which struck Europe
during the fourteenth century; not only did it kill a third of the population,
but it also made people fearful of contact with others and bred a multitude of
superstitions associated with the transmission and cure of the disease that
bring to mind of those spread about AIDS.*

*One question that must be resolved is whose civil rights must be protected
in what ways. Does a person diagnosed as HIV-positive have the right to
keep that fact a secret? Does the government have the right to conduct widespread AIDS tests among at-risk populations? What protection do those suffering from AIDS and related illnesses such as ARC (AIDS-related
complex) have with regard to the confidentiality of their medical records and
availability of insurance and health care?*

*In the following article, Patton makes it clear that these and other ques-
tions are not easy ones to resolve. Patton, the former editor of the* Gay Community News *in Boston, has also been published in the* New York Native,
the Village Voice, The Body Politic, Sojourner, *and* The Women's Review of Books. *She works as an ambulance attendant in Cambridge, Massachusetts. Patton is the author of* Sex & Germs: The Politics of AIDS
(1985), from which this reading was taken, and Inventing AIDS *(1990).*

The U.S. entered the era of AIDS with conflicting demands: enormous cyni-
cism surrounded the very enterprise of medicine, costs were thought to be too
high, and medicine was alternately believed to have caused oppression by in-
appropriately labeling people and to have helped relieve some oppression by
pronouncing blacks the biological equals of whites, admitting that women's reproductive anatomy is compatible with work, and that homosexuality is a "normal" difference, not a biological defect. The arrival of AIDS provoked even
more contradictory demands from both the left and the right. Rightists claimed
that any money spent on AIDS was too much, that AIDS was an elective disease created by homosexuals who might just as well die off. Lesbian and gay activists demanded more responsive funding, and more concerted research, but
cautioned their brothers not to get involved in the research until legal issues
could be sorted out.

AIDS caused a legal crisis as well as a medical one, as patients suffered bad
treatment, research subjects discovered the catch-22 in the fine print, and les-

bians/gay men were subjected to renewed discrimination. The legal problems of the several at-risk communities multiply, since illegal Haitian immigrants, lesbians/gay men, and intravenous drug users are already in legal jeopardy.

Once it was clear that AIDS was actually an epidemic and not just a collection of cases, emergency care personnel, dentists, hospital support services, doctors and nurses, even undertakers began refusing to get anywhere near a person with AIDS. AIDS presented an unforeseen case for medical workers who had grown up and been trained in an age that did not know the constant threat of contracting a deadly illness in their line of work. Other than occasional, isolated cases, most hospital workers only feared contracting hepatitis or tuberculosis, which might cause a short-term illness, but would rarely be fatal. AIDS created a serious crisis in medical care delivery ethics: the image of the tireless and self-sacrificing nurse, doctor, ambulance attendant, or emergency room attendant quickly gave way as workers consulted with their union representatives and refused to treat patients. Although hospitals and professional associations have developed precautions for handling AIDS cases, many workers simply do not believe the protocols are adequate. Each new medical discovery reopens the contagion question. As long as the researchers can provide data that hospital workers who follow precautions do not increase their chances of getting AIDS, the legal and ethical establishments back up the right of the patient. What happens, however, when a health care worker *does* get AIDS at the job? Which way will justice wink then?

The conservative police and prison guard unions continue to maintain that they should not be forced to work with people who might even be suspected of having ("harboring" is the term they generally use) AIDS. The lack of any clear knowledge about who has or might be at risk for AIDS made it immediately evident that these elective injunctions could be construed to include anyone who even *looked* gay, Haitian, or like a prostitute or drug user. Although the medical professionals have uneasily gone back on the job, there are still occasional stories of indigent people left untreated or AIDS patients in hospitals left for several shifts lying in their full bedpans, having their food left at the door, or being shipped off to other care facilities.

A California lawyer is currently suing the city of Los Angeles because paramedics under its jurisdiction failed to touch or assist him when he suffered a heart attack. The attendants refused to treat him, incorrectly believing that he had AIDS. The suit for $1 million is now in Los Angeles County Superior Court.

A man with AIDS who stood trial for a stabbing incident got a taste of "guilty until proven innocent," as prospective jurors were told that the defendant had AIDS. Although jurors were assured that they could not catch the disease by simply being in the courtroom, they were allowed to step down if they feared contracting the disease. Despite doctors' assurances, the defendant and the court marshalls wore surgical masks and gowns. Of course, AIDS was completely irrelevant to the prosecution's case. Even blind justice must have gone home weary after such an obvious, symbolic display of the defendant's "guilt" before the trial had even begun.

Lesbian/gay rights advocates and lawyers set to work, often behind the scenes, to make sure that workers used the precautions dictated by their professional associations. There were two lines of attack used to insure access to services: existing civil rights statues that included sexual preference, and existing disability laws.

Regulations governing hospital admissions vary, but, in general, public hospitals are required to treat patients in immediate need of services without questioning their ability to pay. However, hospitals do not necessarily have to admit everyone who walks in, and may go through a review and admission process. There are no clear-cut standards for admission, especially with a relatively new illness like AIDS where possible outcomes are not well known.

People with AIDS have also encountered difficulty in claiming public benefits, such as SSI and SSA, food stamps, or fuel assistance. AIDS has heavily taxed the public benefits systems in the large cities with a high incidence of the disease, but the problem extends beyond mere numbers. AIDS strikes a previously healthy and quite young population, while many of the public assistance programs are predicated on covering chronic illnesses or disabilities associated with aging. An estimated 40 to 60 percent of the people with AIDS are un- or underinsured for this type of illness and must seek public assistance to cover their medical care. This creates an additional reason to fear job loss if one's homosexuality or AIDS diagnosis becomes known: the insurance benefits extended by the employer may be the only recourse for a person with AIDS. This is particularly a problem for military personnel, who may be discharged if their homosexuality becomes known. Thus, military men who have AIDS may be extremely reluctant to admit to homosexual behavior or intravenous drug use.

Legal advocates have had to use pressure to get AIDS, and later AIDS-Related Complex (ARC), classified as a disability under SSI, SSA, and other program guidelines. These programs are complicated and difficult to apply for under ordinary circumstances, but in the case of AIDS/ARC, with their wide range of clinical manifestations and unusual age distribution, even entering the system can seem insurmountable. Often, applications are turned down and must be appealed, resulting in lost time and the need for expert assistance. AIDS organizations in the larger cities provide technical assistance by social workers experienced in maneuvering their clients through the maze of welfare programs. In addition, considerable efforts at education and negotiation go on behind the scenes to update the various programs' formulas to be responsive to changing needs.

Intravenous drug users, prostitutes, and Haitians with AIDS face additional problems in obtaining benefits since they live in legal limbo. Some of the affected Haitians are in this country illegally and fear deportation if they make any appearance in a government office. Prostitutes and IV drug users have experienced a history of harassment by these very government agencies and may fear legal reprisal or just plain indifference. Intravenous drug users who are on methadone maintenance programs may also fear jeopardizing their relationship to their clinic if their AIDS diagnosis becomes known when they apply for public assistance. Even more than gay men, at least in urban areas, the IV drug and prostitution subcultures and illegal entrants fear anything that makes them visible to government agencies.

Housing law has also come into play. People have been evicted because they were suspected of having AIDS or simply because they were gay. Very few municipalities have housing discrimination codes that cover sexual preference. Perhaps the most spectacular housing case involved the eviction of a New York City doctor whose practice included a number of people with AIDS. Although the doctor and his patients got an injunction against the tenants seeking to evict him, the tenants have appealed.

The Hastings Center is quite right, if dissonant with the new conservatism, in seeing part of the ethical problem in AIDS as a social one: "as a society we must express our moral commitment to the principle that all persons are due a full measure of compassion and respect." Though a bit naive, they rightly see that the people at risk for AIDS will not approach the medical system or its research arms with much trust, and have a well developed interest in less than full compliance. It is not enough for doctors to express the wish to protect their clients or subjects. The doctor or researcher must be prohibited *by law* from releasing names without a good reason. And those reasons must be spelled out clearly, lest a doctor balance the common good against the individual's rights without full understanding of the social, political, and legal ramifications of doing so. In addition, the researcher must have a reasonable assurance that she/he will not be subjected to government or other harassment, as from insurance companies or employers. Some suggest that medical professionals go a step further in their exhibition of "goodwill": they should publicly support policies, such as civil rights measures, that will improve their subjects' ability to pursue legal remedies and free them from social stigma. Only when lesbians/gay people, Haitians, drug users, and prostitutes no longer fear legal or social reprisal can informed consent, confidentiality, and accurate information be assured.

Some people consider the fear of government subpoena of names and medical information to be sheer paranoia, but both Hastings and Lambda Legal Defense address just that possibility. There is no standard set of case law to deal with the problem of confidentiality, since public health laws are by and large left to each state to administer. But with an increasingly conservative Supreme and District Court judgeship, and the rise of rightist legal theorists who propose far more restrictive constitutional theories, it seems reasonable to imagine the worst possibilities. Hastings suggests that a clear and consistent policy of confidentiality will stand an institution in a better light in court than a less thought out rationale. But if gay researchers or institutions ultimately refuse to comply with subpoenas, this might as easily be taken as contempt. Lesbian/gay rights are not protected or widely respected enough for individual gay rights to hold up against the ominous "public good."

There is good reason for paranoia on the part of all the people who have AIDS or who belong to the groups at risk: all are to some degree in violation of law. Homosexuality is illegal in most states; many of the Haitians are illegal entrants to the U.S. and face deportation; and intravenous drug use or ownership of drug injection apparatus is generally illegal. In addition, early in the AIDS epidemic, the Centers for Disease Control several times supplied the names of people with AIDS to other agencies, once by accident. It was clear by the summer of 1983 that the CDC had not taken adequate precautions to insure the confidentiality of those people under its surveillance.

The failure to insure adequate confidentiality measures has many possible consequences. On the most distressing and basic human level, people who need medical treatment may be afraid of going to doctors for fear that their illegal or stigmatized status may become known. While this may vary among those in the major affected groups—gay or bisexual men in the urban gay ghettos, men who have access to gay-sensitive health care and the legal resources of the lesbian/gay community—it is certainly an important factor affecting the decision to seek health care by Haitians and IV drug users.

AIDS became a reportable disease in most states by 1983, placing doctors in jeopardy of legal restraint if they failed to report the disease, and bringing at-risk groups more solidly under the surveillance of the Public Health Service and state public health departments. Many public health officials recognized the need to protect clients' confidentiality if they were to get good compliance. They realized that an early concern over the issue of confidentiality would inspire confidence in their protocols and increase the likelihood that healthy but exposed people would voluntarily seek screening or vaccination if they become available. However, government agencies have not been cognizant of the additional concerns of people in risk groups, and have overlooked the past history of abuse of confidentiality and disregard for the special concerns these people have in seeking medical care.

With the increasing right-wing backlash accelerated by AIDS's connection with homosexuality, the penalties for risking exposure as a homosexual increase as a factor in the individual's willingness to seek appropriate medical assistance. The stereotype of gay men as irresponsible and self-destructive has also resulted in the presumption by public health officials that the lesbian/gay community will not cooperate in sex education or voluntarily stop donating blood. Although the medical establishment has in some ways learned that it must cooperate with gay organizations, the bias against considering gay men as cooperative increases in direct proportion to beliefs about their promiscuity. Like the social ideas about sexual behavior, there is a wide, if not always articulated belief, that gay men will not cooperate in attempts to alter their sexual behavior, with no understanding about how the gay male sexual community functions or what messages have been conveyed by the government in the past.

In reality, the lesbian/gay community has launched massive and sensitive educational campaigns about "safe sex," but sex education is so discouraged in this country that several states have considered them insufficient and have begun to make moves toward exercising public health perogatives to quarantine people with AIDS or establish legal penalties against homosexual acts. California submitted its public health statutes to lawyers, and shortly after that closed all establishments in San Francisco that were believed to have sex on the premises. The bars, baths, and bookstores were allowed to reopen only if they enforced the safe sex guidelines established by a local AIDS organization. Each establishment was required to hire staff to make frequent rounds, and had to insure that a ratio of surveillance staff to clients was maintained.

When faced with the choice of improbable but possible exposure to AIDS versus an almost certain harm resulting from admitting to being gay, it is not surprising that a healthy gay man might reasonably decide not to go to the doctor for screening. For bisexual men whose homosexual activity is hidden, or for gay men who live in smaller towns or regions where homosexuality is highly stigmatized or illegal, the equation tips even further against going to a doctor. A paradoxical corollary applies to this concern about the relative harm of coming out versus finding out about AIDS: with the equivocal HTLV-III blood test, openly gay men, who are unaware of the legal or insurance problems a positive test might cause, may rush out to get tested as soon as the test becomes widely available. The lesbian/gay community will experience a widespread and uncontrollable reaction to test results in individuals, as well as possible inter-community tensions which federal agencies may be able to manipulate to their advantage. As AIDS becomes more prevalent outside the urban gay male community, the many different needs of gay men in other living situations may create conditions where legal strategies are undermined by lack of cooperation of gay men who do not understand or are not aware of their civil rights. The great number of false positives from widespread HTLV-III antibody testing may also create a large pool of "straight," low risk people with even more contradictory concerns.

Privacy and civil rights law has tended, under the influence of the new left, feminist, and lesbian/gay movements, to become more inclusive, to extend to categories of people or activities that were not necessarily originally enumerated. As the political climate shifts, however, and the composition of the Supreme Court changes, there is even greater reason to fear that lists originally procured and protected with the best of intentions may later become weapons against disenfranchised groups. The general social concern expressed about AIDS outside the affected groups is not motivated by a desire to help the homosexual, Haitian, IV drug user, or prostitute—as might have been argued in more liberal times, in spite of a tacit moral sentiment against these people— but to protect the "innocent" victims, allegedly including straight men with no risk other than going to prostitutes, from the social deviants who middle Americans believe "produced" AIDS.

No one in U.S. society has ever been fully equal under the law, fully innocent until proven guilty, especially when public health is balanced against individual liberties. In the current political climate, where abortion rights, First Amendment rights, and the whole notion of a right to privacy (who needs to be private unless they are doing something bad?) are under attack, there is no pretense that anyone other than traditional god-fearing, Christian family members deserves equal treatment under the law. The equation promoting the common good is weighted unapologetically against lesbians/gay men, liberated women, third world people, and anything liberal. In a system that says gay men should sacrifice a little freedom to the Public Health Service to produce a greater social good, the lives saved through faithful and well-intentioned cooperation with AIDS surveillance and research will not and may not be intended to be those whose lives are at risk. 🖎

SUGGESTIONS FOR WRITING

1. What rights to privacy does an AIDS carrier have? Do these rights change once the person develops full-blown AIDS?

2. Examine your responses to the attitudes of the health-care industry (hospitals, clinics, doctors, nurses, social workers) that Patton describes in her article. What responsibility does the health-care industry have to AIDS patients?

3. In some communities, children diagnosed as HIV-positive or as having AIDS have been prevented from attending school, and, in some cases, violence and vandalism have been directed against their families. Respond to these attitudes and behaviors.

4. Agree or disagree that patients have the right to know whether their doctor, nurse, or dentist is HIV-positive.

NOT BY CONDOMS ALONE: SOCIETY AND THE AIDS EPIDEMIC

David R. Carlin, Jr.

Several years ago, C. Everett Koop, then the surgeon general of the United States, suggested that it was imperative that the government undertake a widespread campaign to inform Americans—not only intravenous drug users and male homosexuals, but the general population as well—about the threat of AIDS. His suggestions about condom use and safe sex were met with anger and outrage, particularly by people who were offended by the explicit nature of the information that he wished to convey. They also believed such information would lead to sexual promiscuity, particularly among teenagers and young adults. Koop countered by pointing out that, unless the American public were given information that clearly stated in what specific ways the AIDS virus could be spread, the epidemic would continue to grow at an alarming rate.

David R. Carlin, Jr., *believes that seeing condoms as the answer to the AIDS epidemic is simplistic. In the following article, Carlin outlines his suggestions for bringing the AIDS epidemic under control. Carlin is a columnist for* Commonweal *magazine.*

As I write this, in mid-February, Liberace has been dead for nearly two weeks, *Time* is running a cover story titled "The Big Chill: How Heterosexuals Are Coping with AIDS," and the stock market value of companies that manufacture condoms is skyrocketing.

The AIDS epidemic, which had receded from the front pages for a time, thus giving those of us who measure social crises in terms of front-page headlines a false sense of security, is back with a bang, and the bang is louder than ever. Facts, as the man said, are stubborn things. Unlike certain naughty children, inattention does little to improve them.

The present moment of the AIDS crisis might be titled: "By condoms ye shall be saved." If only Americans would get in the habit of wearing condoms while engaged in sexual intercourse, especially anal intercourse; if only we could remove ridiculous taboos against TV advertising for condoms, thereby unleasing those great public health educators, the condom manufacturers; if only we could go into the high schools, junior high schools, and grade schools of America to teach our dear children the dangers of unsafe sex and the merits of condom use; if only we could do all these things, why, then, our problems would be largely solved. When the Angel of Death visits our street, he will pass over our household if we post evidence at the front door that we own a six-month supply of condoms and have successfully completed a course of instruction on how to use them.

It's not that I doubt the hygienic utility of condom use. I have no doubt that the widespread use of condoms will cut down on the spread of AIDS among those having gay sex, promiscuous sex, sex with intravenous drug users, and so forth. Cultural antediluvian that I am, I confess that I have moments of weakness in which I doubt the wholesomeness of such categories of sexual activity. But these things happen. So mark me down as a condom proponent.

But if anyone really believes that sex education, TV commercials, and a national enthusiasm for condom use will prove anything like sufficient to curb the spread of AIDS, I respectfully submit that individual should have his or her head examined. I suspect, however, that very few people really do believe this. It's just that in the ideological atmosphere surrounding the AIDS epidemic—an atmosphere, I think it is not too harsh to say, of intellectual cowardice and dishonesty (of this, more later)—persons who actually know better feel compelled to pretend that propaganda plus prophylactics will do the job until either a vaccine or an antidote is discovered.

U.S. Surgeon-General C. Everett Koop has compared AIDS with the Black Death, the bubonic plague that killed about 30 percent of the western European population within a few years in the middle of the fourteenth century. To some, this comparison has seemed a bit hysterical; after all, there are only about 30,000 diagnosed AIDS victims in the United States today out of a total population of around 240,000,000. But bear the following in mind: between one and two million persons are carrying the virus that causes AIDS; once someone contracts the virus, it doesn't go away; and of those having the virus, 50 percent or more may eventually develop AIDS. If the present doubling rate keeps up (the number of AIDS victims doubles every eighteen months or so), millions will have the disease by the year 2000, and tens of millions will be carrying the lethal virus. So Dr. Koop is right on target when he makes his comparison with the Black Death. Unless things change drastically, a considerable fraction of the population of the United States will be killed off by AIDS in the next twenty-five years.

If this disease did not have sexual associations, especially homosexual associations, certain perfectly obvious public health steps would have been taken by now. We would have widespread and semi-compulsory blood tests to identify carriers of the AIDS virus (e.g., blood tests are prerequisites for marriage licenses, for all hospital in-patients, for all persons being treated for sexually transmitted diseases, for all drug rehab clients). We would also trace and notify parties who have had sexual contact with infected persons.

Yet there are certain parties who oppose such common-sense measures.

(1) The gay rights movement is opposed. The stated reason for this opposition is a conviction that the measures will not work and might even be counter-productive. The real reason is that such measures will disproportionately affect gays, thus undermining the social legitimacy of homosexuality, the achieving of which remains the chief goal, the truly essential goal, on the gay rights agenda.

(2) Sex education enthusiasts are opposed, since such steps are inconsistent with their fundamental superstition, namely, that all our sex-related problems will be solved if only we can instruct people more thoroughly in sexuality. Such

enthusiasts, in fact, though shedding sincere tears for the victims of AIDS, see the present crisis as a golden moment, a teachable moment, for spreading the evangel of sex education.

(3) A certain kind of civil libertarian is opposed, the kind who tends to see sexual activity as the paradigmatic instance of action protected by the right of privacy. Any government snooping into our sex lives, especially snooping into the sex lives of a hitherto oppressed group like gays, imperils the entire structure of American liberty.

(4) Certain Christians with overdeveloped organs of compassion and underdeveloped organs of good judgment are unhappy with such measures. Their admirable and tender hearts go out to gays who are undergoing the difficult and painful experience of coming to terms with their sexuality; the last thing such Christians want to see is anything that has the potential for thrusting gays back into the pariah status from which they are in the process of emerging.

And what about the rest of us—those who do not belong to any of the above groups, yet have been unwilling to call for obvious public health steps? We are the intellectual cowards I mentioned above. We know what needs to be done, but we fear being called anti-gay or homophobic or intolerant or puritanical or sexually unenlightened or conservative or Falwell-ish or lacking in Christian charity. Better that millions should be infected and die than that we should suffer the anguish of having such dreadful adjectives hurled at us. ✒

SUGGESTIONS FOR WRITING

1. Respond to Carlin's contention that people have not endorsed mandatory AIDS testing because they are afraid to appear to be anti-gay.

2. Compare Carlin's attitude to that of William F. Buckley, Jr., in his piece, "Identify All Carriers."

3. In what ways does Carlin appeal to his readers' emotions in his suggestions for halting the AIDS epidemic?

4. Why does Carlin believe that Koop and those who share Koop's point of view are naive in thinking that condoms are the answer to the AIDS epidemic? Do you agree or disagree?

HOOKERS WITH AIDS—
THE SEARCH

Lynn Hampton

Not everyone who has AIDS or ARC or who is HIV-positive is someone with whom we can easily identify. Because some of the first at-risk groups were male homosexuals, intravenous drug users, prostitutes, and bisexual men, it was easy for many people to dismiss the illness as a plague sent to punish its victims for their way of life. In fact, some people who criticize the U.S. government's handling of the early AIDS epidemic have contended that it was primarily because the at-risk groups consisted of "undesirables" that the government moved so slowly in mobilizing the Centers for Disease Control and the National Institute of Health in the war on AIDS. Fear of the disease, as well as misunderstanding about how it is transmitted and of the consequences of working with infected persons, caused many health-care professionals to refuse to have anything to do with AIDS patients.

In the following essay, **Lynn Hampton,** *who works with a prostitute's rights group in Atlanta, Georgia, describes her work educating female prostitutes about AIDS and safe sex. This is done not simply because their clients were at risk of infection, but also urgently because these women run a very high risk of contracting the disease from their customers. Although Hampton observed that few of the prostitutes in her study tested HIV-positive, in 1990 in countries where follow-up studies have been conducted an overwhelming percentage of prostitutes have tested HIV-positive.*

Cruising down that stretch of Peachtree Street the hippies used to call The Strip, past the taco place, past the old drugstore, down by the Krystal, you'll see them: the remains of the street people. Here are the burnt-out druggies, the winos, the shake-down artists, the pimps and their ladies.

I'm standing on the corner watching a young white hooker change her blouse in a parked car in the Krystal parking lot and wondering whether she's incredibly defiant or just stupid. Everybody knows whores aren't allowed in the Krystal lot. Rumor has it that the fat white rent-a-cop who keeps the women out of the joint shot a black hooker in the spine for mouthing off when he told her to haul her freight. Could be true.

Now the woman gets out of the car and strolls across the lot in my direction. She doesn't look like she's afraid she'll be blown away any minute, and she doesn't look particularly defiant, either. I decide she just doesn't know what she's doing, and I call out, "Hey, mama. What's happening?"

She glances at me with little but disinterest. I'm obviously not a trick, and she doesn't make me for a police woman, either, so whoever I am, I can't be that important. "Not too much," she replies.

I fish in my green canvas shoulder bag and pull out a handful of prophylactics. "Can you use some of these?"

Now she registers some interest. "Sure. Thanks." She's looking at me with vague suspicion, wondering what's the catch.

"It's not real healthy for working girls to be on the Krystal property," I tell her. "And the rent-a-cop gets pretty weird, I've heard." I smile to let her know I'm one of the good guys.

"Oh, wow. Thanks."

I pull out one of my cards and hand it to her. The logo is a woman in a corset wearing fishnet stockings. Underneath, it says, "I'm for H.I.R.E.," and under that, "Hooking is Real Employment." In the bottom left corner is my name, "Sunny" Lynn Hampton, Vice President. We're a prostitute's rights advocacy group in Atlanta, with the decriminalization of prostitution as our goal.

"Far out," she says, and pokes the card into her back pocket.

"I'm the one putting up all these posters about free AIDS testing. You seen 'em?" I ask.

"Yeah. What's the story?"

"Well, the Feds are trying to find out if working girls are carrying the AIDS virus. So far, it doesn't look that way, at least in Atlanta. I've tested about sixty women and nobody's got it so far. Anyway, it's a good chance to get tested, for free and anonymously. We're also testing for hepatitis B and syphilis. Wanna do it?"

"Gee, I don't know, man. How does it work?"

"I ask you a bunch of questions and fill out a questionnaire. Then I draw a tube of blood. That's it. Takes about half an hour."

"I don't know . . . You won't put my name on anything?"

"No. Just a number. Come on. I'll give you more rubbers."

"Okay," she shrugs. I interview her over a beer in the taco place and bleed her in the john.

This job and I were made for each other. The Department of Human Resources lucked out when they found me. What they needed was someone who could establish credibility with the women, someone comfortable with street people, not some tight-assed social worker or nurse with a white coat and a bad attitude. They also needed someone who could draw blood samples, somebody mighty good at it, too, who could tap blood even in a junkie whose veins were long since shot.

When I heard about it, I jumped at the chance, already knowing the job was mine. I was an advocate for hooker's rights, I had ten years of experience as a medical technician, and I knew the street scene from my days as a flower child in the late '60s. Who could ask for more? And the money was great.

I found that nothing had changed much on the streets in the years since bell bottoms and peace signs disappeared. Same dirty streets, same sleazy joints, same drugs, just new faces buying and selling them.

It took a week or so for people to get used to seeing me around, drinking beer in the joints, talking to people, giving condoms to the working girls.

Then I met Sam.

"Ain't you the rubber lady?" she asked.

"Is that what they're calling me?" I laughed. "Yeah, that's me. You need some rubbers?"

"Shoot, yeah. Gimme a bunch."

I gave her a handful of condoms. "You know, I'm not just the good fairy of condoms," I said, "I need some interviews from you ladies, too. Make my day, C'mon. I'll give you more rubbers after the interview."

Later, her blood sample safe in its styrofoam sheath in my bag, we chatted over a beer while she waited for her man, Poochie, to come. She was eager to explain that Poochie was her boyfriend, not her pimp.

"What's the difference?" I wanted to know.

"Well, a pimp says he loves you and makes you work and beats you up if you don't. But Poochie, he really loves me. We been together four years. He don't make me work. I'm just doin' this until he can find a job. He don't hardly ever hit me, either," she beamed.

Sam was white, said she was twenty-seven, but looked thirty-five. I guess it had been a long, hard road.

Suddenly a young black man entered the taco joint and approached us. "You got any money?" he asked Sam.

"Hey, baby! Yeah, I got 80." She handed him a wad of bills. "This here is the rubber lady. She gave me an AIDS test and a whole bunch of rubbers."

He nodded at me. "That's good."

One day I stood in front of the topless bar across the street from the Krystal watching a young black hooker plying her trade. I was just about to approach her when Poochie walked up behind me. "What's happenin,' man?" he said.

"Say, Pooch. Not too much. I was just fixing to hit on that hooker over there." He looked at the woman, then at me and grinned. "I don't think I'd bother," he said. "She ain't no 'ho. She a boy."

"C'mon, man. You kidding me?"

"Nah, I ain't kiddin'. She a 'ho, but she a boy, too. You just doin' real women, right?"

"Yeah. Damn." The woman crossed the street toward me. Sure enough. The Adam's apple always give them away.

Jennifer was the name she gave me. She was twenty-three, blonde and pretty, despite her thinness and the black eye. On the inside of her elbows were bruises ranging from last week's brown to today's deep purple, the unmistakable tracks of a heavy cocaine shooter. She was bright, with a caustic, quick wit and flashing smile. I liked her. "C'mon, Jennifer," I said after the interview, "You've got to start using condoms. If you don't, it's just a matter of time. And your needles. Do you share needles?"

"Honey, when I buy them, sometimes they're at right angles."

"You're not serious."

"Hell yes, I'm serious. What do you think, I just walk into a drugstore and say, 'Excuse me, sir. May I have some sterile points, please? And a half pound of pharmaceutical cocaine, while you're at it?' Shit, I'm lucky to get needles at all. And you're telling me I may get a disease that will kill me five years from now? Honey, I'm amazed I'm alive right now. If I'm alive two weeks from now,

I'll be doubly amazed. I've got to come up with $400 each and every day, just to put in my arm. That doesn't include rent, food and trips to Rome, honey. Just to feed my veins. That's what I have to worry about, not some disease that may kill me in five years. Get real."

Sometimes I worked with a partner. One of them was David, a bright young sociologist. David was gay, and rather small in stature. We were working Ponce de Leon Avenue one night, even sleazier and more dangerous than The Strip, when suddenly, behind us we heard, "You! Wait! Wait for Sherry!"

We stopped and turned to look. Running toward us as fast as her size thirteen pumps could carry her was the ugliest transvestite I'd ever seen: Six-foot-four, about 220 pounds, waving her arms frantically with a look of utter terror on her painted face. She was done up in a blue satin dress, size eighteen at least, with a feather boa flapping behind in her wake. In the dim light of a street lamp, I saw a nasty razor scar from the cheekbone to nostril that no amount of makeup could hide.

"Oh, thank God!" she cried, winded and panting. "There's a car full of rednecks after me. Can I walk with you as far as the Starvin' Marvin to call a cab? I'm afraid they'll get me."

David reached up to pat her shoulder. "Calm down," he said. "We'll take care of you."

And the three of us strolled down that funky, dirty old street, the huge scarfaced black man in a blue dress and feather boa protected by a fat middle-aged woman and a small gay man.

Sometimes you have to laugh.

We went to a halfway house to give a safe sex talk and interview the women. These were women halfway out of prison—not quite in jail, not quite ready for the street. Most of them were in for drug-related offenses, and there's no such thing as a female drug addict who doesn't turn tricks. We got eighteen blood samples that day.

Most of the women were black; a third were white. One of them was twenty-three and had been in prison for four years. Her veins were fine—no scar tissue at all. "You in for a drug offense?" I asked, bending over her arm.

"No."

I untied the tourniquet, looking up. "What, then?"

"Murder. I killed my husband."

I was stunned for a moment. "Well, I hope he needed killing," I said. Her blue eyes didn't waver. "He did," she replied.

Plum Nellie's is a funny kind of a bar. An old woman, with hands twisted from rheumatoid arthritis, plays the piano while gay boys sing Broadway show tunes, camp it up and flirt. In the back, pimps in snakeskin boots and leather coats wait for their ladies.

I'd been waiting, too. Six or seven rum-and-Cokes had made the wait easier, and I was drunk enough to not be aware how truly strange a spectacle I made in the place. The gay boys ignored me; the pimps glanced at me with amused looks and shrugged to each other while I smiled benignly at everyone.

It was 1:00 a.m. and still no whores.

"That's one helluva hunk of gold you got there," I said to a young pimp standing next to me. He detached himself from his friends to glance my way, fingering the gold chain around his neck. The thing must have weighed half a pound.

"Yeah," he said.

"Business must be pretty good," I slurred.

"Not too bad," he replied, his eyes suspicious.

"That's good. That's good. Too bad it won't stay that way." I let my voice trail off.

"What you talkin' about?"

"Well, I've been doing the free AIDS tests for working girls. Maybe you've seen my posters. Anyway, most of them aren't using rubbers regularly."

"So what?" He was vaguely hostile.

"They're all gonna die, man. It's just a matter of time." I sipped my drink, giving him time to digest what I'd said.

It didn't take long.

"But these women ain't fuckin' no faggots. How they gonna get AIDS?"

"Because they're running drugs with other people's points, man. And they're fucking bisexuals. Like I said, it's just a matter of time."

"No shit. Say, why don't you gimme some rubbers? I'm gonna make my chicks use 'em."

I dug into the green bag for condoms.

"What else you got in that bag?"

"Oh, I've got my blood tubes, needles, interview forms, stuff like that. Why?"

He looked at me for a long moment. "You're pretty drunk, ain't ya?"

I thought about it for a second. Everything was kind of fuzzy. "Yeah, I am a wee bit stinko, now that you mention it."

"Why don't you let me call you a cab? There's people around here who'd take you off in a heartbeat just for them needles."

I blinked. "Take me off. You mean . . . off? Oh, wow."

I let him call a cab.

Only about 20 percent of prostitutes are streetwalkers. The other 80 percent are call girls and escort agency workers. In order to make our study representative of the entire spectrum of working women, I needed an equal number of these women. To find them, I advertised in a local newspaper.

One of the women who responded was a forty-five-year-old named Cindy. Cindy ran a massage parlour out of her apartment and not only worked herself, but employed five or six other women, too.

Cindy was a woman with a goal. She had lived in India for twelve years and had put together a project to build model villages there for orphans. She intended to go to India in some comfort, however, and decided that she needed $40,000 to live in style while organizing her orphan village. She had amassed $30,000 in nine months.

Here's to free enterprise and the American way.

Late one night, I interviewed two women, using the dim light of a neon sign in a window to read the questions on my questionnaire. I wasn't too sure about these ladies. They were too well dressed.

One was very attractive and wore a clingy black dress short enough to reveal her very shapely legs; the other was tall and slender, blond and very fair of skin. Her prettiness was spoiled by severe acne scars. She wore tight leather jeans and a lavender halter which defined her bosom. Their makeup was impeccable.

This was early on in the study, and I hadn't yet realized that the women who work Peachtree Street don't look like the stereotypical whore. If you see a woman with a short dress and fishnet stockings with high heels, you can bet she's either a cop or a boy. The RG's (real girls) wear bluejeans and T-shirts. They don't carry purses, many wear no makeup and inevitably they wear sneakers.

You can't run in high heels.

The two were cooperative and honest. I read the questions about numbers of partners, about drug use. No problem. When I got to the section about birth control, I asked what types they had used in the past five years. They each replied that they used condoms occasionally. No birth control pills. No IUD's, no diaphragms.

"How many times have you been pregnant?"

"None."

The light began to dawn. I already knew what the answer to my next question would be.

"How old were you when you started having your periods?"

They glanced at each other nervously. "Uh . . . I don't know . . . Like, thirteen."

"Uh, yeah, about thirteen. Me too."

Right. What could I do? Embarrass them? Say something like, "Gee, ladies, this survey is for RG's only?" Or, "Wow, you really had me fooled! Gosh, what they can do with silicone these days!"

Besides, if they were living as women, working as women, and were in the process of becoming women through surgery and hormones, what the hell was the difference? I finished the interview, drew their blood, gave them condoms and wished them well.

Next day, in the office of the Department of Human Resources, I explained to Terry what had happened.

"You got two blood samples from a couple of transsexuals?"

"Yeah, I did. What can I say. And they were gorgeous, man."

"Well," she thought for a moment. "We'll submit the samples with an explanation. That way, they can still get their results."

The Department and the Centers for Disease Control decided not to use the interviews as part of the data for the study, so even though I drew 125 blood samples all together, 123 was the official count.

The study lasted from February 1986 to February 1987. Of 123 blood samples, one was positive for HIV antibodies. She was a drug addict from Florida, who shared needles. She had never turned a trick in the state of Georgia.

The other cities testing prostitutes had similar results, proving what some of us already knew—prostitutes don't have AIDS, junkies do. Every hooker infected with HIV is a drug user first and foremost, who uses prostitution to support her drug habit, and she got it from an infected needle.

An article in the October 24, 1986 *Journal of the American Medical Association* states, "Since infection is transmitted to only about 10 to 50 percent of steady heterosexual partners, the likelihood of transmission to a partner with a single exposure must be quite low, *probably less than 1 percent per contact.*" (Italics mine.)

With this being true, it's unlikely that a prostitute could infect a client even without the use of a condom, and there is little chance if a condom is used. Still, month by month, toward the end of the study, the numbers of women working Peachtree Street and Ponce de Leon decreased as police sweeps "cleaned up" the area of "disease-ridden" prostitutes.

The Georgia Department of Human Resources, even with only one HIV-positive blood sample from 123 working women, still recommended the mandatory testing of all convicted prostitutes. As a taxpayer, I kind of resent that.

Toward the end of the study, David and I walked the circle from Peachtree to Tenth Street to Juniper and back many times on a Saturday night without seeing a single whore working the street. I guess you could say Atlanta has conquered the "prostitute problem." The street whores of Midtown have been harassed and arrested right out of existence.

To me, it's a little embarrassing. A city as cosmopolitan and sophisticated as Atlanta claims to be with no hookers on Peachtree? New York has 42nd Street. San Francisco has the Tenderloin. Baltimore has The Block, but there's no mo' ho's on Peachtree no mo', y'all.

If a city's sophistication can be judged in part by its view on sexuality, what shall we say about Atlanta? What was it Mammy said to Rhett? "You can put a mule in a race-horse harness, but it still ain't nothin' but a mule."

Poochie and Sam are gone now. Sherry no longer clatters down Ponce in her size thirteen pumps. Jennifer is gone. Plum Nellie's is gone, too. Even Cindy is gone, off to India to build her orphan village.

I guess it's a good thing. The young upwardly mobile couples who rushed to midtown to buy up the fine old houses while they were still cheap can breathe a sigh of relief. Fancy hotels and condos and office high-rises have changed the face of Midtown, and the Strip is now the cultural center.

That's progress.

Still, the hookers took a little of the old flavor and color of Atlanta with them when they went away . . . Oh, well. Git up, mule. 🖋

SUGGESTIONS FOR WRITING

1. How do you respond to the Georgia Department of Human Resources' requirement that all convicted prostitutes take an AIDS test? If such a test were made mandatory, to what use should the test results be put? Compare

this attitude to that expressed in the essay by William Buckley, Jr., "Identify All Carriers."

2. Based on what you know about AIDS, can the yuppies who have moved in to downtown Atlanta really breathe a "sigh of relief"? Explore why or why not.

3. What is your reaction to the fact that a prostitutes' rights activist group had to be the one to initiate AIDS education among hookers?

9

RACISM AND RESISTANCE

One of America's oldest and most persistent problems is racism. Undoubtedly this problem stems from our long history as a slave-holding country. The first African slaves arrived in America shortly after the first European settlers and America was one of the last countries in the world to ban slavery. But the end of slavery did not mean the end of racism. Although it is supposed to be a proud fact of our national life that we are a multiracial country, with African-Americans, Orientals, white Europeans, Native Americans, and Hispanics sharing the social space, white hatred of blacks and other people of color has been a persistent theme.

Although there is intolerance among all of these groups, we will focus in this chapter on writings that deal with the stormy history of African-Americans and whites in America. For many whites, black people are dangerous just by virtue of their difference. Individual uniqueness becomes blurred as all people of one race are lumped together in one category. Stereotypes are taken for truths. Cultural differences are defined as natural inferiorities. Black speech, for example, is often degraded as inarticulate and non-grammatical. Many white people simply fear the differences they cannot understand. In reaction, some black people fear and stereotype white people, developing a counterracism. But it is white racism that has been built into the social system—for a long time, of course, even into the legal system. Considering that we pride ourselves in our national diversity, we nevertheless have not honored differences of race.

It is also true that the history of resistance to racism in this country is almost as old as slavery itself, and this resistance has continued to the present. Slaves resisted and rebelled; whites and blacks fought for the abolition of slavery. In our century, black people and their *white allies peacefully resisted racism and demanded civil rights. Laws of discrimination have been for the most part removed; laws prohibiting discrimination and fostering equal opportunity were established. But racism persists, and the new laws have been perceived by some Americans, white and black, as condoning favoritism toward blacks, ironically contributing to the racism they were supposed to eliminate. In our complex culture, racism is often subtle and hard to define.*

In this section, you will read about racism and resistance to racism. Both have taken many different forms. You will read the accounts of slaves who learned to survive a racist system, and the stories of people who opposed racism in the civil rights movement. We have also included two essays that try to account for the current rise in racist incidents on college campuses. The readings will invite you to write about racism and racial difference. What experiences have you had with racism? What are your own racial attitudes? What accounts for racial difference? How should we as a society respond to these differences? These and other questions will allow you to examine this persistent American problem from many perspectives. ✒

Selections from
LIFE AND TIMES OF
FREDERICK DOUGLASS

Frederick Douglass

Frederick Douglass was the author of the most famous and influential narrative written by a former slave. Douglass, born into slavery in 1817, escaped and became a freeman in 1838. A powerful figure in the movement to abolish slavery, he was an imposing orator and an effective and sophisticated writer. Later in his life Douglass worked for women's rights and for early labor union organizations; he was an important national voice in the struggle for equal treatment of African-Americans, and he served as consul general to the republic of Haiti. He died in 1895. In this section of his Life and Times, *Douglass narrates and analyzes the causes of an act of violence directed at him by a gang of white working men who resented working with a slave, and he describes the response of the legal system.*

. . . Very soon after I went to Baltimore to live, Master Hugh succeeded in getting me hired to Mr. William Gardiner, an extensive shipbuilder on Fell's Point. I was placed there to learn to calk, a trade of which I already had some knowledge, gained while in Mr. Hugh Auld's shipyard. Gardiner's, however, proved a very unfavorable place for the accomplishment of the desired object. Mr. Gardiner was that season engaged in building two large man-of-war vessels, professedly for the Mexican government. These vessels were to be launched in the month of July of that year, and in failure thereof Mr. Gardiner would forfeit a very considerable sum of money. So, when I entered the shipyard, all was hurry and driving. There were in the yard about one hundred men; of these, seventy or eighty were regular carpenters—privileged men. There was no time for a raw hand to learn anything. Every man had to do that which he knew how to do, and in entering the yard Mr. Gardiner had directed me to do whatever the carpenters told me to do. This was placing me at the beck and call of about seventy-five men. I was to regard all these as my masters. Their word was to be my law. My situation was a trying one. I was called a dozen ways in the space of a single minute. I needed a dozen pairs of hands. Three or four voices would strike my ear at the same moment. It was "Fred, come help to cant this timber here,"—"Fred, come carry this timber yonder,"—"Fred, bring that roller here,"—"Fred, go get a fresh can of water,"—"Fred, come help saw off the end of this timber,"—"Fred, go quick and get the crow-bar,"—"Fred, hold on the end of this fall,"—"Fred, go to the blacksmith's shop and get a new punch,"—"Halloo, Fred! run and bring me a cold chisel,"—"I say, Fred, bear a hand, and get up a fire under the steam box as quick as lightning,"—"Hullo, nigger! come turn this grindstone,"—"Come, come, move, move! and bowse this timber forward,"—"I say, darkey, blast your eyes! why don't you heat up some pitch?"—"Halloo! halloo! halloo! (three voices at the same time)"—"Come here; go there; hold on where you are. D—n you, if you move I'll knock your brains out!" Such, my dear reader, is a glance at the school which was mine during the first eight months of my stay at Gardiner's shipyard.

At the end of eight months Master Hugh refused longer to allow me to remain with Gardiner. The circumstance which led to this refusal was the committing of an outrage upon me, by the white apprentices of the shipyard. The fight was a desperate one, and I came out of it shockingly mangled. I was cut and bruised in sundry places, and my left eye was nearly knocked out of its socket. The facts which led to this brutal outrage upon me illustrate a phase of slavery which was destined to become an important element in the overthrow of the slave system, and I may therefore state them with some minuteness. That phase was this—the conflict of slavery with the interests of white mechanics and laborers. In the country this conflict was not so apparent, but in cities, such as Baltimore, Richmond, New Orleans, Mobile, etc., it was seen pretty clearly. The slaveholders, with a craftiness peculiar to themselves, by encouraging the enmity of the poor laboring white man against the blacks, succeeded in making the said white man almost as much a slave as the black slave himself. The difference between the white slave and the black slave was this: the latter belonged to one slaveholder, while the former belonged to the slaveholders collectively. The white slave had taken from him by indirection what the black slave had taken from him directly and without ceremony. Both were plundered, and by the same plunderers. The slave was robbed by his master of all his earnings, above what was required for his bare physical necessities, and the white laboring man was robbed by the slave system of the just results of his labor, because he was flung into competition with a class of laborers who worked without wages. The slaveholders blinded them to this competition by keeping alive their prejudice against the slaves as *men*—not against them as *slaves*. They appealed to their pride, often denouncing emancipation as tending to place the white working man on an equality with negroes, and by this means they succeeded in drawing off the minds of the poor whites from the real fact, that by the rich slave-master they were already regarded as but a single remove from equality with the slave. The impression was cunningly made that slavery was the only power that could prevent the laboring white man from falling to the level of the slave's poverty and degradation. To make this enmity deep and broad between the slave and the poor white man, the latter was allowed to abuse and whip the former without hindrance. But, as I have said, this state of affairs prevailed mostly in the country. In the City of Baltimore there were not unfrequent murmurs that educating slaves to be mechanics might, in the end, give slave-masters power to dispense altogether with the services of the poor white man. But with characteristic dread of offending the slaveholders, these poor white mechanics in Mr. Gardiner's shipyard, instead of applying the natural, honest remedy for the apprehended evil, and objecting at once to work there by the side of the slaves, made a cowardly attack upon the free colored mechanics, saying they were eating the bread which should be eaten by American freeman, and aimed to prevent him from serving himself, in the evening of life, with the trade with which he had served his master, during the more vigorous portion of his days. Had they succeeded in driving the black freemen out of the shipyard, they would have determined also upon the removal of the black slaves. The feeling was, about this time, very bitter toward all colored people in Baltimore (1836), and they—free and slave—suffered all manner of insult and wrong.

Until a very little while before I went there, white and black carpenters worked side by side in the shipyards of Mr. Gardiner, Mr. Duncan, Mr. Walter Price, and Mr. Robb. Nobody seemed to see any impropriety in it. Some of the blacks were first-rate workmen and were given jobs requiring the highest skill. All at once, however, the white carpenters swore that they would no longer work on the same stage with Negroes. Taking advantage of the heavy contract resting upon Mr. Gardiner to have the vessels for Mexico ready to launch in July, and of the difficulty of getting other hands at that season of the year, they swore that they would not strike another blow for him unless he would discharge his free colored workmen. Now, although this movement did not extend to me *in form*, it did reach me in *fact*. The spirit which is awakened was one of malice and bitterness toward colored people generally, and I suffered with the rest, and suffered severely. My fellow-apprentices very soon began to feel it to be degrading to work with me. They began to put on high looks and to talk contemptuously and maliciously of "the niggers," saying that they would take the "country," and that they "ought to be killed." Encouraged by workmen who, knowing me to be a slave, made no issue with Mr. Gardiner about my being there, these young men did their utmost to make it impossible for me to stay. They seldom called me to do anything without coupling the call with a curse, and Edward North, the biggest in everything, rascality included, ventured to strike me, whereupon I picked him up and threw him into the dock. Whenever any of them struck me I struck back again, regardless of consequences. I could manage any of them singly, and so long as I could keep them from combining I got on very well.

In the conflict which ended my stay at Mr. Gardiner's I was beset by four of them at once—Ned North, Ned Hayes, Bill Stewart, and Tom Humphreys. Two of them were as large as myself, and they came near killing me, in broad daylight. One came in front, armed with a brick; there was one at each side and one behind, and they closed up all around me. I was struck on all sides, and while I was attending to those in front I received a blow on my head from behind, dealt with a heavy handspike. I was completely stunned by the blow, and fell heavily on the ground among the timbers. Taking advantage of my fall they rushed upon me and began to pound me with their fists. With a view of gaining strength, I let them lay on for awhile after I came to myself. They had done me little damage, so far, but finally getting tired of that sport I gave a sudden surge, and despite their weight I rose to my hands and knees. Just as I did this one of their number planted a blow with his boot in my left eye, which for a time seemed to have burst my eyeball. When they saw my eye completely closed, my face covered with blood, and I staggering under the stunning blows they had given me, they left me. As soon as I gathered strength I picked up the handspike and madly enough attempted to pursue them but here the carpenters interfered and compelled me to give up my pursuit. It was impossible to stand against so many.

Dear reader, you can hardly believe the statement, but it is true and there-fore I write it down—that no fewer than fifty white men stood by and saw this brutal and shameful outrage committed, and not a man of them all interposed a single word of mercy. There were four against one, and that one's face was beaten and battered most horribly, and no one said, "That is enough," but some cried out, "Kill him! kill him! kill the d—n nigger! knock his brains out! he struck a white person!" I mention this inhuman outcry to show the character of the men and the spirit of the times at Gardiner's shipyard, and, indeed, in Baltimore generally, in 1836. As I look back to this period I am almost amazed that I was not murdered outright, so murderous was the spirit which prevailed there. On two other occasions while there I came near losing my life. On one of these, I was driving bolts in the hold through the keelson, with Hayes. In its course the bolt bent. Hayes cursed me and said that it was my blow which bent the bolt. I denied this and charged it upon him. In a fit of rage he seized an adze and darted toward me. I met him with a maul and parried his blow, or I should have lost my life.

After the united attack of North, Stewart, Hayes, and Humphreys, finding that the carpenters were as bitter toward me as the apprentices, and that the latter were probably set on by the former, I found my only chance for life was in flight. I succeeded in getting away without an additional blow. To strike a white man was death by lynch law, in Gardiner's shipyard, nor was there much of any other law toward the colored people at that time in any other part of Maryland.

After making my escape from the shipyard I went straight home and related my story to Master Hugh, and to his credit I say it, that his conduct, though he was not a religious man, was every way more humane than that of his brother Thomas, when I went to him in a somewhat similar plight, from the hands of his "Brother Edward Covey." Master Hugh listened attentively to my narration of the circumstances leading to the ruffianly assault, and gave many evidences of his strong indignation at what was done. He was a rough but manly-hearted fellow, and at this time his best nature showed itself.

The heart of my once kind mistress Sophia was again melted in pity towards me. My puffed-out eye and my scarred and blood-covered face moved the dear lady to tears. She kindly drew a chair by me, and with friendly and consoling words, she took water and washed the blood from my face. No mother's hand could have been more tender than hers. She bound up my head and covered my wounded eye with a lean piece of fresh beef. It was almost compensation for all I suffered, that it occasioned the manifestation once more of the originally characteristic kindness of my mistress. Her affectionate heart was not yet dead, though much hardened by time and circumstances.

As for Master Hugh, he was furious, and gave expression to his feelings in the forms of speech usual in that locality. He poured curses on the whole of the shipyard company, and swore that he would have satisfaction. His indignation was really strong and healthy, but unfortunately it resulted from the thought that his rights of property, in my person, had not been respected, more than from any sense of the outrage perpetrated upon me *as a man*. I had reason to think this from the fact that he could, himself, beat and mangle when it suited him to do so.

Bent on having satisfaction, as he said, just as soon as I got a little better of my bruises, Master Hugh took me to Esquire Watson's office on Bond street, Fell's Point, with a view to procuring the arrest of those who had assaulted me. He gave to the magistrate an account of the outrage as I had related it to him, and seemed to expect that a warrant would at once be issued for the arrest of the lawless ruffians. Mr. Watson heard all that he had to say, then coolly inquired, "Mr. Auld, who saw this assault of which you speak?" "It was done, sir, in the presence of a shipyard full of hands." "Sir," said Mr. Watson, "I am sorry, but I cannot move in this matter, except upon the oath of white witnesses." "But here's the boy; look at his head and face," said the excited Master Hugh; "*they* show what has been done." But Watson insisted that he was not authorized to do anything, unless white witnesses of the transaction would come forward and testify to what had taken place. He could issue no warrant, on my word, against white persons, and if I had been killed in the presence of a *thousand blacks*, their testimony combined would have been insufficient to condemn a single murderer. Master Hugh was compelled to say, for once, that this state of things was too bad, and he left the office of the magistrate disgusted.

Of course it was impossible to get any white man to testify against my assailants. The carpenters saw what was done, but the actors were but the agents of their malice, and did only what the carpenters sanctioned. They had cried with one accord, "Kill the nigger! kill the nigger!" Even those who may have pitied me, if any such were among them, lacked the moral courage to volunteer their evidence. The slightest show of sympathy or justice toward a person of color was denounced as abolitionism, and the name of abolitionist subjected its hearer to frightful liabilities. "D—n abolitionists," and "kill the niggers," were the watchwords of the foul-mouthed ruffians of those days. Nothing was done, and probably would not have been, had I been killed in the affray. The laws and the morals of the Christian city of Baltimore afforded no protection to the sable denizens of that city.

Master Hugh, on finding that he could get no redress for the cruel wrong, withdrew me from the employment of Mr. Gardiner and took me into his own family. Mrs. Auld kindly taking care of me and dressing my wounds until they were healed and I was ready to go to work again.

While I was on the Eastern Shore, Master Hugh had met with reverses which overthrew his business and had given up ship-building in his own yard, on the City Block, and was now acting as foreman of Mr. Walter Price. The best that he could do for me was to take me into Mr. Price's yard, and afford me the facilities there for completing the trade which I began to learn at Gardiner's. Here I rapidly became expert in the use of calkers' tools, and in the course of a single year, I was able to command the highest wages paid to journeymen calkers in Baltimore.

The reader will observe that I was now of some pecuniary value to my master. During the busy season I was bringing six and seven dollars per week. I have sometimes brought him as much as nine dollars a week, for wages were a dollar and a half per day.

After learning to calk, I sought my own employment, made my own contracts, and collected my own earnings—giving Master Hugh no trouble in any part of the transactions to which I was a party.

Here, then, were better days for the Eastern Shore slave. I was free from the vexatious assaults of the apprentices at Gardiner's, free from the perils of plantation life, and once more in favorable condition to increase my little stock of education, which had been at a dead stand since my removal from Baltimore. I had on the Eastern Shore been only a teacher, when in company with other slaves, but now there were colored persons here who could instruct me. Many of the young calkers could read, write, and cipher. Some of them had high notions about mental improvement, and the free ones on Fell's Point organized what they called the "East Baltimore Mental Improvement Society." To this society, notwithstanding it was intended that only free persons should attach themselves, I was admitted, and was several times assigned a prominent part in its debates. I owe much to the society of these young men.

The reader already knows enough of the ill effects of good treatment on a slave to anticipate what was not the case in my improved condition. It was not long before I began to show signs of disquiet with slavery, and to look around for a means to get out of it by the shortest route. I was living among freemen, and was in all respects equal to them by nature and attainments. Why should I be a slave? There was no reason why I should be the thrall of any man. Besides, I was not getting, as I have said, a dollar and fifty cents per day. I contracted for it, worked for it, collected it; it was paid to me, and it was rightfully my own; and yet upon every returning Saturday night, this money—my own hard earnings, every cent of it—was demanded of me and taken from me by Master Hugh. He did not earn it—he had no hand in earning it—why, then should he have it? I owed him nothing. He had given me no schooling, and I had received from him only my food and raiment, and for these, my services were supposed to pay from the first. The right to take my earnings was the right of the robber. He had the power to compel me to give him the fruits of my labor, and this *power* was his only right in the case. I became more and more dissatisfied with this state of things, and in so becoming I only gave proof of the same human nature which every reader of this chapter in my life—slaveholder, or non-slaveholder—is conscious of possessing.

To make a contented slave, you must make a thoughtless one. It is necessary to darken his moral and mental vision, and, as far as possible, to annihilate his power of reason. He must be able to detect no inconsistencies in slavery. The man who takes his earnings must be able to convince him that he has a perfect right to do so. It must not depend upon mere force—the slave must know no higher law than his master's will. The whole relationship must not only demonstrate to his mind its necessity, but its absolute rightfulness. If there be one crevice through which a single drop can fall, it will certainly rust off the slave's chain. ✒

Suggestions for Writing

1. What lessons do you think Douglass learned about slavery and racism from this experience?

2. Do you think that racism is more common among working-class, middle-class, or upper-class white people? What different forms does racism take in these different classes?

3. If you were one of the workers who witnessed this attack, would you have had the courage to intervene? Why or why not? How can white people now resist the racism of other whites?

4. Describe an act of racial violence that you have been involved in or observed. What was the cause of it? How could it have been prevented?

FIGHT, AND IF YOU CAN'T FIGHT, KICK

Anonymous

This account is part of the oral autobiography of an anonymous ex-slave from Tennessee, collected in the 1940s by a team of researchers from Fisk University in Nashville. The title refers to the wisdom that this slave's mother passed down to her; it suggests a refusal to accept abuse, even in slavery. The speaker's mother clearly does not fit the old stereotype of the happy and compliant slave. She has a very powerful sense of her own dignity, and she resists the dehumanization that her station in the world would seem to impose. This woman's account gives us a picture of life under slavery that challenges the common image of victimization and suffering. Certainly the mother suffers, but she resists her enslavement as fully as possible, just as many slaves resisted in armed and organized slave rebellions.

My mother was the smartest black woman in Eden. She was as quick as a flash of lightning, and whatever she did could not be done better. She could do anything. She cooked, washed, ironed, spun, nursed and labored in the field. She made as good a field hand as she did a cook. I have heard Master Jennings say to his wife, "Fannie has her faults, but she can outwork any nigger in the country. I'd bet my life on that."

My mother certainly had her faults as a slave. She was very different in nature from Aunt Caroline. Ma fussed, fought, and kicked all the time. I tell you, she was a demon. She said that she wouldn't be whipped, and when she fussed, all Eden must have known it. She was loud and boisterous, and it seemed to me that you could hear her a mile away. Father was often the prey of her high temper. With all her ability for work, she did not make a good slave. She was too high-spirited and independent. I tell you, she was a captain.

The one doctrine of my mother's teaching which was branded upon my senses was that I should never let anyone abuse me. "I'll kill you, gal, if you don't stand up for yourself," she would say. "Fight, and if you can't fight, kick; if you can't kick, then bite." Ma was generally willing to work, but if she didn't feel like doing something, none could make her do it. At least, the Jennings couldn't make, or didn't make her.

"Bob, I don't want no sorry nigger around me. I can't tolerate you if you ain't got no backbone." Such constant warning to my father had its effect. My mother's unrest and fear of abuse spread gradually to my father. He seemed to have been made after the timid kind. He would never fuss back at my mother, or if he did, he couldn't be heard above her shouting. Pa was also a sower of all seeds. He was a yardman, houseman, plowman, gardener, blacksmith, carpenter, keysmith, and anything else they chose him to be.

I was the oldest child. My mother had three other children by the time I was about six years old. It was at this age that I remember the almost daily talks of my mother on the cruelty of slavery. I would say nothing to her, but I was thinking all the time that slavery did not seem so cruel. Master and Mistress Jennings were not mean to my mother. It was she who was mean to them.

Master Jennings allowed his slaves to earn any money they could for their own use. My father had a garden of his own around his little cabin, and he also had some chickens. Mr. Dodge, who was my master's uncle, and who owned the hotel in Eden, was pa's regular customer. He would buy anything my pa brought to him; and many times he was buying his own stuff, or his nephew's stuff. I have seen pa go out at night with a big sack and come back with it full. He'd bring sweet potatoes, watermelons, chickens and turkeys. We were fond of pig roast and sweet potatoes, and the only way to have pig roast was for pa to go out on one of his hunting trips. Where he went, I cannot say, but he brought the booty home. The floor of our cabin was covered with planks. Pa had raised up two planks, and dug a hole. This was our storehouse. Every Sunday, Master Jennings would let pa take the wagon to carry watermelons, cider and ginger cookies to Spring Hill, where the Baptist church was located. The Jennings were Baptists. The white folks would buy from him as well as the free Negroes of Trenton, Tennessee. Sometimes these free Negroes would steal to our cabin at a specified time to buy a chicken or barbecue dinner. Mr. Dodge's slaves always had money and came to buy from us. Pa was allowed to keep the money he made at Spring Hill, and of course Master Jennings didn't know about the little restaurant we had in our cabin.

One day my mother's temper ran wild. For some reason Mistress Jennings struck her with a stick. Ma struck back and a fight followed. Mr. Jennings was not at home and the children became frightened and ran upstairs. For half hour they wrestled in the kitchen. Mistress, seeing that she could not get the better of ma, ran out in the road, with ma right on her heels. In the road, my mother flew into her again. The thought seemed to race across my mother's mind to tear mistress' clothing off her body. She suddenly began to tear Mistress Jennings' clothes off. She caught hold, pulled, ripped and tore. Poor mistress was nearly naked when the storekeeper got to them and pulled ma off.

"Why, Fannie, what do you mean by that?" he asked.

"Why, I'll kill her, I'll kill her dead if she ever strikes me again."

I have never been able to find out the why of the whole thing. . . .

Pa heard Mr. Jennings say that Fannie would have to be whipped by law. He told ma. Two mornings afterward, two men came in at the big gate, one with a long lash in his hand. I was in the yard and I hoped they couldn't find ma. To my surprise, I saw her running around the house, straight in the direction of the men. She must have seen them coming. I should have known that she wouldn't hide. She knew what they were coming for, and she intended to meet them halfway. She swooped upon them like a hawk on chickens. I believe they were afraid of her or thought she was crazy. One man had a long beard which she grabbed with one hand, and the lash with the other. Her body was made strong with madness. She was a good match for them. Mr. Jennings came and pulled her away. I don't know what would have happened if he hadn't come at that moment, for one man had already pulled his gun out. Ma did not see the gun until Mr. Jennings came up. On catching sight of it, she said, "Use your gun, use it and blow my brains out if you will." . . .

That evening Mistress Jennings came down to the cabin. "Well, Fannie," she said, "I'll have to send you away. You won't be whipped, and I'm afraid you'll get killed." . . .

"I'll go to hell or anywhere else, but I won't be whipped," ma answered.

"You can't take the baby, Fannie, Aunt Mary can keep it with the other children."

Mother said nothing at this. That night, ma and pa sat up late, talking over things, I guess. Pa loved ma, and I heard him say, "I'm going too, Fannie." About a week later, she called me and told me that she and pa were going to leave me the next day, that they were going to Memphis. She didn't know for how long.

"But don't be abused, Puss." She always called me Puss. My right name was Cornelia. I cannot tell in words the feelings I had at that time. My sorrow knew no bound. My very soul seemed to cry out, "Gone, gone, gone forever." I cried until my eyes looked like balls of fire. I felt for the first time in my life that I had been abused. How cruel it was to take my mother and father from me, I thought. My mother had been right. Slavery was cruel, so very cruel.

Thus my mother and father were hired to Tennessee. The next morning they were to leave. I saw ma working around with the baby under her arms as if it had been a bundle of some kind. Pa came up to the cabin with an old mare for ma to ride, and an old mule for himself. Mr. Jennings was with him.

"Fannie, leave the baby with Aunt Mary," said Mr. Jennings very quietly.

At this, ma took the baby by its feet, a foot in each hand, and with the baby's head swinging downward, she vowed to smash its brains out before she'd leave it. Tears were streaming down her face. It was seldom that ma cried, and everyone knew that she meant every word. Ma took the baby with her. . . .

An uneventful year passed. I was destined to be happily surprised by the return of my mother and father. They came one day, and found me sitting by the roadside in a sort of trance. . . .

"Puss, we've come back, me and pa, and we've come to stay." . . .

She and pa embraced and caressed me for a long time. We went to the cabin, and Master Jennings was there nearly as soon as we were.

"Hello, Fannie. How did you get along?" he asked.

"Why, Mr. Jennings, you know that I know how to get along," she answered.

"Well, I'm glad to hear that, Fannie."

Ma had on new clothes, and a pair of beautiful earrings. She told Aunt Mary that she stayed in Memphis one year without a whipping or a cross word.

Pa had learned to drink more liquor than ever, it seemed. At least, he was able to get more of it, for there were many disagreements between pa and ma about his drinking. Drinkers will drink together, and Mr. Jennings was no exception. Pa would have the excuse that Master Jennings offered him liquor, and of course he wouldn't take it from anybody else. It was common to see them together, half drunk, with arms locked, walking around and around the old barn. Then pa would put his hands behind him and let out a big whoop which could be heard all over Eden. . . .

Our family was increased by the arrival of a baby girl. Ma was very sick, and she never did get well after that. She was cooking for Mistress Jennings one day when she came home and went to bed. She never got up. I guess ma was sick about six months. During that time she never hit a tap of work. She said she had brought five children in the world for the Jennings, and that was enough; that she didn't intend to work when she felt bad.

On the day my mother died, she called pa and said . . . "Go tell Master Jennings to come in, and get all the slaves too."

Pa went and returned in five minutes with old master.

"Fannie, are you any worse?" said old master.

"No, no, Master Jennings, no worse. But I'm going to leave you at eight o-clock."

"Where are you going, Fannie," Master Jennings asked as if he didn't know that ma was talking about dying.

Ma shook her head slowly and answered, "I'm going where there ain't no fighting and cussing and damning."

"Is there anything that you want me to do for you, Fannie?"

Ma told him that she reckoned there wasn't much of anything that anybody could do for her now. "But I would like for you to take Puss and hire her out among ladies, so she can be raised right. She will never be any good here, Master Jennings."

A funny look came over Master Jennings' face, and he bowed his head up and down. All the hands had come in and were standing around with him.

My mother died at just about eight o'clock. 🖋

SUGGESTIONS FOR WRITING

1. What do you know about slavery, and where did you learn what you know? Describe the ways that slaves and slavery are depicted in popular culture.

2. Analyze the speaker's attitude toward her mother. Has she turned her mother into a storybook figure rather than a real person?

3. What does this story tell us about the lives of all women, not just of slave women?

4. Do you think that women should learn how to defend themselves physically in order to resist violence? Why or why not?

5. If you are female, what models did your mother give to you for dealing with the dangers of the world?

THE JEALOUS MISTRESS

Harriet Jacobs

Harriet Jacobs (1813-1897), a slave who escaped from captivity, became part of the movement to abolish slavery and wrote an account of her life that illustrates the harshness of slave life for women. Jacobs worked in slavery as a domestic servant, a condition that saved her from some of the harshest work slaves were condemned to, but one that also put her in the grasp of "Dr. Flint," the name she gives to her master, who constantly tried to subject her to his sexual desires. Jacobs had learned from her own masters the value that her society placed on female chastity, and yet she found herself in the position of being expected to be a sexual slave. In this chapter of Incidents in the Life of a Slave Girl, *she focuses on her relationship with her mistress, who was aware of Dr. Flint's desires but who took out her anger on the slave who was his victim. This passage shows vividly the complex relationships that developed across racial and gender lines in the household.*

I would ten thousand times rather that my children should be the half-starved paupers of Ireland than to be the most pampered among the slaves of America. I would rather drudge out my life on a cotton plantation, till the grave opened to give me rest, than to live with an unprincipled master and a jealous mistress. The felon's home in a penitentiary is preferable. He may repent, and turn from the error of his ways, and so find peace; but it is not so with a favorite slave. She is not allowed to have any pride of character. It is deemed a crime in her to wish to be virtuous.

Mrs. Flint possessed the key to her husband's character before I was born. She might have used this knowledge to counsel and to screen the young and the innocent among her slaves; but for them she had no sympathy. They were the objects of her constant suspicion and malevolence. She watched her husband with unceasing vigilance; but he was well practised in means to evade it. What he could not find opportunity to say in words he manifested in signs. He invented more than were ever thought of in a deaf and dumb asylum. I let them pass, as if I did not understand what he meant; and many were the curses and threats bestowed on me for my stupidity. One day he caught me teaching myself to write. He frowned, as if he was not well pleased; but I suppose he came to the conclusion that such an accomplishment might help to advance his favorite scheme. Before long, notes were often slipped into my hand. I would return them, saying, "I can't read them, sir." "Can't you?" he replied; "then I must read them to you." He always finished the reading by asking, "Do you understand?" Sometimes he would complain of the heat of the tea room, and order his supper to be placed on a small table in the piazza. He would seat himself there with a well-satisfied smile, and tell me to stand by and brush away the flies. He would eat very slowly, pausing between the mouthfuls. These intervals were employed in describing the happiness I was so foolishly throwing away, and in threatening me with the penalty that finally awaited my stubborn disobedience. He boasted much of the forbearance he had exercised towards me, and reminded me that there was a limit to his patience. When I succeeded in avoiding opportunities for him to talk to me at home, I was ordered to come to his office, to do some errand. When there, I was obliged to stand and listen to such language as he saw fit to address to me. Sometimes I so openly expressed my contempt for him that he would become violently enraged, and I wondered why he did not strike me. Circumstanced as he was, he probably thought it was better policy to be forbearing. But the state of things grew worse and worse daily. In desperation I told him that I must and would apply to my grandmother for protection. He threatened me with death, and worse than death, if I made any complaint to her. Strange to say, I did not despair. I was naturally of a buoyant disposition, and always I had a hope of somehow getting out of his clutches. Like many a poor, simple slave before me, I trusted that some threads of joy would yet be woven into my dark destiny.

I had entered my sixteenth year, and every day it became more apparent that my presence was intolerable to Mrs. Flint. Angry words frequently passed between her and her husband. He had never punished me himself, and he would not allow any body else to punish me. In that respect, she was never satisfied; but, in her angry moods, no terms were too vile for her to bestow upon me. Yet I, whom she detested so bitterly, had far more pity for her than he had, whose duty it was to make her life happy. I never wronged her, or wished to wrong her; and one word of kindness from her would have brought me to her feet.

After repeated quarrels between the doctor and his wife, he announced his intention to take his youngest daughter, then four years old, to sleep in his apartment. It was necessary that a servant should sleep in the same room, to be on hand if the child stirred. I was selected for that office, and informed for what purpose that arrangement had been made. By managing to keep within sight of people, as much as possible, during the day time, I had hitherto succeeded in eluding my master, though a razor was often held to my throat to force me to change this line of policy. At night I slept by the side of my great aunt, where I felt safe. He was too prudent to come into her room. She was an old woman, and had been in the family many years. Moreover, as a married man, and a professional man, he deemed it necessary to save appearances in some degree. But he resolved to remove the obstacle in the way of his scheme; and he thought he had planned it so that he should evade suspicion. He was well aware how much I prized my refuge by the side of my old aunt, and he determined to dispossess me of it. The first night the doctor had the little child in his room alone. The next morning, I was ordered to take my station as nurse the following night. A kind Providence interposed in my favor. During the day Mrs. Flint heard of this new arrangement, and a storm followed. I rejoiced to hear it rage.

After a while my mistress sent for me to come to her room. Her first question was, "Did you know you were to sleep in the doctor's room?"

"Yes, ma'am."

"Who told you?"

"My master."

"Will you answer truly all the questions I ask?"

"Yes, ma'am."

"Tell me, then, as you hope to be forgiven, are you innocent of what I have accused you?"

"I am."

She handed me a Bible, and said, "Lay your hand on your heart, kiss this holy book, and swear before God that you tell me the truth."

I took the oath she required, and I did it with a clear conscience.

"You have taken God's holy word to testify your innocence," said she. "If you have deceived me, beware! Now take this stool, sit down, look me directly in the face, and tell me all that has passed between your master and you."

I did as she ordered. As I went on with my account her color changed frequently, she wept, and sometimes groaned. She spoke in tones so sad, that I was touched by her grief. The tears came to my eyes; but I was soon convinced that her emotions arose from anger and wounded pride. She felt that her marriage vows were desecrated, her dignity insulted; but she had no compassion for the poor victim of her husband's perfidy. She pitied herself as a martyr; but she was incapable of feeling for the condition of shame and misery in which her unfortunate, helpless slave was placed.

Yet perhaps she had some touch of feeling for me; for when the conference was ended, she spoke kindly, and promised to protect me. I should have been much comforted by this assurance if I could have had confidence in it; but my experiences in slavery had filled me with distrust. She was not a very refined woman, and had not much control over her passions. I was an object of her jealousy, and, consequently, of her hatred; and I knew I could not expect kindness or confidence from her under the circumstances in which I was placed. I could not blame her. Slaveholders' wives feel as other women would under similar circumstances. The fire of her temper kindled from small sparks, and now the flame became so intense that the doctor was obliged to give up his intended arrangement.

I knew I had ignited the torch, and I expected to suffer for it afterwards; but I felt too thankful to my mistress for the timely aid she rendered me to care much about that. She now took me to sleep in a room adjoining her own. There I was an object of her especial care, though not of her especial comfort, for she spent many a sleepless night to watch over me. Sometimes I woke up, and found her bending over me. At other times she whispered in my ear, as though it was her husband who was speaking to me, and listened to hear what I would answer. If she startled me, on such occasions, she would glide stealthily away; and the next morning she would tell me I had been talking in my sleep, and ask who I was talking to. At last, I began to be fearful for my life. It had been often threatened; and you can imagine, better than I can describe, what an unpleasant sensation it must produce to wake up in the dead of night and find a jealous woman bending over you. Terrible as this experience was, I had fears that it would give place to one more terrible.

My mistress grew weary of her vigils; they did not prove satisfactory. She changed her tactics. She now tried the trick of accusing my master of crime, in my presence, and gave my name as the author of the accusation. To my utter astonishment, he replied, "I don't believe it; but if she did acknowledge it, you tortured her into exposing me." Tortured into exposing him! Truly, Satan had no difficulty in distinguishing the color of his soul! I understood his object in making this false representation. It was to show me that I gained nothing by seeking the protection of my mistress; that the power was still all in his own hands. I pitied Mrs. Flint. She was a second wife, many years the junior of her husband; and the hoary-headed miscreant was enough to try the patience of a wiser and better woman. She was completely foiled, and knew not how to proceed. She would gladly have had me flogged for my supposed false oath; but, as I have already stated, the doctor never allowed any one to whip me. The old sinner was politic. The application of the lash might have led to remarks that would have exposed him in the eyes of his children and grandchildren. How often did I rejoice that I lived in a town where all the inhabitants knew each other! If I had been on a remote plantation, or lost among the multitude of a crowded city, I should not be a living woman at this day.

The secrets of slavery are concealed like those of the Inquisition. My master was, to my knowledge, the father of eleven slaves. But did the mothers dare to tell who was the father of their children? Did the other slaves dare to allude to it, except in whispers among themselves? No, indeed! They knew too well the terrible consequences.

My grandmother could not avoid seeing things which excited her suspicions. She was uneasy about me, and tried various ways to buy me; but the never-changing answer was always repeated: "Linda does not belong to *me*. She is my daughter's property, and I have no legal right to sell her." The conscientious man! He was too scrupulous to *sell* me; but he had no scruples whatever about committing a much greater wrong against the helpless young girl placed under his guardianship, as his daughter's property. Sometimes my persecutor would ask me whether I would like to be sold. I told him I would rather be sold to any body than to lead such a life as I did. On such occasions he would assume the air of a very injured individual, and reproach me for my ingratitude. "Did I not take you into the house, and make you the companion of my own children?" he would say. "Have I ever treated you like a negro? I have never allowed you to be punished, not even to please your mistress. And this is the recompense I get, you ungrateful girl!" I answered that he had reasons of his own for screening me from punishment, and that the course he pursued made my mistress hate me and persecute me. If I wept, he would say, "Poor child! Don't cry! don't cry! I will make peace for you with your mistress. Only let me arrange matters in my own way. Poor, foolish girl! you don't know what is for your own good. I would cherish you. I would make a lady of you. Now go, and think of all I have promised you."

I did think of it.

Reader, I draw no imaginary pictures of southern homes. I am telling you the plain truth. Yet when victims make their escape from this wild beast of Slavery, northerners consent to act the part of bloodhounds, and hunt the poor fugitive back into his den, "full of dead men's bones, and all uncleanness." Nay, more, they are not only willing, but proud, to give their daughters in marriage to slaveholders. The poor girls have romantic notions of a sunny clime, and of the flowering vines that all the year round shade a happy home. To what disappointments are they destined! The young wife soon learns that the husband in whose hands she has placed her happiness pays no regard to his marriage vows. Children of every shade of complexion play with her own fair babies, and too well she knows that they are born unto him of his own household. Jealousy and hatred enter the flowery home, and it is ravaged of its loveliness.

Southern women often marry a man knowing that he is the father of many little slaves. They do not trouble themselves about it. They regard such children as property, as marketable as the pigs on the plantation; and it is seldom that they do not make them aware of this by passing them into the slavetrader's hands as soon as possible, and thus getting them out of their sight. I am glad to say there are some honorable exceptions.

I have myself known two southern wives who exhorted their husbands to free those slaves towards whom they stood in a "parental relation"; and their request was granted. These husbands blushed before the superior nobleness of their wives' natures. Though they had only counselled them to do that which it was their duty to do, it commanded their respect, and rendered their conduct more exemplary. Concealment was at an end, and confidence took the place of distrust.

Though this bad institution deadens the moral sense, even in white women, to a fearful extent, it is not altogether extinct. I have heard southern ladies say of Mr. Such a one, "He not only thinks it no disgrace to be the father of those little niggers, but he is not ashamed to call himself their master. I declare, such things ought not to be tolerated in any decent society!" 🖋

SUGGESTIONS FOR WRITING

1. Who is more dangerous to the slave girl in this narrative, the husband or the wife? Why is the wife not more sympathetic to the girl?

2. Describe the power relationships within this triangle. Are they similar to the power relationships within contemporary love triangles? How much of the girl's problem is a result of her being a slave, and how much is a result of her being the object of a married man's desires?

3. Analyze the moral issues involved for each of the people in this situation.

THE NEGRO QUESTION

This letter was sent to The Locomotive Firemen's Magazine *in 1897 by a member of the Brotherhood of Locomotive Firemen, one of the early railroad labor unions. The writer responds to a call for the acceptance of black workers into the union and states his reasons for opposing integration. What is remarkable in the letter is the openness of the writer's racism. In our time it would be rare to read such overtly racist ideas in print. Certainly some white people would say these same things, but to write them would be to identify themselves publicly and officially as racists, which few people are willing to do, even if they hold strong racist beliefs.*

I notice a great deal in the *Magazine* about the American Federation of Labor and the negro firemen. My sentiments have been spoken in nearly every instance. I object to the proposed federation, principally on account of having to strike the word "white" from our constitution. I don't want to be affiliated with any organization when I have to be on an equality with the negro. When it comes to that I will ask for a final withdrawal, and I will not be alone on this ground, because every true Southern brother will be as I am, and it would be only a short time until every Southern Lodge will have surrendered its charter and I believe a great many Northern Lodges will follow suit.

Look at the Knights of Labor. What became of them after admitting negroes into their ranks? They collapsed, of course, just like the firemen or any other order who will recognize the negro will do.

I was raised in the South, and still live in the South, and will always hold myself above the negro race. I have been running an engine for a little over three years. I have had white firemen and I have had negro firemen. The white firemen will burn less coal than the negro. On the same run a negro will burn from eight to nine tons of coal where the white man will burn about seven tons. The negro gets $1.80 for firing this trip. The man gets $2.25 for the same trip and burns from one to two tons less than the negro. The least cost of coal is $1 per ton at mines. The negro gets 45 cents less than a white man and consumes from $1 to $2 worth more fuel. I wish some one could show me the economy of having a negro fireman. They (negroes) burn more coal and have less steam than white firemen and cause more delay for want of steam which frequently amounts to overtime for the whole crew. I have one (negro) firing for me, not through choice, but because I can't help myself. I wish some of the brothers who favor the proposed plan of federation could smell a sweet-scented negro just one time and I think he would change his mind when he votes. I bought a cake of soap and gave to one of them not long ago to go to the river and wash himself so I could stay on the engine with him. A skunk or a pole-cat would have been perfume for him.

I close by predicting that whenever we have to recognize a negro as a labor organization, that the Brotherhood of Locomotive Firemen will be no more in the South, and will die in the North when our Northern brothers get a little better acquainted with the negro.

A Member of 426.

Birmingham, Ala.

SUGGESTIONS FOR WRITING

1. Do you know people who are as racist as this writer? What explains their racism? Where did they learn those attitudes?

2. Racist attitudes, we would argue, are very rarely expressed in the open fashion of this writer. Is hidden racism as bad as open racism? How does hidden racism express itself?

3. Write a letter that would answer the arguments that this writer raises. What are the advantages of integration to the union that you could point out?

4. Are there still groups that are subjected to open and widely accepted stereotyping? What are these groups? Why are stereotypes about them acceptable?

Selections from
COMING OF AGE IN MISSISSIPPI

Anne Moody

This excerpt from **Anne Moody's** *autobiography is a powerful document from the civil rights movement. It is particularly successful in expressing the spirit of non-violence espoused by Dr. Martin Luther King, Jr. that was at the heart of the movement. It is important to remember that all Moody and her friends wanted was to be served food together with white people. The anger and violence she encountered illustrates the symbolic value that segregation in public places held for many white Southerners. Moody's account gives us an intimate view of that violence. Accounts like Moody's played an important role in the 1960s, helping change the attitudes of white people toward racism and the movement to bring equal rights to all.*

Moody (b. 1940), a native Mississippian, was born into a poor family. She educated herself at Tougaloo College, where she became involved in the civil rights movement.

I had counted on graduating in the spring of 1963, but as it turned out, I couldn't because some of my credits still had to be cleared with Natchez College. A year before, this would have seemed like a terrible disaster, but now I hardly even felt disappointed. I had a great excuse to stay on campus for the summer and work with the Movement, and this was what I really wanted to do. I couldn't go home again anyway, and I couldn't go to New Orleans—I didn't have money enough for bus fare.

During my senior year at Tougaloo, my family hadn't sent me one penny. I had only the small amount of money I had earned at Maple Hill. I couldn't afford to eat at school or live in the dorms, so I had gotten permission to move off campus. I had to prove that I could finish school, even if I had to go hungry every day. I knew Raymond and Miss Pearl were just waiting to see me drop out. But something happened to me as I got more and more involved in the Movement. It no longer seemed important to prove anything. I had found something outside myself that gave meaning to my life.

I had become very friendly with my social science professor, John Salter, who was in charge of NAACP activities on campus. All during the year, while the NAACP conducted a boycott of the downtown stores in Jackson, I had been one of Salter's most faithful canvassers and church speakers. During the last week of school, he told me that sit-in demonstrations were about to start in Jackson and that he wanted me to be the spokesman for a team that would sit-in at Woolworth's lunch counter. The two other demonstrators would be classmates of mine, Memphis and Pearlena. Pearlena was a dedicated NAACP worker, but Memphis had not been very involved in the Movement on campus. It seemed that the organization had had a rough time finding students who were in a position to go to jail. I had nothing to lose one way or the other. Around ten o'clock the morning of the demonstrations, NAACP headquarters alerted the news services. As a result, the police department was also informed, but neither the policemen nor the newsmen knew exactly where or when the demonstrations would start. They stationed themselves along Capitol Street and waited.

To divert attention from the sit-in at Woolworth's, the picketing started at J. C. Penney's a good fifteen minutes before. The pickets were allowed to walk up and down in front of the store three or four times before they were arrested. At exactly 11 A.M., Pearlena, Memphis, and I entered Woolworth's from the rear entrance. We separated as soon as we stepped into the store, and made small purchases from various counters. Pearlena had given Memphis her watch. He was to let us know when it was 11:14. At 11:14 we were to join him near the lunch counter and at exactly 11:15 we were to take seats at it.

Seconds before 11:15 we were occupying three seats at the previously segregated Woolworth's lunch counter. In the beginning the waitresses seemed to ignore us, as if they really didn't know what was going on. Our waitress walked past us a couple of times before she noticed we had started to write our own orders down and realized we wanted service. She asked us what we wanted. We began to read to her from our order slips. She told us that we would be served at the back counter, which was for Negroes.

"We would like to be served here," I said.

The waitress started to repeat what she had said, then stopped in the middle of the sentence. She turned the lights out behind the counter, and she and the other waitresses almost ran to the back of the store, deserting all their white customers. I guess they thought that violence would start immediately after the whites at the counter realized what was going on. There were five or six other people at the counter. A couple of them just got up and walked away. A girl sitting next to me finished her banana split before leaving. A middle-aged white woman who had not yet been served rose from her seat and came over to us. "I'd like to stay here with you," she said, "but my husband is waiting."

The newsmen came in just as she was leaving. They must have discovered what was going on shortly after some of the people began to leave the store. One of the newsman ran behind the woman who spoke to us and asked her to identify herself. She refused to give her name, but said she was a native of Vicksburg and a former resident of California. When asked why she had said what she had said to us, she replied, "I am in sympathy with the Negro movement." By this time a crowd of cameramen and reporters had gathered around us taking pictures and asking questions, such as Where were we from? Why did we sit-in? What organization sponsored it? Were we students? From what school? How were we classified?

I told them that we were all students at Tougaloo College, that we were represented by no particular organization, and that we planned to stay there even after the store closed. "All we want is service," was my reply to one of them. After they had finished probing for about twenty minutes, they were almost ready to leave.

At noon, students from a nearby white high school started pouring in to Woolworth's. When they first saw us they were sort of surprised. They didn't know how to react. A few started to heckle and the newsmen became interested again. Then the white students started chanting all kinds of anti-Negro slogans. We were called a little bit of everything. The rest of the seats except the three we were occupying had been roped off to prevent others from sitting down. A couple of the boys took one end of the rope and made it into a hangman's noose. Several attempts were made to put it around our necks. The crowds grew as more students and adults came in for lunch.

We kept our eyes straight forward and did not look at the crowd except for occasional glances to see what was going on. All of a sudden I saw a face I remembered—the drunkard from the bus station sit-in. My eyes lingered on him just long enough for us to recognize each other. Today he was drunk too, so I don't think he remembered where he had seen me before. He took out a knife, opened it, put it in his pocket, and then began to pace the floor. At this point, I told Memphis and Pearlena what was going on. Memphis suggested that we pray. We bowed our heads, and all hell broke loose. A man rushed forward, threw Memphis from his seat, and slapped my face. Then another man who worked in the store threw me against an adjoining counter.

Down on my knees on the floor, I saw Memphis lying near the lunch counter with blood running out of the corners of his mouth. As he tried to protect his face, the man who'd thrown him down kept kicking him against the head. If he had worn hard-soled shoes instead of sneakers, the first kick probably would have killed Memphis. Finally a man dressed in plain clothes identified himself as a police officer and arrested Memphis and his attacker.

Pearlena had been thrown to the floor. She and I got back on our stools after Memphis was arrested. There were some white Tougaloo teachers in the crowd. They asked Pearlena and me if we wanted to leave. They said that things were getting too rough. We didn't know what to do. While we were trying to make up our minds, we were joined by Joan Trumpauer. Now there were three of us and we were integrated. The crowd began to chant, "Communists, Communists, Communists." Some old man in the crowd ordered the students to take us off the stools.

"Which one should I get first?" a big husky boy said.

"That white nigger," the old man said.

The boy lifted Joan from the counter by her waist and carried her out of the store. Simultaneously, I was snatched from my stool by two high school students. I was dragged about thirty feet toward the door by my hair when someone made them turn me loose. As I was getting up off the floor, I saw Joan coming back inside. We started back to the center of the counter to join Pearlena. Lois Chaffee, a white Tougaloo faculty member, was now sitting next to her. So Joan and I just climbed across the rope at the front end of the counter and sat down. There were now four of us, two whites and two Negroes, all women. The mob started smearing us with ketchup, mustard, sugar, pies, and everything on the counter. Soon Joan and I were joined by John Salter, but the moment he sat down he was hit on the jaw with what appeared to be brass knuckles. Blood gushed from his face and someone threw salt into the open wound. Ed King, Tougaloo's chaplain, rushed to him.

At the other end of the counter, Lois and Pearlena were joined by George Raymond, a CORE field worker and a student from Jackson State College. Then a Negro high school boy sat down next to me. The mob took spray paint from the counter and sprayed it on the new demonstrators. The high school student had on a white shirt; the word "nigger" was written on his back with red spray paint.

We sat there for three hours taking a beating when the manager decided to close the store because the mob had begun to go wild with stuff from other counters. He begged and begged everyone to leave. But even after fifteen minutes of begging, no one budged. They would not leave until we did. Then Dr. Beittel, the president of Tougaloo College, came running in. He said he had just heard what was happening.

About ninety policemen were standing outside the store; they had been watching the whole thing through the windows, but had not come in to stop the mob or do anything. President Beittel went outside and asked Captain Ray to come and escort us out. The captain refused, stating the manager had to invite him in before he could enter the premises, so Dr. Beittel himself brought us out. He had told the police that they had better protect us after we were outside the store. When we got outside, the policemen formed a single line that blocked the mob from us. However, they were allowed to throw at us everything they had collected. Within ten minutes, we were picked up by Reverend King in his station wagon and taken to the NAACP headquarters on Lynch Street.

After the sit-in, all I could think of was how sick Mississippi whites were. They believed so much in the segregated Southern way of life, they would kill to preserve it. I sat there in the NAACP office and thought of how many times they had killed when this way of life was threatened. I knew that the killing had just begun. "Many more will die before it is over with," I thought. Before the sit-in, I had always hated the whites in Mississippi. Now I knew it was impossible for me to hate sickness. The whites had a disease, an incurable disease in its final stage. What were our chances against such a disease? I thought of the students, the young Negroes who had just begun to protest, as young interns. When these young interns got older, I thought, they would be the best doctors in the world for social problems.

Before we were taken back to campus, I wanted to get my hair washed. It was stiff with dried mustard, ketchup and sugar. I stopped in at a beauty shop across the street from the NAACP office. I didn't have on any shoes because I had lost them when I was dragged across the floor at Woolworth's. My stockings were sticking to my legs from the mustard that had dried on them. The hairdresser took one look at me and said, "My land, you were in the sit-in, huh?"

"Yes," I answered. "Do you have time to wash my hair and style it?"

"Right away," she said, and she meant right away. There were three other ladies already waiting, but they seemed glad to let me go ahead of them. The hairdresser was real nice. She even took my stockings off and washed my legs while my hair was drying.

There was a mass rally that night at the Pearl Street Church in Jackson, and the place was packed. People were standing two abreast in the aisles. Before the speakers began, all the sit-inners walked out on the stage and were introduced by Medgar Evers. People stood and applauded for what seemed like thirty minutes or more. Medgar told the audience that this was just the beginning of such demonstrations. He asked them to pledge themselves to unite in a massive offensive against segregation in Jackson, and throughout the state. The rally ended with "We Shall Overcome" and sent home hundreds of determined people. It seemed as though Mississippi Negroes were about to get together at last.

SUGGESTIONS FOR WRITING

1. Analyze why the white people became violent when the black people began to pray.

2. What are Anne Moody's feelings about white people at the end of this experience? Are her responses justified?

3. Describe this event from the perspective of one of the white people in the crowd. How would this account differ from Moody's?

4. Consider what it would be like to live in a time when racial segregation of the kind described by Moody was rigidly enforced. In what ways would your life be different?

WE DIDN'T NONE OF US
EAT THERE

Audie Lee Walters

*Audie Lee Walters was a white woman in the segregated South who sup-
ported a strike that her husband was committed to. The strike also involved
black women whose husbands did the same kind of work, hauling wood.
This account tells us about how these working-class white women reacted to
the racism encountered by the black women traveling with them. During the
era of segregation, actions that we take for granted, like eating or using the
bathroom, were subject to legal restriction. Walters is an example of the
many white people who engaged in quiet acts of solidarity with black people
who were demanding their rights.*

My husband is 53 years old. He's been hauling wood since way before we were
married. And we've been married 37 year. Fred makes about fifteen hundred
dollar a year. We got four boys and two girls. When we was raising our kids, my
husband hauled wood a lot of times barefooted.

What shoes we did have, they had holes in the feet. But he had to work,
even when he didn't have no shoes, to keep all the bills paid. I never did go out
with him to cut wood. He never would let me. I always had a baby to tend to.
I don't know how we've kept our young'uns in school, but we have, some way
or another. . . .

Some days Fred didn't bring in but one load, then other days he'd get two,
three loads. Sometimes, they didn't haul at all. Them's the days we didn't eat.
You know, a wood hauler, they live from today until tomorrow. So if you haul
a load of wood today, you eat today. But if you don't haul a load of wood tomorrow, you don't eat.

So, when Fred quit hauling wood, went out on strike, I didn't know what to
think. We got to talking about it and now I realize what the strike's all about.
I know they can't haul wood and take a beat of ten or fifteen dollar a load. The
day they went out on strike, one man hauled a load in here and he got a dollar
and a half bring-home pay. A dollar and half. That ain't hardly enough.

So I kept talking to Fred about the strike and I realized what he was trying
to do. And I found out that there was some other way, that we could hope there
was some other way to get better wages for hauling wood.

Fred told me he was going to walk the picket line, get something done so
Masonite wouldn't take everything that belonged to him. He just couldn't haul
wood and let them take his money, what belonged to him. And he convinced
me it was the right thing for him to do.

It don't take a man to walk the picket line. Annie Belle Pulliam, she says
she'd walk the picket line every day if they'd let her. There's a lot of women

that's not afraid of it. Some of the other places that are out in Mississippi have women walking the picket lines. But they're afraid for us to walk it here at Masonite in Laurel.

Me and my daughter, Elaine and Annie Belle and three colored women, we went up to Canton last week to talk to Brother Ralph and some Presbyterian church people about raising something for Christmas for the families that's out on strike.

Well, we started out, it's about a hundred and fifty mile drive, and we got along a ways and we was getting hungry. So we stopped at this little cafe in Bay Springs. The colored women, they told us white women to go on in there and eat and just bring them something out to the car to eat.

We said, no, if they didn't serve all of us we wasn't going to eat there. Well, they wouldn't serve the colored women, so we went on. We didn't none of us eat there.

So we drove on up the road until we come to the next town. That was Raleigh. The colored women said for us white women to go in there and ask if they serve colored folks in there. So me and Annie Belle and Elaine, we went in. The lady in the cafe, she put glasses of water down in front of us. And we asked did they serve colored women in there. The lady said, no, they didn't. She said if they were colored and served on the Grand Jury she'd serve them. She told us if the colored women wanted any service they'd have to go around to the back of the cafe to get their food.

So Annie Belle, she just shoved her water glass at the lady and said we wouldn't eat in no damn place that refused to serve colored folks. Then I asked the lady could I use her bathroom. I says, "I would like to use your bathroom." She told me to go up the street to the courthouse if I wanted to use a bathroom.

Well, we left out of there, went on up the road, still looking for a place to eat. Finally, when we got to Canton, we found a cafe that said they served both white and colored. And we all ate there together. On the way back home, we stopped at a shopping center in Raleigh and there was a place there that had a bathroom.

Annie Belle, she got the key to the bathroom and when she had finished using it, she give the key to one of the colored women. A lady come running out and said, "You can't use it. You're colored." Well, the colored lady just looked at her and said, "Lady, I'm human." And she took the key and went on in and used the bathroom. 🖉

SUGGESTIONS FOR WRITING

1. Why did Walters take the side of the black women rather than the white people who were denying them service?

2. Have you ever been witness to an openly racist act? Did you stand up against it? Do most people have the courage to resist racism?

3. What is the significance of the fact that the people involved in this episode were women? Would a racially mixed group of men be likely to react in the same way?

4. Have you ever been the victim of prejudice of any kind—because of your race, your gender, your sexual orientation, your class, or any other reason? What did the scorn of prejudice feel like?

Selections from
PRISON NOTES

Barbara Deming

This chapter, from **Barbara Deming's** Prison Notes, *recounts some of her experiences in Albany, Georgia, where she was arrested for marching for peace and against racism in 1964. Her narrative shifts back and forth between a scene in the jail, where a drunken white man yells racist insults, and an earlier meeting with a genteel white woman who claims that black people enjoy their subservient position. For Deming, these are two faces of the same racism, one obvious and brutal, the other quiet and condescending.*

Deming (b. 1917), was a major figure in the civil rights and peace movements in the Sixties and in the feminist movement in the Seventies and Eighties. She has written such books as Revolution and Equilibrium *(1971),* We Cannot Live Without Our Lives *(1974), and* Remembering Who We Are *(1981).*

There is a jail within a jail here, hell within hell. The men and women behind these bars are not supposed to exist, but some are supposed to exist even less than others.

A prisoner who has just been brought in screams in panic. An old-timer calls to him from a cage around the corner: "Take it easy!"

"You goddam black sonofabitch," cries the newcomer, "you kiss my ass!"

Silence. Then, "How you know what color I is?" the Negro asks softly.

"Fuck you, chocolate drop, I know you're black. Don't talk shit to me; I'm white, I'm the aristocrat. My God, you wish you could change white, don't you?" His voice speeds up. "All you goddam niggers wish you were white! You don't show me shit, you black bastard. You ain't even a son of God, you son of the Devil!" He erupts in what is supposed to be an imitation of the other man's speech: "Blah blah blah blah blah blah blah—"

The Negro answers him wearily, "I don't give a damn if you *blue;* you in jail."

"I'm in jail and I'm blue," the white man suddenly states blankly—for a moment confronting the facts. Then he begins to rattle the bars in another fit. He yells, "Let my ass out of here, you bastards!" He screams again. And again he turns his attention to the other prisoner, for relief. "Where's Martin Luther King at tonight? He going to get you out of jail? Where's old Martin Luther at?" He offers a few obscene suggestions as to where King might be. "You goddam gob of spit," he suddenly cries. "You would like to be white, you Martin Luther King! *Least* I don't run round wanting to be black and segregating with you sons of bitches. *Least* I don't run round sitting on my knees praying up to heaven: 'Turn me white, turn me white!' Nigger!" he screams; and then with all his breath, "Niggggggaaaaaaaaaaa!"

The cry is like the cry of a man dropping through space. Save me somehow! Save me! I am nothing! It is an invocation shrieked: Damn, damn your soul, be less than I, and I am something! Nigger, nigger, naught, naught, *help!*

The man cries, "Tell that woman in the cell over there she's a nigger, too!" And then he screams again.

None of us can speak. We are at the bottom of the world.

I lean against the cold steel wall, arrange my cramped limbs in a new position, and try to think, try to struggle to the surface again after that cry.

I stare at the wall across from me. A former prisoner has scratched in wide letters: FUCK THE COPS! It should really be UNFUCK THE COPS, one peacewalker has suggested; unlove them is what is meant. But a man who feels violent can imagine the act of love as an act of murder. I consider how many of the threats hurled back and forth in here take the form of coarse invitations to make love. These cries waver sometimes, in weird fashion, between the note of abuse and the note of actual flirtation, the distance between the two notes surprisingly slight. It occurs to me that I shouldn't be surprised. In each case the cry is really the same. It is: Give me your life! I hear again in my head the segregationist's hideous scream, and I think: Yes, at the heart of most violence is this delusion—that one's existence can be made more abundant by it. Just as the act of love can be imagined as murder, murder, or what amounts to it, can be imagined as an act that gives one life. It is a delusion which tantalizes us all, in one extremity or another.

Yes, the easiest way to free ourselves does always seem to be to put certain other people from us. Real or imaginary murder can be swift and apparently simple. For the moment it *is* magic, *can* set one free. It is only in time that the magic fails. In time it is proved that our lives are bound together, whether we like it or not.

I think again of this jail. The man who is cast in here—out of society—remains a member of society and in time returns, more trouble to others and to himself than he was before. The Negro, cast more violently still out of the world of people, remains a person, and the truth of this returns to trouble those who wish him a "nigger" merely, meant for service. I recall how, ironically, for those who try to believe him less than a man, this no-man tends to loom, finally, larger than life. I recall a conversation with one of the cops who has stopped in his rounds to talk with us.

We have got onto the subject of Negroes' being denied their rights. He argues for a while that their rights are not denied. "They have some advantages over us!" he suddenly asserts. "You put a prisoner who won't work into a sweat box. If he's a white man, he'll go to work after three days. A nigger can stay in there as many as thirty days!" He eyes us. "Cut a nigger and maybe he'll bleed just a little, right after you've cut, but then it'll stop. Cut a white man like that, he'll bleed to death!" He shakes his head again. "And syphilis won't drive a nigger crazy! So they have advantages *we* haven't got!" He grins. "I'm going to write to Bobby Kennedy!" I think: Your words are wild, but you are right to say that you, too, live at a disadvantage—for you are haunted. I hear again a young Negro leader addressing a mass meeting in Birmingham: "We're going to win our freedom, and as we do it, we're also going to set our white brothers free."

I remember another person who is haunted, hear again the trembling voice of a white woman two of us met while visiting influential Albany families to try to talk with them about the peace walk. She is a middle-aged woman with a face that is still pretty, but anxieties have creased and crumpled it. "We love our colored people, we love them!" she exclaims, her hand on my arm, urgent, her face peering into mine with such an entreaty that I can't help reassuring her, "Of course you do. I know." Her hand is on my arm again. "They are happy here, with things just as they are! Happy, I know it!" She begs us to leave town. "I can see that you are dedicated people, you mean well, but oh dear, you'll just do harm, you don't understand!" I ask her as gently as I can, "But if they really are happy, how can our coming make any difference?" She stares at me, confused, then just begins to shake her head.

My thoughts of her are interrupted. A cop has come into the room that opens onto the cell blocks, and the man who was yelling before begins again: "Officer! Officer!"

"What?"

"I want to talk with you!"

"What do you want? Some service?"

The man yells, "I want to get out of here!" and the cop yells back, "We all do. We're in jail, too." He gives a snort of laughter and walks off. A door slams.

The prisoner gives a great roar of frustration: "Arrrr! It's the stinkiest dirtiest cell I was ever in!" And he lifts his steel bunk on the chain by which it is slung from the wall, then drops it, lifts it, drops it, lifts it, drops it, *clang, clang, clang*.

The Negro he has been taunting calls out, "I'm just as drunk as you are and I'm not making all that racket!"

The white man cries, "Fuck you, black bastard, I ain't fucking with you! Your ancestors were goddam slaves!" But he stops.

I think myself back into the house of the pleading woman. Sunlight pours through tall windows into the room where we sit—plays on the polished furniture, on the silky rosy-patterned rugs. She offers us, in a graceful glass dish, caramels she has made herself. Her husband is particularly fond of them, she confides; she loves to make them for him, and also to arrange the flowers. She smiles a little girl's smile. I listen for the step of servants in the large house, but hear no sound. They exist, of course; the house and the encircling garden are beautifully cared for. At the mill her husband runs, they exist too, these people whose ancestors were her ancestor's slaves, and whom, without thinking, she still calls "ours"—without thinking, but her face, as she speaks the word, dented by anxieties.

I remember the term so often used against us: We are "outside agitators." Her face before my eyes, I think: Yes, agitators, but it is above all your own doubts about your lives which we agitate; when you insist that we are outsiders, it is because, in fact, we come too close to you.

I remember the cry with which she has met the two of us at her door. At her first vague, inquiring look, we have introduced ourselves as members of the peace walk. "Oh, I'm so distressed!" she exclaims, staring at us, and her cry and her staring look draw us in an instant surprisingly near. I feel almost as though we have been recognized as relatives from out of town, appearing at a time of troubles. She leads us quickly into the house, seats us beside her on a sofa, scanning our faces. Then almost before we can begin to speak, the words leap out: "We love our colored people, love them!"

She clearly needs to have us believe it and to be able to believe it herself. She has a soft heart, has to see herself as a loving person. But clearly, too, she loves with a love that pleads: Don't make it uncomfortable for me to love you. Please don't insist on showing me all that you are, all that you feel. Let me continue to love you as my happy servants.

There pass again in my imagination Negro faces met on the road in our walk, faces of two kinds. A car approaches, goes slowly by us. A Negro family. No glance meets ours. The eyes of all are carefully veiled as they pass. On no face are feelings legible; each countenance has been drained of them as by a blow. Only a seemingly endless patience can be read there. A second car approaches. A young Negro woman is alone at the wheel. At the sight of us, black and white, and the sight of our signs, her eyes open wide, and then her whole face leaps into life, feelings written upon it like skywriting. She flings up her arms, calls out, "Well, all right then!"

The noisy prisoner is shouting again: "Shut your big black mouth. Shut your big black mouth!"

I think: The lady who offered us her caramels would turn in horror from this yelling man. And she would turn in horror from these cages which hold us; she would weep, and mean it, if she could see us in here. And yet the man yells, actually, her own desperate wish, which she cannot bear to acknowledge; and it is the daydream she dreams that holds us between these steel walls. The charge against us could be said to be that we refused to make it easier for her to live with herself. ✒

SUGGESTIONS FOR WRITING

1. Why is the white drunk in the jail so angry at the black people there? Does his anger tell us anything about racism in general?

2. Whose racism is more dangerous, the drunk's or the society matron's? Why?

3. What does Deming have to say about the origins of racism? Why do you think people become racists?

4. Is prejudice ever justified? Are people of color right to resent white people? Are women justified in distrusting men? Are there alternatives to distrust and prejudice for these groups?

TWO VIEWS OF RACISM ON CAMPUS

Many commentators have noted that since the late 1980s, racist incidents have increased on college campuses. One way of explaining these outbursts is that they simply reflect a general increase in racist attitudes in our society. The racist incidents on campuses attract more attention than others, perhaps, because it seems if anyplace should be free of racism, it is the college campus. Colleges, in theory at least, are dedicated to the kind of rational thought that opposes irrational racist responses. The two following essays offer specific and very different explanations of why this increase in racism has occurred.

Thomas Sowell (b. 1930), author of "The New Racism on Campus," is one of the country's leading African-American conservative intellectuals. He is the author of such books as Race and Economics *(1975),* Markets and Minorities *(1981),* Civil Rights: Rhetoric or Reality *(1984), and* A Conflict of Visions *(1987).* Jon Wiener *(b. 1944), author of "Reagan's Children," is a professor of history at the University of California, Irvine, a contributing editor to* The Nation, *and the author of* Social Origins of the New South *(1979),* Come Together: John Lennon in His Time *(1984), and* Professors, Politics, and Pop *(1992).*

THE NEW RACISM ON CAMPUS

Thomas Sowell

Ugly incidents of racial violence, threats, harassment, and open insults of minority students on various college campuses across the country have attracted increasing press attention in recent years. Some have called it "the new racism." In a sense it is new, and yet it has been coming for a long time, casting an ignored shadow before it.

Beneath the surface of episodes bad enough or special enough to attract press attention, there is a broader racial polarization in many places. "The races in the Northern universities have grown more separate since the Sixties," as professor Allan Bloom has pointed out in *The Closing of the American Mind.* In 1987, the dean of students at Middlebury College reported that, for the first time in a long career, she had received requests from white students that they not be assigned black roommates. It has become one of the signs of the times on many campuses that black students eat at separate tables. At too many colleges and universities, "diversity" has become mere academic Newspeak for a larger, segregated minority enclave.

The new racism has provoked no new thinking in academia. On the contrary, it has provoked only a more fervent reiteration of the unexamined beliefs and obligatory clichés about race that have prevailed on most campuses since the 1960s. An article in *The Chronicle of Higher Education* last year referred to the new racism as "vestiges of the 'old' racism." But when a black student at Harvard had his window shattered by a thrown object and is further harassed by racist phone calls, that is not a "vestige" of what happened at Harvard 30 years ago, when such behavior would have been unheard of—and when a black student was elected a marshall of the class of 1958.

Those who are most vocal on campus racial issues depict the new racism as growing out of a new conservative mood in general or the Reagan Administration's philosophy in particular. However, neither the regional pattern of campus racial incidents nor the ideological character of the institutions affected fits this vision. Last March the National Institute Against Prejudice and Violence published a list of 105 incidents of "campus ethnoviolence." Only seven of these occurred in the South. More than that occurred in Massachusetts alone—and Massachusetts has never been Reagan country. On the contrary, vicious racial incidents have been most prominent where the prevailing liberal (or radical) racial vision has been most prominent. The new racism is not a vestige but a backlash.

This backlash has developed on campuses that already have all the things that are supposed to cure it—campuses dominated by racial "representation" or body-count thinking, campuses awash in affirmative action officers, associate deans for minority affairs, ethnic studies faculty, and ethnic student organizations, centers, and even separate residences. These things have not been a solution but an essential part of the problem. However, it is hardly surprising that existing ethnic establishments should use racial incidents as a reason for expansion of their roles and their turf. Indeed, the whole pattern that has emerged over the past 20 years has been quite predictable.

Twenty years ago, I was shocked to learn that half the black students at Cornell University were on some form of academic probation. Yet when I checked into their test scores, I discovered that the average black student at Cornell at that time had higher scores than three-quarters of all American college students. Why was there a problem then? Because black students at the 75th percentile were competing with white Cornell students who were at the 99th percentile. Minority students with every prospect of achieving success were artificially turned into failures by being mismatched with an institution preoccupied with its minority body count.

The same pattern continues to this day at many institutions across the country. The issue is not whether minority students are "qualified" to attend college but whether they are *mismatched*. A recent study showed that the average black student at MIT had math scores in the top 10% of all American students—but these same scores were in the *bottom* 10% among the extraordinary students at MIT. Almost one-fourth of the black students at MIT failed to graduate, and those who did had significantly lower grades than their classmates. Once more, failures were artificially created by preferences.

At the University of California at Berkeley, the attrition rate among black students has exceeded 70%. The black students at Berkeley score above the national average on the Scholastic Aptitude Test (SAT), but not as far above as the other students at Berkeley. This massive attrition is once again due to a mismatch. Yet, at Berkeley as elsewhere, the demand is for still more preferential admissions.

Why does the body-count approach result in such gross mismatches, such widespread academic failure, and such a growing backlash among white students? At the heart of a complex series of reactions is a simple fact: Body-count reasoning and policies ignore the size of the pool of minority students who meet the standards of the institutions in the vanguard of this approach.

Students at top-tier colleges and universities usually have composite SAT scores of 1200 or more. According to a study by professor Robert Klitgaard, then of Harvard's Kennedy School, there were fewer than 600 black students in the entire country in 1983 who met that standard. There has been a modest rise since then in the test scores of black, Hispanic, and American Indian students. But the total number who meet the standards of top-tier institutions is still far short of anything required for proportional representation of these groups.

Among the top engineering schools and departments, there are a dozen or so where the average math SAT score alone is over 700 (out of a possible 800). As of 1988, fewer than 800 black, Puerto Rican, Mexican American, and American Indian students—put together—scored that high. By contrast, there were more than 6,400 Asian Americans who scored in the 700s on the math SAT. Yet minority representation discussions go on in utter disregard of the academic differences in the respective pools of students. Some critics have even singled out engineering schools as especially "racist" because of their "underrepresentation" of minority students other than Asians.

Given these bitter but inescapable facts, lofty talk about statistical representation of minority students at the most demanding colleges, universities, and engineering schools means grossly mismatching students and institutions. Moreover, the mismatching does not stop at the top-tier schools. When the most demanding institutions siphon off minority students whose qualifications match the standards of second-tier and third-tier institutions, these latter colleges, universities, and engineering schools proceed to siphon off minority students who would normally go to institutions whose admissions standards are lower. The net result is an artificially created problem. Even though minority students' qualifications cover a wide range, they are not matched with the institutions across that range but instead are systematically mismatched. The bad academic consequences of this situation have led to worse social consequences, among minority and majority students alike.

The only large group of white students who have a long history of being admitted to leading colleges and universities without meeting the normal admissions standards are big-time varsity athletes. They too have a long history of taking Mickey Mouse courses, receiving grades that they haven't earned—and of failing to graduate nevertheless. Why should anyone be surprised when such patterns have also emerged under preferential admissions for minority students? Why should anyone be surprised that the "dumb jock" stereotype that has followed college athletes for decades under these conditions should now have a racial counterpart, after similar conditions have been created for minority students?

What of the minority students themselves—and the minority faculty, often recruited with the same headlong rush for body count? In both cases, they are faced with two choices: (1) accept the prevailing standards and lose their own self-respect or (2) retain their self-respect by continually attacking, undermining, and trying to discredit the standards that they do not meet, scavenging for grievances and issuing a never-ending stream of demands and manifestoes. Given the alternatives, it is hardly surprising that so many choose the second.

Even on a campus where most minority students concentrate on their academic work, those who engage in bombast and disruption are far more likely to be noticed by white students. This is only one factor in the racial backlash that has led to a White Student Union being formed at Temple University, racist "skinhead" recruiting literature on campus at Stanford, Ku Klux Klan graffiti at Berkeley, and racist notes being left under the doors of black students at Smith College.

There is more than enough blame to go around for the ugly—and worsening—racial atmosphere on many campuses. The central responsibility, however, must go to the college and university administrations that have repeatedly capitulated to the noisiest demands and disregarded the most solemn warnings as to what their policies would lead to.

Many knowledgeable people gave such warnings 20 years ago. Professor Clyde Summers of the University of Pennsylvania—a man who had spoken out against racial discrimination back in the 1940s, long before it was fashionable to do so—was only one who sounded the alarm at the new racial policies in academia in 1969. He called it "irresponsible, if not cruel" to admit minority students to institutions where they would find it difficult to keep up academically, or even to survive. He also saw what he called a "monstrous" danger of increased racism among whites as a result. All this was ignored.

Twenty years ago— in February 1969—then-NAACP executive director Roy Wilkins castigated college administrators who were "ready to buy peace at any price" by creating "sealed-off, black studies centers" for "racial breast-beating." That same year, black educator Kenneth B. Clark resigned from Antioch College's board of directors because Antioch was "permitting a group of students to inflict their dogmatism and ideology on other students and on the total college community," because the college was "silent" while militant black students "intimidate, threaten, and in some cases physically assault the Negro students who disagree with them," thereby "making a mockery of its concern for the protection and development of human dignity." Intimidation continues at other leading colleges today.

Yet another ingredient in the racial tensions on campus are the various ethnic studies programs. There are no inherent reasons why these cannot be first-rate fields of scholarly study—but they seldom are. There have been and still are outstanding scholars researching and writing about a wide variety of American ethnic groups. But the wholesale creation of ethnic studies programs all across the country at the same time ignored completely the size of the pool of scholars available. Here again, this was not an educational decision but another example of what Roy Wilkins called buying "peace at any price."

All too many ethnic studies courses resemble the Afro-American studies courses at Princeton, described in the student-published *Course Guide* as "a three-hour rap session," where "few students" did the assigned readings, where grading was "arbitrary" and "random," where seminars were "a lot of fun" and had a "very light" workload. Nationwide, black-studies programs have shrunk drastically since 1970, as they acquired a reputation for low quality. Twenty years ago black civil rights activist Bayard Rustin warned that "black studies must not be used for the purpose of image-building or to enable young black students to escape the challenges of the university by setting up a program of 'soul courses' that they can just play with and pass."

Increasingly, racial incidents on campus have offered a new lease on life to ethnic studies programs. In the wake of each incident, there are demands for more minority students and more minority faculty on campus—and for expanded ethnic studies programs, sometimes to be made compulsory for all students. To force upon students courses that they have rejected over the years is hardly likely to improve race relations. But it is the expedient thing to do on many campuses, however much it may escalate an already ugly racial polarization.

What is most dangerous about the new racism on campus is that the responses to it set the stage for more of the same. The history of racial conflicts in countries around the world shows that nothing is easier than to start a spiral of racial confrontations—and nothing is harder than to stop it. In India hundreds of lives have been lost in riots over group admissions quotas to medical school in the state of Gujarat alone. In Sri Lanka racial polarization that began over university admissions quotas escalated into a bloody civil war, complete with hideous atrocities on both sides. We in the United States are not at that point, or even close to that point. But there is no sign of anything that stands between our present situation and such tragedies. Certainly neither academic faculties nor administrators have taken either a long view or a courageous stand.

Any real leadership on racial or ethnic issues will have to come from outside academia—and especially from those who control donations and government appropriations. Such leadership will have to be based on a realization that the new racism has grown out of the old dogmatism that still holds sway on campuses across the country.

A central tenet of this racial dogmatism is that preferential admissions are the only way to allow large numbers of minority students to get a college education. In reality, however, a substantial increase in the numbers of black students completing college—a 64% jump between 1940 and 1947—occurred without preferences or quotas. This compares with a 49% increase between 1960 and 1967 with special admissions standards. The earlier increase was due largely to money for college being made available under the GI Bill.

Money is the key, for most minority students depend heavily on financial aid. As long as that financial aid is channeled through colleges and universities, these institutions will use the money to buy themselves protection from trouble on campus and to project a good image off campus by concentrating on racial body count. Only if the money goes to the individual student—wherever he or she attends college—will minority students be able to sort themselves out among institutions according to their own educational qualifications, as they did under the GI Bill.

Money is also the key for those, including business donors, seeking to change current academic policies from outside. Closing a checkbook can be the best way to open a dialogue with academic administrators who take the path of least resistance and give in to the prevailing dogmas.

Many other dogmas—about "role models" or "cultural bias" in tests, for example—reign unchallenged in academia. These dogmas cannot survive any demand for evidence that will stand up to scrutiny. The time is long overdue to insist on hard facts—and to insist that the focus of minority admissions and financial aid policy must be the successful education of minority students, regardless of what that does to the statistical profile of any given campus.

REAGAN'S CHILDREN: RACIAL HATRED ON CAMPUS

Jon Wiener

The Boston Red Sox had just lost the World Series to the New York Mets. At the University of Massachusetts, Amherst, hundreds of students, many of them drunk, poured out of the dorms. White Red Sox fans began shoving Mets fans who were black; soon a white mob of 3,000 was chasing and beating anyone who was black. Ten students were injured. Joseph Andrade recalls thinking, "My God, my life is being threatened here—and it's because I'm black."

The U-Mass explosion—on October 27, 1986—may be the most emblematic outbreak of student hatred of the 1980s. But it is by no means the only one. The upsurge in campus racism is the most disturbing development in university life across the nation during the past decade. More than anything, it reveals how white attitudes toward minorities have changed on campus during the Reagan years, even at institutions that historically have been bastions of liberalism.

At the University of Michigan, Ann Arbor, for example, the campus radio station broadcast a call from a student who "joked": "Why do blacks always have sex on their minds? Because all their pubic hair is on their head. . . . Who are the two most famous black women in history? Aunt Jemima and Mother Fucker." At Dartmouth College, the *Dartmouth Review* attacked a black music professor, William Cole, describing him as "a cross between a welfare queen and a bathroom attendant." Then four *Review* staff members confronted Cole after a class last February and, in front of his students, apparently attempted to provoke him into a fight. Esi Eggleston, a black student who witnessed the confrontation, told PBS's *Frontline*: "That moment let me know that there are people in this world who hate you just because of your color. Not dislike you, or choose not to be friends with you, but hate you."

At the University of Wisconsin, Madison, a fraternity held a "slave auction" as part of a pledge party last October. At U.C.L.A. white and Chicano students fought on campus last spring during a student election. At Purdue, a black academic counselor found "Death Nigger" scratched on her office door. A headline in a recent issue of *The Montclarion*, the student newspaper at Montclair State College in New Jersey, read, "Attention focused on racial tension at M.S.C."

Why is all this happening now? Shelby Steele, a black associate professor of English at San Jose State University, tends to blame the victim. In the February *Harper's*, he argues that the problem on campus is not white racism but rather black "feelings of inferiority," which give rise to "an unconscious need to exaggerate the level of racism on campus—to make it a matter of the system, not just a handful of students." Instead of "demonstrating for a black 'theme house,' " Steele writes, black students "might be better off spending their time reading and studying."

Duchesne Paul Drew, a Columbia University junior who is black, offers a different explanation: "Reagan was President during the formative years of today's students." When Reagan was elected in 1980, this year's freshman class was 10 years old. Their political consciousness was formed while the White House used potent code words and attacked social programs to legitimize a subtle racism. Columbia students report that racist remarks are seldom made to blacks but frequently are heard in conversations among whites. The litany is that black people tend to be criminals, drug addicts and welfare cheats; that they don't work; and that black students aren't as smart as whites.

This, of course, is the image of blacks George Bush sought to project in his campaign to succeed Reagan. The Republicans' Willie Horton television spots suggesting that blacks are rapists and murderers played not just in living rooms but in dormitories and student centers for most of the fall semester. Undergraduate viewers may have been even more vulnerable to the Horton propaganda than was the rest of the TV audience, because most of them lacked the experience and knowledge required to challenge racist imagery—especially after eight years of Ronald Reagan.

The Reagan Administration gave its blessing to the *Dartmouth Review*, the best-known purveyor of campus racism and intolerance. The *Review* (which is not an official Dartmouth publication) boasts that several of its former staff members have gone on to prestigious jobs in Reagan's Washington: One became a speechwriter for President Reagan, another for Vice President Bush. *Review* columnist and president Keeney Jones penned a notorious racist parody, "Dis Sho Ain't No Jive Bro," that purported to quote a black student at Dartmouth: "Dese boys be sayin' that we be comin' here to Dartmut an' not takin' the classics. You know, Homa. . . ." Jones was subsequently hired as a speechwriter for Secretary of Education William Bennett. The editor who published that column, Dinesh D'Souza, went on to a career as a policy analyst in the Reagan White House.

This legitimization of racism has been accompanied by other developments. Admission to top colleges, including some public universities like the University of California, Berkeley, and U.C.L.A., has become fiercely competitive; Berkeley had 21,200 applications to its 1987 freshman class, and enrolled 3,700—14 percent. Many students with straight A averages in high school were denied admission. At the same time, some college campuses are beginning to reflect the diversity of the American population: Berkeley's incoming class in 1987 was 12 percent black, 17 percent Latino, 26 percent Asian and only 40 percent white.

This new alignment comes as a shock to many white students, especially those who grew up in all-white, middle-class suburbs. Some of them respond to campus racial diversity by proclaiming that all blacks and Latinos have been admitted under affirmative action programs and thus are taking places away from "more qualified" whites. That argument is often turned around, however, as a justification for hostility toward Asians, who are criticized for being super-competitive.

University administrators at many campuses prefer to ignore racial incidents or keep them out of the news, but anti-racist student organizations have successfully focused attention on the problem. After the U-Mass incident following the World Series, campus officials at first denied that race had played any part in what the campus police termed a brawl among sports fans. That made it hard for black students to follow Shelby Steele's advice and spend their time "reading and studying." Not until students demonstrated did U-Mass Chancellor Joseph Duffey admit that his campus had a racial problem. At Penn State, eighty-nine students were arrested at a campus sit-in last April. At U-Mass a year ago, 200 students held a five-day sit-in; at Wisconsin in November 1987, 100 protesters marched outside the Phi Gamma Delta ("Fiji") fraternity house, where a racist incident had occurred, chanting, "Hey, Fijis, you can't hide, drop the sheets and come outside!" As a result of dozens of scenes like these, the student campaign against racism has provided the focus for campus politics at many colleges and universities.

Campus antiracist activists have put forward a variety of strategies. One of these identifies the problem as ignorance among white kids, many of whom grew up in isolated lily-white suburbs and need to learn about the diversity of American culture. Advocates of this approach insist that all students should take a course in ethnic studies or cultural diversity, often taught by newly hired minority faculty members. The Universities of Indiana and Minnesota each require two courses in U.S. cultural pluralism; the University of Wisconsin, Madison, has just established a one-course ethnic studies requirement and the University of California, Berkeley, is currently debating a similar measure.

Minority student organizations across the country enthusiastically support an ethnic studies requirement for graduation. Charles Holley, co-president of the Black Student Union of the Madison campus, argues that the courses teach "what minorities are all about, where we came from, what we feel." The student government officers at Berkeley, in a joint statement declared that "students commonly graduate without reading the work of a minority author, studying under a minority professor, or having learned the vital histories of people of color. In a state that will soon have a non-white majority, such an undergraduate experience dangerously perpetuates false stereotypes."

Another strategy focuses on the empowerment of targets of violence. Much racial harassment typically goes unreported, even though it makes life miserable for minority students. When these students have their own campus centers and organizations, they don't have to suffer in isolation; they can—and increasingly do—rally their forces against their antagonists. In the aftermath of racial flare-ups minority students have frequently demanded university support for such centers. At U-Mass, participants in last winter's sit-in called on school administrators to renovate New Africa House as a cultural center for minority students.

A third strategy strives to reduce campus violence in general as a way of thwarting racial violence. Jan Sherrill, director of the Center for Study and Prevention of Campus Violence at Towson State University, in Maryland, argues that American culture condones violent means of resolving disputes as a legitimate form of male self-expression. Reagan's oft-proclaimed "values" glorified the macho response to international problems. Terrorism at a disco in Berlin? Send the Air Force to Tripoli to bomb Qaddafi. Men longed to join the President in saying, "Go ahead, make my day." A media culture of exploding cars, free-swinging cops and bone-crunching sports is reinforced by campus norms that say it's O.K. for young men to get drunk, wreck their dorm rooms and slug it out with one another. A program at Towson State's Richmond Hall has focused on reducing property damage in the dorm and violence of all kinds between students by setting strict rules and giving residents responsibility for enforcing them. As a result, there have been no racist incidents or attacks on gays or women this academic year in the dorm, which has become "a violence-free zone," according to Sherrill. It's not yet clear whether incidents elsewhere on campus will decline.

On many campuses, racism is endemic to the fraternity subculture. The house that held the slave auction at Madison last October, Zeta Beta Tau (Z.B.T.), is predominantly Jewish and had itself been a target of an attack: Members of Fiji crashed a Z.B.T. party, beat three persons and taunted them with anti-Semitic slurs. In another racist incident involving fraternities on that campus, a Kappa Sigma party in 1986 had a "Harlem Room," with white students in blackface, watermelon punch, graffiti on the walls and garbage on the floor.

Racism among fraternities is fostered by the fact that most are completely segregated, and it is exacerbated by rituals of heavy drinking on party weekends. Last November the Chancellor at Madison, Donna Shalala, established a Commission on the Future of Fraternities and Sororities, which is to recommend ways to reduce their racist and sexist behavior. The possibilities, Shalala said, range from attacking "substance abuse" as a cause of "misconduct" to elimination of the Greek system altogether.

A more problematic strategy for reducing campus racism focuses on criminalizing racist speech, which constitutes the most prevalent form of harassment. At the University of Michigan, Ann Arbor, interim president

Robben Fleming implemented a new code last year that allows university administrators to place on probation, suspend or expel students engaged in "discriminatory" behavior, including racist speech. Under the code, the student who told the racist "jokes" over the radio would be put on probation; if he made "other blatantly racist remarks" while on probation he could be suspended or expelled. Most of the university Regents support the code, *The Michigan Daily* reports, as do several deans and professors. But the student representatives of the University Council have denounced the proposal as a "terrible misuse of power," and the United Coalition Against Racism, a student group that has demanded university action against racial abuse, has voiced a similar sentiment.

At Madison, Z.B.T. was cleared by the student government disciplinary committee of all charges of violating university rules against racial discrimination. Committee chair Rana Mookherjee said of the fraternity's slave auction, "There is no rule you can write to eradicate bad taste and insensitivity." Many minority students expressed outrage at the decision; one was in tears. A spokesman for the Madison campus's Minority Coalition, Peter Chen, said, "By hiding behind the issue of free speech, the administration is making this campus safe for racism."

The protection of offensive speech will always cause frustration, but nonetheless provides an important lesson in the meaning of the First Amendment. Campus leaders need not limit themselves to defending the First Amendment just because of constitutional barriers to criminalizing offensive speech, however. On the contrary, they have an obligation to speak out, forcefully and frequently, explaining why racist speech is objectionable. Chancellor Shalala did that: Although fraternity members have a First Amendment right to objectionable speech, she said, "using slavery as a basis for humor should be offensive to every American."

Donna Shalala began her term as chancellor last February by announcing the "Madison plan." It calls for the University of Wisconsin to double the number of minority undergraduates over the next five years; create 150 financial aid packages for low-income students; raise $4 million in private money to increase the scholarship endowment and another $4 million to endow twenty-five new minority graduate and professional fellowships; hire seventy new minority faculty members over the next three years, more than doubling the current number; and require ethnic studies courses in each college. In addition, the university will hire or promote 125 minority academic staff members over the next three years. Shalala has budgeted $4.7 million to implement this program over the next three years, part of which must come from new appropriations, which the Wisconsin Legislature is currently considering.

The Minority Coalition at Madison criticized the plan for failing to establish a strong racial harassment policy, an adequate multicultural center or antiracism workshops during student orientation. But the goals, the budget and the timetable make the Madison plan one of the most far-reaching attempts to overcome institutional racism undertaken by any major university. The University of Wisconsin's effort is important, among other reasons, because of the school's size: It has the fourth largest student body in the nation, numbering almost 44,000. It's especially heartening that Wisconsin is making such an extensive commitment at a time when people feel beaten down and defeated by eight years of losing battles against the Reagan White House.

Unfortunately, the promises made at Madison and at other progressive institutions to hire more black faculty run up against a major obstacle: the small pool of available black college teachers. These men and women are being intensely wooed, and Madison's recruitment successes will inevitably hurt the campaigns on other campuses. The shortage of black faculty is part of a larger problem—the declining number of blacks in higher education, from the undergraduate through the professorial ranks. Most talented black undergraduates opt for law or medicine or business over academia—and why not? The prospect of spending years as an isolated, underpaid, overworked assistant professor is not an inviting one.

The Madison plan addresses this problem in several ways: by pledging that the university will work with local high schools to improve their graduation rates; will in the future recruit twice as many minority students to its freshman class and provide them with financial support to help them stay through graduation; and will double the number of fellowships for graduate and professional schools, to encourage minority students to finish dissertations.

Defensive administrators at colleges and universities across the country argue that the recent spread of racism on campus shows only that the university is a part of American society, which itself seems to be increasingly racist and violent. That's true, but it shouldn't provide an excuse for educators who prefer to wait for the larger society to change. More universities need to make the kind of commitment demonstrated by Chancellor Shalala at the University of Wisconsin if they are going to overcome the racism that has stained the campus during the Age of Reagan. ✒

SUGGESTIONS FOR WRITING

1. What is your reaction to the assertion that there has been an increase in campus racism? Have you observed racism among students on your own campus?

2. If there has been an increase, why do *you* think it has occurred? Is Sowell or Wiener closer to the truth as you see it? Do both of them have part of the answer?

3. What do you think ought to be done about campus racism? How should universities react to students who openly express racist views?

4. Is there racism against whites on the part of black students?

5. Have you observed racist incidents on your own campus? Why did they happen? What was the university's response to them? How did you respond?

10

INTERNATIONAL
PERSPECTIVES

The themes previously explored in this text—learning about and coming to terms with one-self, coming to terms with others, gender and sexuality, race and class relations, or movements of political opposition—all can be pursued in a global context. In expanding our horizons, we could do well to confront some basic assumptions (and their pitfalls) that can improve our understanding of other cultures. One such assumption is that a comparative study of world cultures makes us aware of our common humanity, taking into account the many differences in language, appearance, and geography. This certainly sounds like a noble sentiment (as the strains of "We Are the World" play on our mental soundtracks), but can actually mask a relentless determination to generalize from our own cultural experience, dissolving all contrasting cultures into the essence of one overriding tradition—one that usually flatters our own. At the other extreme (think of the famous Rudyard Kipling lines: "East is East and West is West/And never the twain shall meet"), we can so exaggerate differences between cultures that, where we do not encourage condemnation of an alien culture, we produce a kind of weak relativism that asserts, "That may be suitable for their culture, but not necessarily for ours." Such an attitude may well prevent the serious consideration of what other cultures have to offer us.

The following selections, while not necessarily placed within a spectrum moving from similarity with American experience to radical divergence from it, might still be contemplated in this way. Their order, like that of other sections in Reading for Difference, *more or less follows successive life stages. To some extent, the persons whose experiences are represented (whether as fiction of non-fiction) partake of the contemporary world of electronic commu-*

nications and consumerism. Americans often assume that the world's peoples eagerly await these aspects of our civilization, but the processes by which more and more sectors of the globe are caught up in these networks is sometimes disruptive and painful. In other cases, the persons you will encounter in this section follow a way of life that shares more with the premodern (pre-industrial, agrarian, localized) world than with our own. The first two selections are fictional, and the remaining five are autobiographical. Notice that the writing styles are not clearly separable into fictional or non-fictional varieties.

Relatively lengthier introductions are given to each of these selections. Again, we feel that American readers might need more background on the cultures producing these narratives. They range from accounts of life within a particular cultural tradition to an essay by Jamaican writer Michelle Cliff that shows us what it means to live the way an increasing number of us in this world live: very much between cultures, in constant motion, assuming global interconnectedness, but searching all the while for a sustaining cultural identity. On a shrinking globe, and in the face of the homogenizing tendencies of mass electronic media and consumerism, this very contradiction points to the need to read for difference. ✒

THE WIND HOWLS TOO

John Berger

In Pig Earth (1979), from which "The Wind Howls Too" is taken, **John Berger** *vividly portrays the rhythms of life as it was once lived by the vast majority of European people: agrarian, hard-working (in the sense of taxing physical labor), in close contact with one's extended family and neighbors, and according to the seasons. In the twentieth century, the people of the southern French countryside have clung to this way of life, though it is rapidly disappearing. Berger is its affectionate chronicler. In this story of an adolescent boy coming of age through his participation in family rituals, Berger conveys a great deal about the social—including gender—relations of the people through the smallest details, such as the gnôle (an apple brandy peculiar to this region of France) that the men make and, apparently exclusively, drink.*

Berger (b. 1926) is a British novelist, essayist, screenwriter, and critic who lives in a small village in the South of France. Many of his published books, including The Sense of Sight *(1985),* About Looking *(1980),* The Success and Failure of Picasso *(1965), and* Ways of Seeing *(1972), are about visual arts and experience, including the cultural role and impact of advertising. He has devoted much of his energy to representing the vanishing way of life of French peasant society, in such books as* Another Way of Telling *(with Swiss photographer Jean Mohr, 1982),* Pig Earth, *and* Once in Europa *(1987).*

Sometimes when I listen to the wind howling at night, I remember. There was very little money in the village. During eight months we worked on the land to produce the minimum of what we needed to feed and clothe and warm us for the whole year. But in the winter nature went dead, and it was then that our lack of money became critical. Not so much because we required money to buy things, but because there was so little to work with. This, and not the cold or the snow or the short days or the sitting round the wood stove, is why in winter we lived in a kind of limbo.

Many of the men went from the village to Paris to earn wages as stokers and porters and chimney-sweeps. Before the men left they made sure that there was enough hay and wood and potatoes to last until after Easter. Those who stayed behind were the women, the old and the young. During the winter the fact that I had no father was scarcely remarkable; half the children of my year were temporarily without fathers.

That winter my grandfather was making a bed for me, so that I shouldn't have to sleep any more with my sister who was soon to be married. My mother was making a mattress of *crin. Crin* was the hair of the mare's mane and cows' tails. Every morning, when it snowed in the night, my mother announced the news in the same way. "He has served us some more!" she said. She spoke about the snow as if it were uneatable food.

After the cows had been milked, my grandfather and I cleared the snow from the courtyard. This done, he went to his carpenter's bench and I, before going down to school, made sure that no snow was covering the stone sabot. If it was, I brushed it off.

The stone sabot was in the courtyard near the wall, beside the door to the vaulted cellar where the potatoes and turnips and a few pumpkins were kept. When we cleared the courtyard we did not always clear right to the edges, and so there was a risk that the stone sabot might disappear under the snow. Winter was the season of disappearances. The men went away. The cows were hidden in the stables. Snow covered the slopes, the gardens, the dung-heaps, the trees. And the roofs of the houses, covered by the same snow, became barely distinguishable from the slopes. Not since I first found the stone sabot had I let it disappear.

It looked like this. Its stone was whitish, marked with blue. It was a man's size. It was too large for me if I put my foot on it. The first time I saw it, I tried to pick it up to compare it with the pair of sabots, made from walnut wood, which were at the bottom of the wardrobe. The man who made the wardrobe took a winter making it and my great-grandfather paid him by cutting stones for his new house. The man's initials were A.B. and my great-grandfather carved these above the door to his house. I had seen them. When he was young, A.B. cracked many jokes. Later he was much given to thought, and finally he killed himself in the new house with his initials above the door. When I tried to pick up the sabot, I could not move it.

"Pépé, why is there a stone sabot in the courtyard?" I asked my grandfather. He was my authority about everything which was mysterious. It was several months before he answered my question.

One evening, he told me, his father, my great-grandfather, came through the door from the stable into the kitchen—the same kitchen in which we lived—and announced: "Néra has put my eye out." "Aiee!" screamed his wife, but when she looked at him she said, "No, your eye is not out." He had very blue eyes. "She butted me," he insisted, "as I was feeding her."

Pépé looked into his father's face. Miserably and terribly during the next five minutes one of his blue eyes turned entirely red, blood red, and he never saw out of it again. Nor did he ever recover from the shock of losing this eye. He believed himself repulsively disfigured.

Glass eyes were not easy to find. One day a friend drove by cart to A . . . and there in a barber's shop he found a whole bottle of them. "Give me the bluest you have," said the friend. Pépé's father would not wear it. Instead, Pépé, who was the youngest of three sons and his father's favourite, had to walk in front of him whenever he went out, to warn those they met not to look into his father's eyes.

One year later Pépé announced to the family that he was leaving. He was going to Paris. The family could not live off four cows. His brothers did not argue with him, for it was either him or one of them who had to go. He was fifteen at the time. His father ordered him to stay at home.

As he was packing his bundle, he found a pair of his father's boots. They were the newest and strongest boots in the house, and he put them on. His father was working in a circle of rocks above the house. He climbed the slope to embrace him. Then he pointed to the boots on his feet, and, as he was running down, he shouted: "The good ones are going! The bad ones are staying!"

In Paris he worked for several years without returning. The last job he had was on the building site of Le Grand Palais, which was to house the world exhibition to celebrate the opening of the century.

Whilst he was absent, his father, peering out of one eye, cut the stone cross and headstone for his own grave. On it he carved his name and added the date of his birth, 1840, the year that Napoleon's body was transferred from St. Helena to the Invalides. Then he carved the supposed date of his death. The latter proved correct, for he died before the year was out. I passed the grave in the cemetery. And the date of Napoleon's home-coming I learnt at school.

When Pépé came back from Paris he found the stone sabot in the courtyard. He said his dead father had put it there as a sign that he had forgiven him for taking the boots.

That was all.

"How do you know your father forgave you?" I asked him after a long while.

"Nobody can take the stone sabot," he explained. "It's fixed to the rock. It'll outlast the house. And *that* is what is important. The boots I took were unimportant. He wanted me to know that."

The way Pépé told me this story made me think he had never told it to anybody else. His telling me was a privilege. I kept the stone sabot clear of snow because I recognised this. Whenever he saw me bent over the sabot, he smiled.

The Sundays passed. We became vague about the date. In limbo one loses a sense of time. My mother kept on repeating, "He has served us some more!" Repeatedly we cleared the courtyard. The pile of snow in the corner grew and became as high as a room. Every day two pairs of crows perched on top of the same apple trees. My grandmother hated them because they tried to eat the grain she gave her chickens. Pépé claimed that one of the crows was older than he: "I'd give a lot," he mumbled, "to see all that he has seen—the fights, the legal battles, the zouaves, the inventions, the couples in the forest . . ."

One evening in January my grandfather took the decision. "Tomorrow," he said, "we are going to kill the pig." On the day we killed the pig everybody had a job to do. And from that day onwards we knew that, however distant it still was, the spring was approaching. The mornings would get lighter. Not regularly, but when there were no clouds in the sky.

I went with my grandfather to look at the pig.

"He's as long as a pew," said Pépé with pride.

"He's bigger than last year's," I said, wanting to share in the pride.

"He's the biggest I remember. It's all those potatoes Mémé feeds him. She'd feed him her own dinner if she had to."

He ran his hand along the length of the pig's back, as if celebrating the virtues of my grandmother.

Mémé had found it difficult to make up her mind whether to marry Pépé or not. There was a photograph of the wedding in their bedroom. With the money he had saved whilst working in Paris, he had bought out his brothers, and the family farm became his. In the wedding photograph their two faces were unlined and round like apples. Even in the wedding photograph Pépé looked cunning. He had the eyes of a fox, watchful, canny, with a fire in their darkness. Perhaps it was the look in his eyes which made her hesitate.

Pépé confided to his friend Marius that Mémé couldn't make up her mind whether or not to marry him. After the story of the stone sabot, he told me many stories of his life. The two friends planned a practical joke. Exactly that. A joke that would prove useful.

On the Sunday before Easter, Pépé suggested to his sweetheart that they take a walk together through the forest. By that time the violets and white wood anemones are out. One day it may be warm enough to undress; the next it can snow. The afternoon of their walk it was cold. He led her to a disused chapel where, inside, they were protected from the wind. He kissed her and put his hand on her breast. "The chapel was not consecrated," he said to me gravely. She started to undo her blouse. He didn't say this to me. He said: "I began to caress her." I pictured the breasts to myself when he told me the story.

Suddenly they heard a key turn in the door and the bell above the roof begin to ring a tocsin: the peal used to warn people against fire, or to keep lightning away in a storm. The couple were trapped there in the chapel. Pépé pretended to look for a way out. My grandmother adjusted her chemise, pushed him towards the door and clung to his back. She was convinced that they had been caught by robbers, and could scarcely hear what he said for the noise of the bell.

The neighbours came running through the forest and saw Marius astride the roof of the chapel ringing the bell like a madman. They shouted to him but he couldn't hear. All they could see was that he was either crying or laughing. When he climbed down he solemnly put his finger to his lips and opened the chapel door. When the couple came out, he said: "There are two things nobody can hide—a cough and love!" Next Sunday the banns for their marriage were announced.

Pépé began to talk with the pig in the stable. To each kind of animal Pépé spoke in a different voice, making different sounds. With the mare he spoke softly and evenly, and when he repeated himself, it was as if he was speaking to a companion who had become deaf. To the pig his language was full of abrupt, high-pitched sounds, interspersed with exhaling grunts. Pépé sounded like a turkey when he spoke to the pig.

"Ahir ola ahira Jésus!"

Whilst he made this noise, he fitted a noose round the pig's snout, being careful not to let it tighten. The pig followed him obediently, past the five cows and the mare, through the stable door and into the sudden harsh light of the snow. There the pig hesitated.

All his life the pig had complied. Mémé had fed him as if he were a member of the family. He, for his part, had put on his kilo per day. One hundred and forty kilos. One hundred and forty-one. One hundred and forty-two. Now, for the first time, he hesitated.

He saw four men standing before him, their hands, not in their pockets to protect them from the cold, but held out in front. He saw my grandmother waiting in the kitchen doorway without a bucket of food. Perhaps he saw my mother staring with anticipation through the kitchen window.

In any case, he put his head down and with his four small feet beneath their gigantic hams, he stepped one step back. Pépé pulled the rope and as the noose tightened, the pig screamed and tried to back away. For an instant Pépé held the pig by himself. Nothing could drag him against his will. The next instant the neighbours were there pulling on the rope too.

Pépé's friend Marius and I pushed from behind. Every feature of the pig, except his mouth, is small. His arsehole is no larger than a buttonhole in a shirt. I held him by his tail.

After five minutes of dragging and heaving, we had him across the yard, alongside the large wooden sledge. This was the sledge that killed my father.

Pépé and my grandmother had waited four years for a child. "The weather and the cunt," Pépé said, "do what they want." My father was their first-born. Two years later came my aunt. They had no other children. And so, as soon as he was old enough, Pépé needed my father to work. The sledge killed him when he was thirty and I was two. He was bringing down hay from the *alpage*. The path was steep and about three kilometres long. In places it was cut through the rock, in places it was muddy, in places it was paved with rough stones around sharp, heavily banked corners. We used this path to take the cows up to the *alpage* in June and bring them down at the end of September. When I helped Pépé drive them up, he never stopped at the place where his son was killed. There was an overhanging grey rock there, which bulged outwards like the side of a whale. Not on the way up, on the way down, in the autumn, we always stopped under this rock and Pépé said: "This is where your father lost the heart to go on."

We needed to get the pig up on to the sledge, lying on his right side. During the struggle across the yard, he had planted his feet as hard as he could against the ground in order to resist being pulled by the rope and being pushed from behind. When he felt himself being toppled, his four legs lunged and searched for the ground with desperate speed and force and at the same time he yelled louder. Never before had he discovered his strength as he was discovering it now.

The men threw themselves on him. For a moment he was invisible beneath the heap of men, and he lay still. I could see one of his eyes. The pig has intelligent eyes, and his fear was now intelligent. Suddenly, lunging and kicking, he fought like a man, a man fighting off robbers.

During the next twelve months he was going to give body to our soup, flavour our potatoes, stuff our cabbages, fill our sausages. His hams and rolled breast, salted and dried, were going to lie on the rack, suspended from the ceiling above Pépé and Mémé's bed.

Grunting and using our knees and fists we got him still. Pépé roped three of his feet to the side bars of the sledge. As soon as a foot was tied, the pig struggled with all his strength to tug it from the knot. I climbed up to sit on his haunches. The men were swearing and laughing. As Mémé crossed the courtyard, I waved to her.

The day my father was killed, he had already brought down three loads of hay. It was in November, just before the snow. The hay is piled high on the sledge and tied down. At the top of the path, before the descent, you get between the shafts, tug once, and then brake the sledge as its runners slide down over the stones and the leaves and the dust for three kilometres. You brake it by digging in your heels and leaning backwards against the load. If, at the top, you reckon the load is too heavy, you tie logs to the back of the sledge and let these trail on the path, to act as an additional brake.

Nobody knows what happened when my father brought down his fourth load. He was found dead under the sledge. People said he ought to have been able to push the sledge off his chest. Perhaps that November afternoon, before the winter, his exhaustion or sadness was so great that he could not summon the will. Or perhaps the sledge stunned him.

My grandmother shouted at me: "You be careful he doesn't kick you!" Then she gave Pépé the knife, a small one, no longer than the ones used at table, and she knelt on the ground with her basin.

Low down, Pépé made a very short cut, from which the blood gushed out, as if it had always been waiting to do just that. The pig struggled knowing it was too late. The five of us were too heavy for him. His screams became deep breaths. His death was like a basin emptying.

The other basin was filling up. My grandmother, squatting on her haunches, was stirring and agitating his blood, to prevent it curdling. Every so often she took out and threw away the white fibres forming in it.

His eyes were shut. The space in him, left by the blood, was being filled by a kind of sleep, for he was not yet dead. Above the sledge Marius was gently pumping the left foreleg up and down so as to empty the heart. Pépé looked at me. I thought I knew what he was thinking: one day when I am too old, you will kill the pig!

We fetched the *petrin*. It was long enough for a man to lie down in. Before we rolled him into it, we arranged a chain like a belt for him, so that when he was wet we could still turn him round by pulling on his belt. To fill the *petrin* like a bath took two milk churns of hot water. He lay there almost entirely covered. Scraping his skin with the sides of tablespoons we shaved him, and the more closely we shaved him, the more his skin looked like that of a man. In the hot water his hair came off easily. He did not look like a man from the village, for he was too fat and too untanned, but like a man of leisure. The most difficult parts to shave were his knees, where the skin was calloused.

"He prayed more than a monk," said Marius. "Day and night he prayed to his trough."

When he was perfectly naked, with even the cuticles removed from his toes, Pépé put a hook through his snout and we hauled on the pulley to hoist him up. The pulley was attached to a wooden balcony where I often played as a small child. The only way onto the balcony was through a door from the hayloft; there were no stairs, so my mother knew that when I was there, playing and crawling on all fours above the courtyard, I was out of harm's way. The pig was larger than any of us. The men threw buckets of water over him, and to celebrate, they drank their first glass of *gnôle*.

Once Pépé spoke to me about death. "Last night," he said, "I was dragging some wood down with the mare, when I felt death was behind me. So I turned round. There was the path we'd come down, there was the walnut tree, there were the juniper bushes, there were the boulders with moss on them, a few clouds in the sky, the waterfall in the corner. Death was hiding behind one of them. He hid as soon as I turned round."

The pig's hind legs were ten centimetres off the ground.

"Head from body in ONE!" Pépé shouted and severed the head in one long cut with his small knife.

The body fell.

"The head for you!" he nodded towards me. I knew what I had to do. I took it, and ran up the pile of snow in the courtyard so fast that my feet made footholds and I reached the top. And there on the white summit I placed the pig's head.

The men were drinking their second glass of *gnôle*.

Into each hind leg, between the two bones, Pépé inserted a small hook. This time we hoisted up the carcass, neck down. The crows were too frightened by the men in the courtyard to approach the head on the pile of snow.

Delicately, from anus to neck, down the centre of the stomach, making an insertion with his knife, Pépé folded back the skin and fat. "André!" He said my name between his teeth because he was concentrating so hard.

He had made visible all that makes a pig a living, growing animal. All except the brain and head which were on the snow pile. The arrangement of the warm, steaming organs was the same as inside a rabbit. It was their size which was so impressive. When his belly was opened, it was like the mouth of a cave.

Pépé once admitted to me that he had dug for gold. During one summer he and a friend had got up two hours earlier every morning to go and dig there. They found nothing; but he showed me the shaft, should I ever wish to continue working it. It was hidden in a moraine on a steep wooded slope, where the boulders, the tree roots and the soil itself were all covered with a thick green moss. Whatever you touched there was like the fur of an animal.

I held one side of the zinc pan and Marius held the other, waiting for the guts and stomach to tumble out. Using only the point of his knife, as a woman does when unpicking stitches with the tip of her scissors, Pépé detached them. The grey guts overflowed the pan and we had to hold them in with our hands. They were warm and from them came the smell of killing.

The pig's liver, the pig's lungs, whitish-pink like two sprays of pear blossom, the pig's heart, Pépé removed separately.

I ran to the top of the snow pile again and turned the head round so that it faced its empty carcass. Underneath the head the blood had thawed a little snow, making a red cave. Standing on top of the snow pile, my head was level with the balustrade of the wooden balcony, where I had played when I could first walk. The men down below were throwing buckets of water over the carcass and rubbing it down, inside and out, with a cloth. Then they went in to eat.

Down the centre of the table were loaves of fresh bread and large bottles of cider. There were two kinds of cider, the sweet cider which we had pressed only two months before, and last year's, which was stronger. The older one was easy to distinguish because it was cloudier. Most of the women drank the new cider.

From a large black cast-iron pot on the stove, my mother filled the soup tureen to put on the table. To celebrate the killing of the new pig, we were going to eat what remained of the old.

In the soup, made with parts of the salted backbone, were carrots, parsnips, leeks, turnips. The loaves were passed round and held against each chest in turn, as a slice was cut off. Then, spoons in hand, we entered the meal.

Some of the men started to talk about the war. The body of another German soldier had been discovered a few weeks before in a crevice high up in the forest. This was the winter of 1950.

"If he'd stayed at home, he'd be sleeping today with his wife in his bed."

I was drinking the strong cider and listening to each conversation.

Every year, when the pig was killed, all the neighbours and Monsieur le Curé and the schoolmaster were invited to eat. The schoolmaster was sitting near Pépé at the head of the table. I was anxious in case he told Pépé about the hedgehog. The hedgehog was discovered in the schoolroom cupboard where the schoolmaster kept his coat. We called him The Hedgehog because his hair stood up at the back. He had very small hands too. And he wore glasses. Standing before the class, he invited whoever had put the hedgehog in the cupboard to remove it. Nobody got up. Nobody dared look at me. Then he asked: "Who knows why hedgehogs smell?" Like a fool, I put up my hand and said they made a smell when they were frightened.

"Then since you know more about him than any of the others, please remove him." The others began to laugh and some shouted Bravo! in such a way that he realised he had picked the culprit. As a punishment, he made me learn and recite out loud a page about hedgehogs. He brought the book himself next day, and I had to sit in the schoolroom until I had learnt it. I still remember how it began: "The fox knows many little things and the hedgehog knows one big thing." I wondered whether he had read the text himself, because a few lines further down it explained that, because of their spines, hedgehogs could not mate like other animals, but had to do so standing up, and face to face like men and women.

I was reassured, for the schoolmaster was making Pépé laugh. Opposite me La Fine, who lived below our fields and could take away the pain of burns, was telling a story about Joseph, her brother-in-law. He went to C . . . on a day when there was a fête and a band. He came back late at night convinced that in one of the cafés he had pissed into a golden lavatory! It turned out he had pissed into a bandsman's bassoon!

My mother never sat down. She went round the table serving. When she brought the stuffed cabbages on, we all cheered. "Wait till you taste them!" she cried, full of confidence. They had been cooking since early morning in a net in a deep pot. First she put a plate into the bottom of the net, then on the plate a layer of cabbage leaves, then a layer of stuffing of minced pork and eggs and shallots and marjoram, then a layer of leaves, then a layer of stuffing, until the net was as full and heavy as a goose. When I was younger I had watched her do it. Now I was drinking last year's cider like a man.

"I would like to know what life was like ten thousand years ago," Pépé was saying. "I think of it often. Nature would have been the same. The same trees, the same earth, the same clouds, the same snow falling in the same way on the grass and thawing in the spring. People exaggerate the changes in nature so as to make nature seem lighter." He was talking to a neighbour's son who was on leave from the army. "Nature resists change. If something changes, nature waits to see whether the change can continue, and, if it can't, it crushes it with all its weight! Ten thousand years ago the trout in the stream would have been exactly the same as today."

"The pigs wouldn't have been!"

"That's why I would like to go back! To see how the things we know today were first learnt. Take a *chevreton*. It's simple. Milk the goat, heat the milk, separate it and press the curds. Well, we saw it all being done before we could walk. But how did they once discover that the best way of separating the milk was to take a kid's stomach, blow it up like a balloon, dry it, soak it in acid, powder it and drop a few grains of this powder into the heated milk? I would like to know how the women discovered that!"

At the other end of the table the guests were listening to Mémé who was telling a story. There were two cousins in a nearby village who lived side by side because they inherited the same property . . .

"That is what I would like to know if I was a crow on a tree watching!" Pépé was saying. "All the mistakes which had to be made! And step by step, slowly, the progress!"

The two cousins fall out and start a fight. One of them bites a piece out of the other's nose. Both are too frightened to continue fighting. A few days later the bitten one is digging in his garden, with a cloth over his nose. He sees his cousin coming out of the house on the other side of the fence. "Well, well!" he shouts. "Are you feeling hungry today? Why not come over and finish off the rest of the nose?"

Whenever a plate was empty, my mother piled more stuffed cabbage on to it.

"The thread of knowledge which nature doesn't crush, like a thread of gold in the rock," Pépé was saying.

The faces shone in the heat, and the table became more and more untidy. My mother brought on an apple tart the size of a small cart-wheel.

"And then I would like to go several thousand years into the future."

"There'll be no more peasants."

"Not so sure! I didn't say forty thousand, I said several thousand! I'd look down at them like the old crow looks at us!"

Unless I concentrated on stopping them revolving, the walls of the kitchen would not stay still. On the table with the apple tart were cups of coffee and bottles of *gnôle*. I gulped down some coffee.

"All farms will be on flat plains," pronounced the schoolmaster.

The cold air of the courtyard cleared my head. At the end of the meal the guests left, saying, "Till the next time."

I wanted an excuse not to go down to school. The chances were not good, for the only possible excuse was that I was needed for work, and there was not enough work for me to do. I held the pig's forelegs whilst Pépé sawed the carcass into two from the back.

He put his shoulder under one of the sides, I unhooked it, he adjusted its weight, and he carried it across the courtyard, past the stone sabot, and up the outside wooden stairway to the room above the vaulted cellar. The side of the pig was longer than he was tall. He walked slowly, and on the stairway he stopped once. When he carried the second side, he stopped three times.

The next day he would cut the meat and lay it out neatly, like a flowerbed of pink delphiniums, on the trestle table. Every year he arranged it like this.

Then my mother would salt the meat in the wooden *saloir* and in six weeks Pépé and I would go looking for juniper branches for smoking the hams and the bacon.

The kitchen had been restored to its working tidiness. On the scrubbed table the women were cleaning the pig's guts and preparing to make *boudin* from his blood. Reluctantly I went down the steep path to school.

When I came out I had to screw up my eyes against the falling snow. Mémé did not warn me about bringing snow on my boots into the kitchen, because she was crying. She and my mother had laid Pépé on his bed.

He had collapsed in the courtyard. Tomorrow the same neighbours who had eaten lunch with us would be returning to pay their last respects to him.

No mountain in the world was as still and as cold as his face. I waited for his face to move. I told myself I would wait all night. But its stillness outdid me.

I went out and crossed the courtyard to look at the stone sabot. There was enough moonlight for me to see it.

I heard Pépé saying again: "That is what I'd like to know if I was a crow on a tree watching . . ."

During the night more snow fell, and in the morning, on top of the pile in the courtyard, I saw an unexpected shape, draped in white. I had forgotten the pig's head. Once more I ran full tilt up the side to the top. I brushed off the snow. The eyes were shut and the skin was as cold as ice. It was then that I started to howl. I do not know for how long I sat there, on top of the snow pile, howling. ✐

SUGGESTIONS FOR WRITING

1. Have you ever participated in a major project that demanded the labors of your entire family and perhaps your neighbors? What was your role? How did you feel about it?

2. The French are unsurpassed in making a big production out of a family meal. In "The Wind Howls Too," the prolonged dinner with the unhurried conversation takes on a haunting dramatic aspect, especially considering the way the story turns out. Describe a particularly memorable family meal.

3. Discuss the quite different activities of the men and women.

4. Narrate a "coming of age" story of your own invention or experience.

LITTLE MOUNTAIN

Elias Khoury
(Translation by Maria Tabet)

The name of Beirut, **Elias Khoury's** city, rarely appeared in print in recent years without the modifier "war-torn" preceding it. Lebanon has seen centuries of military, political, and religious conflict. When the Ottoman Turks began their sixteenth-century conquest of the Levantine territory, including what would later be called Lebanon, they were but the latest of a succession of empires dating back thousands of years. With the decline of the Ottoman Empire in the nineteenth century came European, especially French, domination. Lebanon gained its autonomy under a 1920 League of Nations mandate, and it became an independent republic in 1944. Since that time, with the birth of Israel in 1948 and the subsequent waves of Arab nationalism, Lebanon has been rocked by the upheavals of the Middle East. Every regional struggle—from Iranian-backed revolutionary movements to Syrian military action, from Palestinians demanding autonomy from Israel to Israel's strikes against what it calls terrorists, is played out there.

Lebanon's history thus has been multicultural, with the imprint of many ethnic and religious groups. There are the Muslim sects, and equally diverse number of Christian sects, a distinct religious group known as the Druse, and some Jews, all of whose loyalties are dispersed among Arab, Israeli, French, Iranian, and other sponsors. During the past few years, the large number of Palestinian refugees, many living in refugee camps, has had a major impact on Lebanon. Many Americans assume that religious differences provide the major cultural basis for conflict, but regional historians argue that political and economic imbalances—in short, the legacy of colonialism—are far more important. Khoury's novel, in which violence is portrayed matter-of-factly as part of the landscape, was published before the 1982 Israeli invasion. The effects of the invasion are still being felt in terrorism, the taking of hostages, and the awful conditions of the teeming refugee camps.

Khoury, who grew up in Ashrafiyyeh or "Little Mountain" (Christian East Beirut), is one of the most widely acclaimed of the younger authors writing in Arabic, a language whose literary riches began to receive some long-overdue recognition when Egyptian novelist Nahguib Mahfouz was awarded the Nobel Prize in literature in 1988. Khoury, a lecturer at the American University of Beirut (he taught formerly at the Lebanese University in Beirut), is cultural editor of the Beirut daily newspaper al-Safir. His writings appear in literary journals throughout the Arab world, and he has published novels, short stories, and criticism. Little Mountain, his second novel, was published in 1977. Other novels include White Faces (1981), City Gates (1981), and The Travel of Little Gandhi (1989).

They call it Little Mountain.[1] And we called it Little Mountain. We'd carry pebbles, draw faces and look for a puddle of water to wash off the sand, or fill with sand, then cry. We'd run through the fields—or something like fields— pick up a tortoise and carry it to where green leaves littered the ground. We made up things we'd say or wouldn't say. They call it Little Mountain, we knew it wasn't a mountain and we called it Little Mountain.

One hill, several hills, I no longer remember and no one remembers anymore. A hill on Beirut's eastern flank which we called mountain because the mountains were far away. We sat on its slopes and stole the sea. The sun rose in the East and we'd come out of the wheatfields from the East. We'd pluck off the ears of wheat, one by one, to amuse ourselves. The poor—or what might have been the poor—skipped through the fields on the hills, like children, questioning Nature about Her things. What we called a 'eid[2] was a day like any other, but it was laced with the smell of the *burghul* and 'araq[3] that we ate in Nature's world, telling it about our world which subsists in our memory like a dream. Little Mountain was just a tip of rock we'd steal into, wondrous and proud. We'd spin yarns about our miseries awaiting the moments of joy or death, dallying with our feelings to break the monotony of the days.

They call it Little Mountain. It stretched across the vast fields dotted with prickly-pear bushes. The palm tree in front of our house was bent under the weight of its own trunk. We were afraid it would brush the ground, crash down to it, so we suggested tying it with silken rope to the window of our house. But the house itself, with its thick sandstone and wooden ceilings, was caving in and we got frightened the palm tree would bring the house down with it. So we let it lean farther day by day. And every day I'd embrace its fissured trunk and draw pictures of my face on it.

We feared for the mountain and for its plants. It edged to the brink of Beirut, sinking into it. And the prickly-pear bushes that scratched our legs were dying and the palm tree leaning and mountain edging toward the brink.

They call it Little Mountain We knew it wasn't a mountain and we called it Little Mountain.

Five men come, jumping out of a military-like jeep. Carrying automatic rifles, they surround the house. The neighbors come out to watch. One of them smiles, she makes the victory sign. They come up to the house, knock on the door. My mother opens the door, surprised. Their leader asks about me.

—He's gone out.
—Where did he go?
—I don't know.
—Come in, have a cup of coffee.

[1]The popular name for the Ashrafiyyeh area of Beirut.
[2]That is, a feast day, festival, or holiday of religious origin or significance.
[3]*Burghul* is the crushed wheat used in two major national dishes in Lebanon; it is known in the West as bulgar. 'Araq, the national drink, is a distilled grape alcohol, aromatized with anise.

They enter. They search for me in the house. I wasn't there. They search the books and the papers. I wasn't there. They found a book with a picture of Abdel-Nasser[1] on the back cover. I wasn't there. They scattered the papers and overturned the furniture. They cursed the Palestinians. They ripped my bed up. They insulted my mother and this corrupt generation. I wasn't there. I wasn't there. My mother was there, trembling with distress and resentment, pacing up and down the house angrily. She stopped answering their questions and left them. She sat on a chair in the entrance, guarding her house as they, inside, looked for the Palestinians and Abdel-Nasser and international communism. She sat on a chair in the entrance, guarding her house as they, inside, tore up papers and memories. She sat on a chair and they made the sign of the cross, in hatred or in joy.

They went out into the street, their hands held high in gestures of victory. Some people watched and made the victory sign.

We called it Little Mountain when we were small. We'd run along its dirt roads or on the edge of the asphalt which cut into our feet. We'd walk its streets looking for things to play with. And during the holidays, I'd go with my father and brothers to the fields called Sioufi and frolic between the olive and Persian lilac trees. There, we'd stand on top of a high hill overlooking three roads: the Nahr Beirut road, the Karm al-Zeytoun road[2] and the third one, which we called the road to our house. We'd stand on the high open hilltop, run through it and always be afraid of falling off onto one of the three roads.

He stood perched on the high hill. Holding his big father by the right hand, he'd watch the cars far away on the road below and marvel at how small they were. They weren't like the car he rode to his uncle's distant house. Very small cars, one behind the other, like the small car that his father bought him and set in motion by singing to it. There's not a sound to these metal cars going by. Soundless, they move along regularly, one behind the other, in a straight line. They don't stop. Inside are miniature-like people. They aren't children of my age—he'd think to himself—and once, when he asked his father about the secret of the small cars, his father answered in the overtones of a diviner that the reason was that Ashrafiyyeh being a mountain, the Beirutis went and spent the summer there. And compared with Beirut, the mountain is high. The distance between us and the Nahr Beirut is high, like that between us and the Karm al-Zeytoun road. And the farther you are, the smaller things get. Later, when you grow up, you'll see that the cars are very small. Because vision is also related to the size of the viewer. I would nod, feigning comprehension, not understanding a thing. Generally, I'd let my father tell me his story, which he always retold, about distances and cars and distract myself by chasing a golden cicada flitting among the green grasses or perched between the branches of the olive trees.

A long line of small soundless cars. We'd sit on the edge of the hill and watch them go by, waiting for the day when we'd grow up and see that they

[1]The president of Egypt from 1954 to 1970 and the most revered leader of Arab Nationalism.
[2]That is, the Beirut River and Olive Grove roads, respectively.

were very small really, or go down to the road and see that they were very big. They trickled by like colored drops of water of varying size. Trucks, petrol tankers, all sorts of small cars. We could tell the difference between them although we couldn't name them or say what they were for. They were far away and small and we'd hold each other by the hand waiting to grow up so they'd grow even smaller, we'd hold each other by the hand and wait to understand the secret. And I always used to wonder how come cars were small just because they were far away and I would daydream about the stories of dwarfs they told us at school or of the man whom the devil turned into a dwarf, which my grandmother always told me.

Little Mountain where it was, the vegetation that covered its handsome mound was giving way to roads and we rejoiced at the opening of the first cinema in Sioufi. But surprises awaited me. We were growing and what we had been waiting for, so long now, didn't happen. We were getting bigger, we'd go to Sioufi to watch the cars—and see that they'd gotten bigger. We got bigger and the cars got bigger. Hemmed in by the gathering clamor and frenzy. We were getting bigger and the once-straight lines were curving, the clamor getting closer and the spaces narrower. I walk alone. Little Mountain twists and turns. I search for memories of when Palm Sunday[1] was a 'eid and we came out of the church to the sound of Eastern chants: I find only a small, neglected picture in my pocket.

Cars growing, closing in on me. Trees shrinking, disappearing. I was growing bigger and so were the cars, around my neck were their sounds, their colors, their sizes. Now, we can tell the difference between them but we don't understand.

Old expectations and distant memories are merely expectations and memories. At night, the cars climb the three roads to the high hilltop. Bruising my eyes, their lights encircle me. The white of the engines walling me in as they approach my face. The cars are big, they have huge eyes extending filaments of fire that don't burn. They leave the traces of terror, questions and answers, on my face.

The cars were growing—and we were growing. The broad streets were growing and the trees bent low on Little Mountain. What has become of my father's explanations as he told me stories of distance and height and size?

You stand alone amid the flood of lights that blinds you and robs you of your memory. You go looking for your house, alone, memoryless.

Abu George told me the story of the names. Abu George has been my friend since the time I wandered around Little Mountain, alone among the lights, looking for my father's explanations. He'd find me alone, sitting on the edge of a hill overlooking the railroad tracks of the slow train that stands out in my memory, and would tell me his stories of the French and the world war.

He'd relate how Sioufi used to be a huge property owned by a man called Yusef-as-Sagheer.[1] That is why Ashrafiyyeh was called Little Mountain. Then,

[1]In the Eastern church, Palm Sunday is an important festival especially for children.

the brothers Elias and Nkoula Sioufi bought it up dirt-cheap and, after World War I, they built a furniture factory on it. The neighborhood came to be known by their name.

The factory, in reality a large workshop, was an event in itself. It had about fifty workers. They built themselves some shacks nearby, and a small café serving coffee and 'araq opened next door. The factory was a novel sort of undertaking and people began getting used to a novel way of life, for the first time. Modern machines. European-style furniture. They knew neither where it went nor how it would be sold. They collected their wage—or something like a wage—at the end of the month, gave some of it to their women, and drank 'araq with the rest.

As the neighborhood got used to this new kind of life, there arose a new kind of theft. Instead of the old kind of robberies—like those of a man called Nadra who lived at the eastern end of the neighborhood and who, in the ancient Arab tradition of chivalry, extorted money from the rich to give it to the poor—there was now organized robbery. Gang robbery, premeditated and merciless; without a touch of chivalry or any other kind of principle. The most important event which established this new-style thieving was the robbery of the Sioufi factory itself. At the end of each month, the accountant would go to Beirut to fetch the workers' money and come back to the factory to distribute it to them. Once, at a crossroads, some thieves ambushed him; they took the money and left him there, hollering. Alerted by his screams, the workers gathered around. Men, women, and children rushed out and chased the thieves. The thieves ran and people ran behind them, popping out of the dirt roads and alleys. Before anyone had caught up with them, the thieves stopped running, threw the coins to the ground and resumed their race. At that point, bodies doubled up over coins and hands started snatching. People forgot the thieves and let them get away, snatching up the coins from the ground helter-skelter. It was no chivalrous kind of theft, Abu George would say. Why? Because they all forgot their honor and made for the coins. They were lenient with the thieves and took the factory's money. That is when the decline set it. And the story has it, the factory started going bankrupt then, Abu George would continue. Elias Sioufi died of a broken heart and his brother, Nkoula, sold off the property to the people of the neighborhood. And it was split into small holdings.

However, Abu George went on, there was perhaps another reason for the bankruptcy. People who knew Nkoula Sioufi—who had become an errand-runner at the Ministry of Finance—said the reason was that he drank and gambled and associated with foreigners. God only knows, Abu George would say. But the decline set in with the beginning of this new-style thieving. And we now have to deal with things we never knew.

Is the mountain slipping?

The big cars advanced, invading, their whine filling the streets. The mountain was being penetrated from all sides. They cut the trees, erected buildings.

---

[1] As-Sagheer means the little one in Arabic.

The concrete mountain's machines were everywhere. In every street, there was a machine, Syrian and Kurdish workers swarming around it, throwing sand, gravel and water into its entrails. Rotating on itself, spilling out the cement used to build the tall, indomitable buildings. Buildings shot up as though born here and the thick, warm sandstone tumbled to the ground and was replaced by the hollow, cold cement blocks. And the wheel turned. Hundreds of workers came up here from the tin shacks clustered at the eastern entrance of Beirut—called Qarantina[1]—to carry gravel and sand and spread the cement across the squares.

Bulldozers came, flattening the hills to the ground or what was presumed to be the level of the ground. And in front of our house, the palm tree collapsed, locked into the excavator's jaws, its roots which bulged above ground, torn out and cast down, in a pool of gravel and sand. Torn like small arteries by a bombshell. The new buildings soared. Mountains of buildings, roads and squares.

Is the mountain slipping?

I walk its side streets, looking for my childhood. Before me on the hill which I call mountain, a gentle slope separating the mountain from Nahr Beirut. The small cars have grown and I have grown. And the tall buildings now hide the sea. I used to think we had stolen the sea. But the smell of reinforced concrete has stolen the smell of the sea.

The mountain isn't slipping.

The hubbub at its gates, the buildings multiplying and the squares being built. That loud voice is no longer mine. Noise cowering at the gates and frenzy the new sign. This is Little Mountain which isn't slipping.

Concrete soaring and heads soaring. Heavy music soaring and heads soaring. On my body, I bear from those days an ancient tattoo and I wait, on the brink.

1956: the tripartite attack on Egypt. We were at the poor, small neighborhood school. We were little. We'd listen to *Sawt al-Arab*.[2] We went home and rejoiced when Egypt won.

1958: barricades in the neighborhood. Somber faces. The Muslims want to kill us. My mother didn't believe it. She always said that's crazy. They're very much like us.

The tall buildings have become barricades. Things have changed. The gathering clamor. Things have changed. The cars are growing and we are growing.

Abu George would go on with his story about the furniture factory. He'd never weary of recounting his memories of the neighborhood, considering himself a part of its history. And at every turn, he'd ponder with me the use of living. He'd talk at length of how his brother was a soldier with the French army in Hawran,[1] of how he rebelled during the Jabal Druze revolt and paid for it by

---

[1]The area known as Qarantina was the site of a military quarantine hospital under the French Mandate. Later, it became Beirut's principal garbage dump and part of the urban slum area that constituted the city's "belt of misery."
[2]The Cairo-based pan-Arab radio listened to extensively throughout the Arab world in the headier days of Arab Nationalism.

the terrible death he suffered in the dank prison cells. Still, the important thing is that the factory was not torn down after the bankruptcy. The large building stayed there but without machines or workers. We used to go and look at it, enter and find it dark but always clean. Then came the second world war. We didn't experience the horrors of World War I,[2] but we discovered air raids. The French army turned the factory into a military site. A sort of barracks where dozens of French soldiers and others, who I think were Chinese, lived; it was said they came from Indochina: they were short and yellow-skinned and went almost barefoot in rubber shoes that didn't keep the cold out. They were basically orderlies in the service of the French, cooking the food, brewing the coffee. When off-duty, they'd sing their own songs in a language I couldn't understand even though I tried to be on good terms with them.

During the air raids, the soldiers would go out into the fields. And those other short ones, their little feet in the rubber shoes, darted about the hills, scattering among the ears of wheat, talking with the speed of their strange language.

Naturally, Lebanon gained its independence after the war and the French soldiers left and those little short soldiers went off to their own country. And I think I saw them, or people like them, when they showed films about the Vietnam war on TV.

They came. Five men, jumping out of a military-like vehicle. Carrying automatic rifles. They surround the house. The neighbors come out to watch. One of them smiles, she makes the victory sign. They come up to the house. Knock on the door; my mother opens, surprised. Their leader asks about me. He's out. —Where did he go?—I don't know.—Come in, have a cup of coffee.

They enter. They search for me in the house. I wasn't there. They search the books and the papers. I wasn't there. They find a book with a picture of Abdel-Nasser on the back cover. I wasn't there. They overturn the papers and the furniture. They curse the Palestinians. They rip my bed up. They insult my mother and this corrupt generation. I wasn't there. Their leader stood, an automatic rifle across his shoulder, in his hand a pistol, threatening.

—He'd better not come back here.

I wasn't there. My mother was there. Trembling with distress and resentment, pacing up and down the house angrily. She stopped answering their questions and left them. She sat on a chair in the entrance, guarding her house as they, inside, looked for the Palestinians and Abdel-Nasser and international communism. She sat on a chair in the entrance, guarding her house. And they, inside, tore up papers and memories. She sat on a chair. And they made the sign of the cross, in hatred or in joy.

They went out into the street, their hands held high in gestures of victory. And some people watched and made the victory sign.

---

[1] A region of Syria which is part of the larger *Jabal Druze*, i.e., Druze Mountain, area that led a famous revolt in the mid-1920s against the French Mandate.

[2] There was famine in Lebanon during World War I owing to the requisitioning of grain for the soldiers by the Ottoman authorities and to hoarding by grain merchants.

The big cars stream in, filling the streets. Military-like vehicles, painted black, horns blaring as they go by. Men with automatic rifles jump out. One of them looks through the binoculars dangling from his neck, darting from one corner of the street to the other. They shout at people and tremble with hatred. Their leader looks through the binoculars dangling from his neck, stops to answer the questions of passers-by. He tells them about the siege of Qarantina. We'll mop up every last bit of it and throw them out of Lebanon. We'll defeat them and all the beggars trying to plunder our country.

He gets into his military-like Chevrolet and speeds off. The men scuttle in all directions at once. They march down the streets in step. Han-doy, han-doy (a military expression meaning one-two[1] which the militiamen in our neighborhood used. I don't know why, but it was current practice).

Cars roaming the streets. The cars gnaw at the streets with their teeth. The big cars blast their sirens. I stand in front of them: their tires are huge, high, and thick.

Black metal devouring me: roadblocks, they say. I see my face tumbling to the ground. Black metal devouring me: my voice slips down alone and stretches to where the corpses of my friends lie buried in mass graves. Black metal devouring me: the raised hands do not wave banners, they clutch death. Metal on the street, terror and empty gas-bottles, corpses and smuggled cigarette cartons. The moment of victory has come. The moment of death has come. War has come. And my mother shakes her head and tells me about the poor.

They call it Little Mountain. And we called it Little Mountain. We'd carry pebbles, draw faces and look for a puddle of water to wash off the sand, or fill with sand, then cry. We'd run through the fields—or something like fields— pick up a tortoise and carry it to where green leaves littered the ground. We made up things we'd say or wouldn't say. They call it Little Mountain, we knew it wasn't a mountain and we called it Little Mountain.

One hill, several hills, I no longer remember and no one remembers anymore. A hill on Beirut's eastern flank which we called mountain because the mountains were far away. We sat on its slopes and stole the sea. The sun rose in the East and we'd come out of the wheatfields from the East. We'd pluck off the ears of wheat, one by one, to amuse ourselves. The poor—or what might have been the poor—skipped through the fields on the hills, like children questioning Nature about Her things. What we called 'eid was a day like any other, but it was laced with the smell of the burghul and 'araq that we ate in Nature's world, telling it about our world which subsists in our memory like a dream. Little Mountain was just a tip of rock we'd steal into, wondrous and proud. We'd spin yarns about our miseries awaiting the moments of joy or death, dallying with our feelings to break the monotony of the days.

They call it Little Mountain. It stretched across the vast fields dotted with prickly-pear bushes. The palm tree in front of our house was bent under the

[1]A corruption of the French "un-deux," obviously meant ironically by the author.

weight of its own trunk. We were afraid it would brush the ground, crash down to it, so we suggested tying it with silken rope to the window of our house. But the house itself, with its thick sandstone and wooden ceilings, was caving in and we got frightened the palm tree would bring the house down with it. So we let it lean farther day by day. And every day I'd embrace its fissured trunk and draw pictures of my face on it.

We feared for the mountain and for its plants. It edged to the brink of Beirut, sinking into it. And the prickly-pear bushes that scratched our legs were dying and the palm tree leaning and the mountain edging toward the brink.

They call it Little Mountain. We knew it wasn't a mountain and we called it Little Mountain.

When I was three, the parish priest came in his long black cassock and handsome beard. He sat in our house and we all gathered around him in a circle. He started telling us anecdotes and stories. Then, he told us about the achievements of Stalin and the Bolsheviks. He turned to me, ruffled my hair, and told my mother that it was time I was dedicated to Saint Anthony and was given his habit to wear (wearing St. Anthony's habit is a tradition among most of the Eastern Christians in our country; it is worn by children in blessed remembrance of the first Christian monk to have left the city and gone to Sinai to start up the church's first monastic order).

The habit is brown with a white cord dangling from the waist. I walk down the street imitating the gestures of saints. I walk and around me are children who wear or don't wear the habit. We proceed in a long lien to where the golden icons lie and the glass is tinted by the sun. And when I forget that I have become a saint, I run wild, playing in the gravel and the sand. I fall down in the streets. Then, when I go home, my mother looks over the saint's soiled habit and slaps and scolds me. Then orders me to kneel down and pray. I kneel down and pray so that the saints might forget that I abandoned them and went off to play with the other children.

I walk, proud in my beautiful brown habit, imitating the priest's gestures. I go to school, vaunting my clothes and put a round halo of leaves on my head.

The parish priest died all of a sudden. I didn't understand what it meant. I remember crying because my sister wept. Then, about six months later as I recall (maybe I no longer actually remember the event but have it imprinted in my memory because of the dozens of times my mother told me the story), I went to church with my mother and father. It was the custom to take off the monk's beautiful garment in church, where it was placed at the alter and candles were lit in offering.

We went to church. I was feeling joyful and rapturous. We reached the heavy door that was always open. It was shut. My father knocked on the door, no one opened. My mother knocked, no one opened. My father said what shall we do. I knocked on the door, kicked it. Leave the habit at the door, answered my mother.

—And the candles?

—We'll light them next week.

I knocked on the door, kicked it. No one opened. My father helped me out of the habit. I began to cry. My mother took the habit, placed it at the door and made the sign of the cross. I was in tears. My father held me by the hand and we walked home. No one opened the church door. We left the habit at the door and I went home miserable. No candles were lit the following week.

They came.

Five men, jumping out of a military-like jeep, carrying automatic rifles. Five men wearing big black hats with big black crosses dangling from their necks. They surround the house. They ring the church bells and bang on the door.

Five long black crosses dangling before my mother as she opens the door. She mutters unintelligible phrases. She slams the door shut in their faces and cries.

Five men break down the door and ask for me. I wasn't there. They find a book with a picture of Abdel-Nasser on the back cover. I wasn't there. My mother was there, trembling with distress, resentment, and fear. My mother was there. She sat on a chair in the entrance, guarding her house as they, inside, looked for the Palestinians and Abdel-Nasser and international communism. She sat on a chair in the entrance, guarding her house as they, inside, tore up papers and memories.

My mother was there.

I wasn't there.

I was in the East, searching with short, almost barefoot men in rubber shoes that didn't keep the cold out. I was in the East, looking for Little Mountain stretched across the frames of men, the sea surging out of their beautiful eyes. ✒

SUGGESTIONS FOR WRITING

1. Why, since the young man's family is Christian, are the Christian militia—all the while denouncing Palestinians and Arab nationalists—looking for him? Why do you think so much emphasis is placed on the repetition of the scene where the troops entered his home when he was away?

2. Even in times and places of extreme violence, life must go on. In what ways are these people able to continue with their lives despite the violence? Are you aware of similar examples from other times and other places? Describe one.

3. What things do you think of when you think of Lebanon or the Middle East? How do such impressions, assumptions, or stereotypes affect your reading of "Little Mountain"? Where do your ideas come from?

IF I COULD WRITE THIS IN FIRE, I WOULD WRITE THIS IN FIRE

Michelle Cliff

Jamaica, a Caribbean nation that gained its independence from Great Britain in 1962, provides a striking example of the legacy of colonialism. A white minority historically controlled the black population, many of them descended from slaves. There have also been a number of Asian immigrants, especially from India. As in most colonies, natives who received an education were taught the virtues of the English way of life and, by extension, that they had no culture of their own. During much of the twentieth century, American influence has been strong. The reggae music for which Jamaica is known today represents an amalgam of Jamaican folk styles (including African influences) and American rock 'n' roll. Today, large Jamaican immigrant communities exist in London and New York.

Michelle Cliff, the author of this autobiographical essay, moves about from Jamaica to England to the United States, experiencing the diversity of postcolonial life. Aware of the racial and cultural contradictions in her own background, her ambivalence toward the First World education she has received leads her to explore the black separatism of Marcus Garvey and to appreciate the Rastafarian subculture of Jamaica, much to the consternation of her more "proper" family. She has mastered the language of Milton, Wordsworth, and Keats, but she expresses the wish to write as much as possible in the Jamaican patois.

Cliff, born in 1946 in Jamaica, was educated there and in England, where she received her Ph.D. in English literature at the University of London. She has taught at the University of California, Santa Cruz. Her books include No Telephone to Heaven *(1987),* The Land of Look Behind *(1985),* Abeno *(1984), and* Claiming an Identity They Taught Me to Despise *(1980).*

I

We were standing under the waterfall at the top of Orange River. Our chests were just beginning to mound—slight hills on either side. In the center of each were our nipples, which were losing their sideways look and rounding into perceptible buttons of dark flesh. Too fast it seemed. We touched each other, then, quickly and almost simultaneously, raised our arms to examine the hairs growing underneath. Another sign. Mine was wispy and light-brown. My friend Zoe had dark hair curled up tight. In each little patch the riverwater caught the sun so we glistened.

The waterfall had come about when my uncles dammed up the river to bring power to the sugar mill. Usually, when I say "sugar mill" to anyone not familiar with the Jamaican countryside or for that matter my family, I can tell their minds cast an image of tall smokestacks, enormous copper cauldrons, a man in a broad-brimmed hat with a whip, and several dozens of slaves—that is, if they have any idea of how large sugar mills once operated. It's a grandiose expression—like plantation, verandah, out-building. (Try substituting farm, porch, outside toilet.) To some people it even sounds romantic.

Our sugar mill was little more than a round-roofed shed, which contained a wheel and woodfire. We paid an old man to run it, tend the fire, and then either bartered or gave the sugar away, after my grandmother had taken what she needed. Our canefield was about two acres of flat land next to the river. My grandmother had six acres in all—one donkey, a mule, two cows, some chickens, a few pigs, and stray dogs and cats who had taken up residence in the yard.

Her house had four rooms, no electricity, no running water. The kitchen was a shed in the back with a small pot-bellied stove. Across from the stove was a mahogany counter, which had a white enamel basin set into it. The only light source was a window, a small space covered partly by a wooden shutter. We washed our faces and hands in enamel bowls with cold water carried in kerosene tins from the river and poured from enamel pitchers. Our chamber pots were enamel also, and in the morning we carefully placed them on the steps at the side of the house where my grandmother collected them and disposed of their contents. The outhouse was about thirty yards from the back door—a "closet" as we called it—infested with lizards capable of changing color. When the door was shut it was totally dark, and the lizards made their presence known by the noise of their scurrying through the torn newspaper, or the soft shudder when they dropped from the walls. I remember most clearly the stench of the toilet, which seemed to hang in the air in that climate.

But because every little of piece of reality exists in relation to another little piece, our situation was not that simple. It was to our yard that people came with news first. It was in my grandmother's parlor that the Disciples of Christ held their meetings.

Zoe lived with her mother and sister on borrowed ground in a place called Breezy Hill. She and I saw each other almost every day on our school vacations over a period of three years. Each morning early—as I sat on the cement porch with my coffee cut with condensed milk—she appeared: in her straw hat, school tunic faded from blue to gray, white blouse, sneakers hanging around her neck. We had coffee together, and a piece of hard-dough bread with butter and cheese, waited a bit and headed for the river. At first we were shy with each other. We did not start from the same place.

There was land. My grandparents' farm. And there was color.

(My family was called *red*. A term which signified a degree of whiteness. "We's just a flock of red people," a cousin of mine said once.) In the hierarchy of shades I was considered among the lightest. The countrywomen who visited my grandmother commented on my "tall" hair—meaning long. Wavy, not curly.

I had spent the years from three to ten in New York and spoke—at first—like an American. I wore American clothes: shorts, slacks, bathing suit. Because of my American past I was looked upon as the creator of games. Cowboys and Indians. Cops and Robbers. Peter Pan.

(While the primary colonial identification for Jamaicans was English, American colonialism was a strong force in my childhood—and of course continues today. We were sent American movies and American music. American aluminum companies had already discovered bauxite on the island and were shipping the ore to their mainland. United Fruit bought our bananas. White Americans came to Montego Bay, Ocho Rios, and Kingston for their vacations and their cruise ships docked in Port Antonio and other places. In some ways America was seen as a better place than England by many Jamaicans. The farm laborers sent to work in American agribusiness came home with dollars and gifts and new clothes; there were few who mentioned American racism. Many of the middle class who emigrated to Brooklyn or Staten Island or Manhattan were able to pass into the white American world—saving their blackness for other Jamaicans or for trips home; in some cases, forgetting it altogether. Those middle-class Jamaicans who could not pass for white managed differently—not unlike the Bajans in Paule Marshall's *Brown Girl, Brownstones*—saving, working, investing, buying property. Completely separate in most cases from Black Americans.)

I was someone who had experience with the place that sent us triple features of B-grade westerns and gangster movies. And I had tall hair and light skin. And I was the granddaughter of my grandmother. So I had power. I was the cowboy, Zoe was my sidekick, the boys we knew were Indians. I was the detective, Zoe was my "girl," the boys were the robbers. I was Peter Pan, Zoe was Wendy Darling, the boys were the lost boys. And the terrain around the river—jungled and dark green—was Tombstone, or Chicago, or Never-Never Land.

This place and my friendship with Zoe never touched my life in Kingston. We did not correspond with each other when I left my grandmother's home.

I never visited Zoe's home the entire time I knew her. It was a given: never suggested, never raised.

Zoe went to a state school held in a country church in Red Hills. It had been my mother's school. I went to a private all-girls school where I was taught by white Englishwomen and pale Jamaicans. In her school the students were caned as punishment. In mine the harshest punishment I remember was being sent to sit under the *lignum vitae* to "commune with nature." Some of the girls were out-and-out white (English and American), the rest of us were colored—only a few were dark. Our uniforms were blood-red gabardine, heavy and hot. Classes were held in buildings meant to recreate England: damp with stone floors, facing onto a cloister, or quad as they called it. We began each day with the headmistress leading us in English hymns. The entire school stood for an hour in the zinc-roofed gymnasium.

Occasionally a girl fainted, or threw up. Once, a girl had a grand mal seizure. To any such disturbance the response was always "keep singing." While she flailed on the stone floor, I wondered what the mistresses would do. We sang

"Faith of Our Fathers," and watched our classmate as her eyes rolled back in her head. I thought of people swallowing their tongues. This student was dark—here on a scholarship—and the only woman who came forward to help her was the gamesmistress, the only dark teacher. She kneeled beside the girl and slid the white web belt from her tennis shorts, clamping it between the girl's teeth. When the seizure was over, she carried the girl to a tumbling mat in a corner of the gym and covered her so she wouldn't get chilled.

Were the other women unable to touch this girl because of her darkness? I think that now. Her darkness and her scholarship. She lived on Windward Road with her grandmother; her mother was a maid. But darkness is usually enough for women like those to hold back. Then, we usually excused that kind of behavior by saying they were "ladies." (We were constantly being told we should be ladies also. One teacher went so far as to tell us many people thought Jamaicans lived in trees and we had to show these people they were mistaken.) In short, we felt insufficient to judge the behavior of these women. The English ones (who had the corner on power in the school) had come all this way to teach us. Shouldn't we treat them as the missionaries they were certain they were? The creole Jamaicans had a different role: they were passing on to those of us who were light-skinned the creole heritage of collaboration, assimilation, loyalty to our betters. We were expected to be willing subjects in this outpost of civilization.

The girl left school that day and never returned.

After prayers we filed into our classrooms. After classes we had games: tennis, field hockey, rounders (what the English call baseball), netball (what the English call basketball). For games we were divided into "houses"—groups named for Joan of Arc, Edith Cavell, Florence Nightingale, Jane Austen. Four white heroines. Two martyrs. One saint. Two nurses. (None of us knew then that there were Black women with Nightingale at Scutari.) One novelist. Three involved in whitemen's wars. Two dead in whitemen's wars. *Pride and Prejudice*.

Those of us in Cavell wore red badges and recited her last words before a firing squad in W. W. I: "Patriotism is not enough. I must have no hatred or bitterness toward anyone."

Sorry to say I grew up to have exactly that.

Looking back: To try and see when the background changed places with the foreground. To try and locate the vanishing point: where the lines of perspective converge and disappear. Lines of color and class. Lines of history and social context. Lines of denial and rejection. When did *we* (the light-skinned middle-class Jamaicans) take over for *them* as oppressors? I need to see when and how this happened. When what should have been reality was overtaken by what was surely unreality. When the house nigger became master.

"What's the matter with you? You think you're white or something?"

"Child, what you want to know 'bout Garvey[1] for? The man was nothing but a damn fool."

---

[1]Marcus Garvey (1887–1940) was a Jamaican nationalist leader.

"They not our kind of people."

Why did we wear wide-brimmed hats and try to get into Oxford? Why did we not return?

Great Expectations: a novel about origins and denial. about the futility and tragedy of that denial. about attempting assimilation. We learned this novel from a light-skinned Jamaican woman—she concentrated on what she called the "love affair" between Pip and Estella.

Looking back: Through the last page of *Sula*.[2] "And the loss pressed down on her chest and came up into her throat. 'We was girls together,' she said as though explaining something." It was Zoe, and Zoe alone, I thought of. She snapped into my mind and I remembered no one else. Through the greens and blues of the riverbank. The flame of red hibiscus in front of my grandmother's house. The cracked grave of a former landowner. The fruit of the ackee which poisons those who don't know how to prepare it.

"What is to become of us?"

We borrowed a baby from a woman and used her as our dolly. Dressed and undressed her. Dipped her in the riverwater. Fed her with the milk her mother had left with us: and giggled because we knew where the milk had come from.

A letter: "I am desperate. I need to get away. I beg you one fifty-dollar."

I send the money because this is what she asks for. I visit her on a trip back home. Her front teeth are gone. Her husband beats her and she suffers blackouts. I sit on her chair. She is given birth control pills which aggravate her "condition." We boil up sorrel and ginger. She is being taught by Peace Corps volunteers to embroider linen mats with little lambs on them and gives me one as a keepsake. We cool off the sorrel with a block of ice brought from the shop nearby. The shopkeeper immediately recognizes me as my grandmother's granddaughter and refuses to sell me cigarettes. (I am twenty-seven.) We sit in the doorway of her house, pushing back the colored plastic strands which form a curtain, and talk about Babylon and Dred. About Manley and what he's doing for Jamaica. About how hard it is. We walk along the railway tracks—no longer used—to Crooked River and the post office. Her little daughter walks beside us and we recite a poem for her: "Mornin' buddy/Me no buddy fe wunna/Who den, den I saw?" and on and on.

I can come and go. And I leave. To complete my education in London.

II

Their goddam kings and their goddam queens. Grandmotherly Victoria spreading herself thin across the globe. Elizabeth II on our t.v. screens. We stop what we are doing. We quiet down. We pay our respects.

1981: In Massachusetts I get up at 5 a.m. to watch the royal wedding. I tell myself maybe the IRA will intervene. It's got to be better than starving themselves to death. Better to be a kamikaze in St. Paul's Cathedral than a hostage

[2] A novel by Toni Morrison.

in Ulster. And last week Black and white people smashed storefronts all over the United Kingdom. But I really don't believe we'll see royal blood on t.v. I watch because they once ruled us. In the back of the cathedral a Maori woman sings an aria from Handel, and I notice that she is surrounded by the colored subjects.

To those of us in the commonwealth the royal family was the perfect symbol of hegemony. To those of us who were dark in the dark nations, the prime minister, the parliament barely existed. We believed in royalty—we were convinced in this belief. Maybe it played on some ancestral memories of West Africa—where other kings and queens had been. Altars and castles and magic.

The faces of our new rulers were everywhere in my childhood. Calendars, newsreels, magazines. Their presences were often among us. Attending test matches between the West Indians and South Africans. They were our landlords. Not always absentee. And no matter what Black leader we might elect— were we to choose independence—we would be losing something almost holy in our impudence.

WE ARE HERE BECAUSE YOU WERE THERE
BLACK PEOPLE AGAINST STATE BRUTALITY
BLACK WOMEN WILL NOT BE INTIMIDATED
WELCOME TO BRITAIN . . . WELCOME TO SECOND-CLASS
CITIZENSHIP
(slogans of the Black movement in Britain)

Indian women cleaning the toilets in Heathrow airport. This is the first thing I notice. Dark women in saris trudging buckets back and forth as other dark women in saris—some covered by loosefitting winter coats—form a line to have their passports stamped.

The triangle trade: molasses/rum/slaves. Robinson Crusoe was on a slave-trading journey. Robert Browning was a mulatto. Holding pens. Jamaica was a seasoning station. Split tongues. Sliced ears. Whipped bodies. The constant pretense of civility against rape. Still. Iron collars. Tinplate masks. The latter a precaution: to stop the slaves from eating the sugar cane.

A pregnant woman is to be whipped—they dig a hole to accommodate her belly and place her face down on the ground. Many of us became light-skinned very fast. Traced ourselves through bastard lines to reach the duke of Devonshire. The earl of Cornwall. The lord of this and the lord of that. Our mothers' rapes were the thing unspoken.

You say: But Britain freed her slaves in 1833. Yes.

Tea plantations in India and Ceylon. Mines in Africa. The Cape-to-Cairo Railroad. Rhodes scholars. Suez Crisis. The whiteman's bloody burden. Boer War. Bantustans. Sitting in a theatre in London in the seventies. A play called West of Suez. A lousy play about British colonials. The finale comes when several well-known white actors are machine-gunned by several lesser-known Black actors. (As Nina Simone says: "This is a show tune but the show hasn't been written for it yet.")

The red empire of geography classes. "The sun never sets on the British empire and you can't trust it in the dark." Or with the dark peoples. "Because of the Industrial Revolution European countries went in search of markets and raw materials." Another geography (or was it a history) lesson.

Their bloody kings and their bloody queens. Their bloody peers. Their bloody generals. Admirals. Explorers. Livingstone. Hillary. Kitchener. All the bwanas. And all their beaters, porters, sherpas. Who found the source of the Nile. Victoria Falls. The tops of mountains. Their so-called discoveries reek of untruth. How many dark people died so they could misname the physical features in their blasted gazetteer. A statistic we shall never know. Dr. Livingstone, I presume you are here to rape our land and enslave our people.

There are statues of these dead white men all over London.

An interesting fact: The swearword "bloody" is a contraction of "by my lady"—a reference to the Virgin Mary. They do tend to use their ladies. Name ages for them. Places for them. Use them as screens, inspirations, symbols. And many of the ladies comply. While the national martyr Edith Cavell was being executed by the Germans in 1915 in Belgium (called "poor little Belgium" by the allies in the war), the Belgians were engaged in the exploitation of the land and peoples of the Congo.

And will we ever know how many dark peoples were "imported" to fight in whitemen's wars. Probably not. Just as we will never know how many hearts were cut from African people so that the Christian doctor might be a success— i.e., extend a whiteman's life. Our Sister Killjoy observes this from her black-eyed squint.

Dr. Schweitzer—humanitarian, authority on Bach, winner of the Nobel Peace Prize—on the people of Africa: "The Negro is a child, and with children nothing can be done without the use of authority. We must, therefore, so arrange the circumstances of our daily life that my authority can find expression. With regard to Negroes, then, I have coined the formula: 'I am your brother, it is true, but your elder brother.'" (On the Edge of the Primeval Forest, 1961)

They like to pretend we didn't fight back. We did: with obeah, poison, revolution. It simply was not enough.

"Colonies . . . these places where 'niggers' are cheap and the earth is rich." (W.E.B. DuBois, "The Souls of White Folk")

A cousin is visiting me from Cal Tech where he is getting a degree in engineering. I am learning about the Italian Renaissance. My cousin is recognizably Black and speaks with an accent. I am not and I do not—unless I am back home, where the "twang" comes upon me. We sit for some time in a bar in his hotel and are not served. A light-skinned Jamaican comes over to our table. He is an older man—a professor at the University of London. "Don't bother with it, you hear. They don't serve us in this bar." A run-of-the-mill incident for all recognizably Black people in this city. But for me it is not.

Henry's eyes fill up, but he refuses to believe our informant. "No, man, the girl is just busy." (The girl is a fifty-year-old white woman, who may just be following orders. But I do not mention this. I have chosen sides.) All I can manage to say is, "Jesus Christ, I hate the fucking English." Henry looks at me. (In the family I am known as the "lady cousin." It has to do with how I look. And the fact that I am twenty-seven and unmarried—and for all they know, unattached. They do not know that I am really the lesbian cousin.) Our informant says—gently, but with a distinct tone of disappointment—"My dear, is that what you're studying at the university?"

You see—the whole business is very complicated.

Henry and I leave without drinks and go to meet some of his white colleagues at a restaurant I know near Covent Garden Opera House. The restaurant caters to theatre types and so I hope there won't be a repeat of the bar scene—at least they know how to pretend. Besides, I tell myself, the owners are Italian *and* gay; they *must* be halfway decent. Henry and his colleagues work for an American company which is paying their way through Cal Tech. They mine bauxite from the hills in the middle of the island and send it to the United States. A turnaround occurs at dinner: Henry joins the whitemen in a sustained mockery of the waiters: their accents and the way they walk. He whispers to me: "Why you want to bring us to a battyman's den, lady?" (*Battyman* = *faggot* in Jamaican.) I keep quiet.

We put the whitemen in a taxi and Henry walks me to the underground station. He asks me to sleep with him. (It wouldn't be incest. His mother was a maid in the house of an uncle and Henry has not seen her since his birth. He was taken into the family. She was let go.) I say that I can't. I plead exams. I can't say that I don't want to. Because I remember what happened in the bar. But I can't say that I'm a lesbian either—even though I want to believe his alliance with the whitemen at dinner was forced: not really him. He doesn't buy my excuse. "Come on, lady, let's do it. What's the matter, you 'fraid?" I pretend I am back home and start patois to show him somehow I am not afraid, not English, not white. I tell him he's a married man and he tells me he's a ram goat. I take the train to where I am staying and try to forget the whole thing. But I don't. I remember our different skins and our different experiences within them. And I have a hard time realizing that I am angry with Henry. That to him—no use in pretending— a queer is a queer.

1981: I hear on the radio that Bob Marley is dead and I drive over the Mohawk Trail listening to a program of his music and I cry and cry and cry. Someone says: "It wasn't the ganja that killed him, it was poverty and working in a steel foundry when he was young."

I flash back to my childhood and a young man who worked for an aunt I lived with once. He taught me to smoke ganja behind the house. And to peel an orange with the tip of a machete without cutting through the skin—"Love" it was called: a necklace of orange rind the result. I think about him because I heard he had become a Rastaman. And then I think about Rastas.

We are sitting on the porch of an uncle's house in Kingston—the family and I—and a Rastaman comes to the gate. We have guns but they are locked behind a false closet. We have dogs but they are tied up. We are Jamaicans and know that Rastas mean no harm. We let him in and he sits on the side of the porch and shows us his brooms and brushes. We buy some to take back to New York. "Peace, missis."

There were many Rastas in my childhood. Walking the roadside with their goods. Sitting outside their shacks in the mountains. The outsides painted bright—sometimes with words. Gathering at Palisadoes Airport to greet the Conquering Lion of Judah. They were considered figures of fun by most middle-class Jamaicans. Harmless—like Marcus Garvey.

Later: white American hippies trying to create the effect of dred in their straight white hair. The ganja joint held between their straight white teeth. "Man, the grass is good." Hanging out by the Sheraton pool. Light-skinned Jamaicans also dred-locked, also assuming the ganja. Both groups moving to the music but not the words. Harmless. "Peace, brother."

III

My grandmother: "Let us thank God for a fruitful place."
My grandfather: "Let us rescue the perishing world."

This evening on the road in western Massachusetts there are pockets of fog. Then clear spaces. Across from a pond a dog staggers in front of my headlights. I look closer and see that his mouth is foaming. He stumbles to the side of the road—I go to call the police.

I drive back to the house, radio playing "difficult" piano pieces. And I think about how I need to say all this. This is who I am. I am not what you allow me to be. Whatever you decide me to be. In a bookstore in London I show the woman at the counter my book and she stares at me for a minute, then says: "You're a Jamaican." "Yes." "You're not at all like our Jamaicans."

Encountering the void is nothing more nor less than understanding invisibility. Of being fogbound.

Then: It was never a question of passing. It was a question of hiding. Behind Black and white perceptions of who we were—who they thought we were. Tropics. Plantations. Calypso. Cricket. We were the people with the musical voices and the coronation mugs on our parlor tables. I would be whatever figure these foreign imaginations cared for me to be. It would be so simple to let others fill in for me. So easy to startle them with a flash of anger when their visions got out of hand—but never to sustain the anger for myself.

It could become a life lived within myself. A life cut off. I know who I am but you will never know who I am. I may in fact lose touch with who I am.

I hid from my real sources. But my real sources were also hidden from me.

Now: It is not a question of relinquishing privilege. It is a question of grasping more of myself. I have found that in the real sources are concealed my survival. My speech. My voice. To be colonized is to be rendered insensitive. To have those parts necessary to sustain life numbed. And this is in some cases—in my case—perceived as privilege. The test of a colonized person is to walk through a shantytown in Kingston and not bat an eye. This I cannot do. Because part of me lives there—and as I grasp more of this part I realize what needs to be done with the rest of my life.

Sometimes I used to think we were like the Marranos—the Sephardic Jews forced to pretend they were Christians. The name was given to them by the Christians, and meant "pigs." But once out of Spain and Portugal, they became Jews openly again. Some settled in Jamaica. They knew who the enemy was and acted for their own survival. But they remained Jews always.

We also knew who the enemy was—I remember jokes about the English. Saying they stank. saying they were stingy. that they drank too much and couldn't hold their liquor. that they had bad teeth. were dirty and dishonest. were limey bastards. and horse-faced bitches. We said the men only wanted to sleep with Jamaican women. And that the women made pigs of themselves with Jamaican men.

But of course this was seen by us—the light-skinned middle class—with a double vision. We learned to cherish that part of us that was them—and to deny the part that was not. Believing in some cases that the latter part had ceased to exist.

None of this is as simple as it may sound. We were colorists and we aspired to oppressor status. (Of course, almost any aspiration instilled by western civilization is to oppressor status: success, for example.) Color was the symbol of our potential: color taking in hair "quality," skin tone, freckles, nose-width, eyes. We did not see that color symbolism was a method of keeping us apart: in the society, in the family, between friends. Those of us who were light-skinned, straight-haired, etc., were given to believe that we could actually attain whiteness—or at least those qualities of the colonizer which made him superior. We were convinced of white supremacy. If we failed, we were not really responsible for our failures: we had all the advantages—but it was that one persistent drop of blood, that single rogue gene that made us unable to conceptualize abstract ideas, made us love darkness rather than despise it, which was to be blamed for our failure. Our dark part had taken over: an inherited imbalance in which the doom of the creole was sealed.

I am trying to write this as clearly as possible, but as I write I realize that what I say may sound fabulous, or even mythic. It is. It is insane.

Under this system of colorism—the system which prevailed in my childhood in Jamaica, and which has carried over to the present—rarely will dark and light people co-mingle. Rarely will they achieve between themselves an intimacy informed with identity. (I should say here that I am using the categories light and dark both literally and symbolically. There are dark Jamaicans who have achieved lightness and the "advantages" which go with it by their successful pursuit of oppressor status.)

Under this system light and dark people will meet in those ways in which the light-skinned person imitates the oppressor. But imitation goes only so far: the light-skinned person becomes an oppressor in fact. He/she will have a dark chauffeur, a dark nanny, a dark maid, and a dark gardener. These employees will be paid badly. Because of the slave past, because of their dark skin, the servants of the middle class have been used according to the traditions of the slavocracy. They are not seen as workers for their own sake, but for the sake of the family who has employed them. It was not until Michael Manley became prime minister that a minimum wage for houseworkers was enacted—and the indignation of the middle class was profound.

During Manley's leadership the middle class began to abandon the island in droves. Toronto. Miami. New York. Leaving their houses and businesses behind and sewing cash into the tops of suitcases. Today—with a new regime—they are returning: "Come back to the way things used to be" the tourist advertisement on American t.v. says. "Make it Jamaica again. Make it your own."

But let me return to the situation of houseservants as I remember it: They will be paid badly, but they will be "given" room and board. However, the key to the larder will be kept by the mistress in her dresser drawer. They will spend Christmas with the family of their employers and be given a length of English wool for trousers or a few yards of cotton for dresses. They will see their children on their days off: their extended family will care for the children the rest of the time. When the employers visit their relations in the country, the servants may be asked along—oftentimes the servants of the middle class come from the same part of the countryside their employers have come from. But they will be expected to work while they are there. Back in town, there are parts of the house they are allowed to move freely around; other parts they are not allowed to enter. When the family watches the t.v. the servant is allowed to watch also, but only while standing in a doorway. The servant may have a radio in his/her room, also a dresser and a cot. Perhaps a mirror. There will usually be one ceiling light. And one small square louvered window.

A true story: One middle-class Jamaican woman ordered a Persian rug from Harrod's in London. The day it arrived so did her new maid. She was going downtown to have her hair touched up, and she told the maid to vacuum the rug. She told the maid she would find the vacuum cleaner in the same shed as the power mower. And when she returned she found that the fine nap of her new rug had been removed.

The reaction of the mistress was to tell her friends that the "girl" was backward. She did not fire her until she found that the maid had scrubbed the teflon from all her new set of pots, saying she thought they were coated with "nastiness."

The houseworker/mistress relationship in which one Black woman is the oppressor of another Black woman is a cornerstone of the experience of many Jamaican women.

I remember another true story: In a middle-class family's home one Christmas, a relation was visiting from New York. This woman had brought gifts for everybody, including the house-maid. The maid had been released from a mental institution recently, where they had "treated" her for depression. This visiting light-skinned woman had brought the dark woman a bright red rayon blouse and presented it to her in the garden one afternoon, while the family was having tea. The maid thanked her softly, and the other woman moved toward her as if to embrace her. Then she stopped, her face suddenly covered with tears, and ran into the house, saying, "My God, I can't, I can't."

We are women who come from a place almost incredible in its beauty. It is a beauty which can mask a great deal and which has been used in that way. But that the beauty is there is a fact. I remember what I thought the freedom of my childhood, in which the fruitful place was something I took for granted. Just as I took for granted Zoe's appearance every morning on my school vacations—in the sense that I knew she would be there. That she would always be the one to visit me. The perishing world of my grandfather's graces at the table, if I ever seriously thought about it, was something else.

Our souls were affected by the beauty of Jamaica, as much as they were affected by our fears of darkness.

There is no ending to this piece of writing. There is no way to end it. As I read back over it, I see that we/they/I may become confused in the mind of the reader: but these pronouns have always co-existed in my mind. The Rastas talk of the "I and I"—a pronoun in which they combine themselves with Jah. Jah is a contraction of Jahweh and Jehova, but to me always sounds like the beginning of Jamaica. I and Jamaica is who I am. No matter how far I travel—how deep the ambivalence I feel about ever returning. And Jamaica is a place in which we/they/I connect and disconnect—change place. *

SUGGESTIONS FOR WRITING

1. Analyze Cliff's adolescent friendship with the girl from less exalted social circumstances.

2. Why, after the scene in the London bar, does Cliff feel bad about refusing to sleep with her cousin Henry?

3. Describe the nature of the feelings and attitudes Cliff expresses toward the British cultural traditions she has absorbed.

4. What is the significance of the title of this essay?

Selections from
THE THIEF'S JOURNAL

Jean Genet
(Translated by Bernard Frechtman)

*Jean Genet (1910–1986) was a French playwright whose plays are among
the most original and controversial of the modern French theater. They include* The Maids *(1952),* Deathwatch *(1954),* The Balcony *(1957),*
The Blacks *(1960), and* The Screens *(1962). They combine modern
themes of crime, sexual transgression, racial conflict, and class oppression
with ritualistic elements that incorporate aspects of ancient Greek drama.
Genet was also a novelist (*Our Lady of the Flowers*, 1949, and* Funeral
Rites, *1968), and the author of an autobiography,* The Thief's Journal
*(1954), from which this excerpt is taken. Occasionally a journalist, he cov-
ered the ill-fated 1968 Chicago Democratic National Convention for Esquire* magazine.

*An acknowledged thief and a homosexual, Genet was in legal trouble for
most of his early life. At the age of nine, caught in the act of stealing, he was
told by a relative: "You are a thief!" Genet said later that this was a pivotal
moment; it was as if a divine utterance had given him his calling. In many of
his writings,* The Thief's Journal *in particular, Genet represents criminals
as saints, enumerating a pantheon of infamous criminals on whom he be-
stows his adoration. This theme of the outlaw as religious icon is central to
modern French literature, and no one did more than Genet to establish it. Indeed, the French philosopher Jean-Paul Sartre (1905–1980) devoted one of
his best books,* Saint-Genet *(1963), to an appreciation of this reverse morality in Genet's life and work. It was because of Sartre and the testimony of
a number of other prominent French writers that Genet was granted a pardon by President Vincent Auriol in 1949 for theft.*

Convicts' garb is striped pink and white. Though it was at my heart's bidding
that I chose the universe wherein I delight, I at least have the power of finding
therein the many meanings I wish to find: *there is a close relationship between
flowers and convicts.* The fragility and delicacy of the former are of the same nature as the brutal insensitivity of the latter.[1] Should I have to portray a convict—or a criminal—I shall so bedeck him with flowers that, as he disappears
beneath them, he will himself become a flower, a gigantic and new one. Toward what is known as evil, I lovingly pursued an adventure which led me to
prison. Though they may not always be handsome, men doomed to evil possess

---

[1] My excitement is the oscillation from one to the other.

the manly virtues. Of their own volition, or owing to an accident which has been chosen for them, they plunge lucidly and without complaining into a reproachful, ignominious element, like that into which love, if it is profound, hurls human beings. Erotic play discloses a nameless world which is revealed by the nocturnal language of lovers. Such language is not written down. It is whispered into the ear at night in a hoarse voice. At dawn it is forgotten. Repudiating the virtues of your world, criminals hopelessly agree to organize a forbidden universe. They agree to live in it. The air there is nauseating: they can breath it. But—criminals are remote from you—as in love, they turn away and turn me away from the world and its laws. Theirs smells of sweat, sperm, and blood. In short, to my body and my thirsty soul it offers devotion. It was because their world contains these erotic conditions that I was bent on evil. My adventure, never governed by rebellion or a feeling of injustice, will be merely one long mating, burdened and complicated by a heavy, strange, erotic ceremonial (figurative ceremonies leading to jail and anticipating it). Though it be the sanction, in my eyes the justification too, of the foulest crime, it will be the sign of the most utter degradation. That ultimate point to which the censure of men leads was to appear to me the ideal place for the purest, that is, the most turbid amatory harmony, where illustrious ash-weddings are celebrated. Desiring to hymn them, I use what is offered me by the form of the most exquisite natural sensibility, which is already aroused by the garb of convicts. The material evokes, both by its colors and roughness, certain flowers whose petals are slightly fuzzy, which detail is sufficient for me to associate the idea of strength and shame with what is most naturally precious and fragile. This association, which tells me things about myself, would not suggest itself to another mind; mine cannot avoid it. Thus I offered my tenderness to the convicts; I wanted to call them by charming names, to designate their crimes with, for modesty's sake, the subtlest metaphor (beneath which veil I would not have been unaware of the murderer's rich muscularity, of the violence of his sexual organ). Is it not by the following image that I prefer to imagine them in Guiana: the strongest, with a horn, the "hardest," veiled by mosquito netting? And each flower within me leaves behind so solemn a sadness that all of them must signify sorrow, death. Thus I sought love as it pertained to the penal colony. Each of my passions led me to hope for it, gave me a glimpse of it, offers me criminals, offers me to them or impels me to crime. As I write this book, the last convicts are returning to France. The newspapers have been reporting the matter. The heir of kings feels a like emptiness if the republic deprives him of his anointment. The end of the penal colony prevents us from attaining with our living minds the mythical underground regions. Our most dramatic movement has been clipped away: our exodus, the embarkation, the procession on the sea, which was performed with bowed head. The return, this same procession in reverse, is without meaning. Within me, the destruction of the colony corresponds to a kind of punishment of punishment: I am castrated, I am shorn of my infamy. Unconcerned about beheading our dreams of their glories, they awaken us prematurely. The home prisons have their power: it is not the same. It is minor. It has none of that elegant, slightly bowed grace. The atmosphere there is so heavy that you have to drag yourself about. You creep along. The home prisons are more stiffly erect, more darkly and severely; the slow, solemn agony of the penal colony was a more perfect blossoming of abjection.[1] So that now the home jails, bloated with evil males, are black with them, as with blood that has been shot through with carbonic gas. (I have written "black." The outfit of the convicts—captives, captivity, even prisoners, words too noble to name us—forces the word upon me: the outfit is made of brown homespun.) It is toward them that my desire will turn. I am aware that there is often a semblance of the burlesque in the colony or in prison. On the bulky, resonant base of their wooden shoes, the frame of the condemned men is always somewhat shaky. In front of a wheelbarrow, it suddenly breaks up stupidly. In the presence of a guard they bow their heads and hold in their hands the big straw sun bonnet—which the younger ones decorate (I should prefer it so) with a stolen rose granted by the guard—or a brown homespun beret. They strike poses of wretched humility. If they are beaten, something within them must nevertheless stiffen: the coward, the sneak, cowardice, sneakiness are—when kept in a state of the hardest, purest cowardice and sneakiness—hardened by a "dousing," as soft iron is hardened by dousing. They persist in servility, despite everything. Though I do not neglect the deformed and misshapen, it is the handsomest criminals whom my tenderness adorns.

Crime, I said to myself, had a long wait before producing such perfect successes as Pilorge and Angel Sun. In order to finish them off (the term is a cruel one!) it was necessary for a host of coincidences to concur: to the beauty of their faces, to the strength and elegance of their bodies there had to be added their taste for crime, the circumstances which make the criminal, the moral vigor capable of accepting such a destiny, and, finally, punishment, its cruelty, the intrinsic quality which enables a criminal to glory in it, and, over all of this, areas of darkness. If the hero join combat with night and conquer it, may shreds of it remain upon him! The same hesitation, the same crystallization of happy circumstances governs the success of a pure sleuth. I cherish them both. But if I love their crime, it is for the punishment it involves, "the penalty" (for I cannot suppose that they have not anticipated it. One of them, the former boxer Ledoux, answered the inspectors smilingly: "My crimes? It's before committing them that I might have regretted them") in which I want to accompany them so that, come what may, my love may be filled to overflowing.

I do not want to conceal in this journal the other reasons which made me a thief, the simplest being the need to eat, though revolt, bitterness, anger or any similar sentiment never entered into my choice. With fanatical care, "jealous care," I prepared for my adventure as one arranges a couch or a room for love; I was *hot* for crime.

---

[1]Its abolition is so great a loss to me that I secretly recompose, within me and for myself alone, a colony more vicious than that of Guiana. I add that the home prisons can be said to be "in the shade." The colony is in the sun. Everything transpires there in a cruel light which I cannot refrain from choosing as a sign of lucidity.

I give the name violence to a boldness lying idle and enamoured of danger. It can be seen in a look, a walk, a smile, and it is in you that it creates an eddying. It unnerves you. This violence is a calm that disturbs you. One sometimes says: "A guy with class!" Pilorge's delicate features were of an extreme violence. Their delicacy in particular was violent. Violence of the design of Stilitano's only hand, simply lying on the table, still, rendering the repose disturbing and dangerous. I have worked with thieves and pimps whose authority bent me to their will, but few proved to be really bold, whereas the one who was most so—Guy—was without violence. Stilitano, Pilorge and Michaelis were cowards. Java too. Even when at rest, motionless and smiling, there escaped from them through the eyes, the nostrils, the mouth, the palm of the hand, the bulging basket, through that brutal hillock of the calf under the wool or denim, a radiant and somber anger, visible as a haze.

But, almost always, there is nothing to indicate it, save the absence of the usual signs. René's face is charming at first. The downward curve of his nose gives him a roguish look, though the somewhat leaden paleness of his anxious face makes you uneasy. His eyes are hard, his movements calm and sure. In the cans he calmly beats up the queers; he frisks them, robs them, sometimes, as a finishing touch, he kicks them in the kisser with his heel. I don't like him, but his calmness masters me. He operates, in the dead of night, around the urinals, the lawns, the shrubbery, under the trees on the Champs-Elysées, near the stations, at the Porte Maillot, in the Bois de Boulogne (always at night) with a seriousness from which romanticism is excluded. When he comes in, at two or three in the morning, I feel him stocked with adventures. Every part of his body, which is nocturnal, has been involved: his hands, his arms, his legs, the back of his neck. But he, unaware of these marvels, tells me about them in forthright language. From his pockets he takes rings, wedding bands, watches, the evening's loot. He puts them in a big glass which will soon be full. He is not surprised by queers or their ways, which merely facilitate his jobs. When he sits on my bed, my ear snatches at scraps of adventure: An officer in underwear whose wallet[1] he steals and who, pointing with his forefinger, orders "Get out!" René-the-wise-guy's answer: "You think you're in the army?" Too hard a punch on an old man's skull. The one who fainted when René, who was all excited, opened a drawer in which there was a supply of phials of morphine. The queer who was broke and whom he made get down on his knees before him. I am attentive to these accounts. My Antwerp life grows stronger, carrying on in a firmer body, in accordance with manly methods. I encourage René, I give him advice, he listens to me. I tell him never to talk first. "Let the guy come up to you, keep him dangling. Act a little surprised when he suggests that you do it. Figure out who to act dumb with."

Every night I get a few scraps of information. My imagination does not get lost in them. My excitement seems to be due to my assuming within me the role of both victim and criminal. Indeed, as a matter of fact, I emit, I project at night the victim and criminal born of me; I bring them together somewhere,

[1]He says: "I did his wallet."

and toward morning I am thrilled to learn that the victim came very close to getting the death penalty and the criminal to being sent to the colony or guillotined. Thus my excitement extends as far as that region of myself, which is Guiana.

Without their wishing it, the gestures and destinies of these men are stormy. Their soul endures a violence which it had not desired and which it has domesticated. Those whose usual climate is violence are simple in relation to themselves. Each of the movements which make up this swift and devastating life is simple and straight, as clean as the stroke of a great draftsman—but when these strokes are encountered in movement, then the storm breaks, the lightning that kills them or me. Yet, what is their violence compared to mine, which was to accept theirs, to make it mine, to wish it for myself, to intercept it, to utilize it, to force it upon myself, to know it, to premeditate it, to discern and assume its perils? But what was mine, willed and necessary for my defense, my toughness, my rigor, compared to the violence they underwent like a malediction, risen from an inner fire simultaneously with an outer light which sets them ablaze and illuminates us? We know that their adventures are childish. They themselves are fools. They are ready to kill or be killed over a card game in which an opponent—or they themselves—was cheating. Yet, thanks to such guys, tragedies are possible.

This kind of definition—by so many opposing examples—of violence shows you that I shall not make use of words the better to depict an event or its hero, but so that they may tell you something about myself. In order to understand me, the reader's complicity will be necessary. Nevertheless, I shall warn him whenever my lyricism makes me lose my footing.

Stilitano was big and strong. His gait was both supple and heavy, brisk and slow, sinuous; he was nimble. A large part of his power over me—and over the whores of the Barrio Chino—lay in the spittle he passed from one cheek to the other and which he would sometimes draw out in front of his mouth like a veil. "But where does he get that spit," I would ask myself, "where does he bring it up from? Mine will never have the unctuousness or color of his. It will merely be spun glassware, transparent and fragile." It was therefore natural for me to imagine what his penis would be if he smeared it for my benefit with so fine a substance, with that precious cobweb, a tissue which I secretly called the veil of the palace. He wore an old gray cap with a broken visor. When he tossed it on the floor of our room, it suddenly became the carcass of a poor partridge with a clipped wing, but when he put it on, pulling it down a bit over the ear, the opposite edge of the visor rose up to reveal the most glorious of blond locks. Shall I speak of his lovely bright eyes, modestly lowered—yet it could be said of Stilitano: "His bearing is immodest"—over which there closed eyelids and lashes so blonde, so luminous and thick, that they brought in not the shade of evening but the shade of evil. After all, what meaning would there be in the sight that staggers me when, in a harbor, I see a sail, little by little, by fits and starts, spreading out and with difficulty rising on the mast of a ship, hesitantly at first, then resolutely, if these movements were not the very symbol of the movements of my love for Stilitano? I met him in Barcelona. He was living among beggars, thieves, fairies and whores. He was handsome, but it remains to be seen whether he owed all that beauty to my fallen state. My clothes were dirty and shabby. I was hungry and cold. This was the most miserable period of my life.

1932. Spain at the time was covered with vermin, its beggars. They went from village to village, to Andalusia because it is warm, to Catalonia because it is rich, but the whole country was favorable to us. I was thus a louse, and conscious of being one. In Barcelona we hung around the Calle Mediodia and the Calle Carmen. We sometimes slept six in a bed without sheets, and at dawn we would go begging in the markets. We would leave the Barrio Chino in a group and scatter over the Parallelo, carrying shopping baskets, for the housewives would give us a leek or turnip rather than a coin. At noon we would return, and with the gleanings we would make our soup. It is the life of vermin that I am going to describe. In Barcelona I saw male couples in which the more loving of the two would say to the other:

"I'll take the basket this morning."

He would take it and leave. One day Salvador gently pulled the basket from my hands and said, "I'm going to beg for you."

It was snowing. He went out into the freezing street, wearing a torn and tattered jacket—the pockets were ripped and hung down—and a shirt stiff with dirt. His face was poor and unhappy, shifty, pale, and filthy, for we dared not wash since it was so cold. Around noon, he returned with the vegetables and a bit of fat. Here I draw attention to one of those lacerations—horrible, for I shall provoke them despite the danger—by which beauty was revealed to me. An immense—and brotherly—love swelled my body and bore me toward Salvador. Leaving the hotel shortly after him, I would see him a way off beseeching the women. I knew the formula, as I had already begged for others and myself: it mixes Christian religion with charity; it merges the poor person with God; it is so humble an emanation from the heart that I think it scents with violet the straight, light breath of the beggar who utters it. All over Spain at the time they were saying:

"Por Dios."

Without hearing him, I would imagine Salvador murmuring it at all the stalls, to all the housewives. I would keep an eye on him as the pimp keeps an eye on his whore, but with such tenderness in my heart! Thus, Spain and my life as a beggar familiarized me with the stateliness of abjection, for it took a great deal of pride (that is, of love) to embellish those filthy, despised creatures. It took a great deal of talent, which came to me little by little. Though I may be unable to describe its mechanism to you, at least I can say that I slowly forced myself to consider that wretched life as a deliberate necessity. Never did I try to make of it something other than what it was, I did not try to adorn it, to mask it, but, on the contrary, I wanted to affirm it in its exact sordidness, and the most sordid signs became for me signs of grandeur.

I was dismayed when, one evening, while searching me after a raid—I am speaking of a scene which preceded the one with which this book begins—the astonished detective took from my pocket, among other things, a tube of vaseline. We dared joke about it since it contained mentholated vaseline. The whole record office, and I too, though painfully, writhed with laughter at the following:

"You take it in the nose?"

"Watch out you don't catch cold. You'd give your guy whooping cough."

I translate but lamely, in the language of a Paris hustler, the malicious irony of the vivid and venomous Spanish phrases. It concerned a tube of vaseline, one of whose ends was partially rolled up. Which amounts to saying that it had been put to use. Amidst the elegant objects taken from the pockets of the men who had been picked up in the raid, it was the very sign of abjection, of that which is concealed with the greatest of care, but yet the sign of a secret grace which was soon to save me from contempt. When I was locked up in a cell, and as soon as I had sufficiently regained my spirits to rise above the misfortune of my arrest, the image of the tube of vaseline never left me. The policemen had shown it to me victoriously, since they could thereby flourish their revenge, their hatred, their contempt. But lo and behold! that dirty, wretched object whose purpose seemed to the world—to that concentrated delegation of the world which is the police and, above all, that particular gathering of Spanish police, smelling of garlic, sweat and oil, but substantial looking, stout of muscle and strong in their moral assurance—utterly vile, became extremely precious to me. Unlike many objects which my tenderness singles out, this one was not at all haloed; it remained on the table a little gray leaden tube of vaseline, bro-ken and livid, whose astonishing discreteness, and its essential correspondence with all the commonplace things in the record office of a prison (the bench, the inkwell, the regulations, the scales, the odor), would, through the general indifference, have distressed me, had not the very content of the tube made me think, by bringing to mind an oil lamp (perhaps because of its unctuous char-acter), of a night light beside a coffin.

In describing it, I recreate the little object, but the following image cuts in: beneath a lamppost, in a street of the city where I am writing, the pallid face of a little old woman, a round, flat little face, like the moon, very pale; I cannot tell whether it was sad or hypocritical. She approached me, told me she was very poor and asked for a little money. The gentleness of that moon-fish face told me at once: the old woman had just got out of prison.

"She's a thief," I said to myself. As I walked away from her, a kind of intense reverie, living deep within me and not at the edge of my mind, led me to think that it was perhaps my mother whom I had just met. I know nothing of her who abandoned me in the cradle, but I hoped it was that old thief who begged at night.

"What if it were she?" I thought as I walked away from the old woman. Oh! if it were, I would cover her with flowers, with gladioluses and roses, and with kisses! I would weep with tenderness over those moon-fish eyes, over that round, foolish face! "And why," I went on, "why weep over it?" It did not take my mind long to replace these customary marks of tenderness by some other gesture, even the vilest and most contemptible, which I empowered to mean as much as the kisses, or the tears, or the flowers.

"I'd be glad to slobber over her," I thought, overflowing with love. (Does the word glaïeul [gladiolus] mentioned above bring into play the word glaviaux [gobs of spit]?) To slobber over her hair or vomit into her hands. But I would adore that thief who is my mother.

The tube of vaseline, which was intended to grease my prick and those of my lovers, summoned up the face of her who, during a reverie that moved through the dark alleys of the city, was the most cherished of mothers. It had served me in the preparation of so many secret joys, in places worthy of its discrete banality, that it had become the condition of my happiness, as my sperm-spotted handkerchief testified. Lying on the table, it was a banner telling the invisible legions of my triumph over the police. I was in a cell. I knew that all night long my tube of vaseline would be exposed to the scorn—the contrary of a Perpetual Adoration—of a group of strong, handsome, husky policemen. So strong that if the weakest of them barely squeezed his fingers together, there would shoot forth, first with a slight fart, brief and dirty, a ribbon of gum which would continue to emerge in a ridiculous silence. Nevertheless, I was sure that this puny and most humble object would hold its own against them; by its mere presence it would be able to exasperate all the police in the world; it would draw down upon itself contempt, hatred, white and dumb rages. It would perhaps be slightly bantering—like a tragic hero amused at stirring up the wrath of the gods—indestructible, like him, faithful to my happiness, and proud. I would like to hymn it with the newest words in the French language. But I would have also liked to fight for it, to organize massacres in its honor and bedeck a countryside at twilight with red bunting.[1]

The beauty of a moral act depends on the beauty of its expression. To say that it is beautiful is to decide that it will be so. It remains to be proven so. This is the task of images, that is, of the correspondences with the splendors of the physical world. The act is beautiful if it provokes, and in our throat reveals, song. Sometimes the consciousness with which we have pondered a reputedly vile act, the power of expression which must signify it, impel us to song. This means that treachery is beautiful if it makes us sing. To betray thieves would be not only to find myself again in the moral world, I thought, but also to find myself once more in homosexuality. As I grow strong, I am my own god. I dictate. Applied to men, the word beauty indicates to me the harmonious quality of a face and body to which is sometimes added manly grace. Beauty is then accompanied by magnificent, masterly, sovereign gestures. We imagine that they are determined by very special moral attitudes, and by the cultivation of such virtues in ourselves we hope to endow our poor faces and sick bodies with the vigor that our lovers possess naturally. Alas, these virtues, which they themselves never possess, are our weakness.

Now as I write, I muse on my lovers. I would like them to be smeared with my vaseline, with that soft, slightly mentholated substance; I would like their muscles to bathe in that delicate transparence without which the tool of the handsomest is less lovely.

When a limb has been removed, the remaining one is said to grow stronger. I had hoped that the vigor of the arm which Stilitano had lost might be con-

---

[1] I would indeed rather have shed blood than repudiate that silly object.

centrated in his penis. For a long time I imagined a solid member, like a black-jack, capable of the most outrageous impudence, though what first intrigued me was what Stilitano allowed me to know of it: the mere crease, though curiously precise in the left leg, of his blue denim trousers. This detail might have haunted my dreams less had Stilitano not, at odd moments, put his left hand on it, and had he not, like ladies making a curtsey, indicated the crease by delicately pinching the cloth with his nails. I do not think he ever lost his self-possession, but with me he was particularly calm. With a slightly impertinent smile, though quite nonchalantly, he would watch me adore him. I know that he will love me.

Before Salvador, basket in hand, crossed the threshold of our hotel, I was so excited that I kissed him in the street, but he pushed me aside:

"You're crazy! People'll take us for mariconas!"

He spoke French fairly well, having learned it in the region around Perpignan where he used to go for the grape harvesting. Deeply wounded, I turned away. His face was purple. His complexion was that of winter cabbage. Salvador did not smile. He was shocked. "That's what I get," he must have thought, "for getting up so early to go begging in the snow. He doesn't know how to behave." His hair was wet and shaggy. Behind the window, faces were staring at us, for the lower part of the hotel was occupied by a café that opened on the street and through which you had to pass in order to get up to the rooms. Salvador wiped his face with his sleeve and went in. I hesitated. Then I followed. I was twenty years old. If the drop that hesitates at the edge of a nostril has the limpidity of a tear, why shouldn't I drink it with the same eagerness? I was already sufficiently involved in the rehabilitation of the ignoble. Were it not for fear of revolting Salvador, I would have done it in the café. He, however, sniffled, and I gathered that he was swallowing his snot. Basket in arm, passing the beggars and the guttersnipes, he moved toward the kitchen. He preceded me.

"What's the matter with you?" I said.

"You're attracting attention."

"What's wrong?"

"People don't kiss that way on the sidewalk. Tonight, if you like . . ."

He said it all with a charmless pout and the same disdain. I had simply wanted to show my gratitude, to warm him with my poor tenderness.

"But what were you thinking?"

Someone bumped into him without apologizing, separating him from me. I did not follow him to the kitchen. I went over to a bench where there was a vacant seat near the stove. Though I adored vigorous beauty, I didn't bother my head much about how I would bring myself to love this homely, squalid beggar who was bullied by the less bold, how I would come to care for his angular buttocks . . . and what if, unfortunately, he were to have a magnificent tool?

The Barrio Chino was, at the time, a kind of haunt thronged less with Spaniards than with foreigners, all of them down-and-out bums. We were sometimes dressed in almond-green or jonquil-yellow silk shirts and shabby sneakers, and our hair was so plastered down that it looked as if it would crack.

We did not have leaders but rather directors. I am unable to explain how they became what they were. Probably it was as a result of profitable operations in the sale of our meager booty. They attended to our affairs and let us know about jobs, for which they took a reasonable commission. We did not form loosely organized bands, but amidst that vast, filthy disorder, in a neighborhood stinking of oil, piss and shit, a few waifs and strays relied on others more clever than themselves. The squalor sparkled with the youth of many of our number and with the more mysterious brilliance of a few who really scintillated, youngsters whose bodies, gazes and gestures were charged with a magnetism which made of us their object. That is how I was staggered by one of them. In order to do justice to the one-armed Stilitano I shall wait a few pages. Let it be known from the start that he was devoid of any Christian virtue. All his brilliance, all his power, had their source between his legs. His penis, and that which completes it, the whole apparatus, was so beautiful that the only thing I can call it is a generative organ. One might have thought he was dead, for he rarely, and slowly got excited: he watched. He generated in the darkness of a well-buttoned fly, though buttoned by only one hand, the luminosity with which its bearer will be aglow.

My relations with Salvador lasted for six months. It was not the most intoxicating but rather the most fecund of loves. I had managed to love that sickly body, gray face, and ridiculously sparse beard. Salvador took care of me, but at night, by candlelight, I hunted for lice, our pets, in the seams of his trousers. The lice inhabited us. They imparted to our clothes an animation, a presence, which, when they had gone, left our garments lifeless. We liked to know—and feel—that the translucent bugs were swarming; though not tamed, they were so much a part of us that a third person's louse disgusted us. We chased them away but with the hope that during the day the nits would have hatched. We crushed them with our nails, without disgust and without hatred. We did not throw their corpses—or remains—into the garbage, we let them fall, bleeding with our blood, into our untidy underclothes. The lice were the only sign of our prosperity, of the very underside of prosperity, but it was logical that by making our state perform an operation which justified it, we were, by the same token, justifying the sign of this state. Having become as useful for the knowledge of our decline as jewels for the knowledge of what is called triumph, the lice were precious. They were both our shame and our glory. I lived for a long time in a room without windows, except a transom on the corridor, where, in the evening, five little faces, cruel and tender, smiling or screwed up with the cramp of a difficult position, dripping with sweat, would hunt for those insects of whose virtue we partook. It was good that, in the depths of such wretchedness, I was the lover of the poorest and homeliest. I thereby had a rare privilege. I had difficulty, but every victory I achieved—my filthy hands, proudly exposed, helped me proudly expose my beard and long hair—gave me strength—or weakness, and here it amounts to the same thing—for the following victory, which in your language would naturally be called a come-down. Yet, light and brilliance being necessary to our lives, a sunbeam did cross the pane and its filth and penetrate the dimness; we had the hoarfrost, the silver thaw, for these elements, though they may spell calamity, evoke joys whose sign, detached in our room, was adequate for us: all we knew of Christmas and New Year's festivities was what always accompanies them and what makes them dearer to merrymakers: frost.

The cultivation of sores by beggars is also their means of getting a little money—on which to live—but though they may be led to this out of a certain inertia in their state of poverty, the pride required for holding one's head up, above contempt, is a manly virtue. Like a rock in a river, pride breaks through and divides contempt, bursts it. Entering further into abjection, pride will be stronger (if the beggar is myself) when I have the knowledge—strength or weakness—to take advantage of such a fate. It is essential, as this leprosy gains on me, that I gain on it and that, in the end, I win out. Shall I therefore become increasingly vile, more and more an object of disgust, up to that final point which is something still unknown but which must be governed by an aesthetic as well as moral inquiry? It is sad that leprosy, to which I compare our state, causes an irritation of the tissues; the sick person scratches himself; he gets an erection. Masturbation becomes frequent. In his solitary eroticism the leper consoles himself and hymns his disease. Poverty made us erect. All across Spain we carried a secret, veiled magnificence unmixed with arrogance. Our gestures grew humbler and humbler, fainter and fainter, as the embers of humility which kept us alive glowed more intensely. Thus developed my talent for giving a sublime meaning to so beggarly an appearance. (I am not yet speaking of literary talent.) It proved to have been a very useful discipline for me and still enables me to smile tenderly at the humblest among the dregs, whether human or material, including vomit, including the saliva I let drool on my mother's face, including your excrement. I shall preserve within me the idea of myself as a beggar.

I wanted to be like that woman who, at home, hidden away from people, sheltered her daughter, a kind of hideous, misshapen monster, stupid and white, who grunted and walked on all fours. When the mother gave birth, her despair was probably such that it became the very essence of her life. She decided to love this monster, to love the ugliness that had come out of her belly in which it had been elaborated, and to erect it devotedly. Within herself she ordained an altar where she preserved the idea of Monster. With devoted care, with hands gentle despite the calluses of her daily toil, with the willful zeal of the hopeless, she set herself up against the world, and against the world she set up the monster, which took on the proportions of the world and its power. It was on the basis of the monster that new principles were ordained, principles constantly combated by the forces of the world which came charging into her but which stopped at the walls of her dwelling where her daughter was confined.[1]

But, for it was sometimes necessary to steal, we also knew the clear, earthly beauties of boldness. Before we went to sleep, the chief, the liege lord, would

---

[1] I learned from the newspapers that, after forty years of devotion, this mother sprayed her sleeping daughter, and then the whole house, with gasoline—or petroleum—and set fire to the house. The monster (the daughter) died. The old woman (age seventy-five) was rescued from the flames and was saved, that is, she was brought to trial.

give us advice. For example, we would go with fake papers to various consulates in order to be repatriated. The consul, moved or annoyed by our woes and wretchedness, and our filth, would give us a train ticket to a border post. Our chief would resell it at the Barcelona station. He also let us know of thefts to commit in churches—which Spaniards would not dare do—or in elegant villas; and it was he himself who brought us the Dutch and English sailors to whom we had to prostitute ourselves for a few pesetas.[1]

Thus we sometimes stole, and each burglary allowed us to breath for a moment at the surface. A vigil of arms precedes each nocturnal expedition. The nervousness provoked by fear, and sometimes by anxiety, makes for a state akin to religious moods. At such times I tend to see omens in the slightest accidents. Things become signs of chance. I want to charm the unknown powers upon which the success of the adventure seems to me to depend. I try to charm them by moral acts, chiefly by charity. I give more readily and more freely to beggars, I give my seat to old people, I stand aside to let them pass, I help blind men cross the street, and so on. In this way, I seem to recognize that over the act of stealing rules a god to whom moral actions are agreeable. These attempts to throw out a net, on the chance that this god of whom I know nothing will be caught in it, exhaust me, disturb me and also favor the religious state. To the act of stealing they communicate the gravity of a ritual act. It will really be performed in the heart of darkness, to which is added that it may be rather at night, while people are asleep, in a place that is closed and perhaps itself masked in black. The walking on tiptoe, the silence, the invisibility which we need even in broad daylight, the groping hands organizing in the darkness gestures of an unwonted complexity and wariness. Merely to turn a doorknob requires a host of movements, each as brilliant as the facet of a jewel. When I discover gold, it seems to me that I have unearthed it; I have ransacked continents, south-sea islands; I am surrounded by negroes; they threaten my defenseless body with their poisoned spears, but then the virtue of the gold acts, and a great vigor crushes or exalts me, the spears are lowered, the negroes recognize me and I am one of the tribe. The perfect act: inadvertently putting my hand into the pocket of a handsome sleeping negro, feeling his prick stiffen beneath my fingers and withdrawing my hand closed over a gold coin discovered in and stolen from his pocket—the prudence, the whispering voice, the alert ear, the invisible, nervous presence of the accomplice and the understanding of his slightest sign, all concentrate our being within us, compress us, make of us a very ball of presence, which so well explains Guy's remark:

"You feel yourself living."

But within myself, this total presence, which is transformed into a bomb of what seems to me terrific power imparts to the act a gravity, a terminal oneness—the burglary, while being performed, is always the last, not that you think you are not going to perform another after that one—you don't think—but because such a gathering of self cannot take place (not in life, for to push it further would be to pass out of life); and this oneness of an act which devel-

[1]Spanish unit of currency.

ops (as the rose puts forth its corolla) into conscious gestures, such of their efficacy, of their fragility and yet of the violence which they give to the act, here too confers upon it the value of a religious rite. Often I even dedicate it to someone. The first time, it was Stilitano who had the benefit of such homage. I think it was by him that I was initiated, that is, my obsession with his body kept me from flinching. To his beauty, to his tranquil immodesty, I dedicated my first thefts. To the singularity too of that splendid cripple whose hand, cut off at the wrist, was rotting away somewhere, under a chestnut tree, so he told me, in a forest of Central Europe. During the theft, my body is exposed. I know that it is sparkling with all my gestures. The world is attentive to all my movements, if it wants me to trip up. I shall pay dearly for a mistake, but if there is a mistake and I catch it in time, it seems to me that there will be joy in our Father's dwelling. Or, I fall, and there is woe upon woe and then prison. But as for the savages, the convict who risked "the Getaway" will then meet them by means of the procedure briefly described above in my inner adventure. If, going through the virgin forest, he comes upon a placer guarded by ancient tribes, he will either be killed by them or be saved. It is by a long, long road that I choose to go back to primitive life. What I need first is condemnation by my race.

Salvador was not a source of pride to me. When he did steal, he merely filched trifles from stands in front of shop windows. At night, in the cafés where we huddled together, he would sadly worm himself in among the most handsome. That kind of life exhausted him. When I entered, I would be ashamed to find him hunched over, squatting on a bench, his shoulders huddled up in the green and yellow cotton blanket with which he would go out begging on wintry days. He would also be wearing an old, black woolen shawl which I refused to put on. Indeed, though my mind endured, even desired, humility, my violent young body rejected it. Salvador would speak in a sad, reticent voice:

"Would you like us to go back to France? We'll work in the country."

I said no. He did not understand my loathing—no, my hatred—of France, nor that my adventure, if it stopped in Barcelona, was bound to continue deeply, more and more deeply, in the remotest regions of myself.

"But I'll do all the work. You'll take it easy."

"No."

I would leave him on his bench to his cheerless poverty. I would go over to the stove or the bar and smoke the butts I had gleaned during the day, with a scornful young Andalusian whose dirty white woolen sweater exaggerated his torso and muscles. After rubbing his hands together, the way old men do, Salvador would leave his bench and go to the community kitchen to prepare a soup and put a fish on the grill. Once he suggested that we go down to Huelva for the orange picking. It was an evening when he had received so many humiliations, so many rebuffs while begging for me that he dared reproach me for my poor success at the Criolla.

"Really, when you pick up a client, it's *you* who ought to pay *him*."

We quarreled in front of the proprietor of the hotel, who wanted to put us out. Salvador and I therefore decided to steal two blankets the following day and hide in a south-bound freight train. But I was so clever that that very evening I brought back the cape of a customs officer. As I passed the docks where they mount guard, one of the officers called me. I did what he required, in the sentry box. After coming (perhaps, without daring to tell me so, he wanted to wash at a little fountain), he left me alone for a moment and I ran off with his big black woolen cape. I wrapped myself up in it in order to return to the hotel, and I knew the happiness of the equivocal, not yet the joy of betrayal, though the insidious confusion which would make me deny fundamental oppositions was already forming. As I opened the door of the café, I saw Salvador. He was the saddest-looking of beggars. His face had the quality, and almost the texture, of the sawdust that covered the floor of the café. Immediately I recognized Stilitano standing in the midst of the ronda players. Our eyes met. His gaze lingered on me, who blushed. I took off the black cape, and at once they started haggling over it. Without yet taking part, Stilitano watched the wretched bargaining.

"Make it snappy, if you want it," I said. "Make up your minds. The customs man is sure to come looking for me."

The players got a little more active. They were used to such reasons. When the general shuffle brought me to his side, Stilitano said to me in French:

"You from Paris?"

"Yes. Why?"

"For no reason."

Although it was he who had made the first advance, I knew, as I answered, the almost desperate nature of the gesture the invert dares when he approaches a young man. To mask my confusion, I had the pretext of being breathless, I had the bustle of the moment. He said, "You did pretty well for yourself."

I knew that this praise was cleverly calculated, but how handsome Stilitano was amidst the beggars (I didn't know his name yet)! One of his arms, at the extremity of which was an enormous bandage, was folded on his chest as if in a sling, but I knew that the hand was missing. Stilitano was an habitué of neither the café nor even the street.

"What'll the cape cost me?"

"Will you pay me for it?"

"Why not?"

"With what?"

"Are you scared?"

"Where are you from?"

"Serbia. I'm back from the Foreign Legion. I'm a deserter."

I was relieved. Destroyed. The emotion created within me a void which was at once filled by the memory of a nuptial scene. In a dance hall where soldiers were dancing among themselves, I watched their waltz. It seemed to me at the time that the invisibility of two legionnaires became total. They were charmed away by emotion. Though their dance was chaste at the beginning of "Ramona," would it remain so when, in our presence, they wedded by exchanging a smile, as lovers exchange rings? To all the injunctions of an invisible clergy the Legion answered, "I do." Each one of them was the couple wearing both a net veil and a dress uniform (white leather, scarlet and green shoulder braid). They haltingly exchanged their manly tenderness and wifely modesty. To maintain the emotion at a high pitch, they slowed up and slackened their dance, while their pricks, numbed by the fatigue of a long march, recklessly threatened and challenged each other behind a barricade of rough denim. The patent-leather vizors of their képis kept striking together. I knew I was being mastered by Stilitano. I wanted to play sly:

"That doesn't prove you can pay."

"Trust me."

Such a hard-looking face, such a strapping body, were asking me to trust them. Salvador was watching us. He was aware of our understanding and realized that we had already decided upon his ruin, his loneliness. Fierce and pure, I was the theater of a fairyland restored to life. When the waltz ended, the two soldiers disengaged themselves. And each of those two halves of a solemn and dizzy block hesitated, and, happy to be escaping from invisibility, went off, downcast, toward some girl for the next waltz.

"I'll give you two days to pay me," I said. "I need dough. I was in the Legion too. And I deserted. Like you."

"You'll get it."

I handed him the cape. He took it with his only hand and gave it back to me. He smiled, though imperiously, and said, "Roll it up." And joshingly added, "While waiting to roll me one."

Everyone knows the expression: "to roll a skate."[1] Without batting an eyelash, I did as he said. The cape immediately disappeared into one of the hotel proprietor's hiding places. Perhaps this simple theft brightened my face, or Stilitano simply wanted to act nice; he added: "You going to treat an ex-Bel-Abbès boy to a drink?"

A glass of wine cost two sous. I had four in my pocket, but I owed them to Salvador, who was watching us.

"I'm broke," Stilitano said proudly.

The card players were forming new groups which for a moment separated us from Salvador. I muttered between my teeth, "I've got four sous and I'm going to slip them to you, but you're the one who'll pay."

Stilitano smiled. I was lost. We sat down at a table. He had already begun to talk about the Legion when, staring hard at me, he suddenly broke off.

"I've got a feeling I've seen you somewhere before."

As for me, I had retained the memory.

I had to grab hold of invisible tackle. I could have cooed. Words, or the tone of my voice, would have not merely expressed my ardor, I would not have merely sung, my throat would have uttered the call of indeed the most amorous of wild game. Perhaps my neck would have bristled with white feathers. A catastrophe is always possible. Metamorphosis lies in wait for us. Panic protected me.

I have lived in the fear of metamorphoses. It is in order to make the reader fully conscious, as he sees love swooping down on me—it is not mere rhetoric which requires the comparison—like a falcon—of the most exquisite of frights

---

[1] *Rouler un patin* (to roll a skate) is French slang meaning to kiss with the tongue.—Translator's note.

that I employ the idea of a turtle dove. I do not know what I felt at the moment, but today all I need do is summon up the vision of Stilitano for my distress to appear at once in the relationship of a cruel bird to its victim. (Were it not that I felt my neck swell out with a gentle cooing, I would have spoken rather of a robin redbreast.)

A curious creature would appear if each of my emotions became the animal it evokes: anger rumbles within my cobra neck; the same cobra swells up my prick; my steeds and merry-go-rounds are born of my insolence. . . . Of a turtle dove I retained only a hoarseness, which Stilitano noticed. I coughed.

Behind the Parallelo was an empty lot where the hoodlums played cards. (The Parallelo is an avenue in Barcelona parallel to the famous Ramblas. Between these two wide thoroughfares, a multitude of dark, dirty, narrow streets make up the Barrio Chino.) Squatting on the ground, they would organize games; they would lay out the cards on a square piece of cloth or in the dust. A young gypsy was running one of the games, and I came to risk the few sous I had in my pocket. I am not a gambler. Rich casinos do not attract me. The atmosphere of electric chandeliers bores me. The affected casualness of the elegant gambler nauseates me. And the impossibility of acting upon the balls, roulettes and little horses discourages me, but I loved the dust, filth and haste of the hoodlums. When I bugger . . . ,[1] as I bend farther forward I get a profile view of his face crushed against the pillow, of his pain. I see the wincing of his features, but also their radiant anguish. I often watched this on the grimy faces of the squatting urchins. This whole population was keyed up for winning or losing. Every thigh was quivering with fatigue or anxiety. The weather that day was threatening. I was caught up in the youthful impatience of the young Spaniards. I played and I won. I won every hand. I didn't say a word during the game. Besides, the gypsy was a stranger to me. Custom permitted me to pocket my money and leave. The boy was so good looking that by leaving him in that way I felt I was lacking in respect for the beauty, suddenly become sad, of his face, which was drooping with heat and boredom. I kindly gave him back his money. Slightly astonished, he took it and simply thanked me.

"Hello, Pépé," a kinky, swarthy-looking cripple called out as he limped by.

"Pépé," I said to myself, "his name is Pépé." And I left, for I had just noticed his delicate, almost feminine little hand. But hardly had I gone a few steps in that crowd of thieves, whores, beggars and queers than I felt someone touching me on the shoulder. It was Pépé. He had just left the game. He spoke to me in Spanish:

"My name is Pépé."

"Mine is Juan."

"Come, let's have a drink."

He was no taller than I. His face, which I had seen from above when he was squatting, looked less flattened. The features were finer.

---

[1]Since the hero, whom at first I called by his real name, is my current lover (1948), prudence advises me to leave a blank in place of his name.

"He's a girl," I thought, summoning up the image of his slender hand, and I felt that his company would bore me. He had just decided that we would drink the money I had won. We made the round of the bars, and all the while we were together he was quite charming. He wore a very low-necked blue jersey instead of a shirt. From the opening emerged a solid neck, as broad as his head. When he turned it without moving his chest, an enormous tendon stood out. I tried to imagine his body, and, despite the almost frail hands, I imagined it to be solid, for his thighs filled out the light cloth of his trousers. The weather was warm. The storm did not break. The nervousness of the players around us heightened. The whores seemed heavier. The dust and sun were oppressive. We drank hardly any liquor, but rather lemonade. We sat near the peddlers and exchanged an occasional word. He kept smiling, with a slight weariness. He seemed to be indulging me. Did he suspect that I liked his cute face? I don't know, but he didn't let on. Besides, I had the same sly sort of look as he; I seemed a threat to the well-dressed passer-by; I had his youth and his filth, and I was French. Toward evening he wanted to gamble, but it was too late to start a game as all the places were taken. We strolled about a bit among the players. When he brushed by the whores, Pépé would kid them. Sometimes he would pinch them. The heat grew more oppressive. The sky was flush with the ground. The nervousness of the crowd became irritating. Impatience prevailed over the gypsy who had not decided which game to join. He was fingering the money in his pocket. Suddenly he took me by the arm.

"Venga!"

He led me a few steps away to the one comfort station on the Parallelo. It was run by an old woman. Surprised by the suddenness of his decision, I questioned him:

"What are you going to do?"

"Wait for me."

"Why?"

He answered with a Spanish word which I did not understand. I told him so and, in front of the old woman who was waiting for her two sous, he burst out laughing and made the gesture of jerking off. When he came out, his face had a bit of color. He was still smiling.

"It's all right now. I'm ready."

That was how I learned that, on big occasions, players went there to jerk off in order to be calmer and more sure of themselves. We went back to the lot. Pépé chose a group. He lost. He lost all he had. I tried to restrain him; it was too late. As authorized by custom, he asked the man running the bank to give him a stake from the kitty for the next game. The man refused. It seemed to me then that the very thing that constituted the gypsy's gentleness turned sour, as milk turns, and became the most ferocious rage I have ever seen. He whisked away the bank. The man bounded up and tried to kick him. Pépé dodged. He handed me the money, but hardly had I pocketed it than his knife was open. He planted it in the heart of the Spaniard, a tall, bronzed fellow, who fell to the ground and who, despite his tan, turned pale, contracted, writhed and expired in the dust. For the first time I saw someone give up the ghost. Pépé had disappeared, but when, turning my eyes away from the corpse, I looked up, there, gazing at it with a faint smile, was Stilitano. The sun was about to set. The dead man and the handsomest of humans seemed to me merged in the same golden dust amidst a throng of sailors, soldiers, hoodlums and thieves from all parts of the world. The Earth did not revolve: carrying Stilitano, it trembled about the sun. At the same moment I came to know death and love. This vision, however, was very brief, for I could not stay there because I was afraid I might have been spotted with Pépé and lest a friend of the dead man snatch away the money which I kept in my pocket, but as I moved off, my memory kept alive and commented upon the following scene, which seemed to me grandiose: "The murder, by a charming child, of a grown man whose tan could turn pale, take on the hue of death, the whole ironically observed by a tall blond young-ster to whom I had just become secretly engaged." Rapid as my glance at him was, I had time to take in Stilitano's superb muscularity and to see, between his lips, rolling in his half-open mouth, a white, heavy blob of spit, thick as a white worm, which he shifted about, stretching it from top to bottom until it veiled his mouth. He stood barefoot in the dust. His legs were contained in a pair of worn and shabby faded blue denim trousers. The sleeves of his green shirt were rolled up, one of them above an amputated hand; the wrist, where the resewn skin still revealed a pale, pink scar, was slightly shrunken.

Beneath a tragic sky, I was to cross the loveliest landscapes in the world when Stilitano took my hand at night. What was the nature of that fluid which passed with a shock from him to me? I walked along dangerous shores, emerged into dismal plains, heard the sea. Hardly had I touched him, when the stairway changed: he was master of the world. With the memory of those brief moments, I could describe to you walks, breathless flights, pursuits, in countries of the world where I shall never go.

SUGGESTIONS FOR WRITING

1. What do you think of Genet's style? How does knowing that the author was a convict affect your reading?

2. Does Genet believably portray the humiliation he feels at the hands of the authorities, or is he being exaggeratedly paranoid?

3. Genet is obviously comfortable with himself. How do you react to his tone or stance?

4. Have you read works of other writers who have been imprisoned? How would you characterize prison writings? What value for society results from the publication of prison writings?

Selections from
DETAINED: A WRITER'S
PRISON DIARY

Ngugi wa Thiong'o

Kenya was at one time a shining example of the historic African rebellion against the colonial system. Known to the British colonizers as British East Africa, Kenya gained its independence, along with its new name, in 1963, as a result of the famous Mau Mau uprising led by the visionary African revolutionary Jomo Kenyatta, known to his followers as the "Burning Spear." Revolutions have a way of turning sour, however, of disappointing their most fervent followers. Under the leadership of Jomo Kenyatta and his successor, Daniel Arap Moi, Kenya quickly became what the author of Detained *calls a "neo-colonialist" society, that is, one that cultivates close ties with its former colonial oppressor. Done to secure foreign investments, this guaranteed that what remained of the revolution would be embodied in the charismatic leader; the revolution was reduced to "cult of personality."*

__Ngugi wa Thiong'o__ (b. 1938), a Kenyan writer, spoke out against Kenyatta's neo-colonialism in favor of moving Kenya further away from the colonial legacy. In his own practice as a writer, this has meant the gradual abandonment of English in favor of the Gikuyu language, a principal language in Kenya. He says this step is necessary for "decolonising the mind," a phrase that also serves as the title of one of his books (1986). In December 1977, Ngugi was arrested for his anti-government statements, and he spent nearly a year in prison without ever coming to trial. He has written about this experience in Detained: A Writer's Prison Diary *(1981).*

Ngugi's many writings must be discussed in relation to his decision to abandon English in favor of Gikuyu. In 1977 he published a novel called Petals of Blood, *his last in English. His first novel in Gikuyu was translated as* Devil on the Cross *(1982). He continued to use English for his non-fiction works, such as* Detained, *until he announced in the preface to his collection of essays in* Decolonising the Mind *that henceforward he would write exclusively in Gikuyu. From time to time he does publish English translations of these works. Ngugi's plays are also highly regarded. Perhaps the best known is* I Will Marry When I Want *(1982), which originally appeared in the Gikuyu language. Ngugi today lives in exile from Kenya.*

I

Warũ̃ nga ngatha ya wĩra . . . Warĩĩnga heroine of toil . . . there she walks haughtily carrying her freedom in her hands . . .

12 December 1978: I am in cell 16 in a detention block enclosing eighteen other political prisoners. Here I have no name. I am just a number in a file: K6,77. A tiny iron frame against one wall serves as a bed and a tiny board against another wall serves as a desk. These fill up the minute cell.

It is past midnight. Unable to face the prickly bristles of three see-through blankets on a mattress whose sisal stuffing has folded into innumerable lumps as hard as stones, I am at the desk, under the full electric glare of a hundred-watt naked bulb, scribbling words on toilet-paper. Along the passageway which separates the two lines of Kenyatta's tiger cages, I can hear the heavy bootsteps of the night warder. He is going on his rounds.

At the one end, the passageway leads into a cul-de-sac of two latrines, a wash-room with only one sink and a shower-room for four. These are all open: no doors. At the other end, next to my cell, the passageway opens into a tiny exercise-yard whose major features are one aluminium rubbish-bin and a falling apart tenniquoit-cum-volleyball net hung on two iron poles. There is a door of iron bars at this opening—between the exercise-yard and the block of cells—and it is always shut and locked at night. The block of 'tiger cages' and the yard are enclosed by four double stone walls so high that they have completely cut off any part of the skyline of trees and buildings which might give us a glimpse of the world of active life.

This is Kamītī Maximum Security Prison, one of the largest prisons in post-colonial Africa. It is situated near three towns—Rūirū, Kīambu and Nairobi—and literally next-door to Kenyatta University College but we could as easily have been on the moon or on Mars. We have been completely quarantined from everything and everybody except for a highly drilled select squad of prison guards and their commanding officers.

Maximum security: the idea used to fill me with such terror whenever I met it in fiction, Dickens mostly, and I have always associated it with England and Englishmen and with Robben Island in South Africa: it conjured up images of hoards of dangerous killers always ready to escape through thick forests and marshes, to unleash yet more havoc and terror on an otherwise stable, peaceful and godfearing community of property-owners that sees itself as the whole society. A year as an inmate in Kamītī has taught me what should have been obvious: that the prison system is a repressive weapon in the hands of a ruling minority determined to ensure maximum security for its class dictatorship over the rest of the population, and it is not a monopoly exclusive to South Africa and England.

The menacing bootsteps come nearer. But I know that the prowling warder cannot enter my cell—it is always double-locked and the keys in turn locked inside a box which at five o'clock is promptly taken away by the corporal on duty to a safe somewhere outside the double walls—but of course he can look into the cell through an iron-barred rectangular slit in the upper half of the door. The slit is built so as to only contain the face.

The bootsteps stop. I take my time in turning to the door although I can feel in my bones that the warder is watching me. It is an instinct that one develops in prison, the cunning instinct of the hunted. The face of the warder fills the whole slit: I know nothing so menacingly sinister in its silent stillness as that trunkless face glaring at you through the iron bars of a prison cell.

'Professor . . . why are you not in bed?' the voice redeems the face. 'What are you doing?'

Relief! I fall back on the current witticism in the detention block.

'I am writing to Jomo Kenyatta in his capacity as an ex-detainee.'

'His case was different,' the warder argues back.

'How?'

'His was a colonial affair.'

'And this, a neo-colonial affair? What's the difference?'

'A colonial affair . . . now we are independent . . . that's the difference . . .' he says.

'A colonial affair in an independent country, eh? The British jailed an innocent Kenyatta. Thus Kenyatta learnt to jail innocent Kenyans. Is that the difference?'

He laughs. Then he repeats it. 'The British jailed Kenyatta. Kenyatta jails Kenyans.' He laughs again, adding:

'Take it any way you like . . . but write a good petition . . . you might get a hearing this time . . . Your star shines bright in the sky . . . ex-detainee . . .' he chuckles to himself. 'Does "ex-" mean the same thing as "late"—*hayati?*'

'What do you mean?'

'Can I say the late detainee instead of the ex-detainee?'

The tone tells me that he knows the difference and he is trying to communicate something. But tonight I feel a little impatient.

'You know I no longer teach English,' I say to him.

'You never can tell the language of the stars,' he persists. 'Once a teacher, always a teacher,' he says, and goes away laughing.

In his prison notes, *The Man Died*, Wole Soyinka[1] aptly comments that 'no matter how cunning a prisoner, the humanitarian act of courage among his gaolers plays a key rôle in his survival.' This warder is a good illustration of the truth of that observation. He is the one who in March told me about the formation of the London-based *Ngũgĩ Defence Committee* and the subsequent picketing of the Kenya Embassy on 3 March 1978. He enjoys talking in riddles and communicating in roundabouts. It's a way of protecting himself, of course, but he enjoys seeing a prisoner grope for the hidden meanings.

Tonight, his laughter sounds more direct and sympathetic, or perhaps it is another kind of riddle to be taken any way I like.

Two warders guard the passageway in turns. One sleeps, the other guards. At one o'clock they change places. They too cannot get out because the door between the passageway and the exercise-yard is locked and the keys taken away. Night warders are themselves prisoners guarding other prisoners. Only they are paid for it and their captivity is self-inflicted or else imposed by lack of alternative means of life. One very young warder—a Standard Seven drop-out—tells me that his ambition is to be a fighter pilot! Another, a grandfather, tells me his ambition once was to become a musician.

---

[1]Noble prize winning African author.

To hell with the warders! Away with intruding thoughts! Tonight I don't want to think about warders and prisoners, colonial or neo-colonial affairs. I am totally engrossed in Warĩĩnga, the fictional heroine of the novel I have been writing on toilet-paper for the last ten months or so![2]

Toilet-paper: when in the sixties I first read in Kwame Nkrumah's autobiography, *Ghana*, how he used to hoard toilet-paper in his cell at James Fort Prison to write on, I thought it was romantic and a little unreal despite the photographic evidence reproduced in the book. Writing on toilet-paper?

Now, I know: paper, any paper, is about the most precious article for a political prisoner, more so for one like me, who was in political detention because of his writing. For the urge to write:

> *Picking the jagged bits embedded in my mind,*
> *Partly to wrench some ease for my own mind,*
> *And partly that some world sometime may know*

is almost irresistible to a political prisoner. At Kamĩtĩ, virtually all the detainees are writers or composers. Wasonga Sijeyo has volumes of notes on his life, Kenyan history, botany, zoology, astronomy and Luo culture. Koigi wa Wamwere has many essays on politics and culture, several political fables, a short novel, an autobiography, and a long poem on his prison experience. Gĩcerũ wa Njaũ has a novel in Kiswahili. Thairũ wa Mũthĩga has a few poems. Simba Ongongi Were composes heart-rending songs; while Mahat Kuno Roble, though illiterate, is a highly accomplished poet. And from Shimo-la-Tewa Prison, I have received two huge manuscripts of two novels by Mwangi wa Mahiinda. These prisoners have mostly written on toilet-paper. Now the same good old toilet-paper—which had been useful to Kwame Nkrumah in James Fort Prison, to Dennis Brutus on Robben Island, to Abdilatif Abdalla in G Block, Kamĩtĩ, and to countless other persons with similar urges—has enabled me to defy daily the intended detention of my mind.

> *A flicker, pulse, mere vital hint*
> *which speaks of the stubborn will*
> *the grim assertion of some sense of worth*
> *in the teeth of the wind*
> *on a stony beach, or among rocks*
> *where the brute hammers fall unceasingly*
> *on the mind.*

I now know what Dennis Brutus meant. Writing this novel has been a daily, almost hourly, assertion of my will to remain human and free despite the Kenya African National Union (KANU) official government programme of animal degradation of political prisoners.

---

[2]The novel has now appeared in Gĩkũyũ as *Caitaani Mũtharaba-inĩ* (Heinemann, Nairobi, 1980) and the English translation will appear in 1981 under the title *Devil on the Cross*.

Privacy, for instance. I mean its brutal invasion. Thus, I was daily trailed by a warder for twenty-four hours, in waking and sleeping. It was unnerving, truly unnerving, to find a warder watching me shit and urinate into a children's chamberpot in my cell, or to find him standing by the entrance to the toilet to watch me do the same exercise. The electric light is on the night long. To induce sleep, I had to tie a towel over my eyes. This ended in straining them so that after a month they started smarting and watering. But even more painful was to suddenly wake up in the middle of the night, from a dreamless slumber or one softened by sweet illusion or riddled with nightmares, to find two bodiless eyes fixed on me through the iron bars.

Or monotony: the human mind revolts against endless sameness. In ordinary social life, even the closest-knit family hardly ever spends a whole day together in meaningless circles on their compound. Man, woman and child go about their different activities in different places and they only meet in the evening to recount their different experiences. Experiments done on animals show that when they are confined to a small space and subjected to the same routine they end up tearing each other. Now the KANU government was doing the same experiment on human beings.

At Kamītī, we daily saw the same faces in the same white kūūngurū prison uniforms; we daily fed on unga and beans in the morning, at noon and at three o'clock; we daily went through the same motions, and this, in a confined space of reliefless dust and grey stones. The two most dominant colours in the detention block were white and grey and I am convinced these are the colours of death.

The government could not have been ignorant about the possible results of these experiments in mental torment: valium was the most frequently prescribed drug in Kamītī Prison. The doctor expected a detainee to be mad or depressed unless proved otherwise.

There was a history to it. I was told a harrowing story about one detainee before my time who had a mental breakdown in that very block. The authorities watched him going down the drain until he was reduced to eating his own faeces. Yet the regime kept him in that condition for two years. This is normal practice in regimes with no popular roots in the masses, and Kenyatta's KANU government was one: but this did not make the horror easier to contemplate.

A week after my incarceration, Wasonga Sijeyo, who had been in that block for nine years but had managed to keep a razor-sharp mind and a heart of steel, eluded the vigilant eyes of the warders then guarding me and within seconds he told me words that I came to treasure:

'It may sound a strange thing to say to you, but in a sense I am glad they brought you here. The other day—in fact a week or so before you came—we were saying that it would be a good thing for Kenya if more intellectuals were imprisoned. First, it would wake most of them from their illusions. And some of them might outlive jail to tell the world. The thing is . . . just watch your mind . . . don't let them break you and you'll be all right even if they keep you for life . . . but you must try . . . you have to, for us, for the ones you left behind.'

Thus in addition to it being an insurrection of a detained intellect, writing this novel has been one way of keeping my mind and heart together like Sijeyo.

Free thoughts on toilet-paper! I had deliberately given myself a difficult task. I had resolved to use a language which did not have a modern novel, a challenge to myself, and a way of affirming my faith in the possibilities of the languages of all the different Kenyan nationalities, languages whose development as vehicles for the Kenyan people's anti-imperialist struggles had been actively suppressed by the British colonial regime (1895–1963) and by the neo-colonial regime of Kenyatta and his comprador KANU cohorts. I had also resolved not to make any concessions to the language. I would not avoid any subject—science, technology, philosophy, religion, music, political economy—provided it logically arose out of the development of theme, character, plot, story, and world view. Further I would use any and everything I had ever learnt about the craft of fiction—allegory, parable, satire, narrative, description, reminiscence, flash-back, interior monologue, stream of consciousness, dialogue, drama—provided it came naturally in the development of character, theme and story. But content—not language and technique—would determine the eventual form of the novel. And the content? The Kenyan people's struggles against the neo-colonial form and stage of imperialism!

Easier said than done: where was I to get the inspiration? A writer needs people around him. He needs live struggles of active life. Contrary to popular mythology, a novel is not a product of the imaginative feats of a single individual but the work of many hands and tongues. A writer just takes down notes dictated to him by life among the people, which he then arranges in this or that form. For me, in writing a novel, I love to hear the voices of the people working on the land, forging metal in a factory, telling anecdotes in crowded matatus and buses, gyrating their hips in a crowded bar before a jukebox or a live band, people playing games of love and hate and fear and glory in their struggle to live. I need to look at different people's faces, their gestures, their gait, their clothes, and to hear the variegated modulations of their voices in different moods. I need the vibrant voices of beautiful women: their touch, their sighs, their tears, their laughter. I like the presence of children prancing about, fighting, laughing, crying. I need life to write about life.

But it is also true that nobody writes under circumstances chosen by him and on material invented by him. He can only seize the time to select from material handed to him by whomever and whatever is around him. So my case now: I had not chosen prison, I was forced into it, but now that I was there, I would try and turn the double-walled enclosure into a special school where, like Shakespeare's Richard II, I would study how I might compare:

This prison where I live unto the world . . .
My brain I'll prove the female to my soul,
My soul the father; and these two beget
A generation of still-breeding thoughts,
And these same thoughts people this little world,
In humours like the people of this world,
For no thought is contented.

In this literary target I was lucky to have for teachers, detainees and a few warders, who were very co-operative and generous in sharing their different mines of information and experience. For instance, Thairū wa Mūthīga, Gīcerū wa Njaū and Koigi wa Wamwere taught me a lot of Gīkūyū vocabulary, proverbs, riddles and songs; Wasonga Sijeyo was an expert on the nationalist anti-imperialist struggles before 1963 and on the beginnings of land grabbing and foreigners' bribery of former nationalists with token shares in their companies; Gīkonyo wa Rūkūūngū gave me books on rituals of Catholic worship; Simba Ongongi Were taught me some Zairean tunes and words; Mūhoro wa Mūthoga, Koigi wa Wamwere and Adamu Matheenge gave me topographical details of Nakuru; while Gīcerū wa Njaū, Thairū wa Mūthīga and I often discussed women of different careers, especially barmaids, secretaries and engineers, as well as different aspects of social life and bourgeois rivalry in Nairobi. I learnt a lot about business acumen and the whole practice and culture of accumulation from stories and real-life anecdotes narrated to us by the only millionaire in detention, Mahat Kuno Roble.

Not only from conscious discussions and direct inquiries: whispered news of happenings outside the walls would often provide me with material that I would later weave into the fabric of the novel. For instance, the main theme and story line emerged when I learnt that two members of parliament were serving sentences after being convicted of coffee theft. The shocking news of Professor Barnard's visit and the generous provision by his Kenya hosts of public platforms to air his racist pro-apartheid views prompted the philosophical discussion in a matatu about 'life to come' and the problems of rival claims to the same heart on the day of resurrection; it also prompted the satirical depiction of a vision of one robber character, for a world in which a rich few would ensure their immortality through the purchase of spare organs of the human body, thus leaving death as the sole prerogative of the poor.

In the daytime, I would take hasty notes on empty spaces of any book I might be reading, I would scribble notes on the bare walls of my cell, then in the evening I would try to put it all together on toilet-paper.

Sometimes I would be seized with the usual literary boredom and despair— those painful moments when a writer begins to doubt the value of what he is scribbling or the possibility of ever completing the task in hand—those moments when a writer restrains himself with difficulty from setting the whole thing on fire, or tearing it all into pieces, or abandoning the whole project to dust and cobwebs. These moments are worse in prison because there are no distractions to massage the tired imagination: a glass of beer, a sound of music, or a long walk in sun and wind or in a starry night.

But at these very moments, I would remind myself that the KANU-led comprador ruling class had sent me here so that my brain would turn into a mess of rot. The defiance of this bestial purpose always charged me with new energy and determination: I would cheat them out of that last laugh by letting my imagination loose over the kind of society this class, in nakedly treacherous alliance with imperialist foreigners, were building in Kenya in total cynical disregard of the wishes of over fourteen-million Kenyans.

Because the women are the most exploited and oppressed section of the entire working class, I would create a picture of a strong determined woman with a will to resist and to struggle against the conditions of her present being. Had I not seen glimpses of this type in real life among the women of Kamĩrĩĩthũ Community Education and Cultural Centre? Isn't Kenyan history replete with this type of woman? Me Kitilili, Muraa wa Ngiti, Mary Mũthoni Nyanjirũ? Mau Mau women cadres? Warĩĩnga will be the fictional reflection of this resistance heroine of Kenyan history. Warĩĩnga heroine of toil . . . there she walks . . .

I am now on the last chapter. I have given myself 25 December as the deadline. 25 December 1978 has a special significance to me. In February or March I had told the other detainees that we would all 'eat' Christmas at home. I had even invited them to a Christmas goat-meat roasting party at my home in Gĩtogoothi, Bibirioni, Limuru. It was said half-in-joke, like so many other prison wagers related to dreams of eventual liberty, but I secretly believed it and inwardly clung to the date though becoming less and less openly assertive about it as days and nights rolled away. Now only twelve days are left. Twelve days to eat Christmas at home. Twelve days to meet my self-imposed literary deadline!

But tonight something else, an impulse, a voice, is urging me to run this last lap faster. The voice is not all that secret. Maybe it is born of the feverish expectation of early release which has been building up in the block for the last four months, though nobody is now sure of its 'ifs' and 'whens'. Maybe it is also born of a writer's usual excitement at seeing the light at the end of a long hazardous tunnel. Or maybe it is a combination of both. But whatever its source, the voice remains insistent.

The heart is willing. The hand which has been scribbling non-stop since about seven o'clock is weak. But the voice is relentless: Write On!

I rise to stretch my legs. I walk to the iron-barred rectangular slit and peer into the passageway. Neither of the two warders is asleep. They are playing draughts, but they are murmuring more than they are playing. I ask the same warder about the time.

'Half-past twelve,' he says, and then adds: 'Why do you want to know the time, Professor?'

'I wanted to know if my star is still shining the sky,' I answer back.

'You better have some sleep. You might need it.'

No. I don't feel like any sleep tonight. I go back to the desk to resume the race to the literary tape only a couple of paragraphs away.

II

In front of me is a photograph of my daughter Njooki, meaning she who comes back from the dead; or Aiyerubo, meaning she who defies heaven and hell; or Wamũingĩ, meaning she who belongs to the people. Later when I am out of Kamĩtĩ, I will see her and hold her in my arms and learn that she was named Wamũingĩ by the peasant women of Limuru, and Aiyerubo by the Writers of African Peoples in Nigeria, but just now she is only a name and a photograph sent through the post.

She was born on 15 May 1978, five months after my abduction and subsequent incarceration. When her photograph arrived in Kamĩtĩ some time after that defiant break from the chains of heaven or hell, one detainee, Thairũ wa Mũthĩga, had nicknamed her *Kaana ka Boothita*, a post-office baby.

Thairũ spoke a truth. Deep inside me I know that Njooki was a message from the world. A message of hope. A message that somewhere outside these grey walls of death were people waiting for me, thinking about me, perhaps even fighting, with whatever weapons, for my release. A protest, a hastily muttered prayer from the lips of a peasant, a groan, a sigh, wishes of helpless children: such gestures and wishes may today not be horses on which seekers of freedom may ride to liberty, but they do reflect a much needed moral solidarity with a political prisoner, or with the issues for which he has been jailed. One day these very wishes will be transformed by the organized power and united will of millions from the realm of morality into people's chariots of actual freedom from naked exploitation and ruthless oppression. But just now the mere expression of solidarity and my knowledge of it through Njooki's photograph is a daily source of joyful strength.

In a neo-colonial country, the act of detaining patriotic democrats, progressive intellectuals and militant workers speaks of many things. It is first an admission by the detaining authorities that their official lies labelled as a new philosophy, their pretensions often hidden in three-piece suits and golden chains, their propaganda packaged as religious truth, their plastic smiles ordered from abroad, their nationally televised charitable handouts and breast-beating before the high altar, their high-sounding phrases and ready-to-shed tears at the sight of naked children fighting it out with cats and dogs for the possession of a rubbish heap, that these and more godfatherly acts of benign benevolence have been seen by the people for what they truly are: a calculated sugar-coating of an immoral sale and mortgage of a whole country and its people to Euro-American and Japanese capital for a few million dollars in Swiss banks and a few token shares in foreign companies. Their mostly vaunted morality has been exposed for what it is: the raising of beggary and charity into moral idealism. There is a new-found dignity in begging, and charity for them is twice-blessed; it deflates the recipient and inflates the giver. Nyerere once rightly compared those African regimes who dote on their neo-colonial status to a prostitute who walks with proud display of the fur coat given to her by her moneyed lover. Actually the situation of a comprador neo-colonial ruling class is more appropriately comparable to that of a pimp who would proudly hold down his mother to be brutally raped by foreigners, and then shout in glee: look at the shining handful of dollars I have received for my efficiency and integrity, in carrying out my part of the bargain!

But recourse to detention is above all an admission by the neo-colonial ruling minority that people have started to organize to oppose them, to oppose the continued plunder of the national wealth and heritage by this shameless alliance of a few nationals and their foreign paymasters.

Thus detention more immediately means the physical removal of patriots from the people's organized struggles. Ideally, the authorities would like to put the whole community of struggling millions behind barbed-wire, as the British colonial authorities once tried to do with Kenyan people. But this would mean incarcerating labour, the true source of national wealth: what would then be left to loot? So the authorities do the simpler thing: pick one or two individuals from among the people and then loudly claim that all sins lie at the feet of these few 'power hungry' 'misguided' and 'ambitious' agitators. Note that any awakening of a people to their historic mission of liberating themselves from external and internal exploitation and repression is always seen in terms of 'sin' and it is often denounced with the religious rhetoric of a wronged, self-righteous god. These agitators suddenly become devils whose removal from society is now portrayed as a divine mission. The people are otherwise innocent, simple, peace-loving, obedient, law-abiding, and cannot conceivably harbour any desire to change this best of all possible worlds. It is partly self-deception, but also an attempted deception of millions. Chain the devils!

But political detention, not disregarding its punitive aspects, serves a deeper, exemplary ritual symbolism. If they can break such a patriot, if they can make him come out of detention crying 'I am sorry for all my sins', such an unprincipled about-turn would confirm the wisdom of the ruling clique in its division of the populace into the passive innocent millions and the disgruntled subversive few. The 'confession' and its corollary, 'Father, forgive us for our sins', becomes a cleansing ritual for all the past and current repressive deeds of such a neo-colonial regime. With a few titbits, directorship of this or that statutory body, the privilege of standing for parliament on the regime's party ticket, such an ex-detainee might even happily play the rôle of a conscientious messenger from purgatory sent back to earth by a father figure more benevolent than Lazarus' Abraham, 'that he may testify unto them (them that dare to struggle), lest they also come into this place of torment'. The forgiving father sits back to enjoy international applause for his manifold munificence and compassionate heart. But even when they find that such a detainee is not in a position to play the rôle of an active preacher against the futility of struggle (they may have damaged him beyond any exploitable repair), they can still publicize this picture of a human wreck or vegetable as a warning to all future agitators: he could not stand it, do you think you are made of sterner steel? The former hard-core patriot is physically or intellectually or spiritually broken and by a weird symbolic extension, the whole struggling populace is broken. All is now well in imperialist heaven for there is peace on neo-colonial earth, policed by a tough no-nonsense comprador ruling class that knows how to deal with subversive elements.

The fact is that detention without trial is not only a punitive act of physical and mental torture of a few patriotic individuals, but it is also a calculated act of psychological terror against the struggling millions. It is a terrorist programme for the psychological siege of the whole nation. That is why the practice of detention from the time of arrest to the time of release is deliberately invested with mystifying ritualism. My arrest, for instance.

This could have been effected by a single unarmed policeman or even by a simple summons to Tigoni Police Station. I had nothing to hide. I had done nothing to which I would plead guilty in my patriotic conscience or in a democratic court of law. Indeed I had done nothing that I could not publicly and proudly own up to before the nation and the world. But the police who must have followed me over the years and who must therefore have noted and recorded my mostly solitary, non-violent deeds and habits, nevertheless chose to steal into my house at night with an incredible show of armed might.

It was at midnight on 30–31 December 1977 at Gītogoothi, Bibirioni, Limuru. Two Land-Rovers with policemen armed with machine-guns, rifles and pistols drove into the yard. A police saloon car remained at the main gate flashing red and blue on its roof, very much like the Biblical sword of fire policing the ejection of Adam and Eve from the legendary Garden of Eden by a God who did not want human beings to eat from trees of knowledge, for the stability of Eden and his dictatorship over it depended on people remaining ignorant about their condition. Behind the saloon car were others which, as I later came to learn, carried some local administrative officials and the local corps of informers. These latter remained lurking in the shadows for fear that, even at such a dark hour, the peasants around might recognize them and denounce them to the people.

Armed members of the special branch who swarmed and searched my study amidst an awe-inspiring silence were additionally guarded by uniformed policemen carrying long range rifles. Their grim determined faces would only light up a little whenever they pounced on any book or pamphlet bearing the names of Marx, Engels or Lenin. I tried to lift the weight of silence in the room by remarking that if Lenin, Marx or Engels were all they were after, I could save them much time and energy by showing them the shelves where these dangerous three were hiding. The leader of the book-raiding squad was not amused. He growled at me, and I quickly and promptly took his 'advice' to keep quiet and let them do their work. But I kept on darting my eyes from one raider to the other in case they did something illegal. I soon realized the futility of my vigilance since I was alone and they were all over the study. They could very easily have put banned books or pamphlets if they had wanted to, like the description in a poem entitled 'It's No Use', by Victor Jacinto Flecha. (The translation, by Nick Caistor, appeared in *Index on Censorship*, VIII, 1, London, January/February 1979.)

It's no use
Your hiding deep in the dark well of your house
Hiding your words
Burning your books
It's no use.

They'll come to find you
In lorries, piled high with leaflets,
With letters no one ever wrote to you
They'll fill your passport with stamps
From countries where you have never been

They'll drag you away
Like some dead dog
And that night you'll find out all about torture
In the dark room
Where all the foul odours of the world are bred
It's no use
Your hiding
From the fight, my friend.

Nevertheless, I kept on looking from one to the other and I saw them fer-reting among the books by Lenin, Marx and Engels without any more verbal interruptions from me. To the list of the Dangerous Three, they now added Kim Chi Ha, and any book that bore the words 'scientific socialism', plus about twenty-six copies of the offending play, *Ngaahika Ndeenda*. But even then, I could not help musing over the fact that the police squadron was armed to the teeth with guns to abduct a writer whose only acts of violent resistance were safely between the hard and soft covers of literary imaginative reflections.

Abduction. The word needs an explanation. The police took me away under false pretences. The conversation in the sitting-room went something like this:

NGŨGĨ: Gentlemen, can I request that we sit down and record all the books and pamphlets you have taken?
POLICE: We shall do all that at the police station.
NGŨGĨ: Tell me quite frankly: am I under arrest?
POLICE: Oh, no.
NGŨGĨ: In that case, I'll provide you with a table, pen and paper and we can record everything before it leaves the house.
POLICE: We shall do it at the station and you are coming with us.
NGŨGĨ: What for?
POLICE: To answer a few questions.
NGŨGĨ: Am I under arrest?
POLICE: No.
NGŨGĨ: In that case, can't the questions wait until morning?
POLICE: No.
NGŨGĨ: Can you please give me a minute with my wife to sort out one thing or two?
POLICE: It is not necessary. We promise that you'll be back in the morning. Just a few questions.
NGŨGĨ: Can you tell me where you are taking me so that my wife here can know?
POLICE: Kĩambu!

At Kĩambu police station I was pushed into an empty room with bare walls where I was guarded by only one member of the abducting team. Now he smiled rather slyly and he asked me: 'How come that as soon as we knocked at the door, you were already up and fully dressed?'

I had neither the time nor the necessary energy to tell him that I had had a premonition; that I had just returned home from Nairobi after saying a rather elaborate farewell to my lawyer friend, Ndeere wa Njugi—a strange thing this farewell since he was only going to Langata and I to Limuru; and also, after firmly and repeatedly refusing a beer from another friend, Solomon Kagwe— again a strange thing because he worked in Morocco and I had not seen him for many years; that I had driven from Impala Hotel, Nairobi, to Limuru at a snail's pace, literally not more that fifty kilometres an hour the whole way; that on arrival home, instead of putting on my pyjamas and slipping into bed, I just lay on the cover fully clad, staring at the ceiling and turning over the recent events since the public performances of *Ngaahika Ndeenda* had been banned; that when I heard the knocking at the door and I put on my shoes and went to the window and saw uniformed policemen, I felt as if I had been expecting the scene all along! This I could not tell him, even had I the necessary energy or desire, because a few seconds after his query, a tall slim man came in and standing, staring straight ahead, almost past me, he made the formal announcement: 'I am Superintendent Mbūrū attached to Kīambu Police Station and I am under instructions to arrest you and place you in detention. Have you anything to say?' The whole exercise, executed in a emotionless tone, had a slightly comic side: so between Limuru and Kīambu I was not under police arrest? 'Do your duty!' was all I said.

It was only during the journey to Kilimani Police Station, Nairobi, in a yellow Volvo driven by Superintendent Mbūrū himself, that I experienced respite from the show of armed terror! Mbūrū even managed to start a conversation:

'Did your family originally come from the Rift Valley?' he asked.

'No!' I said.

'I have had that impression from reading your books.'

'I only write about it,' I said.

If one had overheard that conversation, one would have assumed that Mbūrū was only giving me a lift to Nairobi instead of taking me to an unknown destination.

Temporary respite: Mbūrū did not harass me; he at least had executed his duty decently.

The following morning—it was now Saturday, and the last day of 1977— soon after being served with detention orders by Mr. Mūhīndī whom I later came to learn was an assistant commissioner of police in charge of Nairobi area and also the detainees' security officer, I was suddenly grabbed by some police and roughly put in chains. I was then pushed from behind into the back seat of a blue car with blinds between two hefty policemen armed with a machine-gun and a rifle while a third one, equally well equipped, sat in the front seat beside the driver. I was driven through the heavy traffic in Nairobi streets—Haile Selassie, Ronald Ngala, Race Course, Thika Road, Kamītī Road—to the gates of the infamous Kamītī Maximum Security Prison.

The driver almost smashed his way through the heavy closed outer doors of the giant prison. But realizing his mistake, he quickly backed into a small bush, under a tree, car blinds still drawn, so that none of the people walking about could see who or what was inside the black maria.

It was then that I witnessed something which I had last seen in colonial Kenya during the barbaric British imposed State of Emergency when similar terror tactics were a daily occurrence. The whole area around Kamĩtĩ was immediately put under curfew—and this in the noon of the day. I saw innocent men, women and children drive for cover pursued by baton waving warders and within seconds there was not a single civilian standing or walking in the vicinity of Kamĩtĩ Prison. The poor folk had unknowingly made the mistake of peacefully going about their daily chores during the ceremony of detention and no doubt had paid for the pleasure with a few bruises here and there.

The huge prison gates, like the jaws of a ravenous monster, now slowly swung open to swallow me within its walls, which still dripped with the blood of the many Kenyan patriots who had been hanged there for their courageous Mau Mau guerrilla struggle against British imperialism. These had for ever lost their names. They had died as mere numbers on prison files. Up to now, still belonging to nameless numbers, their bones, including Kĩmaathi's, lie in that foul place, unwept and unremembered by ungrateful inheritors of the power they paid for with their lives.

Ironies of history: now my turn had come. From Saturday 31 December 1977 I had died to my name of Ngũgĩ. Henceforth I would only answer to a lifeless number of a file among many files. I was later to learn that for a whole two weeks after my abduction, my family and virtually the whole nation were kept in ignorance of my fate. Every police and every government official would plead equal ignorance until my detention was announced in the *Kenya Gazette* of 6 January 1978 (though this issue was held, and not released until 14 January).

Even then my place of detention, as in the case of all other detainees, remained a top secret known only to an initiated few. The KANU government would in fact go to ridiculous lengths to mystify people about our whereabouts: like convening the Detainees' Review Tribunal in Mombasa and flying the detainees there. Yet virtually all the members of the tribunal came from Nairobi, only ten minutes' drive from Kamĩtĩ. Or the whole mystery surrounding a detainee's meeting with his family at Embakasi Airport, giving the impression of a flight from afar. And whenever a detainee went out and came in, a curfew was clamped on the whole prison. Why all the mystery, the suspense, the secrecy? Did they really fear that people would storm Kamĩtĩ Prison to free detainees by force?

Of course not: The ruling clique in Kenya has the monopoly of all the instruments of anti-people coercive violence, and this they know. But they also know that no force on earth—not even nuclear weapons—can finally put down the organized power of an awakened people. Hence the imperative to bring up people in a culture of silence and fear to make them feel weak before the state. This state assumes the malevolent character of a terrifying supernatural force that can only be placated by supplications of a people on their knees or be appeased by unavengeable gifts of human flesh such as a Pinto or a JM.

The rituals of mystery and secrecy are calculated exercises in psychological terror aimed at the whole people—part of the culture of fear—and at the individual detainee—part of the strategy of eventually breaking him. The first is harder to see, for it can only be understood by delving into history, our history, to trace the roots of current ruling-class culture. That will come later. It is to understand it that I am writing this account. But the latter is easier to see, for it is part of the daily trials of a political prisoner.

The rituals, seemingly petty and childish but rigorously followed to the letter by bemedalled officers and decorated warders, serve to make a detainee feel that he has been completely cut off from the people and hence from that group solidarity—the sense of being one with the people—which alone keeps men and women going even when menaced by truncheons, nailed boots, tear-gas and deathly whistling bullets. He must be made, not just to know, but to actually feel that with the links cut, he is now adrift in an ocean of endless fear and humiliation. He is not introduced into the ocean gradually. He is thrown into it to swim and stay afloat in any way he knows how, or else to plunge into the depths and drown.

During the first month of my prison life, I was daily locked in cell 16 for twenty-two hours. The remaining two hours were distributed to cover the daily chores of emptying the chamberpot topful with shit and urine; of gulping down the breakfast, lunch and supper of porridge, ugali, worm-infested beans and rotten vegetables; and of sunshine and exercise. The other detainees had lived under these conditions for the previous two years; precisely, from September 1975. Everyday I would ask myself: how have they managed to stay afloat?

For the first three weeks of the same month I was also under internal segregation. This simply meant that no detainee was allowed near me. During meals, I would be made to sit apart from the others, often with a warder between us. During my ration of sunshine, I had to sit in my corner often with a watchful warder to ensure that there was no talking contact between me and any of the others.

But since we were all in the same block, it was not easy for the warders to enforce total segregation. The other detainees would break through the cordon by shouting across to me; or by finding any and every excuse for going past where I was sitting and hurriedly throwing in one or two words; or by stopping outside my cell—the other detainees were let out for sunshine in groups of twos or threes, though there were three detainees permanently out under doctor's orders—and through the iron-bar opening they would assure me of their human solidarity. This was always very touching coming from people who were in no better conditions. Sometimes two detainees would stand just far enough away not to be accused of being with me, but near enough for me to hear everything. They would talk to one another about various aspects of prison life, sometimes offering one another advice or hints on how to cope with prison life, but I knew that this was meant for me. And at night, or when inside our cells in the day, there was of course no way of preventing the other detainees from shouting messages and anecdotes through the walls, and I shouting back news of what had been happening in the world up to the time of my arrest.

Despite the efforts of my fellow detainees to break the walls of segregation, the feeling of being alone would often steal into me and I would be seized with the momentary panic of a man drowning in a sea of inexplicable terror. I often felt like those lepers in medieval Europe who had to carry small bells around their necks to announce their leprous presence to the healthy, or those *osu* untouchables in Achebe's novels who had to jump into the bush to let a freeborn pass. In my case I was being denied the social fellowship of even the other political untouchables.

Months later, when I told the other detainees about my feelings during those weeks of January, they laughed and assured me how lucky I was to have had them around me, that the sense of isolation is thousand times more intense for those in solitary confinement.

Mūhoro wa Mūthoga, popularly known as Fujika, told me that his own initiation into prison life at Kamītī was through a six-month solitary confinement in a ghostly cell in what was known as the Isolation Block. Every effort was exerted to make him live and feel the reality behind that name. His only contact was with the warders who brought him food, let him out for an hour of sunshine and exercise, and who guarded the empty silent corridors. One warder always walked on tiptoe. Another would open the cell door, push food inside, and then jump back quickly, shutting the door as if the inmate was a dangerous animal in a cage. Yet another warder, the most liberal, would speak to him words through clenched teeth as if they were being painfully pulled out of his tongue at some cost, and even then the words would come out as whispers. Otherwise the others communicated with him only in gestures. He started doubting himself: could he possibly, unknowingly, have done something more terrible than just asking for application forms from the attorney-general to legally register a new democratic political party? Could he have misread the Kenya constitution, which on paper at least, allowed multi-party formations? The application forms had been sent to him all right. He had sent back the forms plus the constitution of the intended party. In answer, he was arrested and sent to Kamītī Maximum Security Prison. Maybe *intentions* to form new political parties to represent classes other than the comprador bourgeoisie to whom KANU now belonged had been banned and he had failed to read the relevant gazette!

The detainee told me that he always felt as if he was under a death sentence and he was only awaiting its execution. Gradually he grew into the habit of also speaking in whispers or gesturing whenever he wanted to ask for something. On a few occasions he caught himself walking on tiptoe. When he was finally let out of the six months' ordeal and met the others in the main detention block, he was really scared of them as if they were beings from another world. He started speaking to them in whispers!

I was never myself subjected to this form of torture. I was lucky that my own initiation into prison life took the more mild form of internal segregation. Nevertheless, the constant reminder of my social apartness, this cruel human isolation in the midst of fellow humans, a case really of water everywhere and not a drop to drink, began to tell on me. I became edgy. Voices of warders, even when friendly, would grate on my nerves unpleasantly, and I would suddenly be seized with murderous thoughts. Fortunately for me these thoughts found no physical expression. But they soon had an outlet in words!

III

The first verbal 'victim' was the prison chaplain who one morning came into cell 16 staggering under the weight of two huge Bibles—*The Living Bible* in English and *Ibuku Rĩa Ngai* in Gĩkũyũ—plus a bundle of revivalist tracts from the American-millionaire-supported evangelical missions. He was in a prison officer's uniform of khaki trousers and jumper-coat lined with aluminium buttons and a decoration of two or three stones on the shoulder flaps. He also carried the hallmark of all prison officers and warders—a cord over the left shoulder carrying a whistle hidden in the breast-pocket. But underneath these symbols of oppression, he wore the holy uniform of a reverend: a black cloak ending in a white collar round the neck. He appeared to me, at the moment, the very embodiment of an immense neo-colonial evil let loose over our beautiful Kenya.

I let him talk and simply held back my tongue in anger.

'Sometimes,' he said, after sitting on the edge of the desk seat with me on the bed, 'God chastises us for our own good . . . Take Mau Mau for instance . . . Mau Mau was God's scourge with which he lashed Kenyans to teach them a good lesson . . . the fruit of this lesson, well learnt, is the stability we now enjoy and which is the envy of our neighbours.'

I could hardly believe my ears: Mau Mau, the most glorious chapter in our nation's long history of struggle was, to this man with the cloak of a priest beneath a prison officer's uniform, a huge *sjambok*[1] with which God had flagellated Kenyans into humble submission to his eternal will.

'We have all sinned and come short of the glory of God,' he said. 'Who knows, maybe this is a unique God-created chance for you to meet with Christ. God works in mysterious ways, his wonder to perform,' he went on.

He did not see the anger seething inside me. He only could see in my silence a being about to be smitten to the ground by the thunderbolt of the Lord, like Saul in the New Testament. But to me, his attempts at word comfort sounded like prayers of thanksgiving for being chosen to be the earthly instrument of God's mysterious ways of performing his wonders, and his attempts at converting me, were trumpets of victory over a fallen foe of imperialist Christendom.

My silence lured him on. He now presented me with the two Bibles.

'The Bible is the only book in the world containing within its hard covers a complete library,' he said, fingering each Bible lovingly as he placed it on the desk. 'Twenty-eight books in one . . . how many people can boast of a home library that big?'

He then handed to me two religious tracts—*God's City in Heaven* or some such title—with obvious awe at the American manufactured weightless leaves of holiness.

Despite my seething anger, I made a hasty retreat before this onslaught and actually took the leaves. I really felt weak before the moral certainty of a man who had walked the same path over and over again and hence knows every

---

[1]A policeman's club.

sharp corner and dangerous bend, every nook and brook on the way, and who knows clearly, from years of experience, where this path lead to: a prisoner's acceptance to forever carry a fascist cross without a murmur of discontent because he has now the spiritual satisfaction of having Christ for a personal saviour.

The visit had been beautifully timed. For over two weeks now I had not engaged in any debate, indeed I had hardly talked to anyone at any length since the night I was abducted form home. I had been denied human company. At the time of his visit, all the older detainees, except Shikuku, had gone to Shimo-la-Tewa Prison in Mombasa to meet the review tribunal. I was totally alone. I felt as if I had been on the run, relentlessly pursued by an invisible silent malignant force which, despite my every effort to outdistance it, had finally caught up with me, and was now transforming me, a free agent able to take decisions, into a passive creature panting and cringing for mercy at the feet of the twin warders of body and soul. My hard anger had now melted into a kind of spiritual lethargy and intellectual torpitude: What's the point of answering back? Isn't it easier, for me, for everybody, but mostly for me, to buy peace with silence?

The priest sensed the uncertainty in his quarry: he now took out his spiritual dagger and went for the kill.

'Let us kneel down and ask God for forgiveness for all our sins,' he commanded, but in a voice tear-bathed in infinite pity and compassion.

Then suddenly, from somewhere in the depths of my being, rose a strong rebellious voice.

'Wake up from your spiritual lethargy and intellectual torpor. Don't let them drug you with this opium, don't let them poison your system with it. It was to make you acutely hunger and thirst for a compassionate human voice that they have kept you near and yet far from human company. If you let him get away with this, you are going to be his prisoner for the rest of your stay here and possibly for ever.'

I felt life astir.

'Hold it!' I cried out. 'Who needs your prayers, your Bibles, your leaves of holiness—all manufactured and packaged in America? Why do you always preach humility and acceptance of sins to the victims of oppression? Why is it that you never preach to the oppressor? Go. Take your Bibles, your prayers, your leaves of holiness to them that have chained us in this dungeon. Have you read Ngaahika Ndeenda? Did you ever go to see the play? What was wrong with it? Tell me! What was wrong with Kamīrīīthū peasants and workers wanting to change their lives through their own collective efforts instead of always being made passive recipients of Harambee charity meant to buy peace and sleep for uneasy heads? Tell me truthfully: what drove you people to suppress the collective effort of a whole village? What has your borrowed Christianity to say to oppression and exploitation of ordinary people?'

I found myself getting worked up as I went along. A few warders had now crowded the door but I did not care. I flayed, right to its rotten roots, his spiritual dependence on imperialistic foreigners. What had made him bring me tracts written by Billy Graham? Did he know that this was the same man who used to bless American soldiers in their mission to napalm, bomb, murder and massacre Vietnamese men, women and children in the name of an anti-communist holy crusade? Were there no Kenyans who could write sermons? Why had he not at least paid homage to Kenya's spiritual independence by bringing into prison sermons by the likes of Reverend John Gatū and Bishop Henry Okullu, men whose liberal sincerity and concern had led them to a measure of patriotism?

The denunciatory vehemence in my voice shook him. The moral certainty had gone. He now became defensive. Avoiding the more earthly issues of oppression, exploitation and foreign control, he said that as a man of God he never indulged in politics. To justify that stand, he quoted the Biblical exhortation to believers to render unto Caesar things that were Caesar's and to God things of God. I quickly quoted back to him the Biblical scene where Jesus had whipped out of God's earthly temple the Pharisee and Sadducee collaborators with Caesar's oppressive conquest.

A little game started. He would refer me to Biblical passages which talked of faith, sin, salvation, grace, life to come; I would in turn refer him to alternative passages where God is cited as having sent his prophets to denounce earthly misrule and oppression of innocents.

'Anyway, we could go on arguing for ever,' he abruptly cut short the heated discussion, 'but I have others to see. You educated people like arguments too much. But remember that you cannot argue your way to Heaven.' He stood up, took back the two huge Bibles and the bundle of Billy Graham and staggered toward cell 11 where Martin Shikuku was on hunger strike.

The second verbal 'victim' was a warder. He was on leave when I was brought to Kamītī. This was his first shift since resuming work. Suddenly, out of the blue, he shouted at me and accused me of dragging my feet in returning to my cell. 'We know what you are trying to do, but don't be too clever. This is not the university,' he added, wagging a warning finger at me. This was soon after our supper usually eaten at 3:00 p.m.

The detainees and even the other warders turned their heads. They knew that he had deliberately picked on me as an object on which to display his talents in bullying. Total silence in Kamītī. Everybody froze into his position to watch the drama.

The kind of lethargy I had earlier felt before the spiritual warder again crept in to still my trembling anger: 'I am new in this place . . . shouldn't I buy peace by simply swallowing my anger and pride and slink into my cell? I am down. I must avoid confrontation.'

But another voice, the other voice, quickly intervened: 'You may now be down. But you must always struggle to rise. Struggle for your rights. If you don't pick the glove, if you don't stand to your full height now and stare injustice in the face, you'll never be able to raise you head in this place. It is now, or never!'

I stood up. But instead of going back to the cell, I walked toward the new warder in slow measured steps. I held back my anger. I tried to speak in a controlled voice but loud enough for everybody to hear. I wanted to be firm without shouting:

'You know very well that you did not tell me to go back to my cell. You also know that it is not yet time to go in. To me, even a second of my ration of sunshine is precious and it is my right. I am not begging for more than my due and I have no intention of doing so in the future. But whatever the case, never, never shout at me or abuse me. If I have broken any regulation, do our duty, and tell me so politely. I will hear. If I refuse to obey, you should report me to your superiors: the corporal, the sergeant, the chief, officer one, the superintendent or the senior superintendent. But don't add tyranny to the insult and injury of lies and falsehoods.'

He looked about him for support from the other warders. No voice came to his rescue. Suddenly noise and movement returned to the compound. We severally went back to our cells. It was an unwritten rule among detainees never to loudly comment on the results of a showdown between a detainee and a warder, especially when the detainee had won, for fear of uniting the warders into a common determination of vengeance. But I knew, from the relaxed tone of their voices and the ease of their laughter, that they were happy I had stood up to him.

Later, in fact, Koigi was to tell me: 'That warder is a well known bully. If you had not answered him, he would have gone on to spit at you and shit on you. I would like you to watch how he treats Detainee X who in order to avoid conflict dances to their every whim and caprice . . .'

Those two small incidents, and my own internal struggles to know how to react, brought home to me the real message behind what Wasonga Sijeyo had told me about my not letting them break me. They also showed me the tactical meaning behind all those mystificatory rituals.

This: detention and conditions in detention, including the constant reminder of one's isolation, can drive, in fact are meant to drive, a former patriot into a position where he feels that he has been completely forgotten, that all his former words and actions linked to people's struggles, were futile gestures and senseless acts of a meaningless individual martyrdom; yes, reduce him to a position where he can finally say: *The masses have betrayed me, why should I sacrifice myself for them?*

For a detained patriot, breaking through the double-walls of grey silence, attempting, if you like, a symbolic link with the outside world, is an act of resistance. And resistance—even at the level of merely asserting one's rights, of maintaining one's ideological beliefs in the face of any programmed onslaught—is in fact the only way a political detainee can maintain his sanity and humanity. Resistance is the only means of resisting a breakdown. The difficulty lies in the fact that in this resistance he has to rely first and foremost on his own resources (writing defiance on toilet-paper for instance) and nobody can teach him how to rely on them.

But all messages of solidarity, even though through a silent photograph, or through the unwritten word in a letter, are important contributions to his struggle to stay afloat. To a person condemned to isolation, such messages from the outside sound like Joshua's trumpets that brought down the legendary walls of Jericho.

True for me too: Njooki, a picture sent through the post; and Warĩĩnga, a picture created on rationed toilet-paper, have been more than a thousand trumpets silently breaking through the fortified walls of Kamĩtĩ Maximum Security Prison to assure me that I am not alone; Warĩĩnga, by constantly making me conscious of my connection with history, and Njooki, by constantly making me aware that I am now in prison because of Kamĩrĩĩthũ and its people.

But Warĩĩnga and Njooki also keep on reminding me that my detention is not a personal affair. It's part of the wider history of attempts to bring up the Kenyan people in a reactionary culture of silence and fear, and of the Kenyan people's fierce struggle against them to create a people's revolutionary culture of outspoken courage and patriotic heroism. ✑

SUGGESTIONS FOR WRITING

1. What are the principal emotional responses and reactions Ngugi displays toward his imprisonment? Are they unique to his situation, or common to all prisoners?

2. What are the reasons for some of the specific features of his prison regimen (for example, the light being left on at night and his being observed while defecating)? How do they affect him?

3. Contrast this "prison writing" with the selection from Genet's *The Thief's Journal*.

4. What is your response to Ngugi's debate with the evangelist who visits him in prison?

WHERE DO WHITES FIT IN?

Nadine Gordimer

*Few issues have commanded as much attention in recent years as South
African apartheid. In 1990, opponents of apartheid worldwide rejoiced when
Nelson Mandela, founding member and principal theorist of the outlawed
(from 1962 to 1990) African National Congress gained his release from
prison after 27 years.* **Nadine Gordimer,** *a white South African sympathetic to Mandela's cause, wrote "Where Do Whites Fit In?" shortly before
the events that led to Mandela's imprisonment. These events included the
Sharpeville massacre of 1960, at which South African security forces opened fire
on unarmed anti-apartheid demonstrators, killing dozens and prompting
Mandela to call for armed struggle (which led to his trial and imprisonment
for treason).*

*Gordimer's voice has been important in the debate over the way to dis-
mantle the apartheid system. While sympathetic white allies are welcomed by
the movement, blacks resent whites who seek to overshadow their leadership.
Gordimer is mindful of this problem, compounded as it is by an even more
elaborate system of racial separation than the American type that persisted for
decades in the South. She expresses an uneasiness about the kind of political role
she and like-minded whites can or should have in the struggle against apartheid.*

*Gordimer (b. 1924) is one of the most highly regarded African writers of
the twentieth century. Her subject, by and large, is the corrosive effect of
apartheid on South African society. Gordimer's fiction and essays focus on
the seemingly doomed attempts people make to live normal lives. She is best-
known for her novels, including* My Son's Story *(1990),* July's People
(1981), Burger's Daughter, *(1979),* The Conversationist *(1974),* A
Guest of Honour *(1970), and* The Late Bourgeois World *(1966). She
has published collections of stories including* Jump and Other Stories
*(1991), as well as works of non-fiction. One of the most important non-
fiction collections is* The Essential Gesture: Writing, Politics and Places
*(1988), from which "Where Do Whites Fit In?" is taken. In 1991,
Gordimer won the Nobel Prize for literature.*

Where do whites fit in in the New Africa? *Nowhere,* I'm inclined to say, in my
gloomier and least courageous moods; and I do believe that it is true that even
the gentlest and most westernised Africans would like the emotional idea of
the continent entirely without the complication of the presence of the white
man for a generation or two. But *nowhere,* as an answer for us whites, is in the
same category as remarks like *What's the use of living?* in the face of the threat
of atomic radiation. We are living; we are in Africa. *Nowhere* is the desire to
avoid painful processes and accept an ultimate and final solution (which

doesn't exist in the continuous process that is life itself); the desire to have over and done with; the death wish, if not of the body, at least of the spirit.

For if we're going to fit in at all in the new Africa, it's going to be sideways, where-we-can, wherever-they'll-shift-up-for-us. This will not be comfortable; indeed, it will be hardest of all for those of us (I am one myself) who want to belong in the new Africa as we never could in the old, where our skin-colour labelled us as oppressors to the blacks and our views labelled us as traitors to the whites. We want merely to be ordinary members of a multi-coloured, any-coloured society, freed both of the privileges and the guilt of the white sins of our fathers. This seems to us perfectly reasonable and possible and, in terms of reason, it is. But belonging to a society implies two factors which are outside reason: the desire to belong, on the one part, and acceptance, on the other part. The new Africa may, with luck, grant us our legal rights, full citizenship and the vote, but I don't think it will accept us in the way we're hankering after. If ever, it will take the confidence of several generations of jealous independence before Africa will feel that she can let us belong.

There is nothing so damaging to the ego as an emotional rebuff of this kind. (More bearable by far the hate-engendered hate that the apartheiders must expect.) And you don't have to be particularly thin-skinned in order to feel this rebuff coming in Africa. Africans are prickling with the desire to be off on their own; the very fact that you welcome the new Africa almost as fervently as they do seems an intrusion in itself. They have had so much of us—let's not go through the whole list again, from tear-gas and taxes to brotherly advice—that all they crave is to have no part of us.

You'll understand that I'm not speaking in economic or even political, but purely in human or, if you prefer it, psychological terms. For the purposes of what I have to say it may be true that in South Africa, for example, foreign capital and skills would have to be retained, in order to keep the mines and industry going, by wide concessions given by any black independent government with its head screwed on the right way. But the fact that we might go on living in our comfortable houses in the suburbs of Johannesburg under a black republic just as we do under a white near-republic, does not mean that we should feel ourselves accepted as part of the homogeneous society of the new Africa. For a long time to come any white South African must expect to find any black man, from any African territory, considered by the black South African as more of a brother than the white South African himself. No personal bonds of loyalty, friendship or even love will change this; it is a nationalism of the heart that has been brought about by suffering. There is no share in it we can hope to have. I for one can read this already in the faces, voices and eloquently regretful but firm handclasps of my own African friends.

Make no mistake, those moderate African political leaders who offer us whites—with sincerity, I believe—full participation in the new life of Africa offer us only the tangibles of existence. The intangibles that make up emotional participation and the sense of belonging cannot be legislated for.

What are we to do? Shall we go? Shall we leave Africa? For those small white communities who are truly foreign to the African territories in which they live, 'sent out' from a homeland in Europe for a spell of duty on administrative jobs or as representatives of commercial firms, there can't be much question of staying on. But in those territories, such as South Africa and the Rhodesias, where there is a sizeable and settled white population whose *home* is Africa, there is no easy answer; sometimes, it seems no answer at all. I do not attempt to speak, of course, for the stubborn mass that will continue, like a Napoleon in a mad house, to see itself as the undisputed master and make no attempt to consider the reality of living another role. I do not even try to guess what will happen to them; what *can* happen to them in a situation that they find unthinkable. I can only fear that events will deal with them grimly, as events usually do with people who refuse to think. I speak for people like myself, who think almost too much about the whole business and hope to arrive at an honest answer, without self-pity for the whites or sentiment about the blacks.

Some of us in South Africa want to leave; a few of us have gone already. And certainly, when one comes to Europe on a visit, one becomes a little uneasy at the number of friends (well-informed friends with a good perspective on the swerves and lurches of the way the world is going) who take one aside and ask whether one isn't planning to leave Africa? Which brings me to the reasons why some people have left and why these friends in Europe think one should pack up, too. A few have left because they cannot bear the guilt and ugliness of the white man's easy lot here; a few have left because they are afraid of the black man; and most, I should say, have left because of a combination of the two. I doubt if any consciously have left for the long-term reason I have elaborated here—the growing unwelcomeness of the white man in Africa. Yet I feel that if the white man's lot were to become no better and no worse than anyone else's tomorrow and the fear of violence at the hands of the black man (which we all have) were to have been brought to the test and disproved, unwelcomeness might still remain as the factor that would, in the end, decide many of us to give up our home and quit Africa.

I myself fluctuate between the desire to be gone—to find a society for myself where my white skin will have no bearing on my place in the community—and a terrible, obstinate and fearful desire to stay. I feel the one desire with my head and the other with my guts. I know that there must be many others who feel as I do, and who realise that generally the head is the more sensible guide of the two. Those of us who stay will need to have the use of our heads in order to sustain the emotional decision that home is not necessarily where you belong ethnogenically, but rather the place you were born to, the faces you first saw around you, and the elements of the situation among your fellow men in which you found yourself and with which you have been struggling, politically, personally or artistically, all your life.

The white man who wants to fit in in the new Africa must learn a number of hard things. He'd do well to regard himself as an immigrant to a new country; somewhere he has never lived before, but to whose life he has committed himself. He'll have to forget the old impulses to leadership, and the temptation to give advice backed by the experience and culture of Western civilisation— Africa is going through a stage when it passionately prefers its own mistakes to successes (or mistakes) that are not its own. This is an absolutely necessary stage in all political, sociological and spiritual growth, but it is an uncomfortable and disillusioning one to live through. And giving up the impulse to advise and interfere and offer to resume responsibility may not be as easy as we whites think. Even those of us who don't want to be boss (or *baas*, rather) have become used to being bossy. We've been used to assuming leadership or at least tutorship, even if it's only been in liberal campaigns to secure the rights of the Africans to vote and speak for themselves. Out of our very concern to see Africans make a go of the new Africa, we may—indeed, I know we shall—be tempted to offer guidance when we haven't been consulted. The facts that we'll be well-meaning and that the advice may be good and badly-needed do not count; the sooner we drum that into our egos the better. What counts is the need of Africa to acquire confidence through the experience of picking itself up, dusting itself down, and starting all over again; and the quickening marvel of often getting things right into the bargain.

It's hard to sit quiet when you think you can tell how a problem may be solved or a goal accomplished, but it may be even harder to give help without recriminations or, worse, smugness when it is sought. If we want to fit in anywhere in Africa, that is what we'll have to teach ourselves to do; answer up, cheerfully and willingly, when we're called upon and shut up when we're not. Already I notice that the only really happy whites I know in Africa—the only ones who are at peace with themselves over their place in the community—are some South African friends of mine who have gone to live in Ghana, and who have an educational job to do on contract from the Government. They are living as equals among the Africans, they have no say in the affairs of the country for the Africans to resent and they are contributing something useful and welcome to the development of Africa. In other words, they are in the position of foreign experts, employed at the Government's pleasure. I can positively feel my fellow-whites in Africa swelling with indignance at this extreme picture of the white man's future life on the continent; and it makes me feel rather indignant myself. But I think we've got to accept the home truth of the picture, whether we like it or not, and whether or not what we see there seems fair. All that the new Africa will really want from us will be what we can give as 'foreign experts'—the technical, scientific and cultural knowledge that white civilisation has acquired many hundreds of years before black civilisation, and on which, whether the Africans like it or not, their own aspirations are based.

I suppose we may get over being a minority minority instead of the majority minority we've been used to being all these past years, but I don't know whether that valuable change of attitude will actually bring us much nearer the integration we seek. Will intermarriage help us? It would, of course, on a large scale, but personally I don't believe that it will happen on a large scale in Africa. Intermarriage has always been regarded as a social stigma by whites, even in those territories where, unlike South Africa, it is not actually a crime, but I have never been able to find out whether, among blacks, it is regarded as a stigma or a step up in the world. (Most whites assume it is regarded as a deeply desired privilege, of course.) I know that, for example, in South Africa many Africans who are not Bechuanas, and have nothing whatever to do with the people of Bechuanaland, have on their walls a picture of Ruth and Seretse Khama. It is difficult to say whether this means that they take pride in the fact that a white woman chose to marry an important African, or whether the picture simply gives them a chance to identify themselves with the ex-chief's successful defiance of white taboo and authority.

Once the social stigma is removed—in the new Africa marriage with an African will be marrying into the ruling class, remember, and no one can measure how much of colour-prejudice is purely class-prejudice, in a country where there has been a great gap between the living standards of black and white—and once (in the case of South Africa) there are no legal disabilities in mixed marriages, I think that intermarriage will increase at two extreme levels of the social scale, but scarcely at all in between. Intellectuals will intermarry because they feel closer to intellectuals, whatever their race or colour, than to the mass, and the humbler and poorly-adjusted fringes of both the black and white masses, who have not found acceptance in their own societies, will intermarry in order to find a home somewhere—if not within the confines of their own background, then in someone else's. But I don't think we can hope for intermarriage on an effective scale between ordinary people, and I shouldn't be surprised if independent black Africa frowned upon it, in an unofficial but firm way. Especially in a country like South Africa, where there might remain whites in sufficiently large numbers to create an unease at the possibility that they might try to close their hands once again on those possessions of power from which their fingers had been prised back one by one. It is quite likely that there will be a social stigma, among ordinary people whose sense of nationalism is well stoked up, attached to marrying whites; it may be considered un-African. (Nkrumah has set the official precedent already, by choosing not a Ruth Williams, but a girl who "belongs" to the continent—a bride from Nasser's Egypt.) If white numbers do not dwindle in those areas of the continent which are heavily white-populated, and there is integration in schools and universities and no discrimination against white children, the picture will change in a few generations, of course. I do not see those young people as likely to regard parental race prejudice on either side as anything but fuddy-duddy. But will the whites remain, stick it out anywhere in Africa in sufficient numbers for this to come about? Isn't it much more likely that they will dwindle to small, socially isolated communities, whites in the diaspora?

If one will always have to feel white first, and African second, it would be better not to stay on in Africa. It would not be worth it for this. Yet, although I claim no mystique about Africa, I fear that like one of those oxen I sometimes read about in the Sunday papers, I might, dumped somewhere else and kindly treated, continually plod blindly back to where I came from. 🖋

SUGGESTIONS FOR WRITING

1. To what extent are Gordimer's concerns justified? Evaluate her sincerity.
2. As a white minority citizen of South Africa, what kinds of feelings does Gordimer seem to have toward her own ethnic heritage?

3. Do you think you could reach a point in your friendship with a person of another race where you would actually lose sight of the racial difference? Or could close friendship exist with full recognition of the difference?

Selections from
DON'T BE AFRAID GRINGO:
A HONDURAN WOMAN SPEAKS
FROM THE HEART

Elvia Alvarado
(Translated by Medea Benjamin)

*Medea Benjamin, of the San Francisco-based Institute for Food and De-
velopment Policy, met and interviewed **Elvia Alvarado** in Honduras.
The book* Don't be Afraid Gringo: A Honduran Woman Speaks
from the Heart *(1987) is based on Benjamin's translations of her edited
transcriptions of interviews with Alvarado. It is to Benjamin's credit that
she has allowed Alvarado's voice to emerge so forcefully. This selection
focuses on love and marriage among the Honduran peasant class.*

*Alvarado, a campesina, or peasant woman from Honduras, is repre-
sentative of the majority of her region's population. She lacks formal education, but she has learned a great deal from life, including the dramatic
lesson that she can speak out about her condition and thus embolden others to seek redress of their grievances. Before the early 1980s, Honduras
had been able to avoid the social dislocation produced by the military conflicts in neighboring nations. But because of U.S. President Ronald
Reagan, whose chief foreign policy goal was to topple the revolutionary
Sandinista government of Nicaragua, neighboring Honduras became the
leading base for the U.S.-sponsored* contra *war. Small guerrilla forces
would infiltrate Nicaragua, inflict whatever damage they could, and return to their base camps in Honduras. Almost overnight, Honduras became swollen with* contra *troops, weapons, landing strips, and U.S.
"military advisors." All this meant increased aid to the government of
Honduras, but it failed to benefit the Elvia Alvarados of the country.*

MARRIAGE CAMPESINO STYLE

One day, early in the morning, my oldest daughter Celia came and told me,
"Mommy, I'm going to the river to bathe with Chela." Chela was one of her
girlfriends. She took a bucket and some soap to wash with, and she left.
What I didn't know is that she had already snuck her suitcase out of the
house.

When it was noon I started to get worried, because she should've been back
long ago. I sent one of the other girls to see if her friend Chela was home yet,
but she wasn't. "I don't know why she's taking so long," I said. "She's got chores
to do here in the house, so she better get back soon." Since Celia was the old-

est, she was the one that ground the corn for tortillas. When she didn't show up, I sent my daughter Clara to do the grinding.

A few hours later, Chela appeared. "Didn't you go to the river with Celia?" I asked her. "Me?" she said. "No, Celia was with Tila, not with me." Tila was another one of Celia's girlfriends.

Later on one of the boys passed by the house and said, "Left you with the birdcage but no bird, huh?" "What are you talking about?" I asked him. "What's that supposed to mean?"

"You don't know?" he laughed. "Celia's gone off with her boyfriend." "No," I said. "She went to the river with Tila."

He laughed again. Then I knew it was true.

"OK," I thought, "if she doesn't want to stay with me, then let her go. If she wants to be with a man already, that's her choice."

I was mad, because Celia was only 15 years old. Besides, she was the oldest, and I needed her to help in the house. But I knew that getting mad wouldn't do any good.

For three days she didn't show up. Then the boy's father came to the house. I was inside grinding corn. "Good morning," he said. "Come in and sit down," I told him. "I'm busy and don't have time to waste." That was to let him know that I wasn't very happy about the situation.

He said, "I came to ask your forgiveness. A father doesn't know what his son is up to. And I want to know if you want them to get married or what."

"Don't worry," I said. "It's all the same to me. If your son wanted to marry her, he wouldn't have stolen her from my house. He would've made a decent wedding. But instead of a legal marriage, he stole her. I'm not going to force him to marry her. Let them live together as long as they like, and if he gets tired of her he can send her back home."

Celia's been with him ever since.

Among campesinos, men and women hardly ever get married—legally, that is. They just live together. My older son got married in the church, because his girlfriend insisted. She wouldn't give him anything until he agreed to marry her, so what could he do? When my son got married, his wife was still a *niña*, a girl—that's what we say here in Honduras when a woman hasn't been tried out by a man yet.

You see, the boys here are really bad. If the girl is loose and will give him what he wants without getting married, why bother? But sometimes the girl says, "No, I want to get married. And if you don't marry me then nothing doing." So he tells her that he wants to marry her. But if she gives in and lets him try her out, forget the marriage. If she holds out, then if he really wants her he'll have to get married.

None of my other children got married. It's all the same to me. Married or not married, it's the same life. Married women have more rights—for example, · if the husband dies all his possessions go to his wife. But us poor people, what possessions do we have? None. So what difference does it make?

The church wants us to get married. Some priests go around trying to convince couples who are living together to get married. Some people give in, but most don't.

Look at me with Alberto. We lived together for 18 years. The priest that used to come here to give mass would tell us to get married. And my mother, who's a devout Catholic and spends her life praying, told us to get married. One of my brothers even tried to convince Alberto to marry me.

At first Alberto refused. He simply said no, he didn't want to be married. But after I started working with the church and getting liberated, that's when he wanted to get married. And then I was the one who didn't want to. I wanted my freedom.

Most men don't want to get married because they say that marriage ties them down. They say that if they get married, they can't have a woman on the side. But if they don't get married, they say they're free and have the right to have two women.

We Hondurans are very respectful of the church. We say, "You don't fool around with God." So once you're married, you're married. Marriage means responsibility. Because when you get married the priest says, "So-and-so, you want this woman to be your wife?" And the man says, "Yes, I want this woman to be my wife." The woman says the same thing. And then the priest pronounces them married for the rest of their lives. So if you get married in the church then you can't get divorced.

We don't have anything like a honeymoon, either. The honeymoon is running away with a woman and sleeping out in the fields together the first night. And the next day back to work. That's the campesino's honeymoon.

When a boy decides he wants to live with a girl and she agrees, he steals her from her parents' house—just like what happened with my daughter Celia, except they usually do it at night. During the day the boy tells her that he's going to take her away that night. So she goes home and pretends to go to sleep, but she's really up waiting for him. When he gets there, she makes sure everyone is sleeping. She grabs her suitcase full of clothes and quietly sneaks out the window or out the door. Then they go out to the fields to sleep together.

In the morning they go to his parents' house. When the parents see him coming home with a girl, and the girl is carrying a suitcase, they get scared. "Oh no," say the parents, "he's got himself hitched." You see, once a boy starts going with a girl, the girl moves into his parents' house.

They accept the girl whether they like it or not. A campesino family would never reject a girl their son brings home. Never.

When the parents of the girl figure out what happened, they have to decide what to do. They can go to the boy's house and ask him to marry the girl; they can wait for the boy's parents to come to them; or, if they don't like the boy, they can take their daughter back home.

But if they take her home, a few days later the boy usually steals her again. And he keeps doing that until the girl's parents agree to let her stay with him.

The boy's parents wait about three days. If the girl's parents don't come for her, then the boy's father goes to the girl's house to make an agreement. The girl's parents might say they want them to get married, or they might say it doesn't matter to them. They might say, "Let them be free and live together as long as they love each other." That way if they want to separate they can, and they don't have to worry about getting divorced.

Alejandro was a poor campesino in one of the villages I work in. He had two wives—one was named Martina and the other Marina—and he had children with both of them.

I was close to him, because he was part of the campesino group. So I said to him, "Alejandro, you have to take a good look at your life. You can't have two women—you can barely afford to support one!" "Here the men don't support the women," he laughed. "It's the women who support the men. So having two women is better than one."

The problem was that these two women fought over him. If you ever saw Alejandro, you'd wonder what the hell they saw in him. He's a skinny little man who's nothing to look at. And besides that, he's dirt poor.

One day there was a big scandal in the village, because Martina and Marina were fighting over who would get what portion of Alejandro's corn. Marina shouted, "The corn is mine, because I fed Alejandro all the time he was working in the fields. You didn't give him anything." "That's not true," Martina shouted. "What's Alejandro's is mine!"

In front of all the neighbors, Martina jumped on Marina and started pulling her hair. Marina tore Martina's dress and pulled down her underwear. Then they started rolling around in the dirt, tearing at each other.

I was in another house at the time. The daughter of one of them ran to get me, because the women have a lot of respect for me. For the campesinos, we leaders are like authorities; they count on us to give advice and act as intermediaries.

When I got there the neighbors had already torn them apart. But they were still shouting at each other and sobbing.

"Why are you two fighting?" I asked them. "Marina, you know that Alejandro lives with Martina. And Martina, you know that Alejandro lives with Marina. If you both love him, then don't fight. Now as for the problem of the corn," I said joking around, "you have to share it like you share Alejandro—one night a meal for one, the next night for the other." And everyone started laughing, including Marina and Martina.

"But seriously," I said, "we have to discuss this problem at our next meeting. We're going to ask Alejandro what he proposes and we'll come up with a solution. The important thing is to stop fighting, because it gives a bad impression. If the rich folks find out that the women here are at each other's throats, they'll be delighted. We can't fight with each other like this. It's not good for the community."

I calmed them down and they divided the corn equally. Martina went off carrying the corn on her back, while Marina loaded her horse and went home.

Two weeks later we had a meeting of the whole village, and we discussed the problem. "Don't worry," Alejandro grinned. "I can take care of this problem. I know what these women want, and I can make them both happy." Everyone laughed.

"Look, Alejandro," I told him. "You've got to solve this problem." But there wasn't much I could do, because Alejandro had been carrying on with his two families for years. His children with Marina and Martina were all in their teens already. And for Alejandro the arrangement is great. Both women work—because he has no money to give them—and both feed him. So what could we do about it at this point, except hope that he manages to keep them both happy?

When men and women start living together, there's a tremendous double standard. Because the women have to be faithful to the men, but the men don't have to be faithful to the women. If a woman lives with one man and sleeps with another, it's a terrible scandal. Men kill their wives for sleeping with another man.

But campesino men are free to sleep with other women. They usually don't go to bordellos, because they can't afford them and because they're afraid of getting some disease. But they sleep with other campesinas who don't have husbands. Some campesinas just do it because they want to. Others get paid; but we don't consider them prostitutes, because they just do it when they need some money.

It's also very common for campesinos to simply leave their wives and children and start a new family elsewhere. I'd say that about half the women in Honduras have no husbands. The men are very irresponsible. That's part of the double standard.

There are even men who keep two families going at the same time, like Alejandro. But that usually causes lots of problems, because the women start fighting with each other.

The fighting is a lot more serious when it's a woman that's sleeping around. There was a case recently right in the hotel in San Pedro. She was a married woman who had a lover on the side. Somehow her husband found out and decided to catch her in the act.

So one day he told her he had to work that evening and would be home late. Then he took the car and pretended he left, but he was really around the corner watching.

The wife called her boyfriend and made a date in the hotel. She got all dolled up and left the house in a taxi. After she'd been in the hotel about a half hour, the husband broke down the door, found them there in bed, and shot them both.

Sometimes the men just kill the wife, because they say it's the woman's fault. A man will sleep with any woman he gets a chance to sleep with, so they say it's the woman's fault if she goes with him.

That happens in the middle and upper classes—these crimes of passion. But I haven't heard of any cases among campesinos, because we campesina women just wouldn't do that. It's not in our blood. Or maybe we're too smart, because we know our husbands would kill us.

I've heard that there are men and women who make love in all different ways, but we campesinos don't know anything about these different positions. We do it the same all the time—the man gets on the woman and goes up and down, up and down, and that's it. Sometimes the woman feels pleasure and sometimes she doesn't.

We don't have any privacy either, because our houses are usually one big room. So we have to wait until everyone is asleep and then do it very quietly. We just push down our underpants and pull them back up again.

We like to have sex, but we don't let the men see us nude. That's just how we are. As soon as girls are born, their vaginas have to be covered all the time.

We never change in front of men; we even take baths with our bras, panties, and slips on. And that's how we sleep, too. Take me and Alberto. We lived together for 18 years and never once did he see me naked.

Not many campesina women use birth control. They just keep having babies, babies, and more babies. I only have six children, which might be a lot in your country but it isn't a lot here. Most campesinas have eight, ten, even twelve children.

I've thought a lot about why we have so many children, and I really don't know why. The men want their wives to have as many children as they can. And most women want a lot of children, too. They think it's only natural.

Part of the reason might be the Catholic church. Most of us are Catholics, and the church tells us that it's natural to have children and that going against nature is going against God.

We campesinas don't have abortions, either. Middle and upper class women have abortions when they don't want the child or when they're afraid of gossip because they're not married. It's illegal, but they have their ways. But the only time campesinas abort is when they're sick and lose the child by accident. We don't abort on purpose; it's not part of our culture.

I never talk about family planning in the campesino meetings. There's one campesino group, ANACH, that gets involved in family planning, because it's a government organization and the government tells it to. They go around telling the campesinos not to have so many children. But the campesinos get mad; they don't like anyone telling them that.

So our group doesn't talk about it. First of all because the campesinos say it's a personal matter, and secondly because there are plenty of other groups that teach about family planning. The church teaches people the rhythm method. The health clinic gives talks about IUDs and pills and all that stuff. And the government has programs on the radio. So we don't have to get involved in those questions.

I personally don't think it's good to have lots of children if you can't maintain them. It breaks my heart to see children suffering because their parents can't afford to feed them. So I think it's good to plan.

My daughters take birth control. I told my daughter Clara that her husband is too poor for her to have another child right now. She has one child, and I think she should wait a few years before having another one—and that's it. Two children are plenty these days.

But to tell you the truth, I don't like my daughters using that birth control, because of all the problems it causes. Those pills do a lot of harm to women here. Maybe they don't affect the gringas so much, because they're more resistant than we are. They're stronger and better fed. But not Honduran women; many of them get sick.

The worst thing we get is cancer. Here in my village six women died recently from vaginal cancer. Before we never had that kind of sickness. At least I'd never heard of it before. But now lots of my friends are dying from it. Some were using pills, others were using IUDs. My sister's in the hospital right now dying of cancer of the uterus.

I once asked a doctor friend of mine, Dr. González, if it's true that birth control causes cancer. He said they haven't been able to prove it yet, but that he was worried about the big increase in women's cancer. All the women I know are scared to death about getting cancer.

Some women think that having your tubes tied causes cancer. I did it because I had to—I had high blood pressure, and it would have been dangerous for me to have more children. But most women are afraid to do it. Other methods like the IUD give lots of infections. And you have to remember that when we get sick it's hard for us to get to a doctor. The nearest clinic is far away. And even if we could see a doctor, we can't afford to buy the medicine. I know a woman who had to pay $60 to get rid of an infection in her vagina. That's more than most of us make in a month!

It's also hard for poor women to find out if they have cancer. If a woman goes to a private doctor to get one of those exams, it ends up costing her $25. And if you go to the health center to get it free, it's a long hassle. First you have to go there to get a number. Then you go back the next day and wait in line. And even then they might not see you.

When they finally take the test, they send it to the capital and it takes months to get the results. If you really do have cancer, it keeps getting worse and you don't even know. That's why so many poor women die of cancer, and that's why we're so afraid of birth control.

A lot of this money for family planning comes from the United States. What I want to know is why the United States sends us all these birth control gadgets without sending us anything to protect us against the diseases they cause? Why don't they send any medicine to stop us from getting cancer? And if there is no medicine to stop it, then they should stop sending the birth control. How can the United States go around pushing a program without thinking it through? That's just not right.

The United States gives millions of dollars to stop Hondurans from having children. I don't understand why they're so interested in our personal lives. Some say the gringos just want to get rid of poor people. Others say that the United States sees poor people as potential guerrillas, so the fewer children they have, the fewer guerrillas. I don't know, but that's what they say.

TAMING MACHO WAYS

When I started working with the mothers' clubs in the Catholic church, it was the first time I realized that we women work even harder than the men do.

We get up before they do to grind the corn and make tortillas and coffee for their breakfast. Then we work all day—taking care of the kids, washing the clothes, ironing, mending our husband's old rags, cleaning the house. We hike to the mountains looking for wood to cook with. We walk to the stream or the well to get water. We make lunch and bring it to the men in the field. And we often grab a hoe and help in the fields. We never sit still one minute.

It's true that there are some jobs that require a lot of strength and that women can't do as well as men. For example, when we have to clear a piece of forest, it's the men who go out with the axes and cut down the trees. Other work we consider "men's work" is chopping firewood and plowing the land with a team of oxen. These are things that men do better than women, because they're stronger. I don't know if it's a physical difference from birth, but the fact is that here in Honduras women are usually either pregnant or nursing, and that takes a lot of energy out of you.

Men may be out working during the day, but when they come home they usually don't do a thing. They want their meal to be ready, and after they eat they either lie down to rest or go out drinking. But we women keep on working—cooking the corn and beans for the next day's meal, watching the children.

Even when we go to sleep, we don't get to rest. If the babies wake up crying, we have to go take care of them—give them the breast if they're still breast-feeding, give them medicine if they're sick. And then if our husbands want to make love, if they get the urge, then it's back to work again.

The next morning, we're up before the sun, while our husbands are still sleeping.

In some families, like the workers in the city, I've seen men help women in the house. But I've never seen it in a campesino home. Even if the man has no work and sits at home, he won't help out.

I have a friend in the city who works in a factory. If he comes home from work and the meal isn't ready—maybe his wife is busy watching the children or washing clothes—he just grabs the pots and pans and gets to work. I've seen it with my own eyes. He actually cooks the meal for the whole family. You'd never see that in a campesino house!

I don't think it's fair that the women do all the work. Maybe it's because I've been around more and I've seen other relationships. But I think that if two people get together to form a home, it should be because they love and respect each other. And that means that they should share everything.

The problem some campesina women have is even worse. Not only do their husbands refuse to help, but they don't even support the family. They don't give her money to put food on her children's plates.

When the men find work, they earn a few dollars a day. The campesino with better habits gives all his money to his wife; maybe he keeps 50 cents to buy cigarettes. The campesino with bad habits gives his wife less. If he earns $2.50, he gives her one dollar and keeps $1.50 for himself.

If the woman complains and asks why she only gets one dollar while he gets $1.50, he says, "That's none of your business. I earned the money and it's mine to spend as I please." What can the woman say? If she still complains, she's asking for a fight.

That's why so many campesina women have to work. They fatten pigs or raise chickens, bake bread or sell tortillas in the market—anything to make a few pennies to feed their children.

Some of the women are sharp, though, and get money from their husbands without them knowing.

Take my friend Zenaida. She waits until her husband is fast asleep. When she hears him snoring, she gets up very, very quietly and searches through his pants pockets. Whatever money she finds, she takes. Then she crawls back into bed while the poor man is still snoring away.

The next day he gets up, puts on his pants, and goes out to work in the field. He doesn't yet realize his money is gone. But when he comes home from work, he says, "Hey, did you take some money out of my pocket?"

"Are you crazy?" Zenaida asks. "Why would I look through your pockets?"

"You did, didn't you?" he says, still not sure.

"Why? What happened?" she asks.

"I had some money I'd been saving up to buy some clothes, and it's gone," says her husband.

"You probably lost it when you were out drinking last night," Zenaida answers. "It probably fell out of your pocket while you were drunk. Because I surely didn't take your money."

He's all upset because he lost the money. Meanwhile, Zenaida's in the kitchen, laughing with her children. "Hah. Your father says he was saving the money for clothes, but he wanted it to get drunk with. I fixed him. But don't you dare tell him, because with this money I can go to the market and buy you good things to eat." So the children keep their mouths shut.

I never did that to my husband, because I always worked. I had more money than he did. But lots of women do it. They tell me about it, and we have a good laugh. It serves the men right, we say.

Another problem women have is that their husbands often beat them. Say a campesino comes home late after drinking or sleeping with a woman he has on the side. If his wife yells at him, he hits her. Sometimes he leaves her all black and blue or with a bloody nose, a black eye, or a busted lip.

The neighbors can hear everything. But since it's a fight between the two of them, no one interferes. Unless the woman starts to yell, "Help! So-and-so's trying to kill me." Then the neighbors come over and tell him to stop hitting the poor woman.

"No," the campesino says. "This no-good woman is yelling about things she has no right to stick her nose into. I'm the man in this family, and nobody tells me what to do."

He usually stops hitting her when the neighbors get involved. But if no one comes to help her, she wakes up the next morning all black and blue.

The woman never says what really happened. She's too embarrassed. So she says she fell down or had an accident. She doesn't even tell her friends or her own mother what happened. Because if she tells her mother, her mother says, "You knew what he was like when you went to live with him. So why did you go with him in the first place?" Or if the mother tells her to come home and live with her and she does, a few days later they get back together again and the other's the one that looks bad.

If the woman can't take it any more, she leaves him. But even after the woman leaves, the man usually follows her and keeps harassing her.

We know it's against the law to beat someone like that, but the police don't get involved in fights between couples. They say it's none of their business. They say it's something for the man and wife to figure out by themselves.

Machismo is a historical problem. It goes back to the time of our great-grandfathers, or our great-great-grandfathers. In my mind, its connected to the problem of drinking. Drinking is man's worst disease. When men drink, they fight with everyone. They hit their wives and children. They offend their neighbors. They lose all sense of dignity.

How are we going to stop campesinos from drinking? First of all, we know the government isn't interested in stopping it, because it's an important source of income. Every time you buy a bottle of liquor, part of that money goes to the government.

That's why the government doesn't let the campesinos make their own liquor, because the government doesn't make any money off homemade brew. So a campesino can go into town any time, day or night, spend all his money, and drink himself sick. But if he gets caught making *choruco*—that's what we call homemade spirits made from corn and sugar—they throw him in jail. The government wants the campesinos to drink, but only the liquor that they make money off of.

If we're ever going to get campesinos to stop drinking, we first have to look at why so many campesinos drink. And for that we have to look at what kind of society we have. We've built up a society that treats people like trash, a society that doesn't give people jobs, a society that doesn't give people a reason to stay sober. I think that's where this vice comes from.

I've seen what happens when campesinos organize and have a plot of land to farm. They don't have time for drinking any more, except on special occasions. They spend the day in the hot sun—plowing, planting, weeding, irrigating, cutting firewood for the house, carrying the produce to market. Most of them are very dedicated to their work and their families.

So I've noticed that once the campesinos have a purpose, once they have a way to make a living and take care of their families, they drink less. And they usually stop beating their wives, too. And I've seen that once the women get organized, they start to get their husbands in line.

I know that changing the way men and women treat each other is a long process. But if we really want to build a new society, we have to change the bad habits of the past. We can't build a new society if we are drunks, womanizers, or corrupt. No, those things have to change.

But people *can* change. I know there are many things I used to do that I don't do any more, now that I'm more educated. For example, I used to gossip and criticize other women. I used to fight over men. But I learned that gossip only destroys, it doesn't build. Criticizing my neighbors doesn't create unity. Neither does fighting over men. So I stopped doing these things.

Before, whenever I'd see the slightest thing I'd go running to my friends, "Ay, did you see so-and-so with what's-his-face?" I'd go all over town telling everyone what I saw. Now I could see a woman screwing a man in the middle of the street and I wouldn't say anything. That's her business.

If someone is in danger, then, yes, we have to get involved. For example, I heard a rumor that a landowner was out to kill one of the campesino leaders I work with. I made sure to warn the campesino so he'd be careful. That kind of rumor we tell each other—but not idle gossip.

I also used to flirt with married men, just for the fun of it and to make their wives jealous. Now I'm much more responsible, much more serious. That doesn't mean I don't joke around and have a good time. I just make it clear that we're friends.

We all have to make changes. Campesino men have to be more responsible with their women. They have to have only one woman. Because they have a hard enough time supporting one family, let alone two. Campesinos who drink have to stop drinking. And campesinos who fight with their wives have to stop fighting. Our struggle has to begin in our own homes.

SUGGESTIONS FOR WRITING

1. What surprises you most about the life Alvarado describes?

2. How much are the tensions between women and men described by Alvarado specific to her class? On the other hand, do these conflicts between the sexes transcend class lines?

3. Elsewhere in *Don't Be Afraid Gringo*, Alvarado expresses the belief that, whatever the motives of U.S. leaders, the American people—if they but knew of her plight and that of other Central Americans—would want to help, and would demand a different policy from the U.S. government. What do you think of the faith she places in the people of the United States?

COPYRIGHTS AND ACKNOWLEDGMENTS

For permission to use the selections reprinted in this book, the author is grateful to the following publishers and copyright holders:

AMERICA PRESS INC. For "Abortion, Lies and Videotape" by Thomas H. Stahel. From *America*, November 11, 1989, Vol. 161, No. 14. Reprinted with the permission of America Press Inc., 106 West 56th St., New York, New York 10019. Copyright © 1989.

ARTE PUBLICO For "Like Mexicans" by Gary Soto, reprinted with permission of the publisher from *Small Faces*, by Gary Soto (Houston: Arte Publico Press, University of Houston, 1986). For "An Awakening ... Summer 1956" by Nicholasa Mohr. Reprinted with permission of the publisher from *Woman of Her Word: Hispanic Women Write*, ed. by Evangelina Vigil (Houston: Arte Publico Press, University of Houston, 2d ed., 1987).

E. DIGBY BALTZELL For "Blue Blood Blues" from *The New Republic*, April 3, 1989. Reprinted by permission of *The New Republic*.

CAPRA PRESS For "Tell the Women We're Going" by Raymond Carver. From *Fires*, copyright © 1983 by Raymond Carver. Reprinted by permission of Capra Press.

CLEIS PRESS For "An Open Letter to Mothers Whose Daughters Happen to Be Lesbians" by D. Clarke. From *Different Daughters: A Book by Mothers of Lesbians*, ed. by Louise Rafkin, Cleis Press, 1987. For "Being Positive Is Positive" by Elisabeth. From *AIDS: The Women*, ed. by Ines Rieder and Patricia Ruppelt, Cleis Press, 1988. For "Hookers with AIDS—the Search" by Lynn Hampton. From *AIDS: The Women*, ed. by Ines Rieder and Patricia Ruppelt, Cleis Press, 1988.

COMMONWEAL FOUNDATION For "Not by Condoms Alone: Society and the AIDS Epidemic" by David R. Carlin, Jr. From *Commonweal*, March 13, 1987. Copyright © Commonweal Foundation, 1987.

THE CONDE NAST PUBLICATIONS INC. For "Only Daughter" by Sandra Cisneros. From *Glamour*, November 1990. Courtesy *Glamour*. Copyright © 1990 by The Conde Nast Publications Inc.

THE CROSSING PRESS For "Daddy" by Jan Clausen. From *Mother Sister Daughter Lover*, Crossing Press, 1980. Copyright © Jan Clausen, The Crossing Press, 1980.

JOHN DEADLINE ENTERPRISES, INC. For "Bar Wars" by Bob Greene. From *Esquire*, November, 1986. Reprinted with permission by John Deadline Enterprises, Inc.

DOUBLEDAY For "Playboy Joins the Battle of the Sexes" by Barbara Ehrenreich from *The Hearts of Men* by Barbara Ehrenreich. Copyright © 1983 by Barbara Ehrenreich. Used by permission of Doubleday, a division of Bantam Doubleday Dell Publishing Group, Inc. For "The Movement" by Anne Moody from *Coming of Age in Mississippi* by Anne Moody. Copyright © 1968 by Anne Moody. Used by permission of Doubleday, a division of Bantam Doubleday Dell Publishing Group, Inc.

EXQUISITE CORPSE For "My Abortion" by Deborah Salazar. From *Exquisite Corpse*, October/ December, 1989. Reprinted with permission of *Exquisite Corpse*.

FIREBRAND BOOKS For "Confessions of a Closet Baptist" by Mab Segrest. From *My Mama's Dead Squirrel: Lesbian Essays on Southern Culture* by Mab Segrest, Firebrand Books, Ithaca, New York. For "If I Could Write This in Fire, I Would Write This in Fire" by Michelle Cliff. From *The Land of Look Behind: Prose and Poetry* by Michelle Cliff, Firebrand Books, Ithaca, New York.

FISK UNIVERSITY LIBRARY SPECIAL COLLECTIONS For "Fight, and If You Can't Fight, Kick." From *Unwritten History of Slavery: Autobiographical Accounts of Ex-Slaves*, ed. by Ophelia Settle Egypt, J. Masouka, and Charles Johnson, Social Science Documents, No. 1, Social Science Institute, 1945. Reprinted by permission of Beth M. House, Fisk University Library Special Collections.